THE
ELEMENTS
OF STYLE

THE ELEMENTS OF STYLE

AN PRACTICAL ENCYCLOPEDIA OF INTERIOR
ARCHITECTURAL DETAILS FROM 1485 TO THE PRESENT

REVISED EDITION

STEPHEN CALLOWAY
GENERAL EDITOR

ELIZABETH CROMLEY
CONSULTANT EDITOR

SIMON & SCHUSTER

SIMON & SCHUSTER
Simon & Schuster Building
Rockefeller Center
1230 Avenue of the Americas
New York, New York 10020

For the first edition

Senior Executive Editor **Robert Saxton**
Senior Executive Art Editor **Jacqui Small**
Project Editor **Sarah Polden**
Senior Art Editor **Mike Brown**
Editor **Lydia Seagrave**
Editorial Assistant **Jaspal Bhangra**
Designers **Geoff Fennell,
Rozelle Bentheim**
Production **Ted Timberlake**

Illustrations **Dennis and Sheila Curran**
Location Photography **Kim Sayer**
Archive Photography **Ian B. Jones**
American Editor **Elizabeth Cromley**
Americanization **Carol Hupping**
Directories **Carol Hupping,
Fayal Greene**

For the revised edition

Executive Editor **Alison Starling**
Executive Art Editor **Vivienne Brar**
Editor **Elisabeth Faber**
Designers **Mark Richardson, Geoff Borin**
Production **Dawn Mitchell**

Biographies **Valerie Clack**
American Directory revised by **Fayal Greene**
British Directory revised by **Emma Shackleton**

Edited and designed by Mitchell Beazley,
an imprint of Octopus Publishing Group Ltd,
2–4 Heron Quays, Docklands
London E14 4JP

Color reproduction by Scantrans Pte. Ltd, Singapore
Production by Toppan Printing Co., Ltd
Printed and bound in China

10 9 8 7 6 5

Library of Congress Cataloging-in-Publication Data

The Elements of Style: a practical encyclopedia of interior
architectural details, from 1485 to the present / Stephen Calloway,
general editor. Elizabeth Cromley, American editor
p. cm.
Includes bibliographical references and index.
1. Interior architecture. 2. Architecture – Details. 3. Interior
architecture – United States. 4. Architecture – United States –
Details. I. Calloway, Stephen. II. Cromley, Elizabeth C.
NA2850.E44 1991
721–dc20   91-8764
                              CIP
ISBN 0-684-83521-5

General Editor's Acknowledgments

The creation of *The Elements of Style* has been very much a collaborative effort; a task rather like the building of a house, in which, from the initial planning stages through to the completion of the project, the learning and skill of many individuals have been called upon. The essential foundation of the work has been the deep and detailed knowledge that each of the individual authors has brought to bear in the compilation of his or her chapter(s). All have given much more than duty alone could require, and without their enthusiasm, expertise and patience such a book could not have been achieved. The publisher's creative team, including the illustrators and the photographers, also deserve grateful thanks. Particular mention should be made of those who have been with the project throughout, helping with the research and marshalling a vast body of material, textual and visual, with both efficiency and an unfailing cheerfulness. I should like to thank very warmly the many curators, public institutions and organizations and, above all, the owners of private houses who kindly allowed us access to take photographs, often at considerable inconvenience to themselves. (Detailed photo credits appear on pages 560-63.) Finally, it is a pleasure to record our immense gratitude to one friend, whom at his own request I shall not name, who most generously made available for study and photography his unrivalled collection of architectural treatises, pattern books and trade catalogues.

The engraving above shows the origin of the
Corinthian capital. The Athenian sculptor
Callimachus is said to have come across a woven
straw basket containing the few possessions of a
poor girl from Corinth who had died tragically. The
basket had been covered with a slab or roof tile,
and acanthus leaves had grown up around it, and
curled beneath the overhang. Moved by the pathos
and simple charm of the composition, Callimachus
sketched it and later carved it in stone with such
skill that it became part of the classical language of
architecture – one of the Five Orders that have
fashioned the aesthetic of building from the
Renaissance to the present day. (From John
Evelyn's translation of Roland Fréart's A Parallel
of the Antient Architecture with the Modern,
published in England in 1664; second edition
1707).

CONTENTS

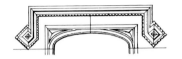

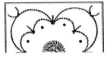
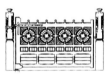

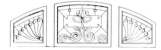

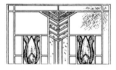

FOREWORD

J. JACKSON WALTER, FORMER PRESIDENT, NATIONAL TRUST FOR HISTORIC PRESERVATION

On the shore of the Ashley River outside Charleston, South Carolina, stands Drayton Hall, the preeminent surviving example of Georgian Palladian architecture in the United States. This historic house, a National Trust property whose construction was completed in 1742, is justly famous because it has never been restored; rather it is preserved – untouched by plumbing, electricity or central heating – a unique reflection of pre-Revolutionary American culture, frozen in time.

But while the house itself is one-of-a-kind, the collection of components that were assembled in its fabrication is widely known. All of them, the walls, doors, windows, floors and fireplaces, were created according to the principles of design that together make up the Georgian style. They hold another distinction, as well. They are all here in *The Elements of Style*.

The genius of this book is that it joins in one volume many snapshots of architectural history. It is a source book indispensable for owners of historic houses and those who work on them because it permits and encourages both identifying architectural detail and placing it in the context of a centuries-long evolution.

This is especially important because contemporary architectural styles are quite different, both in technology and in the materials used, from earlier eras. The quality and craftsmanship of artisans creating individual ornaments often have been replaced by factories using mass-production techniques, which first were introduced in the mid-19th century. Quality and richness of detail may have suffered in the process, but the trade-off has provided a much broader population the opportunity to enjoy good design.

The Elements of Style takes the mystery out of this evolution. It is a book, for example, that will be equally worthwhile to those interested in Georgian Drayton Hall, and to those who happen for the first time upon Woodrow Wilson House, another National Trust property located in Washington D.C., where the kitchen authentically preserves the appliances and the ambience of the early 1920s. Visitors to all of the National Trust's collection of 17 historic house museums will find much to think over, to understand and to use in these pages. The sheer magnitude of America's, and Britain's, architectural heritage comes alive here.

For the preservationist, whether homeowner or professional, telling the story that lies behind bricks and mortar, woodwork and window is a constant challenge. As George McDaniel, the director of Drayton Hall, puts it, his historic site is a "small postage stamp of history", an intact survivor from a society of the past.

The Elements of Style places a large magnifying glass into the hands of anyone who wants to understand why things look as they do inside, and outside, our historic architectural structures. It brings the continuity of design over the last 500 years into sharp focus. And it shows in great and satisfying detail the enormous ingenuity succeeding cultures have brought to bear on creating a hospitable environment, both practically and aesthetically, in which to live.

Jack Walter

PREFACE

STEPHEN CALLOWAY

"For a man's house is his castle", wrote Sir Edward Coke at the beginning of the 17th century. The phrase has become a cornerstone of the way we think and live. Yet, by a stroke of historic irony, the great lawyer's memorable line was penned at the very time when Inigo Jones was building the first modern house in England, the Queen's House at Greenwich – that precocious expression of polite taste and perfect monument to a new domestic ideal. From this date on people cared for their houses not merely as strongholds of safety and domestic wealth: they loved them for their architecture. Today we are heirs to a legacy of fine building and to a continuing fascination with the details and stylistic elements which give our houses their character. In Britain, and in the United States too, that interest in old houses has become something of a national obsession. The desire to know and understand the history of our homes has never been stronger. We are, perhaps more than ever before, aware of the crucial importance of our great architectural traditions and the central position they occupy in what we have come to call our heritage.

At the heart of this concept of heritage lies our idealized image of the period house, which, great or small, ostentatious or plain, has come to epitomize so many of our notions of civilization. The study of the architectural evolution of the country house in England and the United States, and of urban and village building, has a long and distinguished history. But in recent years, academic interest in the planning, stylistic development and detailing of historic houses has increasingly become linked with the more passionate and practical enthusiasms of the conservation movement. As a result, the houses we live in have become a major concern – the subject of both a large body of scholarly and investigative endeavour and often intense public discussion and debate.

One of the foremost defenders of traditional values in design and workmanship, the Prince of Wales, has repeatedly stressed the influential role which fine architecture can play in our everyday existence. As the protagonist of a humane architecture based on human scale and sound techniques and materials, he has championed the idea that good building is not only an index of civilization, but also an important contributory factor in the quality of life which we enjoy.

Today, those who value the best of the old in our heritage are convinced of its relevance to the new. But there is, it has to be said, a great deal that must be learned or re-learned. In recent decades more modern tendencies have prevailed, and we have come perilously close to losing much of the rich vocabulary and even the grammar which gave our architectural language in previous ages its subtlety and fluent charm. What we need now is a return to visual literacy, an understanding of all the elements and details of the house as they have changed through five centuries. To promote such an understanding, which alone can be the only proper basis for conservation, restoration and sensitive design, is one of the main aims of this book.

We have sought to create within the compass of a single volume a practical sourcebook for all those who care about our heritage of domestic architecture in Britain and the United States. The vast body of illustrative material that has been drawn together here includes specially commissioned photographs of houses, reproductions of engraved plates from the key architectural publications of each period, and draw-

ings based on a wide variety of archival material, including old photographs and measured drawings (often of buildings now demolished), rare prints and builders' pattern books. The images used to illustrate each chapter have been selected by the individual authors, each of whom has made a particular study of his or her period. For each chapter the chief aim has been to show the development of standard forms but also to illustrate some of the influential high-points of architectural achievement and something of the variety that has always characterized domestic buildings.

Primarily, *The Elements of Style* is intended as a visual and documentary resource for people concerned with the details of houses, whether as owners, conservators, architects, interior decorators or designers. For the student and the interested general reader the book can also be used as way to trace the history of the British and American house. Between the practical approach and the academic there is no real division of interests: a chief desideratum in each case is sympathy for matters of detail, a belief in the importance of accuracy at the most meticulous level.

The overall plan of this book is a simple chronological one, period by period, style by style. The main chapters deal with what we may define as polite architecture: that is, buildings which aim, with whatever degree of success, at observing the architectural rules and at being fashionable, or in later periods buildings which conform to nationally prevalent types. Houses which fall outside this rather general definition – modest country dwellings, traditional structural types in use over a long period, and distinct regional variations on standard forms – are dealt with separately in chapters devoted to vernacular building. British vernacular is treated separately from the end of the Tudor period: before then the two strands have been combined, for the distinctions between vernacular and polite in that era are so blurred as to be misleading, even meaningless. Under American vernacular, the coverage is of rustic and regional features from Colonial times to the mid-19th century. Inevitably, these chapters are highly selective: given the multiplicity of localized styles, *The Element of Style* can do no more than illustrate some of the highlights of vernacular architecture.

Similarly, although Britain and the United States are treated separately in the first half of the book, the chapters on Arts and Crafts, Art Nouveau, the Twenties and Thirties, and the Modern and Beyond Modern styles combine material from both sides of the Atlantic, in order to emphasize the close connections that exist in an age of international influences. This approach has brought about some interesting juxtapositions, such as the work of Charles Rennie Mackintosh in Glasgow and the early houses of Frank Lloyd Wright.

The Elements of Style is not a book about great architects; although inevitably their names and works appear among these pages, their stories are told elsewhere, and the interested reader will have no difficulty in tracking down more information. Nor is it a study of grand houses to the exclusion of the more modest. We have chosen to place the greatest emphasis on that category which the 18th-century architect and his builder called the "good middling sort of house"; for in such houses we may discern much of the genius of each age and in full measure those qualities which the first architectural writer in English, Sir Henry Wotton, required of all fine building: "Firmness, Commodity and Delight".

Stephen Calloway

HOW TO USE THIS BOOK

The Elements of Style may be used in two ways: as a guide to styles, and as a guide to the development of individual features over the centuries. The second of these two approaches is facilitated by the colour tabs on the edges of the right-hand pages. Each tab, in its colour and position, relates to one of the thirteen features covered by the book; this makes it easy to compare the features of one period with those of earlier or later periods. For example, on every double-page spread on Windows there is a yellow tab in the second position from the top of the page; so by looking for the yellow tabs as you flip through the book you will quickly be able to compare how windows looked in different periods. Where a double-page spread deals with two features (one page for each), two colour tabs are given, one above the other. For the reader's information, all the coloured feature tabs are shown opposite, in the position in which they are used throughout the book.

Code letters after the picture captions refer to the Acknowledgments on pages 560-563.

A NOTE ON BRITISH/AMERICAN TERMINOLOGY

Throughout this book both British and American terminology have been given wherever there is a possibility of misunderstanding. The British term is given first, followed by its American equivalent after an oblique stroke, thus: tap/faucet.

The main differences between British and American architectural usage are as follows:

British:	American:
Skirting board	Baseboard
Ceiling rose	Ceiling medallion
Terraced house	Row house
Letterbox	Mailslot
Hopper head	Leader head

In Britain the "first floor" refers to the floor above the ground floor – in the United States this would be termed the second floor. To avoid complication, it has been thought preferable to refer to "the floor above the entrance level".

ARCHITECTURAL TERMS THE ANNOTATED DRAWINGS ILLUSTRATE SOME OF THE PRINCIPAL SPECIALIST TERMS.

MOULDINGS The profiles derived from the classical Orders:

torus   scotia   ovolo   echinus   cyma reversa   cyma reversa, or ogee   cyma recta   cavetto   fillet   astragal

The mouldings as used in joinery work/millwork in the 17th-19th centuries:

torus   scotia   ovolo   ovolo   quadrant bead   ogee (architrave)   bolection   fillet   astragal

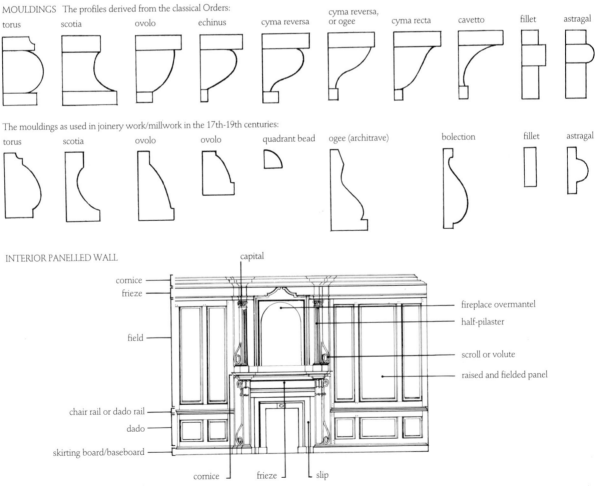

INTERIOR PANELLED WALL

capital

cornice
frieze

field

chair rail or dado rail
dado

skirting board/baseboard

fireplace overmantel
half-pilaster

scroll or volute
raised and fielded panel

cornice   frieze   slip

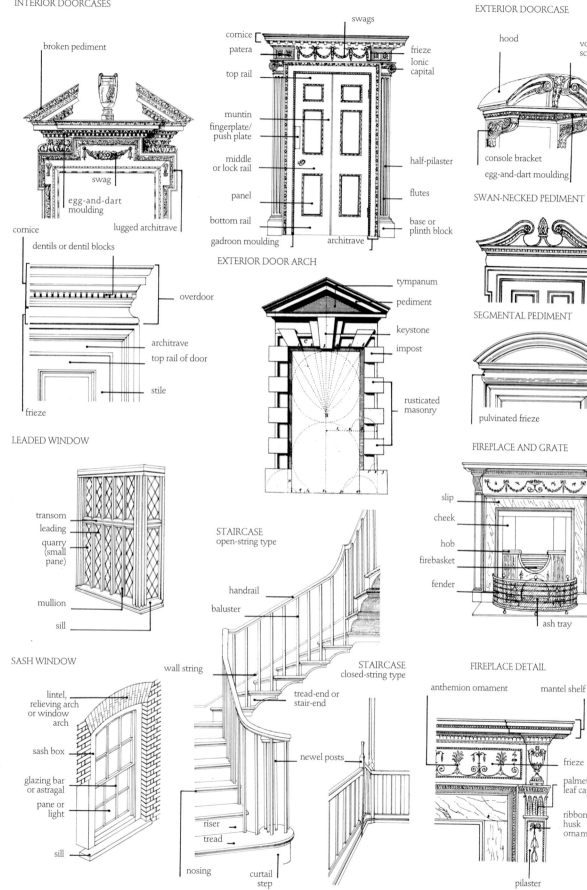

INTERIOR DOORCASES

broken pediment

swag

egg-and-dart moulding

lugged architrave

cornice

dentils or dentil blocks

overdoor

architrave

top rail of door

stile

frieze

LEADED WINDOW

transom

leading

quarry (small pane)

mullion

sill

SASH WINDOW

lintel, relieving arch or window arch

sash box

glazing bar or astragal

pane or light

sill

cornice

patera

top rail

muntin

fingerplate/ push plate

middle or lock rail

panel

bottom rail

gadroon moulding

swags

frieze

Ionic capital

half-pilaster

flutes

base or plinth block

architrave

EXTERIOR DOOR ARCH

tympanum

pediment

keystone

impost

rusticated masonry

STAIRCASE open-string type

handrail

baluster

wall string

tread-end or stair-end

newel posts

riser

tread

nosing

curtail step

STAIRCASE closed-string type

EXTERIOR DOORCASE

hood

volute or scroll

console bracket

egg-and-dart moulding

SWAN-NECKED PEDIMENT

SEGMENTAL PEDIMENT

pulvinated frieze

FIREPLACE AND GRATE

slip

cheek

hob

firebasket

fender

ash tray

FIREPLACE DETAIL

anthemion ornament

mantel shelf

frieze

palmette leaf capital

ribbon-and-husk ornament

pilaster

DOORS

WINDOWS

WALLS

CEILINGS

FLOORS

FIREPLACES

KITCHEN STOVES

STAIRCASES

BUILT-IN FURNITURE

SERVICES

LIGHTING

METALWORK

WOODWORK

TUDOR AND JACOBEAN

1485–1625

① Chastleton House in Oxfordshire, c.1602-10, is a perfect example of a large stone gentry house from the end of the period. The solid, symmetrical form of the building and the large transomed and mullioned windows are typical of better houses from the third quarter of the 16th century. The house is very little altered. C
② The ground-floor plan of Chastleton House, Oxfordshire. It is a square courtyard plan

with projecting staircase towers at either side. The entrance front has two symmetrical towers forming a porch. The plan may owe something to the work of Robert Smythson, the most important Elizabethan architect.
③ A ground-floor plan of a simple house, common in both town and country. The floor is divided into two rooms by a back-to-back fireplace which formed a central stack rising up through the house. There is a rear staircase projection.

The Tudor and Jacobean periods can be seen as a turning point in British domestic architecture. Fashionable building gradually moved away from the styles and tastes of medieval building toward more sophisticated structures with classicized decoration.

After the Wars of the Roses (1455-85), the accession of the Tudor dynasty ushered in an era of strong rule, political stability and prosperity, and a new age of building and rebuilding. It was not only the first two Tudor monarchs, Henry VII and Henry VIII, who were prolific builders, but also their subjects. The wealthy and the less wealthy rebuilt, re-modelled or extended their houses. Timber-framed buildings were reconstructed or rebuilt in stone or brick; there was a rise in both the quality and quantity of new dwellings.

The construction of more durable houses has led to a greater survival rate, and the large number of houses built has created a greater stock of examples from which to make generalizations. With the dawning of the 16th century it becomes possible for the first time to write the history of the English interior with any accuracy. This great advance is tempered by the fact that subsequently there have been four to five hundred years in which alterations can be and have been made. Important original elements such as floor and wall decorations were changed according to fashion. In an 18th or 19th century house original walls, ceilings and floors can often be found, whereas in 16th- and 17th-century houses they are far rarer. An additional complication is that some elements of the English interior scarcely change between the 17th and the 19th centuries. It is

often impossible, for example, to date ironwork accurately, as practical designs, once they had evolved, endured for hundreds of years.

Where original elements from the period survive unaltered, this is due either to their exceptional quality or to some freak of building history. Original floors are sometimes revealed in areas where new floorboards have been laid over old ones. Wall decoration can be found under later panelling, hangings or paint layers. Thus, our view of the early domestic interior is coloured by the patchy evidence which has been left to us.

Certain overall developments during the period help us to unravel the appearance of the Tudor and Jacobean interior. Houses became markedly more comfortable than their medieval forebears. The central hearth, which had been the sole means of heating a room in a medieval house, had been replaced by the wall fireplace in almost all sizes of dwelling by the end of the period. In terms of construction and interior decoration, this change was radical. The abandonment of the central hearth removed the need for single-story houses with holes in the roof; floors were introduced above the entrance level, and as ceilings were no longer obscured or damaged by smoke they could now be decorated. Perhaps more importantly, the wall fireplace became a focus for decorative treatment. From the Tudor period right through to the mid-20th century the fireplace was a dominant element in the style of a room.

Another development which was to have a major impact on the form of the interior was the increasing availability of glass. By the end of the period glass was

The Great Chamber at Chastleton House, Oxfordshire, c.1602-10. It is a very fashionable Jacobean interior: every surface is decorated. The room is dominated by an enormous stone fireplace which carries the arms of the original owner on the overmantel. The plaster ceiling is covered with strapwork designs incorporating pendants and bosses. C

not only typical in larger houses but had become common in smaller houses too. This affected the size, number and design of windows. Moreover, bigger windows and those without shutters admitted more light and provided the incentive for carved or painted decoration inside the room.

A more fundamental development was the increasing specialization of room functions within a house. In the Middle Ages even the King would live in one big room, where he would eat, sleep and conduct affairs of state. From the beginning of the 16th century, first the royal palaces, then courtier houses and finally gentry houses developed a series of specialized rooms. Separate withdrawing rooms, dining rooms, parlours, bedrooms, closets and even libraries and studies became commonplace. Each of these rooms had its own functional requirements and sometimes a code of decoration. Fabric hangings, for example, were considered inappropriate for rooms in which people ate, as they tended to retain the smell of food: plaster was thought to be more suitable.

A further factor which affected the style of the interior was regional variation. Building materials are on the whole heavy and bulky items which were expensive to transport in an era before the creation of an efficient road or rail network. Thus the style and form of houses varied widely accross the country. The three principal building materials were timber, brick and stone. All-timber buildings were found only in areas without supplies of local stone or brick-earth, such as the West Midlands. Stone was almost universal in the great limestone belt which stretches across England from Bath to

Lincoln and it was the standard building material throughout Scotland and Wales. The Thames valley and East Anglia produced suitable brick-earth. Different building materials were reflected in different architectural effects. Although some forms, especially window and door styles, could be reproduced in brick, stone or timber, other elements of decoration were greatly affected by the material in which they were executed. Stone houses, for example, tended to have less decoration than timber ones, as stone was more difficult and expensive to carve. Areas of good building stone such as the Cotswolds or Northamptonshire tend to have houses with more sober decoration than, for example, the highly decorated timber-framed houses of Lancashire or Cheshire. Brick was increasingly used in areas without good stone. It varied as much as stone in quality and colour: much depended on the nature of the clay from which it was made and on the manufacturer. Brick had its own limitations and advantages: it could be carved (rubbed) but more often the individual bricks were laid in patterns, which took local forms.

Another variable in terms of style was the location of the building, whether in a town or in the countryside. Rapid increases in population made for a period of urban expansion – so rapid that in 1580 a royal proclamation forbade new building within three miles of the gates of the city of London. The early Stuarts, James I and Charles I, placed further restrictions on building in London. This meant that houses built in the centre of the capital (and other towns followed suit) were generally tall and narrow and had external decoration, such

① A timber-framed town house. It is well built and has fairly large windows: indications of a comfortable but not an extraordinary house. (The frames contain 20th-century metal windows.) LV

② A late 15th-century merchant's house with a jettied upper floor, a fashionable feature of town houses at this date. LV

③ Paycocke's in Coggeshall, Essex, is an elaborately fenestrated late 15th-century

house, with mullioned oriel windows on the upper story. P

④ Two 15th-century timber framed houses. The door and window frames form an integral part of the structure. LV

as carved timbers and pargeting, concentrated on their cramped facades. In the countryside, where land was less expensive, buildings could sprawl outward and facade decoration could afford to be looser.

Through most of the period the principal foreign influences were from the Low Countries and Germany, but as the 16th century wore on the influence of Italy began to make itself felt, rarely directly from the Italian peninsula but more often through the medium of northern European countries. This process led to the gradual adoption of classical motifs and the classical Orders –

that is, the systems of ornament, derived from ancient Greece and Rome, based on the Doric, Ionic, Corinthian, Tuscan and Composite styles of columns and entablatures. The desire of clients for these novelties was probably less strong than the enthusiasm of the craftsmen who sold the designs. From c.1560 a stream of books and engravings began to come to England from Antwerp, widening the craftsmen's decorative vocabulary. When the Duke of Alva began to persecute Protestants in the Netherlands in the late 1560s, the flow of printed matter was augmented by the craftsmen and artists

① *Three brick chimneys of the early 16th century. Chimneys were often grouped together on a single base with joined heads. These examples with octagonal shafts have fairly plain heads although many were more decorative, with rubbed brickwork.* DM

② *The main entrance to Chastleton House, Oxfordshire, shows a typical applied doorcase of the early 17th century. The shallow stone staircase with ball finials is also representative.* C

③ *External decorative effects were achieved in a number of ways. This house in Puddletown, Dorset, late 15th century, has alternating bands of knapped flints and stone blocks which form a black and white striped pattern.* SP

④ *A detail of a carved bressumer (a massive, structural beam) on the leading edge of a jetty, late 15th century. The lively carving runs the width of the building and demonstrates the effective use of concentrated decoration.* P

⑤ *The gable ends of many houses, whether timber-framed or not, were decorated by carved timber fascias called bargeboards. The one shown here dates from c.1621 and is decorated with a diamond (or diaper) pattern.* DM

themselves who fled to England to escape the dangers.

One of the most important decorative imports from Antwerp in this period was strapwork, a dominant form of interior decoration on ceilings, fireplaces and woodwork. Many of the newest decorative fashions, including strapwork, were first adopted at Court or in court circles, but the speed at which ideas diffused down the social scale was remarkable. This inevitably led to the misunderstanding of decorative motifs by lesser craftsmen.

The imagination of local craftsmen played a central part in the style of domestic buildings. Certain features were universal – the shapes of door and window heads, the overall configuration of a fireplace, the creeping influence of the Italian Renaissance – but the final product was infinitely varied. With the additional complication of regional variations in materials, the period 1485-1625 seems to be one of considerable stylistic freedom. This is especially apparent when the period is compared with the age of Baroque, which saw the introduction of the rules of classical architecture, as well as the beginnings of mass production.

Doors

An early 16th-century doorway with a four-centred head and carved spandrels. Windows were inserted above the door head at a later date, replacing the original plaster nogging (infill). Note the foliate decoration in the spandrels. LV

The dimensions and position of a doorway were dictated by the practical requirements of access and construction. Whether of wood, stone or brick, Tudor door heads tended to be flat or four-centred (that is, in the form of a shallow arch that rises to a central point). Four-centred heads sometimes had carved spandrels. The jambs often had stopped, chamfered mouldings, to protect and decorate the frame. Hoodmoulds or projecting cornices are common over front doors and, during the 16th century, porches became popular.

Internal doorways, protected from the weather, are often more elaborate than external doorways. Their decorative development is similar to that of the fire-place. Classical details such as pillars and cornices appeared c.1550, but the late medieval style remained dominant throughout the period.

External doors were made from planks up to 26 inches (65cm) wide and were usually oak. The planks were either fastened by horizontal battens on the reverse or by a second set of planks, laid at right angles to the first (a double-boarded or cross-boarded door). The heads of nails were sometimes left exposed to give a decorative finish. Ordinary internal doors were usually battened. Grander doors were often lighter, comprising a framework with an infill of wooden panels. Door fittings were basic, except in the grandest houses.

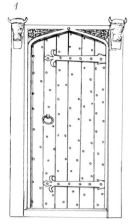
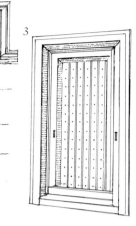

All the doors and details shown on this page, except ⑧, are exterior.
① The front door to a merchant's house in Stratford-upon-Avon, dated 1596. The timber surround has a four-centred arch and a typical leaf pattern carved into the spandrels.
② This grand stone doorway, c.1530, has richly moulded jambs that sit on a block plinth, a moulded hood and spandrels carved with an ornate foliate design. Such a surround could contain a door or provide the entrance to a porch.
③ An early 17th-century square-headed stone doorway with chamfered lintel and jambs.
④ Brick was a versatile building material and it was often given an ornamental treatment. Mid-16th century.

⑤ A four-centred timber doorhead, with Gothic quatrefoils and tracery. Early 16th century.
⑥ Early 16th-century stone doorhead with a hoodmould.
⑦ Only the grandest houses had terracotta ornament. This group – doorhead, hoodmould and overdoor frieze with hoodmould – is made from light and dark terracotta. It was constructed c.1525 for Sutton Place in Guildford, Surrey.
⑧ A common form of late 16th- and early 17th-century doorhead has a pediment and obelisks. This example is from York. The use of such motifs, in a restrained composition, reflects the growing influence of classical forms.

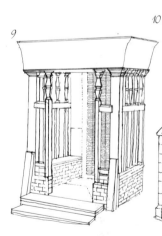

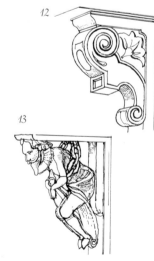

⑨ A single-story timber porch, typical from the late 16th century on. The inside supports are turned, like contemporary balusters.
⑩ and ⑪ Two-story porches from the early 16th century. The first is a stone porch with hoodmoulds over door and window. The buttressed form looks back to medieval models. The second is an elongated, crenellated brick porch, common during most of the period.
⑫ and ⑬ Projecting doorhoods were often supported on corbels. These examples are from the late 16th/early 17th century. The top one is a classical design; the bottom one is a vernacular exercise in craftsmanship.

① *A highly elaborate 15th-century door and doorcase from Lavenham, Suffolk. The door contains a wicket (a small, secondary door) with an ogee arch. By contrast, the main doorhead is four-centred with decorated spandrels.* LV

② *This door has ribbed surface decoration in the form of blank arcading, covering the gaps between the planks of wood from which the door is constructed.* LV

③ *A stone door surround with four-centred head and stop-moulded jambs. The surround dates from the early years of the 17th century. The door is later.* C

④ *The rows of nails on this door indicate that its back has five battens securing the vertical planks. An alternative method for securing the outer boards was to have a second set of planks nailed the full width of the door at right-angles to the first.* LV

⑤ *A detail of a mid-16th-century internal door. The spandrels are of an unusual, asymmetrical design. This kind of imaginative approach resulted from the free hand most carvers were given by their clients.* SU

⑥ *A typical spring latch from an internal door of a grand house. It dates from the first years of the 17th century.* C

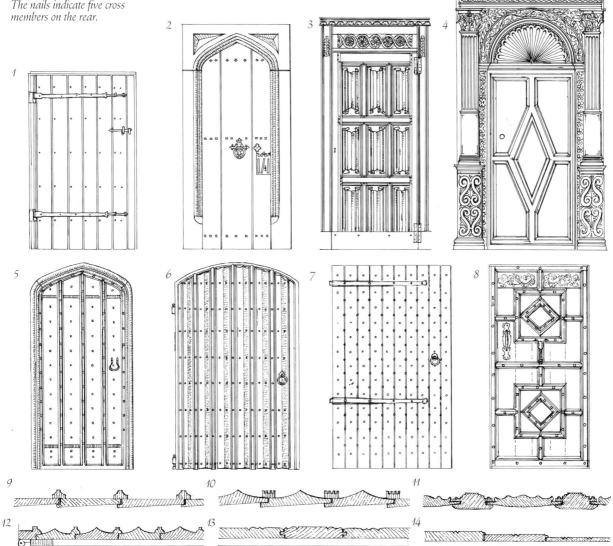

① *A boarded internal door, typical throughout the period. The nails indicate five cross members on the rear.*

② *An early 16th-century internal door in a stone surround.*

③ Some internal doors from the early to mid-16th century had linenfold panelling.
④ This late 16th-century doorway combines classical elements with traditional details.
⑤ to ⑧ Door panelling. All but the last are cross-boarded.
⑤ and ⑥ Large external doors with ribbed and moulded faces were common to better houses in the 16th century.
⑦ A simple front door, enlivened by staggered nails.
⑧ An external door from a Jacobean town house in York. The panelling is formed by applied battens.
⑨ to ⑭ Sections of door panelling. Profile ⑨ is the section of the fifth door above, ⑩ the section of the sixth door and ⑪ the section of the third door. These and profile ⑫ show elaborate schemes; ⑬ and ⑭ are typical of vernacular and service doors.
⑮ Strap hinges were secured either by a pintle (a hook) sunk into the door jamb, or, on lighter doors, by a pivot and a plate which was nailed into the jamb.
⑯ A wooden latch, lock and bolt, 17th century. The latch was operated externally by a piece of string.
⑰ An iron latch, very common throughout the period and well into the 19th century.
⑱ Wrought-iron or brass box locks were luxury items. Early 16th century.
⑲ to ㉑ Typical handles. The first is the most common form; the last is from an internal door.

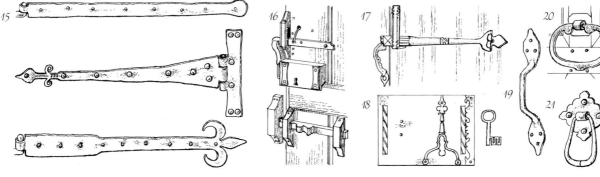

Windows

① *A wooden oriel window with narrow mullions from Lavenham, Suffolk. It is directly beneath the eaves of a timber-framed house that dates from the early 16th century. The glazing, consisting of rectangular panes, is a later modification; the original window would have had diamond-shaped panes. LV*
② *A typical timber-framed town house from the early 16th century, with three groups of mullioned and transomed windows. The lower part of the wall would originally have been wood, but it has rotted away over time and been replaced with more durable brick.*

The simplest windows in this period comprise unglazed square openings, divided by a series of wooden or stone mullions (vertical posts). Most had internal shutters. The mullioned window was standard in the early part of the period; by the late 16th century mullioned and transomed windows were more common: that is, windows with upright posts and horizontal bars. This rule applies across the whole spectrum of building. However, window heads underwent changes during the period. Grand houses from the beginning of the century had foiled tracery window heads but for much of the 16th century the four-centred arch was standard for all but the poorest houses. By the end of the century square heads were the norm. Stone or brick hoodmoulds were common throughout the period.

The grandest buildings always had glazed windows, but glazing only became standard in larger farmhouses and town houses from the late 16th century onward. Smaller houses had to wait until the late 17th century. Glass was generally very thin and rather grey and was cut from blown disks (crown glass). During the 16th century the individual panes (quarries) were arranged diagonally; during the 17th century larger panes were made and arranged in rectangles. If windows opened, and not all did, it was by means of iron or wooden casements, hinged to the masonry mullions.

① A simple wooden window frame with a single mullion and two iron standards. These were common to small houses and quite large farmhouses alike.
② An early 16th-century timber frame with deeply moulded mullion and jambs.
③ A wooden bay window with deeply cut mouldings on the transom and mullions, c.1530.
④ A detail of an eight-light stone window of the early 16th century with four-centred arches.

⑤ A typical late 16th-/early 17th-century stone window. The stone dressing echoes the decoration on the edges of the porch where the window is located.
⑥ A six-light window in terracotta from Sutton Place, Guildford, Surrey, c.1525. Both sets of lights have trefoiled heads, slightly old-fashioned at this time. Note the hoodmould.
⑦ A two-light window from the middle of the 16th century: effects originally cut in stone could be reproduced in brick.
⑧ A brick oriel window of the late 16th century, constructed from cut and moulded bricks.

⑨ to ⑪ Plan sections.
⑨ A simple wooden window. The standards and the glass are indicated.
⑩ A stone bay window, showing the different thicknesses and mouldings of the mullions.
⑪ A timber bay window, similar to ③, with structural corner posts and thinner glazing mullions.

⑫ These window details show mullion profiles, grooves for the glazing and the small panes of glass. The glass is set into the glazing slots in lead. Most mullions are symmetrical (as in the first example) but some are flat on the external surface and angled on the inside of the window. Wood allowed for more complicated mouldings than stone; stone mullions tend to be more angular in less fashionable districts. The first two details are wood, the last is stone.

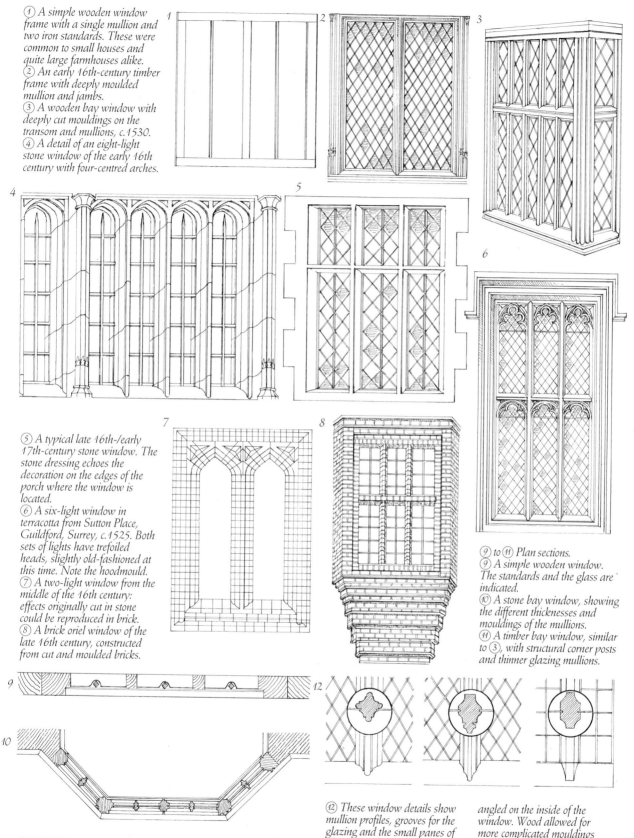

① *A much-restored transomed and mullioned window of the early 16th century. The window is supported by wooden brackets to form an oriel.* P

② *The simplest vernacular windows in timber-framed buildings were framed by the structural members of the house and divided into lights by mullions. In poorer houses there was originally no glass.* LV

③ *In a timber-framed house with herringbone brick nogging (infill), the window is framed by the structural timbers, divided by thin mullions and glazed with diagonal panes.* LV

④ *A projecting oriel window in which the outside mullions and the transom are structural members. The glazing is of a later date than the late 15th-century timberwork.* LV

⑤ *A detail of an iron casement, hinged on pintles that are sunk into a stone frame. An iron runner with a decorative stop prevents the window from swinging open too far.* C

⑥ *A grand mullioned and transomed stone window with a rectangular glazing pattern. It dates from the first part of the 17th century.* C

1

2

① A pair of iron casements set in a stone surround, 17th century. The casements swing out and are held by the fixed restraints. Note the decorative curling hinges.
② A wrought-iron casement showing the catch, handle, pintle hinges, elaborate glazing pattern and a ventilation quarry.
③ Examples of pierced lead ventilation quarries. Some bear the initals of the original owner.
④ to ⑥ Various Tudor wrought-iron casement fixtures.
④ Iron stays were often included to hold the window open. These could be fixed to the window and hooked into the wall, or vice versa.

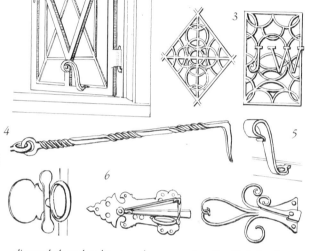

3

4

5

6

⑤ A simple handle.
⑥ Casement catches could twist, have a spring mechanism or function as a simple latch.

⑦ There was a great variety of glazing patterns, particularly in grander houses. In the 16th century panes were usually diamond-shaped and measured little more than 5½ x 3 inches (14 x 8cm). During the 17th century larger panes were made, up to about 8 x 5½ inches (20 x 14cm) and rectangles became more usual. Top, late 16th-century; bottom, 17th-century.

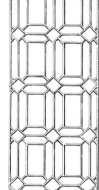

7

8

9

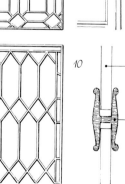

10

Glass

Lead

Window lights were filled with small panes of glass which were held together by cames (grooved bars of lead). These were wired to iron standards (vertical rods) and staybars (horizontal rods) which were set, at intervals, into the window surround.
⑧ A detail of a window head showing a locket (a staybar with a loop to hold the standard). The glass would be wired to the ironwork.
⑨ Part of a window showing the staybars and standards. Note the trefoil heads, a popular late medieval motif, used in grander buildings.
⑩ A diagrammatic section through a came, showing the glass in situ.

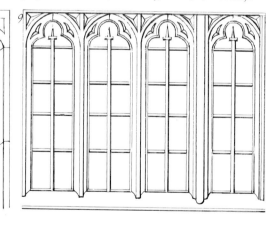

Walls

A highly decorated interior from Chastleton House, Oxfordshire, c.1602-10, showing excellent panelling. The field is divided by pilasters, a fashionable detail in Jacobean houses. C

The most common interior wall surface in this period was flat plasterwork, laid on brick, stone or a skeleton of oak or chestnut laths, and painted with limewash (whitewash).

In more elaborate buildings timber panelling was applied to a brick or stone wall as a decorative cladding or to stud work (the timber framework of a house) to form a wall in itself. When applied to existing walls the panelling could be full height or to frieze or dado level. Dado panelling was usually surmounted by wall hangings (tapestry or painted cloth), or occasionally painted decoration in imitation of fabrics or panelling. Wallpaper was rare in this period. Frieze-height panelling (wainscot) was sometimes surmounted by a painted or plaster frieze.

Panelling comprises thin boards let into grooves in solid timber uprights and cross members. The boards were generally of oak, measuring no more than 24 inches (60cm) square and split as thin as possible. Carved decoration was popular; early in the 16th century a linenfold pattern (derived from wall hangings) was fashionable. Later on, arabesques, strapwork and foliate forms were used, as well as busts in roundels. Geometric shapes were often formed using applied battens. In grander houses a design of panelling might encompass the fireplace and door surrounds.

① *An elevation and section of an early 17th-century wall showing good-quality wainscotting with a plaster frieze.*
② *Typical 16th- or early 17th-century panelling. The framing is jointed and pegged.*
③ *Linenfold panelling, the most fashionable form of carved* decoration early in the period.
④ *Larger panels with applied geometric shapes were popular in the early 17th century.*
⑤ *Crudely carved panels such as these were widespread during the later 16th century.*

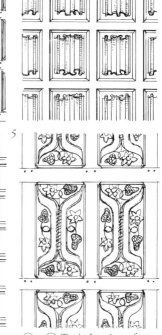

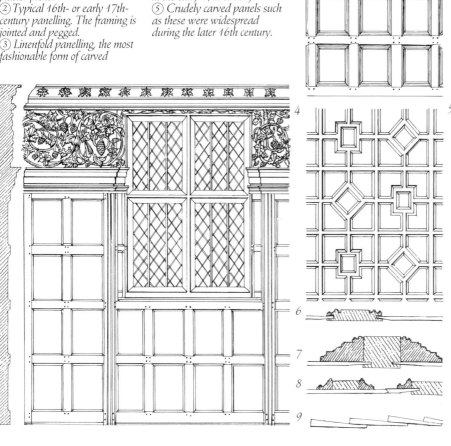

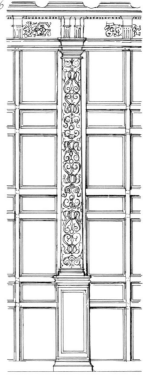

⑥ *to* ⑨ *Typical sections of panelling;* ⑥ *is a section of the first wall (left),* ⑦ *of the second wall and* ⑧ *of the fourth wall. The last shows clapboarding, where tapering boards are used with the overlapping face or the smooth face exposed.*
⑩ *Two methods of attaching panels into a framework. The first shows a mason's mitre, where cross-panels are chamfered.*

⑪ *and* ⑫ *Carved timber friezes. The group with arms and initials is from Haddon Hall, Derbyshire. The simpler example is from a Suffolk town house.*
⑬ *Part of a grand early 17th-century plaster frieze from York.*
⑭ *Framed plaster motifs are typical of simple ornament.*
⑮ *A high-quality plaster frieze with strapwork and arabesques, popular Jacobean motifs.*
⑯ *This fashionable Jacobean panelling is divided into bays by pilasters; the carved foliate decoration on this one is typical.*

① This wall would probably have been covered with a fabric hanging. The addition of a picture was a much later development in merchants' houses such as this. P

② Panelling was often re-used and rearranged. This wall, made up of well executed linenfold panelling, shows signs of alteration to the right of the door. P

③ Linenfold panelling, carved in imitation of fabric wall hangings, was a highly popular wall treatment throughout the 16th century. P

④ A detail of an early 16th-century carved beam. Wood was the most versatile material for internal decoration: it was less expensive and easier to carve than brick or stone. P

⑤ This plaster wall from the late 16th century has been painted to resemble textile wall hangings. It gives a clear idea of the elaborate effects that were achieved in paint. TY

⑥ Strapwork was an infinitely flexible motif which could be translated into a variety of media. Here, painted decoration of c.1630 adorns a stairwell. A trompe l'oeil painted pendant can be seen, top right. SU

⑦ A painted wall in the Governor's House, Newark-on-Trent, Nottinghamshire, from the mid-16th century. The decoration, resembling a hanging, enlivens a stud partition. TY

Ceilings

① This ceiling, c.1500, from Paycocke's, Coggeshall, shows the decorative effect achieved by moulding the underside of the main floor joists of the story above. P
② A detail of the mouldings on the main beams and the elegant foliate stops. P

In the 15th century the ceiling was simply the underside of the floor above; this continued to be the case in humble houses for much of the period. In this case the structural floor members were sometimes decorated. However, in the early 16th century the underside of the floor joists in better houses began to be covered with boarding or laths which were plastered. These suspended flat ceilings could be left plain or sometimes were carved or decorated with plaster mouldings. Even quite poor houses had some kind of ceiling ornament, often in the form of chamfered and stopped mouldings on the joists.

On decorated ceilings the main beams, which are the principal structural elements, divide the ceiling into compartments which can be left plain, be painted, or filled with carved timber or plaster ribs. Early compartmented (coffered) ceilings are grid-like, but those from the later 16th century have a more fluid form and often contain organic motifs or strapwork. At the points where ribs or straps intersect moulded bosses or, in grander houses, pendants are sometimes fixed. Plaster mouldings were at first worked in situ but later the more elaborate patterns were made in wooden or wax moulds and then fixed in place.

Ceilings were not always flat: those on the upper floors of large houses were often coved or hipped.

① to ④ *Typical sections through timber-framed roofs. Many variations on these standard forms can be found.*

① *A simple arch-braced roof.*
② *A king post roof, where the structure is supported by a single post from the tie-beam and does*

not have a collar beam.
③ *A crown post roof is supported by a collar-beam carried on a single post from the*

tie-beam.
④ *A queen post roof, where the collar-beam is supported by two posts from the tie-beam.*

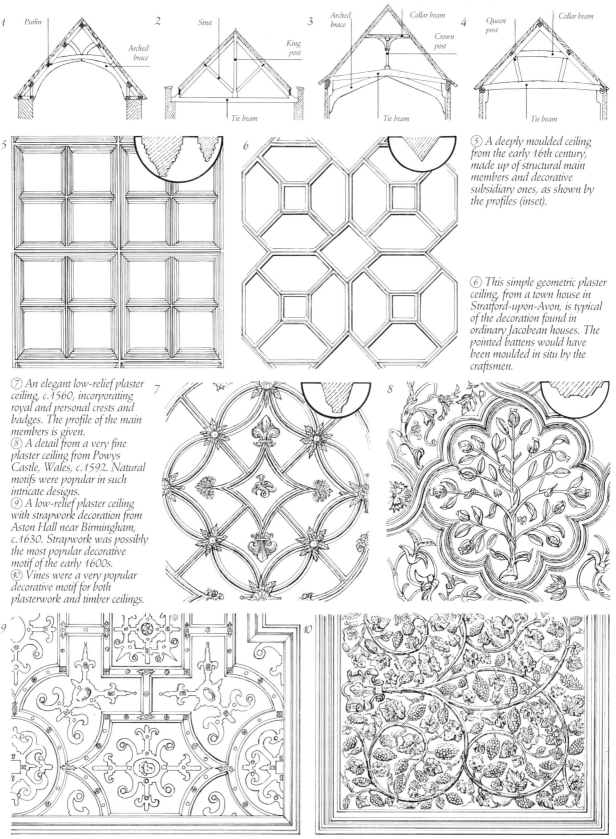

⑤ *A deeply moulded ceiling from the early 16th century, made up of structural main members and decorative subsidiary ones, as shown by the profiles (inset).*

⑥ *This simple geometric plaster ceiling, from a town house in Stratford-upon-Avon, is typical of the decoration found in ordinary Jacobean houses. The pointed battens would have been moulded in situ by the craftsmen.*

⑦ *An elegant low-relief plaster ceiling, c.1560, incorporating royal and personal crests and badges. The profile of the main members is given.*

⑧ *A detail from a very fine plaster ceiling from Powys Castle, Wales, c.1592. Natural motifs were popular in such intricate designs.*

⑨ *A low-relief plaster ceiling with strapwork decoration from Aston Hall near Birmingham, c.1630. Strapwork was possibly the most popular decorative motif of the early 1600s.*

⑩ *Vines were a very popular decorative motif for both plasterwork and timber ceilings.*

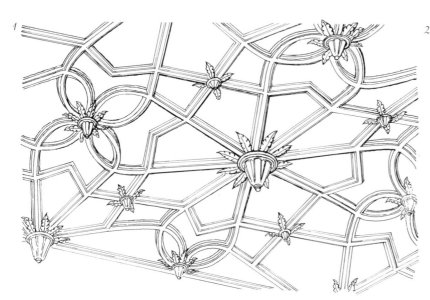

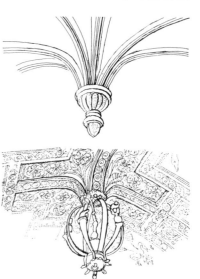

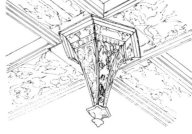

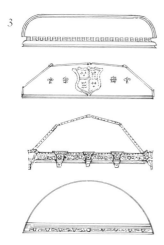

① A late 16th-century plaster ceiling with bosses and pendants at the intersections of the ribs.

② Ceiling pendants, common in grand houses from the 1530s, became increasingly popular in manor houses and large town houses. Plaster pendants usually had wooden frames. Most were solid, although fretted designs were desirable.

③ Common profiles of more elaborate suspended ceilings. The first is the earliest and dates from c.1537. The next two date from the 1570s and reflect more closely the shape of the roof structure above. The last shows a barrel ceiling, popular throughout the period where roof space allowed.

④ An early 17th-century ceiling showing some of the most important decorative elements of the period 1560-1610: strapwork, vine trails, pendants and organic motifs. C

⑤ This carved oak cornice comes from the base of a coved ceiling, early 16th-century. (The profile directly above shows the position of such cornices.) The twisting, interwoven motifs are typical of late medieval decoration.

⑥ A ceiling beam from a mid-16th-century house in Lavenham, Suffolk. Such vigorous designs are typical of merchants' houses.

⑦ The simplest ceilings were made from the decorated undersides of the floor joists of the room above. P

Floors

1

2

① *Flagstones were common in all classes of house throughout the British Isles during the Tudor and Jacobean period, and long after. The passageway floor shown here is from a house in Devon.* PS

② *This original rush matting is from Hampton Court Palace, Surrey. It survived for 300 years under floorboards. Matting was used in all levels of house, from the humblest cottage to the grandest palace.* TY

The simplest ground-level floors were beaten earth; better ones were brick, laid on edge, or tile; the best were flagged in stone. Brick floors were common, but as brick is a soft material most brick floors found today are later replacements. In grand houses brick was normally restricted to service areas. Tiles can be boldly patterned, glazed or left plain; the colours and sizes vary from region to region. Stone slabs were the most favoured ground level flooring; once they had become worn they were turned over and re-used before being replaced. Local stone was usually laid; types commonly found today include York stone, granite, slate, many sandstones and even marble. Cobblestones can be found in rural houses where animals were kept inside.

Upper stories have wooden floors, mostly of oak, although elm is found. Boards are much wider than modern planks: 24 inches (60cm) is not unusual.

Many floors were plastered, particularly in northern England. The mix usually contained a high proportion of straw for greater strength. In grand houses the floors could be painted but most were covered in rush matting. Matting was a universal floor covering. It was sometimes laid when the plaster was damp so that it fused into the floor or it was laid in loose strips on the dry surface. Lengths were often stitched together and nailed down at the edges. Carpets were a luxury.

Fireplaces

An early 16th-century stone fireplace with a four-centred arch and carved and painted spandrels. Note the brick relieving arch, revealed by the removal of the wall panelling. This took some of the weight of the brick chimney stack, which allowed the fireplace lintel to be wider. SU

At the beginning of the period the central hearth was common, but during the 16th century the wall fireplace came into the ascendant. The re-location of the fireplace made it the focus of architectural interest.

The simplest fireplaces were brick or stone stacks built against an outside wall or placed on one of the central, internal walls. In the latter case a number of fireplaces could share the same flue (back-to-back and on different floors). Such fireplaces had timber or stone lintels which could be plain, chamfered, moulded or carved.

In grander houses, the fireplace opening could be conceived as one timber, brick or stone structure. Those from the early 16th century were usually spanned by a four-centred arch with chamfered or moulded decoration. A frieze often surmounted the lintel. From the 1540s fashionable fireplaces had Renaissance details, such as classical Orders on the jambs. Overmantels had niches, coats of arms, decorative panels or strapwork.

Hearths were of stone or brick; those of brick were regularly re-laid. The back wall was often finished with thin bricks or tiles, on edge, or was protected by a wrought-iron fireback. The simplest hearths had small brick walls which supported the burning logs, but most had iron andirons (fire dogs). During the 16th century wood became more expensive and increasingly coal was burned in firebaskets.

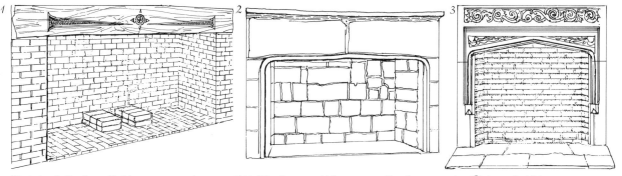

① A simple fireplace of brick with a carved oak lintel, a type common throughout the period.
② A simple stone fireplace from

a townhouse, c.1600. The deep lintel is typical.
③ A more sophisticated stone fireplace from the first half of the

16th century, with a four-centred arch, stop-chamfered jambs and a foliated overmantel. The hearth projects into the room.

④ An early 16th-century stone surround with a four-centred arch, embellished spandrels and quatrefoils on the lintel. Spandrels often contained badges or mottoes.
⑤ A four-centred surround from the 1590s with geometric painted decoration.
⑥ Dating from the early years of the 17th century, this marble example combines a Corinthian column with incised foliage and strapwork decoration.

⑦ Thin bricks or tiles, laid on edge, were often inserted into the back of a fireplace. The tiles in this example form a herringbone pattern.
⑧ The back walls of hearths were often protected by an iron fireback. This example is from Cowdray House, Sussex, early 16th century.

⑨ Local building materials were used to line the fireplace. Stone was used where it was readily available, although it was not very durable against great heat.

Iron firebacks reflect the work of local craftsmen and, at a grand level, the status and allegiances of the owner.
⑩ A simple Sussex fireback, decorated with a cable twist.
⑪ A detail of a rectangular fireback, 16th century. The birds

could be a pun on the name Fowles, a family of ironmasters.
⑫ The date of manufacture,

the initials of the owner and a crest are typical of better firebacks.

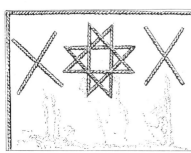

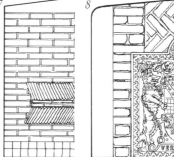

① An unusual combination of rubbed-brick jambs and a carved wooden lintel makes up this early 16th-century fireplace. P
② A detail of a carved fireplace spandrel. A shield is coupled with a running vine motif with bunches of grapes. SU
③ Heraldic badges and shields, which today appear blank, were often brightly gilded and painted, as in this detail from an early 16th-century fireplace. SU
④ A surround flanked by half-columns with an overmantel comprising a decorative panel similarly flanked is a typical arrangement of the late 16th/ early 17th centuries. C
⑤ The lower part of this chimneypiece is 18th-century but the wooden overmantel with an armorial and figures is typical of the late 16th century. C

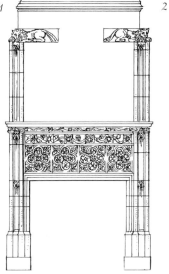

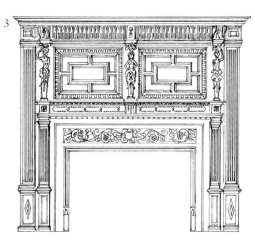

① A very grand pre-Reformation fireplace, with typical late medieval motifs. The broken form of the overmantel shows that it has been altered.

② The four-centred arched surround of this chimneypiece, c.1600, is conservative while the overmantel with its strapwork and pilasters is very fashionable.

③ Columns, half-columns and pilasters feature in grand Elizabethan and Jacobean chimneypieces. The overmantel continues the cornice from the wall. Wood, early 17th century.

④ This fashionable wooden chimneypiece from Bromley-by-Bow Palace, London, c.1603, has decorative pilasters on the jambs and half-columns and niches on the overmantel.
⑤ A grand stone chimneypiece with caryatids, strapwork and

allegorical scenes in relief. Built for a member of the court circle in Greenwich, London, c.1607-12.
⑥ A stone and oak chimneypiece from a London townhouse, c.1620.
⑦ All firebaskets were wrought-iron. This example, late 16th

century, has receptacles for jugs of wine.
⑧ This is a spear-headed firebasket from Haddon Hall, Derbyshire, early 16th century.
⑨ A cast-iron andiron, 30 inches (75cm) high, c.1610, with a female bust on a pedestal.

⑩ Hooks on andirons held cross-bars which retained the logs.
⑪ An andiron with a stand for a jug of wine. Late 16th century.

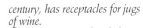

Staircases

This is the principal staircase at Chastleton House, Oxfordshire, 1602. It is of the framed type (without a central newel). The newel posts and pendants are of a common obelisk-like form. C

The most common form of staircase during this period was the straight flight. In small houses it was squeezed into a narrow space and was often hidden behind a partition. The dog-leg stair is a variation, comprising two adjacent flights with balustrades on the same vertical plane. In better houses the staircase was an object of status; it was often placed to the side of the central hall, with elaborate, weighty decoration. Many houses, including quite grand ones, had external staircases and galleries.

Spiral staircases (vice stairs) can be found in better houses early in the period. These developed massive square central newels of brick or stone, which by the mid-16th century had evolved into the framed newel stair.

Here, the solid central newel is replaced by a timber-framed tower surrounded by a stone or brick stairwell.

Most Elizabethan balusters are turned to resemble columns or they are waisted. Some carved or pierced flat balusters are found from the middle of the 16th century, but they are more typical of Jacobean staircases. They are curvaceous or tapering shapes, mostly based on strapwork. All stairs are closed-string: that is, the balusters are set on a diagonal brace rather than on the stairs themselves. A wide variety of mouldings was adopted for the handrail. The *pièce de résistance* was the newel post, which could be elaborately turned and carved in even quite humble houses.

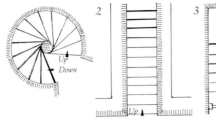
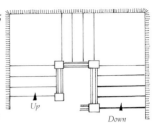

① *The spiral staircase was in use throughout the period, in timber, stone or brick.*
② *The straight flight is the simplest and most common form*

of staircase in this period.
③ *The dog-leg stair is found in modest houses throughout the period.*
④ *A central solid square newel*

became a common staircase form in larger houses of the mid- and late 16th century. The newel rises from the bottom of the building to the top.

⑤ *The framed newel staircase offered the greatest opportunity for display. It first appeared in larger houses in the middle of the 16th century.*

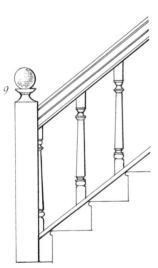
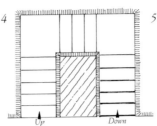
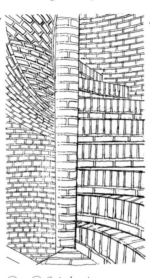
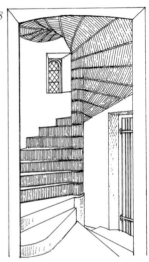

⑥ *to* ⑧ *Spiral staircases were sometimes contained in the thickness of the wall of grand houses. The finest are brick but most are stone or timber. Either*

the steps are integral to a central newel, building it up, as in the detail of a stone staircase, left (c.1620), or they are keyed into a solid newel. PS

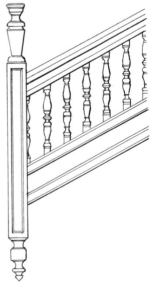

⑨ *This staircase from Warwick has a simple newel post with plain turned balusters that resemble columns. It is typical of ordinary houses, of*

the mid-16th century.
⑩ *A Somerset staircase, c.1560, with more elaborate turned and carved members. The balusters are held between*

the handrail and a diagonal strip, the closed-string type.
⑪ *The obelisk was a popular form for newel posts in the early 17th century, as seen on this*

elaborate staircase, c.1620.
⑫ *This upper story flight from Northamptonshire, c.1580, has a pendant hanging from the newel.*

① A staircase with a turned newel post and carved pilaster balusters. Late 16th century.
② Part of a very elaborate framed newel staircase with sloping pilaster balusters and strapwork embellishments, early

17th century.
③ In this 17th-century example from Shropshire, openwork strapwork is placed below the handrail instead of balusters. Such designs were very popular during the Baroque period.

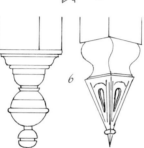

④ A profile of an inset, rubbed brick (carved out) handrail from a spiral staircase, early 16th century.
⑤ Wooden handrails from the late 16th century onward are chamfered or, as in these examples, moulded.
⑥ Newel posts on upper stories often had pendants. Pendant

and finial designs are interchangeable: most are simple, turned shapes. Pierced obelisk forms are Jacobean.
⑦ A wooden newel staircase from Totnes, Devon, constructed at the end of the period. The treads are equally supported by the central newel and the timber framing of the internal wall. PS
⑧ Dog gates prevented hounds from going upstairs. This example shows the original hinges and catch, c.1620.
⑨ A turned oak newel post, typical from the late 16th century onward.

⑩ Square-section newel posts. The first, early 17th-century example has a pyramidal finial with a vase and foliage. The second has Ionic details on the finial. The last newel, c.1564-8, is topped with the patron's crest. Note the strapwork.

Built-in furniture

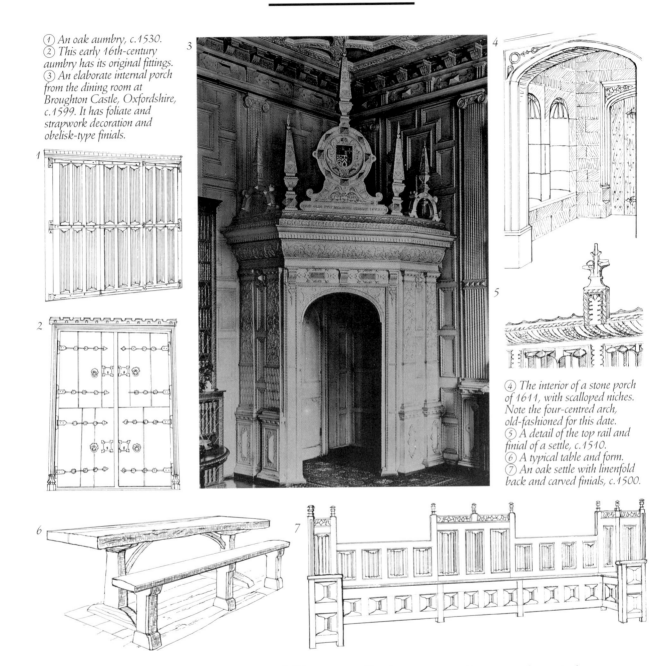

① An oak aumbry, c.1530.
② This early 16th-century aumbry has its original fittings.
③ An elaborate internal porch from the dining room at Broughton Castle, Oxfordshire, c.1599. It has foliate and strapwork decoration and obelisk-type finials.

④ The interior of a stone porch of 1611, with scalloped niches. Note the four-centred arch, old-fashioned for this date.
⑤ A detail of the top rail and finial of a settle, c.1510.
⑥ A typical table and form.
⑦ An oak settle with linenfold back and carved finials, c.1500.

Built-in furniture was a significant feature of all houses during the early 16th century and continued to be so in poorer houses throughout the period. Much furniture built *in situ* was for storage, especially the safe keeping of clothes, silver and archives. The most common form is the wall aumbry which was created by attaching a frame and doors to a wall recess. The recess might be in a masonry wall or worked into a wooden partition. Aumbries can be very elaborate or, in small cottages, merely small cupboards for the storage of spices or candles. In smaller houses they were often located close to the fireplace to keep the contents dry. Sometimes kitchens were provided with similar cupboards or top-lifting bins which protected food from rodents.

Fixed seats were often created in window recesses, porches or even within great fireplaces. These might be of wood but more often were part of the masonry construction of the house. Settles (high-backed wooden benches often with arms) could be built into walls and were common to all grades of houses. The seat of the bench was sometimes hinged and doubled as a storage chest. Trestle tables and benches were sometimes built into the floor in kitchens and halls and were usually plain.

Internal porches appear in some (but not the poorest) late 16th- and 17th-century houses. They served as insulators and were usually attached to external doors, although some large rooms also had an internal porch.

Services

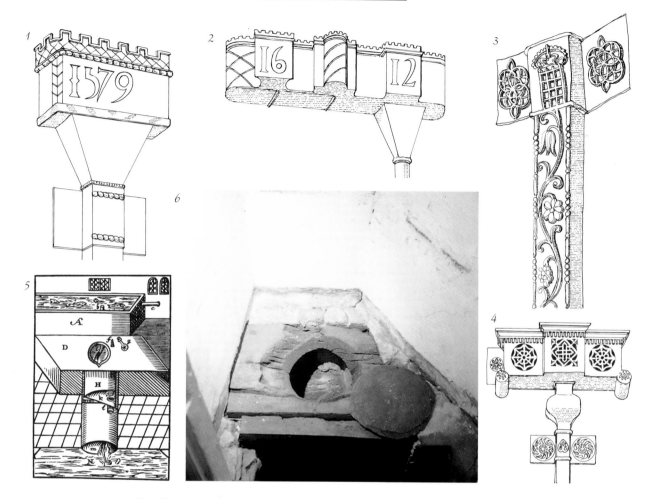

① to ④ *Ornate lead hopper heads/leader heads and down pipes/downspouts from Sherborne in Dorset, Bramshill in Hampshire, Bramhall in Cheshire and Haddon Hall in Derbyshire. These were fed by wooden gutters lined with lead or by plain lead gutters. The down pipes/downspouts could be of square or round section. They were luxury items so the date of installation is often recorded, as on the first two examples. Some simpler heads were made but they have a poorer survival rate as they tended to be replaced.*

⑤ *The water closet from Sir John Harington's* The Metamorphosis of Ajax; a Cloacinean Satire, *published in 1596. A is the cistern; D is the stone seat with a hole in it; H is the flushing pipe; and N is the collecting vault. It is a highly sophisticated system for its day.*
⑥ *A garderobe, c.1610, from a large town house in Newark-on-Trent, Nottinghamshire. It is now located in a cupboard. The seat has a wooden cover and rests on a shaft which leads to a pit at ground level. Its survival is remarkable.* TY

Standards of sanitation varied according to the status and location of a house. Houses near rivers had ready-made waste disposal facilities and those near springs an easy water supply. Andrew Boorde in his book *The Dietary of Health* (1540) rates a supply of water as the primary factor in choosing the location of a house.

Water supply to the grandest houses, and in some towns such as the city of London, was by conduit. Wooden or lead pipes fed the water from springs to conduit heads. More commonly houses were served by either communal or private wells. Internal lead plumbing was restricted to grand houses, as was the external network of lead gutters, rainwater heads and down pipes/downspouts which directed rainwater to cisterns. Highly decorated heads and pipes survive at some great Jacobean houses such as Knole and Hatfield House.

Most households were served by outside privies (houses of office), although built-in garderobes (water closets) were not uncommon during the late 16th and 17th centuries. These were usually sited in recesses and comprised a wooden seat with a hole and a shaft. The shaft was often located next to a chimney-stack to allow upward ventilation. It either led to a conduit which could be flushed from below or, more commonly, to a garderobe pit which was periodically dug out and cleared.

BAROQUE

1625–1714

Educated Englishmen of the 17th century were humbled by the belief that their own culture was inferior to that of the ancient world. Their architecture was one of many examples of such inadequacy. Over the previous hundred years the English had been gradually introduced to ancient ornament, but it had been applied in a relatively unsystematic way, although with some erudition, and often at great expense. The artistic achievement of the Court of the first two Stuart kings (James I, 1603-25, and Charles I, 1625-49) was the introduction of a universally applicable system of ornament in the ancient manner, an important component of an official ideology which maintained authority in part through visual display. Highly influential in this respect were the designs of the Court architect Inigo Jones (1573-1652).

The basic principle of the courtly style was the theory of *decorum*, re-discovered by Italian theorists from ancient writings about art. *Decorum* is the Latin word for appropriateness. For architects it meant that ornament appropriate for one type of building, or for one position in the building, should not be used elsewhere. It could be achieved by using the classical Orders appropriately – for example, feminine Corinthian for the Queen's House, Greenwich (1616-30), by Inigo Jones; and Doric for a stable. *Decorum* could also be achieved if the general outline of a building respected the building's purpose. Thus, the designs for a new palace for King Charles are advertised by the use of a triumphal arch motif dominating the centre, while a row of houses occupied by people of roughly equal

status has scarcely any points of emphasis at all.

The courtly style also introduced one principle of enduring effect. This was the structural and practical metaphor by which the stories were divided into basement (really the ground floor), piano nobile (main reception floor), and attic (top floor). The basement's supportive role (structurally) and servile purpose (functionally) are expressed by rusticated masonry and absence of ornament. The piano nobile's ceremonial purpose is expressed by its height and by its pedimented windows. The insignificance of the attic is expressed by its smallness. This system of arranging an elevation can be seen in designs for the Prince of Wales' lodging at Newmarket Palace, Suffolk (c.1619), which may have influenced houses of the neighbouring gentry such as Raynham Hall, Norfolk (c.1635).

The other novelty introduced by the Court was the concept of unity. Like *decorum*, unity filtered from ancient writings on art via the work of the Italian theorists. It required a design system so comprehensive that the alteration of any element would require adjustments throughout the design. The simplest method of achieving unity was by providing a single dominant feature. This could be a dominant piano nobile, as at Wilton House, Wiltshire (c.1632), an applied central portico, as at The Vyne, Hampshire (1654), or a projection or recession in the plan, as at Stoke Bruerne, Northamptonshire (before 1634). It could be a central tower in the elevation, as at Coleshill House, Berkshire (c.1650, now demolished), or a central room in the plan. It could be a zone of orna-

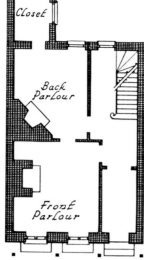

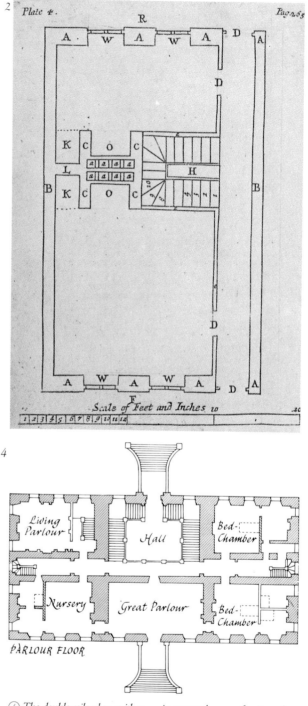

① *The elevation and plan of a London townhouse type built by Nicholas Barbon from c.1670. The deeper windows on the piano nobile answer the requirements of* decorum. SUM

② *The ground floor plan of a terraced/row house, c.1700. The position of the chimney flue (0) and staircase (H) are unusual: generally, there was a dog-leg stair in one corner.* MX

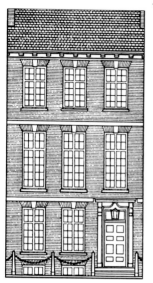

③ *Reputedly the first regular terrace/row in London, these houses in Great Queen Street*

show the early use of a facade with giant pilasters based on the classical Orders. SUM

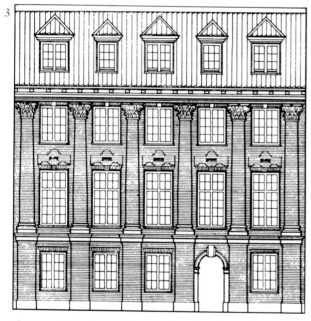

④ *The double-pile plan, with a central corridor dividing two ranges of rooms, was influential*

in country houses after its early appearance at Coleshill, Berkshire (1649). OUP

ment on an otherwise plain wall, as at Beningbrough Hall, Yorkshire (1715), or of richer ornament on a sparsely ornamented wall.

These principles were fully realized only in the circles where state influence was most assertive. Elsewhere, designers were less troubled by these abstract ideas. Although the role of *decorum* came to be influential, it was often broken, perhaps by an extravagant window surround, or by a pompous door frame

leading to a room of little consequence. Many examples of such rule-breaking will be found illustrated in these pages, reflecting a superficial familiarity with Court architecture, but little understanding of its principles. For the Court found that it had to repress the underlying aesthetic urge of the period, which is dynamic. Frames burst outward, ornament spills over, architraves do not adhere to a straight course, mouldings are fat and voluptuous, carving is coarse

1

3

2

4

and expressive, colour is bold and simple.

The exile of the Court from 1642 to 1660 dissolved the adherence to theory, while the dynamism of non-courtly architecture thrived. The theoretical basis of early Stuart Court architecture was restored with King Charles in 1660, although its practical expression was enriched by study of courtly architecture in the places of exile, particularly France and the Netherlands. The former influence is more easily recognized in public buildings, but it can also be seen in courtier's houses like the Duke of Montagu's at Boughton, Northamptonshire (1683), and the Duke of Somerset's at Petworth, Sussex (1688). The impact of the Netherlands upon Court architects can be seen at Eltham Lodge, Kent (1663), a derivative of Pieter Post's Mauritshuis at The Hague; but it can also be seen at a lower social level in the brick houses with shaped gables in the eastern counties of England.

After 1690 the ancient idea of unity became less influential. Architects became even more interested in re-creating the appearance of ancient Roman buildings, or at least of Italian Renaissance buildings (which seemed to have an authentically ancient appearance), but at the expense of theory. Thus, Easton Neston Hall, Northamptonshire (c.1685) has different (and irregular) numbers of stories on different elevations: its

The grand carved staircase of Moulton Hall, Yorkshire. Such vigour of expression, with scrolling acanthus leaves, bulging fruit and other symbols of natural abundance, was a Baroque characteristic. A more delicate form of wood carving can be seen in the work of Grinling Gibbons (1648-1751). MU

composition is not unified, despite the fact that it has some similarity with a Renaissance palace. The fashion for buildings copied from the antique did not produce unified designs either. And although Castle Howard, in Yorkshire (1699-1726, Nicholas Hawksmoor and Sir John Vanbrugh), is a unified composition, other great houses such as Blenheim Palace, Oxfordshire (1705, by the same architects), are composed of elements which are in distinct conflict. One of the most extreme examples of this is Vanbrugh's Seaton Delaval Hall, Northumbria, whose component parts seem to have little or no relationship with each other. The architects of this post-1690 school were evidently more interested in purely visual effects, and therefore have more in common with the 18th-century Picturesque movement than with the Baroque.

Doors

The entrance was the most important feature of the exterior and was thus emphasized by an extensive use of ornament. Such decoration could be increased by multiplication as much as by addition: here, a concentric series of mouldings with dentillated infill is used to dramatic effect. It is an excellent provincial example. MO

The formality of life in the Baroque period was nowhere more theatrically expressed than at the front door, which was made to look simultaneously as festive as the backdrop of a stage, and as imposing as the gates of a citadel. It might be flanked by columns, or (less expensively) pilasters. The columns might be plain Doric, to look forbidding, or ornamental, to look expensive. If ornamental, they could be fluted, twisted, or enriched with ornate panels of decoration. The doors were often positioned at the top of steps, and could be canopied by a shell or placed in a porch. Above it there could be a pious inscription, a carved achievement of arms, or a pediment, depending on whether the owner wished to stress his morals, his blood or his learning. The pediment could be simple, it could terminate in scrolls, or it could be double-curved and scrolled (the swan's-neck type); it could be filled with carved ornament, which sometimes took over and obscured the underlying shape. However, as knowledge of antiquity became more common, enrichment was increasingly confined to particular areas, such as capitals or friezes.

Doors were ornamented with hinges in L-shaped, butterfly or "cock's-head" patterns. Massive wooden box locks were used by most people, but the rich bought intricate and expensive iron and brass locks to advertise their patronage of ingenious mechanics.

① *The front door was made to look both festive and imposing. This surround is from Aston Hall, Warwickshire, 1618-35.*

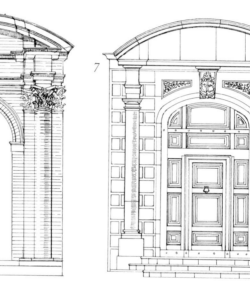

② *Columns were a desirable but expensive frame to a door; pilasters were a less expensive alternative. Ham House, Surrey, 1610.*

③ *A run of steps allowed the owner to descend in style. This*

example is early 1580s.

④ *The growing importance of classical proportions and motifs in fashionable architecture is illustrated by this engraving from an English edition of Andrea Palladio's* First Book

of Architecture (1729). It compares the decoration and proportions of a door and a window. AP

⑤ *Where classical allusions were appropriate, the door might have a pediment. The*

Judge's House in Salisbury, Wiltshire, is enriched with ornament in the tympanum.

⑥ *and* ⑦ *The Corinthian Order looks most expensive but the Doric is more imposing. The first surround here, c.1677, is from King's Bench Walk, London. The projections of the engaged columns and pilasters are continued into the pediment. The second, stone surround dates from c.1695.*

⑧ *The alternative to a pediment was a cornice, here enriched with scrolls. 1717.*

⑨ *The Ionic Order gave elegance to a surround. This garden door from Wolvesey Palace, Winchester, 1684, is tall and well proportioned.*

⑩ *Classical learning and wealth are brought together in an exceptionally expressive design. The elongated form of this surround from Mark Lane, London, early 18th century, is typical of Baroque taste.*

① *Tall porches such as this (1623) were fashionable on grand houses early in the period.*
② *Until the English Civil War (1642-51) columns were often enriched by panels of ornament, usually strapwork, as on this porch. King's Manor, York, 1635.*
③ *A porch could resemble an aedicule (a niche framed by two columns). This example from Nether Lypiatt Manor, Gloucestershire, 1702-5, is made grander by a flight of steps.*
④ *Twisted columns, inspired by those of King Solomon's Temple, Jerusalem, were even more showy.*

⑤ *and* ⑥ *The pedimented form and the temple portico were the main variations of the porch during this period. GBV*
⑦ *Country houses sometimes had wide porticoes. Groombridge Place, Kent, c.1660.*

⑧ *and* ⑨ *Roman arches and swan's-neck pediments were fashionable in the late 17th/early 18th centuries.*
⑩ *Ornate door hoods often took the form of shells.*
⑪ *Pediments or hoods could be segmental and enriched with scrolls, as in this hood, c.1655.*
⑫ *This mighty hood, 1699, is supported on foliate brackets.*
⑬ *Rectangular hoods are typically Queen Anne.*

① The front door to Kimbolton Castle, Cambridgeshire, 1680s, is a grand classical ensemble, approached by a flight of steps. The door is set within a courtyard, a consequence of recasing a medieval house. AQ
② By the end of the 17th century, pattern books from Continental Europe were being published in England. This doorway from Beningbrough Hall, Yorkshire, c.1715, was designed by William Thornton who copied details from Domenico De Rossi's Studio d'Architettura Civile of 1702; these, in turn, were based on Roman remains. AQ
③ A typical Queen Anne town house from Albury Street, Deptford, south London. The narrow proportions are characteristic, reflecting the narrow passage within the house leading from the door to the stairs. AQ

④ The rich decorations on this doorway from Thorpe Hall, Northamptonshire, designed c.1653, are indications of the importance of the room. The entablature and pilasters of the doorcase and the wreath motif on the doors are worked in high relief. TH
⑤ A great variety of panel arrangements was used in the 17th century. Doors with two square panels were common. MO
⑥ By the mid-17th century fashionable London doors had square and rectangular panels, but in more remote areas joiners continued to create more imaginative designs, as here. Yorkshire, c.1654-60. MO
⑦ Nail-head ornament (of medieval origin) and geometrical panel patterns (fashionable in the 16th century) were used until the English Civil War (1642-51). MU

Internal doors
① *Baroque doors are large and often have only two panels.*

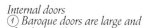

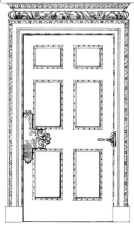

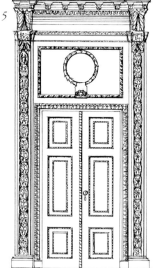

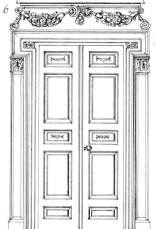

② *and* ③ *The classical formula for door surrounds – architrave, pilasters and frieze – attained prodigies of elaboration but the door itself was often very simple. The four-panelled door evolved*

from double two-panelled doors.
④ *The six-panelled door, like this one from Eltham House, Kent, 1664, was to become the standard Georgian door.*
⑤ *Doorways were made to*

harmonize with the architecture of a room. The pilasters that frame this double door of the mid-1650s reach the cornice.
⑥ *and* ⑦ *Five-panelled doors and ten-panelled double doors*

were among a number of experimental forms of the time.
⑧ *In particularly important locations the height of the doorway could be increased by the use of an overdoor, as in this example from Ashburnham House, London, c.1660.*
⑨ *Panelling could be very imaginative and elaborate.*
⑩ *Sections of moulded door panels, from c.1640 to c.1695. Doors were moulded in much higher relief by the end of the 17th century than in the middle.*

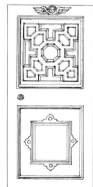

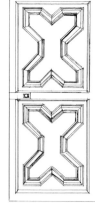

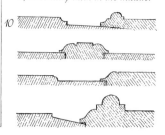

① *Joiners were accustomed to framing doors in whatever shapes were determined by the bricklayers or masons.* WH

② *Fashionable tall doors needed many framing members. They often had more than the six panels typical of Georgian doors.* WH
③ *Arched doors were inspired by Roman prototypes. The spandrels are customarily filled with facetted triangular shapes.*

④ *The thin joinery on internal doors prevented locks from being cut into the woodwork. Box locks were therefore mounted on front surfaces, on the inside of rooms (top). The reverse had mounting bolts, handles and keyhole plates (bottom).* WH

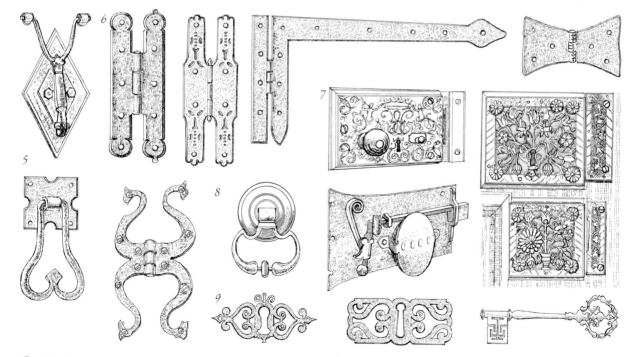

⑤ *A door knocker, c.1650 (top). By 1700 more ornate, scrolled knockers had appeared (bottom).*
⑥ *Hinges were mounted on the door face, rather than being cut into the inside edge as they were from the Georgian period. The three*

standard forms of hinges are illustrated here: H-shaped, L-shaped and butterfly.
⑦ *Locks were prestige items, even in simple houses. The mechanism was often ingenious and the box could be highly chased (engraved).*

⑧ *Cock's-head hinges and drop handles are used on Baroque furniture and doors alike.*
⑨ *A decorative keyhole escutcheon plate on the back of a door complemented the box lock; an elaborate key would complete the set.*

Windows

① *Far from London and the fashionable Court circle, provincial designers combined the new taste for classical forms with traditional styles. This window from Moulton Manor, Yorkshire, has a hoodmould, a feature of Tudor windows, but it has an almost antique profile. The mullions and transoms have traditional hollow chamfers but, again, the* architrave profile is classicized and fashionable. MO
② *An asymmetrical provincial house from Dorset, c.1660. The hipped roof is fashionable, but the service end of the house (right) destroys the symmetry of the design.*
③ *A fashionable hunting lodge from Berkshire, c.1660. The whole composition is centralized, with hierarchical fenestration.*

Window surrounds, particularly those on the entrance front, were styled with as much pomp as front doors. Those in the middle of the middle floor were especially elaborate and were designed to impose unity by centralizing the whole composition. Even the owner of a relatively unostentatious town house would be prepared to spend money on an ornate serliana (Venetian window) with an arched centre light.

Large window openings were at first supported by mullions and transoms. As the period progressed these were reduced both in quantity and bulk. Initially the central king mullion remained substantial while the others were reduced in size. Then, as the numbers of windows increased and became narrower, king mullions became dispensable. Transoms were positioned relatively high in the opening and were reduced from two to one. The moulded profiles of early mullions were replaced by plain square sections.

Hinged casements filled the space between mullions and transoms. The development of counter-weighted vertically sliding sashes in the 1670s eliminated the need for mullions and transoms while allowing much larger areas of glass to be moved. By 1700 sashes were common, and the fashionable ones were as tall and narrow as possible. Casements remained in smaller houses and in the service areas of many larger ones.

WINDOWS

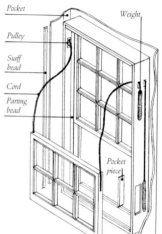

① and ② Until the English Civil War (1642-51) most windows differed little from those of the 16th century. These windows are from the 1620s. The second example has a large central king mullion, commonly used at this date to reinforce a wide window. ③ From mid-century, mullions acquired unmoulded profiles. ④ and ⑤ Pattern books with classical designs were consulted in fashionable circles. They illustrated correct elements, motifs and proportions. AP, GBV ⑥ Narrower windows, which eliminated the need for king mullions, appeared in the 1630s.

7 Pocket
Weight
Pulley
Staff bead
Cord
Parting bead
Pocket piece

⑦ The sash window was the great innovation of the 1670s. It operated on a system of weights and balances which allowed large areas of glass to be moved.

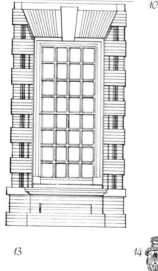

⑧ and ⑨ Decorative scrollwork or rustication framed principal windows on late 17th-century facades – that is, those above the front door or on the piano nobile. ⑩ Tall and narrow proportions were highly desirable. This resulted in the elimination of mullions and transoms. The orangery window illustrated, c.1704, is 14 feet (4.2m) tall. ⑪ This attenuated window is one of a pair flanking a front door in Sussex, c.1712. The thick glazing bars are typical.

⑫ Round-headed windows similar to this were introduced by Hugh May at Windsor Castle, Berkshire, c.1672.

⑬ Simple round relieving arches, in the Netherlandish style, were popular in the 1650s and 60s.

⑭ A late 17th-century window head, with classical details. ⑮ The keystone became fashionable from the 1640s.

① and ② *Provincial designers combined traditional and classical forms, although classical features were often misunderstood. The pediment (left) does not span the opening, and the frieze above the mullioned and transomed window (right) has cyma (double-curved) profiles which have been inverted. The round window is an archetypal Baroque form.* MO, MU

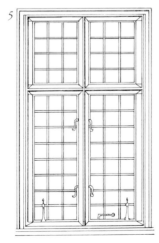

③ *Hierarchical fenestration in the classical style is treated in an eccentric, somewhat exaggerated fashion at Moulton Hall, Yorkshire, 1654–60, a house remote from fashionable London.* MU
④ *Sash windows from Winslow Hall, Buckinghamshire, 1698-1702, designed by Sir Christopher Wren. Their elongated forms and the use of the counter-balanced sash typify windows of high Baroque and Queen Anne houses.* WH
⑤ *Hinged casements filled the spaces between mullions and*

transoms. The bottom lights in this four-light window, c.1703, would open. Most windows had internal

shutters; curtains were less usual.
⑥ *Iron latches often display the blacksmith's craft. This highly*

decorative pair is from a house in Guildford, Surrey, c.1680.
⑦ *Some latch-plate patterns were popular over a very long period. The so-called cock's head pattern (left) is found from the 16th to the 18th centuries. Other zoomorphic shapes were used.*
⑧ *Iron springs and small pivots were common latch mechanisms.*

WINDOWS

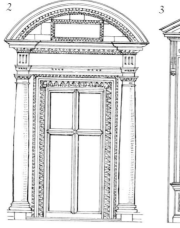

① to ③ The expressive possibility of windows was considerable. Those on the entrance front, particularly those on the middle floor, were styled with as much pomp as the front door. The brick window frame here dates from c.1655, while the stone surrounds were constructed between 1674 and 1679. The later pair are a purer expression of classical forms.

④ A town house of some standing could have a serliana (Venetian window), usually made more conspicuous by being set in a projecting bay or oriel. This example from Sparrowe's House, Ipswich, Suffolk, a late 17th-century merchant's house, is further enhanced by pargeting. Both the window and the decorative plaster pilasters are free interpretations of classical originals: this is typical of much provincial building at this date.

⑤ Balconies reflected the status of a house and its owner. They sometimes surmounted the front door and were used for watching the hunt, to view the garden, or, in towns, to enjoy the spectacle of the street.

⑥ Elaborately ornamented windows in the centre of the middle floor imposed unity on a facade by drawing the eye towards the centre. A fine example

from Barnell Hill, Surrey.

⑦ Unity could also be imposed by the repetition of decorative forms, vertically, horizontally or both. The cornice of one window

becomes the sill of the other in this group from Petworth House, Sussex, 1690s. It is a variation on the fashionable group of a window above a front door.

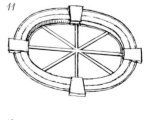

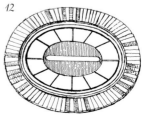

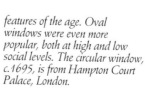

⑧ Windows were simpler on top floors, although even the attic dormers of a very classical composition had pedimented gables, as in this example from the 1650s/early 1660s.

⑨ This less classical dormer of 1684 has a hipped slate roof. Note the old-fashioned diamond-shaped quarries.

⑩ to ⑫ The circular window is one of the most characteristic

features of the age. Oval windows were even more popular, both at high and low social levels. The circular window, c.1695, is from Hampton Court Palace, London.

Walls

A detail of the east wall of the dining room at Thorpe Hall, Northamptonshire, c.1654-6. The bold lines of the wainscotting and the doorcase are impressive. Their austerity is somewhat relieved by the limited use of swags and other carved details. The whole design shows a strict observance of classical proportions and parts, with a clearly defined dado (chair) rail and a simple cornice. The ten-panelled double doors complement the wainscotting. TH

Walls were patterned, except in the poorest houses, usually by means of painted stencils. In the later 17th century stencilled patterns began to be replaced by block printed papers, the first wallpapers. Both these forms of decoration are liable to decay and their survival is very rare. Richer owners would cover their walls with woven or painted fabric hangings. Tapestries for the wealthy were produced in England or were imported from Continental Europe. The most extravagant covering was leather which was stamped, sometimes tooled and occasionally gilded. It was attached to battens.

Wood panelling, termed wainscot, was a fashionable form of wall lining; it was often regarded as furniture and could be removed from its original house as a result of a bequest. It was formed into panels which increased in size as joinery skills advanced. Wainscot was painted with patterns determined by the shape of the panels: usually geometric and abstract designs were used, with the occasional addition of figurative detail. Heraldry, moral themes and classical architecture (which became more effective as panel size increased) were depicted on the walls of wealthy householders. The tendency was to simulate a more expensive material: deal (pine or fir) was painted to resemble oak, oak to resemble walnut, and many woods were treated to simulate marble or tortoiseshell.

WALLS

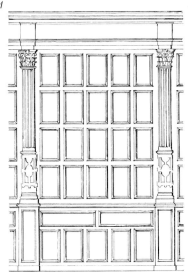

① In the first half of the 17th century wainscot was divided into small units. This wainscot from a merchant's villa of 1631 is ornamented with the classical Orders. The panels were painted, often with geometric patterns.
② Later, joinery skills increased and panels became larger. This allowed a more convincing classical elevation, as in this example from 1700. The profile of this wainscot (right) shows how classical Orders were also able to meet practical needs: the column plinth became a chair rail and a classical cornice attached the wainscot to the ceiling.

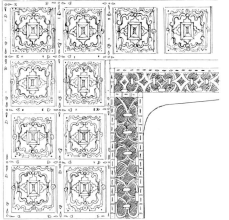

③ An early 17th-century example of figurative carving in oak, a form of ornamentation which could be found in better houses.
④ Painted geometric patterns decorate the plasterwork on the wall and fireplace surround of this early 17th-century house.
⑤ The late 17th century was the heyday of naturalistic carving. This detail, c.1677, from a picture surround at Sudbury Hall, Derbyshire, shows the virtuosity of Grinling Gibbons. His reputation is such that the talents of contemporaries like Edward Pierce and John Selden have become overshadowed.
⑥ Strapwork decoration was popular early in the period. Here it is used on an oak pilaster.
⑦ Two examples of wood cornicing. The top one (c.1690) is decorated with acanthus leaf carving in the cove. The early 17th-century example below has dentils and geometric carving.
⑧ In this carved overdoor detail Honour and Dignity are conveyed in the palms and the cloths of state.

① Inigo Jones and his pupil John Webb produced designs for interior ornament correctly modelled on ancient Roman examples, such as this frieze, early 1630s. The original Roman designs were for open-air use, in stone. AM

② It took time for Jones' ornament to become known. Meanwhile, the more inventive Romanized ornament of the 16th century continued in use, much of it taken at second or third hand from the Italian archaeologists who had studied remains of Roman interiors, lost before Jones could see them.

③ Beds were sometimes recessed into alcoves, which could be architecturally incorporated into the wall surface. Jean Le Pautre, c.1660.

④ and ⑤ The principal type of plant ornament was the acanthus, with its deeply cut leaves. Here it is used to form a running pattern the full height of the pilasters framing a mirror. TH

⑥ The older style of classical wall panelling: small panels rebated into their frame. MO

⑦ The large panels of the second half of the 17th century were simply butted up to the frame, or to each other. Strips of moulded ornament were applied over the gaps where the panels met. The popular profile for such moulding was the bolection type, shown here. TH

Ceilings

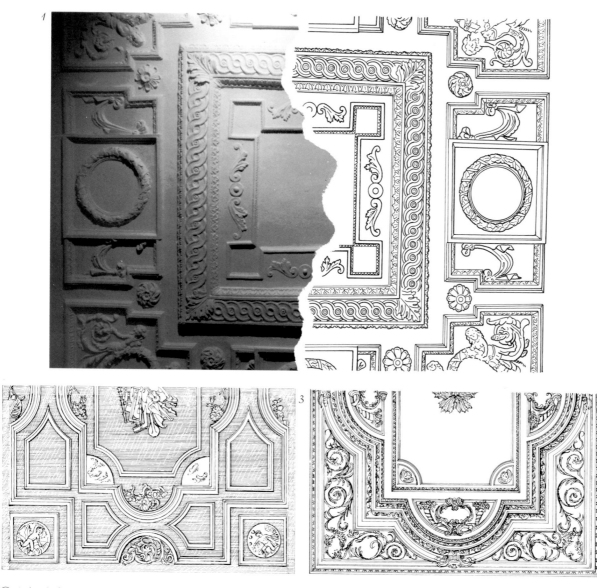

① *A detail of a grand plastered ceiling, Thorpe Hall, Northamptonshire, c.1653.*

Vigorous moulded ornament against a plain ground divided by a grid. TH

② *A variant of the grid-plus-oval formula: a grid forming a central rectangle, with semi-*

circular breaks, c.1685.
③ *A more elaborate design, of c.1695.*

Most ceilings of the period were not plastered. Ornament was provided by chamfering the beams, and sometimes the joists supporting the floor above. The only feature that distinguishes ceilings of this type from similar constructions of the 16th century or earlier is that the timbers became narrower – a reflection of the fact that wood was increasingly competed for. By way of compensation, the stops at the ends of the chamfers became increasingly complex.

Better houses had plaster ceilings suspended from the undersides of the floor above, as previously. However, the style of plaster ornament changed greatly, although not until c.1640. There was a desire to emulate ancient architecture. As walls were gradually organized into ancient architectural forms, their junction with the ceiling was marked by a cornice – even when ceiling and wall were plain. If this point had been emphasized at all in the 16th century, it would have been with a frieze. There was also an increasing systematization of the ornament. The 16th- and early 17th-century ceiling was an impenetrable maze of ornament. The Baroque ceiling, although retaining densely ornamented areas, had them divided from each other, and even from some areas that were entirely plain, by a grid which imposed a clearly centralized, and sometimes hierarchical system.

① A ceiling from a house in Houndsditch, London, c.1630. Until nearly 1640 ceilings were ornamented with dense strapwork, as here. If there were any breaks or any emphatic features, they were usually repeated; thus, much of their distinction was lost. Sometimes the ornament centred on framed armorial or emblematic devices; commonest were the four seasons, five senses, seven sins, and nine virtues.

② A half-ceiling design by Inigo Jones. It was Jones who introduced the simplified type of ceiling, based on a grid of deeply moulded beams. The spaces could be painted, filled with ornament, or left blank in order to emphasize other parts of the design. *RIBA*

③ Later, the basic grid was omitted, leaving only the ovals or circles which had formerly been framed. Whether or not the designer enriched these patterns, they remained simple, forceful and large. From Hamstead Marshall, Berkshire, c.1686.

④ The oval was the favoured central ceiling form in the second half of the 17th century. This detail is from a ceiling of c.1655.

⑤ and ⑥ Plasterwork corner ornament of c.1680. Towards the end of the late 17th century, classical stories, such as scenes from Ovid's Metamorphoses, a long poem on myths and legends (AD 1-8), began to be illustrated on ceilings.

⑦ A cherub: a central ceiling panel of c.1695.

Floors

① A selection of the many patterns obtainable by paving in different coloured marbles. These geometric designs are taken from a French source, C. A. d'Aviler's Cours complet d'architecture, (1691). They were influential in England where marble was used in the grandest houses.
② A rare surviving detail of a painted wooden floor at Hanbury Hall, Worcestershire (c.1700). The pattern, taken across the floorboards, is known as broderie and is similar to the designs for contemporary garden parterres.
③ Two patterns for parquet floors laid in the apartments of Queen Henrietta Maria at Somerset House, London, in 1661 after her return from exile in France. They reflect the latest French tastes. The skill required to produce illusionistic designs made this an expensive technique. AP

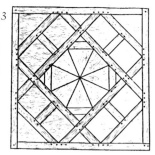

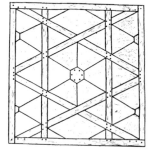

Baroque houses would have stone flags in the principal and service rooms at entrance level when stone was available; alternatively bricks or tiles would be used. The installation of modern damp-proofing has reduced the numbers of surviving original floors. In houses of exceptional quality, floors using stone or marble in two or more colours were laid in such a way that they created illusionistic patterns: the surface appeared to vary in depth.

On the upper levels, floors were made of wooden boards, except in the East Midlands of England where they were made of lime putty laid on laths. The most expensive wooden floors were laid in patterns and were executed in woods of several colours. Again, elaborate illusionistic designs were the most prized, and effects similar to those produced in stone could be achieved by using parquet or even marquetry. A less expensive form of decoration was achieved by painting patterns on floorboards. This technique may have been quite common but few such floors have survived.

Woven carpets, usually imported from the eastern Mediterranean, were considered to be too expensive to walk on. They were placed beneath the best furniture, and beneath the owners themselves when their portraits were painted. In less formal rooms, floors would sometimes be covered with rush matting.

Fireplaces

Overmantels were reserved for major rooms of major houses. Sometimes they took the form of an achievement of arms. This grand marble example, with sumptuous sculpture, is from Thorpe Hall, Northamptonshire, 1654-6. TH

Many fireplaces were little more than a hole in the wall, framed with moulded wood or stone, like a simple classical door. However, in houses of any pretension it was usual to give fireplaces prestigious treatment. They could be dignified with a frieze and cornice, and in a very grand room the cornice would be supported by pilasters.

The decorative arrangement of the surrounding wall could be altered or interrupted to emphasize the fireplace. The most momentous version of this was the overmantel, an architectural composition above the chimneypiece, usually framed by pilasters and sometimes pedimented. Early in the period the most superb cornices projected on corbels, forward of the pilasters, transforming the overmantel into a sculptural feature; by 1700 such effects were only possible when the fireplace was set across a corner. Naturalistic carving offered further expressive possibilities. After the Restoration, carved frames became enlarged, while the panels they framed were diminished. There was also a fashion for mirror glass (very expensive). These trends culminated, c.1710, in overmantels wholly of sculpture with inset mirrors.

Firebacks were cast with ornamental designs. The fire dogs which held the logs in place were given ornamental finials or styled as classical columns.

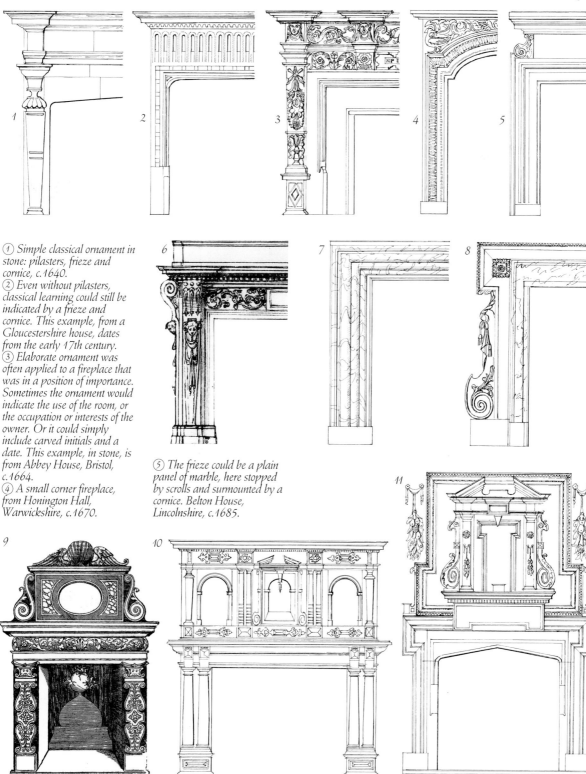

① Simple classical ornament in stone: pilasters, frieze and cornice, c.1640.
② Even without pilasters, classical learning could still be indicated by a frieze and cornice. This example, from a Gloucestershire house, dates from the early 17th century.
③ Elaborate ornament was often applied to a fireplace that was in a position of importance. Sometimes the ornament would indicate the use of the room, or the occupation or interests of the owner. Or it could simply include carved initials and a date. This example, in stone, is from Abbey House, Bristol, c.1664.
④ A small corner fireplace, from Honington Hall, Warwickshire, c.1670.

⑤ The frieze could be a plain panel of marble, here stopped by scrolls and surmounted by a cornice. Belton House, Lincolnshire, c.1685.

⑥ A sketch by Inigo Jones for a bedchamber chimneypiece in the Queen's House, Greenwich, c.1637. The draped heads (herms) come from a French source, but other details are of Italian inspiration. There would certainly have been an overmantel. RIBA

⑦ A much simpler but still luxurious treatment, with a fine bolection moulding in black and white marble. Designed by Hugh May for Eltham Lodge, Kent, 1664.
⑧ A fireplace with lugged architrave, marble slips and Baroque scrolls, c.1700.

⑨ This fireplace is by the Italian architect, painter and theorist Sebastiano Serlio (1475-1554), from a translation published in England in 1611. His designs were influential in fashionable circles. SE
⑩ An oak chimneypiece of c.1640, with double pilasters

and an overmantel reminiscent of court cupboards of the period. This is an old-fashioned type, with limited concessions to classicism.
⑪ A more complex design of c.1632, showing an individualistic ransacking of classical ornament.

① *Although simple in design, this fireplace is dignified by a contrast of different marbles. Mid-17th century.* TH
② *Bizarre use of ornament suggests a provincial designer who has inaccurately* memorized antique detail seen in London. Yorkshire, mid-17th century.* MO
③ *Another provincial fireplace, more elegant but still not entirely harmonious. The pilasters support the cornice alone, not* the frieze; and the architrave seems to run on behind them. TH
④ *An arched pediment breaks forward of the cornice. This is another fireplace that depends on a contrast of marbles.* TH
⑤ *By multiplying the* mouldings in the architrave, the designer here has achieved greater richness without seriously jeopardizing the unity of the composition. MU
⑥ *A cast-iron fireback, 17th century, in situ.* C

① Hoods, used to induce smoke to ascend the chimney, survived into the 17th century. They could be combined with pilasters, frieze and cornice to form an imposing composition, rather like a tomb. This is an early 17th-century example.
② Corner fireplaces were a common feature of smaller rooms in the late 17th century, when space was at a premium. Usually they were set into a diagonal section of wall. This example dates from 1701.
③ Another corner fireplace, with bold marble mouldings, 1630s. The upper part is ingeniously worked into the panelling. Note the receding shelves, for displaying china.

④ A marble fireplace accentuated by a decorative treatment of the surrounding panelling, c.1700.

⑤ In the later 17th century, chimneypieces could include mirror glass panels – an indication of wealth.
⑥ The overmantel could be richly sculpted with mythological figures, fruit, foliage and dead game birds. This example is c.1690.
⑦ A simple chimneypiece could have a discreet ornamental panel, perhaps carved in the Grinling Gibbons manner.
⑧ A more elaborate picture frame built into the overmantel, dating from c.1650.
⑨ The sculpture could be lavish and vivid, like that of a church monument. Hampton Court Palace, Surrey, c.1700.

① *This is a sketch by Sir Christopher Wren, with a detail of carving drawn in by the great woodcarver Grinling Gibbons. The architectural framework is relatively simple, and greatly enriched with naturalistic carving. The cornice is supported by* atlantes *(figures of Atlas), and graced by a lolling cherub and ho-ho birds. Fruit, leaves and trumpets frame the overmantel panel.* SO

② *Another design by Wren, with detail drawn in by Grinling Gibbons. The chimneypiece is as simple as possible, but the two-tier overmantel expresses the symbolism of the Stuart monarchy, from the bust of* Charles I below to the Garter badge above. SO
③ *A palatial chimneypiece design of 1666 by John Webb, showing a full classical treatment with swags, crowns and imperial eagles.* LHT
④ *A fireplace with a fine* chimneyboard – a board fitted into the opening to stop draughts when the fire was not in use. Chimneyboards were decorated as lavishly as possible, usually in paint. This is a design by the Frenchman Jean Le Pautre, published in 1661.

⑤ *Two cast-iron firebacks in the typical arched form. The first example is decorated with a Phoenix, symbol of the Commonwealth. The second is an allegorical figure of Spring. Other favourite ornamental themes from the Bible or classical mythology were the Nativity, the Woman of Samaria, Neptune, Charity, and Hercules slaying the Hydra. Rich floral borders are characteristic.*
⑥ *Four andirons (firedogs). These were used in pairs. Two posts at the front of the fire were all that was needed to prevent logs from falling on to the floor. Some andirons had brass or even silver mounts.*
⑦ *An early example of a raised grate, Jean Le Pautre, 1665.*
⑧ *The andiron lost its importance to the basket grate in the early 18th century, when sea coal began to replace wood as a fuel. This is an early example of a grate, from the late 17th century.*

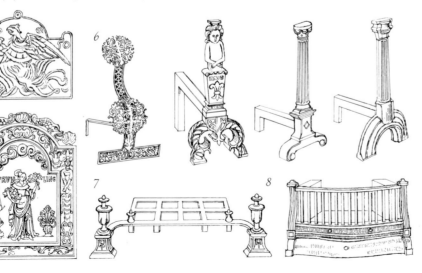

Staircases

The secondary staircase at Thorpe Hall, Northamptonshire, 1654-6, is almost as ornate as the main staircase, suggesting that the two had complementary functions of almost equal status. It is evidently not a back stair for the use of servants only: in the Baroque period the gentry and their staff would have mingled in the public spaces. TH

The Baroque staircase is often a massive affair. The stairs are usually of wood, commonly oak, and until the end of the period are of the "closed string" form, with a diagonal beam enclosing the ends of the treads and risers and supporting the balustrade. The grandest stairs are of stone with elaborate wrought-iron balustrades. Because stone stairs could not rest on a diagonal beam and had to be cantilevered, engineering skills were needed. Such staircases were reserved for the wealthy, but with ingenuity less expensive wooden stairs could be made to imitate stone: either they were cantilevered or they appeared to be so by setting the beam back out of sight.

The most expensive wooden balustrades were continuous pierced panels, at first of strapwork and later of acanthus scrollwork, sometimes with additional carved figures. Individual turned balusters are more common. At first these were waisted but by the mid-17th century their centre of gravity had dropped so that they became vase-shaped; the more expensive ones have carved acanthus enrichments. After 1660 twisted balusters became fashionable. Newels are usually square-sectioned with a finial on top. From c.1660 they were sometimes also braced from the floor by a carved console. Square-sectioned newels were eventually replaced by a form of classical column.

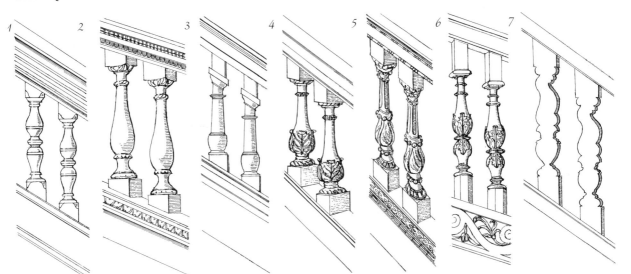

① In the 1620s and 30s balusters were waisted and were vertically symmetrical.

② As classical prototypes were sought, mid-century balusters were given a vase-shaped profile.

③ These balusters from Farnham Castle, Surrey, show how some joiners were unsure whether details should line up with the balustrade or with the treads.

④ Their greater bulk distinguishes Baroque balusters from their Georgian successors.

⑤ Elaborately carved balusters from Shropshire, 1670.

⑥ Acanthus leaves were carved on expensive balusters in mid-century.

⑦ Less expensive versions were obtained by cutting the profile from a flat piece of wood.

⑧ Grand balustrades were composed of continuous pierced panels rather than of individual balusters. This example, dated 1641, shows the use of strapwork.

⑨ By mid-century, strapwork was being replaced by continuous scrolls of acanthus foliage.

⑩ The balustrade was a vehicle for display, and ambitious stairs were planned around a generous well to let it be seen.

⑪ The features of this Baroque staircase might be taken for Georgian but for their boldness (c.1650). MO

⑫ Balusters were usually housed in a continuous diagonal beam or "closed string".

⑬ By 1700 joiners could produce "open strings", shown here with acanthus ornamentation at the base of the stems and fluted newel.

① *Exceptional skill is shown in the engineering of the early 17th-century cantilevered stone staircase in the Queen's House, Greenwich Palace. Known as the "tulip" staircase, the wrought-iron balustrading is in fact ornamented with fleurs-de-lis.*
② *Although the great stone staircase at Chatsworth, Derbyshire (1688-91), appears to be cantilevered, the outer ends of the treads are actually resting on a recessed diagonal beam. The finely executed scrolled carving is of a form more usually found in wooden staircases.*
③ *This late 17th-century Scottish wrought-iron balustrade panel has been worked into a pattern of flowerheads, foliage and coiled scrollwork.*
④ *A detail from a cantilevered wooden staircase, c.1714. The scrolled moulding on the stair-ends is extended to the soffits with acanthus ornamentation.*

⑤ *The quality of the upper stair linking the gallery to the cupola of Thorpe Hall, Northamptonshire (c.1650), indicates the importance of the upper stories.* TH

⑥ *Four handrail cross-sections dated, from left to right, 1701, 1618-35, 1684 and 1632. The later handrails would be used with iron or wooden balustrading.*

STAIRCASES

⑦ *Until the mid-17th century grander newels were turned and ornamented with carved finials.*
⑧ *Square-sectioned newels were less expensive to produce. This ball finial has typical acanthus leaf decoration, c.1630.*
⑨ *A plain newel and ball finial.*
⑩ *From the mid-17th century grander ornamented newels also became square-sectioned. This example, c.1655, is topped by a carved flower basket. It became fashionable to brace newels with carved consoles at floor level.*
⑪ *In the 18th century newels and balusters became slighter. On this stair landing, c.1700, the newel posts are styled as classical columns.*
⑫ *By the end of the 17th century the quality of ironwork greatly improved. This landing balustrade panel (c.1706) is from a grand staircase in Northamptonshire.*

Built-in furniture

① *Towards the end of the 17th-century, bookcases became a fixed item of furniture, and grand houses aspired to a built-in library such as this impressive one, designed by Daniel Marot, c.1690.*

② *This handsome recessed display cabinet is built into the panelled wall of a manor house in Dorset, 1712. The scalloped shelves curve to fit the niche; the fielded panel cupboard door at the top slides down to conceal them. The cupboard beneath provides additional storage space.*

③ *A dated oak spice cupboard from the Lake District in northwest England, with a panelled door, complete with lock. Spice cupboards often contained a set of small drawers to store individual items.*

The definition of furniture was wider than it is today and could include such items as panelling: a man might bequeath his wainscot, for example, independently of his house.

Where houses had very thick walls it was always possible to contrive built-in cupboards. Ventilated food cupboards were sometimes recessed. Their doors, which were generally oak, would vary in style from region to region. Some were relatively plain with pierced perforations; others, where owners were prosperous, might be panelled and ornamented. Spice cupboards used for storing spices and medicines could also be set into a wall.

Built-in buffets, which were used for the display of silver and glass, became fashionable late in the 17th century. In the grandest houses these could be set into arched niches in the dining room. Less affluent households might have a built-in corner cupboard, usually with shaped shelving and shell-head decoration. These popular fixed cupboards were often incorporated into the wall panelling.

As books became more available, libraries were furnished with built-in bookcases. Originally, the books were housed behind cupboard doors but these were replaced by open shelving as it became increasingly conventional to display spine bindings.

Services

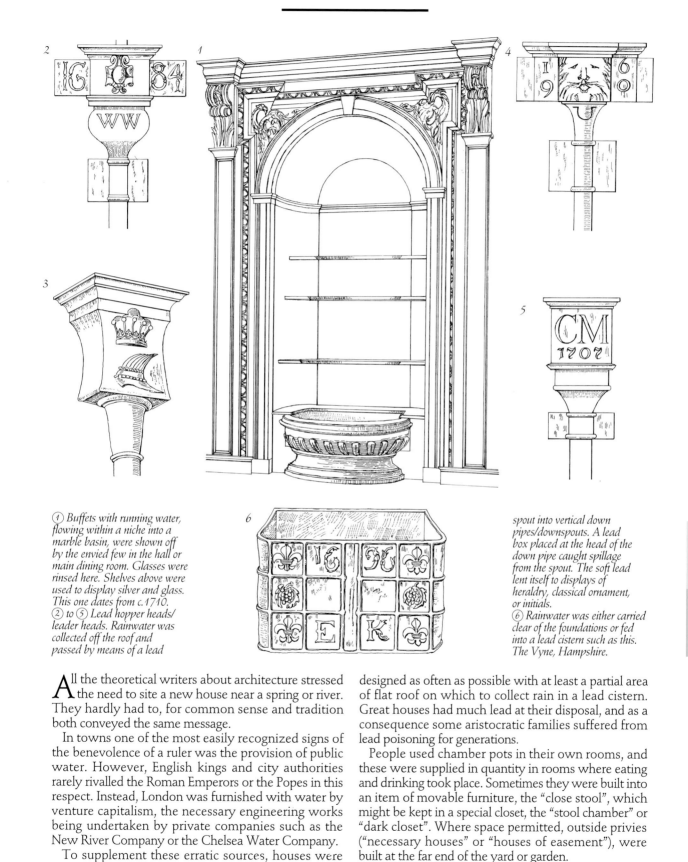

①　Buffets with running water, flowing within a niche into a marble basin, were shown off by the envied few in the hall or main dining room. Glasses were rinsed here. Shelves above were used to display silver and glass. This one dates from c.1710.
②　to ⑤ Lead hopper heads/ leader heads. Rainwater was collected off the roof and passed by means of a lead

spout into vertical down pipes/downspouts. A lead box placed at the head of the down pipe caught spillage from the spout. The soft lead lent itself to displays of heraldry, classical ornament, or initials.
⑥　Rainwater was either carried clear of the foundations or fed into a lead cistern such as this. The Vyne, Hampshire.

BUILT-IN FURNITURE

SERVICES

All the theoretical writers about architecture stressed the need to site a new house near a spring or river. They hardly had to, for common sense and tradition both conveyed the same message.

In towns one of the most easily recognized signs of the benevolence of a ruler was the provision of public water. However, English kings and city authorities rarely rivalled the Roman Emperors or the Popes in this respect. Instead, London was furnished with water by venture capitalism, the necessary engineering works being undertaken by private companies such as the New River Company or the Chelsea Water Company.

To supplement these erratic sources, houses were designed as often as possible with at least a partial area of flat roof on which to collect rain in a lead cistern. Great houses had much lead at their disposal, and as a consequence some aristocratic families suffered from lead poisoning for generations.

People used chamber pots in their own rooms, and these were supplied in quantity in rooms where eating and drinking took place. Sometimes they were built into an item of movable furniture, the "close stool", which might be kept in a special closet, the "stool chamber" or "dark closet". Where space permitted, outside privies ("necessary houses" or "houses of easement"), were built at the far end of the yard or garden.

Lighting

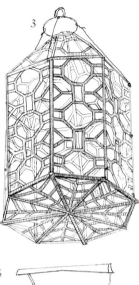

① *Fanlights with lanterns were seen at the end of the period.*
② *This branched light, c.1660, has typical serpentine arms.*
③ *A hexagonal lantern from Hardwick Hall, Derbyshire, c.1600.*
④ *An elaborate sconce, c.1700: 18 inches (45cm) high.*

⑤ *A wooden chandelier, c.1710, with a typical oviform finial.*
⑥ *A wall lantern from the early 18th century, shown open.*
⑦ *The framed mount of this sconce, c.1700, could contain mirror glass or embroidery.*
⑧ *An embossed sconce of 1684.*

During the Baroque period even a single candle was an expensive item. The fire lit most indoor activities after sunset, and a candle would be carried up to bed. The poor used rushes, dipped in fat and held by a clip. The middle classes had tallow candles and the rich had wax. Candle stands were usually made of turned wood, although brass and pewter were more desirable. The very rich had silver stands, but only in the best locations and not until the end of the 17th century.

Where people were on the move – in passages and on the stairs – a constant but dim light could be provided by a lantern. Staircase lanterns were often suspended from an iron branch that was hinged from the landing;

the lantern was pulled across and lit from the staircase.

Rooms of ceremony could have a branched fixture, suspended by a cord from a hook in the ceiling. It would hang quite low for ease of lighting (chains and pulleys were an 18th-century innovation). It was usually made of brass, with a central reflective globe to enhance the candlelight. Chandeliers were grander still. Most were made from carved and gilded wood; the best were rock-crystal. Sconces (demi-girandoles) were another luxury. For most of the period these were mounted on brass plates which were sometimes decorated with *repoussé* work; by c.1700 mirror glass was used and the ornament was transferred to richly carved and gilded frames.

Metalwork

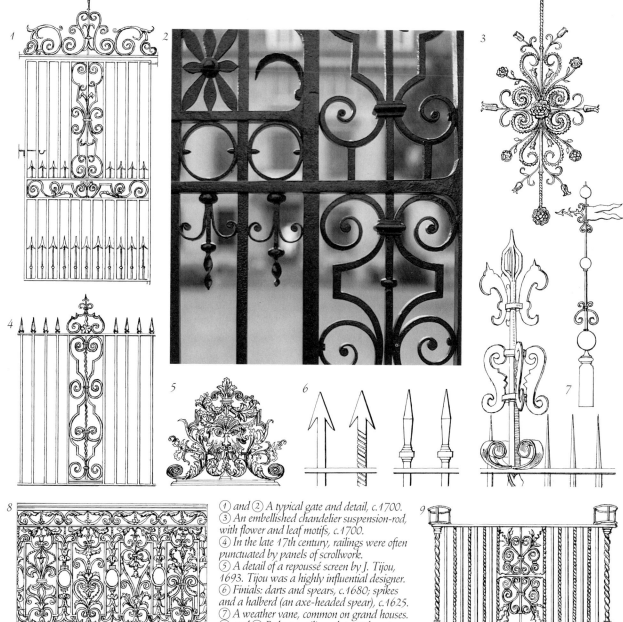

① and ② *A typical gate and detail, c.1700.*
③ *An embellished chandelier suspension-rod, with flower and leaf motifs, c.1700.*
④ *In the late 17th century, railings were often punctuated by panels of scrollwork.*
⑤ *A detail of a repoussé screen by J. Tijou, 1693. Tijou was a highly influential designer.*
⑥ *Finials: darts and spears, c.1680; spikes and a halberd (an axe-headed spear), c.1625.*
⑦ *A weather vane, common on grand houses.*
⑧ and ⑨ *Balcony railings, late 17th century. The second example has torch-stands.*

During the 17th century, technical improvements resulted in the production of highly sophisticated ironwork. Iron was supplied in bars as little as half an inch (1cm) thick and was worked into ornamental forms: darts, twists, leaves, waves, frets, scallops, and even masks, bird and animal heads and cloths of estate (heraldic emblems). Sometimes repoussé work was used – hammered, relief ornament. Wrought-iron gates and railings include the full repertoire of decorative devices. Finials ceased to be simply spikes and became balls, leaves and spears; some bulbous shapes were supplied ready-cast and were welded on. Bars were held together by either rivets or collars. Full-height bars in a

gate are often interspersed with shorter spear-headed bars which prevented dogs from slipping through. Panels of double-curved arabesques were fashionable at plinth height and on the top of gates.

From 1650, iron balconies became fashionable. Prominently positioned over front doors, they often have alternating plain and twisted bars and panels of foliage and scrollwork. They were always painted, probably blue or green, and sometimes gilded. Clairvoyées (openings in boundary walls) were often situated at the end of walks; viewers on the outside enjoyed a fine vista of grounds and house. These openings were usually fitted with ornamental wrought-iron grilles.

EARLY GEORGIAN

1714–1765

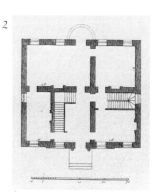

① *With its restrained and carefully proportioned facade, Marble Hill House, Twickenham, west of London, is typical of Palladian taste. The house is based on a design by* Colen Campbell and was constructed between 1724 and 1729 by Roger Morris, under the supervision of the amateur architect Henry Herbert, 9th Earl of Pembroke. MR

② *and* ③ *The elevation and plan of a typical villa from Abraham Swan's* A Collection of Designs in Architecture. *Although this house is based upon the ideal of the Italian* palazzo facade, the proportion of window to solid wall is greatly increased. The plans of such houses also reflected Italian practice, following in particular Palladio's Vicenzan villas. ASA

Gentlemen amateurs, the new breed of professional architects, and confident if largely untutored speculative builders all made a distinctive contribution to the development of the English house in the first half of the 18th century. By the time of the death of Queen Anne (1714), at the grandest level of taste, a new architecture of subtle forms and details had all but supplanted the Baroque vigour of the later 17th century. The fashionable circle led by Lord Burlington (1694-1753) and the architects Colen Campbell (1673-1729) and William Kent (1685-1748) espoused the ideals of the Italian architect Andrea Palladio (1508-80). Their fine town and country houses reveal Palladio's influence in their planning and proportions (which were based in turn on ancient Roman architecture), in their symmetry and regularity of fenestration and in their detailing, which stemmed from 16th-century Italian models. Palladio's palazzi around Vicenza in northern Italy had a profound effect on Georgian architecture, inspiring the emphatic height and richness accorded to the piano nobile, the main floor of a house which was either the raised ground floor or the floor above the entrance level. Outside offices and stable-blocks of grand country houses were also given the most elaborate architectural treatment, but in the arrangement of kitchens (often in a separate pavilion) and the other humbler domestic quarters, anything approaching modern notions of convenience was cheerfully sacrificed to the achieving of grandeur.

In London, the grandest and most fashionable houses also aspired to the Palladian values, but further down the scale there was an explosion of speculative building which hastened the creation of that dense pattern of streets and squares which grew outward from the city in the Georgian era. As a result, the brick-built, terraced/row house, which had first appeared in the 17th century, rapidly became the most characteristic and important building type. Its size, proportions, detailing and the methods of construction were governed by the informal rules of taste propounded in the professional architects' and builders' pattern books and by a series of Building Acts. The latter had their origin in the legislation that followed the Fire of London (1666) which had decreed that houses in central London should be flat-fronted and of brick or stone. An Act of 1707 proscribed the use of the popular wooden eaves cornices and required the use of full-height party-walls (that is, shared walls between houses which extended through the roof) and parapets, to prevent flames spreading at rooftop level. Similarly, to increase fire safety, a 1709 Act required that the sash-box of windows should be set back by the thickness of one brick (4 inches/10cm). Previously windows had been set flush with the wall, so the new legislation radically altered the visual effect of the fenestration, thereby changing building aesthetics. Both these Acts technically governed only building in the City of London; but whilst an Act of 1724 extended their scope, it was the wish of provincial builders to keep up with architectural fashion that led them to adopt the new precepts, even in small towns and in the country.

The rapidly rising cost of building plots in towns and

① *An elevation and plan for a terraced/row town house from* The Modern Builder's Assistant *by William Halfpenny, 1742. The ample proportions of mid-century architect-designed houses were gradually squeezed by the economic pressures on speculative building. The*

planning was always constrained by the limitations of the site, normally forcing all rooms to be lit by windows on either the back or the front; staircases were often very dark. WHP
② *A drawing room on the floor above the entrance level in a*

1720s house in Spitalfields, east London. The panelling is composed of standard, simple mouldings. Such deal (fir or pine) panelling was always painted. Dull and muted colours predominated, although stronger dark colours such as this shade of red were also popular. DC

cities (often made available by landowners on a lease-hold basis) account for the dense planning of the Georgian town house. In terraced/row houses in particular every effort had to be made to ensure that as many rooms as possible were lit by windows and considerable ingenuity went into the disposition of the main rooms and their attendant closets, which were either "light" (with a window) or "dark". These secondary rooms fulfilled a number of service functions and often provided sleeping accommodation for servants, for the average town house in the 18th century was lived in by a large number of people by today's standards.

Services became rather more civilized during this period, though for a limited section of the population. Piped water reached a good proportion of the better sort of houses in towns and the need for adequate drainage was recognized. Away from the urban centres things remained much more basic. Artificial lighting continued to be a very simple matter throughout the period and was mostly provided by candles in movable stands. The grander class of house would have had an enclosed lantern in the main spaces such as the entrance hall and chandeliers in the principal rooms; such lights were often supplemented by wall fixtures. However, throughout the period the provision of a great deal of illumination was a costly luxury.

The decoration of houses was a similar indicator of

wealth and status. Elaborate plaster and stucco work, woodcarving and specialist paint effects and gilding were very expensive both in terms of materials and labour and were reserved for the houses of the gentry and the richer merchant classes who wished to ape them. Most ordinary houses had plain paintwork, whose function was as much practical as cosmetic: it protected the structure from wear and tear. Exterior joinery was almost invariably preserved with paints compounded from white lead which were extremely resilient. Interior paintwork was given some variety by the addition of muted, earth-based pigments. The painter's work became increasingly important as the 18th century progressed and the use of less expensive imported Baltic fir and pine (generically termed "deal") supplanted native woods such as oak. These softwoods were less durable than the indigenous woods and so paintwork became increasingly important. In the early decades of the period, bright, strong colours were extremely expensive and they were difficult to apply evenly, but by the middle of the 18th century technological improvements brightened paintwork. Parallel advances in papermaking and printing saw the refinement of wallpapers and printed textile hangings, so that by mid-century even the middle-class English house had become much more colourful and sophisticated than its counterpart of fifty years before.

Doors

The handsome doorcase of a provincial town house of c.1730. The older type of hood on carved brackets is integrated with the upward breaking cornice and a fashionable round doorhead. From Colchester, Essex.

The main door is the principal ornamental feature of the Georgian facade. It was, except in costly buildings with stone details, the work of the joiner, who kept abreast of fashion by studying pattern books.

In the earlier decades of the 18th century, Baroque doorcases have elaborately carved elements including heavy brackets supporting a hood, sometimes formed as a shell. These brackets are usually carved with stylized animals, foliage or cherubs, or designed as classical consoles with scrolls. In the 1720s and 30s, Palladian designs based on the temple form became popular. Columns and pilasters followed exact rules of proportion.

The door itself is always panelled, often with heavy fielded panels in two vertical rows. Early doors were tall, filling the entire opening, but have often been cut down later to accommodate a fanlight. All front doors were painted in dark colours or grained to imitate wood.

The evolution of internal doors follows a similar pattern. In grand houses doors on the principal floors are often double, and set in deep reveals. They have handsome ring handles to the rim-locks. Ordinary doors were fitted into plain doorcases with architrave mouldings and other joinery details en suite with the room. Upper floors, below stairs areas and all lesser houses have simpler varieties of the fashionable panel door. Plank construction hangs on in country areas.

① *Two variations on the standard Ionic doorcase from* The Builder's Jewel, *1746, by Batty Langley. The arch-topped opening would be suitable for a fanlight.* BJ

② *A heavily rusticated doorcase from James Gibbs'* Book of Architecture, *1728. Emphatic keystones are typical of Gibbs' designs but were widely copied.* BA

③ *and* ④ *Two designs from William Salmon's* Palladio Londiniensis *of 1734: a sober Doric doorcase and an enriched Corinthian doorcase.* PL

In the first half of the 18th century external door heads developed from projecting hoods to complex pediments.

⑤ *A carved shell hood with small brackets, from Essex, c.1710.*
⑥ *An Ionic segmental broken pediment with carved inset, 1717.*

⑦ *An incised flat architrave on consoles in cut brick, 1717.*
⑧ *A typical composite form of the 1720s, Rugby Street, London.*

⑨ *A broken flat pediment by John Wood, Bath, 1729.*
⑩ *A deep pediment on full columns. London, c.1755.*

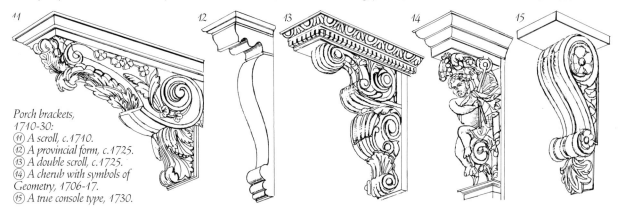

Porch brackets, 1710-30:
⑪ *A scroll, c.1710.*
⑫ *A provincial form, c.1725.*
⑬ *A double scroll, c.1725.*
⑭ *A cherub with symbols of Geometry, 1706-17.*
⑮ *A true console type, 1730.*

① *A finely proportioned doorcase, c.1720.*
② *A good Doric doorcase with a segmental pediment. The door contains later glazing.* OC

③ *A doorcase of c.1740-50 in which the arched top of the door void breaks into the pediment.* MN
④ *The pediment often has a carved cartouche (panel) inset.*

⑤ *and* ⑥ *More correct classicism ousted freer forms on a straight entablature.*
⑦ *Some pediment mouldings had continuous carved ornament.*

⑧ *Pattern books reproduced the most commonly used classical motifs: these grotesque and egg-and-dart mouldings were used on the lintel or jambs of a door.* TA

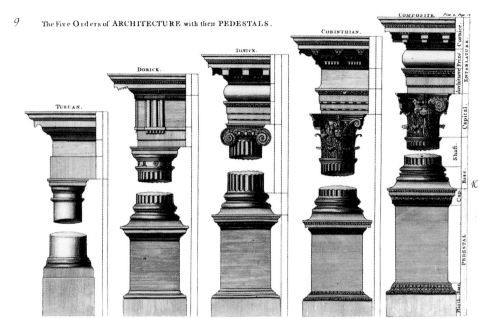

The Five Orders of ARCHITECTURE with their PEDESTALS.

TUSCAN.   DORICK.   IONICK.   CORINTHIAN.   COMPOSITE.

⑨ *The Five Orders, from Isaac Ware's* A Complete Body of Architecture, *1756. All the pattern books begin with the Orders, which dictated decorative detail and proportions. Most doorcases and porches derive their design from the Orders.* IW
⑩ *Classical paterae (small circular motifs decorated with leaves or petals) were commonly used on doorcases and porches.* DE

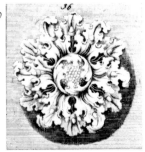

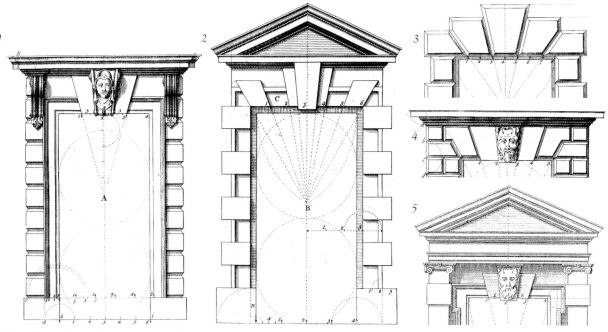

① to ⑤ Five designs for doorcases (or window surrounds) by Batty Langley from his City and Country Workman's Remembrancer, 1745. Langley issued several small pattern books as practical guides for speculative builders who needed clear directions about proportions and details, such as the placing of keystones. These designs for heavily rusticated and solid doorcases recall those of James Gibbs (see page 75), but all such ideas derive from Italian 16th-century sources, for example the treatise by Sebastiano Serlio, Tutte l'Opere d'Architettura, 1584. The finest buildings had carved stone rustication; less grand ones had wooden doorcases, carved and often painted white or stone-colour. BL

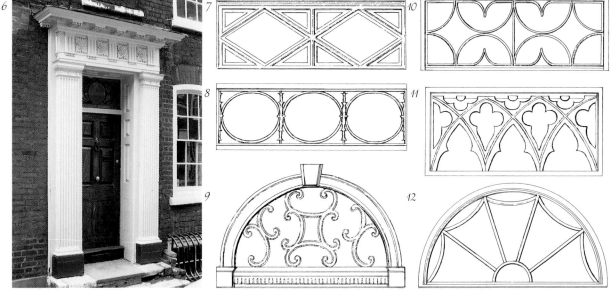

⑥ This fine Doric doorcase, c.1725, from Spitalfields, London, with triglyphs and metopes in the usual pattern of five and four on the frieze, is based on pattern book designs. As often happened in the later 18th century, the door has been shortened to allow the introduction of a fanlight/transom light. The upper panels of the reveals (the inner surfaces of the doorcase) indicate the proportions of the missing part of the door.

The fanlight became an increasingly important element in the design of the front door as the 18th century progressed. In the first two decades the entire door void was usually filled with a tall door. Gradually it became more popular practice to reduce the height of the door, replacing its upper register of panels with a fixed glazed panel that admitted light to the hallway. The new arrangement was so beneficial that nearly all doors of the older arrangement were altered during the mid-century: this makes precise dating of the various types of fanlight quite difficult. The simple forms are usually the earliest. Later fanlights have an inner arch divided into segments.
⑦ Early fanlights/transom lights are of simple, geometric forms with rather thick glazing bars.
⑧ Later on, wooden bars give way to thin iron frames with decorative details in cast lead.

⑨ Heavier ironwork offered security, as well as extra interest above the door.
⑩ Fanlight/transom light forms become increasingly fanciful as doorcases become more sober after c.1730.
⑪ The doorway of an older house could be given a new touch of fashionable detail, such as this Gothick panel, c.1750.
⑫ The classic form, with radiating panes resembling the leaves of a fan.

① A doorcase in Fournier Street, Spitalfields, London. This is the grandest door in a street of fine houses erected between 1725 and 1728. The Ionic columns with bases and segmental pediments, combined with a richly carved projecting porch, are unusually elaborate features.

② A Doric doorcase of the early 1720s from Twickenham, Middlesex. Note how the shallow hood breaks forward to form a correct cornice.
③ A doorcase of the early 1720s in which slight, fluted Doric pilasters are rather clumsily combined with carved hood brackets.

④ An imposing Baroque composition from Montpelier Row, Twickenham, early 1720s. The complex panel pattern of the door is rare.
⑤ A transitional type of doorway which unites the earlier heavy hood on brackets with an arch-topped, rusticated door void. Mid-1720s.

⑥ This Ionic doorcase has fluted columns supporting a frieze and dentillated pediment. A good Gothick detail fanlight/transom light of the mid-18th century surmounts the door.

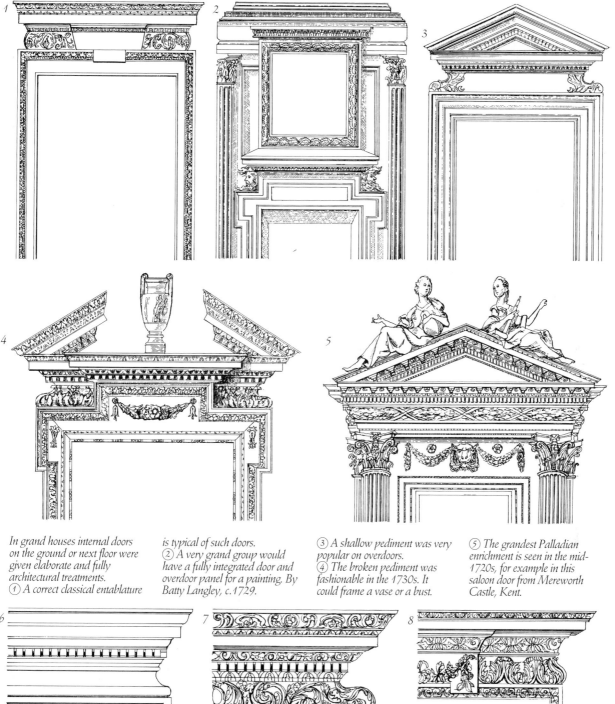

In grand houses internal doors on the ground or next floor were given elaborate and fully architectural treatments.

① A correct classical entablature is typical of such doors.

② A very grand group would have a fully integrated door and overdoor panel for a painting. By Batty Langley, c.1729.

③ A shallow pediment was very popular on overdoors.

④ The broken pediment was fashionable in the 1730s. It could frame a vase or a bust.

⑤ The grandest Palladian enrichment is seen in the mid-1720s, for example in this saloon door from Mereworth Castle, Kent.

Door heads in middle-status houses are elegant. The basic form is that of a classical entablature.

⑥ Plain door heads, such as this one from York, c.1730, often have tiny dentil ("toothed") blocks.

⑦ This richly carved doorhead from Rainham Hall, Essex, has the "eared" lintel typical of doors and chimneypieces in the 1730s.

The architrave mouldings around the door frame at this date are frequently enriched with carving. Variations on egg-and-dart and beaded rope patterns are common, but continuous floral or leaf ornament was also popular.

⑧ A prominent central tablet ("label") often added enrichment, as in this York door, c.1735.

① *A simple two-panel door; a type common throughout the 18th century for upper floors of good houses and in more modest dwellings.* DC

② *This six-panel arrangement was the standard pattern for internal doors of the first half of the 18th century. This example has flat panels and simple mouldings.* DC

③ *A simple pair of double doors in a 1720s house in Spitalfields, London; they run to the full height of the room and match the panel detail.* DC

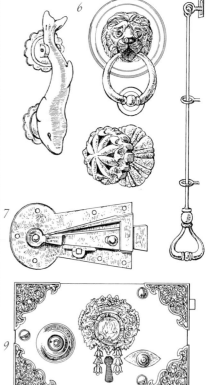

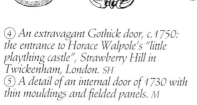

④ *An extravagant Gothick door, c.1750: the entrance to Horace Walpole's "little plaything castle", Strawberry Hill in Twickenham, London.* SH
⑤ *A detail of an internal door of 1730 with thin mouldings and fielded panels.* M

⑥ *A front door would have a large fixed knob and possibly a knocker. A bell-pull could be attached beside the doorcase. There are no letterboxes/mailslots at this date.*
⑦ *A wrought-iron latch.*
⑧ *Drop-handles are typical of interior doors*

of the period, although door knobs became increasingly popular.
⑨ *Plain rim-locks of brass or iron (left) were standard in most houses. A very grand lock (right) would be brass or gilt and engraved or chased after designs in pattern books.*

Windows

① Built on a site first leased in 1736, this house in South Audley Street, London, has a remarkable facade which illustrates the Palladian ideal of the hierarchy of the classical Orders, as applied to the ascending stories of a town house. The Venetian windows are ornamented with a rusticated Doric Order on the ground floor and Ionic on the floor above; the top story has a plain pedimented tripartite window.
② On the facade of this fine house of 1717 in Hanover Square, London, the emphatic keystones and dropped aprons below the windows merge to create an overall fenestration pattern of great subtlety and Baroque vigour. The hierarchy of the floors is reflected in the proportions of the windows, ranging from the two principal floors to the servants' quarters in the mean attic.

Whilst casement windows with glazing bars or leaded panes are still usual in vernacular buildings, fashionable houses have sash windows. The principle of the double-hung sash, with pulleys and counterweights in sash-boxes, remained unchanged, as did the arrangement of internal folding shutters.

Sashes were originally placed flush with the outside wall surface, but the Building Act of 1709 (which covered the City of London and was extended in scope by the Act of 1724) required them to be inset by the depth of one brick (4 inches/10cm). This radically changed the appearance of sashes from the outside.

The preferred pattern of panes for sash windows was always six-over-six, unless the proportions of the house dictated another arrangement. The glazing bars of the early decades are thick and of blunt profile, while later they become more attenuated. The crown glass (early window glass that was blown and spun) was held in place with metal "sprigs" and putty. From the beginning of the 18th century Baltic softwood was increasingly used and had to be protected by white-lead paint. This distinctive paintwork is now regarded as typical of Georgian fenestration.

The inner leaves of shutters tend to be of flush construction, but the outer face and the window surround are usually panelled en suite with the other woodwork.

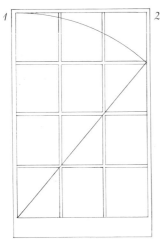

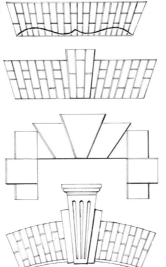

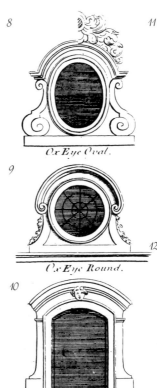

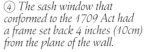

① The most usual arrangement of panes in the double-hung sash window is six-over-six – that is, with one horizontal and two vertical astragals (glazing bars) dividing each sash into upright rectangular panes.
② Typical patterns for cut brick

and stonework lintels. The bottom three show decorative emphasis of the keystone.
③ A diagram of a sash

window from before the 1709 Building Act. The frame is set flush with the wall, with the sash boxes revealed.

④ The sash window that conformed to the 1709 Act had a frame set back 4 inches (10cm) from the plane of the wall.

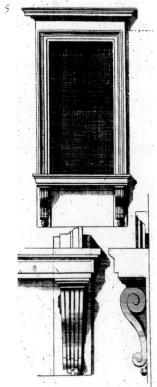

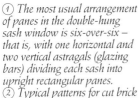

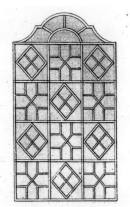

Ox Eye Oval.

Ox Eye Round.

A Lanthorn with a Scheme Arch.

Lanthorns Flemish.

⑤ and ⑥ Two windows from the English edition of Sebastien le Clerc's A Treatise of Architecture, an influential pattern book of 1724, which made French models available to British architects and builders. These designs are for windows on the piano nobile and have substantial console brackets:

those shown in detail have plain, robust mouldings. The use of casement-type windows, though customary in Continental Europe, was old-fashioned by this date in England. TA
⑦ to ⑩ Four designs for dormer or gable windows from le Clerc's Treatise, 1724. Dormers were placed above the

cornice or parapet to light rooms within the roof-space. Particularly popular in the late 17th century, they are more apt for deep hipped roofs of the mansard type than the discreet, shallower roof pitches favoured by the Palladians. TA
⑪ and ⑫ Two designs "for windows in the Chinese Taste"

from The Gentleman's and Builder's Repository, 1738, by Edward Hoppus. Designs for ornamental lattice windows proliferated in this period; they were inserted in houses, as well as being used in the construction of tea pavilions, gazebos and other garden frivolities in the Chinese or Gothick styles. EH

① The classic early Georgian double-hung sash window. The sash boxes, which are fully revealed, are set flush with the wall surface. The typical six-over-six panes have relatively slim glazing bars.

② A good example of a sash window of the 1720s, in the English Baroque style. The elaborate keystone emphasizes the curved head. Brackets support the sill. Note the fire insurance plaque, to the left.

③ The spectacular fenestration of James Gibbs' Octagon, the only surviving part of Orleans House, Twickenham, c.1720, is a splendid interpretation of Baroque forms. Arch-topped rusticated windows and oculi (round openings) light a single tall room. OC

④ Fanciful window shapes of the 1740s inspired by medieval forms. The quatrefoil window on the left includes a rectangular casement.

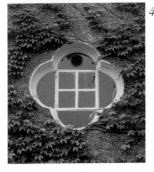

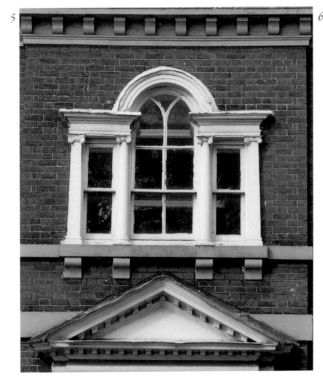

⑤ The Venetian window was a favoured motif of the early 18th century. It was employed to give emphasis to the centre of a facade. This window, from the 1730s, is from Colchester, Essex.

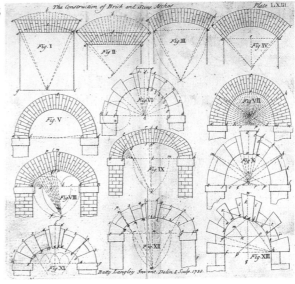

⑥ A diagram of the proportions of arches from Batty Langley's The Builder's Compleat Assistant, 1738. Constructing door and window heads correctly was vital to the structural integrity of the wall. B

① *The same window is illustrated, top and bottom left. It has typical 18th-century domestic window shutters. When not in use, the leaves of the shutters fold back into shutter boxes in the jambs (bottom picture). The outer leaves have decorative panels while the inner leaves are of flush panel construction, of a single plank width. Early hinges are H-shaped. Butterfly forms (top picture) come next, followed by rectangular hinges. Flat bars with catches are often supplemented by iron bars that fit into sockets in the reveals. Knobs can be wood or metal. Shutter boxes often have original paint finishes.* DC*

② *Exterior shutters were never as popular in Britain as in Continental Europe. Some early 18th-century houses, such as a group in Spitalfields, London, do retain authentic examples. Provincial vernacular use of exterior shutters was more common.* DS*

③ *Mid-18th-century shutters have refined profiles. The panel details and mouldings often match the other joinery in the room.* OC*

④ *A Gothic Revival window of the late 1740s with fragments of 16th- and 17th-century stained glass set in the heads.* SH*

Walls

A typical panelled and painted wall treatment of the early Georgian period, reconstructed in a house in Spitalfields, London, *built in the 1720s. This is one of a pair of shallow-arched alcoves formed at each side of the chimney breast.* DS

At the beginning of the century, walls in fashionable buildings tended to observe a three-part division into frieze, field and dado, deriving from the proportions of the architrave, column and base of the classical Orders.

Wooden panelling to the full height of the room was fashionable until c.1740. As a result of less expensive woods being used, panelling came more usually to be painted in this era, in flat oil paint or various fancy effects such as marbling. Decorative carved elements could be picked out in contrasting colours or gilded.

Walls could be panelled or plastered up to the dado rail and the field hung with tapestry or decorated with stretched silk brocade, supported on a structure of

battens or cheap timber boards. Wallpapers too became increasingly available. At this date they came in individual sheets (about 3 × 2 feet/90 × 60cm), which were pasted onto a fabric backing nailed to the battens. Silk and paper hangings were usually finished with a carved or moulded fillet, often elaborately pierced.

Plaster or stucco walls were thought appropriate for dining rooms (fabric absorbed smells) and halls. Stucco walls were left plain, or scored to resemble masonry. Cornices and other features could be elaborately ornamented. Ordinary builders' plastering was widely used in belowstairs areas and in modest dwellings. It was often colour-washed or limewashed.

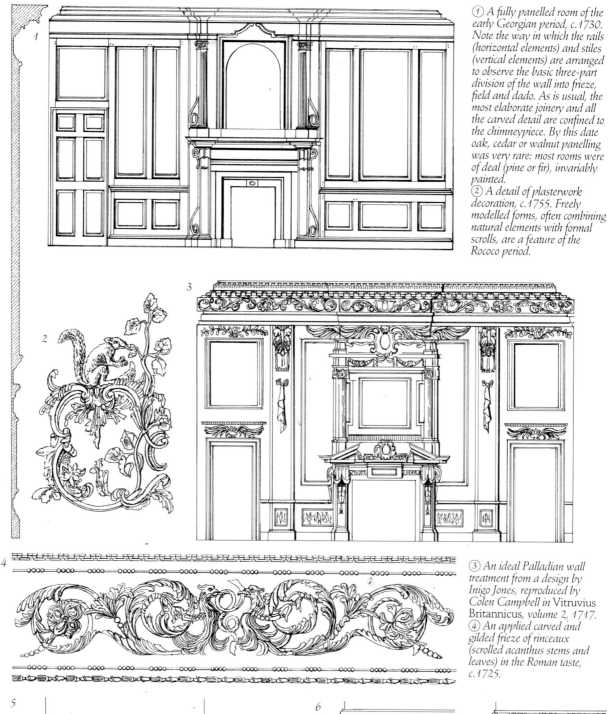

① A fully panelled room of the early Georgian period, c.1730. Note the way in which the rails (horizontal elements) and stiles (vertical elements) are arranged to observe the basic three-part division of the wall into frieze, field and dado. As is usual, the most elaborate joinery and all the carved detail are confined to the chimneypiece. By this date oak, cedar or walnut panelling was very rare: most rooms were of deal (pine or fir), invariably painted.

② A detail of plasterwork decoration, c.1755. Freely modelled forms, often combining natural elements with formal scrolls, are a feature of the Rococo period.

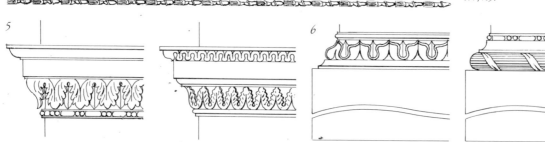

③ An ideal Palladian wall treatment from a design by Inigo Jones, reproduced by Colen Campbell in Vitruvius Britannicus, volume 2, 1717.

④ An applied carved and gilded frieze of rinceaux (scrolled acanthus stems and leaves) in the Roman taste, c.1725.

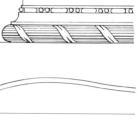

⑤ Two profiles of dado rails of the type commonly to be found in houses of some pretension toward the end of the first half of the 18th century. The flat upper edge is characteristic. Although early examples are usually carved in wood, this form of ornament was later applied as a strip of press-moulded composition.

⑥ Two profiles of skirting boards/baseboards derived from the detailing of classical column bases. The enrichment was often picked out in contrasting colours or gilded.

① The dividing wall between front and back rooms in a typical 1720s town house. The tall doors are detailed en suite with the other panelling. DC

② A plain panelled dado, showing the simple mouldings and pronounced base and dado rail characteristic of the early 18th century. M

③ and ④ Details from the upper and lower walls of James Gibbs' Octagon Room at Orleans House, Twickenham, showing rich use of the Orders and other ornament. The picking out in colour is not original. OC

⑤ Designs from the third edition of Thomas Chippendale's The Gentleman and Cabinet Maker's Director, 1762, for fillets to edge either wallpaper or fabric stretched on walls. Fillets were made of wood, metal or composition and were usually gilded. TCH

⑥ The dividing wall of the Holbein Chamber at Strawberry Hill, Twickenham, 1758-9, with pierced Gothic tracery, copied from the old choir-screen at Rouen cathedral. SH

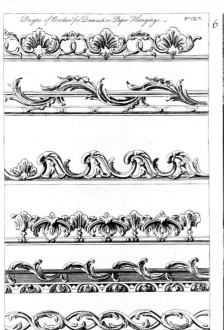

Ceilings

The painted ceiling in the State Dining Room at Grimsthorpe Castle, Lincolnshire, c.1724. It was possibly painted by Francesco Sleter, one of a number of Italian artists working in England at this time, and is an allegorical representation of the Arts and Sciences. Such broad, well-balanced compositions were highly fashionable in the early decades of the 18th century. The trompe l'oeil painted plasterwork forms an effective foil to the lively central subject.

Simple ceilings are formed from the underside of the floor timbers above, perhaps with the spaces between roughly plastered. Many more sophisticated ceilings follow this pattern, with the basic elements plastered over and enrichments added in the gaps. Coffered ceilings are of this type, with the compartments made regular. The standard early Georgian ceiling is of rather more intricate construction, comprising light battens that are nailed to the joists and covered with a uniform layer of plaster. This surface is usually decorated with mouldings around the edge, often with a circular element at the centre. The heavy ornament popular in the late 17th century gave way to Palladian detail worked in much shallower relief. Modillion cornices and other "correct" friezes were composed of classical motifs. By the 1730s and 40s asymmetrical Rococo designs, with freely modelled leaf, shell and bird forms, had become fashionable, only to be ousted by strict Neo-classical detailing in the 1750s and 60s.

The fashion at the beginning of this period for elaborate painted ceilings was confined to palatial buildings, but small painted insets with scenes or coats of arms remained popular. There is insufficient evidence about ceiling colours. Whitewash predominated but picking out may have been quite common, with details reserved in white against "sky tones", grey, yellow or pink.

① A ceiling with heavily enriched plasterwork, by Batty Langley from The City and Country Builder's and Workman's Treasury, 1745. The 17th-century penchant for massive ceiling motifs gave way to more refined mouldings and a Roman splendour. The richest ones were gilded and painted in various colours. However, a unifying design of broken white accorded well with the chaste Palladian principles of decoration. BL

② Modillion cornices from Batty Langley, A Sure Guide to Builders, 1729. Modillions (brackets formed as enriched scrolls) alternate with panels, each of which contains a patera or rosette. This remained one of the most popular options for grand ceiling cornices. A

③ Another cornice design. This type, with dentil ("toothed") blocks, is lighter in effect than the modillion cornice. The leaf-scroll anticipates the Rococo in feel. A

④ A design for a cartouche of plasterwork from James Gibbs' Book of Architecture, 1728. Gibbs' cartouches with their sturdy symmetrical forms remain firmly anchored in the grand Baroque tradition. They had many applications, from ornaments for wall panels and friezes to adaptation as the corner pieces of coved ceilings. BA

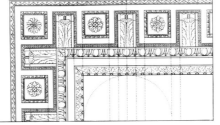

⑤ A decorative corner cartouche in moulded and modelled plasterwork, c.1725, representing Spring, from a set of the Four Seasons. The detail comes from a ceiling at Pierrepont House, Bath.

⑥ Another cartouche design from James Gibbs' Book of Architecture, 1728. BA

① *A ceiling with simple geometric panels executed in plaster. The mouldings were shaped with hand-held forming tools. The modillions are mould-made.*

② *A "box-cornice" of the 1720s in Elder Street, London. The box-cornice, here with tiny dentil blocks, topped the panelling. It is joiner's work made up with wooden mouldings.* DC

③ *A modillion cornice of simple and unornamented form, c.1735. Such cornices can be of wood or plaster.*

④ *Heraldic Gothick ceiling in the library at Strawberry Hill, Twickenham, 1753-4, executed by Andien de Clermont, a specialist decorative painter.* SH

⑤ *A Gothic Revival ceiling of 1758 at Strawberry Hill, carried out with ornamental elements of moulded papier mâché, fixed with pins.* SH

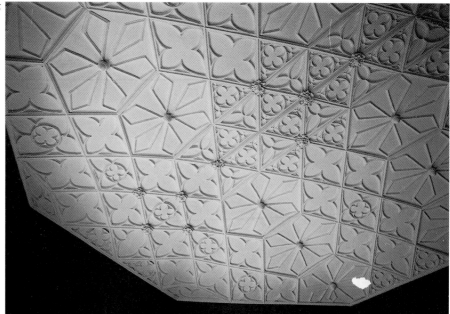

Floots

① A rare surviving example of a painted floor of the mid-18th century in the Tyrconnel Room at Belton House, Lincolnshire. Painted and stencilled floors are more common in The Netherlands than in England. They probably derive from the once popular practice of painting canvas floorcloths. BHL

② This fine stone paving is laid in the pattern carreaux d'octagones, *the most popular design for halls throughout the 18th century.*

The lowliest flooring found in early Georgian houses was beaten earth, used in country cottages and even in the basements of some town houses. Bricks bedded edge-on or thick slate tiles were better, but the preferred finish for areas below stairs was plain stone paving.

Stone floors laid on joists are typical of entrance halls. Elaborate paving, including inlaid marble work, is confined to grander houses with strong brick-vaulted cellars. Several pattern books of the period give designs for geometric paving and these were widely adopted.

Wood plank floors, laid over joists, were the norm elsewhere in the house. Oak floorboards are common in houses built early in the period; later houses have elm boards or, by the mid-18th century, boards of Baltic fir or pine (collectively termed "deal"). Planks from the early decades are often more than 12 inches (30cm) wide: these were left untreated and were regularly scrubbed or scoured with sand. Later boards are narrower (8–10 inches/20–25cm) and, in the principal rooms, were stained and polished at the margins to frame a carpet.

Oriental carpets and English "Turkey" and floral carpets were fashionable floor coverings. Druggets protected stairs and main thoroughfares; ornamental painted and varnished canvas floorcloths were resilient and considered suitable for dining rooms.

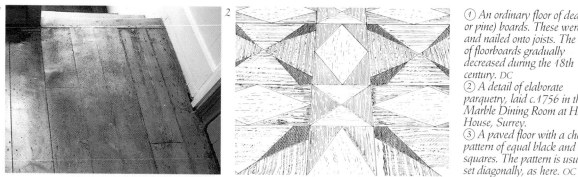

① *An ordinary floor of deal (fir or pine) boards. These were laid and nailed onto joists. The width of floorboards gradually decreased during the 18th century.* DC
② *A detail of elaborate parquetry, laid c.1756 in the Marble Dining Room at Ham House, Surrey.*
③ *A paved floor with a checked pattern of equal black and white squares. The pattern is usually set diagonally, as here.* OC

④ *A design for geometric paving from John Carwitham's important treatise* Various Kinds of Floor Decorations Represented Both in Plano and Perspective, *1739. Carwitham shows many geometric patterns which could be carried out in stone, both indoors and outside on terraces. He also suggested that they were suitable models for painted* floorcloths. *Trompe l'oeil patterns, such as this one, were popular.* JC
⑤ *and* ⑥ *Two pages of designs for paved and inlaid floors from the Builder's and Workman's* Treasury of Designs *by Batty Langley, 1739. The most complex of the motifs is the central design on the first page. It is described as a "pavement of parallelopipedons interwov'd".* BL

Fireplaces

This fireplace has a simple incised pattern on the jambs and the lintel. The form is a common one from the 1720s, used with or without a heavy keystone. DC

The fireplace forms the visual centrepiece of an early Georgian room. Ornate fireplace surrounds reflect the great variety of pattern book designs, which were tailored to the class of house and the importance of the room. The finest examples are of carved white statuary marble, often with inlays of coloured marbles or rare materials such as porphyry. Scagliola work is an inexpensive imitation of marble. All the most popular designs were made in wood, in sections, with carved or applied composition details. Figured marble cheeks or slips (strips that fill the space between the surround and the grate) are a standard feature of fashionable fireplaces. The simple country fireplace has a stout wooden lintel and often a brick hearth, with a freestanding cast-iron fireback and andirons for the logs.

Coal became widely used in town houses. Early in the period it was placed in the fire basket (dog grate) which was intended for wood. This stood on a stone or marble hearth slab within the open brick arch of the fireplace. However, to burn efficiently, coal needs a smaller grate than wood, and the grate must be raised to draw the fire and to collect ash. New coal-firing grates appeared from the 1720s in the form of stove grates, hob grates and early types of enclosed or register grates.

Kitchen fires began to be supplemented by primitive cast-iron ranges, some with fan-driven spits (jacks).

① *A variegated marble chimneypiece, c.1726. The cusped lintel is typical.*
② *A design by William Jones, 1739. The lintel with a frieze of Vitruvian scrolls rests on vast*
consoles that span the uprights.
③ *A favourite Palladian form with flanking herms (busts on pillars), often used by William Kent.*
④ *Console jambs and a richly carved lintel, after a design by*
William Kent. 1744.
⑤ *A stepped and eared lintel with inset carved panel and simple scrolls. William Jones, 1739.*
⑥ *From B. Langley's Builder's Director or Bench-Mate, 1751,*
with enervated Ionic columns.
⑦ *A fanciful Gothick chimneypiece from the same source.*
⑧ *A break-front pattern with a carved head and sun-burst panel on the lintel. From Bath, c.1730.*

⑨ *A detail of the richly carved lintel from a chimneypiece in Castlegate House, York, c.1730s. The symmetrical stems and scrolling acanthus leaves emerging from the central basket are still wholly in the Baroque style.*
⑩ *A finely carved Palladian lintel from a chimneypiece in Redland Court, Bristol. The mask and swags are typical motifs.*
⑪ *A characteristic central motif from a chimneypiece of the late 1730s, in the form of a lion mask.*
⑫ *Two "Gothick Cornices" suitable for use as fireplace mantel shelves, from Batty Langley's Builder's Director or Bench-Mate, 1751. Langley's Gothick chimneypieces are among his most successful inventions.*

① An exceptionally pure and austere surround in veined marble, 1720s. The "swan's nest" grate is c.1770 or later. DC

② An elegant example of a surround with a flat lintel and jamb, typical of the mid-1720s. The lintel is embellished by a serpentine profile. DS

③ This type of surround was popular in the 1720s. It usually had more robust details. The attenuation of this example was necessitated by the modest scale of the room and the corner location of the fireplace. The grate is from the second half of the 18th century. DC

④ This surround, with robust decorative details, typical of the period 1720-30, is from the drawing room of a house in Spitalfields, London. DS

⑤ The brick jambs and the arch of the hearth are revealed in this fireplace of the 1720s. The firedogs with bottle warmers are more typical of country areas at this date. DS

⑥ This chimneypiece is of very high quality. It is from the Octagon at Orleans House, Twickenham, and was designed by James Gibbs. OC

⑦ A Gothick chimneypiece based on a medieval tomb. It is in the Great Parlour at Strawberry Hill, Twickenham, and was designed by Richard Bentley in 1753-4. SH

① *A detail of a chimneypiece from
John Vardy's book of designs by
Inigo Jones, 1744, typical of
Jonesian proportions.*
② *An elaborate overmantel
designed by E. Hoppus, 1737.*
③ *A carved ornamental frame,
dating from c.1740-50.*

④ *An ingenious design for an
integrated chimneypiece and
overmantel with a frame for a
mirror or painting, 1737.*
⑤ *This rather coarse design for a
chimneypiece and overmantel,
1745, typifies Batty Langley's taste.*
⑥ *A finely carved example of a*

chimneypiece, dating from c.1735.
⑦ *A chimneypiece and
overmantel, of a rare type with full-
blown asymmetrical shell and leaf
forms in the Rococo style, 1738.* AS
⑧ *and* ⑨ *Two designs by W.
Ince in the manner of Thomas
Chippendale for Rococo fantasies*

*in the Gothick and Chinese
tastes. The juxtapostion of
alternative designs, as in the first
example here, is thought to be
the origin of the asymmetry
typical of the Rococo style. Note
the grates, which are designed to
be in character.* IN

FIREPLACES

① *This detail of a fine fireplace, c.1750-53, has "C"- and "S"-scrolls on the wooden surround, typical of the Anglicized version of the French Rococo style, popular in the mid-18th century. The design of the overmantel panel reflects the lines of the surround.* RS

② *This bracket is a very pure interpretation of a classical form. It is from the carved chimneypiece designed by James Gibbs for the Octagon room of Orleans House, Twickenham, Middlesex, 1720. The work is carried out in a fashionable, lightly figured grey marble.* OC

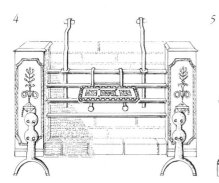

③ *A detail of the Gothick fireplace from the China Closet at Strawberry Hill, Twickenham. This room was completed by Horace Walpole in 1755. The surround was based on "a chimney from Hurstmonceaux (Sussex)", presumably of the late medieval period. The paint colours probably follow Walpole's original design.* SH

④ *This grate, c.1750, shows the origin of the hob grate: the fire bars are supported by two cast-iron sidepieces or hobs. The hobs became much more substantial in the late 18th/ early 19th centuries.*

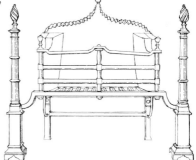

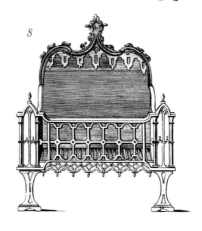

⑤ *and* ⑥ *Two examples of the most usual early and mid-18th century grate, the dog grate, which is a freestanding construction of bars. The front legs reflect current fashions. Genuine period examples stand high off the ground.*

⑦ *and* ⑧ *These designs for dog grates in the Rococo and Gothick tastes are by Thomas Chippendale, from the third edition of* The Gentleman and Cabinet Maker's Director, *1762.* TCH

Staircases

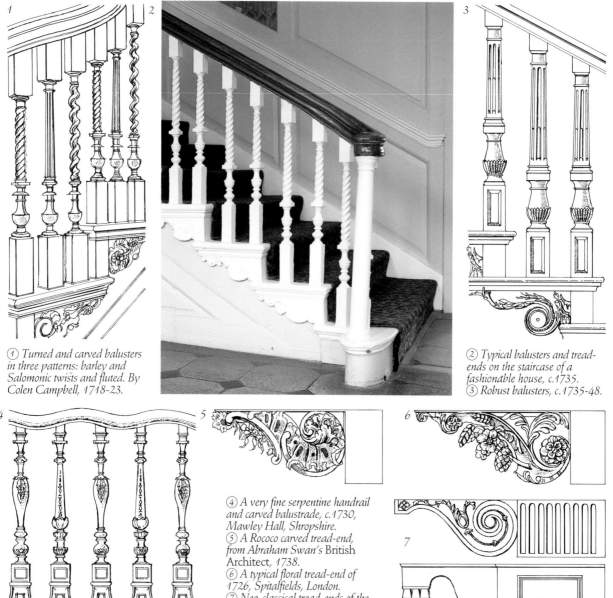

① Turned and carved balusters in three patterns: barley and Salomonic twists and fluted. By Colen Campbell, 1718-23.

② Typical balusters and tread-ends on the staircase of a fashionable house, c.1735.
③ Robust balusters, c.1735-48.

④ A very fine serpentine handrail and carved balustrade, c.1730, Mawley Hall, Shropshire.
⑤ A Rococo carved tread-end, from Abraham Swan's British Architect, 1738.
⑥ A typical floral tread-end of 1726, Spitalfields, London.
⑦ Neo-classical tread-ends of the mid-18th century.

Fashionable houses have a main staircase and a secondary "backstairs" for servants. Ordinary houses have one wooden staircase of straight flights joined by landings, or a winding flight for each story. The most elaborate decoration is reserved for the main flight from the entrance hall to the floor above. Staircases become plainer as they climb the building and are at their simplest up to the attic and down to the basement.

During this period the "closed string" staircase, with balusters spaced along a continuous diagonal board masking the steps, was supplanted by the "open string" for main flights. In this type the balusters are fixed into the treads, which are exposed: this allows for carved or fretted decoration on the tread-ends. The turned balusters of the first half of the century are usually placed two or three to a step. Cantilevering is rare until the end of the period.

Apart from the handrail which was polished, the woodwork, including the treads, was wood-grained in oil paint or finished in a flat colour such as chocolate. The treads were protected by a narrow strip of carpet, or drugget, tacked to the steps.

Particularly fine houses with stone staircases have wrought-iron or, from the end of the period, cast-iron balustrading. The very best examples are in steel, finished with gilt details.

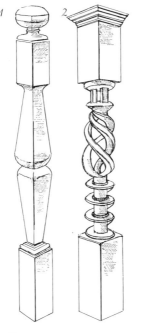
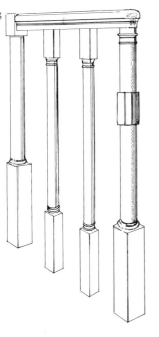
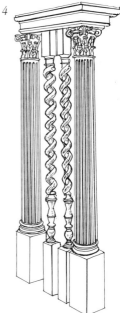
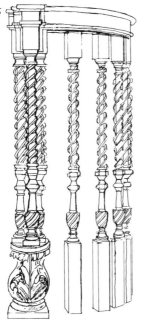

① *A newel post of simple, heavy baluster form carved into facets.*
② *A sophisticated and very finely carved double-twist newel, dating from the late 1720s, Castle House,*

Lewes, East Sussex.
③ *A characteristic arrangement of two newels and balusters on the turn of the stair or half-landing in a mid 18th-century house in Bath.*

④ *A similar arrangement, but here showing architectural detailing and carving and joinery of a very superior order. From 6 Cheyne Walk, Chelsea, London,*

a very good terrace of 1717-18. The newels are Corinthian columns.
⑤ *The terminal sweep of the main staircase in 15 Queen Square, Bristol.*

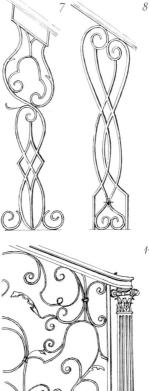

⑥ *to* ⑧ *Patterns for ironwork balustrading from Welldon's pattern book, The Smith's Right Hand, 1756. The best examples are wrought-steel.*
⑨ *A staircase with carved tracery at Strawberry Hill, Twickenham, completed c.1754. Though tricked out with Gothick details, the basic form of the*

staircase is 17th-century. SH
⑩ *A continuous scrolling balustrade of ironwork with mahogany newels and rails from a fine London town house of 1736 by James Gibbs.*
⑪ *A detail of balustrading in the form of a continuous Chinese fret. This was a craze of the mid-century; few examples survive.*

STAIRCASES

Built-in furniture

The highly influential Gothick library in carved and painted wood at Strawberry Hill, Twickenham, designed for writer Horace Walpole by Richard Bentley and completed in 1754. Each section of tracery opens on hinges for access to upper shelves. SH

There is a clear distinction to be made between the below-stairs fixtures of grand houses (and the very similar built-in furniture in more modest houses), and the fashionable fitments in the best rooms of town and country houses. Kitchens contain sturdy oak and elm dressers, surmounted by graduated shelving, and fixed work surfaces supported by stout turned balusters. Housekeepers' rooms are often fitted with ranks of drawers and shelves and similar cupboards are placed on upstairs corridors for the storage of linen. The joinery is plain but elegant; the wood was commonly painted in drab colours and the drawers and cupboards lined with old wallpaper. In modest panelled rooms the chimneybreast is usually flanked by built-in cupboards; these were used for dry storage.

Of the fixtures in elegant rooms the library would generally be the most elaborate, often with arrays of shelves above cupboards, topped by a cornice that is continuous with the wall joinery. The best pieces are made from mahogany or oak; lesser examples are pine. Shelved alcoves may incorporate a built-in bureau or a simpler flap-down writing slope. Niches and corner cupboards with shaped shelves were popular at the beginning of the period. Those with panelled doors were used for storage; glazed doors were intended for display. The latter often had carved shell-heads.

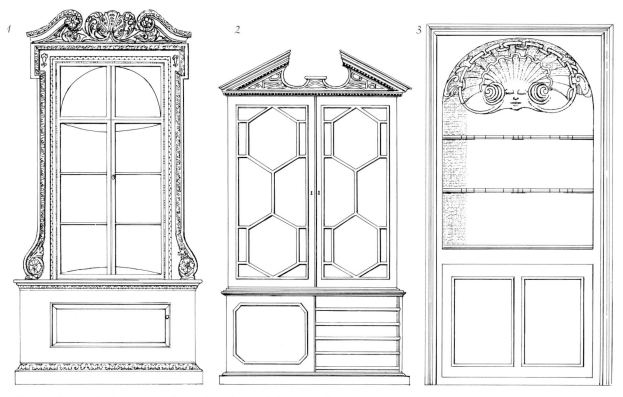

1   2   3

4   5

① One of a pair of niches
flanking the chimneypiece in a
London breakfast room. It has
glazed doors.
② A design of c.1750 from a
series by W. Ince showing
"Bookcases for Recesses".

③ A niche with open shelves
for glasses and crockery at 1
Pierrepont Place, Bath. The
carved shell head was a
favourite motif in the first half of
the 18th century.

④ A shallow cupboard with
double doors built in front of the
flue of a canted (corner) fireplace
of the mid-1720s. DC

⑤ The built-in dresser in the
kitchen of a house in
Spitalfields, east London, of the
1720s. Note the graduated
shelves and baluster supports
and the open storage below. DC

Services

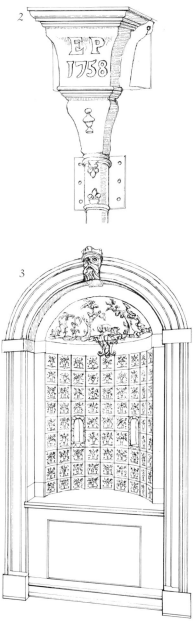

① *A lead cistern or tank for water. These essential items usually stood in the area (the sunken yard in front of the house) or inside the basement of town houses. Early 18th-century examples were often highly ornate; this example has cast ornament. Today they are often found as plant containers. AL*

② *A lead hopper head/leader head for storm water. Its function was to join the gutter and the pipe. Many of these bear dates, initials and decorative motifs.*
③ *Tiled niche with plumbed wash basin, from a house in Bath. A conspicuous luxury feature of the period, in an entrance hall or dining room.*

The services available in early 18th-century English towns were not as primitive as is often imagined. Storm water drained along roof valleys and gutters and was carried into down pipes/downspouts via lead hopper heads/leader heads. Water was carried by pipe to soak-aways or into butts for use. Some houses had fresh water piped in by water companies. Supply was by wooden pipes, with insufficient pressure to rise above ground-level and only at specified times of the day. This made large lead storage cisterns essential.

Throughout the period, most urban households relied upon the services of the night-soil men and the dust-men for the disposal of domestic waste. By the 1730s a few very fashionable houses had water pumped to the upper floors and this made flushing water closets possible, though they remained a rare luxury until much later. Another luxury was a plumbed wash basin; these sometimes took the form of a wall fountain in a niche. Household drainage went into septic tanks dug under the back yard. These had to be emptied regularly. More usual in modest houses was the use of earth closets (privies or offices), located as far from the house as possible.

Kitchens had wide, flat sinks, made of stone or of lead sheet dressed over a wooden framework, and coppers (large vessels for heating water).

Lighting

① *A hanging exterior lantern of elongated "bullet" form, 1722.*
② *and* ③ *Lanthorns (hanging candle lanterns) for hallways or other interior spaces. The first is in the French style, the second in the Gothick taste (1750s).*
④ *A mid 18th-century lantern with domed storm cowl.*
⑤ *An ironwork standard for an oil lantern. This would rise from area railings outside a terraced/*

row house. Alongside is a link-extinguisher, which could be part of the standard or wall-mounted.
⑥ *An ornamental bracket with a hoop for a lantern, c.1740. From Church Row, Hampstead, London.*
⑦ *A mid-century type of lantern on straight rod support, from Castlegate, York, 1761.*
⑧ *A spherical lantern mounted on a projecting curved bar from a flat doorcase.*

Lighting in the early Georgian house was an important indicator of status, with elegant fixtures for fine beeswax candles at one end of the social scale and filthy tallow dips and dim rush-lights at the other. Simple oil-burning lamps were confined to outside lamp brackets and standards (which were often provided with link-extinguishers, a link being a long torch) and, occasionally, hanging lanterns in the hall. Refined oils and improved burners for indoor use had yet to appear.

A grand room of the period would have a central chandelier, which hung only just above head height. These were made of wood or metal and could have glass or crystal drops. They were very varied in form,

usually with six or more curved arms supporting candle holders. Wall brackets, or girandoles, were also widely used, in sets of two, four or more. These would be of brass, silver, gilded or silvered wood, or, in a more modest house, pewter or even tin. Some examples incorporate reflective panels of glass or polished metal, while others are found en suite with the chandelier.

Enclosed lanterns were popular. These came in a great variety of fancy shapes but simple cylindrical types were favoured for hallways and staircases.

Direct illumination by which to read, write, play cards, eat or go up to bed was invariably provided by movable candlesticks and candelabra.

Metalwork

This house of the 1730s in Berkeley Square, London, has typical simple iron railings with cast spiked finials. The railings are enlivened by a lantern supported on an elegant

"overthrow", composed of elaborate wrought-iron curlicues. Note the link extinguishers on the standards, used to put out the torches which were carried through dark streets.

At the beginning of the 18th century all architectural ironwork, such as gates, railings and lamp brackets, were handcrafted in wrought iron. The cast-iron railings commissioned for Sir Christopher Wren's St Paul's Cathedral (1714) and James Gibbs's church of St Martin's in the Fields (1726) in London set a new fashion and popularized the robust baluster forms and elaborate spearhead finials which prevailed well into the next century. Wrought work became a luxury, generally confined to panels for specific spaces such as fanlight grilles; these were gradually supplanted by cast units.

Railings with a main gate, sometimes surmounted or flanked by lanterns, became a standard feature of town houses. A secondary gate would either close off the area steps, which were guarded by a simple handrail, or open into a void, in which case a pulley would be used to lower goods into the basement. All exterior ironwork was protected by paint, usually black. Dark green was also popular early in the period, a paler green later, but a strong bright blue was the favourite. On the best work, finials and details were often picked out in gold leaf.

Circular, cross- or X-shaped plates may still be seen on some facades. These anchor internal tie-rods which were added after construction to strengthen the structure. Small lead plaques, that identified properties covered by fire insurance, may also survive.

① *A grille or panel of symmetrical curlicues in wrought iron above a door on the main staircase at 6 Cheyne Walk, Chelsea, London, 1717-18. The central raised panel is painted*

with a coat of arms.
② *An elaborate pair of wrought-iron gates in the Baroque style, from the forecourt of an early 18th-century Bristol house. Note the centrally placed*

motif above the gates.
③ *Pairs of wrought-iron brackets for a simple porch could be used in place of the conventional carved wooden scroll supports. This example is from Bath.*

④ *Two details of elaborate front railings from a house in Stamford, Lincolnshire, with Baroque curls and small decorative finials and leaves of wrought and cut work.*
⑤ *Plain forged railings with flat hammered finials and split shafts, from Bath.*

⑥ *Finials from Hampstead, London.*
⑦ *These details, from front area*

railings of the 1720s, in Fournier Street, Spitalfields, London, feature hammered spikes and cut

and hammered decorative finials.
⑧ *A selection of ornamental cast finials from front railings of*

houses including the popular thistle, pineapple and baluster designs, c.1726.

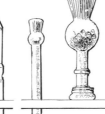

COLONIAL

1607–1780

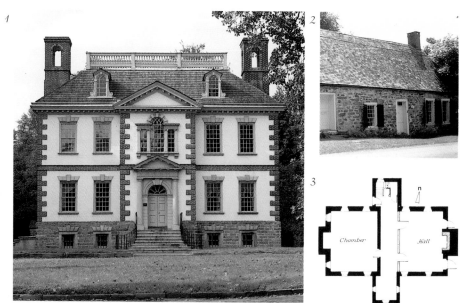

① *Mount Pleasant in Fairmount Park, Philadelphia, 1761-2, is a prime example of Georgian architecture. The imposing front door, symmetrical fenestration and decorative use of materials are all notable features.* MP

② *The Dutch Colonial Abraham Hasbrouck House, New Paltz, New York, 1692, is a single-story building with typically low walls and a deep roof. Originally, it probably had two windows and a single door on this side.* AHH

③ *The ground-floor plan of Bacon's Castle, Surry County, Virginia, c.1655. This was a Tudor-Baroque style manor house, built on the hall-parlour plan. A partition was added in the 18th century, under the influence of Georgian plans.*

The term "American Colonial" is a very broad one, covering the buildings of nearly two centuries, from the first settlement of 1607 to the founding of the new nation after the revolution of the 1770s and 80s. It is helpful to divide this period into two phases: the frontier or settlement phase and the Georgian (or classical or Palladian) phase. The transition came around 1720-30, which also saw the flowering of a consumer society.

The basic forms of American architecture were imported from Continental Europe, England and Africa. However, the evidence shows that unique American styles emerged almost immediately after the settlement began and grew more distinctive by the middle of the 18th century. The differences between the Colonies in climate and social and economic structures and the intermingling of cultures produced less an architectural "melting pot" than a mosaic of regional styles.

The first settlers in the New World enjoyed a plentiful supply of wood and land, but the overriding need to provide rudimentary shelters as quickly as possible meant that their building efforts were modest. The earliest settlements comprised roofed dugouts, pallisaded huts, wigwams, or garrisoned forts surrounding thatched half-timbered cottages. As the colonists became more established they began to build more substantial dwellings. Some of the earliest "manor houses" were almost devoid of style; they could be one-room clapboard structures, with a frame chimney at the gable end and a single battened door and one shuttered window on the main facade. These houses had an aesthetic of sturdy craftsmanship that is characteristic of American vernacular building.

All but the finest Colonial buildings were wood, since wood was more readily available, less expensive and faster to build with than brick or stone. Bricks were generally reserved for foundations and chimneys. In broad terms, masonry was more common in the southern colonies than in the New England states. The settlers used their native systems of timber-frame construction and the ornamentation popular in their home villages. But in the first few decades of settlement they added new features that were more suitable to the harsher weather: sawn weatherboards or split clapboards covered the timber framing, and shingles replaced thatched roofs. Swedish settlers are thought to have introduced log construction in the early 18th century. Most colonists, not just the poor, lived in one-room houses, ranging from hovels to well-built, refined cottages. Larger houses were in a small minority but they were potent symbols of prestige and as such exerted a great influence. It is these exceptionally well-built houses which have survived although they have often been altered and enlarged.

There were marked regional differences from the first. In the southern Colonies the typical house had a main ground floor and a single-space loft. It had steeply pitched gables, sometimes with dormers, and brick chimneys at one or both ends. Most houses were roughly constructed of wood, but better buildings were larger and could be brick, with panelled interiors. The hall-parlour plan was the most common multi-room type of house. Such houses were one room deep with a

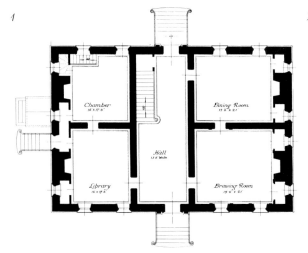

① *The entrance-floor plan of Wilton-on-the-James, Virginia, c.1760. This is a classic Georgian house plan, with more rooms than 17th-century houses, grouped either side of a central hallway.*

② *The dining room of the Hammond-Harwood House, Annapolis, Maryland, c. 1774. This house was designed by William Buckland in a highly refined Georgian style. The decorative plasterwork defines the divisions of the wall into dado, field and frieze. The main decorative emphasis is on the window architraves and fine shutters. The room has a jib window (illustrated on page 114), which looks like*

a window from the inside but is actually a doorway. HHH

③ *The kitchen in the southwest wing of the Hammond-Harwood House contrasts with the sophistication of the dining room. The kitchen in Georgian houses differed*

little from the family room of 17th-century houses. It was dominated by a large, plain fireplace which had substantial andirons, sometimes fitted with a roasting spit, as here. All cooking was done on the fire. Implements would be hung around the opening. The only other furnishings in the kitchen would be a table and a dresser, which could be built-in; in earlier, general-use halls, these were supplemented by chairs or settles and beds. The brick floor is typical of service areas of better houses and of ground-level floors in ordinary houses. HHH

front door that opened directly into the hall. This was the main living room of the house. To the left, partitioned off, was the parlour, a more private room. A staircase would be located at the back of the house.

Most New England houses of the period present a marked contrast. They tend to resemble English medieval post-and-beam houses. In the later 17th century substantial houses became more common and had Tudor and Elizabethan features, such as jettied overhangs with pendant drops and massive central chimneys. The "saltbox" house developed at this time, evolving from rear extensions which were covered by steep, sloping roofs. Windows were small and few in number and ceilings were low. Internal flourishes include chamfered ceiling beams and joists, turned or sawn balusters on staircases and panelled doors and walls. This type of house continued to be built in New England throughout the 18th century. The two-room plan is quite different from the southern arrangement. A small entrance hall would contain a staircase that led to a single-space upper floor. A central chimney and a parlour were located beyond the hall.

German and Dutch settlers usually built stone or half-timbered houses with a three-room plan of a kitchen, hall and parlour on the ground floor. The facade had four

bays and often an off-centred door which opened directly into the kitchen.

The introduction of the symmetrical Georgian facade, typically fronting a plan of four rooms surrounding a central stair hall, was revolutionary. It was introduced in the second quarter of the 18th century by wealthy merchants and planters who had access to English pattern books by James Gibbs, William Salmon and others, and often had first-hand experience of England. The earliest Georgian houses, particularly those in the South, were large mansions, meticulously based on published designs. There were few architects in the 18th-century Colonies and most houses were designed by builders, with advice from the patron. These larger houses quickly exerted an influence on the style of smaller dwellings. The large middle class of merchants, craftsmen and yeomen-farmers created a demand for well-built and stylish dwellings. Often, the builders who erected the mansions also built the more modest villas. They were given a free hand in these designs and adapted fashionable forms to their traditional methods and materials, thus creating distinctly American buildings. Existing houses were updated and given Georgian facades or interiors. Eventually, the style influenced houses of nearly every region, ethnic group and class.

Doms

The front door from Cliveden, Germantown, Philadelphia, Pennsylvania, 1763. Cliveden exemplifies the high Georgian style in the Philadelphia region, here finding a rare expression in stone. One of the hallmarks of the Georgian facade is the focus on a centred front entry, and the elaboration of openings in general. Cliveden's doorway is designed in very correct classical form, but exhibits regional characteristics in the door panelling. CV

American doors from the 17th century are generally battened; that is, constructed of vertical boards nailed together with two or more horizontal battens on the rear. German and Dutch colonists used dovetailed battens. Doors were decorated with scratched designs on the vertical boards, chamfering on the battens or sponge painting. Surrounds are simple, comprising the structural timbers of the house, which are usually chamfered. Door fittings tend to be simple and chunky, made of wrought iron or wood. Batten doors continued in use throughout the Colonial period, and beyond in smaller houses and secondary rooms.

Panelled doors began to appear in better houses by the late 17th century. Two panels in low relief are typical. Heavily moulded doors are a development of the early 18th century, but it was not until the 1730s and the advent of the Georgian style that the door reached its fullest elaboration. At this time the raised-panel door became increasingly common and, under the influence of immigrant craftsmen and imported architectural pattern books, classical surrounds became popular. In most cases patterns were used freely; this gave rise to strong regional variations. The plantation houses of the South have the strictest designs. Classical porches were popular throughout the country and were often added onto older houses. Door fittings became more refined.

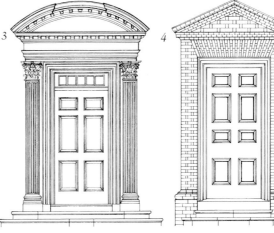

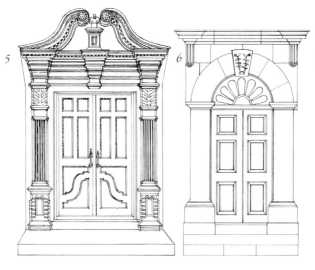

① *A batten door from New England, c.1670. The nailing pattern is exceptional.*
② *A classical doorway from Rhode Island, c.1730.*
③ *A fashionable surround, early/mid-18th century.*
④ *A classic early Georgian brick surround, c.1750.*
⑤ *The unique Connecticut River valley doorways depart radically from pattern book forms. This example is c.1758.*
⑥ *An unusual surround with a keystone, fanlight and Tuscan columns. Virginia, c.1770.*
⑦ *More rectilinear, flat forms appeared in the late 18th century. Massachusetts, c.1770.*

Door hoods were common in both towns and rural areas. They gave an accent to the main entry without the expense of a porch.
⑧ *An unusual and elaborate hood from Maryland, c.1730. It is wood with a plastered cove.*
⑨ *This door hood from Newport, Rhode Island, 1740, is modelled closely on late Baroque/early Georgian English prototypes.*
⑩ *A more typical, unbracketed type from Chester County, Pennsylvania, c.1740.*

Porches became popular in the mid-18th century for grander, particularly plantation houses. They are based on classical temple portico forms, with columns and pediments.
⑪ *A simple classic porch from Goochland County, Virginia, c.1730. The central door panel is related to a design shown in William Salmon's Palladio Londinensis, 1734.*
⑫ *and* ⑬ *Two Doric porches. The first is by William Buckland, Virginia, c.1758. The second is from Massachusetts, c.1770.*

① The front door of Hunter House, Rhode Island, c.1758. The broken, segmental arch and pineapple finial recall the top of a Chippendale-style high chest. NHH

② This front door of 1759 is inspired by the designs of the Scottish architect, James Gibbs. It is rendered in wood. The heavy mouldings stand out against the delicate beaded weatherboards. LH

③ The front door of the Hammond-Harwood House, Annapolis, Maryland, 1773-4. It is representative of the most fashionable Georgian doorways of the day. HHH

④ A fine Palladian interior door from Drayton Hall, South Carolina, 1738-42. DH

⑤ An interior view of the front door at Mount Pleasant, Philadelphia, 1761-62. The decoration is restrained when compared with the exterior, which is similar to that at Cliveden (p. 108). MP

⑥ This interior door from Cliveden, Philadelphia, c.1763-64, has a lugged or "eared" architrave and a broken pediment. Such details mark it as the doorway to a principal room. CV

⑦ A more restrained door, although the architrave and panelling are still elegant. Note the box lock. CV

⑧ A heavily moulded and elaborately panelled interior door. It has walnut wood-grain paintwork. NHH

1

2

3

4

① to ⑥ Interior doors.
① Broken pediments were popular in American architecture for some time after they had gone out of fashion in Britain. This is a fairly early example on an interior door, c.1730, from Charles City County, Virginia.
② and ③ Wall panelling was used to enhance the framing of a doorway. The first, elegant doorway, c.1720, from New Hampshire, has a deeply moulded surround. The second is from Annapolis, Maryland, c.1740.
④ The dining room door from Gunston Hall, Fairfax County, Virginia, c.1758, designed by William Buckland. An elaborate doorway, which reflects the importance of the room.
⑤ and ⑥ Two New England panelled doors. The first, c.1650, has moulded rails and

stiles and thin panels. The second, c.1710, is an early raised-panel door with applied mouldings. Note the hinges.
⑦ A doorway from Odessa, Delaware, late 18th century, with louvered door shutters. The main hall of an American

Georgian house was often used as a room, and the shutters acted as a screen door during the summer.

⑧ Knockers, 1661 and c.1730.
⑨ A typical handle and latch.
⑩ A typical iron bolt, 1768.
⑪ Box locks were made of wood, iron or, as here, brass.
⑫ A wrought-iron lock, c.1750.
⑬ A brass box lock and detail of the knob, c.1722.
⑭ An escutcheon and handle, c.1768.
⑮ A Moravian box lock, 1773.
⑯ A front door latch-lock, mid-18th century.
⑰ A brass doorknob, North Carolina, late 18th century.
⑱ A typical brass escutcheon plate, late 18th century.
⑲ to ㉔ Hinges: a tulip-finialed strap hinge; an H-hinge, early 17th century; an early butterfly hinge with leather washers and iron nails; a typical H-L hinge; a New Mexico-American Indian H-hinge, late 18th century; an early cock's-head H-hinge.

5

6

7

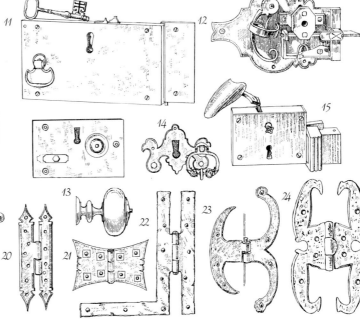

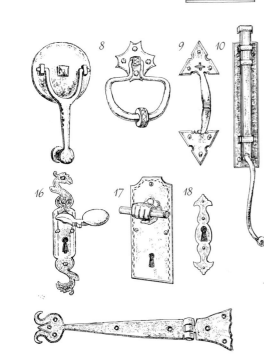

8   9   10   11   12

14   15

16   17   18   13   22   23   24

20   21

Windows

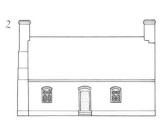

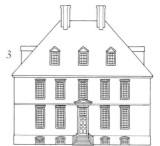

① *A sash window on the entrance level at Cliveden, Philadelphia, Pennsylvania, 1763. It exemplifies the Georgian style in the Colonies. The panelled shutters, simple classical detailing, flat keystoned-arch and the twelve-over-twelve pane arrangement all contribute to the elegance of the facade. CV*
② *An elevation of a typical*
17th-century house showing the limited fenestration of early houses. The casement windows were few in number, and small.
③ *This elevation of the early 18th century shows far more developed fenestration. The house is in the style of an English Baroque mansion and the large sash windows are evenly distributed across the facade, in a hierarchical pattern.*

Early American windows are small in size, few in number, and usually placed asymmetrically. Many of the earliest houses had no windows at all, but most had small openings covered with oiled paper or wooden shutters. The earliest substantial houses have small casement windows with leaded panes, sometimes set in elaborate patterns, or fixed transom windows. The structural timbers form the frames, which can have chamfers and decorative stops.

Sash windows appeared in the early 18th century but it was not until the 1730s that true wooden-framed weighted sash windows were in common use, and then only in better houses. These became more elabo-

rately finished as the century progressed. Flat, gabled or clip-gabled dormer windows were also introduced at this time. Windows were now symmetrically placed, in greater numbers: this is the most characteristic element of Georgian architecture. The Georgian period also introduced the Palladian (Venetian) window, usually located centrally above the front door.

Inside, the windows were generally framed by an ogee moulding on a beaded back band. Toward the second half of the 18th century, glazing bars became thinner and panes larger. The panes were generally set six-over-six, nine-over-nine, or twelve-over-twelve. Shutters for windows were also increasingly popular.

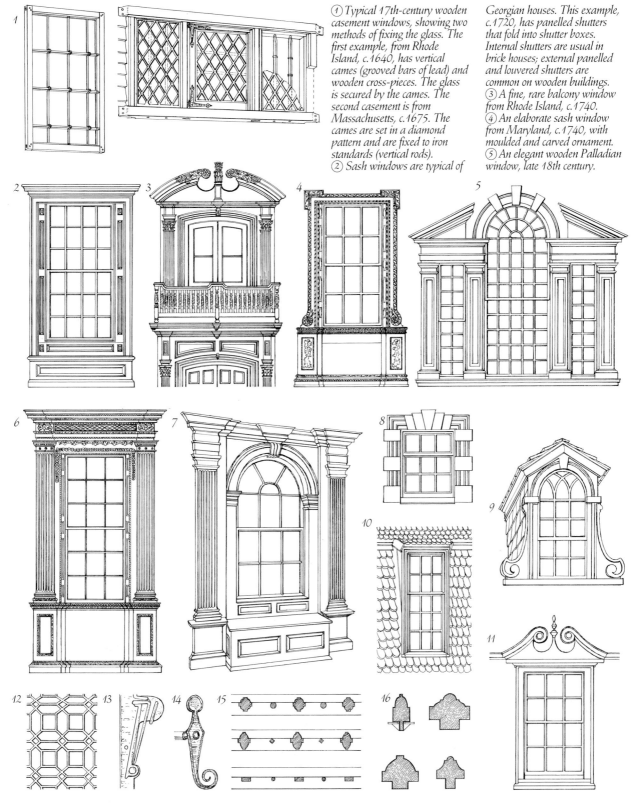

① Typical 17th-century wooden casement windows, showing two methods of fixing the glass. The first example, from Rhode Island, c.1640, has vertical cames (grooved bars of lead) and wooden cross-pieces. The glass is secured by the cames. The second casement is from Massachusetts, c.1675. The cames are set in a diamond pattern and are fixed to iron standards (vertical rods).
② Sash windows are typical of Georgian houses. This example, c.1720, has panelled shutters that fold into shutter boxes. Internal shutters are usual in brick houses; external panelled and louvered shutters are common on wooden buildings.
③ A fine, rare balcony window from Rhode Island, c.1740.
④ An elaborate sash window from Maryland, c.1740, with moulded and carved ornament.
⑤ An elegant wooden Palladian window, late 18th century.

⑥ and ⑦ Two elaborate sash windows, from Fairfax County, Virginia, c.1755, and North Andover, Massachusetts, late 18th century. The influence of English pattern books is evident in the ornament. The second example has a window seat.
⑧ An upper-story rusticated window from Virginia, c.1770.
⑨ to ⑪ Dormer windows carried the fenestration pattern into the roof. The first example is gabled, while the others are set into the roof.
⑫ Elaborate leaded glass was found in better houses from the late 17th century.
⑬ A typical casement fastener.
⑭ An iron shutter dog, used to hold louvered shutters open.
⑮ Three plan sections of windows with wooden mullions and iron standards, c.1637.
⑯ Profiles of typical glazing bars (top to bottom) of the 1770s, 1750, 1740-60 and 1735.

① *One of the two impressive Palladian windows that light the central hall on the main upper floor of Mount Pleasant, Philadelphia, 1761-62. It has Ionic pilasters, a pulvinated frieze capped with a dentilled cornice, supporting brackets at the base and voussoirs (wedge-shaped blocks flanking the keystone) to the arch.* MP
② *The interior of the same window, which spans the width of the hallway. The architecture echoes that of the exterior.* MP
③ *A jib window from the Hammond-Harwood House, Annapolis, Maryland, 1773-74. This window doubles as a door when the sash is raised and the lower panels are opened. From the exterior it appears to be a door, from inside a window,*

thereby maintaining the symmetry of the exterior without sacrificing the symmetry of the dining room interior. HHH
④ *Part of the carved shutters and soffit panel of a companion window from the same room. The extension of detail to this level of complexity is uncommon.* HHH
⑤ *An elaborate Rococo bullseye window from a front gable pediment. This is an unusually rich window treatment for the Colonies at this period.* HHH
⑥ *An interior view of a sash window from Cliveden, Philadelphia, 1764-67. Although Cliveden and the Hammond-Harwood House are at the same social level, this simple architrave surround is in marked contrast to the windows of the other house.* CV

⑦ *An interior view of a casement window with pocket shutters (one open and one closed back into the shutter box) and a window seat.* MP
⑧ *A window with battened wood shutters hung on iron strap hinges, typical of poorer houses and service areas of grand houses.* CV

Walls

This wall of c.1740 in the Great Hall of Drayton Hall, Charleston, South Carolina, represents the earliest instance of Palladianism in American architecture. Builders of southern plantation houses stuck closer to English architectural ideas than did their northern contemporaries. The triglyph and metope frieze just below the cornice was probably unique in the country at the time. Although the grain of wood was not meant to show under the paint, it is evident that the Colonists enjoyed the use of large, old trees. The large panels, low chair rail and fluted pilasters all contribute to the grandeur of the room. DH

Early in the period, the walls in finer houses were usually plastered, with the exception of fireplace walls which were often sheathed with wooden boards. In many smaller houses and some substantial ones, the structural framing is left exposed, particularly on upper floors. Walls generally had no skirting boards/baseboards or cornice mouldings, although the broad expanse of plaster could be interrupted by a post supporting a ceiling beam.

Decoration became more elaborate in the 18th century. The advent of lath-and-plaster ceilings coincided with the introduction of cornices and base mouldings. Chair rails appeared in the early 18th century. In some cases the dado was wainscotted, and in the most elaborate rooms of the finest houses panelling could run from floor to ceiling. In general, the more formal the room, the more elaborate the wainscotting.

Paint was used from an early date on all walls except wainscotting of the finest woods. The palette included earth tones of yellow, almond, red and brown, and very bright blues, greens and yellows. Walls were usually decorated with a flat coat of a single colour although graining and marbling were popular. Abstract patterns and murals were rare until the 19th century. Wallpaper was used in some American houses in the 18th century, particularly block-printed and flocked types.

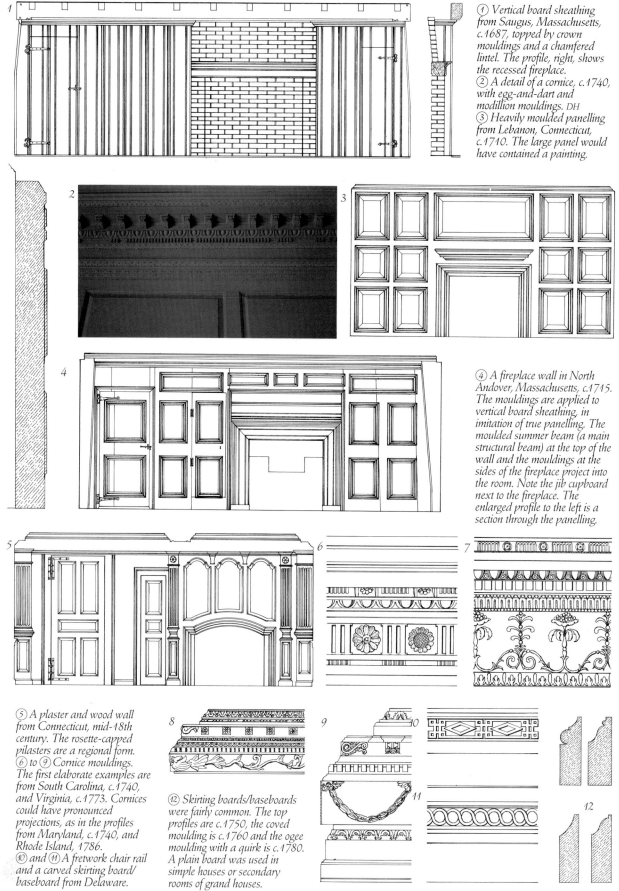

① Vertical board sheathing from Saugus, Massachusetts, c.1687, topped by crown mouldings and a chamfered lintel. The profile, right, shows the recessed fireplace.
② A detail of a cornice, c.1740, with egg-and-dart and modillion mouldings. DH
③ Heavily moulded panelling from Lebanon, Connecticut, c.1710. The large panel would have contained a painting.

④ A fireplace wall in North Andover, Massachusetts, c.1715. The mouldings are applied to vertical board sheathing, in imitation of true panelling. The moulded summer beam (a main structural beam) at the top of the wall and the mouldings at the sides of the fireplace project into the room. Note the jib cupboard next to the fireplace. The enlarged profile to the left is a section through the panelling.

⑤ A plaster and wood wall from Connecticut, mid-18th century. The rosette-capped pilasters are a regional form.
⑥ to ⑨ Cornice mouldings. The first elaborate examples are from South Carolina, c.1740, and Virginia, c.1773. Cornices could have pronounced projections, as in the profiles from Maryland, c.1740, and Rhode Island, 1786.
⑩ and ⑪ A fretwork chair rail and a carved skirting board/baseboard from Delaware.

⑫ Skirting boards/baseboards were fairly common. The top profiles are c.1750, the coved moulding is c.1760 and the ogee moulding with a quirk is c.1780. A plain board was used in simple houses or secondary rooms of grand houses.

① *This columnar screen separates the entrance hall from the stair hall at Cliveden, Philadelphia, 1764-67. The Doric details echo the architectural surround of the front door. The hall itself is a rare instance of a T-shaped hall in the Colonies.* CV

② *The panelled wall of the great drawing room at Drayton Hall, South Carolina, c.1740. It is accented by fluted Corinthian pilasters, which support an elaborate, deep cornice with egg-and-dart and modillion mouldings.* DH

③ *The stair hall at Mount Pleasant, Fairmount Park, Philadelphia, 1761-62, is L-shaped and the corner is marked with this bold fluted Doric pilaster. Note how the simple dado is continued up the staircase wall.* MP

④ *Painted walnut-grain panelling from the southeast parlour of the Hunter House, Newport, Rhode Island, c.1758.* NHH

⑤ *The stair landing at the Hunter House, Rhode Island, c.1758, has wainscotting beneath a plain plaster field. The dado has shadow mouldings which echo the lines of the staircase balusters.* NHH

⑥ *This dado wainscotting with very deeply moulded panels is from the central hallway of the Hunter House. It has been restored to a period shade of blue.* NHH

⑦ *This blue floral flocked wallpaper fragment is from an upstairs room in the Peyton Randolph House in Williamsburg, Virginia. The blue strip on the edge is the original, unfaded colour.* CWF

Ceilings

The "Apollo" drawing room ceiling on the ground floor at Kenmore in Fredericksburg, Virginia, c.1775. It is an elaborate ensemble of swags and roundels, with a central sunburst and head of the god, as seen in the half-view (bottom). The detail of the sunburst (top)

illustrates the lively and refined use of plasterwork. The substantial but relatively plain exterior of Kenmore belies the magnificence of its interiors. The spectacular ceilings are thought to be the work of immigrant craftsmen from Hesse in Germany. KF

Following precedents in Britain and Continental Europe, early houses have very low ceilings with exposed joists and summer beams (main, structural beams). The treatment of the exposed undersides of the floorboards is a fair measure of the quality of the building. In the simplest houses, joists and beams have rough adze or saw marks or even unstripped timbers with the bark intact. Such ceilings are often found on upper stories of finer houses as well. In slightly better houses, the framing is planed and squared. Further refinement consisted of chamfering the joists and beams and terminating the chamfers with decorative stops. A simple planed cornice moulding was a final touch. The ceiling could be left untreated or it could be whitewashed or painted decoratively, although surviving evidence for the latter is scant.

In the later 17th and early 18th centuries, plaster ceilings became more popular in new houses, and many earlier open ceilings were closed in. Usually, the joists were simply lathed and plastered, resulting in a slightly undulating surface. The juncture of ceiling and wall could be marked with a planed or carved cornice moulding. Occasionally, but more often in the later 18th century, the plaster ceiling was elaborately moulded. A completely different, Germanic tradition is seen in heavily moulded Baroque-style ceilings.

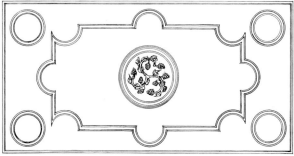

CEILINGS

① *A detail of the small drawing room ceiling at Drayton Hall, South Carolina,* c. 1738, probably the most sophisticated house of its day. DH

② *An early 18th-century plaster ceiling, moulded in situ rather than applied. It reflects a Baroque European tradition, as executed by German craftsmen of southeastern Pennsylvania.*

③ *and* ④ *Part-plans of the library and dining room ceilings in Kenmore, Virginia, c. 1775. These plaster ceilings illustrate the variety of motifs used in the best work.*

⑤ *The hand-carved central medallion on the small drawing room ceiling at Drayton Hall, South Carolina, c. 1738.* DHH

⑥ *The banquet hall ceiling from Mount Vernon, near Alexandria, Virginia, c. 1773, with a detail, right, of the curling vine motif that surrounds the central medallion panel. The ceilings are thought to be the work of the same craftsmen who executed the Kenmore ceilings.*

Floors

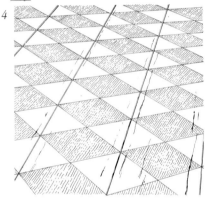

① *Apart from earth floors, plain wooden floors were by far the most common throughout the Colonial period. Americans enjoyed an abundant supply of slow growth pine, with very tight and straight grain that stands up to years of wear. Generally, these floors were neither stained nor varnished but left with a smooth, untreated surface.* NHH
② *Brick floors were usually laid in a herringbone pattern. They were common in cellars and hearths, and were occasionally used in porches or entryways, remaining much the same into the 19th century.* DH
③ *18th-century paving stones from Drayton Hall, South Carolina, in Portland limestone and Welsh redstone.* DHH

④ *Pine floors were sometimes painted in imitation of more expensive materials. The most common paint treatment was a simple checked pattern, to suggest tile or stone pavers.*
⑤ *The most common floor covering was the painted floorcloth. Made from canvas, it was the precursor to linoleum. The most usual pattern was a check, set on the diagonal. The earliest floorcloths were probably imported from Britain. They were used in places that received hard wear: entrance halls, passages, staircases and under sideboards.*
⑥ *By the late 18th century, some floors had more elaborate painted patterns. Either paint was spattered on a flat base colour, or, for fancier designs such as these, stencils were used. Black, greens and reds were popular.*

Most Colonial floors are of close-grained, wide, smooth pine boards, without stain or varnish. Small but significant variations in quality include random or matched widths, revealed or hidden nailing, the degree of smoothing and the method of joining the edges. Butting square edges, the least expensive method, leaves cracks. Better methods included half-lap, tongue-and-groove or spline joints (where the grooved boards are connected by a strip of wood). Many early houses had compacted earth floors, enlivened with scratched designs or covered with straw. Brick floors were most common in cellars. In the later 18th century some floors were painted in imitation of stone. Real stone floors are

rare but can be found in covered porches or in halls, usually laid diagonally in a checked pattern.

Painted floorcloths were the most common forms of covering. Marbleized diamond patterns are typical but more elaborate designs existed. They were usually found in the central hall, dining room or parlour of Georgian-style houses. Inexpensive rag-strip rugs are also typical and were even employed in some of the best houses. Rush matting was used occasionally. Carpets were rare: fine woven or knotted carpets of European or Oriental origin were reserved for the richest houses during the early 18th century but became far more common after the American Revolution.

Fireplaces

As the social centre of the household, the fireplace always received some decorative emphasis in Colonial houses, but the promotion of the hearth to the most important architectural feature of a house did not occur until the early 18th century. An important factor in this evolution was the separation of the kitchen and social rooms, which left the parlour fireplace unconstrained by the needs of cooking. This example, from the Great Hall on the second floor of Drayton Hall, Charleston, South Carolina, c.1740, reflects the popularity of English styles in the southern Colonies, where most of the gentry class were English, and the plantation lifestyle seemed to demand a grand country house. The decorative motifs in the overmantel are typical of a fireplace of this status. (The family crest is believed to be a 20th century addition.) DH

The simplest, earliest fireplaces were wooden frames with mud or plaster infill. These were used in slave houses up to the Revolutionary period. The earliest substantial houses had a large open brick hearth in the main living area, sometimes with a bake oven at the back. Such fireplaces were dirty and inefficient. Decoration was limited to a moulded lintel or rough surround and patterns laid in the brickwork. By the late 17th century surrounds with heavy bolection mouldings were common. The fireplace wall was the decorative focus in the halls, parlours, dining rooms and chambers of finer houses. Panelled cupboards, closets or stairway doors were grouped around the hearth.

During the 18th century the fireplace opening became smaller and the design of the flue was refined. Surrounds became more elaborate, inspired by the classical designs in British pattern books. The fanciest chimneypieces had pilasters or mouldings surmounted by carvings of fruit, flowers, Aesop's fables or classical motifs. Brick or tile slips complete the ensemble. A common alternative to an overmantel was to hang a painting or print above the fireplace, or to paint a landscape directly onto the central panel. The hearth contained andirons. These were often imported, although examples were made in the Colonies from the earliest days. Grates were rare and stoves quite rare during this period.

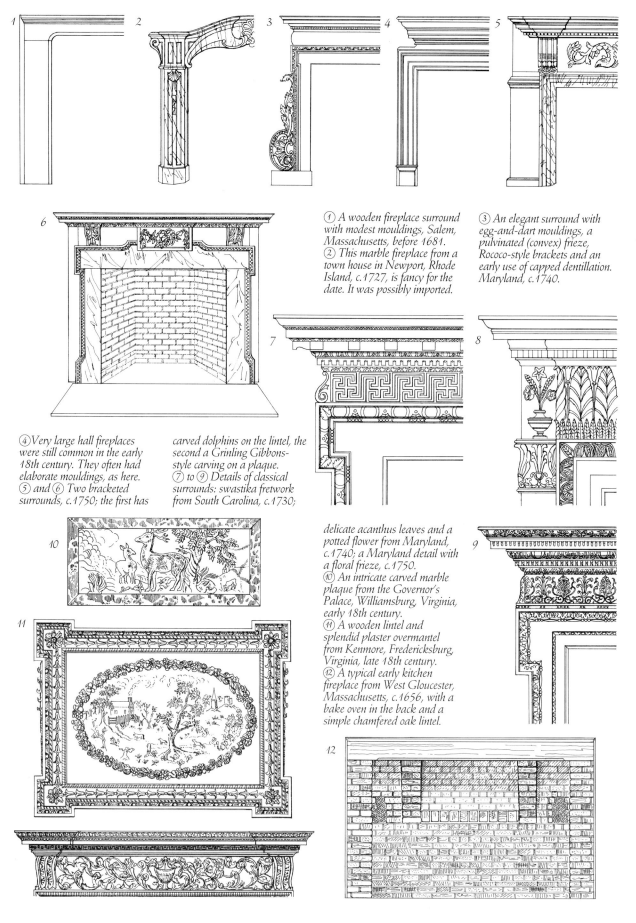

① *A wooden fireplace surround with modest mouldings, Salem, Massachusetts, before 1681.*
② *This marble fireplace from a town house in Newport, Rhode Island, c.1727, is fancy for the date. It was possibly imported.*

③ *An elegant surround with egg-and-dart mouldings, a pulvinated (convex) frieze, Rococo-style brackets and an early use of capped dentillation. Maryland, c.1740.*

④*Very large hall fireplaces were still common in the early 18th century. They often had elaborate mouldings, as here.*
⑤ *and* ⑥ *Two bracketed surrounds, c.1750; the first has*
carved dolphins on the lintel, the second a Grinling Gibbons-style carving on a plaque.
⑦ *to* ⑨ *Details of classical surrounds: swastika fretwork from South Carolina, c.1730;*
delicate acanthus leaves and a potted flower from Maryland, c.1740; a Maryland detail with a floral frieze, c.1750.
⑩ *An intricate carved marble plaque from the Governor's Palace, Williamsburg, Virginia, early 18th century.*
⑪ *A wooden lintel and splendid plaster overmantel from Kenmore, Fredericksburg, Virginia, late 18th century.*
⑫ *A typical early kitchen fireplace from West Gloucester, Massachusetts, c.1656, with a bake oven in the back and a simple chamfered oak lintel.*

① The parlour chimneypiece in the Hunter House, Newport, Rhode Island, 1758. No expense has been spared in the marbleized Corinthian pilasters and the rich, complex mouldings of the panelling and the surround. NHH

② In private, family rooms decoration is less important. Here, ornament is restricted to the panelled chimney breast and to the eight-panelled doors (not illustrated) on the same wall. A deep Italian moulding frames the fireplace opening. NHH

③ This fireplace in the Hunter House, Rhode Island, is restrained but impressive, with grain-painted panelling, a landscape overmantel and delft tile slips. Note also the elegant wrought-iron andirons with brass finials. NHH

④ The parlour chimneypiece in Cliveden, Germantown, Philadelphia, 1764-67, is of an elegant design. The carving is restricted to the egg-and-dart moulding around the

imposing marble surround and to the foliated consoles which support the moulded mantel shelf. Both the overmantel and the surround are "eared", a fashionable embellishment at this date. CV

⑤ The chimneypiece in the dining room of Mount Pleasant, Fairmount Park, Philadelphia, 1761-62, is similar to the last example, but has a more ornate, elongated chimney breast. This is distinguished by its

Chippendale-style pediment and by the carving, which is very similar to that on fine Philadelphia furniture of the period, and was possibly executed by one of the same craftsmen. MP

⑥ The marble surround and simple moulding give an accent to this fireplace which is placed on a plainly panelled wall. The fanciest fireplaces of middle-class houses often looked much like this. MP

① *This large hall fireplace has typical heavy bolection mouldings. The wood panelling and surround have marbled paintwork. It is from the Joseph Reynolds House, Bristol, Rhode Island, c.1698, and is 7 feet (2.10m) wide and more than 4 feet (1.20m) high.*

② *Italian mouldings around fireplaces were popular. This elegant example, c.1720, is coupled with a narrow pulvinated frieze and with panelled pilasters in the overmantel.*
③ *This classically inspired wooden chimneypiece, c.1725, has a rather shallow overmantel. The inner surround is marble.*
④ *A dramatic chimneypiece, from the small drawing room in Drayton Hall, Charleston, South Carolina, c.1738. It illustrates an early use of the broken pediment.*
⑤ *The elegant panelling around this fireplace is typical of middle-class or rural upper-class houses of the mid-18th century.*
⑥ *A plate from Abraham Swan's* The British Architect, *1745. Swan's book was a source of inspiration for several fine houses during this period.* AS
⑦ *A restrained fireplace with a pulvinated frieze. The chimney breast projects into the room. Delaware, mid-18th century.*
⑧ *Another projecting chimney breast from Portsmouth, New Hampshire, c.1755-65, with unrestrained Chippendale carvings.*

① to ③ *Three variations on the classical Georgian chimneypiece. The first is an early example of highly developed architecture from Shirley Plantation, Charles City, Virginia, c.1725-35. The second and third chimneypieces are both from Massachusetts, c.1760, and have fluted Doric pilasters, but the interpretation and emphasis differ dramatically, showing the differences that can occur even in a comparatively small region.*
④ *Three cast-iron firebacks. These could be simple iron plates or much more elaborate cast types, as here, bearing dates and places of manufacture.*

⑤ *Wood-burning stoves did not come into use until the late 18th century, except in some German and Dutch settlements. These examples are basically open iron fireplaces. The first is Benjamin Franklin's design, which helped popularize the stove.*
⑥ *A selection of andirons. Brass, or brass and iron andirons were reserved for the best rooms of the finest houses. The first example is early 18th-century and has penny feet; the second is later and is from Paul Revere's foundry in Boston, Massachusetts. Cast-iron figures were popular in formal or semi-formal rooms of middle- and upper-class houses. These may have been painted. The third andiron, early 18th century, is cast in the form of a woman; the fourth is a Hessian soldier, probably cast by immigrant German craftsmen in the late 18th century. Finally, a wrought-iron andiron, common in most households and in the secondary rooms of more pretentious homes.*

⑦ *Delft tiles, usually Dutch, were fashionable for fireplace slips. Amusing figures and religious or moralistic themes were popular.*

Staircases

The double mahogany stairway in Drayton Hall, Charleston, South Carolina, 1738-42. Reminiscent of English Palladianism, it is an expression of the colonists' striving to recreate *their homelands on American soil. This was probably the most elaborate staircase in the Colonies at the time of its construction and was highly influential.* DH

Most early staircases were rudimentary, consisting of a simple ladder or open tread up to the loft in single-story houses. Some 17th-century New England houses have a joined and moulded staircase leading from the lobby-like entryway, while turned balustrades are more common in Virginia. A common Colonial stairway was the box winder, usually contained in the space next to the chimney flue and hidden behind a door in the fireplace wall. This was often balanced by a cupboard or pantry door on the other side of the hearth. Such an arrangement is typical of small but often fine houses of the 18th and well into the 19th centuries. Box winders were also frequently used as a back stair in the service wing of substantial Georgian houses. The handrail was often attached to the outside wall.

In classically designed houses the stairway was conceived as a showpiece. Central hall staircases tend to be open-string (with the stair-ends visible) and have moulded, turned and carved decorations. Newel posts and handrails are the pinnacle of the turner's art. Some balustrades have a repeated pattern of three different turnings, typical of early Georgian designs. The sides of staircases are decorated with carved stair-ends and panelling. Cantilevered and double staircases are rare; open circular staircases were not found until the post-Revolutionary period.

① A steep rise and closely spaced balusters were common on early staircases. c.1675.
② Early 18th-century turned balusters. Massachusetts.
③ Less expensive flat balusters had stark silhouettes, c.1720.
④ Attenuated, closely spaced balusters show classical influence. Connecticut, c.1740.
⑤ to ⑦ Georgian staircases, with balusters fixed into the treads and decorative stair-ends: North Carolina, c.1780; Virginia, 1753-59; Connecticut, c.1750-60.

⑧ The degree of complexity of handrail mouldings depended on the class of the house and the status of the staircase. These examples date from the early 17th to the mid-18th centuries.
⑨ Stair-ends were a favourite location for carved decorative detail on later Colonial staircases. These typical examples are from Maryland (1729 and c.1740) and Delaware (late 18th century).

⑩ The staircase at Hammond-Harwood House, Annapolis, Maryland, 1773-4 was designed by William Buckland. Its simple, flowing lines look toward Federal elegance. HHH
⑪ The central stair hall is typical of American Georgian architecture. The details vary, but the pattern of a long hall with a bracketed arch and a staircase to the rear was very popular. NHH

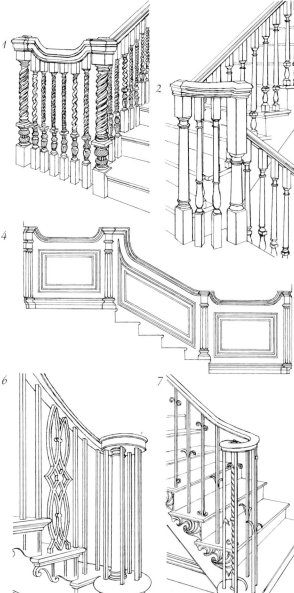

① A detail of the elaborate staircase at the Jeremiah Lee House, Marblehead, Massachusetts, 1768. Landings in grander houses like this often had emphatic baluster displays.
② A less elaborate, more common landing rail. Charleston, South Carolina, mid- to late 18th century.
③ This staircase is typical of middle-class merchant, artisan and farm houses of the late 18th century.
④ Inner walls on staircases were often given a treatment complementary to the balustrade. This "shadow" railing with wainscotting and pilasters, c.1720, is representative.

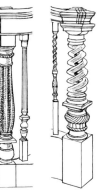

⑤ Newel posts provide structural support to the ends of stair rails. They also give visual stability and become the logical focus of decoration when staircases are no longer hidden behind walls. The examples shown are from Connecticut, late 17th century; South Carolina, c.1730; Virginia, early 18th century; Maryland, c.1740 (a Germanic board newel post); New Hampshire, 1760;

Massachusetts, 1770.
⑥ An early example of the Federal style, with mostly square balusters and restrained ornament on the handrail and stair-ends. Massachusetts, late 18th century.
⑦ An even lighter effect is obtained in the William Gibbes House at Charleston, South Carolina, c.1780, through the unusual use of iron balusters in an interior setting.

⑧ The staircase at Hunter House, Newport, Rhode Island, 1758, has elegant and expensive twist-turned balusters in sets of three, a typical Georgian treatment. Note the panelled stair-ends and the shadow rail with wainscotting on the wall behind the staircase. *NHH*

⑨ A detail of the staircase at Cliveden, Germantown, Philadelphia, 1764-7, a highly refined, classical composition. The baluster turnings are elegantly attenuated and the stair-ends are simple sawn and applied profiles, with no carved ornament. *CV*

Built-in furniture

A fine built-in cupboard, one of a pair flanking the fireplace in the dining room at Mount Pleasant, Philadelphia, 1761-62. The doors were often left open to display the ceramics and silver. Alternatively, many cupboards had glass doors, particularly later in the 18th century as glass became less expensive. MP

Built-in furniture in a Colonial house was a sign of quality and permanence. Early settlers and later frontiersmen had good movable furniture but only rudimentary shelving or roughly-framed built-in bedsteads. As people became more settled, built-in furniture improved. Cupboards were the most common type. The few surviving examples from the early 17th century tend to be small shelved spaces behind panelled doors, built into the fireplace wall, although some houses had more sophisticated dresser walls or hanging wall cupboards. By the second quarter of the 18th century the built-in cupboard had become an important feature of American architecture. Most were divided into a formal display space above and a less visible, everyday storage area below. A shelved alcove behind panelled or glazed doors, above or beside the fireplace, is most typical. Corner or wall cupboards are more elaborate. Here, pewter, ceramics, and silver were displayed, set off by some of the richest architectural detailing in the house. The shelves can be scalloped and occasionally the niche has a shell-head.

Beds built into a wall are characteristic of German and Dutch Colonial houses, as are built-in benches, usually found in porches. Most Colonial kitchens had movable furniture but some were fitted with dressers, shelving, cupboards and occasionally work surfaces.

① and ② Two New England cupboards. The first is from Salem, Massachusetts, c.1720; the single door is unusual. The second is from Lime Rock, Connecticut, c.1720-30. Both have shell-head interiors.
③ An elegant corner cupboard. Fairly narrow at two feet (60cm) wide, it has a moulded cornice and shaped shelves.

Massachusetts, c.1750-70.
④ A glazed corner cupboard, Connecticut, late 18th century.
⑤ A late 18th-century cupboard from Delaware with double doors above and below.
⑥ An early 18th-century cupboard from Connecticut, with a regional, rosette motif.
⑦ A corner cupboard from Virginia, c.1725. The form may

be compared to the first two cupboards, but the marbleized paintwork and the rare early use of swags are extraordinary.
⑧ A corner cupboard from Laurel, Maryland, c.1750. It has remarkable window tracery and Corinthian capitals.
⑨ This cupboard from Virginia is unusually located in the middle of a wall, opposite the

fireplace. Late 18th century.
⑩ A late 17th/early 18th-century built-in dresser. Massachusetts.
⑪ A typical mid-18th-century fireplace wall with storage closets behind panelled doors.
⑫ A cupboard built into the wall above a fireplace, Rhode Island, c.1760. It is typical of the southern states as well.

Services

① *Guttering became popular on larger houses in the late 18th century. The top and middle hopper heads/leader heads are from Connecticut. The bottom example, from New Jersey, is of a type still seen today.*
② *A six-plate stove, cast with moralizing emblems. The fancy legs are unusual. 1760s.*
③ *A Pennsylvanian jamb stove, dated 1760, bearing a Low German Biblical quotation.*
④ *A Dutch ten-plate stove, possibly imported.*
⑤ *A detail of Lord Botetourt's Stove, imported from London, c.1770, for the Governor's Palace, Williamsburg, Virginia.*

BUILT-IN FURNITURE

SERVICES

It was unusual for Colonial houses to have any specialized services apart from fireplaces and bake ovens. When better facilites are found, they are usually indicative of higher status. Most houses, for example, had no guttering system, and rain water simply ran straight off the roof shingles. A very few, grand houses had gutters and capped down pipes/downspouts in the British style. Gutters became more common after the Revolution. In urban areas, houses could have a brick or stone drain at ground level which directed water away from the building.

Some of the most advanced services were in German-Dutch settled communities. They were among the first to use wood-burning stoves, which could be very elaborate ceramic plate structures. Winston-Salem, North Carolina, a Germanic Moravian settlement, supplied cold running water to several houses and public buildings through a gravity-fed system of wooden pipes. Some of the Winston-Salem kitchens had heated surfaces or stoves not unlike range tops. These were also found in the French settlements of Louisiana and Quebec.

A detached privy was the most advanced system of waste disposal. These were often moved about, although more permanent large brick privies were used on some plantations. A few kitchens had stone sinks. These were hand-filled but sometimes had a drain.

Lighting

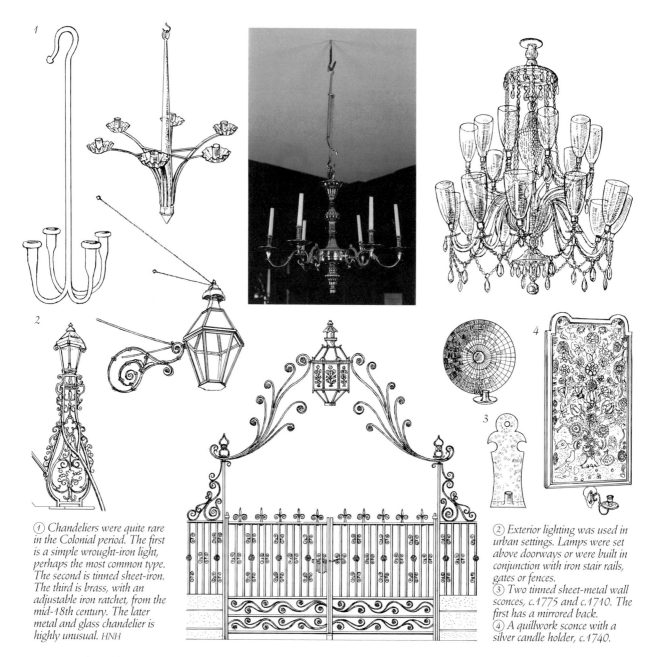

① *Chandeliers were quite rare in the Colonial period. The first is a simple wrought-iron light, perhaps the most common type. The second is tinned sheet-iron. The third is brass, with an adjustable iron ratchet, from the mid-18th century. The later metal and glass chandelier is highly unusual.* HNH

② *Exterior lighting was used in urban settings. Lamps were set above doorways or were built in conjunction with iron stair rails, gates or fences.*
③ *Two tinned sheet-metal wall sconces, c.1775 and c.1710. The first has a mirrored back.*
④ *A quillwork sconce with a silver candle holder, c.1740.*

Few Colonial houses had any sort of built-in lighting. Colonists relied on rush lights, oil lamps, Betty lamps (boat-shaped or saucer-shaped lamps filled with grease or oil), candles, and the glow of the fireplace for nighttime illumination. Chandeliers and hanging lamps were exceptional in domestic buildings prior to the third quarter of the 18th century. These were only rarely the elaborate glass types often displayed in restored Colonial houses. Usually they were much more modest hanging candleholders made of wood and iron, iron, or tinned sheet-iron.

Sconces may have been much more common. The simplest type was of tinned sheet-iron. More elaborate examples used small pieces of mirrored glass on a concave reflecting surface, which cast interesting patterns of light on the walls. Perhaps the rarest and most elaborate were quillwork pictures, made by young girls as school projects. These were scenic pictures built up from small pieces of scrolled paper and wax dusted with mica (lustrous minerals). The picture was set in a deep frame with an iron or glass candleholder in front.

By the mid- to late 18th century some finer houses began to have exterior lanterns, either attached near the front door or as part of a fence or gate. These usually consisted of an iron framework with glass sides which contained a cup for a candle or oil lamp.

Metalwork

① A high-quality wrought-iron gateway with a lamp: a mark of status. Charleston, South Carolina, late 18th century.
② An elegant iron stair railing

from Drayton Hall, South Carolina, c.1740. DH
③ The iron entrance gate from Westover, Charles City County, Virginia, 1730-34. It was

imported from England; similar designs were American-made.
④ Chunky cast-iron balustrading from the entrance to a house in Libertytown, Maryland, late 18th century.
⑤ Balustrades of iron stems with applied wrought-iron scrolls were popular in the early to mid-18th century.
⑥ Pronged and bud-like iron finials decorated fences and gates. Mid- to late 18th century.
⑦ Weather vanes are important examples of Colonial folk art as they allowed blacksmiths and tinsmiths a free rein. Fretted dates were common, as on the first example from Pennsylvania. The second vane, from Albany, New York, mid-17th century, takes the popular cock form. It is brass. The last vane is a Germanic design of 1670 from Pennsylvania.
⑧ Bootscrapers were used in towns and on some farms. Most were plain bars, but these 18th-century examples are more imaginative.

Aside from lamps, andirons, and hardware, the ironwork commonly found in American architecture includes bootscrapers, weather vanes, fences and gates.

Bootscrapers were often placed near the entrance of Colonial houses, particularly in towns and cities where the streets could be especially muddy. They were wrought, or cut out of sheet iron, and set in masonry or in the ground. Usually, they were quite plain, but some are flanked with scrolls, knobs or finials.

Weather vanes were most often found on public buildings but were occasionally added to domestic structures. Many are considered examples of folk art, since there were few guidelines for their forms, and local ironworkers made them in fairly fanciful shapes. They were wrought or cut out, like scrapers, and decorated with arrows, scrolls, letters, dates and sometimes figures of animals or people. Some of the fanciest had a brass or copper ball pierced by the shaft of the vane.

Iron gates and fences, like weather vanes, were most often a feature of public buildings, but their mark of grandeur made them popular on pretentious domestic buildings. The fanciest work was generally reserved for front gates which included very elaborate scrolled and foliated wrought or cast ironwork, sometimes including a lamp to illuminate the entry. Porches often had wrought-iron balustrades.

LIGHTING

METALWORK

Woodwork

① *A reconstruction of an early 17th-century settlement house from St Mary's City, Maryland. The English colonists drew on the vernacular traditions of their homeland and built expedient shelters with earth-set posts, riven (hand split) clapboards and shingles, and wood-framed chimneys. The large size, glass casement windows and stylish flared roof line of this example set it apart as one of the more substantial early structures. While usually intended to be temporary, such houses often ended up being maintained and altered over a period of years or even decades. HSMC*

② *The Vassall-Longfellow House, Cambridge, Massachusetts, 1759, is a fine example of Palladianism in the New England colonies. The wooden pilasters, pediment, doorway and later piazzas at the sides give the house a classical appearance, reminiscent of designs by the Scottish architect, James Gibbs. These Georgian features have been combined with traditional clapboarding. The house has a typical Georgian floor plan, with rooms arranged around a central hall. LH*

The most common building material by far in the Colonial period was wood, whose qualities were important in shaping the early Colonial style. Whereas brick nogging or wattle-and-daub infill left English timber frames exposed, American houses were covered with weatherboards, and instead of thatched roofs they had shingles. Even brick and stone houses had wooden roofs, porches, window and door frames and fences. In the Georgian period the properties of wood were often hidden. Wooden sidings would imitate ashlar masonry.

Designs for brick and stone buildings and details illustrated in European pattern books were adapted for wood by American artisans. In many cases the result was flatter but more ornate. The artisans also introduced ideas from furniture design; they were not constrained by the rigid guild systems of their native countries and could practise more than one trade. Thus, early American architectural woodwork enjoys contributions from chair turners, cabinetmakers, carvers and joiners. Trades grew more specialized in the early 18th century.

Perhaps the rarest survivals of the woodworkers' craft are fences. Split-rail fences, pale fences and ornamental garden fences were an important element of the Colonial landscape. The less utilitarian the fence, the more elaborate the pattern. Like doors on facades, gates were the most decorative sections of fences.

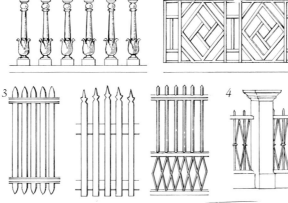

① A balcony and window surround from
Rhode Island, c.1760: a distinctly American
mix of classicism and traditional carpentry.
② Three balcony railings of the late 18th
century. The first comprises turned rails; the
others are "Chinese Chippendale" railings,
popular in the later 18th century.
③ Three typical fences, late 18th-century:
two pale or "picket" fences and a fence
showing Chinese Chippendale influence.
④ Typical 18th-century wooden gates
continued the fence pattern.
⑤ and ⑥ Elaborate gateways have piers
that resemble pillars topped by urns.

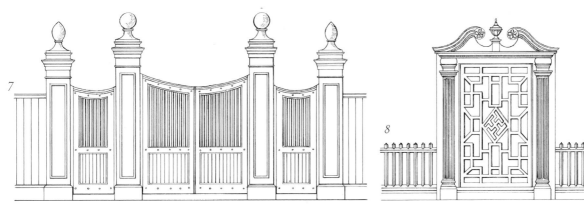

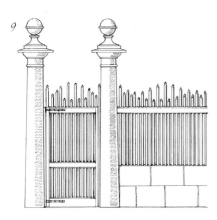

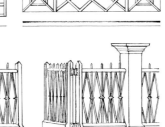

⑦ A triple gateway from Charleston, South
Carolina, for carriages and pedestrians. The
stone piers have fashionable ball finials.
⑧ A Chippendale gate from Farmington,
Connecticut, from the second half of the 18th
century. The surround resembles a doorcase.
⑨ A gate and fence from Charleston, South
Carolina, with diamond-shaped finials.
⑩ A detail from the landing in the William
Randolph House, Tuckahoe, Virginia,
c.1712-30, showing the quality of the interior
carving.
⑪ A carved cherub from the spandrel of a
cupboard in the parlour of the Hunter House,
Rhode Island, c.1758, one of four: perhaps
the most famous features of the house. NHH

LATE GEORGIAN

1765–1811

① *The Adelphi development on the River Thames in London, 1768-72, initiated the reign of Robert and James Adam as the leading architects of the late 18th century. This original drawing shows how the development was conceived as a whole, wharf and terraces/rows together. RA*
② *A ground floor plan of a typical gentleman's country retreat of the late 1790s. Although simple and small, the house is very comfortable and has an internal water closet. JM*
③ *A gentleman's country house*

by John Plaw, 1794, showing the attention that was paid to the proportion and symmetry of rural villas. JNP
④ *A detail of Moray Place, Edinburgh, a development of terraced/row houses built on a duodecagon (twelve-sided) plan around a garden in the early 19th century. The deeply carved, crisp rustication is characterisitc of Edinburgh architecture at this period. Note the authentic lamp standard. SP*
⑤ *The entrance front to Home House, London, c.1775, by the Adam brothers. The fine porch takes the form of a temple portico, a very fashionable feature of large town houses.*

Following the Peace of Paris, which ended the Seven Years' War with France and her allies in 1763, building in Britain gathered momentum and the 1770s and 80s were boom decades. The Palladian principles of proportion which had governed domestic architecture in the first half of the 18th century continued to be applied to almost all houses, but the detailing of terraces/rows and villas became more delicate and more uniform.

The uniformity recommended in Palladian pattern books for terraces/rows and squares of private houses was rarely achieved in the first half of the century, owing to the profiteering of developers. However, the "palace" facade, in which the centre of a terrace/row is marked by pilasters and a pediment, was increasingly preferred after 1760, not only by architects and theorists but by speculative builders who found that this new magnificence helped to sell property. The first such developments were the Circus and the Royal Crescent in Bath, parts of the grandest conception of unified urban planning seen in Britain. The architects Robert

Adam (1728-92) and Sir William Chambers (1723-96) made these monumental facades fashionable and introduced to Britain a grandeur derived from Roman precedents, which had already inspired the Neo-classical style in Continental Europe.

Adam was the most successful British architect of the second half of the 18th century. He built some of the grandest town and country houses of the period, but his development of the Adelphi, overlooking the River Thames in London (1768-72), was perhaps his most influential work. The terraces/rows of brick houses were united by the treatment of the facade, with swags, ribbons and arabesques on the exterior walls, echoing the treatment of the interior. This must have appeared revolutionary to eyes accustomed to the propriety of Palladian design. The pattern books of the 1770s and 80s rapidly translated these devices to more modest houses.

The 1774 Building Act defined the architectural standards within which the new ornament could be employed. This ambitious Act laid down categories or

① *Sculpture galleries were an integral part of the best houses in this age of connoisseurship. This detail from Newby Hall, Yorkshire,* *early 1770s, shows classical statues and busts in a complementary setting, complete with highly decorated alcoves.* NH

② *The stairwell at Home House, London, c.1775, is an exercise in light and space: Robert and James Adam at their best.* HH

"rates" for houses, ranging from first to fourth rate. These grades were determined by a combined calculation of the value and the volume of the property. Among the structural requirements, the Act introduced revised fire regulations concerning sash windows. Following legislation in 1709 these had to be set back from the building line by 4 inches (10cm); now they had to be sunk within the wall face. This meant that only a fine line of wooden frame was visible from the street, a necessity which sat comfortably beside the prevailing taste for sinuous, elegant lines.

In tandem with the development of the city terrace/row, the later 18th century saw the construction of large numbers of small suburban houses. Developers took advantage of the less expensive land to erect houses on larger plots. These owed something to the Palladian villas of the 1750s, which were modest country houses without porticoes or basements. Many of the later villas were plain classical boxes, which aped in miniature the symmetrical country house facade. Others were built in semi-detached pairs, usually unified by simple applied ornament to suggest a single house. However, the Gothic Revival house, with ogee-arched windows and doors, or "Gothic" tracery inserted into conventional round topped windows, was also considered suitable for a more rustic setting. At the end of the century the Picturesque fashion in architecture led to the introduction of asymmetrical villa plans, with small houses sporting "Tuscan" towers and eaves, reminiscent of the follies and towers seen in the paintings of Claude Lorrain. Other fashions and fads were adopted, such as the taste for Egyptian motifs, which touched even speculative building at the turn of the century.

Brick remained the staple building material. In London grey stock brick, darkened by the smoke of sea-coal fires, gave the city a grimy patina. The grandest houses could be finished with stone. In Bath the local soft stone was the universal facing for the facades of walls built of stone rubble, although the dressed ashlar had a tendency to crumble. By contrast, the hard stone used in Edinburgh was structural and finely tooled.

Lime mortars had been used as a finish since the time of Inigo Jones and were known generically as stucco, from the Italian term for plaster. A patent "Roman cement" was introduced in 1796. Both materials were used to simulate stone and modified architectural features in the last thirty years of the 18th century. They were applied over brick and were generally marked out in horizontal and vertical lines to resemble ashlar blocks. Stucco was then painted a warm yellowish tone, in imitation of Bath stone. Houses were either stuccoed through the basement and ground floor facade or fully stuccoed; the latter is especially found on grander developments from the end of the period. John Nash's terraces at Regent's Park, London (1811-28), are the apogee of this taste. An invaluable innovation was Coade stone, an artificial stone composed of a terracotta-like material but white in colour. This could be cast and so the effect of carved ornament came within the budget of the popular builder. A huge diversity of Coade stone details was marketed, but it is perhaps the keystones with faces in high relief which are the most notable castings. These decorated many facades between c.1775 and 1810.

Other innovations played their part in the period. The hob grate, which had been introduced in the 1750s, ousted the less efficient, dirtier basket grate, and improved oil lamps were introduced to the houses of the rich: thus by 1800 the average house was warmer and cleaner to live in, and the grand house was also better lit. All areas of design fell under the influence of Robert Adam and his associates, and even these grates and lights reflect the prevalent classical taste of the era.

Doors

The black-painted front door of a house in Bedford Square, London, 1775-80, is typical of the discreet uniformity of late Georgian urban design. In this case narrow flanking windows

enhance the light levels in the hall. A Coade stone keystone and Coade stone slabs, in imitation of volcanic rock, add grandeur to an otherwise plain and simple pattern.

The basic carpentry of the Georgian door changed very little in the late 18th century, but detailing was influenced by the prevailing Neo-classical taste.

The casing of the street door was modified by the fanlight. Early in the period fanlights are generally simple and rectangular, but the semi-circular or segmental type, which is particularly well adapted to filigree ornament, became increasingly fashionable. Fanlights were made in wood or, for grander houses, wrought in metal. At the end of the century cast-metal tracery became very general. A Coade stone surround echoes the graceful sweep of the fanlight above some later doors. By contrast, other late doorcases, porches

and porticoes have an angular, Grecian simplicity.

Typical street doors and internal doors remained six-panelled. The modest house door is deal (fir or pine) and has plain fielded panels; grand street doors may be oak. All were painted, black and sometimes dark green. Toward the end of the century the occasional bright blue door relieved the sobre streetscape.

Most internal doors are of painted deal, but the best are mahogany, with polished panels framed by incised ribs or a beaded moulding. Inlays of unusual woods such as ebony, holly and cherry are also used. The vogue for painted Pompeian and Etruscan decoration within the door panels ran from the 1770s onward.

The actual front door tended to be plain: it was the surround that indicated the status of a house.
① A classical pediment supported on engaged columns (partly sunk into the wall) adds dignity to this house in Bath.
② A Coade stone keystone could enliven an austere doorcase. Numerous facial designs existed.

③ and ④The fanlight above the door was an important area of enrichment. The simple semi-circular light within a brick arch, left, follows the same basic form as the more elegant doorcase from a house in Guildford, Surrey, right. The scalloped motif above the door is particularly graceful.

⑤ and ⑥The grandest elaboration of forms incorporated wrought ironwork not only in the fanlight but in the flanking windows. This was particularly fashionable in Dublin. The flamboyant second example shows the fashion for giving the name of the occupant above the front door. BM

⑦This doorcase is from an early London speculation by John Nash, 1777-8. The Ionic pilasters are Greek Revival elements.
⑧ Variations on the simple spoked fanlight include Adamesque Roman detailing, geometric forms and the ogee arched Gothic form.

① *A Bath front door in the Adam style, c.1780, with an elaborately wrought fanlight, is given added scale and dignity by the flanking pilasters.*

② *In contrast, this pair of double doors from the very end of the 18th century exhibits the taste of the Greek Revival in its severe rectilinear elegance. Note the shaped panels which frame the large, original door handles. The letterbox, as elsewhere, is a later insertion.*

③ *The rather narrow proportions of this door from Bath are disguised by rich detailing, in the moulded architrave and in the shaped panels within decorative frames.*

④ *This cottage doorway from the 1780s has almost no detailing. Simplified pilasters terminate in attractive brackets which support a functional, lightly moulded porch.* AH

Interior doors were painted or grained, unless the wood used was of high quality, such as mahogany, which would be polished.

⑤ *A typical six-panelled door and moulded doorcase in Avenue House, Bedfordshire, c.1780.* AH

⑥ *Paintwork is used to dramatic effect on this doorway in Home House, London, c.1775. The panelling on the door is picked out along the mouldings. The escutcheon plate and door handle are contemporary.* HH

⑦ *A handsome moulded architrave with a gilded frieze enriches the surround of these double doors designed by Robert Adam for Home House. Double doors were employed in the principal reception rooms of only the grandest houses.* HH

⑧ *The carved detail of the panel mouldings on this door at Newby Hall, Yorkshire, early 1770s, emphasizes the magnificently grained wood. Fine hardwoods were the preserve of the very rich. Intricate carvings on the surround complete the group.* NH

Internal doorways and details.
① and ② Reeded and incised
decoration enriched door panels.
The surround could incorporate
pilasters and a grand
entablature. The first example,
c.1770, is inspired by the work
of the Adam brothers.

③ An oval room would be
served by a curved doorway, as
here in Sydney Place, Bath.
④ Gothic doorways were freed
from the strict proportions that
applied to classical ensembles,
as seen in this narrow doorway
from the turn of the century.

⑤ In the mid-century the Rococo
style found favour in some of the
grandest houses. This lobby door
of the 1770s is from Abington
Hall, Northamptonshire. It has
side lights that repeat the glazed
panels. Such fantasies contrast
with the plain classical elegance
that prevailed in the 1760s.
⑥ Painted Pompeian and
Etruscan decoration were
fashionable in the 1770s and
80s. This Etruscan door is from
Osterley Park House, London.
The motifs reflect a complete
room theme.

⑦ This doorframe, c.1800,
uses classical motifs rather than
the vocabulary of the classical
Orders. The fielded panels are
as elaborate as the surround.
⑧ At the end of the century
there was a vogue for Egyptian
motifs, inspired by Napoleon's
campaigns in Egypt. These
doors of c.1804-10 are from a
billiard room decorated in the
Egyptian taste.
⑨ Three examples of classical
entablatures from the 1760s. RA
⑩ An overdoor, c.1775-77,
with elegant stuccowork.

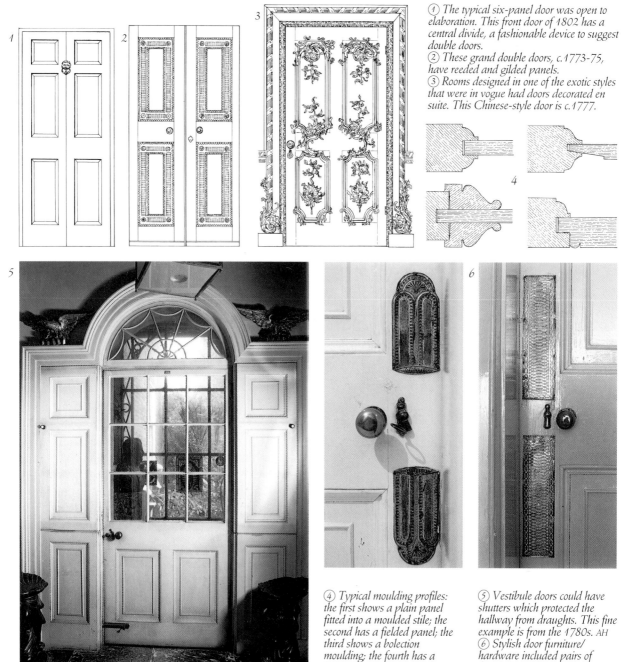

① The typical six-panel door was open to elaboration. This front door of 1802 has a central divide, a fashionable device to suggest double doors.
② These grand double doors, c.1773-75, have reeded and gilded panels.
③ Rooms designed in one of the exotic styles that were in vogue had doors decorated en suite. This Chinese-style door is c.1777.

④ Typical moulding profiles: the first shows a plain panel fitted into a moulded stile; the second has a fielded panel; the third shows a bolection moulding; the fourth has a beaded panel.

⑤ Vestibule doors could have shutters which protected the hallway from draughts. This fine example is from the 1780s. AH
⑥ Stylish door furniture/ hardware included pairs of fingerplates/push plates. AH

⑦ Front door knockers came in a wide variety of cast-iron designs. The Greek lady, left, reflects Neo-classical tastes.
⑧ Fairly simple wrought-iron door latches were still used.
⑨ Robert Adam devised elegant fittings for his interior doors. This knob and escutcheon set epitomizes his best work.
⑩ Ordinary houses had plain metal or wooden door knobs of pleasing, curvaceous forms.
⑪ A set of polished brass fittings, late 18th century.
⑫ A brass box lock with a turned hardwood handle, c.1790.

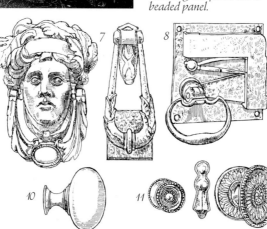

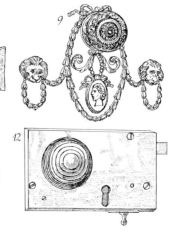

Windows

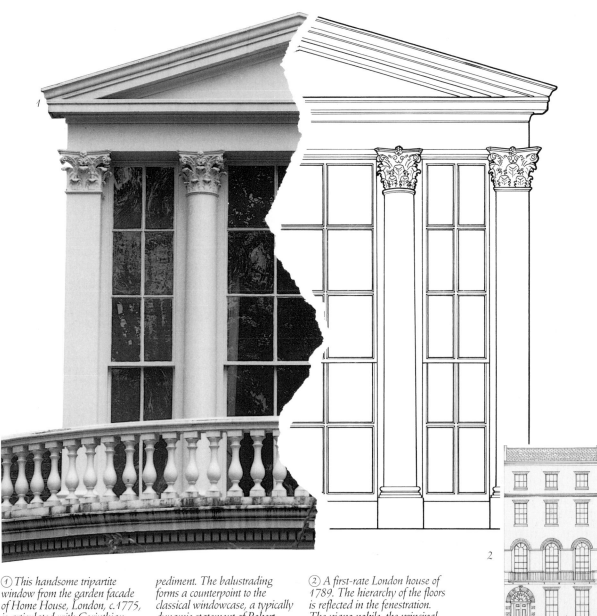

① *This handsome tripartite window from the garden facade of Home House, London, c.1775, is articulated with Corinthian pilasters, engaged columns and a pediment. The balustrading forms a counterpoint to the classical windowcase, a typically dynamic statement of Robert Adam's architectural style. HH*

② *A first-rate London house of 1789. The hierarchy of the floors is reflected in the fenestration. The piano nobile, the principal floor, receives the most attention.*

I n 1774 new fire safety legislation was introduced that required window frames to be rebated within the wall face. This drew the eye away from the frame and toward the proportions of the glazing bars, which became more and more delicate as the century progressed. Rusticated and plain Coade stone surrounds, seen from the 1780s, restored some weight to the frame.

Facades became elegantly attenuated in the 1770s and windows became taller, so that windows on upper floors may be almost as large as those of the ground floor. Building manuals advised that the total window area of a room should be equivalent to the square root of the length times breadth times height of the room.

Drawing room window sills on the floor above the entrance level are often very low, or at floor level, opening onto balconets or onto a balcony that runs across all the windows. To aid access, sash windows were replaced by French doors in the 1780s and 1790s.

Variations on conventional sashes occur at the end of the century. Round-headed window openings become popular, and these have either arched or rectangular sash frames. If the sash box is rectangular, the top of it will be hidden between the exterior and interior masonry and the central glazed panel will follow the curve of the arch. Gothic windows remained popular; these can have ogee-shaped arches and windows.

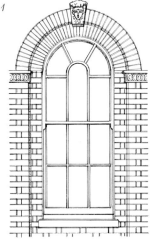

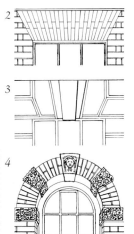

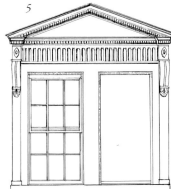

① *A typical window built to the requirements of the 1774 Building Act. The window jambs*

are recessed behind the outer face of the building; this leaves only a thin profile of the sash visible.

② *to* ④ *Brick decoration and rustication remained current, but a highly fashionable window could have textured Coade stone slabs and a Coade stone keystone.*
⑤ *This pediment unites the facades of two terrace/row*

houses; only one house has a window.
⑥ *This shallow elliptical brickwork arch surrounds a provincial window, c.1780. A London window would be more elongated.*

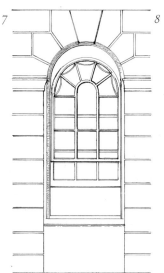

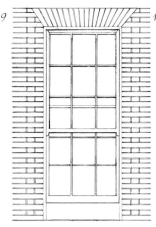

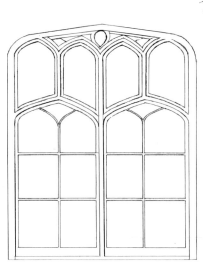

⑦ *and* ⑧ *Sash windows could be round-headed (left, c.1790) or even ogee-headed, in a Gothic vein. Gothic windows were often incorporated into houses of a classical design.*

⑨ *and* ⑩ *In the 1760s and 70s the drawing room on the piano nobile of town houses would have*

long sash windows. By the end of the 18th century French doors were much more fashionable.

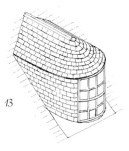

⑪ *This illustration is based on a design by Robert Adam, 1772. It would be suitable for the centre of a very grand facade.*
⑫ *At the turn of the century full-blooded Gothic houses were once again being built. This wall-high window is from Luscombe Castle, Devon, by John Nash, 1800–1804.*
⑬ *Dormers were usually square, but they were occasionally bowed to give animation to the facade.*

① The central pediment draws these three windows together as a group. The string course forms a running sill.
② These windows are united by the architectural enrichment of a shared entablature, engaged pilasters and an engaged carved stone balustrade.
③ A Venetian window, comprising three floor-length sashes. Note the "spider's web" tracery of the round-headed sash.
④ A plainer version of the previous example. This is typical of modest town houses in Bath.
⑤ Deep-cut rusticated stonework was popular at the entrance-level. The dropped keystone is a Palladian motif which dates the window as c.1750-60.
⑥ An attenuated window with a classical stone surround, early 1770s. The shutters are contemporary. NH
⑦ A detail of a shutter at Newby Hall, Yorkshire, showing a guilloche motif. NH

Walls

The Neo-classical style provided a complete architectural vocabulary with which to ornament a wall. At its grandest, as in this example from Home

House, London, c.1775, designed by Robert Adam, such decoration was rich with filigree gold patterns. Here, the gold is offset by the cool greens of

Adam's decorative palette. Pilasters frame mirrored panels, giving elegant spatial ambiguity to the room. The mirrors also reflected and enhanced the

candlelight from the integral girandoles. Note how the wall and ceiling decoration are unified. HH

Most fashionable houses of the 1760s had a panelled dado with fabric hangings stretched on battens between the chair rail and the cornice. Velvets and silks were the most opulent and expensive materials; wool damasks were very popular. Modest houses had plaster walls or they had cotton hangings above the dado: this was an acceptable material in even quite grand houses. Wooden panelling was increasingly eliminated from the dado after 1760. It was replaced by plaster, usually painted in flat white or a stone colour or marbled in a stronger or deeper colour for greater grandeur (this disguised the fugitive nature of the pigments). The chair rail continued to be made of wood. Wallpaper came into

more general use in the 1770s and patterned flock and printed designs supplanted textiles as fashionable field decoration. These was either stuck directly onto the wall or hung from battens; the last method allowed costly papers to be removed. Paper was commonly used to line all walls before painting, except the entrance hall which would be painted plaster. Popular colours were pea green, turquoise, deep pink and Chinese yellow. The surface was varnished if a high finish was required.

Stucco ornament on a plaster ground enlivened the grandest decorative schemes. Motifs such as acanthus leaves, honeysuckle shoots, swags and ribbons were used at the cornice and to frame plaster medallions.

WALLS

Consistent ornament was used throughout an interior to create a unified design. This principle was applied to plain panelling and ornamental plasterwork alike.

① and ② A profile and section of simple panelling from an ordinary house. It would cover the whole wall.

③ This plaster wall with windows, c.1790, shows how the chair rail continued to define the proportions of a room even when there was no panelling. The mirrors between the windows enhance the sense of light and space in the room.

④ This plaster wall, designed by William and James Pain in 1790, has a columnar screen that supports a gallery. Running garlands in the cornice appear also in the doorcases.

⑤ This fluted pilaster form, with additional tongues in the lower portion, was often used in grand plaster designs.

⑥ Painted filigree "grotesque" work was made famous by Robert Adam. It derived in part from original Roman examples and in part from Italian Renaissance prototypes. BM

⑦ Plasterwork often included figurative motifs. A medallion of a woman tending a sacred flame is typical of the Roman taste of the period. Another fashionable motif was crossed arrows.

① The enrichment of the frieze, in conjunction with the cornice above, is a vital element of late Georgian wall design. Classical motifs such as urns, crossed weapons with shields or simple wreaths and rosettes are typical of the Adam style. BM

② Pilasters supporting an arch engage with the wall decoration, as shown in the small diagram. The detail shows how the decoration is continuous across the vaulted ceiling. Such ornament would be found in passageways.

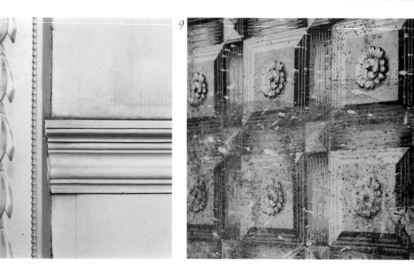

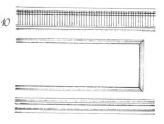

③ Egg-and-dart mouldings were commonly found on the cornice and the dado rail. They are a form of ovolo moulding: that is, quarter-circle sections of convex shape.
④ and ⑤ More elaborate decoration was reserved for the cornice where there was more space than on the dado rail. BM

⑥ and ⑦ Two examples, one Gothic, one classical, of the junction of wall and ceiling. The first is from Brockhall in Northamptonshire, by John Nash, c.1790; the second comes from a house in Bedford Square, London.

⑧ This detail of a wall at Avenue House, Bedfordshire, shows the junction of the moulded dado rail with a doorcase. The vertical member is decorated with simple beading and a laurel motif. AH
⑨ Wallpaper was a luxury,

restricted to the upper-middle and aristocratic classes. It tended to imitate even more expensive materials, such as flocking in place of damask, or, in the case of this typical hand block-printed paper, coffered plasterwork. SU

⑩ Ribbed decoration was typical of both the cornice and the dado rail. This example of a panelled dado with plain wooden ribbing is from Barbreck House in Argyll, Scotland, and dates from 1790.

Ceilings

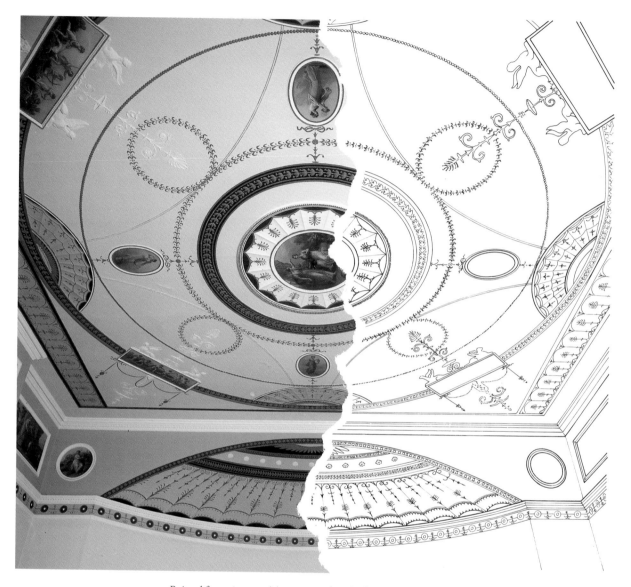

Painted figurative roundels within the plasterwork of a ceiling would have been painted on paper or card and pasted into

place. Delicate tones of grey-blue give harmony to this fine design (early 1770s) setting off the darker mythological scenes. NH

Modest houses had plain plaster ceilings through-out the 18th century, with only the simplest of cornices. In houses one step up the social scale, the cornice might have simple dentils (series of blocks) or an egg-and-dart moulding, but little more.

Heavy coffering and robust Palladian ornament fell from favour in the 1760s and were replaced by the balanced Neo-classical plasterwork espoused by Robert Adam. Adam divided the ceiling into segments and panels, arranged around a centrepiece. Humbler ceilings had moulded rectangular or circular frames.

Halls and stairwells of grand houses might have barrel and quoin vaulting, embellished with classical details.

A shallow saucer dome on pendentives (concave trian-gular corner vaults that support a dome above a square room) is a hallmark of the architect Sir John Soane, the chief exponent of the Greek Revival style which became fashionable at the end of the 18th century.

Figurative decoration was generally painted on canvas or paper and fixed to the ceiling. Robert Adam employed a number of artists such as Biagio Rebecca and Angelica Kaufmann, who painted mostly mytho-logical scenes as ceiling inserts. The framing plaster-work was painted in delicate palettes: pea greens with pinks, and lilacs with greys were characteristic of the 1770s and 80s.

① Ceilings in grand houses were often highly enriched. The recessed octagonal coffering of this dining room ceiling, designed by Robert Adam in 1772, is nobly Roman in feeling. The curved ceiling above the serving niche is decorated with wreaths and rosettes. RA

② This richly detailed ceiling panel harmonizes with the motifs and colours of the wall frieze. The whole group evokes ancient Rome in the spirit of the Adam brothers. NH

③ More modest than the first example on this page, but still highly elegant, is this plaster ceiling from Barbreck House, Argyll, Scotland, of 1790. The central circular pattern complements the curving ornament in the rectangular panels at either side, creating a unified design in a rectangular space.

④ This ceiling from 2 Bedford Square, London, has very simple decoration. The ground plan of the room is reflected in the outer moulding; the oval moulding and the rosette focus attention on the centre of the ceiling.

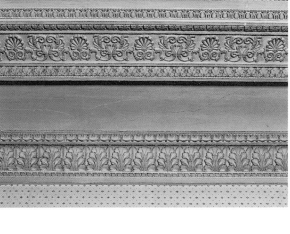

⑤ A running acanthus motif supports the cornice of a handsome ceiling from the 1780s. The use of anthemion and egg-and-dart mouldings and beading in the cornice creates a sense of dignity appropriate to a reception room. AH

① *This ceiling by Robert Adam is composed of strictly geometric compartments, within which more naturalistic ornament of swags relieves the austerity of the architectural forms. The colour choice of white, blue and cream is a modern restoration, based on the evidence of the original design of the early 1770s.* NH
② *The elegance and Roman nobility of the Adam style were universally popular. However, other styles developed in the last quarter of the 18th century, such as the Gothic and Greek Revival styles. The latter was championed by Sir John Soane. This ceiling from his country house, Pitshanger Manor in Ealing, London (1800-1804), is innovative in form and style. It is a shallow dome supported on pendentives (curved triangular sections). The pendentives and*

the dome are decorated with an incised elongated Greek key motif.
③ *A simpler and more everyday manifestation of Greek style appears in this guilloche motif on a cornice from a house in Grove Lane, Camberwell, London.*
④ *and* ⑤ *Applied Gothic detail was used on flat ceilings, as in these two examples at Kentchurch, Herefordshire, and Brockhall, Northamptonshire (John Nash, 1790s).*
⑥ *This design for a plaster centrepiece by Robert Adam, c.1772, has classical emblems representing Glory.* RA
⑦ *By contrast, this Gothic ceiling (shown in plan and two elevations) is very austere. It is a hall ceiling from a house in Edinburgh and represents the fullest application of the Gothic style: a ribbed vault.*

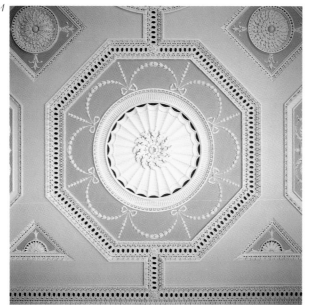
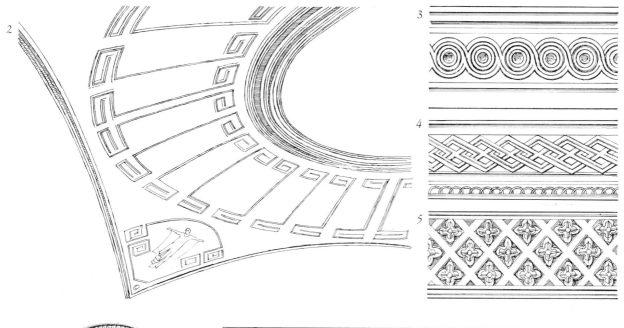

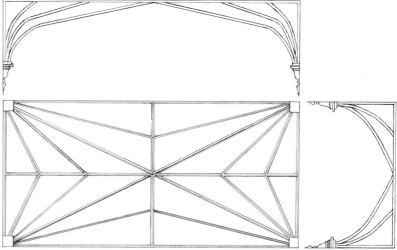

Floors

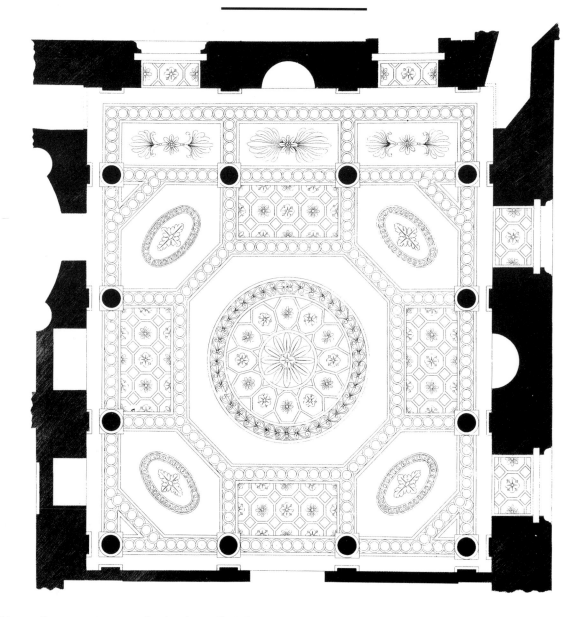

This magnificent engraving illustrates the paved floor of the anteroom at Syon House,

London, designed by Robert Adam by the end of 1760. The floor has the popular centralized

design, with a symmetrical pattern stretching out from a circle. The finished version was

executed in marble, but similar, if simpler designs were made in less expensive stones. RA

There is very little development in flooring during this period. Stone, brick and wood remain the raw materials universally employed. Parquet and stone slab floors show great continuity of design, although simpler patterns become more popular.

Unvarnished fir or pine floorboards were used for most floors in most houses. Grander houses might have polished oak planking on the main staircase, which would complement the narrow turkey carpets laid over the stairs. Entrance halls continue to be stone-flagged.

Carpets became more common from the mid-18th century and were mostly English, with geometric patterns, or from the East, with floral designs. They were usually laid loose on the floor boards, although in the 1760s wall-to-wall carpets appeared in some principal rooms. But the most significant development was the introduction of carpets designed en suite with the ceiling plasterwork. Such groups sprang from the Neo-classical taste for harmony and unity of design. Robert Adam composed the best examples, which were instilled with a strong architectural sense. These designs were reserved for the reception rooms of the grandest houses. Few survive intact.

Flagstones were preferred for kitchen floors. The chill of the stone in winter was ameliorated by painted floor-cloths. A crumb cloth protected the floorcloth.

1

① *This black and coloured marble inlay from Newby Hall, Yorkshire, is an example of the grandest and most costly kind of flooring.* NH

② *Black diamonds mark the intersections of the stone floor of the hall at Home House, London. This design, known as* carreaux d'octagones, *was popular throughout the 18th century.* HH

③ *A geometric paved hall floor of the last quarter of the 18th century. This floor is typical of more modest interpretations of grand inlaid marble flooring.*

2

3

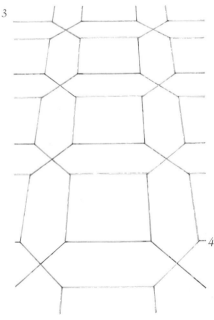

4

④ *Plain, humble flagstones, cut and set square, are typical of the practical flooring adopted for kitchens and other service rooms and passageways.* AH

Fireplaces

The decoration on the marble surround and the fine painting of a classical subject on the central panel mark this as an

Adam fireplace of the greatest elegance, c.1775. The fine freestanding grate is of a similar quality and date. HH

The simplest fireplace surround is a plain wooden frame, of two uprights and a beam: this arrangement formed the basis of almost all chimneypiece designs in the period and encouraged a strictly rectilinear treatment. Chimneypieces were made in marble, stone or wood, and their enrichment with medallions and classical motifs is one of the most characteristic features of late Georgian architectural decoration. That this should be so speaks for the profound influence of Robert and James Adam, the chief exponents of such classical designs. Fine stone chimneypieces are often enriched with inlays of different marbles, and the grandest usually have overmantel mirrors. Surrounds became more austerely classical in the latter part of the 18th century, as seen in the strict geometric lines of Sir John Soane's Greek Revival designs.

The cast-iron hob grate saw improvements from the 1750s. It became universal in smaller houses and also featured in the simpler rooms of mansions. But the hob grate was still inefficient for the burning of coal, mainly because of the size of the chimney flue. Sir Benjamin Thompson, Count von Rumford, designed a reformed hob grate in the late 1790s with canted sides and a narrow flue. This was altogether better, giving out much more heat with less smoke. The grandest rooms have architect-designed hob or dog grates.

FIREPLACES

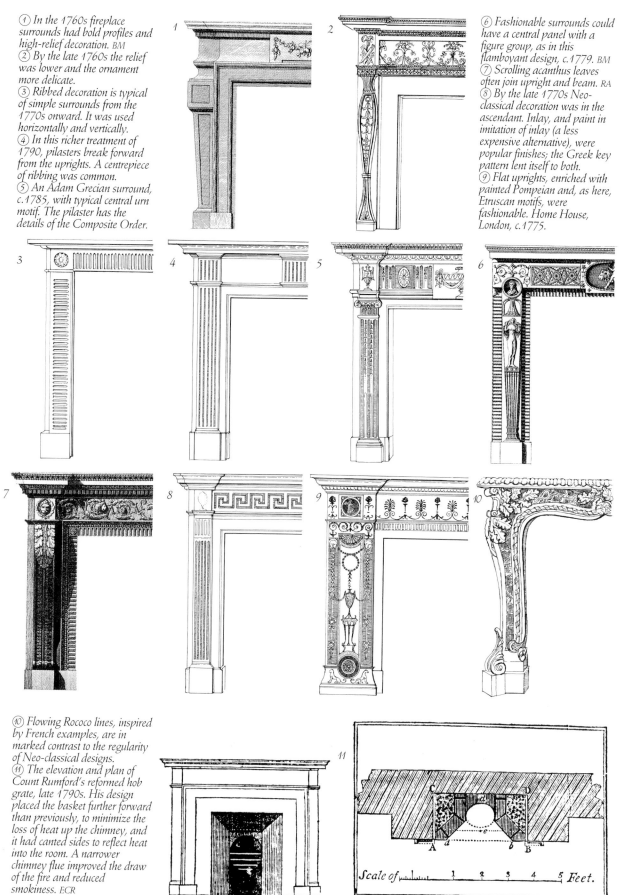

① In the 1760s fireplace surrounds had bold profiles and high-relief decoration. BM
② By the late 1760s the relief was lower and the ornament more delicate.
③ Ribbed decoration is typical of simple surrounds from the 1770s onward. It was used horizontally and vertically.
④ In this richer treatment of 1790, pilasters break forward from the uprights. A centrepiece of ribbing was common.
⑤ An Adam Grecian surround, c.1785, with typical central urn motif. The pilaster has the details of the Composite Order.

⑥ Fashionable surrounds could have a central panel with a figure group, as in this flamboyant design, c.1779. BM
⑦ Scrolling acanthus leaves often join upright and beam. RA
⑧ By the late 1770s Neo-classical decoration was in the ascendant. Inlay, and paint in imitation of inlay (a less expensive alternative), were popular finishes; the Greek key pattern lent itself to both.
⑨ Flat uprights, enriched with painted Pompeian and, as here, Etruscan motifs, were fashionable. Home House, London, c.1775.

⑩ Flowing Rococo lines, inspired by French examples, are in marked contrast to the regularity of Neo-classical designs.
⑪ The elevation and plan of Count Rumford's reformed hob grate, late 1790s. His design placed the basket further forward than previously, to minimize the loss of heat up the chimney, and it had canted sides to reflect heat into the room. A narrower chimney flue improved the draw of the fire and reduced smokiness. ECR

Scale of 1 2 3 4 5 Feet.

① *A painted wooden surround with a classically decorated hob grate en suite. A simple but stylish fireguard fits onto the bars of the grate. Fanned papers were arranged in the hearth when the fire was not lit, as shown here. During the summer months a painted chimneyboard would fill the hearth. NH*

② *This handsome white marble surround turns at the corners on quarter columns. The simplicity of the line illustrates the taste of the early 1800s. The register grate is Regency. AH*

③ *The Pompeian style was adopted in highly fashionable houses in the 1770s. This elegant example is decorated in an effective palette of white, blue and gold. The dog grate is typical of the best work of the period. HH*

④ *Classical restraint is abandoned in fancy or exotic styles such as Chinoiserie or Hindu. The scrolls and leaf forms of this striking Chinoiserie fireplace of the 1770s look back to Rococo precedents. HH*

⑤ *The simple lines of this elegant white marble fireplace mark it as a product of the period 1800-1815. The walls are marbled to match the slips surrounding the grate. HH*

⑥ *This simple wooden surround with delicate floral swags is typical of the 1780s. AH*

⑦ *A detail from a fireplace of the 1780s. The influence of the Adam style is clear in such motifs as the urn and ribbons. AH*

⑧ *Blue and white earthenware tiles, in imitation of Delftware, were often used to line the slips or cheeks of the fireplace. AH*

① *and* ② *Grand chimneypieces feature classical motifs, such as the sphinx, or Helios, the sun god, in his chariot.*
③ *Carved or painted corner medallions could include swags and ribbons, honeysuckle or sheaves of wheat. Lyres, masks and heads of gods could also decorate classical surrounds.*

④ *Mirror glass was a great luxury at this time, but also a practical necessity in large rooms as it reflected light. This design by Robert Adam, c.1773, has a filigree frame.* RA
⑤ *This chimneypiece from Wilbury Park, Wiltshire, c.1755, has the gravity of the Palladian designs from earlier in the century.*

⑥ *The plain lines and weighty forms of Sir John Soane's mirrored chimneypiece at Wimpole Hall, Cambridgeshire, 1791, are lightened by girandoles. The mirror doubled the light of the candles.*
⑦ *Rococo designs were popular in the 1750s; this overmantel mirror frame from Charlotte Square, Edinburgh, stands on a later, classical surround of the 1770s.*
⑧ *Robert Adam's chimneypiece composition in the hall at Kedleston, Derbyshire, c.1765, combines an alabaster chimneypiece with delicate, classicized plasterwork. This presents a contrast to the near-contemporary Rococo overmantel.*

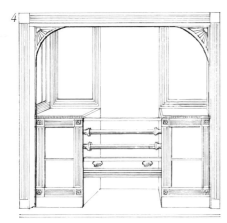

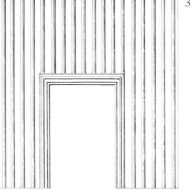

1 Many grates had shutters, to close the hearth when the fire was not in use and to minimize draughts.

2 A reeded frame between hearth and surround was a fashionable feature of fireplaces from the 1770s onward.

3 This engraving from The Builder's Magazine, 1778, illustrates a highly decorated register grate. These occupied the entire hearth and had adjustable iron plates in the flue to regulate the draught. BM

4 An elegant register grate from the Royal Crescent, Bath.

5 This cast-iron register grate has a decorative plaque and reeding and is framed by Flemish tiles. Hatton Garden, London, late 18th century.

6 Hob grates became increasingly common. The chunky design lent itself to ornamentation, and fashionable and richly wrought examples like this one from The Builder's Magazine, 1778, were copied in simplified forms in cast iron for the popular market. BM

7 The freestanding basket grate (dog grate) continued to be installed in grand houses. The best are polished steel with applied and engraved classical motifs, as in this example in the Adam style, c.1770.

8 Fluted decoration and chevrons were commonly used as ornament on simpler hob grates, c.1790.

9 This large kitchen fireplace has an open grate over which pots were hung when cooking. This crude system remained current in many poorer homes into the 19th century. Kitchen ranges, incorporating ovens and roasting spits, were appearing in the most advanced, larger kitchens. They continued to have open grates: the kitchen fire was not enclosed within a stove until the turn of the century.

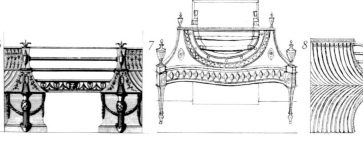

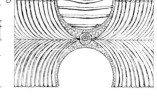

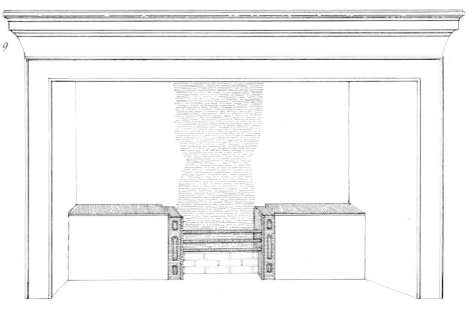

Staircases

Grand houses can have large staircases hung along two or three sides of the entrance hall.

A more dramatic architectural feat is seen at Home House, London, c.1775, where the

exceptional width of the entrance hall allowed the architect, Robert Adam, to create a grand

centralized flight that splits at the half landing and returns to the floor above on either hand. HH

The plan of the standard town house allowed for little change in the position or structure of the staircase during this period. The greatest development is in the form of balusters and newel posts. Wood continues to be the chief material used and almost all staircases are now open-string, with a stepped profile rather than a straight one. The barleytwist balusters of the earlier Georgian period go out of fashion after 1760, replaced by simple tapering uprights, turned for a circular profile and planed for a square profile. The handrail is flatter and finishes in a smooth turned circle of wood; this tops a simple newel post. Tread-ends are similarly restrained and have often no more than a plain

curve as decoration. Most staircases were fir or pine, painted in flat drab; the grandest were polished oak.

Cast-iron balustrading comes more to the fore because casting techniques improved in the middle of the century. Acanthus leaves, wreaths and Greek key patterns abound. Stone staircases are found only in grand town houses. Both William Chambers and Robert Adam designed dramatic imperial staircases, which rise in a single cantilever flight from the entrance hall to a half landing, then divide into a double sweep.

Area steps, leading from the street to the basement, were adopted in many new town houses, providing ready access for tradesmen and services.

FIREPLACES

STAIRCASES

① *The staircase in ordinary town houses rose through a narrow stairwell. This was particularly pronounced on service stairs which, out of necessity, could incorporate beautiful steep curves as here.* HH

② *In grand houses, the handrail on main stairs was finely moulded and terminated in a spiral, be it a tight coil or, as here, a loose curve.* NH

③ *Elegant lines were the priority in stair-ends, as seen in this fine marble detail, c.1775, where the decoration is secondary to the profile.* HH

④ *The interest in modest staircases often lay in the form of the tread-ends, as seen in the curved lines of this staircase in York, early 1760s. The sweep of the handrail enhances the effect.*

⑤ *Much of the interest in better houses centred upon the newel post. The first example is a turned post from Mottram Hall, Cheshire. A variation on the single post was a central post surrounded by balusters, as in the second and third examples.*

⑥ *Although most wooden balusters were square, some delicately turned designs can be found. These fine balusters are from a house in Castlegate, York.*

Cast-iron balusters tended to be more elaborate than wooden ones. The material was something of a luxury and lent itself to ornamental treatment.

① This stone staircase with simple iron balusters is from an upper floor of a grand house. The higher up the house, the plainer the flight. But despite its utilitarian purpose, the flight has a graceful, curving form.

1

2

3

② The restrained sophistication of this balustrade from Sydney Place, Bath, incorporates two different treatments, with curling forms on the flight and latticework on the landing. Note the simple, curved stair-ends.

4

5

6

7

8

③ This balustrade from a house in Charlotte Square, Edinburgh, late 1790s, has a flowing, curvilinear design which does not conform to the strict Neo-classical style of the time.
④ and ⑤ These patterns are from I. and J. Taylor's Ornamental Iron Work,

c.1795. The first shows how delicate and ornate railings could be at the end of the century. The second design is simpler and employs the popular S-shape. The textured ornament and flowers could be gilded. These designs would have been used in grand town houses.

⑥ A detail of the distinctive Greek key balustrade from Steine House, Brighton, c.1800. The railing runs on both sides of an imperial staircase: that is, one which rises centrally and returns in two flights to a landing. The newel post resembles a turned wooden type.

⑦ and ⑧ Even fairly ordinary houses had decorative balustrades and newel posts. The first example is similar to the second staircase on this page, with a curling motif at intervals between straight balusters. The second design alternates straight and curved balusters.

Built-in furniture

An elegant dining room cupboard within a niche, c.1775, which would have been used as a side table and for storage. The top is inlaid rosewood. The brass rail running around the niche would originally have been hung with fabric to protect the wall. Note the jib door (a disguised door flush with the wall): this was inserted later to give servants better access to the room. HH

Built-in furniture became more sophisticated in the late Georgian period, appealing as it did to the Neo-classical taste for balance and unity of design. Built-in cupboards would follow the lines of apsidal rooms and oval ante-rooms. Such cupboards, glazed above and panelled below, would be used to display china, silver and glass. Dining room pieces might include a built-in sideboard or a serving table, cut to fit into a niche. These would usually be confined to one end of the room, near to the service door. The wine cooler beneath the serving table or sideboard would be designed en suite and so was considered to be part of the architecture.

Libraries achieve a restrained magnificence. Book-cases are sunk within a niche, their cornices flush with the wall, or stand proud of the walls, picking up the motifs from the cornice. Dining room and library pieces would probably be made of high-quality woods such as mahogany, which would be polished. In other good rooms, built-in furniture would be painted in flat grey or colours evoking stone. Some very grand, fashionable hallways have console tables, made of wood or stone.

Built-in furniture was also used below stairs and in modest houses. Simple china cupboards and built-in shelving were standard, as were kitchen cupboards and dressers. These would in all cases have been painted; dark or sage green and drab were popular.

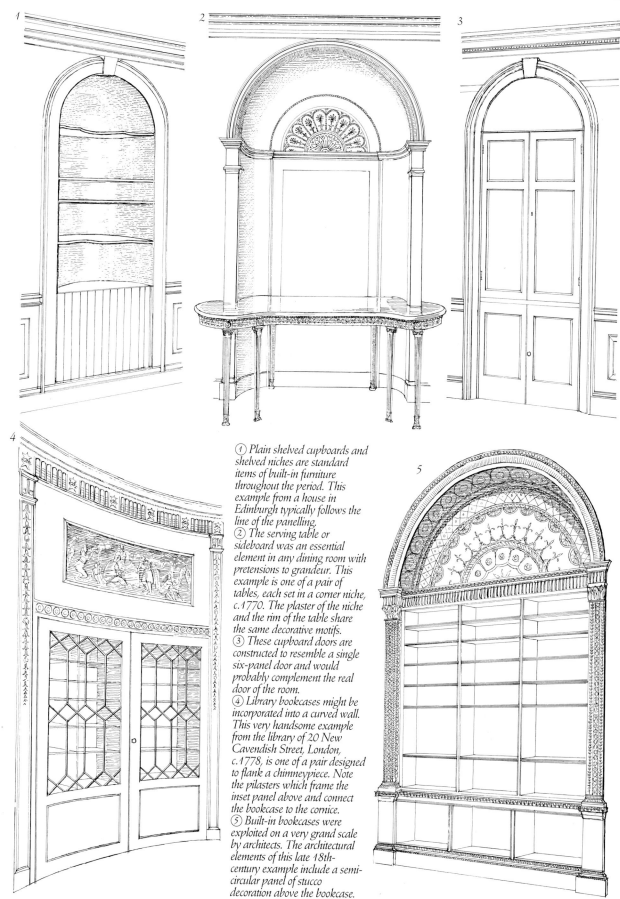

1 Plain shelved cupboards and shelved niches are standard items of built-in furniture throughout the period. This example from a house in Edinburgh typically follows the line of the panelling.

2 The serving table or sideboard was an essential element in any dining room with pretensions to grandeur. This example is one of a pair of tables, each set in a corner niche, c.1770. The plaster of the niche and the rim of the table share the same decorative motifs.

3 These cupboard doors are constructed to resemble a single six-panel door and would probably complement the real door of the room.

4 Library bookcases might be incorporated into a curved wall. This very handsome example from the library of 20 New Cavendish Street, London, c.1778, is one of a pair designed to flank a chimneypiece. Note the pilasters which frame the inset panel above and connect the bookcase to the cornice.

5 Built-in bookcases were exploited on a very grand scale by architects. The architectural elements of this late 18th-century example include a semi-circular panel of stucco decoration above the bookcase.

① *Window seats were often set within the panelled embrasure (splayed recess) of a window. They sometimes had a hinged seat, allowing the boxed-in space below to be used for storage. This combined duty is particularly found in modest houses.* SCY

② *A cupboard built into the recess beside the chimney breast served as a wardrobe, a linen cupboard or for general storage. The proximity of the fire would keep dampness at bay.* AH

③ *An elegant design for a grand library. Sphinxes and busts are typical embellishments.* BM

④ *Grand bookcases had shelves below the dado rail for large folio volumes on art and architecture, as seen in this example, early 1770s.* NH

⑤ *This cupboard sunk within the wall has metal grilles on the top doors, backed with pleated fabric. Latticework was a more expensive alternative to glazing. It was employed in libraries, usually without the fabric, to keep bookcases secure without obscuring the spines of the books.* HH

⑥ *The dresser was a feature of middle-class and grander kitchens. This example, at Avenue House, Bedfordshire, shows the simple construction of drawers and shelving, relieved by a decorative carved profile to the uprights.* AH

Services

① *This conical rainwater head has fine cast detailing.* AH
② *Stoves were essential in large, flagged entrance halls; this example was made c.1800 for Pencarrow House near Bodmin, Cornwall. It provides a plinth for a double colza oil lamp.*

③ *Rainwater was collected and stored in large lead cisterns, located in the area of a town house or on the back wall of a country house. Here, the date of manufacture is recorded.*
④ *Lead hoppers/leader heads often bore the initials of the occupant of the house and the date of installation. Note the Adamesque decoration (right).*

After the introduction of steam pumping in the 1760s it might be assumed that water supplies in Britain improved dramatically. But this was not the case, as steam power was rarely used for domestic purposes. Almost all households received their water at ground level, and no higher. A very few iron pipes were provided by water companies, but wooden piping (installed in some places as early as the 17th century) remained the chief conduit for water until the 19th century. Because of the inadequacies of this system, rainwater was still funnelled down pipes and stored in lead cisterns.

Piped sewerage, like piped water, required considerable capital investment, which was rarely entertained in the congested areas of cities, and was certainly not seen as a public duty by the government. A few landowners supplied new London houses with sewerage pipes, but drainage was primitive and could only cope with liquid waste; this did not make the privy, the standard earth closet, any more sanitary. There were a few internal water closets in the first half of the century, and many more after the 1760s; but because of the low pressure in the pipes they required special pumping to make them work and they remained the privilege of the rich.

One innovation was the wood- or oil-burning stove, used in the centre of a hallway.

Lighting

① *A Neo-classical wall sconce from the staircase hall at Home House, London, c.1775.*
② *This colza oil lamp, c.1790, has a reservoir in the shape of a Roman urn. These freestanding lamps could sit on wall brackets, as illustrated, top.*
③ *A typical hall lantern.*
④ *Chandeliers were the most sumptuous lights. This glass example, c.1790, is typical.*
⑤ *This hall lantern, c.1776-79, shows Roman influence.* BM
⑥ *Householders were obliged to light their front doors from dusk to dawn. This lamp, c.1810, is fitted within a fanlight.*

⑦ *Girandoles could be fixed to mirrored overmantels. This design is by Robert Adam, 1773.*
⑧ *Railings often supported lamp brackets. This elaborate example, 1779, holds an oil lamp.* BM
⑨ *An alternative was the overthrow. This example is from Bath, late 18th century.*
⑩ *Another imaginative lamp standard, c.1795.* IJT
⑪ *Link boys guided people through dark streets and extinguished their torches (links) at the destination. Snuffers were provided on railings for this purpose; this dragon's-head example is from Edinburgh.*

The great breakthrough in lighting technology was the colza lamp (or Argand burner), fuelled by rape-seed oil. This was invented by Aimé Argand, a Swiss physicist, and patented in England in 1784. It had a cylindrical wick, housed between two concentric metal shafts; this arrangement encouraged air flow and produced a brighter flame. The colza lamp gave ten times the light of an ordinary oil lamp of comparable size, and it was less dirty, which meant that it could be used indoors. It was a luxury item and lent itself to elegant metalwork and sober Roman design. After the turn of the century magnificent central fixtures with five, six or eight lamps were made.

Candlelight remained the general source of light for all, and sconces and individual candlesticks were the usual accessories. Elegant Neo-classical silver candelabra provided light for dinner parties, but even the three branches of a candelabrum would have been considered extravagant for a middle-class family dining alone. Chandeliers, even in the most opulent households, were used only on showy occasions. Girandoles became integral to many grand chimneypiece designs; they were built into the overmantel so that their light would be reflected in the mirror glass and brighten the room. Interior lanterns and outside lamp standards took on the more delicate lines and ornamentation of the period.

Metalwork

(1) *The railings of the Circus in Bath are very plain, their austerity relieved only by the overthrows which support lamps.*
(2) *and* (3) *Balconets fronted floor-length windows on raised entrance levels and upper floors. The first example incorporates ovoid forms within the handrail, with anthemion-like shapes depending from it. The second example uses similar motifs, but within a quirky composition reminiscent of late 18th-century Gothic forms.*
(4) *An impressive anthemion motif was used by Robert Adam at Newby Hall, Yorkshire, to lend grandeur to the railings flanking a principal entrance. NH*

One element stands out above all others from late Georgian ironwork, and this is the balconet, or guard iron. These small railings, fronting windows one and sometimes two floors above street level, prevented people from falling through deep sashes and provided a light and stylish miniature balcony. Cast-iron balconets come in numerous designs, including diagonal patterns with rosettes, crossed spears and Gothic tracery. Many were added to earlier houses, but from the 1770s onward they were often installed when the house was built.

Balconies also came into fashion. These are shallow, rectangular, and usually run across the width of three drawing room windows on the floor above the entrance level. At the very end of the century a delicate cast-iron canopy might surmount such a balcony. Such structures are partly glazed and partly roofed in copper or zinc. They developed in the early years of the 19th century into the elaborate two- and three-story verandas seen to best advantage in Brighton, Sussex.

Designs for cast-iron railings and arched lamp supports become rather lighter from the 1770s. Smart little urns and other classical motifs supplement the existing spear-headed finials. Gates display a similar development, with increasingly sophisticated lines and ornament.

Ordinary rural houses have little ironwork; a simple cast-iron porch might be fitted to a front door.

LIGHTING

METALWORK

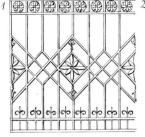

① to ④ *Balconet fronts display the high quality of cast work. The last example shows the*

anthemion – a frequently used motif which became the standard decoration on Regency balconets.

⑤ and ⑥ *A similar delicacy appears in railings from the 1780s; these examples from* The

Builder's Magazine, *1778, are typical of the best designs in their lightness and intricacy.* BM

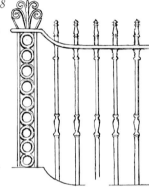

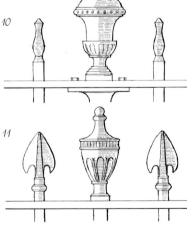

⑦ *Plain street railings retain the spear-head motif of the early 18th century.*
⑧ *Railings that support lights are more elaborate. This elegant upright, at the junction between steps and pavement, would have supported an oil lamp.*
⑨ to ⑫ *A wide variety of finials and spikes appeared on London railings and gates of the 1770s and 80s. The scrolled*

details come from the gates of Syon House, designed by Robert and James Adam. More typical are spear heads punctuated by small urn motifs, as in these examples from Tavistock Place, c.1810.
⑬ and ⑭ *These finials typify the imaginative ironwork of Edinburgh.*
⑮ *Finials from Bath exhibit more restraint.*

⑯ *The geometric forms of this balcony railing from Bath are in the Chinoiserie manner, popularized in furniture by Thomas Chippendale in the 1760s and then adopted in*

architecture. The central panel is flanked by Greek key motifs, highly popular in the late 18th century.

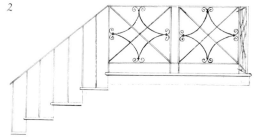

① and ② *Steps to the front door, or to French doors on the garden side, would have fine balustrading; the principal entrance would have the more ornate, curvaceous forms, as seen in the first example.*
③ *At the end of the 18th century, modest terraced/row houses with gardens often had gazebo-like porches. These would act as a trellis for climbing plants.*
④ *This elegant balcony in Bedford Square, London, takes the outline of the anthemion and transforms it into a sinuous, almost Gothic running pattern.*

⑧ *Vulnerable windows or areas might be covered by crossed arrows on a circle. The device is purely decorative when it sits in a niche on the property line between terraced/row houses.*
⑨ *Brackets were used to support lamps, balconies and porches. They came in fine and weighty cast forms; their profiles were usually scrolled and some had foliate elements.*

⑤ *Grand country houses had double gates at the head of the driveway; the gateposts might carry handsome oil lanterns, as shown in this plate from* The Builder's Magazine, *1778.*
⑥ *These double gates with honeysuckle motifs close the street entrance to a house in Norwich.*
⑦ *Gates to area steps were made en suite with railings.*

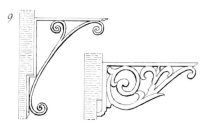

REGENCY AND EARLY 19TH CENTURY

1811–1837

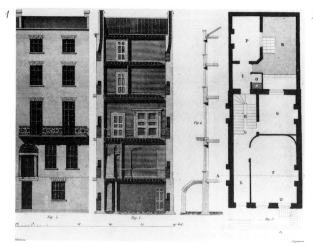

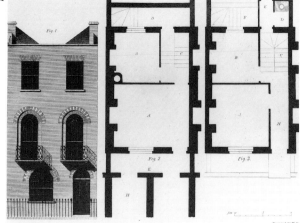

(1) *The elevation, section and plan of a "Second Rate House" from The New Practical Builder and Workman's Guide, 1823, by Peter Nicholson. The raised-* *ground floor and the floor directly above are the most elegant; the latter has front and back drawing rooms which are divided by double doors, and the front room* *has full-length windows that give onto a balcony. NN* (2) *Designs by Nicholson for a "Fourth Rate House". Such houses were run up in vast* *numbers at the beginning of the 19th century. Although modest in scale, they have good basic proportions and interesting and often refined details. NN*

Regency is the term generally accepted to denote the period 1811-20, when George, Prince of Wales, acted as Regent for his mad father, George III, and the decade of his own reign as George IV, from 1820 to 30. Often, too, it is taken, with reasonable justification, to include the short reign of his younger brother William IV, who died in 1837. It is a fascinating transitional period in English domestic architecture, at once the culmination and final, most sophisticated expression of the classical trends which had been current for a century, and an era highly self-conscious of its own modernity.

The Prince's own tastes were important at the smarter level of patronage, and his early espousal of French styles in architecture and decoration and his later love of the exotic were both influential. Fashionable architects of the period such as Sir John Soane (1753-1837) or the Regent's favourite, John Nash (1752-1835), took as their starting point the crisp and correct Neo-classicism of the 1770s and 80s, but treated its accepted canons with an almost Mannerist wit and wilfulness.

Similarly, ordinary architects and even the speculative builders of terraces/rows of town houses played with the established forms and proportions of the Georgian house. Windows were elongated, mouldings attenuated and areas of rich decoration, such as ironwork balconies with late-Roman or Greek motifs, were contrasted against plain areas of brick or fashionable stucco. Stucco and the similar patented "Roman Cement" were widely used as less expensive imitations

of the classic London building material, Portland stone.

Since the Building Act of 1774 all new town houses had had to conform to one of four ratings, applicable to domestic buildings. Fourth-rate houses were the lowliest and first-rate the grandest. These grades were firmly established in the minds and practices of builders and architects by the early 19th century. Aside from differences in scale dictated by the importance of the street, facades tended to bear features which could be read as marks of status. First- and second-rate houses had an order and proportions which third- and fourth-rate houses could not attain. These distinctions are marked in the design of terrace/row houses, as is well illustrated by the different rates of houses shown in Peter Nicholson's influential publication *The New Practical Builder and Workman's Guide* of 1823.

In the interiors of the Regency period there is a striking emphasis on architectural elements, with strongly accented mouldings, a great deal of crisp, linear detailing, such as reeded or incised patterns, and a liking for lean-profiled arches. A clever use of subtly varied planes is also characteristic; for example, wide doorcases, flush with the wall surface, and enclosing doors with shallow but complex panel details were highly fashionable. Often the same spatial games are repeated in niches or blind arches, which are set back only a few inches from the wall-surface. Decoration reflected the boldness of the architecture. In grand houses a certain flashiness of taste can be discerned. Bright gilding, rich silks in high colours and lavish

①"Elevations of a Series of First and Second Rate Houses". This plate by Richard Elsam appears both in his Practical Builder's Perpetual Price Book *of 1825 and in later editions of Nicholson's* The New Practical Builder and Workman's Guide. *Many fine terraces, especially in South London, were erected on this pattern.* RE
②The garden front of the Romantic poet John Keats' house in Hampstead, London. Verandas were typical of refined "village" houses such as this. KH

③A rather grand cottage orné *in the "Elizabethan" style, c.1843, showing the garden front in perspective and the main facade in elevation. Many books offered such designs for gentlemen's rural residences in a Romantic style.* FG

curtain treatments are conspicuous in the furnishing manuals of the day, such as the works of George Smith or the colour plates from Rudolf Ackermann's *Repository of Arts, Literature, Fashions Etc.* (published in parts throughout the period). Even in more modest houses there seems to have been a strong emphasis on rather graphic effects and a definite preference for sharp colours in unusual combinations, such as acid yellow with lilac.

With a widespread increase in wealth throughout the period (in spite of the Napoleonic Wars of 1801-15) came a noticeable broadening of the base of middle-class patronage. Many new areas of the major cities and prosperous towns – including London, Liverpool, Bristol, Cheltenham and Edinburgh – were developed as genteel residential districts. At the same time the rise in popularity of villas and houses in semi-rural areas engendered several new forms of building. Highly characteristic of the Regency is the rapid development of seaside towns, of which Brighton on the south coast of England was the most fashionable. Houses planned for leisure, with spacious reception rooms and tall, curved bays, from which elegant windows opened onto balconies and verandas, enjoyed a well-deserved vogue. Similarly, houses in inland areas which commanded pleasing prospects were, it seems, more or less planned around their fenestration.

Changes in taste in the fine arts and literature toward a new, Romantic sensibility are fully reflected in Regency architecture, decoration and garden design. The delight in the rustic and the picturesque gave rise to a novel form, the *cottage orné,* a pretty and elegant house which represented an idealized conception of a country dwelling. Most of these houses were asymmetrical in plan and many had thatched roofs and weatherboarding. The entire village of Blaise Hamlet, Gloucestershire, consisted of *cottages ornés,* designed by John Nash in 1811. This same Romantic sensibility is reflected in the growth of new kinds of suburban villas, which were often built in semi-detached pairs, or village houses planned as the centrepiece of a miniature estate: a charmed world in which flower-gardens and rustic seats, trellis arches and summer pavilions all contributed to the delights of life, protected by pleasingly irregular fences of twig-work or painted wooden planking.

The revival of historic styles of architecture and decoration was a potent influence upon contemporary practice. The most serious and lastingly influential of these revivals was that of Greek styles and motifs, which joined the more familiar Roman forms and details in the Neo-classical repertoire. The purity of Greek architecture gave an unsurpassed austerity to the final phase of Georgian classicism. However, a Byronic love of the exotic and dramatic is a strong thread

The South Drawing Room on the floor above the entrance level of Sir John Soane's London house in Lincoln's Inn Fields. As originally planned in 1812, the windows led out onto an open loggia. This was glazed-in in 1832, thus enlarging the room and allowing the insertion of extra bookcases. The furnishings are original to the room and the decoration follows that seen in early watercolour views. LIF

running right through the story of Regency taste, and many forms of "Fancy" architecture and decoration enjoyed either brief or more long-lived popularity. Chinoiserie was given the Royal imprimatur by the Pavilion at Brighton (1815-23), but the Egyptian and Turkish styles also had their day. Gothic, which had been intermittently popular as a style for frivolous building since the 1740s, continued to be used in this way, but also began to be treated with a new-found respect and archaeological strictness when its appropriateness for religious or institutional uses started to be explored. It is a development which presages the increasing seriousness which came over English building from the 1830s onward, weighing down the essential lightness of touch of the great Regency architects and designers with a new and ponderous gravitas.

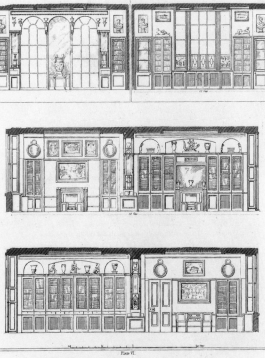

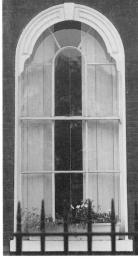

GEOMETRICAL SECTIONS OF LIBRARY AND DINING ROOM.

① *The extent of Sir John Soane's collection of architectural books, models and curiosities led him to insert a very large number of built-in bookcases and cabinets into his house in Lincoln's Inn Fields, London. The library cases of 1812 are typical of the very high standard of detailing which he lavished on his fixtures and the finish which he required of his craftsmen.* LIF

② *A window (formerly part of an open loggia) from the South Drawing Room of the same house. The incised linear motif is in the Greek taste.* LIF

③ *Elevations of the library and dining room of Sir John Soane's house: one of the most inventive exercises in domestic architecture of the period.* HJS

④ *A finely detailed window, dating from 1824, from the ground floor of the house. Note the typical narrow glazing bars, the original internal shutters, and the elegant curved fascia of the folding sun blind/shade which is fixed into the curved head of the window.* LIF

Doors

A classic late Regency street door from the area developed around King's Cross, London, 1815-30. The raised ground floor entrance hall is approached by stone steps. The heavily panelled door and the fanlight/transom light are united by an arch.

The front door remains the principal decorative feature on the facade of the English town house, but the elements are usually confined within the limits of the door void (opening), which is defined by a brick or stucco arch. Elaborate architectural doorcases give way to plainer entrances in which pilasters or stylized console brackets flank the door. Shallow porches, unfashionable since the mid-18th century, enjoyed a return to vogue: they are supported on scrolled brackets and often have classical details on the architrave. Also popular were deeper porches with lead or copper roofs in "pagoda" forms. Fanlights/transom lights are less extravagant than those of the 1790s; by contrast, the doors themselves are richer and more inventive, with reeded mouldings defining geometric panelling, or with studs, in imitation of Ancient Greek or Roman forms. Most doors were painted black or bronze-green.

Internal doors follow a four- or six-panel division, with crisp, attenuated panel mouldings. Surrounds are wide and shallow. In grand houses the doorcases sometimes have an architectural head in the Neo-Grecian taste or details in one of the "Fancy" styles of the day: Gothic, Chinoiserie or Egyptian. A notable feature was the introduction of tall double doors into ordinary houses. These would divide front and back reception rooms on the ground floor and the floor above.

① A street door, c.1825, with
fluted quarter-columns set in
splayed jambs below a simple
fanlight. The door, made to
resemble a narrow pair, has

flush panels at the bottom.
② A reeded door-arch with
typical roundels enclosing an
elaborate fanlight and door,
c.1810. The anthemion leaf

details on the door are in the
Greek Revival style.
③ A decorative panelled door
in a plain door-arch, c.1820.
④ The Regency Gothic

revivalists favoured the late
Perpendicular style. This door
from Clifton Place, Brighton,
has both good-quality
stonework and intricate joinery.

⑤ A porch with a panel of
anthemion ornament, c.1820.
⑥ A segmental arched doorhead from Brighton, c.1820.
⑦ A pagoda porch of lead over
a wooden frame, 1830.
⑧ "Grecian and Roman
Ornaments" from Peter
Nicholson's manual of 1825,
The New Practical Builder.
These include the standard
running patterns and architrave
ornaments used on doorcases
and porches. NN

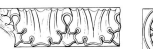

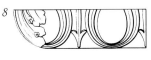

⑨ The preferred forms of the
classical Orders in the early
19th century. The first three are
the Doric, Ionic and Corinthian.
These are more correct forms of
the Greek Orders than had been
used in the 18th century: the
Georgian Orders had been
based on Roman interpretations
of the earlier Greek models.
Eccentric, original forms were
also popular in Regency
England: a Corinthian pilaster
and the "Amonite Order"
(introduced by Amon Wilds) are
illustrated. These decorated
facades of the 1820s.

①*A subtle version of the usual early Regency London doorcase, by Sir John Soane.*
②*A superb Regency door inserted in an 18th-century Edinburgh house. The detailing implies a pair of doors. The richly moulded panels and their corner roundels are Neo-Grecian.* SP

③*A well-proportioned internal door. It has six panels and a reeded frame with corner blocks. The door is made from softwood with a wood-grained paint finish.* KH
④*A fine pair of tall double doors dividing the drawing rooms in Sir John Soane's house, London. The frame is very plain and* narrow. *The doors are flush, without raised or sunken panels, and are made of mahogany with decorative dark bands.* LIF
⑤*A detail of a typical internal door with a mortice lock and brass door knobs and key escutcheons. Extravagant wood-graining to imitate rosewood or flame-mahogany was* very popular in this period. *This is a very good example of the desired effect.* GV
⑥*A curved internal door at Dickens' House, London. The wide, flat architrave profiles echo the shallow fielded panels which are edged with a quirk mould (a V-shaped incision).* DK

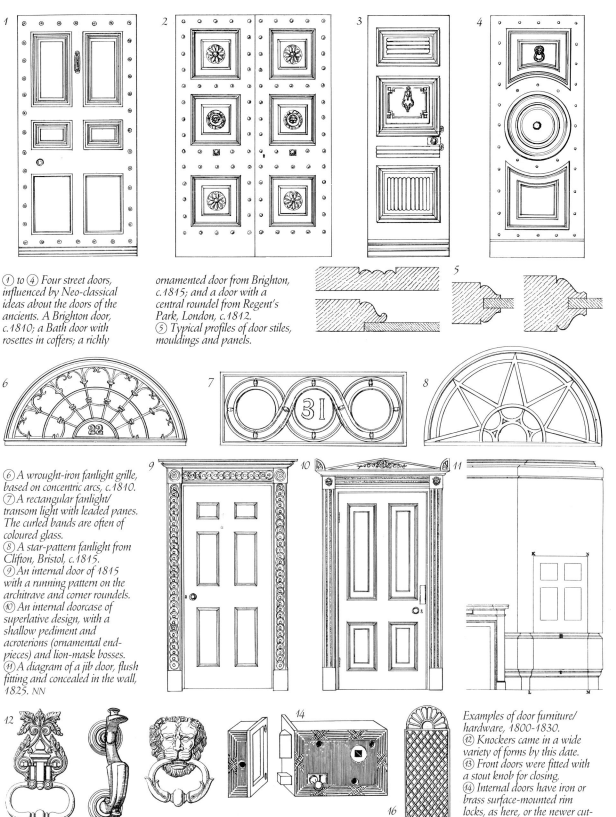

① to ④ *Four street doors, influenced by Neo-classical ideas about the doors of the ancients. A Brighton door, c.1810; a Bath door with rosettes in coffers; a richly ornamented door from Brighton, c.1815; and a door with a central roundel from Regent's Park, London, c.1812.*
⑤ *Typical profiles of door stiles, mouldings and panels.*

⑥ *A wrought-iron fanlight grille, based on concentric arcs, c.1810.*
⑦ *A rectangular fanlight/ transom light with leaded panes. The curled bands are often of coloured glass.*
⑧ *A star-pattern fanlight from Clifton, Bristol, c.1815.*
⑨ *An internal door of 1815 with a running pattern on the architrave and corner roundels.*
⑩ *An internal doorcase of superlative design, with a shallow pediment and acroterions (ornamental end-pieces) and lion-mask bosses.*
⑪ *A diagram of a jib door, flush fitting and concealed in the wall, 1825. NN*

Examples of door furniture/ hardware, 1800-1830.
⑫ *Knockers came in a wide variety of forms by this date.*
⑬ *Front doors were fitted with a stout knob for closing.*
⑭ *Internal doors have iron or brass surface-mounted rim locks, as here, or the newer cut-in mortice type.*
⑮ *Doorknobs, which began to supersede drop-handles, are generally of brass, though china examples appear c.1830.*
⑯ *Fretted, brass fingerplates/ push plates were typical.*

Windows

① *A typical plain arched, ground-floor window of 1815-30, here enlivened by Gothic detailing to the very thin glazing bars.*
② *The fenestration pattern of an early 19th-century town house, taken from John Reid's* The Young Surveyor's Preceptor. *Measurements are given for the width of the* building *and the dimensions of the windows.* YS
③ *Country and coastal houses tended to be much freer in design than city terraced/row houses. The emphasis falls on the group of bow windows rather than the doorway to this house in Exeter, Devon. A delicate cast-iron balcony allows for the enjoyment of the view.*

The 18th-century ideals of uniformity and regularity continue to govern the fenestration of Regency Britain. Proportions, at their most mannered in the years around 1800, gradually become less extreme towards the 1830s, although very elongated drawing-room windows on the floor above the entrance level are one of the chief delights of houses of the period. This taste for refined forms is reflected, too, in the attenuation of the glazing bars, thinner at this time than in any other period and characterized by sharp and often complex profiles. From about 1815 the conventional glazing of sashes or casements in plain squares was often varied by the addition of narrow edges or "margin-lights"; these were frequently of red or other coloured glass.

New notions of charm and grace led to the widespread use of full-length French doors, leading into flower gardens at the rear of both town and country houses. Houses with fine views often have very sophisticated bow windows with wood or ironwork verandas.

Window shutters were still almost universal during this period, and the contemporary pattern books vied to illustrate an ever-increasing variety of ingenious systems. Rising or sliding panels remained rare; the standard folding multi-leaf type, fitted in either flush or canted boxes, continued until shutters began to fall out of use in the later 1840s.

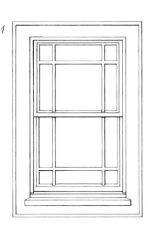

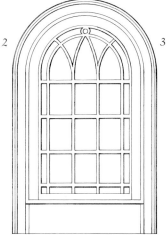

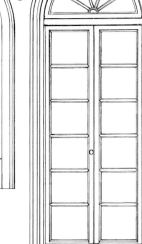

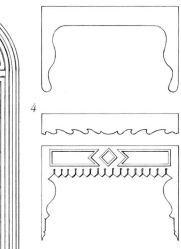

① and ② *Distinctive new glazing patterns of the early 19th century. The narrow margin lights often had red or blue glass.*

③ *A full-length glazed casement, generally termed a French window.*
④ *Wooden fascias of folding canvas sun blinds, 1820-35.*

⑤ *A design for a Gothic window of 1823. Revivalists of the Regency favoured Perpendicular Gothic forms.* AT

⑥ *Typical astragal (glazing bar) profiles from the early 19th century.* NN

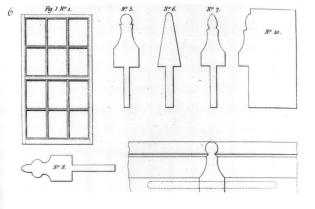

⑦ *An elevation, plan and section of one of the standard arrangements of shutters for a large double-hung sash window. The shutters fold back into shutter boxes in splayed reveals.* YS

⑧ *A detailed diagrammatic representation of the arrangements of folding shutters, usual in the first half of the 19th century. The plate is from Peter Nicholson's* New Practical Builder, *1825. The pattern on the left, with two or three leaves folded at right-angles to the window when not in use, is the most common. An alternative arrangement had splayed shutter boxes, which were thought to admit more light than the deep square-set boxes. The other system illustrated (bottom), where the shutters fold around parallel to the window beside them, is less often found in town houses; it is more usual in country areas.* NN

ELEVATION   SECTION

PLAN

① *The classic town house of the period 1815-35 has two or three full-length sash windows to the front drawing room, which would be found on the floor above the entrance level at this date. The cast-iron balcony is a standard mass-produced pattern.*

② *Raised ground-floor garden fronts or facades facing pleasing prospects were often provided with full-length casements which opened onto a balcony or terrace. A folding sun blind/shade with a decorative fascia is fitted into the window head.*

③ *The drawing room of Sir John Soane's house, London. The original building had full-length windows which opened out onto a loggia. He added glass to the loggia in 1832 and removed the original windows to increase the size of the room.* LIF

④ *Full-length casements or French doors to a garden, c.1820. The margin lights, once glazed in coloured glass, were thought to add charm to the view.* M

⑤ *A garden door of the 1820s at John Keats' House, Hampstead, London. It is provided with shutters set in shallow, splayed boxes and retains rare coloured and acid-etched glass in the margin lights.* KH

⑥ *A bow window of a type popular in the late 18th/early 19th centuries in country towns and seaside areas. This example is from Christchurch, Dorset.* SP

Walls

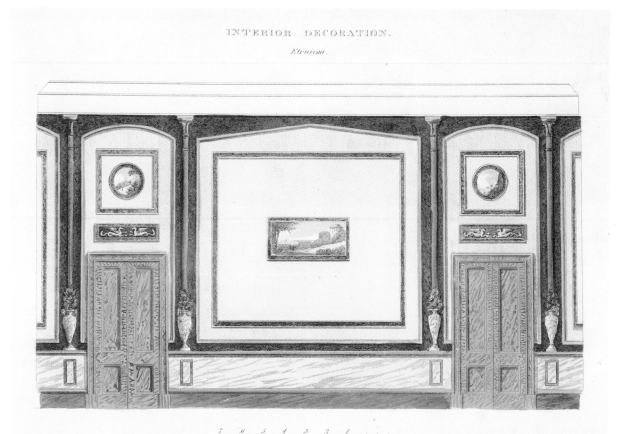

INTERIOR DECORATION.

Etruscan.

A design for the treatment of a wall from George Smith's Cabinet Maker's and Upholsterer's Guide, *1826. This decoration, labelled Etruscan, is loosely based on late Roman painted designs of panels and columns found at Pompeii, but it is also influenced by contemporary French taste.* CU

British architects and builders of the Regency period were the last generation who automatically subscribed to the architectural rules for the division of the wall into cornice, field and dado – a set of rules of proportion which ultimately derives from the five classical Orders. Throughout the period, in houses of any pretension to grandeur, correct detailing of the cornice, dado rail and skirting board/baseboard is observed. Decorative emphasis will usually be in the area of the main field, whether it is treated with plain or fancy plasterwork, painted with a flat coat of paint or specialist paintwork, or hung with wallpapers. These last became far more popular and widely available during this period;

silk and other fabrics remained a conspicuous luxury.

Themes based on carefully detailed architectural forms in either a generalized classical manner or in the fashionable Neo-Grecian taste were carried out either in relief or as painted trompe l'oeil effects. Contemporary pattern books featured colour plates illustrating whole walls. Designs based on the surviving wall paintings at Pompeii, first excavated in the mid-18th century, enjoyed a particular vogue, but many other exotic or historical styles provided inspiration. Among these fancy styles, rooms in the Chinese, Turkish, Egyptian or Gothic tastes were quite common; sadly, few of these survive.

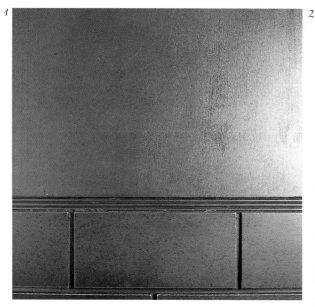

① *and* ② *A superior dado treatment much favoured for halls and staircases was to paint the wall surfaces in imitation of stone blocks or marble. These good examples of both forms are preserved in Sir John Soane's London house.* LIF

③ *A typical plain dado of the period 1815-40. The skirting board/baseboard is formed from a single horizontal plank, usually about 8 inches (20cm) wide, topped with a moulding. The dado itself is still often of wood at this date, while the field of the wall is plastered above the dado rail. Pale stone colours, contrasting with the field, were most popular for dadoes, though darker greens and chocolates were often preferred for their practicality in hallways.* DK

④*An elevation of a wall from John Goldicutt's treatise* Specimens of Ancient Decorations from Pompeii, *1825. Goldicutt's illustrations were prepared with archaeological precision and were much used by designers and decorators. In ordinary houses the proportions of dado and field would have been observed, but the frieze would have been reduced, to fit the standard height of English rooms.* JG

⑤ *A proposal for the end wall of a grand, columniated dining room in the Roman style. The arrangement of pilasters and panels above a dado could be carried out in real marble or painted in trompe l'oeil. Large niches filled with sculpture would complete such a room.* CU

Ceilings

The Breakfast Room in Sir John Soane's house in Lincoln's Inn Fields, London, built 1812. The spherical ceiling, springing from four segmental arches, is one of the most inventive of Soane's "fanciful effects which constitute the poetry of architecture". Convex mirrors fill the corner roundels. LIF

The Regency saw a marked change from the taste of the grander late 18th-century architects for elaborate, all-over decoration of the ceiling toward a new austerity in which ornament was more usually confined to the cornice, to the border of the ceiling plane and to a central rose/medallion. At the same time, however, the forms and motifs that were favoured tend to become bolder. In place of attenuated leaf forms for borders or the running ornament of cornices, the fashion was established for the use of heavy, classical motifs based on the richer forms of late Roman architecture, or stylized anthemion and other motifs of the Greeks. Similarly the central rose/medallion, from which the chandelier or other, more modest light fixture depended, displays a rich variety of forms: the most popular are based on combinations of rosette and patera motifs with radiating palmettes or other leaves. Toward the end of the period and in the very early years of Queen Victoria's reign, there was another noticeable shift in taste, in favour of more naturalistic ornament.

A surprising range of good, architecturally correct mouldings was available from the commercial suppliers of the day and many excellent examples survive, although, all too often, the exquisite detail of the casting has been coarsened by layer upon layer of later whitewash and paint.

① Plasterwork roses/medallions increasingly became the only decorative element on the ceiling. The first here is a rich palmette pattern from a Regency scheme at Belvoir Castle, Nottinghamshire. The others are from Bath, c.1830, and show a formal Greek pattern and a more sinuous leaf design.
② A plasterwork cornice with Greek motifs, from the same room as the last rose/medallion.
③ A coffered arch, c.1820. Each compartment is cast with egg-and-dart mouldings.

④ A diaper cornice (one with an all-over pattern of small repeated motifs) in the French taste by John Nash. From a house in Carlton House Terrace, St James's, London, 1827-32.
⑤ Plasterwork cornice mouldings with Greek elements from Belvoir Castle.
⑥ Part of a page of "roses" and other floral motifs published by L.N. Cottingham in his very influential Smith and Founder's Director of 1824. Primarily intended as cast-iron ornaments, these designs were adapted readily to plasterwork. SF
⑦ A typical cornice detail of the period 1800-1830. The motifs, which would have been crisper before layers of paint began to obscure their detail, are derived from classical precedents: lozenges with a formal flower device alternate with panels of "guttae" (small projections, usually seen on Doric architraves). From Charles Dickens' house in Doughty Street, London. DK

Floors

Drawn by John Goldicutt.

CEILINGS

FLOORS

A mosaic pavement illustrated by John Goldicutt in his Specimens of Ancient Decorations from Pompeii, *1825. The combination of delicate and bold motifs in this design would have appealed to Regency taste. The southern Italian town had been covered with lava when Mount Vesuvius erupted in AD 79, and its treasures were only revealed when excavations began in 1748. JG*

Wooden planks laid across joists remained the standard flooring for most stories of most houses. Deal (fir or pine) boards, stained, polished, or even painted and varnished were the norm; the use of better timbers or parquetry and inlay work in the French taste was confined to the very richest of rooms.

Grander town houses and some on a more modest scale continued to have stone-flagged entrance halls. Stone was considered the most appropriate material for kitchens and basement areas in terraced/row houses and for the service areas of village or country houses. Several of the pattern books of the period give designs for mosaic floors for halls; these enjoyed a vogue lasting well beyond the mid-19th century. The favoured motifs derived from archaeological sources and often included words such as *Salve* (welcome).

The variety of carpets available to even more modest purses increased enormously. English-made "Turkey" and other traditional patterned, pile rugs and carpets competed with looped-weave and flat "Brussels" types. Less expensive pileless or "Scotch" carpeting and druggets were also popular. The most fashionable interiors were now laid with all-over patterned wall-to-wall carpeting (stitched from narrow widths) or "body-and-border" carpets, which were made up from conventionally woven strips to fit the architecture exactly.

① *Common deal (fir or pine) floorboards are typical of all stories of ordinary houses. Narrower than in the 18th century, the average width is 7–9 inches (18–23cm).*

② *A design of 1820-30 by James White for an elaborate border of parquetry work which would have surrounded a carpet specially woven to size.*

③ *Scagliola (a hardened and polished paste of marble dust with plaster and colouring) imitated inlaid marble. Burghley House, Stamford, Lincolnshire, c. 1801-1803.*

④ *Mosaic panels from John Goldicutt's Specimens of Ancient Decorations from Pompeii, 1825. These could be adapted to fit a given space. The "SALVE" (welcome) panel was for an entrance hall.* JG

Drawn by John Goldicutt.

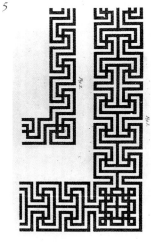

⑤ *Border designs for decorative floors to be carried out in inlaid mosaic work from Peter Nicholson's* Practical Builder, *1822.* PB

⑥ *Carpets assumed a new importance during the Regency period with the advent of specially woven wall-to-wall carpets. These would have an all-over pattern or they would be trimmed with a border which followed the plan of the room. These designs by Woodward Grosvenor and Company are for "Brussels" carpets and are dated 1827 and 1834 respectively. "Brussels" carpets have a looped pile, which is cut for a softer finish in "Wilton" carpets. At their best, both types are highly durable.* WO

Fireplaces

This fireplace surround in white marble was designed by Sir John Soane for the dining room of his own house in Lincoln's Inn Fields, London. Soane relied in this mannered but extremely effective design upon simple lines of reeded decoration. It was carried out in the building phase of 1812. LIF

In comparison with 18th-century types, Regency fireplace surrounds became simpler both in outline and profile. Flat jambs rising from plain, squared base blocks support straight lintels which are also flat-surfaced. The most characteristic type of the period has attenuated reeded decoration along the members and corner tablets with roundels. The mantel shelf, now a distinctly separate thin shelf, often with a reeded edge, gradually increases in depth and projects further at the sides; its greater dimensions were influenced by the increased availability of mantel-clocks and other paraphernalia such as candlesticks and candle-shades. Creamy-white statuary marble or lightly veined grey or white marble

were preferred, while more extravagant designs occasionally introduced luxurious materials such as porphyry or other rare, coloured marbles. In more modest houses, surrounds are wood, often painted in imitation of marble, or ornamented with composition (amalgams that incorporated paper or wood pulp, whiting and glue which could be moulded and set to a hard finish).

Steel grates became rare other than in the very finest rooms, and the manufacturers of cast iron, such as the Carron Company, supplied almost every need. Elegant hob grates continued in fashion, but the better performance of the newer register grates had made these all but universal, certainly in the towns, by the later 1820s.

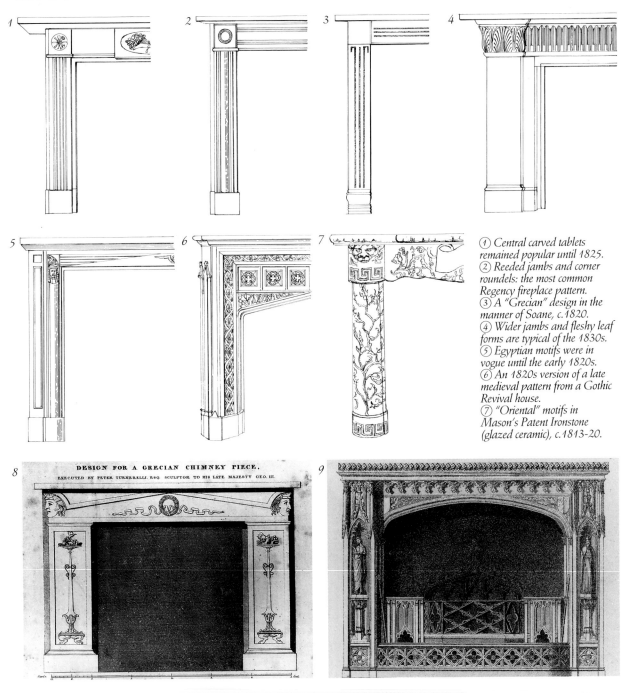

1. Central carved tablets remained popular until 1825.
2. Reeded jambs and corner roundels: the most common Regency fireplace pattern.
3. A "Grecian" design in the manner of Soane, c.1820.
4. Wider jambs and fleshy leaf forms are typical of the 1830s.
5. Egyptian motifs were in vogue until the early 1820s.
6. An 1820s version of a late medieval pattern from a Gothic Revival house.
7. "Oriental" motifs in Mason's Patent Ironstone (glazed ceramic), c.1813-20.

8. Peter Nicholson's *Practical Builder* of 1822 was the bible of all speculative contractors and builders (who built developments in the hope of profitable sales). But it gives very few designs for fireplaces; this presumably is because they were generally bought complete from suppliers. Only if something out-of-the-ordinary was required would it be designed and made specially. This "Design for a Grecian Chimneypiece" was carried out by the royal sculptor, Peter Turnerelli. PB

9. A handsome ensemble in the Gothic Revival manner, using details of the 15th century grafted onto a typical Regency structure. AK
10. A superior fireplace with its furniture (grate and fender) of 1820-30. This composition reveals the influence of the French taste for reviving the style of the Louis XIV period. The massive projecting surround would be of marble, usually plum-coloured, and ornamented with gilt-bronze appliqués. The elegant grate is steel. AK

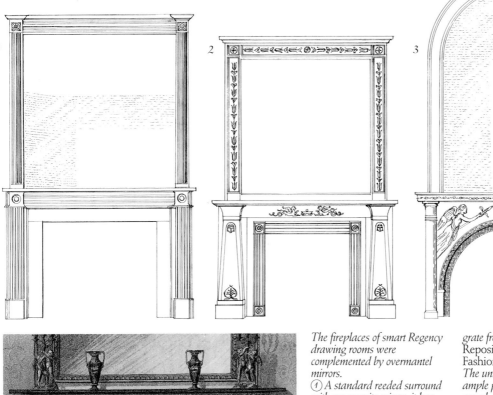

The fireplaces of smart Regency drawing rooms were complemented by overmantel mirrors.

① A standard reeded surround with an en suite mirror; it has standard corner roundels.

② A surround with Greek and Egyptian elements, topped with a gilded mirror frame, c.1810.

③ A subtle design in which the French-inspired arch of the mantel is echoed by the shape of the mirror frame. From T. Hope's Deepdene, Surrey, c.1806-20.

④ A chimneypiece and matching grate from Rudolf Ackermann's Repository of Arts, Literature, Fashions Etc., early 19th century. The unity of the motifs and ample proportions are typical of grand drawing room fireplaces. The surround is of black marble and the grate of steel; all the mounts are gilded. AK

⑤ This example features an "improved" fireplace opening with canted sides to increase burning efficiency. AK

⑥ From Ackermann, an Egyptian ensemble of great grandeur. AK

① A surround of pale, veined marble from a house in St Chad's Street, King's Cross, London. The wide jambs and heavy scrolled brackets gained popularity in the 1830s. GV

② A cast-iron hob grate: the restrained type of the 1820s and 30s. The gentle curve of the fire-bars with three balls is related to chair-backs of the day. GV

③ A simple, rather pretty surround in the Gothic Revival style of the 1830s. (The inset brick arch is later and the gas fire dates from the 1920s.) GV

④ The idiosyncratic Sir John Soane designed this surround in black fossiliferous (containing fossils) marble with inset classical reliefs for the breakfast room of his house, 1812. LIF

⑤ From the late 1820s to the early 1840s a revived Rococo style enjoyed a vogue. KH

⑥ A fine ensemble of cast-iron fireplace furniture, c.1835. The grate has a fixed fireback with Rococo detail. The lion and unicorn are andirons.

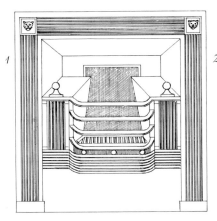

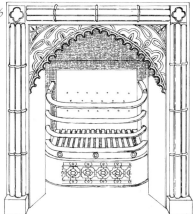

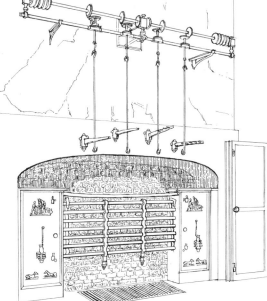

① "A Convex Reed Elliptic Register Stove, with Bright framed Fire, Double Rail, Balls, Bright Heads, Bevil Cheeks, falling Back, and Valve" from M. and G. Skidmore's pattern book of 1811.

② A finely cast "swan's-nest" hob grate with oval panels decorated with Prince-of-Wales Feathers which make it probably datable to not later than 1820.

③ A handsome freestanding grate in the bold Neo-classical manner of the 1820s. From Mallock House, Exeter, where it had been added to an earlier room to update the decoration.

④ This example of c.1830 is a muddled design in which a Gothic Revival front plate and jambs are unsuccessfully combined with enervated Rococo details.

⑤ A small hob grate of c.1820, probably by the Carron Company of iron founders. The side-pieces have fleshy leaf ornaments, while the basket has a band of Gothic detail.

⑥ A small early 19th-century grate in the Gothic Revival style. This could be inset in a fireplace or used, as here, without any surround.

⑦ An ensemble of a cast-iron grate with a fixed fireback, andirons, diapered cheek-pieces and a fender in the Baronial style, designed c.1825 for Aston Hall, Birmingham.

⑧ A large country house kitchen range with cast-iron hobs set within a stone surround. Above are turning pot hooks driven by a "jack", a vane in the chimney flue.

FIREPLACES

Staircases

The principal staircase in Sir John Soane's house in Lincoln's Inn Fields, London, 1812. It is boldly cantilevered around an irregular space. Note the dark marble wall string. LIF

The staircase continued to be one of the great indicators of status in a British house. The construction, workmanship and materials conformed to a precise scale of values. In the grandest houses the main flights of the staircase would be built of stone, cantilevered from the wall, with steps defined by a bold moulding or "nose" and the stair-ends either plain or ornamented with a carved detail. Stone stairs were provided with a graceful mahogany handrail, supported on metal railings or balusters. By this date wrought iron and steel were largely superseded by a great variety of cast-iron elements. Pattern books make it clear that classical motifs were most highly regarded.

The stairs of more modest houses (and the upper flights and secondary staircases of better houses) were of wood, similar to the austerely elegant type of the latter part of the 18th century. Generally of "open-string" construction, these have a handrail, usually of mahogany, which flows sinuously from top to bottom. The plain square-section balusters are placed two to a step. Ornamentation is usually confined to simple mouldings below the nosing and to turned detailing on the newel posts, which take the form of attenuated columns. All the parts except the handrail were painted in dull tones or in a wood-grain finish. A plain, narrow drugget was usually nailed to the steps.

① *Three typical staircases in modest houses of the 1820s and 30s. All have simple joinery details and mahogany handrails that are supported on plain square-section wooden balusters. The first example is the most modest and is of closed-string construction (the balusters are secured into a diagonal board). The last has steps with a moulded nosing and vestigial stair-end ornament based on 18th-century models.* DK, GV, GV

② *The stone steps on the principal staircase in Sir John Soane's London house have deep "nosings" that are also seen on the*

stair-ends. The mahogany handrail is supported on metal railings which are decorated with a lozenge design. LIF

③ *Designs for staircases from Nicholson's* New Practical Builder, *1825. Nicholson devotes many pages to the geometric problems raised by staircases and their rails.* NN

④ *A page of "staircase railings" to be made in cast-iron, from the pattern book* Examples of Ornamental Metal Work *by Henry Shaw, 1836. Shaw gives designs for both simpler balusters, to be used two to a step, and for more complex types which fill a whole step-width.* EO

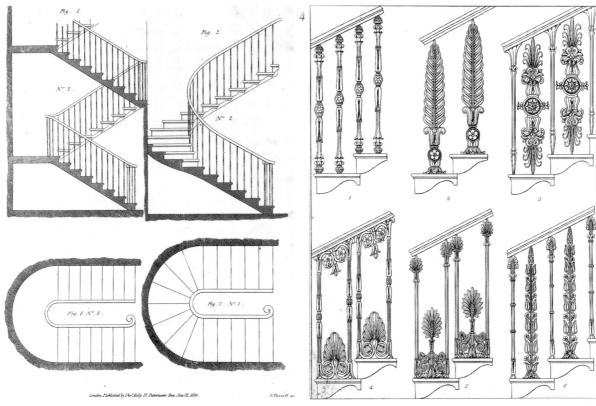

① *Staircases in ordinary houses have the refined simplicity of late Georgian types. Here, ornamentation is confined to the tapered newel post and the elegant profiles on the stair-ends.*

② *Throughout the late 18th and early 19th centuries the construction of staircases was carefully considered. Here, on a winding staircase, the rails sweep up steeply to gain height.*

③ *A plain staircase of c.1800 from Camberwell, London. The rail and square-section balusters of the rising flight "die" into the one above.*

④ *An unusual stair in the Greek Revival manner from Doric House, Sion Hill, Bath, after 1800. Each stair has elegant pairs of wrought-iron supports.*

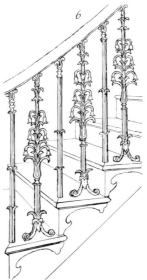

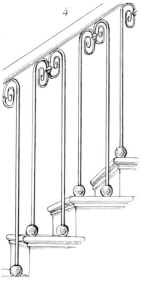

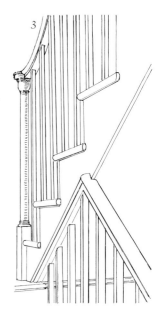

⑤ *Plain railings alternate with ornamental castings which combine Greek key and Gothic motifs. From Bath, c.1815.*

⑥ *A superior set of cast-iron railings with stylized lilies, c.1830. It is similar to designs published by Henry Shaw (see page 193).*

⑦ *A detail of the continuous cast-iron rail of the great circular staircase, added to Devonshire House, London, by the sixth Duke in the 1840s.*

⑧ *The staircases of the Royal Pavilion, Brighton, were added by John Nash in 1815-22; they are trompe l'oeil bamboo in painted cast iron.*

⑨ *A richly carved mahogany staircase in a late classical taste, c.1845, from Osborne Lodge, Cheltenham.*

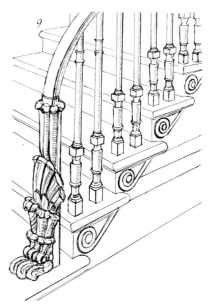

Built-in furniture

① *An engraving showing a variety of built-in shelves in a Neo-Grecian taste. This is one of the three rooms fitted out c.1807 by Thomas Hope for his collection of ancient vases. Other rooms of this house in Duchess Street,* London, *had built-in seats and shelving.* HF
② *A built-in cupboard, c.1820-30. The central door is pierced to allow ventilation for linen stored inside.*
③ *The library at Cassiobury Park, drawn* by John Britton, 1837. A typical Regency use *of a library as a family sitting room.* CP
④ *Wine-cellar shelving: this is one of several service areas which changed very little from the 18th until the late 19th century.* KH

In marked contrast to the taste of subsequent eras, austerity was admired during the Regency; this, coupled with a general paucity of personal possessions by modern standards, meant that there was relatively little need for storage space in the houses of the period. Cupboards are few, especially in town houses. Shallow cupboards about 12–15 inches (30–38cm) deep, with panelled doors, were sometimes fitted in the recesses that flank fireplaces in bedrooms. These were provided with pegs for clothes that would be hung flat rather than edge-on, as is the practice today. Similarly, on the main floors, recesses held built-in china cupboards and bookcases which sometimes incorporated a small writing flap or even a built-in bureau.

In grander houses the library had built-in bookcases, usually of an architectural character. During this period the library tended to become one of the most used family rooms in the house. More artistically minded gentlemen such as Thomas Hope or Sir John Soane also had elaborate built-in pieces made for the reception and display of their collections of antiquities; these two favoured a classical idiom, while others preferred Gothic detail for libraries and private museums.

The built-in furniture of servants' areas such as kitchens and housekeepers' rooms remained as plain and utilitarian as it had been in the 18th century.

STAIRCASES

BUILT-IN FURNITURE

Services

① *A rainwater hopper head/leader head of cast lead, with personal initials and the date of completion, 1811.*
② *A rare survival of the 1820s: a "copper", a large vessel built into a brick hearth, the standard method of heating water throughout the period. Note the wooden lid to conserve heat. DK.*
③ *A sink could be made from sheet lead dressed over a wooden box-shaped framework; this required strongly dovetailed corners.*

④ *A stone kitchen sink, hollowed from a single slab and supported on substantial brick piers. It is supplied with cold water from a tap/faucet and drains to an exterior gully. The lead pipes have "wiped" joints; that is, bulbous soldered connections.*
⑤ *An illustration and working diagram of the earth closet, which continued to be common in areas without a plentiful water supply and public sewers. "Privies" were sited as far from the house as possible. SB*

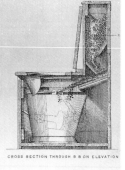

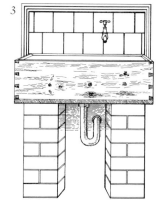

In all essential respects, the services in most British houses changed little from those of the late 18th century. There was a slow improvement in the provision of water, mainly owing to the gradual replacement of wooden pipes with iron ones. These leaked less and could sustain a higher water-pressure, which allowed water to reach taps above ground level. The frequency of supply improved greatly in fashionable quarters of cities and many larger towns, and became constant in the best streets in London. Elsewhere, notably in poor areas, a single outlet often served many households.

A similar pattern of good services for the rich and rudi-mentary provision, or none at all, in slum areas characterizes the system of drainage in the period. As before, storm water flowed through gutters and pipes into storage tanks or to soak-aways. A greater problem was posed by the increasing volume of sewage in towns and cities, which threatened to overwhelm such sewers as existed; these problems were only addressed by civil engineers in Queen Victoria's reign.

In the average house the kitchen still had a single water tap/faucet, fed by public supply or tank water; this was positioned near the shallow stone or lead sink. A "copper" was used for heating water as required, for cooking and washing.

Lighting

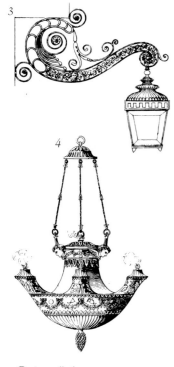

① *A candle-lantern incorporated into a fanlight. From Bristol, 1800-10.*
② *A fine crystal chandelier, c.1815, hung with diamond-shaped drops.*
③ *to* ⑧ *Designs for exterior and interior light fixtures from L. N. Cottingham's* Smith and Founder's Director, *1824. The first is a bracket-lamp for a grand facade; the second is a hanging oil lamp based on classical sources and suitable for a hallway; another hall lamp is flanked by grand exterior lamp standards, for oil, or later, gas lighting; the last is a staircase standard – note the two designs for cast-iron balustrading. SF*

One of the first houses in Britain to be lit by gas was Abbotsford in Roxburgh, Scotland, the mansion of the Romantic novelist Sir Walter Scott. The lighting was installed in 1823. Such extravagance remained very rare until later in the 19th century. The Regency in general saw the transition from candlelight and crude oil-burning lamps to improved oil lamps, mainly invented in Continental Europe. These were brighter and cleaner and used whale or colza oil (rape-seed oil) which smelled less than animal fats. These oil lamps, often based upon antique models, were popular for halls and entrances of grand houses, where they hung by chains or were supported on brackets or on standards at the foot of staircases. The variety of designs increased enormously, as is seen in contemporary pattern books. In more modest houses candle-lanterns fulfilled a similar function.

The colza-burning Argand lamp (see page 166) was freestanding. Its bright light transformed social patterns. However, candle sconces remained the essential lighting fixtures, and also played an important decorative role in the Regency interior.

In more modest dwellings and on the bedroom floors of smart houses hand-held chamber sticks and simple brackets remained the norm.

Metalwork

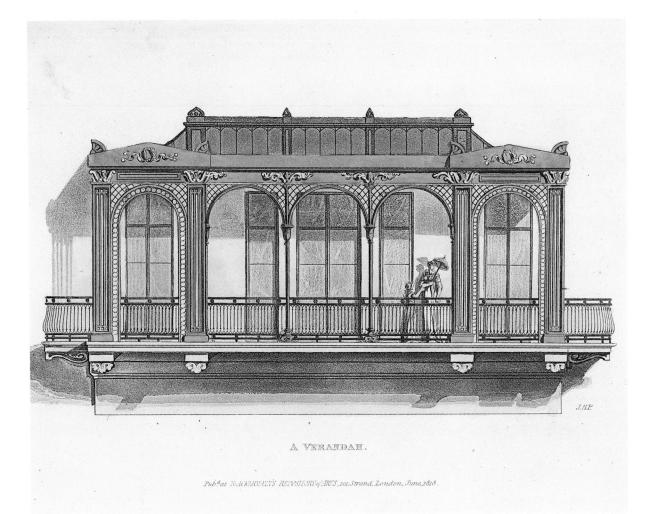

A VERANDAH.

Pub.d at R.ACKERMANN'S REPOSITORY of ARTS, 101.Strand, London, June,1818.

A design for a veranda from J.B. Papworth's Rural Residences, *1818. Such verandas were constructed mainly from standard cast-iron elements supplied by foundries. The most popular finish was a bronze-green, as here; suitable for gardens but with classical allusions. RR*

One of the chief glories of Regency Britain is its ironwork, which gives such a distinctive feel to the facades of terraces/rows and villas of the period. By this date cast iron had almost completely superseded wrought work, which is found only in special cases such as the individually shaped handrails for area steps. These had to be hammered to fit the needs of the staircase. The rest, including most railings for entrance steps and boundary fencing, light brackets, balconies, with their rails and brackets, and even vast multi-arched verandas, are all the work of foundries, great and small. These sprang up in the north of England and also in Kent in southeast England during the later 18th and early 19th centuries. Though in a sense standardized, the range of the castings bought "off the peg" by builders is enormous, and regional variations or even preferences for particular patterns within small districts are observable. For example: balcony patterns are very distinctive and a particular "cake basket" form is popular on the south coast, classical patterns predominate in Cheltenham, Gloucestershire, and a small repeating Gothic design is prevalent in Islington and other London areas. Nearly all the common designs occur in one pattern book of the period, the architect Lewis Nockalls Cottingham's *The Smith and Founder's Director*, first published in 1824.

① *A pretty hand-wrought porch c.1820, at Grafton Street, Cheltenham, Gloucestershire.*
② *A richly ornamented veranda in cast iron with classical motifs, from Leamington Spa, Warwickshire, c.1825.*
③ *and* ④ *Panels of cast iron for balconies, c.1815-25, incorporating simple geometric forms and floral details derived from the classical repertoire. The scrolled foliate pattern is a "rinceau" design.*
⑤ *A balconette in wrought iron with a floor of bars, c.1820.*
⑥ *This iron balcony is of bellied form, increasingly popular after 1830.*
⑦ *Bold cast-iron anthemions, from the top of a boundary wall in Cheltenham, c.1820.*

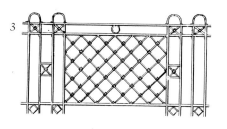

⑧ *A balcony of "cake-basket" form, common in south coast areas in the 1820s.*

⑨ *Cast-iron balcony brackets, one geometric, the other serpentine, from Bristol, Avon.*

⑩ *A typical gate to area steps. From Clifton, Bristol.*
⑪ *Geometric cast-iron fencing from Camberwell New Road,* London, c.1815-25.
⑫ *An elaborate iron entrance gate from York, c.1830.*
⑬ *Typical finial forms, 1810-* 30. The first and second groups have Greek overtones. The central "bud", urn and acorn would punctuate the run.

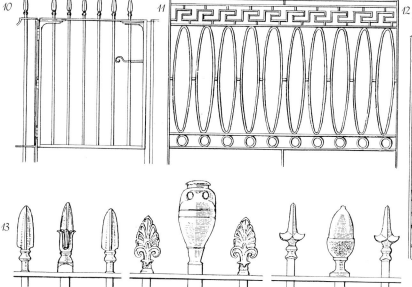

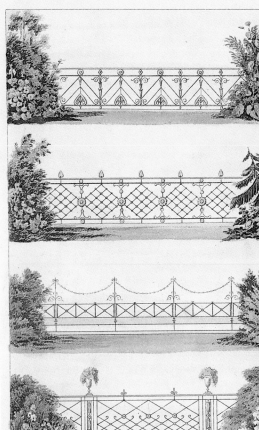

① *An elaborate veranda, similar to a design of 1818 by Papworth. The pagoda form roof was popular.* AA

② *A balcony in Clifton, Bristol, c.1820. The rail features one of the most widespread of all Regency patterns – a Gothic arch and quatrefoil.* SP

③ *Designs from J.B. Papworth's Rural Residences, 1818 for ornamental railings in iron. These would be found on grand estates with parks. Note the gilded details.* RR

④ *A simple hoop-form porch with metal pole supports and a copper roof, from Kensington, London, c.1820.* AA

⑤ *A detail of front-step railings of c.1825, with a sinuous leaf motif. From Kensington.* AA

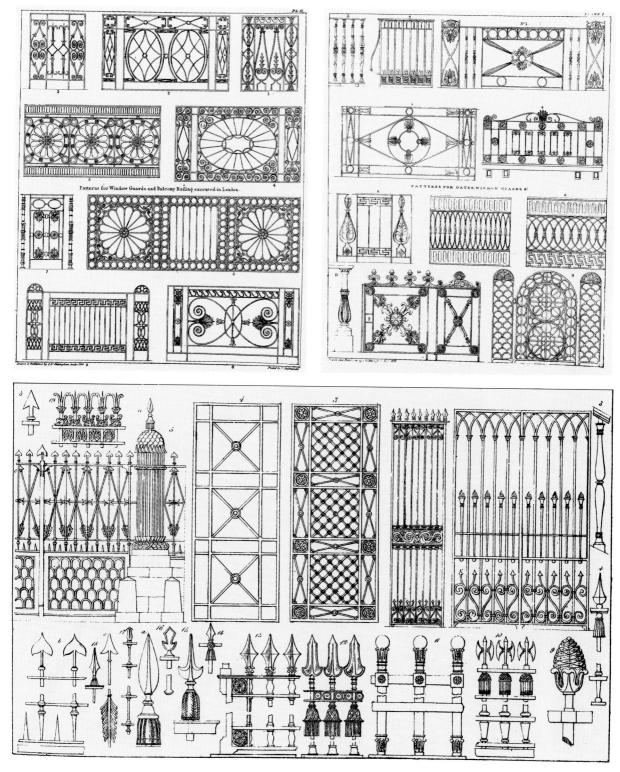

Three pages of designs for cast-iron balconies, railings, finials and stanchions (supporting members) from L.N. Cottingham's The Smith and Founder's Director, 1824. Cottingham's influential publication reveals the extent to which nearly all Regency cast ironwork was ornamented with classical motifs. The railing finials particularly reflect the widespread fascination with Neo-Grecian design. The anthemion balcony design in the bottom right-hand corner of the first plate was one of the most commonly used patterns and is found all over Regency Britain. SF

Woodwork

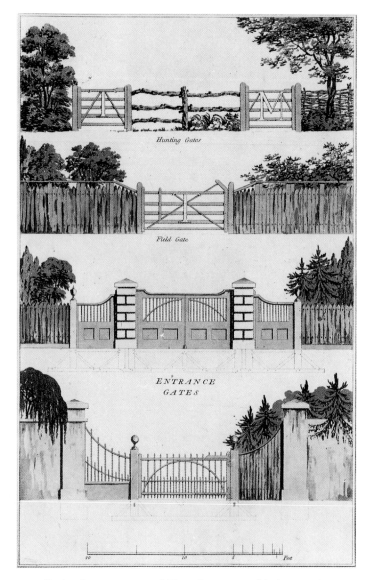

Designs for entrance gates, field gates and formal and rustic fencing. From J. Plaw's Ferme Ornée, *1795. The initials of the occupant of the house and owner of the land were often added to gates, as seen in the top two illustrations.* JP

Before the 18th century, decorative woodwork was used extensively on the facades of British houses. The building regulations of the Georgian period increasingly forbade the use of wooden doorcases, cornices and other elements which would fuel a fire. These had to be made of brick or stone. Also, with the growing availability of cast-iron fixtures in the late 18th century, woodwork ceased to mark property boundaries to town houses.

Woodwork detailing remained rather out of fashion in smart buildings until architects and garden designers such as J.B. Papworth and Humphry Repton introduced a new taste for the picturesque and rustic at the beginning of the 19th century. Initially intended for the most part for the enhancement of country estates, the pretty woodwork fences, gates and cottage details, such as porches of twig- or fret-work, were rapidly adopted for small-town and suburban villas. Some of the designs of these garden-orientated architects seem also to have been taken up in grander town houses, where it became fashionable for the first time to enhance backyards or gardens with trellis-work, tiered stands for pot plants and other charming features. It is to these Regency ideals of *rus in urbe* ("the country in the city") and to the associated designs for rustic woodwork that we may trace many of the intellectual and aesthetic origins of more modern concepts of suburbia.

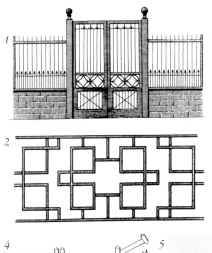

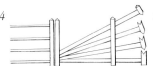

① *A gate and fence. The framework is wooden while the decorative and security details are iron. Such arrangements were common in village houses.* MD

② *Ornamental fencing in a Chinese fret pattern, from C. Middleton's* Designs for Gates and Rails, *1806.* MD

③ *Designs for gates and fences published by J. B. Papworth in* Rural Residences, *1818. These are intended for estates, but the patterns were rapidly assimilated into use for suburban villas.* RR

④ *An ingenious stile: the rails are not fixed on the left-hand side and the post on the right is cut into chevrons which slot together. The rails pivot on the middle post and can be pushed down. The segmented post acts as a counterbalance and pulls the rails up once released.*

⑤ *Designs by Papworth for ornamental fencing in the popular rustic romantic style, incorporating twig-work.* RR

⑥ *and* ⑦ *Designs for trellis-*

work, which was normally painted green. CM

⑧ *A design by Papworth for an ambitious wood and glass structure, suitable as an*

orangery, camellia house or winter garden. RR

⑨ *A simple wooden porch, probably of the 1820s, from Southwell, Nottinghamshire.* RS

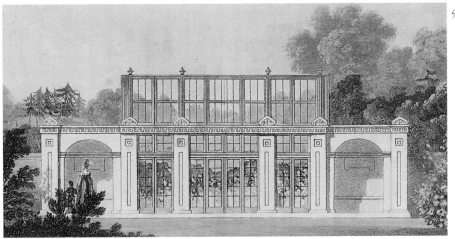

WOODWORK

FEDERAL AND EMPIRE

1780–1850

① *The weatherboarded Sam Brown house in Oregon, 1858, is a simple Greek Revival residence with a square-columned portico and six-over-six windows.* PD

② *The Gaillard-Bennett House, Charleston, South Carolina, includes early Federal details, 1800, certain alterations in 1819, and the addition of a portico and other features, c.1850. There are Doric columns on the first tier of the portico, and Corinthian columns with cast-iron capitals on the second. An elliptical fanlight is also featured.* GB

③ *The English Regency mixed with southern Classical Revival is evident in the Patrick Duncan House, Charleston, South Carolina, c.1816. This suburban villa is attributed by many authorities to William Jay. It has a pedimented portico, supported by Composite columns, a doorway set within an apse, and various details showing Moorish, Gothic and other eclectic influences of the period.* AL

Although English architects after 1760 were designing new structures in the Neo-classical manner, American builders did not adopt this style to any advanced degree before the Revolution began in 1775. The "Neo-classical" movement was the reinterpretation of classical architecture. Ponderous Palladian elements derived from Roman public buildings were abandoned; inspiration instead came from recent archaeological finds, particularly of Roman domestic buildings. A few new dwellings planned in the 1770s indicate some translation of English Neo-classicism in certain details, but economic downturns in certain Colonies, as well as a colonial conservatism which often venerated the "neat and plain" in buildings, prevented acceptance of the movement until after 1782. As late as the early 19th century, an important English émigré architect in the United States, Benjamin Henry Latrobe (1764-1820), complained about the craftsmen who were still tied to the traditional styles of the early Georgian period.

After 1783 and the conclusion of the American Revolution, some wealthy merchants in Providence, Rhode Island, and in other cities built houses that still reflected earlier Georgian tastes. However, some leaders of the new Republic were looking for an architecture that was philosophically appropriate for the nation. Many applauded the work of Robert and James Adam and their followers in England as a suitable model, while others, venerating simple and utilitarian ideals, searched for a style more related to Continental European versions of Neo-classicism and Classical Revivalism.

The Federal or "Adamesque" style became familiar by the end of the 1780s. This architecture achieved elegance through attenuated forms, curved or elliptical features and sophistication of detail: polygonal or curvilinear bays, concealed hipped roofs behind balustrades, elongated windows with large panes and thin glazing bars, decorated cornices, and entry porches with thin, tapered columns in the "ancient taste". Rooms tended to be open and airy, with occasional use of oval shapes on walls, vaulted or shaped ceilings, and flat plaster walls decorated by en suite fireplace surrounds, door surrounds, dadoes and cornices. Grand rooms were often further

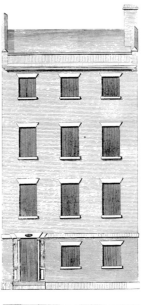

① *A group of Boston townhouses built in the 1840s around a private garden. These houses, with their curvilinear bays, represent a progression from the designs of Asher Benjamin. Note the elegant doorways, hierarchy of windows and simple details which were to be found in such dwellings all along the Eastern seaboard.* RS

② *Asher Benjamin's elevation and ground floor plan for terraced/row houses, from the sixth edition of* The American Builder's Companion, *1827.* ABA

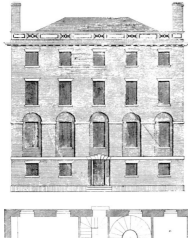

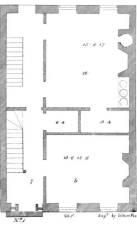

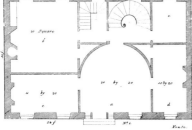

③ *Asher Benjamin's elevation and ground floor plan for a large city house. The plan provides some unusual room shapes and a circular rear staircase.* ABA

④ *and* ⑤ *Two houses from Salem, Massachusetts, with similar fenestration, 1800-1810. The first example has a two-tiered portico: Ionic columns support the second tier which has had glazing added. The lower example has six-over-six sash windows and a pedimented porch.* RS

embellished by ornamental plaster ceilings, and wallpapers with festoon borders. The Adam brothers' work was translated to the United States largely through the pattern books of other designers, especially those of William Pain, whose *Practical House Carpenter* (1766) and *Practical Builder* (1774) may not have reached the Colonies before the 1780s. The spread of this fashion was also related to the presence of newly arrived craftsmen from England, and especially by the rise of the architect, replacing the predominance of the house carpenter of the previous generation. Regional and nationally prominent designers included classically trained aristocrats such as Charles Bulfinch (1763-1844) in Boston and Gabriel Manigault (1758-1809) in Charleston, and former craftsmen, such as Samuel McIntire (1757-1811) in Salem

and John McComb (1758-1853) in New York. Knowledgeable patrons pressed for the Neo-classical style when remodelling earlier houses, George Washington's changes to Mount Vernon, Virginia, in the 1780s being a supreme example. New houses such as Gore Place in Waltham, Massachusetts, and terrace/row houses in Boston, particularly those designed by Bulfinch, reflected the new Federal taste.

A nearly concurrent movement in American architecture was the Classical Revival. This style, usually associated with Thomas Jefferson (1743-1826), rejected the Neo-classicism of the Adam brothers, and looked to French models and to renewed inspiration from Palladio and Roman public buildings. Immigrant architects who were familiar with the later English Neo-classicism were

① *An opulent late Neo-classical interior from the Patrick Duncan House, Charleston, South Carolina, c.1816. The use of stylized fluted columns and palmettes with ovolo mouldings on the panelling provides an elegant and decorative screen to the anteroom behind.* AL

② *A detail from a bedroom in the Morris-Jumel Mansion, New York, originally built in 1765 and restyled in 1810. The wallpaper has festoons at frieze-height and an imaginative pattern on the dado. The festooned curtain pelmets/valances are appropriate to a bedroom.* MJ

encouraged by Jefferson; young students such as Robert Mills (1781-1855) of South Carolina and William Strickland (1788-1854) of Philadelphia also began their careers under Jefferson's aegis. At least one English architect practising in the United States, however, pursued a purer version of the English Regency – William Jay (1793-1837) in Savannah, Georgia.

The movement presaged an American classicism of a more robust sort which relied more on form than applied detailing. The houses feature round or lunette windows, fanlights/transom lights, and prominent one- or two-story porticoes. They reflect a classicism of a unique type, sometimes termed Roman Revival but actually a little more individualistic than this would suggest; followers were versatile enough to eventually embrace the Greek Revival movement as well.

Enthusiasm for the simple elegance and monumentality of Greek remains in Italy inspired the Greek Revival movement, although detractors deplored the emphasis on the Greek temple form. Early practitioners who admired the simplicity and functionalism of the style included the English architect George Hadfield (c.1764-1826), and native American architects such as William Strickland, Ithiel Town (1784-1844) and Thomas U. Walter (1804-87). This period marked the real emergence of the influence of American rather than English pattern books. The earliest of these, such as *The Young Carpenter's Assistant* (1805) by Owen Biddle, and *Modern Builder's Guide* (1797) by Asher Benjamin (1773-1845), were based

on Federal architecture, but Benjamin's work kept pace with the times in a series of revisions. *The Builder's Assistant* (1819), a pattern book by John Haviland (1792-1852), was an early attempt to adapt Greek forms to construction needs.

Houses of the Greek Revival movement reflected the view that the real or imagined Greek temple was the most perfect creation. They were block-like buildings, with low hipped or temple-form gable roofs, and usually featured porticoes of single or double height with columns of various Orders, including Doric and especially Ionic with oversized capitals. Detailing, particularly on masonry examples, could be rather austere: wide cornice trims and some door and window surrounds were decorated in the Greek manner with anthemions (honeysuckle), key frets, or egg-and-dart mouldings. Windows and fanlights/transom lights were no longer rounded but square or rectangular. Townhouse forms were particularly dependent on columnar door surrounds and entablatures for decoration. Uniform brickwork with clean, narrow joints, and stone for lintels and steps added to the handsome simplicity. Inside, the same decorative devices were applied. Wainscotting was no longer used but decorative papers, carpets and furniture contrasted with the simplicity of architectural ornamentation in door surrounds, ceiling decoration and fireplace surrounds. The Greek Revival style was still favoured by some prominent patrons until the 1850s, and later still in vernacular buildings.

Doors

An ornate six-panelled Neo-classical doorway from the Morris-Jumel Mansion, New York, 1810. Embellishments

include a delicate elliptical fanlight, side lights with decorative tracery, and carved paterae in the panels beneath. MJ

In a Federal or Adamesque house the entrance door provides the main emphasis of the facade. In a high-style house the addition of a semi-circular or elliptical fanlight derived from pattern books identifies the building as Classical Revival or Adamesque. Federal doorways are often framed by pilasters and surrounded by delicate wood carvings of oval paterae and classical motifs. In terrace/row houses the door architrave might serve as the only exterior ornamentation. Porticoes of large houses gradually increased in size; in the South they eventually took the form of multi-storied galleries.

Exterior and interior doors are usually made of pine, with some regional use of maple, poplar and cypress.

Interior doors are frequently grained to look like mahogany. Neo-classical door casings are decorated with wooden tracery and applied stuccowork.

Before the end of the Federal period most doors were six-panelled, sometimes with ovolo mouldings. However, Greek Revival doors were usually of the two- or four-panelled form which became standardized through the pattern books of Asher Benjamin and Minard Lafever. Exterior door mouldings, which became heavier, featured classical motifs; pilasters supported a simple entablature or plain lintel with corner blocks and a central panel. Internal doorcases were framed by flat Doric pilasters, with classical mouldings in grander houses.

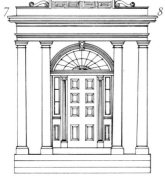

① Two late 18th-century doors.
The first from c.1790 illustrates
the transition from Colonial
Georgian to Neo-classical. The
second is similar but its
delicately fluted pilasters
support a broken pediment; the
oval paterae are distinctly Neo-
classical in style.
② Two patterns from William
Pain's The Practical Builder,
1774. Ionic columns support the
broken pediment of the first
design; a volute and a console

are suggested as architrave
decorations for the second. WPB
③ An ornamented doorway
with elliptical fanlight and side
lights with tracery, c.1809.
④ An early Classical Revival
doorway. The fanlight is semi-
circular; the spokes are elegant
but less attenuated than
Adamesque forms, c.1817.
⑤ A Greek Revival door
framed by Ionic columns,
c.1830.
⑥ An eight-panelled front door

from Minard Lafever's The
Modern Builder's Guide,
1833. ML/B
⑦ An early 19th-century
Classical Revival temple-front
doorway. Tuscan columns
support an entablature
surmounted by a pediment
which is decorated with a Greek
fret.

⑧ An elliptical Corinthian-
columned portico designed by
Samuel McIntire in 1805.
⑨ A two-tiered porch featuring
anachronistic Chinese
Chippendale railings and plain
columns, 1803.
⑩ The classic Greek temple
front: four Ionic columns support
a full entablature.

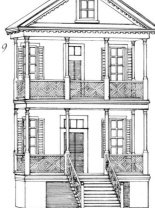

① *The entrance door to the Old Merchant's House, New York, 1832. Classical Revival features include Ionic columns, stone quoins and keystone, a boldly spoked fanlight, and the detailing on the architrave.* OM

② *The interior of a Neo-classical entrance at the Morris-Jumel Mansion, New York, c.1810. Coloured glass is featured in the tracery of the fanlight and side lights.* MJ

③ *Ionic columns frame the sliding double mahogany doors at the Old Merchant's House. The use of sliding doors was a device employed by some Greek Revival architects, notably Asher Benjamin, Ithiel Town and his partner Alexander Davis, and later by lesser-known architects.* OM

④ *to* ⑥ *Three examples of Greek Revival interior door surrounds from the Bartow-Pell Mansion, 1842. The cherub and eagle doorhead decorations are unusually elaborate for this style.* BW

⑦ *An interior six-panelled door (c.1808) at upper floor level with typical H-L hinges and a box lock.* NR

⑧ *Shown from the interior, this fanlight surmounting the entrance door of the Old Merchant's House, 1832, has a delicacy that reflects earlier classical styles.* OM

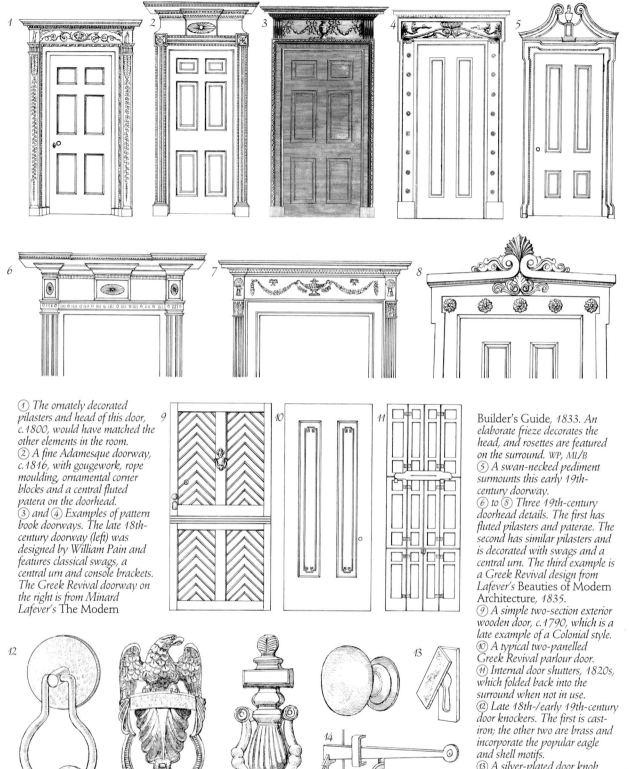

① *The ornately decorated pilasters and head of this door, c.1800, would have matched the other elements in the room.*
② *A fine Adamesque doorway, c.1816, with gougework, rope moulding, ornamental corner blocks and a central fluted patera on the doorhead.*
③ *and* ④ *Examples of pattern book doorways. The late 18th-century doorway (left) was designed by William Pain and features classical swags, a central urn and console brackets. The Greek Revival doorway on the right is from Minard Lafever's* The Modern

Builder's Guide, *1833. An elaborate frieze decorates the head, and rosettes are featured on the surround. WP, MI/B*
⑤ *A swan-necked pediment surmounts this early 19th-century doorway.*
⑥ *to* ⑧ *Three 19th-century doorhead details. The first has fluted pilasters and paterae. The second has similar pilasters and is decorated with swags and a central urn. The third example is a Greek Revival design from Lafever's* Beauties of Modern Architecture, *1835.*
⑨ *A simple two-section exterior wooden door, c.1790, which is a late example of a Colonial style.*
⑩ *A typical two-panelled Greek Revival parlour door.*
⑪ *Internal door shutters, 1820s, which folded back into the surround when not in use.*
⑫ *Late 18th-/early 19th-century door knockers. The first is cast-iron; the other two are brass and incorporate the popular eagle and shell motifs.*
⑬ *A silver-plated door knob and escutcheon plate from a Greek Revival house.*
⑭ *A cast-iron thumb latch of the type used in service areas well into the 19th century.*
⑮ *A typical H-hinge.*
⑯ *to* ⑱ *Two spring locks and a box lock; both types were in use from the late 18th to the early 19th century.*

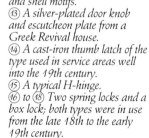

Windows

① *A Neo-classical pedimented window with a six-over-six sash and louvered exterior shutters from the Gaillard-Bennett House, Charleston, c.1800. The larger panes of glass indicate that this is a luxurious house for the period.* GB
② *A Boston town house designed by Charles Bulfinch, c.1812, shows Neo-classical main floor windows set into recessed arches with garlands and fanlights above.*
③ *Greek Revival sash windows are plainer in style. Here, an elliptical window is set into the tympanum, 1836.*

Several features distinguish Federal windows from those of the preceding Colonial period. Glazing bars are thinner with ovolo-shaped profiles; glass panes are larger; and window heads (often with a central keystone), made from marble, stone or wood, are flat. Entablatures may include delicate Adamesque decoration. The nine-over-nine configuration of panes predominated in many areas until the early 19th century when it was gradually replaced by six-over-six double sashes, and sometimes triple sashes.

Adamesque architrave detailing is minimal; however, some windows are set in recessed arches for added interest. In grand houses main floors often have floor-to-ceiling windows, opening on to balconies; the detailing of elaborate interior surrounds matches that of the doors and fireplace. Late 18th-century Palladian windows have delicately moulded pilasters and fanlight tracery. Semi-circular and oval windows are used on the upper stories. Dormer windows are generally gabled or pedimented. A feature of early Jeffersonian classicism is the use of round and semi-circular lunette windows. As the style progresses to full Greek Revival, window forms become simpler: for example, Palladian windows evolve into rectangular tripartite forms. Lintels are plain, a simple central panel and corner blocks being the only embellishment. French doors remain popular.

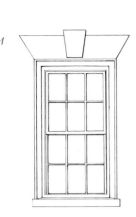
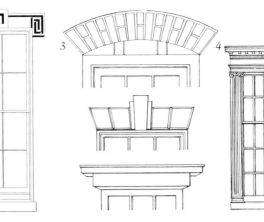

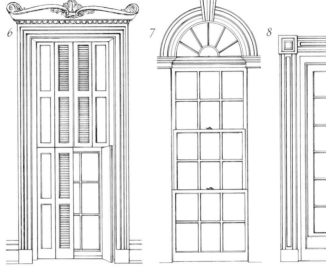

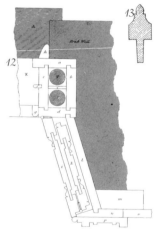

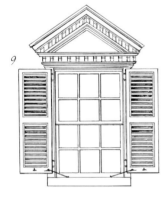

① *A typical classical six-over-six sash window with a stone or stucco window head. It could have louvered shutters.*

② *A window design from Asher Benjamin's* The Architect, or Practical House Carpenter, *1830. Note the thin side portions of the surround, and the plain central panel with Greek key motifs.*

③ *Three Federal window heads. The top and middle examples are from the late 18th century and show a segmental or relieving arch, and a stone or stucco lintel with a central keystone. The third is a 19th-century flat-headed example.*

④ *A Venetian or Palladian window, c.1800. Note the attenuation of the mouldings compared with Colonial windows.*

⑤ *A Neo-classical tripartite window with louvered shutters.*

⑥ *to* ⑧ *Three floor-length windows. The first, with interior louvered shutters, is in the Greek Revival style (1830); note the*

cresting on the architrave. The second is a good example of Thomas Jefferson's Roman Revival style (c.1817). Note the triple sash, lack of architrave mouldings and semi-circular fanlight and keystone. The third example, French doors (1838), has a Greek Revival surround typical of this time.

⑨ *A late 18th-century pedimented dormer window with louvered shutters.*

⑩ *From the same period, a detailed drawing for a more*

elaborate arched surround with a keystone and capped by a broken-bed pediment.

⑪ *Three window architraves, 1820–40. The top example is Neo-classical in style, and the other two Greek Revival.*

⑫ *The construction of a sash frame and shutter, from Asher Benjamin's* The Architect, or Practical Carpenter *(1830). AB*

⑬ *A typical glazing bar profile.*

① *Marble is used to form the lintel and the keystone at the centre of a rubbed brick overarch, 1808.* NR

② *Neo-classical pilasters and richly applied composition mouldings form this window surround, 1808.* NR

③ *Full-length casement windows with a Greek Revival architrave. The pilasters have anthemion mouldings and support a pediment embellished with an eagle. New York, c.1842.* BW

④ *A Palladian (Venetian) window designed by Charles Bulfinch. Ionic pilasters separate the central sash from the side lights which are decorated with fine tracery. Boston, Massachusetts, c.1806.* RS

⑤ *A plain Greek Revival window surround. New York, 1842.* BW

⑥ *A sash window with a cornice window head. Salem, Massachusetts, 1782.* RS

⑦ *Tracery emphasizes the shape of these arched windows in a Gothic Revival portico, 1816.* AL

Walls

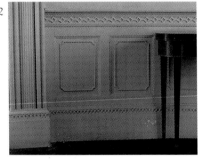 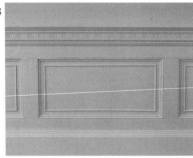 

① *Joseph Dufour's "Monuments of Paris"*
paper was printed in 1815 and is a good
example of the popular French-imported
scenic wallpapers. CT
② *Beading edges this wainscot, 1816.*

Ovolo moulding on the panels and a carved
guilloche enrichment at skirting board/
baseboard level are typical features. AL
③ *A gougework pattern (1808) created by*
the use of a hollow bladed chisel. It was a

popular form of wainscot decoration. NR
④ *Typical of the Federal period, this*
hallway wallpaper (c.1810) features a
variety of Neo-classical architectural motifs.
The main colour is grey, in two shades. MJ

During the Federal period the greatest change in wall treatment is the elimination of full panelling in fashionable rooms, other than on fireplace walls. The wainscot on the remaining walls is taken to dado level only. The field between the dado and cornice is usually plain-plastered with a whitewash finish.

In the best houses the walls of the finest rooms would be papered. Until the end of the 18th century, wallpapers were often plain but with elaborate festoon borders at cornice level and around the wainscotting and doors. After 1800 wallpapers were floral or striped, and geometric and Neo-classical motifs were common. Houses of the wealthy displayed scenic wallpapers

imported from France. Dadoes and entablatures are decorated with gougework, carved foliage and frets, together with Adamesque applied composition designs; ancient motifs are featured on the early Classical Revival walls. The panelling and composition work was often painted, or grained to look like mahogany.

By the 1830s wainscotting generally had been eliminated in favour of heavily moulded grained or marbleized skirting boards/baseboards. Walls are painted in terracotta, stone colours, deep pinks or grey, or are hung with wallpapers reflecting the interest in Greek Revival architecture, with cornice friezes either left plain or decorated with anthemions and key patterns.

WALLS

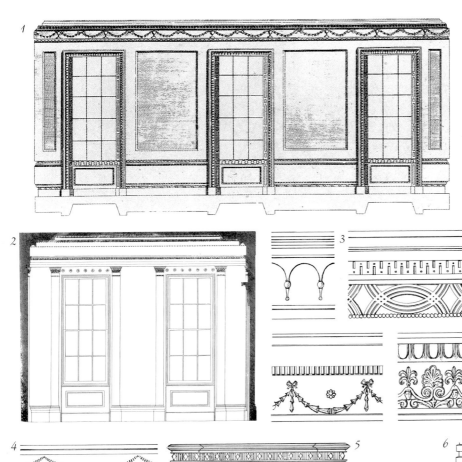

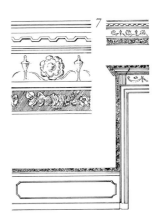

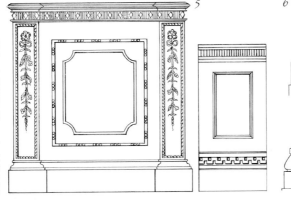

① and ② *Two wall pattern treatments. The first, from William Pain's* Practical House Carpenter, *1766, shows Adamesque interpretations of Neo-classical details. The lower example, from Minard Lafever's* The Modern Builder's Guide, *1833, shows the simplicity of a Greek Revival wall treatment.* WP, MI/B

③ *Four complete entablatures showing cornice and frieze decorations. The first (top left) is a wooden arcaded cornice, c.1818. The interlace and dentil pattern (top right) closely resembles a version by William Pain. On the frieze of the example bottom left, c.1800, a dentillated cornice surmounts the stuccowork garlands. The fourth example is a Greek Revival plaster treatment with egg-and-dart and anthemion mouldings.*

④ *Chair rail mouldings with gougework decoration.*

⑤ *Neo-classical wooden panelled dadoes with gougework decoration on the chair rails. Applied composition mouldings decorate the pilasters*

of the example on the left, 1820, and form the inset panels. The dado on the right, 1796, has additional detailing at skirting board/baseboard level.

⑥ *Two skirting board/ baseboard moulding profiles from Asher Benjamin's pattern book* The Architect, or Practical Carpenter, *1830.*

⑦ *A detail (left) of a ceiling cornice and frieze, with a floral wallpaper border beneath. A narrower border is used to edge doorways and dadoes (right).*

⑧ *An early 19th-century stencilled wall from the Stencil House, Shelburne, Vermont, c.1790.* ST

⑨ *Painted murals were also popular.*

Ceilings

① *Neo-classical plasterwork at its most splendid. This ceiling section from the entry hall at the Gaillard-Bennett House, Charleston, South Carolina, c.1800, has an abundance of* plaster decoration, including urns, anthemions, garlands, rosettes and foliage. GB
② *A simple Greek Revival moulded cornice and floral band surround an oval ceiling at the* Nathaniel Russell House in Charleston. The house was built c.1808 but this decoration probably dates from a period of minor alterations made to the interior in the 1850s. NR ③ *From the same house, a more elaborate cornice and ceiling treatment includes bands of beading and guilloche, with floral motifs set into geometric shapes.* NR

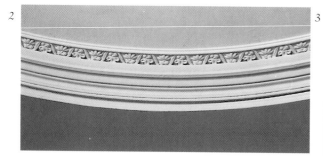

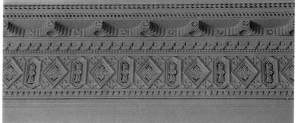

During the Federal period simple houses had boarded ceilings which were usually whitewashed; middling houses had flat-plastered ceilings; and grander houses progressed from plain flat plaster to English-influenced decorative plasterwork. As new technology spread these ceilings were decorated with leaves, swags, garlands, sunbursts and other Neo-classical motifs. Decorations were made of lime-enriched plaster of Paris, a lime putty "stucco" or, in some cases, papier mâché; they were moulded on site (wet plaster was moulded with a template or stamped with dies) or were applied ready-moulded to the ceiling.

In the late 18th century, ceilings were often painted in a strong colour and the plaster enrichments were picked out in white paint or occasionally gilt. English fashion encouraged a taste for segmented ceilings. In the Greek Revival period, grand houses would sometimes have coffered ceiling divisions in one room and a dome in another. Less elaborate houses would have a simple plaster roundel with inner concentric circles and a flat plaster moulding bordering the room.

Pattern books provided a variety of designs for ceiling roses/medallions and borders using guilloche, Greek key and other motifs. Greek Revival designs incorporated combinations of acanthus leaves, anthemions, rosettes and sometimes a Greek key border.

① The early Neo-classical style is shown in this detail of the coved ceiling of George Washington's New Dining Room at Mount Vernon, Virginia. It is thought to have been designed by the London immigrant plasterer John Rawlins in 1787.

② Fret and guilloche patterns from William Pain's The Practical Builder (1774). They were widely used for wood and plaster ornamentation. WPB

③ A ceiling design for plaster ornamentation from South Carolina, c.1800. The fashion for segmented ceilings reflected an English influence.

④ English architect William Jays designed this Regency ceiling at Savannah, Georgia, 1819. His Neo-classical decoration is held to be reminiscent of Sir John Soane's work.

⑤ to ⑦ Three plaster ceiling roses/medallions. The first predates the others and is from the Gibbes House, Charleston, South Carolina, 1780. The middle example dates from c.1824, and the third is from South Carolina and is copied from Minard Lafever's Beauties of Modern Architecture, 1835.

⑧ Moulded plaster ornament with corner rosettes used as a ceiling border, c.1815.

Floors

① *A patterned carpet from the Morris-Jumel Mansion, New York, 1820. The Greek anthemion motif is combined with a late Neo-classical design. Such wall-to-wall carpets, usually woven in strips and tacked to the floor, were indications of prosperity.* MJ
② *Tongue-and-groove pine floorboards, c.1800. Such floors were usually scrubbed and bleached.* GB
③ *The border of this floor has a stencilled Greek Revival motif. New York, 1842.* BW
④ *Parquet floors were rare. This design shows Thomas Jefferson's*

celebrated example at Monticello, Virginia, 1804. Cherry was used to form the central squares with beech for the borders.
⑤ *to* ⑦ *Three examples of designs for painted floorcloths which were popular both as protection for carpets and as summer floor coverings. The first shows a marbleized illusionistic pattern, 1802. The second example has a starred pattern and dates from the early 19th century. The third floorcloth was laid in a hallway and dates from the first half of the 19th century.*

Flooring materials changed little between 1780 and 1840. In the New England states white pine was often used until the end of the 18th century. Then there was a gradual shift to the use of yellow pine which had long been employed in the mid-Atlantic and southern states. In better houses floorboards are tongued-and-grooved; more modest houses have random-width boards nailed to joists. Wooden floors were sometimes painted in diamond patterns or were stencilled; some floors were painted in solid colours. Parquet was rare.

In the grandest houses, entry halls are often white marble or sometimes patterned with alternating white marble and blue stone; flag stones were also used.

Kitchens and servants' quarters usually have brick floors.

Floor coverings became more plentiful and varied: plain or dyed straw-matting was used. Painted canvas floorcloths were stencilled or marbleized; they were sometimes used as a protection for a good carpet. For the wealthy, carpets became more available after 1790. Carpets, usually imported and patterned with scroll-work, polygonal shapes or floral and Neo-classical motifs, were often laid wall-to-wall and tacked to the floor. After 1800 carpets increasingly reflected various Classical Revival styles with gold star and laurel wreath motifs; in the 1830s and 40s patterned rugs offered a vivid contrast to the architectural austerity.

Fireplaces

A black marble fireplace with simple mouldings from an upper room at the Bartow-Pell Mansion, New York, 1842.

The figuring on the marble inner surround offsets the otherwise rather austere appearance of the chimneypiece. BW

The pattern book designs of the Adam brothers strongly influenced the transition from the Colonial style of fireplace to the Neo-classical form. Moulded urns, swags, garlands, paterae and figures are applied to wooden surrounds and overmantels. The central panel often includes a mythological scene. Plainer examples feature gougework, with simple alternating patterns.

Imported marble fireplaces were restricted to the wealthy and often featured engaged columns supporting decorated entablatures. A less expensive treatment was the use of marble slips in a wooden surround. By the 1830s chimneypieces became bolder in style. Classical Revival features such as Ionic and Tuscan columns,

and Greek key motifs, were worked in white, grey or black marble. The same forms and detailing were used for wooden chimneypieces.

Cast-iron liners were a feature of some fireplaces. They were designed to radiate heat. The Franklin stove, which often incorporated a grate with the liner, was in common use by 1785, as were various types of British-imported hob grates (Bath stoves).

Iron andirons were used by the less wealthy and in service areas; brass andirons, embellished with classical urns or spherical finials, were usual in grander houses. Cast-iron firebacks feature Neo-classical patterns or sometimes the popular eagle motif.

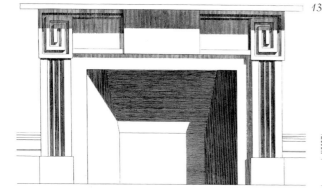

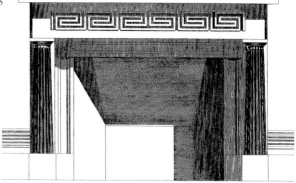

① to ③ *Three typical Neo-classical fireplace surrounds. The first, from a 1790s South Carolina plantation, features simple reeded pilasters and square panels; the second is of the same form but with the addition of carved paterae, fan motifs and dentil mouldings. The third is a late 18th-century undecorated version.*
④ *Neo-classical column and pilaster designs from William Pain's* Practical House Carpenter *(1766).* WP
⑤ *to* ⑦ *Fireplace surround details, including examples of*

gougework *(where wood is cut with a rounded chisel). Applied motifs, dentil work and moulded panels feature in the first. The second shows stucco swags. The third, a design by the influential English architect William Pain, uses applied composition mouldings.* WP

⑧ *An applied composition classical figure on the panel above a pilaster.*
⑨ *to* ⑪ *Three contrasting central panels from Federal fireplaces. The first features two sphinxes and a floral motif. The second example is an elaborate tableau from the Harrison Gray*

Otis House in Boston and depicts Neptune drawn in his chariot by lions. No less attractive is the third, back-country Carolina example from the 1830s.
⑫ *Two designs from William Pain's* Practical Builder *(1774), with anthemion and diaper motifs.* WPB
⑬ *Attesting to the popularity of the pattern books, these two Greek key designs from Asher Benjamin's* The Architect, or Practical House Carpenter *were among the most popular designs from 1830 to 1850.* AB

FIREPLACES

① and ② *Two fireplaces,*
c.1808. On the left, Ionic
columns support a dentillated
entablature with swags and
composition figures. The
example on the right has reeded
wood consoles, a marble slip
and a central panel depicting
Bacchic figures. NR
③ *A typical mid-19th century*
Greek Revival black marble
fireplace with Ionic columns.
New York, 1832. OM
④ *A late Empire influence is*
evident in this marble fireplace.
1842. BW
⑤ *to* ⑦ *Restoration of the*
fireplaces at the Gaillard-
Bennett House, Charleston,
South Carolina, c.1800, has
revealed classical details in
stucco and gougework. Work is
in progress on this overmantel
(left); a detail of the surround is
shown top right. Another
surround (bottom right) shows a
mythological scene. GB

① A fine Neo-classical fireplace and overmantel from Rhode Island, 1780s: fluted pilasters, Grecian urns and floral devices are surmounted by a swan-neck pediment.

② Two overmantels from the coastal Carolinas. The first has carved fanwork, an oval panel and applied composition mouldings, 1786; the second has a bowed entablature supported by Tuscan columns and carved wooden mouldings, 1818.

③ A marble surround and overmantel with carved Grecian floral and acanthus leaf devices, dating from the 1830s.

④ Two coal grates. The mid-19th-century example on the left developed from the Franklin stove (c.1785) on the right.

⑤ Patriotic American motifs. The 19th-century cast-iron and brass fireplace surround features an eagle on the lintel and cheeks; the same emblem appears on the fireback (not to scale).

⑥ Federal andirons. The top set is made of iron. The other examples are made of brass and iron. The Boston andiron (centre left) has ball finials set on pedestals, 1820-30. The Neo-classical example (centre right) features an urn finial, spur legs and ball-and-claw feet, c.1800. The robust "turned" andiron (bottom left) contrasts with the attenuated example (right).

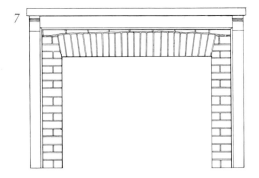

⑦ A simple wooden surround frames this 19th-century brick fireplace. From a southern kitchen, unusually located in the cellar of a house.

Staircases

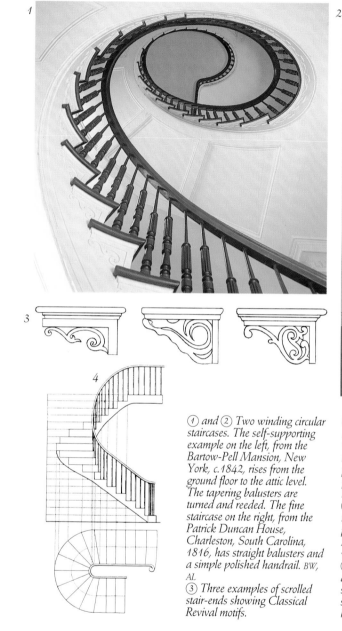

1

2

3

4

5

6

① *and* ② *Two winding circular staircases. The self-supporting example on the left, from the Bartow-Pell Mansion, New York, c.1842, rises from the ground floor to the attic level. The tapering balusters are turned and reeded. The fine staircase on the right, from the Patrick Duncan House, Charleston, South Carolina, 1816, has straight balusters and a simple polished handrail. BW, AL*
③ *Three examples of scrolled stair-ends showing Classical Revival motifs.*

④ *Asher Benjamin's The Architect, or Practical House Carpenter, 1830, was one of several English and American pattern books to supply plans for curved staircases, without landings. AB*
⑤ *Three handrail profiles, typical of the period. The pattern books of Asher Benjamin and others supplied a variety of designs.*
⑥ *Reeded pilasters and a decorated arch lead to this staircase with a half-landing, straight balusters and simple handrail. c.1815.*

Straight, quarter-turn and dog-leg staircases were the common form in the late 18th and early 19th centuries. The pattern books of William Pain and others introduced sweeping elliptical and circular main staircases to grander houses: these were often located in the curvilinear or polygonal projections of houses. In Neo-classical architecture the staircase was a significant feature of the entrance floor, whereas in Classical Revival houses it was considered a waste of space and was less prominently displayed.

In most houses simple turned or square balusters supported a thin handrail; newels could be twisted or attenuated columns or tapering square posts. The motifs

decorating the stair-ends were plainer than those of the Colonial period. In grander houses the balustrade would be mahogany or, less usually, wrought iron which would be in attenuated Neo-classical form. There are rare instances of cantilevered stairs.

Grand Greek Revival houses occasionally had double staircases or generously proportioned single stairs which rose from the entrance hall and were crowned by domes or skylights. Separate servants' stairs led to the upper floors. Detailing generally was well-crafted but heavier: turned or tapered balusters and handrails were thicker and newels were heavily turned or decorated with acanthus leaf scrolls.

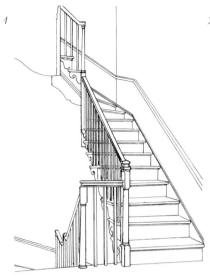

① and ② *A compact winding back stair (left) and a grander example from the Morris-Jumel Mansion, New York, 1765 (right), share common Neo-classical features, including straight balusters, attenuated columnar newels and simple decorations to the stair-ends.* MJ
③ *The handrail of the staircase from the Gaillard-Bennett House, Charleston, South Carolina, c.1800 terminates in a spiral with a decorative central button.* GB

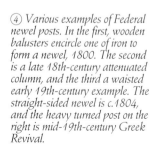

④ *Various examples of Federal newel posts. In the first, wooden balusters encircle one of iron to form a newel, 1800. The second is a late 18th-century attenuated column, and the third a waisted early 19th-century example. The straight-sided newel is c.1804, and the heavy turned post on the right is mid-19th-century Greek Revival.*

⑤ *The termination of the basement stair of the Bartow-Pell Mansion, New York, 1842, is formed by a newel shaped in a heavy and elaborate S-scroll. The attenuated balusters are delicately turned.* BW

⑥ *The robust newel post of the Old Merchant's House, New York, 1832, is turned and richly embellished with carved acanthus leaves; the curved handrail receives the same treatment. The turned and waisted balusters are slender and attenuated. The scrollwork decorating the stair-ends is characteristic of the Greek Revival style.* OM

⑦ *This entrance hall staircase is made of marble and has an ornate cast-iron balustrade decorated with acanthus leaves. Fluted columns support the landing which has a balustrade decorated with roundels, c.1836.*

Built-in furniture

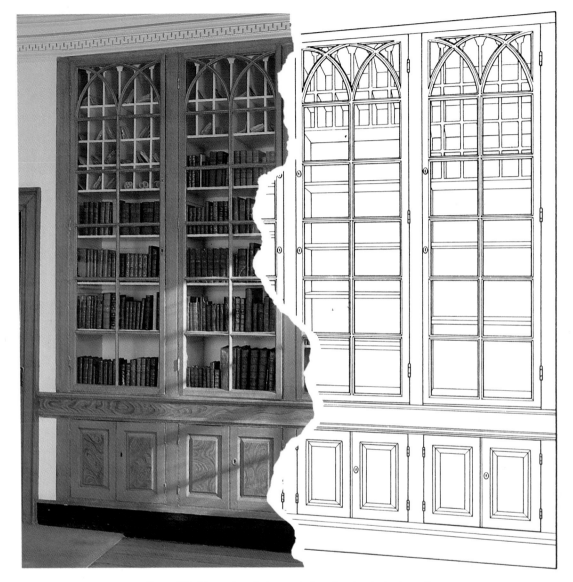

George Washington installed these bookcases at Mount Vernon, Virginia, in the late 1780s. They are Neo-classical in form, but the glazing bars also show a Gothic influence. The panelled cupboard doors have recently been regrained. MV

Built-in furniture is mainly found in dining rooms and formal parlours where the fireplace wall provided space for shelved cupboards. Here, valuable items such as china, silver and books could be stored securely.

As the period progressed, less regular room shapes allowed built-in furniture to become more varied: niches, for example, could be built into oval rooms. Occasionally break-fronted cabinets and cupboards were made of walnut or mahogany but usually they were in plain woods painted or grained to match the architectural features of the room. Glass-fronted bookcases gained popularity. The pattern books of William and James Pain provided designs for floor-to-ceiling bookcases with side pilasters and entablatures decorated with garlands and other applied composition ornament.

Various innovative devices were introduced in the first decades of the 19th century: Thomas Jefferson constructed a revolving door with shelves that connected the dining room with the pantry, and William Jay, influenced by English taste, designed hall console tables.

Built-in mirrors became fashionable. In Greek Revival houses their frames are decorated with classical motifs to match the woodwork of the room, and after 1820 the architraves to cupboards and bookcases are similarly detailed. Throughout this period simple built-in pine kitchen cupboards were often painted dark red or green.

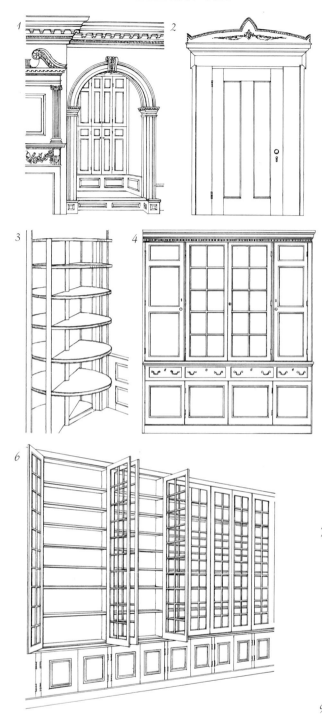

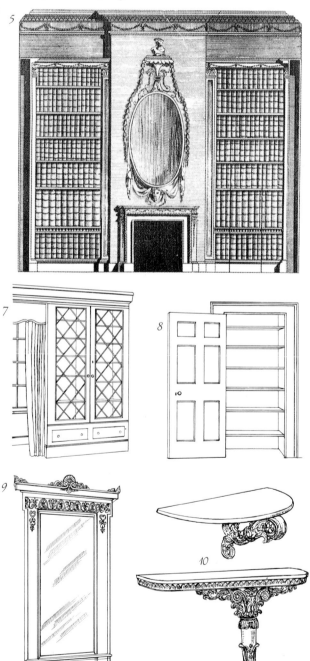

① Fireside seating is provided by this late 18th-century arched shuttered window recess.

② The detailing of this two-panelled Greek Revival built-in dining room cupboard is identical to pattern book plates showing doors of the same date (1855).

③ An early 19th-century revolving "Beaufait" door which acted as a rotating food server. Jefferson designed a similar model for Monticello, Virginia.

④ A handsome early 19th-century mahogany dining room cupboard. There are central glazed doors for the display of china, four drawers, and solid panelled doors above and below.

⑤ An attenuated Neo-classical design for bookcases uses to full advantage the space created by the chimney breast; from William Pain's Practical House Carpenter, 1766. WP

⑥ Built-in floor-to-ceiling bookcases with glazed doors and a panelled base, c.1800. Bookcases of this quality were a luxury item and would only be found in wealthy households.

⑦ Late Federal finely built bookcases with diamond glazing and drawers beneath.

⑧ A shelved cupboard with a panelled door used for storing china and glass, typical of the 18th and early 19th centuries. These cupboards usually flanked a fireplace.

⑨ A Greek Revival built-in full-length mirror, 1832.

⑩ Two examples of late Neo-classical marble console tables. The carved wooden brackets could be gilded.

Services

① *An elaborate stove from the Bartow-Pell Mansion, New York, 1842, with Classical Revival motifs, columns and pilasters.* BW
② *A small parlour stove topped by an urn (in some models this contained water for humidification), c.1850.*
③ *A late 18th-century Moravian-type tile-faced stove.*

④ *The acme of Greek Revival bathroom luxury: a curtained and canopied bath, water closet and sinks are included in this plumber's advertisement.* MY
⑤ *An 1830s stone kitchen sink with an attached pump; lever-handled brass taps/faucets are set into the panel behind.* OM

BUILT-IN FURNITURE

SERVICES

Freestanding six-plate heating stoves were popular towards the end of the 18th century. Made up of six heavy sections of cast-iron, they stood on legs and had a fuel door and smoke hole. They were often embellished with classical motifs, and some models were topped with an urn; a few were tile-faced. Many houses were heated by a combination of a stove placed in a central location such as a hall, and coal fires which burned in parlours and upstairs rooms. In areas where winters were severe, the procurement of sufficient wood stocks for the stoves was an important task. By the 1830s, urban houses had larger coal-fuelled furnaces.

At the beginning of the period, major residences had a dressing room with portable close stools (chamber pots built into a moveable piece of furniture), washstands and moveable iron or tin baths; these baths were more generally available a decade later. Outdoor privies were common: elaborate multi-seated models with classical and Gothic architectural details could be found in houses of the wealthy.

Running water was rare and restricted to grander houses. Outdoor cisterns were used for trapping rainwater, and a very few houses had indoor storage tanks. By the 1820s the kitchens of most of the better houses had stone or metal sinks supplied with running water. Modest households continued to use well water.

Lighting

1 *A rolled and tinned iron chandelier, pre-1800.*
2 *A design for a French Empire-style chandelier, 1810.*
3 *A hanging stamped brass and glass lantern, 1790-1820.*
4 *A gilt brass gas chandelier with etched glass shades, c.1840.*
5 *Glass chandeliers were rare before 1820.*
6 *A double Argand lamp with etched glass chimneys.*
7 *A mid-period rolled and*

tinned iron sconce.
8 *A wooden sconce with an American eagle motif, c.1800.*
9 *Exterior oil lanterns were a feature of town houses.*
10 *Two exterior wrought-iron lamp standards.*
11 *A girandole with a marble base and glass drops, c.1840.*
12 *Late 18th-century rolled and tinned iron lanterns.*
13 *A turn-of-the-century cresset (cage-like iron lamp).*

During the 18th century most houses continued to be dimly lit by a few single candles, rush lamps or by grease (Betty) lamps which burned oil, lard or tallow. Lanterns, sometimes with reflectors, were used indoors and outdoors.

The patented Argand light (1782) was increasingly available by the 1790s. It had a hollow wick which allowed more oxygen to reach the flame (protected by a glass chimney), which resulted in a brighter and cleaner light; whale and lard oil were generally used. Argand lamps, produced expensively in silver or more affordably in Sheffield plate, began to replace candles in the houses of the wealthy; hanging hall lamps in stamped brass remained

popular with the middle and upper classes.

Whale oil was commonly used as a fuel for the many types of brass and glass lamps available in the early 1800s. These were produced as freestanding examples with shades, and as chandeliers and wall brackets. The term "girandole" at this period refers to candlesticks and candelabra with crystal drops, as well as to candle sconces attached to mirrors. By the early 1800s, glass chandeliers and gilt bronze chandeliers were imported by the wealthy from France or England, or in rare cases were made by American craftsmen. They were reserved for the best parlour.

During the 1830s, gas lighting was gradually installed in urban areas as public supplies were provided.

Metalwork

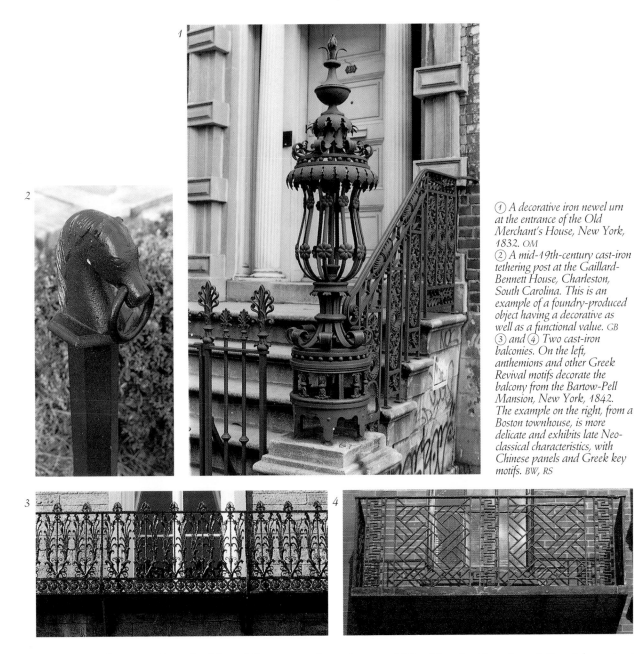

1 A decorative iron newel urn at the entrance of the Old Merchant's House, New York, 1832. OM
2 A mid-19th-century cast-iron tethering post at the Gaillard-Bennett House, Charleston, South Carolina. This is an example of a foundry-produced object having a decorative as well as a functional value. GB
3 and 4 Two cast-iron balconies. On the left, anthemions and other Greek Revival motifs decorate the balcony from the Bartow-Pell Mansion, New York, 1842. The example on the right, from a Boston townhouse, is more delicate and exhibits late Neo-classical characteristics, with Chinese panels and Greek key motifs. BW, RS

The use of ironwork in the United States greatly expanded during the Federal period, especially in southern cities, such as New Orleans, Savannah and Charleston. Cast iron increasingly appears, first as applied ornamentation to wrought iron, then, with improved technology, progressing to the ambitious structural and decorative castings of the 1840s.

Iron production increased towards the end of the 18th century as iron ore sources were developed. Craftsmen from Continental Europe were attracted to the new industry and developed forms based on old European styles but with Neo-classical influences. In New Orleans, which already had a strong ironworking tradi-

tion established by the French and Spanish, output increased after Louisiana's entry into the Union in 1803. Craftsmen, particularly those from Germany, began to create delicate scrollwork for fencing, grilles, lunettes, balustrades and balconies which well reflected the attenuated Neo-classical style.

Early motifs included lyres and anthemions. Exterior stair balustrades, embellished with C- and S-scrollwork, provided emphasis to entrance doors, and iron newels also became fashionable. By the end of the period, foundries were producing castings for double balconies, column capitals and window surrounds, but inevitably patterns became more standardized.

LIGHTING

METALWORK

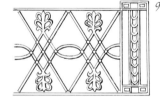

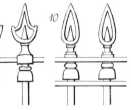

① Elaborate tracery decorates this two-story iron veranda porch, c.1850.
② Two iron balconies. The first example is wrought and dates from c.1800. The other is cast iron and dates from c.1840.
③ A cast-iron balcony railing with lead decorative details.
④ A railing design from Asher Benjamin's Practice of Architecture (1833).
⑤ A Greek Revival style portico railing.
⑥ An intricately worked iron balcony: decorative features include urns, rosettes and delicate scrollwork, c.1800.

⑦ Cast-iron balcony support brackets, c.1840.
⑧ Two sets of wrought-iron double gates. The earlier example on the left leads to a courtyard; the other dates from the end of the period and uses the classical lyre motif.
⑨ Sections of cast-iron railings, 1830-60, incorporating anthemions, lyres and Greek key designs.
⑩ Forged points or spear heads for iron railings.
⑪ Early 19th-century iron entrance balustrades. Three include a bootscraper. A separate scraper is shown on the left.

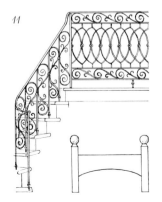

Woodwork

① *An early Neo-classical portico, c.1765, with tapering Tuscan columns, a central Palladian window, and a pediment with dentils and elliptical fanlight. Such two-story wooden porticoes were rare before the 1780s. MJ*

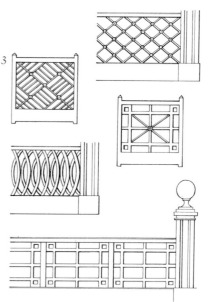

② *A gate with robust posts decorated with oval paterae and floral garlands, surmounted by urns. This example is typical of coastal New England at the height of the Federal period. RS*

③ *Fence and gate sections showing interlacing, diapering and other forms, from Asher Benjamin's* The Architect, or Practical House Carpenter, *1830.*
④ *A single-story 1840s Greek Revival porch*

with fluted Doric columns and flush-boarded pediment.
⑤ *A Neo-classical temple-form house of the 1820s. The whole structure is wood, including the porch and the piazzas.*

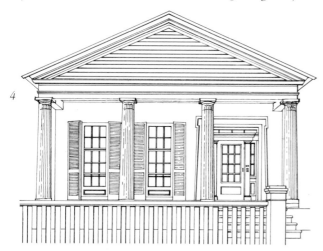

The great number of wooden houses which were built during the Federal period provided many opportunities for exterior detailing, and some achieved great elegance. A typical house will have overlapping weatherboarding, usually of pine, cut in lengths and often beaded along the edges. By the early 1800s, improved saw mills and the availability of machine-cut nails made finely finished houses more common.

Decorative elements included cornices and friezes with swags, dentils, modillions and other ornamentation. The most popular trend was the addition of wooden single-entry porches (New England) or porticoes (mid-Atlantic and southern Colonies). The two-story square-columned portico added in the 1780s by George Washington to Mount Vernon, Virginia, is a notable example. By the 1780s a popular feature of houses in the Carolina Low Country was the double-tiered piazza or veranda which provided shaded outdoor living space.

Neo-classical and Greek Revival houses featured wooden balustrades for piazzas, walls and roofs; and pickets or posts for fencing. Balusters were vase-shaped or straight and square-cut. In both North and South, wooden fencing was more common than iron: the posts were sometimes topped by urns, spheres or other ornaments. Occasionally latticework, Chinese Chippendale and guilloche fencing patterns were used.

METALWORK

WOODWORK

BRITISH VICTORIAN

1837–1901

One of the more influential books brimming with practical advice for the aspiring, and affluent, house-builder was The Gentleman's House *by Robert Kerr, which ran to several editions in the 1860s and 70s.*

Kerr devotes some of his chapters to designs in a variety of styles, all based on the same plan, all distinctly Victorian. Illustrated here are the "Cottage Style", which is somewhat Italianate, and very grand for a cottage; the

"Mediaeval or Gothic Style", with its pointed arches, polychrome brickwork and elaborate cast-iron crestings on the roof ridges; and the "Scotch Baronial" version, with its stepped ("crow-stepped") gables. KE

One third of the houses in Britain date from before 1914, and most by far are Victorian. The building boom experienced in cities in the 1850s, 60s and 70s has been exceeded only by the ribbon developments of the 1920s and 30s.

The British High Victorian style grew out of revivals of the past. Fashionable Victorian town-dwellers were bored by the monotonous classical terraces/rows of plain Georgian houses, by now encrusted in soot and grime. They wanted colour and animation. Such feelings were not peculiar to the landed gentry. In a period of industrialization there was a new generation of nouveaux riches, self-made industrialists, boastful of their success, who in the architecture of their houses advertised their achievements in tangible form. Many favoured the mock Gothic style as a romantic fantasy that implied ancient lineage.

The Gothic Revival had developed from the 18th century, and was boosted in the 19th by the chivalric writings of Sir Walter Scott, Alfred Lord Tennyson and Thomas Love Peacock. Diligent archaeological researches were carried out and published with measured drawings of medieval remains, in the manner of the surveys of classical ruins of one hundred years before. The influential theorist and designer A.W.N. Pugin (1812-52) and some of his contemporaries tried to encourage architects to adopt accurate Gothic detailing. Striped polychromatic brickwork, popularized by G.E. Street in his *Brick and Marble from Northern Italy* and by John Ruskin in *The Stones of Venice*, added colour to the Gothicized exterior.

The vogue for Gothic left its mark not only on many country houses and villas but also on whole suburbs, such as those of north Oxford. It also brought great controversy – the so-called "battle of styles" – to major public building projects such as the new Houses of Parliament (Gothic) and the Foreign Office (classical).

In 1879 William Young, in his book *Town and Country Mansions*, records the Gothicists' belief that in classical architecture "the convenience of the plan, and utility of arrangement, were sacrificed to the architectural effect ... too often, instead of the design growing out of the plan, the plan was adapted for the sake of the elevation". Pugin saw Gothic as "pliable", and classical as "rigid". Speculative builders were uninterested in such academic niceties. They often randomly adopted elements of several styles – including Greek Revival, Romanesque, Tudor, Elizabethan and Italianate. A house could have half-timbered gables, classical sash windows, redbrick and terracotta ornament, and a filigree cast-iron porch.

A true picture of the Victorian house must take-in two extremes: on the one hand, the wonderfully inventive country houses by great architects such as Richard Norman Shaw (1831-1912); on the other, the meanly built flat-fronted terraces/rows of the poor. Between these poles there are various identifiable types: the early Victorian semi-detached villa, based on Regency models; the detached Italianate suburban villa with stuccoed ground floor (popular in the 1830s and 40s); the detached brick villa with asymmetrical plan and Tudor detailing.

The need for services and for privacy expanded the size of the upper middle-class Victorian terraced/row house to unprecedented height and depth. This impression of stuccoed gigantism is striking in such London areas as Belgravia, Bayswater and Pimlico. The grand classical terrace enjoyed a last blossoming in Glasgow with the work of Alexander Thomson, especially his Great Western Terrace of 1869. By the 1880s, the trend toward suburban and rural dwellings among the upper

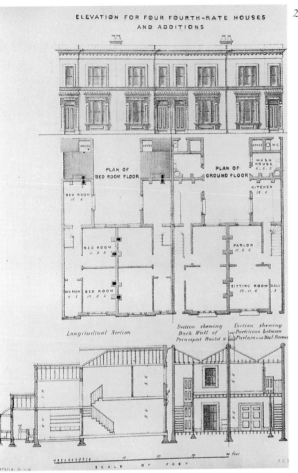

ELEVATION FOR FOUR FOURTH-RATE HOUSES
AND ADDITIONS

PLAN OF BED ROOM FLOOR

PLAN OF GROUND FLOOR

Longitudinal Section

Section sheming Back Wall of Principal Build g

Section sheming Partitions between Parlors and Bed-Rooms

SCALE OF FEET

VILLA AT GRANGE, EDINBURGH
R. THORNTON SHIELLS ARCHITECT EDINB.

FRONT ELEVATION

GROUND PLAN   Window   CHAMBER PLAN

Pillar and Beam of Porch   Porch in Parapteres   Engaged Pillar at Corner

① *A row of modest and very typical terraced/row houses of the mid-19th century, in elevation, plan and cross-section. They maintain something of the classical simplicity of the Regency period, and would be built in stock brick with "Roman cement" dressings, with shallow slated roofs behind the parapets. The plan allows for four small bedrooms, with a parlour and sitting room on the ground floor, and the kitchen and wash house in a wing at the back.* BU

② *A villa of the mid-Victorian period, near Edinburgh, designed by R. Thornton Shiells, 1862. The plan is well organized, with two sitting rooms, five bedrooms (one on the entrance floor), a bathroom and water closet.* VC

middle classes had caused the terrace/row to become déclassé: it was now associated with the lower orders, while the better-off tended to live in villas.

At the end of the 1860s correct English Gothic returned to favour. At the same time the lighter, highly influential Queen Anne Revival style was initiated: its distinctive features include white-painted sash windows, pretty balconies, curly gables and moulded brickwork or terracotta. There are some fine streets in this style around Sloane and Cadogan Squares in London.

Improvements in communications had a big impact on Victorian house building. The rapidly expanding building trade kept up to date with periodicals such as *The Builder* and *The Building News*, both founded in the middle of the century. Well-illustrated building construction books were widely available, and could be purchased in instalments by the less well-off tradesmen. Particularly popular were *The Builder's Practical Director*, *The Encyclopaedia of Practical Carpentry* and *Practical Masonry*, all published between about 1855 and 1870,

with tinted plates. Industrialization, of course, implied mass production. The canals and railways enabled heavy materials to be widely and economically distributed: cast iron from Scotland; terracotta from the English Midlands and the southwest peninsula; slates from Wales and Cumbria. No longer were houses necessarily built of the local vernacular materials, as had been usual in the past. Glass and bricks were less expensive than ever before. Identical terracotta ornament graced exteriors from Scotland to the southwest of England.

By the 1870s a new middleman took centre stage in the burgeoning building industry: the builder's merchant. He acted as agent for the manufacturers, supplying to the builder everything from kitchen ranges to door knobs, illustrated in splendid catalogues which today give a fascinating insight into the late Victorian house.

Health and efficiency were both of great interest to middle-class Victorians, as reflected by the catalogues' descriptions of improved sanitary wares. Ventilation was also important, not only as a way to clear smells from

1

2

3

① *A kitchen from a comfortable Glasgow tenement (apartment) house, with typical large black cooking range, from the end of the period. There were only four rooms in each apartment – parlour, bedroom, kitchen and bathroom. Tenement life ranged from the mean and overcrowded to the comfortable, even luxurious.* TE

② *The parlour from the same tenement. The box bed provided additional sleeping accommodation, but constituted a health risk. Such beds were banned after 1900.* TE

③ *Wood panelling offered an opportunity to revel in a period revival style – in this case, Italian Renaissance.* CR

defective drains, but also to take away the noxious fumes from gasoliers and fires. The great scientist Robert Boyle founded a prosperous company manufacturing and installing ventilation equipment that led to innumerable cowls on rooftops, often disguised as turrets or belfries.

Cleaner air was one of the benefits enjoyed by the thousands who left the cities and penetrated further and further into the countryside in search of salubrious and affordable housing from which they could commute to work by railway. Nostalgia for the countryside fused with the concept of suburbia to form a new ideal – the garden suburb, heralded in the 1870s by Bedford Park in west London, where individually styled houses brought a welcome variety to leafy streets.

Inside the house, the organization of rooms reflected a clearly defined social order. There were the public rooms where guests were received and entertained, the private bedrooms and dressing rooms, and the below-stairs servants' rooms, which for the first time were virtually out of bounds to the family. Such gradations were expressed architecturally, for example in the complexity of mouldings and in the material of the fireplace, ranging from marble through slate to wood. The morning room, at the back of the house, was the feminine equivalent of the study, which was a masculine domain. As well as the dining room, larger houses would have their own breakfast room. Even in the poorest houses there would be an attempt to maintain a parlour, which often had an unlived-in air, as if waiting for a guest important enough to justify its use.

①The living room at Cragside,
Northumbria, shows Arts and Crafts
influence. CR
②The inside of the front entrance doors,
Chelsea House, London: a grand example of
classical revivalism, 1870s. TCM
③A High Victorian drawing room, by Bruce
Talbert, 1876. There is a Gothic influence,
even in the piano. Talbert set the fashion at a
late stage in the Gothic Revival. TAL

Doos

This north London doorway typifies the front entrance to a High Victorian middle-class town house. It is eclectic and debased, with a Gothic bias. The steps lend grandeur; the stained glass panels are showy and illuminate the hall. The house number is incorporated into the fanlight/transom light, a popular Victorian feature. The doors are painted pine and have been woodgrained to simulate hardwood, a treatment totally appropriate to the period.

The porch to a Victorian house was designed not only to protect visitors from the weather but also to convey the social status of the occupants, a projecting porch implying greater wealth than one that was recessed.

Front doors are panelled and sometimes arched in the Gothic style. They were often green or woodgrained. Glazed upper panels or fanlights above allow extra light to enter the hallway. Foundry catalogues were filled with examples of door knockers and knobs and, from the 1840s, letterboxes/mailslots.

The Victorians felt it important to insulate their houses against the cold. In smaller terraced houses, where there is usually an archway across the narrow hall, it was the convention to hang curtains in order to retain heat. Similarly, a portière, or curtain on a swinging pole, would hang behind a door to make a room warmer.

Internal doors are constructed in the traditional frame-and-panel manner. Doors leading to grander principal rooms can be up to 3 inches (7.5cm) thick with numerous panels and applied mouldings. Such features not only indicate the room's importance, but the greater the density of wood the more effective it was as a protection against eavesdropping servants. Doors to more modest rooms are often framed in wood less than one inch (2.5cm) thick with very thin undecorated panels.

Three types of exterior pine battened doors. These were inexpensive to produce and were often used for outbuildings and cottages.
① A ledged and battened door; the "ledges" are the horizontal framing members.
② A ledged, braced and battened door; the diagonal "braces" add extra strength.
③ A framed and battened door.

④ A simple four-panel door without mouldings, popular throughout the Victorian period.

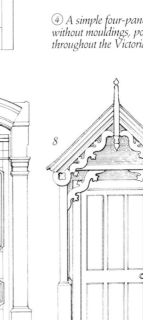

⑤ A modest front door with the vestige of a fanlight/transom light. There is a knocker but no letterbox/mailslot, indicating that the door is probably pre-1840, before the introduction of the penny post.
⑥ and ⑦ These recessed porches are typical of terraced/ row or town houses of the 1870s.

⑧ A rustic wooden porch.
⑨ This grand classical porch could be constructed from stone, or from rendered brickwork to reduce expense. MB

⑩ and ⑪ Polychromatic brickwork reflects the strong influence of John Ruskin's writings about Venice and Italian Gothic, c.1850. CL

① *A front door to a small terraced/row house. The red brick contrasts with the cream galt brick of the facade.* MJB
② *A more elaborate doorway. The porch is enriched with painted cement dressings, with* collars on the column shafts and floriated capitals.
③ *Typical glazed panels for front doorways, 1891.* GF
④ *Letterboxes/mailslots were often small and vertical.*
⑤ *A popular Gothic form for a* front door. The door fittings and the stained glass appear to be original; the painted house number is unfortunate.
⑥ *Twinned doorways from west London, c.1880, with foliated arched heads and* capitals in painted cement rendering. The checked tile paving is authentic but the letterbox/mailslot is modern. RS
⑦ *The side walls of recessed porches often had colourful tiled panels.* RS

1

DESIGNS FOR DOORS AND OVERDOORS EXECUTED IN HARD WOOD BY CABINETMAKERS; ALSO MADE IN PINE, WITH CARTOON-PIERRE ENRICHMENTS, FOR PAINTING.

Grand internal doors will have cornices and pediments above the doorheads. These "overdoors" were popular throughout the period.
① Three "classical" doors with fielded panels and mouldings from the 1892 catalogue of Hampton and Sons. They were available in polished hardwood or in pine with carton-pierre (a form of papier mâché) embellishments ready for painting. HS
② Large panels filled with tongue-and-groove boarding: a form of joinery usually associated with doors to utility rooms.
③ Pointed crenellations decorate this Gothic doorway. The door has raised panelling and elaborate pierced fittings, 1890.

2

3

4

5

④ A shelf for the display of china is included above this "Aesthetic" doorhead. TC
⑤ The panels to this door are decoratively enriched, either with carton-pierre mouldings or trompe l'oeil paintwork. TC
⑥ Nine overdoor designs from Hampton's 1892 catalogue. They were supplied in pine ready for painting or, more expensively, in a polished hardwood such as oak or mahogany. These examples show varying forms of debased classical styles. For example, there is a French influence in the design of the overdoor shown centre right: this incorporates an oil-painted panel with a Rococo frame. Other designs include shelves and alcoves. These were very popular in the late Victorian period for the display of china ornaments. HS

6

① *This wood-grained four-panelled internal door with china knob is a type commonly found in modest houses. Glasgow, c.1890.* TE

② *A grander door with contrasting graining. Bournemouth, Dorset, 1894.* RC

③ *The same door's brass fittings. The S-shaped handle is reflected in the keyhole escutcheon: both are set in a deeply modelled fingerplate/push plate.* RC

④ *An ornate brass fingerplate/push plate with a knob and keyhole.* RC

⑤ *An oak door with cross-grained panels and pierced metal fittings at Cragside, Northumbria, c.1869.* CR

⑥ *A Tudor-style multi-panelled oak door with ebony fittings: the screws are concealed behind raised ebony plugs, c.1869.* CR

Three modest internal doors.
(1) A four-panel door with a "mousemoulded" (double-curved) panel bead. TL
(2) "Borrowed" light is provided by a glazed panel which often has a stained-glass border. BC
(3) A typical six-panel door with square top panels. BC
(4) An escutcheon, handle and knocker make up this brass entrance door set, c.1885. HD
(5) Letterboxes/mailslots became the rule with the introduction of the penny post in 1840. The first here is made from iron and also serves as a door knocker. The other two are made from brass. HD, PP
(6) A quadrant bell pull and a brass bell pull with ebony handle. SE
(7) Three electric bell pushes, c.1890. SC
(8) Decorative wrought-iron exterior hinges with elaborate leafwork, designed by A. W. N. Pugin, 1841. PC
(9) Three designs for entrance door knockers in brass, bronze or special metallic finishes. PP
(10) Ornate Gothic-style polished

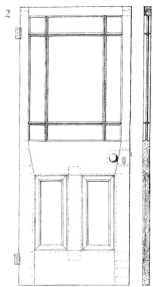

brass interior rimlock by Pugin, 1841. PC
(11) Brass interior door fittings: a handle, escutcheon and fingerplate/push plate. HD
(12) China knobs, usually available in white or black and

often decorated with a gold line. PP
(13) These two brass fingerplates/push plates were supplied by Gratrix of Manchester. SG
(14) Door chains: the one on the left has an electro-bronze finish, the other is cast brass. SE

(15) A stamped-steel cased rim latch with brass bolts and flush slide, 1892. PP
(16) A brass portière pole, fitted to the back of a door for hanging a curtain to provide extra insulation. SG

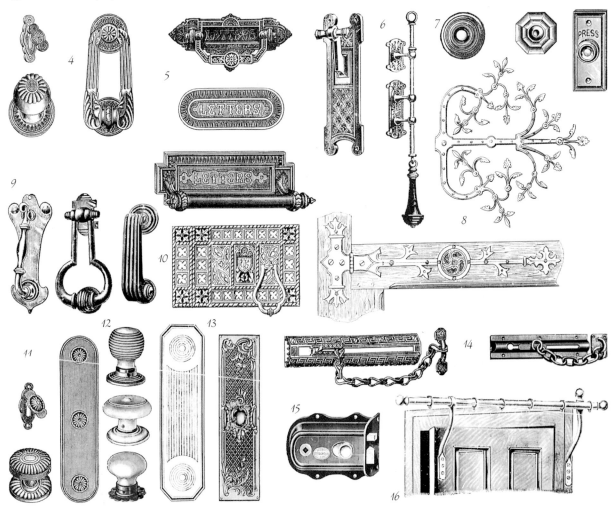

Windows

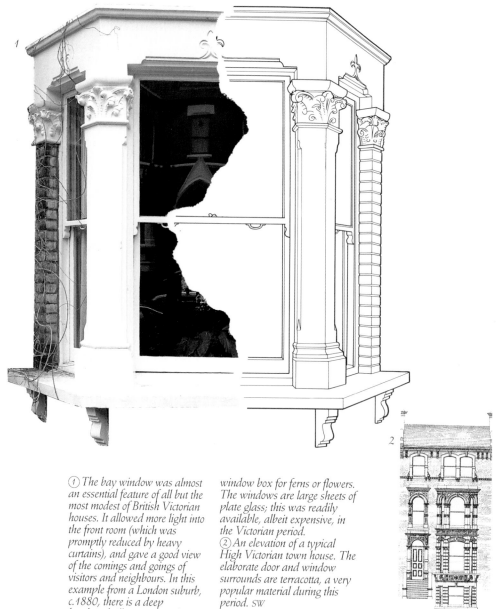

① *The bay window was almost an essential feature of all but the most modest of British Victorian houses. It allowed more light into the front room (which was promptly reduced by heavy curtains), and gave a good view of the comings and goings of visitors and neighbours. In this example from a London suburb, c.1880, there is a deep bracketed sill to accommodate a* window box for ferns or flowers. *The windows are large sheets of plate glass; this was readily available, albeit expensive, in the Victorian period.*
② *An elevation of a typical High Victorian town house. The elaborate door and window surrounds are terracotta, a very popular material during this period. SW*

Improved glassmaking techniques produced larger, stronger and less expensive single panes of glass which needed fewer glazing bars. As Victorian sash windows become plainer, so their openings make increasing use of decorative brickwork, stucco and prefabricated terracotta. By the mid-19th century, sash windows have two small brackets or "horns" at each end of the bottom rail of the top sash. These are to help strengthen the frame and support the heavier panes of glass. The abolition of the window tax in 1851 encouraged the greater use of glass, and the bay window with its wide centre sash and two narrower lights either side is a characteristic feature. Some later sash windows have small panes of glass and thick glazing bars forming the top sash to cut down glare from the sky, with a single sheet of glass below.

Casements, often using leaded lights, return during this period, especially with Gothic-style windows, or "Tudor" (square-headed) in modest houses. In grander houses, the decorative tracery at the tops of the arched windows reduced the amount of sunlight, thus protecting interiors and furnishings from fading; on sashes, exterior blinds served the same purpose. Speculative builders, keen to incorporate the Gothic pattern popularized by John Ruskin's *The Stones of Venice* (1851), inserted sash or casement windows into rectangular openings, with an arch fashioned out of multi-coloured brickwork.

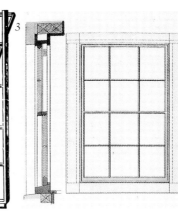

WINDOWS

① A set of shallow-headed sash windows in the debased Gothic style with stone dressings. CL

② An iron-framed fixed window with a top "swing"

casement, sometimes found in service areas. SS

③ A typical mid-Victorian sliding sash window showing a section on the left. EP

④ Glazing bar profiles from The Encyclopaedia of Practical Carpentry and Joinery, c.1860. EP

⑤ Two examples of intersecting

bars. The lower one shows an unusual device for an applied "screw on" bead to hold the glass in place instead of the normal putty. EP

⑥ A brick-arched window from The Stones of Venice (1851) by John Ruskin. The head shows an early example of polychromatic brickwork. SV

⑦ and ⑧ Ruskin's influence is evident in these two examples of Gothic window details: sashes are set into rectangular openings with an arched pattern in the contrasting brickwork above. CL

⑨ Late Victorian prefabricated terracotta window heads from a wide range supplied by Doulton and Company, c.1885. D

⑩ A classical Italianate window opening with stone or rendered dressings. BU

⑪ Another elaborate Italianate window with a wide centre window and two narrow side lights. The balustered balcony is supported by brackets. MB

⑫ A bay window with details of the sash box and shutter in profile on the left. Wooden shutters remained a feature of early Victorian houses: they improved insulation and house security. Depending on the size of the window, they were made up of several hinged, usually panelled, sections which could be folded into a recess when not in use. CL

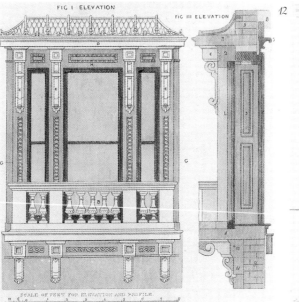

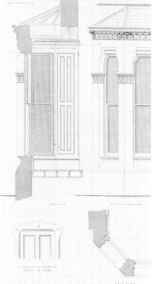

① *This typical upper-story bay window has cement rendered dressings, with banded brickwork on the piers. The treatment of the roof above a bay always presented a problem. Here, the slates have had to be cut and small rolls applied as hips. The finial is terracotta. The roofs of bay windows have become notorious as sources of leaks, as they necessitate the use of small gutters and down pipes/downspouts that are liable to block. RS*

② *This late Victorian Venetian window has a shallow arched head of moulded bricks. The top lights are filled with stained glass. Note the decorative plaster infill panel under the window above. RS*

③ *A simple brick bay with a hipped roof, which is squeezed under the bedroom window directly above. Animation is provided by the bands of red brick (recalling John Ruskin). The central window is divided into quarters – large panes of glass were expensive. MJB*

④ *A projecting window with a slate pitched roof. The down pipe/downspout has been altered as it breaks into the brick jamb. The division of the sashes is probably original. MJB*

⑤ *Twin windows were not especially popular. However, an economy from a builder's point of view was that grouped sash windows could share the counterbalanced weights hung on pulleys hidden within the box frame.*

⑥ *Arch-headed windows were expensive to make. Here, a square-headed window has been used with a segmental brick arch – a popular compromise.*

⑦ *Staircase and landing windows often have stained glass, to ensure privacy or to obscure ugly light-wells and gaps between houses.*

⑧ *The picturesque Gothic style was still popular for estate cottages. It was more robust than it was in the Regency period. Holly Village, London.*

① *A selection of exterior sun blinds supplied by R. Lowther and Company in the 1870s. Furnishings, and women's pale complexions, needed to be protected from the damaging effect of sunlight. Some blind boxes still survive today.* LP

② *An ornamental Wardian fern case illustrated in John Mollisons's* The New Practical Window Gardener *(1877). These self-contained window greenhouses were often installed in urban houses to create a garden effect. They were introduced by Dr Nathaniel Ward.* NP

③ *The dirt and grime of city life made window cleaning a continual task. This patented device allowed a sash window to pivot in such a way that the glass could be cleaned on both*

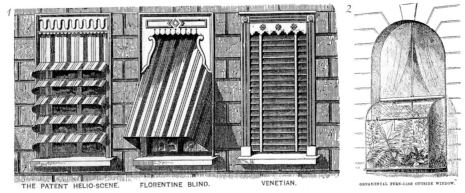

THE PATENT HELIO-SCENE.　　FLORENTINE BLIND.　　VENETIAN.

ORNAMENTAL FERN-CASE OUTSIDE WINDOW.

sides from inside the house. CM

④ *Extensive ranges of window fittings became available. This typical sash furniture is from Selden and Son's 1902 trade catalogue. At the top there is a*

decorated bronzed sash pull, usually used in pairs; the two brass sash drops were to hold an open window in position; the brass sash lift was used to raise the lower half of the window. SS

⑤ *A rack pulley for tightening blinds/shades.* HD

⑥ *A selection of late Victorian patented brass sash fasteners which featured in the 1894 Pryke and Palmer catalogue.* PP

⑦ *Brass casement fasteners; the top two examples could be used on the left or the right.* SS

⑧ *Casement stays. The first has a brass barrel and screw to secure the window.* SS

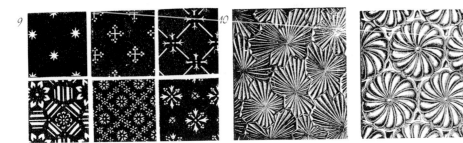

⑨ *Until late in the period glass used for bathroom windows was enamelled or etched, using acid or abrasive methods.* SS

⑩ *In the 1890s this technique was largely superseded by the use of cast or rolled glass, where a roller with an embossed surface was passed over a sheet of molten glass to imprint a pattern. These were two favourite designs.* SS

Walls

Christopher Dresser was an influential designer of the late 19th century. These typically tripartite colour schemes are taken from his Principles of Decorative Design, *1879, and include frieze strips, ceilings and stencil patterns.* TB

Throughout the Victorian period it was still the convention to think of walls as being made up of three basic elements: floor to dado or chair rail level; dado to picture rail or architrave level; and architrave to ceiling level, including the cornice.

Halls and studies are often panelled, as are the dining rooms of grand houses where the dark wood provided an impressive backdrop to the inevitable collection of gilt-framed oil paintings. The drawing room, regarded as the ladies' room and used for taking tea, would have lighter wall decorations.

Wallpaper began to be produced in rolls. A marble design became popular for entrance halls. A robust embossed wall covering, "Lincrusta", was introduced in 1877 for use below the dado rail, and a decade later a less expensive version, "Anaglypta", often with a wood-pattern relief, became popular. A limited range of these "leather papers" (originally they were imitations of 17th-century leather wall hangings) is still available today. Frieze papers were supplied in strips, sometimes with additional stencilling.

Until late in the century it was necessary to mix paint pigment with white oil and lead. The oil tended to darken the colour and application was difficult. Distemper was a less costly alternative but again was difficult to apply and was less durable.

① Two examples of panelling from E. L. Tarbuck's Encyclopedia of Carpentry and Joinery, c.1865. This type of panelling is found in halls, studies and dining rooms and is usually made from oak or pine. The section on the left shows vertically grooved panels; that on the right, plain panels with beaded borders. EP

② Brass bell levers with china furniture. These are found close to fireplaces and were used to summon servants. HD

③ Five typical elaborate wall treatments suggested in Hampton's 1892 catalogue. The first shows a moulded high-relief canvas dado with embossed vellum field covering. The centre top illustration shows a wood panelled dado with embossed leather set into studded panels above, and a handpainted frieze. At top right, a design with printed tapestry hangs beneath a shelf, with a leather-paper frieze above. The Louis XVI-style satin wallpaper panels (bottom left) have a silk lustre finish. Empire-style wall panels (bottom right) are covered in wallpaper, silk or satin with a carton-pierre frieze. HS

④ Four wall stencil patterns designed by A.W.N. Pugin. PC

⑤ This stencil pattern from The Practical Decorator and Ornamentist, 1892, reflects a "Japanese" interest. DO

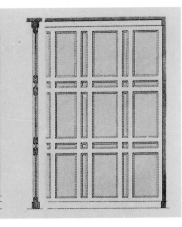

Treatment No. 4. The Dado in Modelled Canvas, in high relief. The filling, embossed vellum.
Treatment No. 5. Wood-panelled Dado. Filling, embossed leather in studded panels. Hand-painted Frieze.
Treatment No. 6. Printed Tapestry, hanging from beneath shelf. Frieze in leather paper.
HAMPTON & SONS,

Treatment No. 7. Louis XVI. Decoration. Panel filling, satin paper with silk lustre. Woodwork in delicate tones to harmonize.
Treatment No. 8. Empire Decoration. Panels covered in paper, silk, or satin. Frieze Enrichments in Carton-pierre.
HAMPTON & SONS,

WALLS

① Wooden brackets support the shelf that forms the cornice above a picture rail. This was a popular way to display collections of china. The stencilling below has a typically Victorian quasi-classical swag pattern. Bournemouth, Dorset, 1894. RC

② The design of this stencilled frieze under a cornice is based on a Greek key pattern. The mouldings above are picked out in contrasting colours. Bournemouth, Dorset, 1894. RC

③ Patterned tiles provided a surface that was durable and easy to clean: they were popular in hallways and passages, as well as in bathrooms. Here the brown, green and blue floral design is edged by a wooden dado rail. 1890s. CR

④ Marbling and stencilling were popular wall treatments, even in poorer households. TE

⑤ Oak panelling with a "castellated" cresting at dado height, with sunflower and animal carvings in the panels Cragside, Northumbria. CR

⑥ Embossed papers such as Lincrusta and Anaglypta were used as wall finishes below dado level. London, c.1880. RG

⑦ This late 19th-century paper has a Tudor rose pattern which would be equally appropriate on a ceiling. RC

Ceilings

① A design for an enriched plaster ceiling from Robert Robson's The Mason's, Bricklayer's, Plasterer's and Decorator's Practical Guide, *1868. There is an 18th-century theme to the ceiling but the foliage treatment is wholly Victorian. Robson also suggests gilding as a finishing touch.* MB
② Catalogue illustrations from George Jackson and Sons showing three designs for ceilings in fibrous plaster, c.1880. GJA

The ceilings of larger Victorian houses offered plasterers great opportunities to demonstrate their skills. Elaborate swags, ribs, flowers and festoons showed evidence of their talents, as did the intricate patterns of the cornices. In the best rooms gasoliers hung from ornate ceiling roses/medallions which would sometimes double as ventilators. Ceilings tended to be high as this encouraged improved air circulation. More modest houses have a plain moulded cornice and a simple central rose/medallion.

A pattern book produced in 1892 by George and Maurice Audsley shows large and impressive stencilled corner designs, but these were not widely employed because the amount of dirt which collected on ceilings – largely due to the use of oil and gas lamps – made frequent redecoration a necessity.

Fibrous plaster was patented in 1856. This contained canvas as a reinforcing agent, and enabled large precast plaster panels to be moulded and then nailed in position on site. Elaborate cornices, roses/medallions and other features could be made by the same method. Papier mâché and composition were acceptable alternatives. "Anaglypta", a compressed lightweight moulded wallpaper, was immensely popular for adding texture to plain ceilings and became an inexpensive substitute for fibrous plaster.

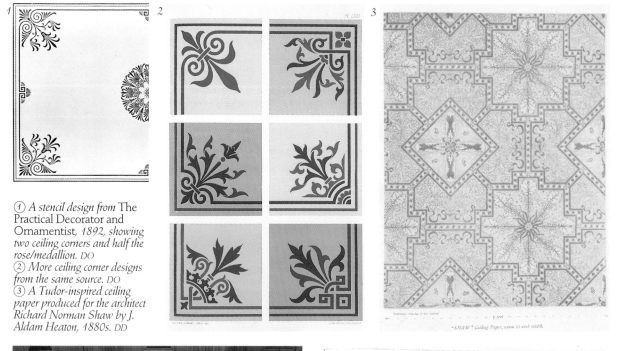

① *A stencil design from* The Practical Decorator and Ornamentist, *1892, showing two ceiling corners and half the rose/medallion.* DO
② *More ceiling corner designs from the same source.* DO
③ *A Tudor-inspired ceiling paper produced for the architect Richard Norman Shaw by J. Aldam Heaton, 1880s.* DD

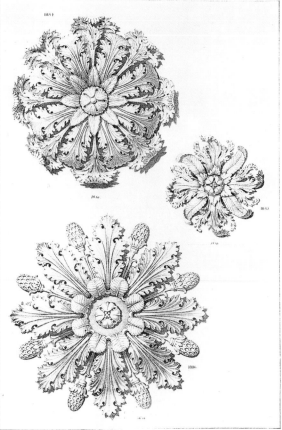

④ *Richard Norman Shaw designed this beamed and coffered ceiling for the library at Cragside, Northumbria, completed in 1872. The elaborate features include walnut panels set in squares with carved bosses.* CR

⑤ *Three papier mâché ceiling roses/medallions from a large range supplied by George Jackson and Sons in 1889. They were also available in fibrous plaster.* GJA

⑥ *Frieze designs from the same Jackson catalogue. The Aesthetic movement has influenced the sunflower design of the first, and the second is in the debased Arts and Crafts style.* GJA

Floors

No. 239.—FLOORCLOTH. No. 1028.—LINOLEUM. No. 80.—INLAID LINOLEUM.

No. 586.—FLOORCLOTH. No. 194.—LINOLEUM. Red. No. 996.—CORK CARPET. Blue.

HAMPTON & SONS, Pall Mall East, and Cockspur Street, Charing Cross, London, s.w.

Hampton and Sons produced a wide range of floor coverings. These six designs from their 1892 catalogue show how effectively expensive floor finishes could be simulated. On the left are two examples of floorcloth: the top one resembles tiles and the lower one has a floral pattern. The centre panels show two examples of decorative linoleum, while at the top right an "inlaid" linoleum (where colour penetrated the full depth) and border simulate encaustic tiling. The cork carpet, bottom right, is like linoleum but the mix of cork and linseed is not so densely compacted. HS

The modest Victorian house usually has plain pine floorboards. It was customary to cover them with rugs and to stain and polish the exposed surround with beeswax and turpentine. Parquetry, where small pieces of different-coloured hardwoods are laid in geometric patterns, was also popular as a border to a central carpeted area.

Sometimes, when a single carpet was laid, a stencil imitating parquetry might be applied to the board surround. An inexpensive substitute for carpets was floorcloth. This was a form of canvas sheeting which was printed to simulate rug patterns, parquet or tiling. It was easy to clean and often used in servants' rooms.

Linoleum, introduced with much success in the latter half of the century, was a more durable alternative to floorcloth. It was made from compressed cork and linseed oil mounted on a stout canvas backing. Again, it was often designed to simulate other superior floor finishes such as parquet but it was considered "better taste" to have plain linoleum in brown or green.

Hall floors are usually tiled with decorative encaustic tiles laid in a geometric pattern. The two foremost commercial suppliers were Minton and Maw; both offered a great variety of patterns. Stone flags or plain red quarry tiles are found in kitchens.

① A design for an elaborate stone and marble floor, suitable for a grand entrance hall (1868). Simplified, less expensive versions could be made in cement with added pigments. MB
② This page from Pryke and Palmer's 1896 catalogue shows a small selection from their large range of encaustic tiling. Easy to maintain and hardwearing, tiles were used in entrance halls and conservatories and also outside on steps and paths. PP

③ Parquetry floors and borders were popular and used a variety of newly imported, different-coloured hardwoods from the Empire. These examples are from 1872. HI
④ Three samples of Axminster carpet (with a knotted weave) illustrated in the 1892 catalogue of Hampton and Sons. Borders were supplied separately. HS

Fireplaces

The cast-iron fireplace with built-in register grate was mass-produced from the late 1850s. It could be used with or without *an additional surround. All but the smallest examples, in servants' rooms, were ornamented with tiled panels.* TE

The fireplace is an essential feature of the Victorian house and appears in virtually every room. It consists of two main parts: the manufactured cast-iron grate and the chimneypiece or surround, generally made from marble, slate or wood.

Large open fireplaces have dog grates, but register grates, which are cast as one piece to combine the grate, fireback and inner frame, are a feature of the main rooms in most town houses. These grates are inserted within the fireplace and the efficiency of the fire is increased by the use of dampers which regulate the supply of air. Panels of coloured patterned tiles on either side of the grate were popular, initially in larger houses.

Towards the end of the 19th century, mass-produced tiled register grates became available.

In fashionable houses fireplace surrounds were often changed when rooms were redecorated. Traditionally, marble and slate and, later, cast iron are found in the principal rooms. Wooden surrounds are more common in smaller houses and in the secondary rooms of grander houses. These would have been varnished or painted, depending on the quality of the wood. The overmantel, with its central mirror and complicated array of columns and shelves for displaying ornaments, became popular later in the period. Gas fires were very gradually introduced in the late 19th century.

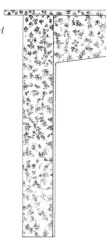

1

2

3

① *A simple cottage-style painted wooden surround.*
② *An elaborate marble chimneypiece suitable for a dining room or library.*
③ *A contrasting style is shown in the simple classical lines of this 1880s Queen Anne Revival chimneypiece designed by Richard Norman Shaw. It is made from pale marble, with the pulvinated (convex) frieze in a darker shade. The curb (hearth surround) has a bolection moulding.*
④ *A Gothic dressed-stone fireplace and integral stone curb, with heraldic decorations in the spandrels.*

⑤ *From the middle of the Victorian period the Carron Company was one of the firms supplying mass-produced cast-iron chimneypieces on a large* scale. *This typical bedroom chimneypiece has a painted oak-grained finish. It came with a register grate; the glazed tiles were an optional extra.* CO

4

5

Carron Company's Mantel and Overmantel

⑥ *Four examples of wooden chimneypieces available in the 1880s from C. Hindley and Sons of Oxford Street, London. They* were supplied in walnut or mahogany or in pine ready for painting. *The designs reflect the popularity of period styles and* current movements. *The first recalls Elizabethan prototypes, while the second is in the Queen Anne Revival style, increasingly popular* at this time. *The other two show the influence of the Aesthetic movement. Note the abundance of ornaments, including Japanese fans.* CH

6

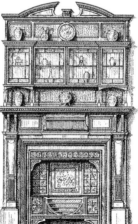
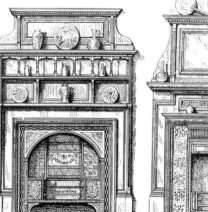

① *A Neo-Georgian surround, using voluted capitals of the Ionic Order. The Adam-style detailing is creditable, though slightly exaggerated, but the squat proportions of the fluted shafts and bases make this fireplace very Victorian. The fender with delicate scrollwork dates from c.1860.* MM

② *A simple marble fireplace surround with plain tiles, such as would be found in a modest house. Glasgow, 1892.* TE

③ *A grander version of a slab surround which would be suitable for a dining room. Slate with a simulated marble finish sets off the cast-iron register grate and floral tiled cheeks. London, c.1880.* RG

④ *The overmantel with a mirror was fashionable. This example is typical of the 1890s Georgian Revival.* RC
⑤ *A polished wooden fireplace surround*

with overmantel. Its bold Baronial style and unusual detailing make it an interesting example. RC
⑥ *Corner fireplaces were a popular*

Victorian feature. This 1890s three-tiered example is resplendent with many "classical" features, bevelled mirrors and a central picture. RC

No. 488. 10s. 6d per pair   No. 489. 7s. 9d per pair   No. 490. 9s. 6d per pair   No. 491. 10s. 6d per pair

No. 492. 13s. 6d. per doz.   No. 493. 24s. per doz.   No. 494. 8s. 6d. per doz.   No. 495. 24s. per doz.

① and ② *Pryke and Palmer supplied tiled register grates in several standard sizes and these two examples from their 1896 catalogue would be suitable for small town houses. The wooden, stone or marble surround would have been supplied separately.* PP
③ *Pryke and Palmer's range of decorative multi-coloured tiles and panels was impressive. Tiles became increasingly popular: they were attractive, durable and easy to clean.* PP
④ *A plain cast-iron standard register grate. The oval flap at the back of the grate could be closed when the fire was not in use to prevent soot from descending the chimney.* SB

⑤ and ⑥ *As foundries became increasingly skilled, so their mass-produced fireplaces gained a sophistication of style: these two late 19th-century register grates were from the William Owen Foundry.* HE
⑦ to ⑩ *Large open fireplaces, such as would be found in the entrance halls of grander houses,* still retained the dog grate. Such grates were originally designed to burn logs, but the Victorians adapted them to suit coal by reducing their size and enclosing them with firebricks. Brass ornamentation was often a feature of these grates. These four examples are from the Carron Company.* CO

① This handsome open fireplace is lined with Italianate majolica tiles and fitted with a substantial dog grate. The turned and carved woodwork of the surround is finished to a high standard. Bournemouth, Dorset, 1894. RC

② A smaller decorated fireplace which would be appropriate for a bedroom. The copper canopy is modelled with a sunburst. The splayed tiles feature swags and cherubs. RG

③ A cast-iron register grate surround: its rather heavy mouldings are relieved by a central panel of fruit. RC

④ Considerable skill is shown in the undercutting of the floral frieze in this Gothic Revival tour de force at Strawberry Hill, Middlesex, c.1860. SH

⑤ A cast-iron surround with a pulvinated (convex) frieze decorated with swags and roundels. An owl is featured on the pilaster. RG

⑥ Gas fires arrived late in the period. Manufacturers were quick to point out their labour-saving advantages: no coals to carry, no ash to empty and no chimneys to clean. However, the response was not immediate as they were expensive to run, tended to blow out and depended on a regular and reliable supply of gas. These are four typical examples, with intricate casings and asbestos heat elements. SS, SS, DG, DI

Kitchen stoves

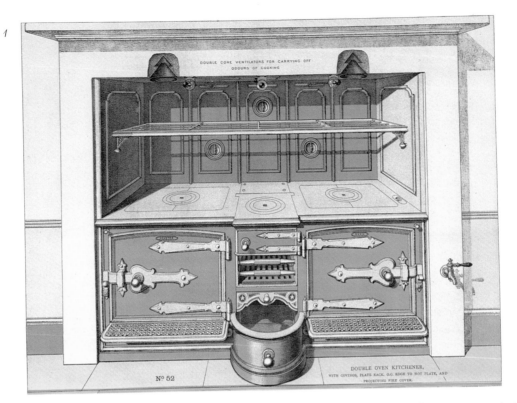

1

DOUBLE CONE VENTILATORS FOR CARRYING OFF
ODOURS OF COOKING

Nº 52

DOUBLE OVEN KITCHENER,
WITH COVINGS, PLATE-RACK, O.G. EDGE TO HOT PLATE, AND
PROJECTING FIRE COVER.

2

3

① *The range was the heart of the Victorian kitchen. This fine representative example has two ovens, a semi-enclosed grate with projecting fire cover and two double cone ventilators for extracting cooking odours above the plate rack (c.1890).* PP

② *and* ③ *Two late 19th-century gas ovens from the Carron Company. Both have grills and ample cooking space. The oven on the left has an additional copper boiler for heating water.* CO

The built-in range was the most commonly used cooker in the Victorian kitchen; it was fuelled by coal and made from cast iron. There was a choice between the "open" and "closed" range; the latter, as the name suggests, has an enclosed rather than open fire grate. The closed range became increasingly popular. Saucepans lasted longer and remained cleaner when heated on a plate rather than on an open fire. Another advantage was that the fire would stay in overnight. Manufacturers offered plenty of choice but most models had a central fire with a water boiler on one side and an oven on the other. Clean and economical fuel consumption was a important selling point.

Freestanding portable "kitcheners" were sometimes preferred because they could be installed further away from the flue, connected by a stove pipe. They were supported on legs but the term "portable" is misleading because they were immensely heavy; however, not being built-in, they could be regarded as tenants' fixtures.

Gas stoves began to make some impact toward the end of the century but they were expensive to run and needed a reliable gas supply. Because they did not provide constant heat they were marketed as ideal for summer use when a cool kitchen would be appreciated. It was some years, however, before they began to seriously rival the traditional range.

Staircases

This substantial polished oak staircase designed by the influential architect Richard Norman Shaw for Cragside, Northumbria, dates from c.1876. Of closed-string form, it has heavy turned balusters and substantial square-sided newel posts. These are surmounted by carved lions, which clasp electric lamp standards – some of the earliest electrical fixtures to survive in England. The stair carpet is held in place by brass stair rods and clips, leaving a portion of the treads exposed on either side. CR

Victorian terraced/row houses usually have "dog leg" staircases because they were inexpensive to construct and economical on space. They are generally made from a softwood, such as pine, and in early-Victorian houses frequently have plain square-sectioned stick balusters. As the period progresses, increasingly elaborate turned balusters and newel posts appear. These were mass-produced and were readily available from builders' merchants, together with broad mahogany or oak moulded handrails.

The edges of stair treads and risers were often painted, stained, or grained and varnished to resemble oak. A strip of carpet was used as a runner up the middle of the stairs, and was held in place by brass or sometimes wooden rods. The carpet was moved up or down a couple of inches at each spring cleaning so that the wear was even. The backstairs and those in modest households would often be covered in floorcloth or linoleum with polished brass protective nosings to the treads.

In large houses the staircase will often be "open well". Such stairs may be made from stone or marble with intricately worked cast-iron balustrades and a polished mahogany handrail. By the late 19th century there was a large range of balustrade castings to choose from. Stair treads are usually cantilevered, and if carpet was used the eyes for stair rods will be set into the stonework.

KITCHEN STOVES

STAIRCASES

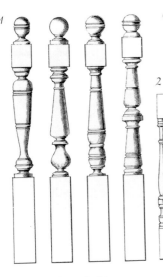

① *and* ② *Steam power made the sawing, planing and turning of wood quicker and less expensive. Balusters and newel posts became increasingly* elaborate. *These four pine newel posts and the selection of balusters (two cross-sections are shown on the right) are typical of a modest late Victorian house.* TL

③ *Speculative builders welcomed the wide choice of mass-produced stair features available from builders' merchants, but an architect-designed house would have its own specially commissioned staircase. This example for a Gothic* villa *is featured in G. A. and W. J. Audsley's Cottage, Lodge and Villa Architecture, c.1860.* CL
④ *to* ⑥ *Cast-iron and bronze balustrades were an expensive but elegant alternative to wood. These three examples come from the* 1882 catalogue of Macfarlane's Castings of Glasgow. *Monograms for the shields featured in the centre example could be supplied to order.* MC
⑦ *The cast-iron spiral staircase was an ingenious device. Unlike the medieval* version which was keyed into the circumference wall, the Victorian spiral was freestanding and often used outside. *This example, supplied by Macfarlane's Castings, has a typically intricate scroll pattern on the treads and stair-ends.* MC

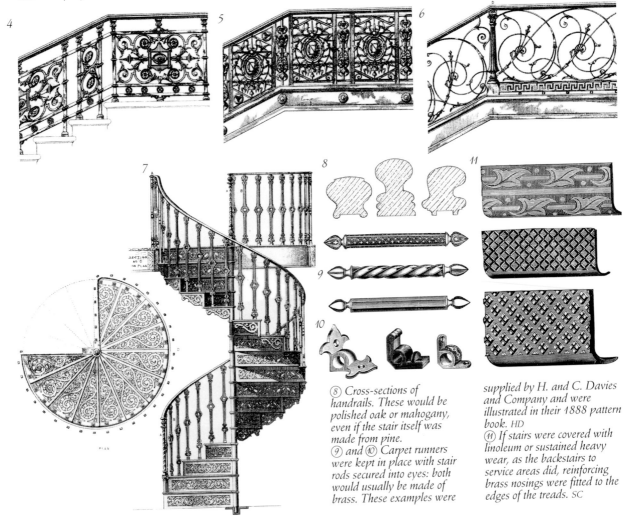

⑧ *Cross-sections of handrails. These would be polished oak or mahogany, even if the stair itself was made from pine.*
⑨ *and* ⑩ *Carpet runners were kept in place with stair rods secured into eyes: both would usually be made of brass. These examples were* supplied by H. and C. Davies and Company and were illustrated in their 1888 pattern book. HD
⑪ *If stairs were covered with linoleum or sustained heavy wear, as the backstairs to service areas did, reinforcing brass nosings were fitted to the edges of the treads.* SC

① Stair balustrades were almost always enriched by turning the stems on a lathe, even in the most modest houses. Painted pine was the least expensive form, but the handrail was often made from a polished hardwood. London, c.1880. RG

② Stone stairs often had cast-iron balustrades. Although more expensive than wood, they were popular and were produced in elegant designs. Here foliage winds its ways up the baluster stems. Glasgow, c.1850. SP

③ This Victorian engraving shows a model plan suggested by the designer Lewis F. Day in 1882 for decorating the hallway and staircase of a typical speculatively built terrace/row house. Stencilling proliferates. The narrow carpet is also characteristic of the period. EA

④ A late 19th-century stencilled design runs up the side of the stairs at dado level. Oil paint finished with a hard varnish made a robust and easily maintained surface. RC

⑤ An unusual carved patera decorates the corner newel of this staircase. The turned and tapered baluster stems are typical of the late Victorian period. RC

⑥ A richly decorated newel post and intricately worked cast-iron balustrade set off this stone staircase. Dating from the 1870s, its detailed and lavish ornamentation is characteristic of late Victorian terrace/row houses. LSH

Built-in furniture

① *This contemporary photograph (1897) shows the white-painted pine fixtures in the boudoir at Wickham Hall, Kent. A classical "Georgian" influence can be discerned, but the crowded shelves and heavy bracketed cornice are distinctly Victorian. The glazed cabinet doors have the appearance of bay windows. The central part makes up the overmantel: the fireplace is obscured by the firescreen. WL*

② *The "Cozy Corner" and "Inglenook" were popular features. This is a combination of the two, although the wooden seat has a decorative rather than functional use as it is some distance from the fire. Bournemouth, Dorset, 1894. RC*

Enthusiasm for built-in furniture stemmed largely from a desire to escape from the cluttered interiors of the early part of the period, together with an expanding trade in mechanized joinery. One large company of household furnishers in their 1880s catalogue claimed to "give special attention to fitted furniture"; they were "pleased to prepare and submit estimates for fitting up libraries, boudoirs and bedrooms in either hard-polished or painted woods".

Publishing was a growing industry and Victorian built-in library bookcases are an impressive feature of larger houses. Their shelves run between pilasters or Gothic shafts. The height usually takes the bookcase to within a few feet of the ceiling where the top, decorated with a cornice, would serve as a display shelf for busts of classical writers and philosophers. Folio volumes would be stored in the lower section of the bookcase, with the shelves above accommodating smaller volumes.

A charming speciality was the "Cozy Corner", an intimate arrangement of built-in seats, often situated next to a fireplace or in the corner of a room.

The kitchen dresser is a standard built-in Victorian fixture. Initially, open shelves were retained for the display of china but later glass doors were added. Food lifts or "dumb waiters" served dining rooms in houses with basement kitchens.

① *Bedroom furniture from C. Hindley and Sons, with a built-in washstand, dressing table and overhead cupboards. "Cozy" fireside seats complete the picture.* CH

② *Food lifts or "dumb waiters" were useful in urban houses with basement kitchens. They ran on a hand-operated system of ropes and pulleys; a wooden cabinet (left) could hide the lift cage.* CM

③ *The library at Cragside, Northumbria, was completed in 1872. The oak bookcases fill the dado: they are elaborately moulded and have glazed doors.* CR
④ *A typical Glasgow kitchen dresser with open shelves above and a built-in coal bunker below.* TE

⑤ *An elaborate example of the popular "Cozy Corner". The glazed cabinet is for displaying china. The silk canopy drapes would match the seats, which would be covered in tapestry or silk, and the woodwork would be painted to match the room.* HS

Plate

HAMPTON & SONS,
PALL MALL EAST, LONDON, S.W.

BUILT-IN FURNITURE

Services

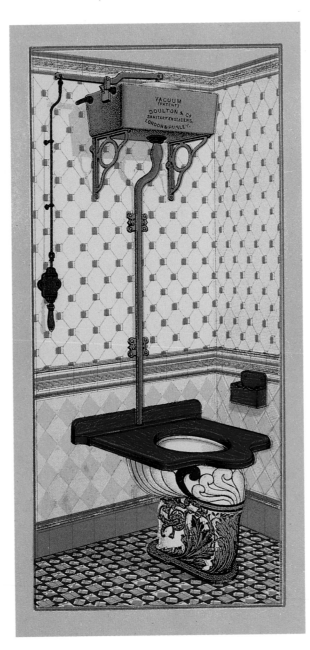

A patent internal closet with transfer-applied pattern, manufactured by Doulton and Company, London (c.1885). D

The Victorians were determined to improve the insanitary conditions which made disease a continual threat. Glazed clay pipes were introduced for underground drains, and the 1884 Public Health Act required all households to have a closet of some kind. In the case of many poorer houses, these were still sited in backyards.

The improved sewerage system encouraged the use of internal water closets. The previously inefficient flushing techniques had been replaced in the 1870s by an overhead cistern which discharged a gush of water. Made of cast iron, it was operated by pulling a chain. At the same time, the trap of the early water closet, which had done little to prevent foul smells escaping, was superseded by the S-bend trap.

Water closet bowls began to be made of glazed earthenware with transfer-applied patterns. The model illustrated was available with a choice of flushing systems: one was operated by raising the wooden seat, the other by pulling the chain. Boxes of paper were included with the purchase. From 1880 rolls of paper were available.

With the arrival of piped water on public supply, portable hip baths were replaced by fixed vitreous enamelled baths. Washstands, formerly filled by hand, were now plumbed in with brass taps/faucets, and plugholes allowed the water to drain away. The ceramic pedestal basin, often decorated with a transfer-printed pattern, eventually overtook the wooden washstand.

Methods of heating water went through several stages of development (including the application of gas flames directly to the underside of the bath) until the invention of the gas geyser in 1868. In spite of problems of noise, smell and a tendency to explode, the geyser attained popularity as a quick, economical way of heating water.

Showers also became popular. They were little more than inverted watering cans operated by a hand pump and chain until pressurized water fed by an overhead tank became available. The water closet increasingly became an indoor feature and the word "lavatory", previously used to describe a wash basin, was adopted as a euphemism for this device. Houses with central heating had large, sometimes decorated, cast-iron radiators. Ornamental ventilators were intended to help the circulation of fresh air. Victorian drain pipes/downspouts and gutters are also made from cast iron, and the hopper heads/leader heads that connect the two are sometimes inscribed with the date of the house.

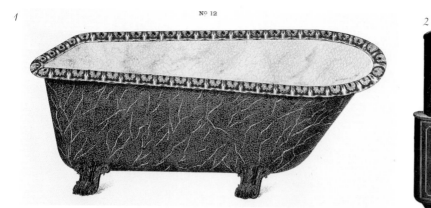

Nº 12

① A cast-iron "Roman" bath (1884), with enamel "marbling" and stencilled rim. HS
② Spray baths combined the bath, shower and screen in one unit and became popular from the 1880s. AE
③ A "Calda" copper gas heater (1890) with a japanned finish. WC
④ Late Victorian bath taps/faucets, available in nickel plate or polished brass with ebony lever handles. AE
⑤ "Universal" gas baths had copper bottoms and incorporated a built-in heating element underneath. GF

C. FARMILOE & SONS

THE REGISTERED "UNIVERSAL" GAS BATH, Tinned Iron, Right Hand, entire Copper Bottom, fitted with Washer and Plug.

⑥ A representative example of a late Victorian "marbled" wash basin which would have been plumbed into the main water supply. The popular shell motif is used to mask the overflow outlet and also to form the soap dishes. The brass taps/faucets are mounted onto a separate wooden panel behind the basin. TE
⑦ A late 19th-century ornamental standard earthenware wash basin with lever taps/faucets, supplied by Emanuel and Son. AE
⑧ The same manufacturer also produced these two wash basins mounted on white enamelled cast-iron frieze brackets. The lower example is designed to fit into a corner. AE
⑨ Hampton's 1892 "Improved Housemaid's Sink" provided a slop sink, wash basin and water closet in one cabinet. HS

SERVICES

1 **No. 8162.** The Plain "Royal" Pedestal Closet.

No. 8163. The "Royal" Pedestal Closet.

Cane & White. White. Printed.
Prices—Centre outlet, 14/6   16/-   20/- each.
P. or L.C.C. S. trap 16/-   17/6 21/6   „

White.
Prices—Embossed as drawn, Centre outlet, 20/6 each.
P. or L.C.C S. Trap, 22/-   „

No. 8165. The "Kodak" Pedestal Closet with Seat Lugs.

No. 8166. The "Trent" Wash-down Pedestal Closet.

With Polished Mahogany, Oak or Walnut Seat, as drawn, Lead P. Trap, and Patent Metal Flush Inlet Coupling with Lead Bend for connecting direct to flush pipe.

Enamelled
White. Printed. in Colours.
Prices—Complete   52/-   57/6   63/- each.

This Closet has been specially designed to replace the "Trent" Wash-out, and can be fixed without disturbing existing fittings.

Cane & White   Printed   Enamelled
or Ivory. as shown. in Colours.
Prices—21/-   26/-   32/-   34/- each.

① *Four typical pedestal closets. "Embossed" models (top right) began to lose favour as they were difficult to clean, but floral transfer patterns continued to be popular. Seats were usually of mahogany or oak; seats in outside closets were pine.* PP

② *A patented concealed urinal designed for either office use or domestic use in the study or billiard room. The case is made of mahogany or walnut. When closed it is described as having "the appearance of a small handsome article of furniture". The lid, when lifted, discloses the white earthenware basin and operates the automatic flushing system.* GF

③ *A hand plunger operates the flush system of this 1890s water closet manufactured by George Jennings; it is set into the lift-up wooden seat.* RC

④ *Rolled perforated toilet paper was introduced in 1880: this is a typical brass holder. Previously, separate sheets would have hung from a hook (right).* AE

⑤ *Privacy became an important factor once the water closet was installed as an indoor feature. Even modest homes would have had brass "indicator" bolts on the door.* AE

⑥ *"Odourless" gas heaters from the 1890s. They were without flues: fumes were discharged into the room.* SC

⑦ *A late Victorian cast-iron coil case, used to disguise a heating pipe.* SB

⑧ *A decorative Gothic-style "Boyles" patent air inlet tube which allowed the ingress of fresh air, c.1890. Fitted to the outside wall of a room, it was designed to combat the fumes of gas appliances.* BV

⑨ *The rainwater hopper head/ leader head is a good example of Victorian cast-iron workmanship and many different styles were manufactured. These four castings from the Steven Brothers and Company range (c.1885) are adapted to fit face-on or into corners. One is inscribed with the house date .* SB

Lighting

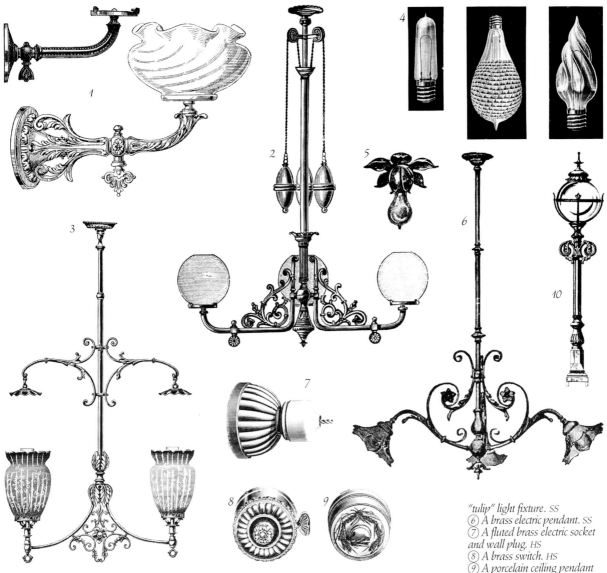

① *Two gas wall brackets.* SS
② *An adjustable brass pendant gas light with a telescopic stem, operated by weighted pulleys.* SS
③ *A ceiling pendant gas light with etched glass shades.* SS
④ *The tube-shaped candle bulb (left), cut-glass ornamental bulb*
(centre) and spiral candle-flame (right) are three examples of early electric light bulbs. HS
⑤ *A brass or copper electric*
"tulip" light fixture. SS
⑥ *A brass electric pendant.* SS
⑦ *A fluted brass electric socket and wall plug.* HS
⑧ *A brass switch.* HS
⑨ *A porcelain ceiling pendant fixture, 1892.* HS
⑩ *A cast-iron external lamp standard, for use with gas or electricity.* MC

Mrs Panton, in her book *From Kitchen to Garret* (1893), writes: "I must impress upon my readers never to have gas anywhere where they can avoid using it, and to pray heartily for that bright day to dawn when the electric light shall be within the reach of all."

This prayer was to be answered, but throughout the Victorian period most houses were lit by candles, oil or gas. A ceiling pendant which could be lowered over the table would be found in dining rooms; those fed by gas incorporated complicated devices to prevent leaks. Wall sconces and wrought-iron or brass standard lamps with copper trim and scrollwork were used to light sitting rooms. Shades were either elaborate silk affairs, which no doubt presented something of a fire risk, or glass, plain or etched. Cut-glass chandeliers were a luxury.

The incandescent gas mantle, introduced in 1887, provided much greater light. However, it was soon challenged by the invention of the electric light. Early bulbs had carbon filaments and produced an inefficient light. Installation was expensive and was confined to grander country houses and a few city areas able to generate their own electricity. Power failures were frequent and even at the end of the period, with the arrival of the superior tungsten filament, a back-up supply of candles was necessary. It was not until the Edwardian era that electricity became generally available and reliable.

Metalwork

A pair of iron gates, enclosed in a Gothic archway leading into Holly Village in Highgate, London, 1865. The gates are likely to be cast at this period, although they are modelled to look like medieval wrought iron. They are more restrained in design than was often the case. The lower rails are interspersed with "dog bars".

Traditionally, architectural ironwork had been the province of the blacksmith, but during the Victorian period the foundry became dominant and the highest skills in the manufacture of cast iron were attained. Great foundries were set up to meet the heavy demand for mass-produced railings, gates, porches, conservatories, fireplaces, baths and whatever else was needed. These foundries published enormous illustrated catalogues offering prompt delivery of stock items.

Cast iron became the prime material for down pipes/downspouts and gutters and lent itself well to the elaborate designs of hopper heads/leader heads. Later in the period, cast iron was used extensively for the manufacture of sanitary fixtures, particularly baths.

In British towns and cities railings were used to enclose squares, parks and the basement areas around terraced/row houses. Modest front garden walls were capped with balustrades; and verandas, conservatories and balcony fronts all became popular. Regrettably, many of these fine features were removed as scrap to "help the war effort" during World War II.

The popularity of cast iron was so overwhelming at this time that the art of wrought ironwork was almost lost. However, there was a renewed interest in handmade ironwork with the development of the Arts and Crafts movement later in the period.

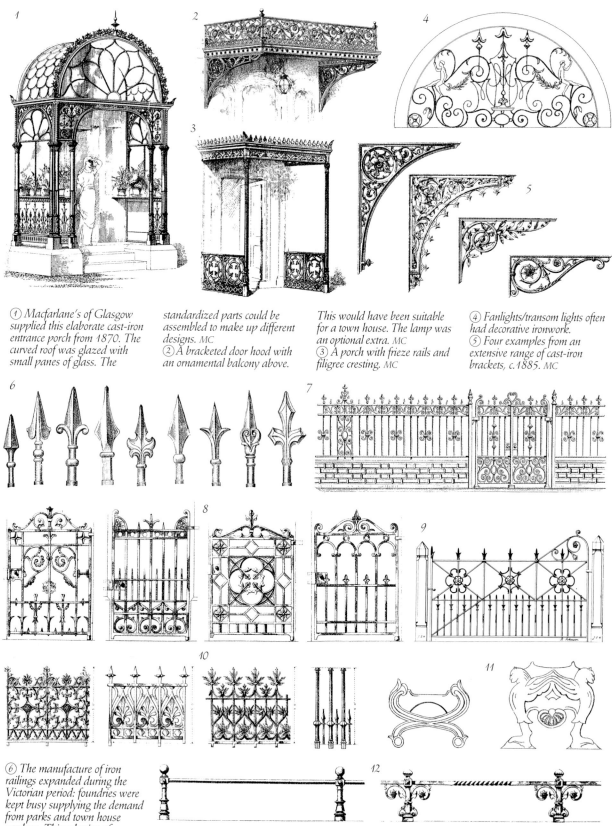

① Macfarlane's of Glasgow supplied this elaborate cast-iron entrance porch from 1870. The curved roof was glazed with small panes of glass. The standardized parts could be assembled to make up different designs. MC

② A bracketed door hood with an ornamental balcony above. This would have been suitable for a town house. The lamp was an optional extra. MC

③ A porch with frieze rails and filigree cresting. MC

④ Fanlights/transom lights often had decorative ironwork.

⑤ Four examples from an extensive range of cast-iron brackets, c.1885. MC

⑥ The manufacture of iron railings expanded during the Victorian period: foundries were kept busy supplying the demand from parks and town house gardens. This selection of standard finials is from a range illustrated in the 1891 catalogue of Bayliss, Jones and Bayliss of Wolverhampton. BJB

⑦ Wrought- or cast-iron palisading was used to enclose the front gardens of villas. BJB

⑧ Four gate patterns from the 1880s Macfarlane's range. MC

⑨ A carriage entrance gate in wrought iron. The finials and some of the enrichments would have been cast. JB

⑩ Four examples of palisade patterns from Macfarlane's. MC

⑪ Bootscrapers were practical and attractive entrance fixtures.

⑫ Low railings were used on sills and parapets, as crestings for walls or as a border to paths. MC

METALWORK

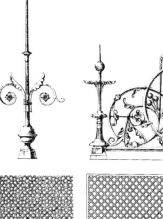

① Decorative chainlink fencing was a pleasing addition to carriage drives. BJB
② A cast-iron finial and cresting suitable for surmounting a turret. MC

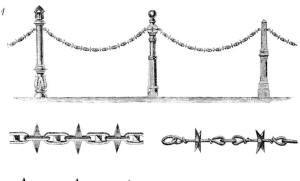

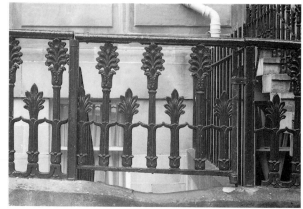

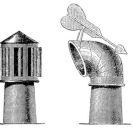

③ Ventilators could often be accommodated attractively inside a turret or belfry. GF
④ Many devices were used in an attempt to prevent chimneys from smoking. These two cowls, one with additional weather vane, were supplied by George Farmiloe and Company in the 1890s. GF

⑤ In grander houses, floor grilles or gratings were incorporated into heating and ventilation systems. MC
⑥ Ornamental cast-iron railings and gates from Glasgow. The example on the left is based on Jacobean strapwork; the other two show a palmette design (top) and scrollwork (below). SP

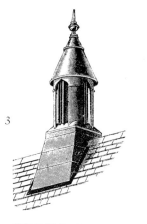

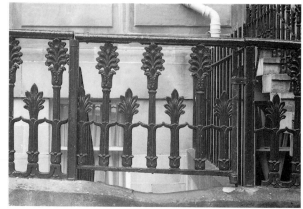

Woodwork

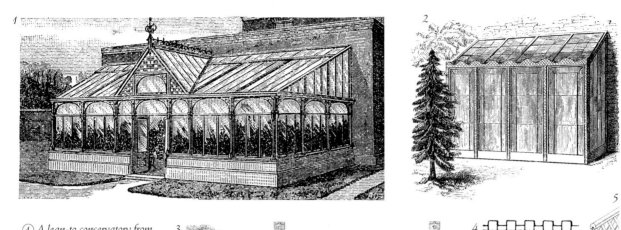

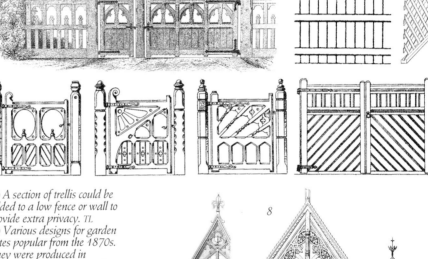

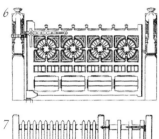

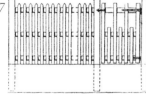

① *A lean-to conservatory from the 1890s pre-fabricated range supplied by William Cooper and Company. The woodwork is seasoned red deal (fir or pine) painted with two coats of white oil paint.* WC

⑤ *A section of trellis could be added to a low fence or wall to provide extra privacy.* TL
⑥ *Various designs for garden gates popular from the 1870s. They were produced in softwood, which was usually painted green or white, or in oak with a stain finish.* BP
⑦ *This palisade fence and gate would suit a rural setting.* BP
⑧ *Machine-carved wooden bargeboards were very much a Victorian feature; porches were decorated in a similarly ornate fashion.* VC

② *Ferns were popular with the Victorians, and ferneries were common.* RU
③ *A late Victorian Gothic-style pattern for gates and fencing.* VC
④ *An example of close boarded fencing with "castellated" top.* BP

The use of wood for external decoration developed apace in the Victorian period. Oak had normally been used for durability outdoors, but it was expensive. Now, less expensive softwoods, such as pine, could be treated with coal tar or oil-based preservatives, and pressure treatment with creosote made them even more weatherproof. Pine was also easy to carve and shape into patterns.

Most large joinery works used steam machinery, and machine sawing and planing made working with timber simpler and less expensive than before. Manufacturers developed extensive ranges of prefabricated functional and ornamental garden buildings, including conservatories, for dispatch by rail. These were delivered in component parts for immediate erection.

Trelliswork, very much a feature of the period, was delivered folded, concertina-style, and when expanded created very effective screens and panels. Dark creosoted shiplap fencing became an alternative to expensive brick walls; open palisade fencing was also popular. Garden entrance gates were painted dark green or white. They had solid lower panels and the tops were openwork panels formed by a variety of spindles.

A.W.N. Pugin's *Ornamental Timber Gables of the Sixteenth Century* (1831) was popular as a pattern book for elaborate machine-carved softwood bargeboards. Wooden porches also reflect this interest in decorative carpentry.

METALWORK

WOODWORK

AMERICAN VICTORIAN

1840–1910

① *Broad gables and a well-integrated porch are key elements of many American late Victorian houses. This example, with overtones of half-timbering, is in Newport, Rhode Island, 1875.* SAL

② *The Hale House, Los Angeles, 1888: a sophisticated essay in wood and paint. This is an elaborate example of the Queen Anne style. The original colours have been restored, following meticulous paint research.* HA

③ *A terrace/row in the Italianate style, in Philadelphia, with roof pediments, elegant porches and ornate eave brackets. Italianate was probably the most prominent townhouse style from the 1850s to the 1880s.* WT

During the second half of the 19th century, architects in the United States began to lose interest in Greco-Roman Classicism, and to adopt new domestic styles based loosely on medieval and other non-classical forms of building. While continuing to be inspired by foreign models both old and new, they developed a robust inventiveness of their own. This was made possible by a combination of new building technologies, an abundance of raw materials, a plethora of architectural and housekeeping publications, and the financial wherewithal of many Americans to build their own homes.

One of the most important technological developments was the advent of balloon framing, whereby the framework of a house could be made out of uniform lumber; this was becoming increasingly available from commercial mills. The framing system comprised inexpensive two-by-four-inch boards, combined as upright studs and cross-members and held together by cheap, mass-produced nails.

Eventually, by the turn of the century, balloon framing replaced traditional hewn timber construction and simplified the making of more complex architectural features, such as overhangs, bay windows and towers.

Advanced manufacturing techniques were also employed to mass-produce finished windows, doors, brackets and decorative turnings, often more elaborate and sometimes less expensive than their handmade counterparts. Along with plentiful building materials,

there was also access to an increasing variety of publications on house building: trade catalogues, pattern books and architectural periodicals.

Industrialization meant that for the first time in the United States, very large houses could be built on a wide scale. Tenements and, later, apartment houses went up in increasing numbers, as the population shifted from country to town and newly arrived foreign immigrants sought accommodation.

At least eight distinct architectural styles developed, along with numerous secondary styles and movements, all of which are now incorporated under the broad heading of "Victorian". These styles overlapped in date and none had a specific beginning or end. To further complicate the analysis of 19th-century American houses, many were built in a combination of styles.

The first post-classical styles, beginning in the 1830s, were the Gothic Revival and the Italianate. The Stick style followed in the 1860s and 1870s, and the late 19th century produced American Queen Anne, Richardsonian Romanesque, Shingle and Colonial Revival styles. At the same time Egyptian and Oriental elements were incorporated into American houses, imitations of Swiss chalets were built, and the octagonal building plan enjoyed renewed interest.

The Gothic Revival and Italianate styles were loosely based on English Regency prototypes, and grew out of an increasing interest in historical architecture. Early

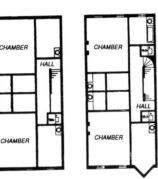

① *The J. J. Glessner House, Chicago, 1885, by H.H. Richardson. The Romanesque style depends on mass and volumes, rather than applied details.* CAF

② *This plan for a cottage of 1881 makes an instructive comparison with the symmetrical Greek Revival plans of forty years before. The rooms are grouped informally. Other common elements of the period are the living hall, and the wrap-around veranda.* CK

③ *Terraced/row townhouse plans, with their parallel party walls, remained fairly static compared with their freestanding counterparts. The major innovations were the introduction of sinks, water closets and baths. Double parlours, or a parlour and dining room, remained a* constant. *This house dates from 1880: the stories are shown in descending order, down to the basement and cellar.*

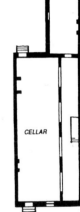

④ *The Gothic Revival style is characterized by steeply pitched roofs, dormer windows, and a curvilinear "gingerbread" trim along the eaves and gable edges. Gothic was greatly popularized by the architectural writings of Andrew Jackson Downing (1815-52). In The Architecture of Country* Houses (1850) *he suggests an interesting geographical basis for the decision between Gothic and Italian: "The former, generally speaking, is best suited to our Northern, broken country; the latter, to the plain and valley surface of the Middle and Southern States – though sites may be found for* each style in all portions of the Union." GE

⑤ *The Shingle style, notable for its plain shingled surfaces, evolved in New England before being disseminated to the rest of the country. It flourished from the 1880s to c.1900. This is a Shingle-style house in Newport, Rhode Island, by* McKim, Mead and White, 1881-2. *Note the veranda on its turned supports, and the two-story open pavilion, which balances the round tower (on the left in this view) containing a study. Asymmetrical planning of this kind is characteristic of the style.* SAL

Gothic Revival houses are characterized by irregular, picturesque massings and plans, sharply pitched roofs and gables, castellated parapets and multi-paned windows sometimes capped with Gothic arches. To enhance their perpendicular appearance, the walls of modestly priced houses were often made with vertical boards and battens. Compared with building in wood, stone or brick construction was always more expensive, and therefore less common.

Italianate houses, somewhat inspired by the northern Italian farm house, feature low-pitched roofs with broad eaves supported by brackets, and windows with tall, narrow proportions. The windows are often surrounded by classically inspired architraves. In the 1850s, Italianate became the most important town house style. Its success was partly due to the fact that it could be successfully applied to a square volume, whereas Gothic demands an irregular volume for full effect.

The Italianate style continued to be used through the rest of the century, while at the same time fashionable circles adopted the Second Empire style, identifiable by the mansard roofs, derived from the 17th-century designs of François Mansart, a Court architect of Louis

XIV. The mansard roof was popular both because it had connections with stylish contemporary France, where it was undergoing a revival at the hands of Second Empire architects, and because its generous width allowed for a large attic story of usable space. Mansard roofs were often used on Italianate houses.

There was also continuing interest in medieval styles, which not only furthered the Gothic Revival but also inspired the Stick and Queen Anne styles. Stick-style houses were loosely based on English half-timbered buildings. Like Gothic houses, they reflected Picturesque philosophies, with their steep gabled roofs and overhanging eaves. However, for decoration the Stick style relied on exposed roof trusses, rafters, and a raised "stick work" pattern on the walls, made by vertical and diagonal arrangements of boards.

Stick, along with elements from Gothic and Italianate, provided the prototypes for the American Queen Anne style. Lasting from the 1880s until 1910, American Queen Anne derived from the style developed by British architect Richard Norman Shaw (1831-1912) and his followers. However, the half-timbered and patterned masonry buildings of the English Queen Anne move-

① *A middle class late Victorian interior: the Villa Montezuma, San Diego, California, 1887. Notable are the lavish use of wood panelling and the rich ceiling. JBE*

② *An early Victorian interior, within an Empire house. The carpet is a reproduction (by Scalamandré) of a tapestry-woven design dating from c.1850. SCA*

ment are only one feature of the American version. American architects added a rich vocabulary of decorative woodwork, enriching the established styles with more complex designs. Roofs, for example, grew even steeper than on Gothic and Stick buildings, and more complicated in shape. The comparatively simple plans and volumes of mid-century houses were compounded by additional projections, overhanging stories, gables and towers. The exterior walls were decorated with wooden shingles, fancy brickwork and terracotta insets.

Some houses in the Stick and Queen Anne styles used elements of the "Eastlake" manner, named after the English designer and critic Charles Locke Eastlake (1833-1906), whose taste in ornament was adopted by Americans for exteriors. Elements in the Eastlake style include robust porch posts, balusters and pendants, as well as the extensive use of spindles for friezes and balustrades.

The Richardsonian Romanesque style, named after its most notable exponent H.H. Richardson (1838-86), began in the late 1880s and continued until the end of the century. This idiom is based on the use of rough-hewn stone facing, composed in asymmetrical volumes and marked by round-arched openings for porches, doors and windows, along with simple details derived from Romanesque, Syrian and Byzantine sources.

The Shingle style, dating from the 1880s to about 1900, contrasts sharply with the rich detailing of the Queen Anne and relates to the Romanesque in its use of continuous, relatively unadorned surfaces. Wooden shingles, usually in plain rows, form a uniform skin for the roof and walls. Ornamental details are simple and based on a modest range of Neo-classical elements taken from American Colonial and Federal houses, such as Doric columns and Venetian (Palladian) windows. Asymmetry is favoured in the planning.

The study of early American buildings from before the Greek Revival led to the construction of houses labelled "Colonial" by their builders. Initially these took the form of Queen Anne houses with generous applications of Neo-classical details. Later, houses more accurately copied from 18th-century models were built.

As all parts of the nation used the same published design sources and similar mass-produced building parts, regional distinctions became subtle. By the 1890s prefabricated Queen Anne houses were transported by rail across the United States. But the relative lack of vernacular distinctions by no means spells a dearth of architectural interest. American Victorian houses are eclectic in their stylistic elements and rich in individual interpretation.

Doors

The main entrance of the Hale House, Los Angeles, 1888. The relatively simple front doors are set within a remarkable portico, featuring an American emblem inside the pediment. The balancing of simple and elaborate elements is characteristic of late Victorian styles. HA

Doors continued to be made as an exterior frame holding thinner panels. This provided strong, lightweight doors receptive to many styles of decoration. For example, Gothic Revival doors supported elements of Gothic tracery, Italianate doors held applied Renaissance-style panels and Colonial Revival doors bore Neo-classical motifs. However, many houses had plain doors, the style of the building being conveyed either by the shape of the door opening or by the portico or porch. Italianate doors were made Italian by their arched openings. Even a worker's cottage door could be Gothicized with a simple bolection moulding or hood.

Wherever feasible, double doors were preferred.

Double front doors first appeared on Gothic houses and continued to be widely used on later styles, often matched with a second pair, forming a vestibule. With the advent of inexpensive glass, more doors were glazed. Fanlights/transom lights over exterior and interior doors were also popular; clear glass in the 1850s, followed by coloured glass and, later, leaded glass panels.

Interior doors, in simple configurations of panels, usually matched the other finished wood in the room. Sometimes simple doors were embellished with decorative carving or paint. Almost every grand house featured a pair of sliding doors between double parlours, or between parlour and dining room.

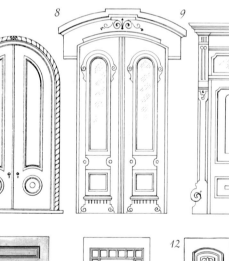

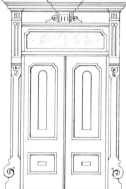

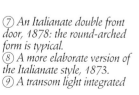

① *A plain hood design for the front door of a working man's cottage, commended by A. J. Downing in* The Architecture of Country Houses, *1850.*
② *An Italianate door canopy, in profile and face-on. From* Woodward's National Architect, *New York, 1869.* WD
③ *An elaborate example of Southern Rococo Revival, this doorway in New Orleans is adorned with carved heads and other ornament in wood. The recessed panels at the sides are shutters which could be closed for protection against rain.*
④ *In the second half of the 19th century emphasis could fall on the door or the porch; this Richardsonian Romanesque porch, with its elaborate Syrian-style arch, contains fairly narrow double doors.*
⑤ *A pair of Gothic entrance doors, published by A. J. Downing in* Victorian Cottage Residences, *1842.*
⑥ *This grander Gothic doorway has a fanlight/transom light. From Oakland, California.*

⑦ *An Italianate double front door, 1878: the round-arched form is typical.*
⑧ *A more elaborate version of the Italianate style, 1873.*
⑨ *A transom light integrated* into a classical design, 1873.
⑩ *This door would be suitable for an Italianate or, with less accuracy, a Gothic house, but it actually appears on a Second Empire design of 1878.*
⑪ *Three glazed doors. The second example has an elaborate etched design. The last is a type used in Queen Anne and Shingle houses.* UD
⑫ *A Renaissance-inspired* group found in Italianate and Queen Anne houses, sold by C.B. Keogh and Co. This illustration combines the front door design (left) and glazed vestibule door (right).

① *An ironwork porch with fairly naturalistic grapevine ornament gives added importance to a relatively simple doorway. With the advent of inexpensive glass, more and more doors were glazed. The screen door first made its appearance during the Victorian period.* GE

② *A doorway and porch from Hanley House, Oregon, 1875. Some builders combined elements from earlier styles with current taste. Here, the type of door lights first used in the Federal period are combined with an Italianate door and portico. The balustrade above gives importance to the front door.* PD

③ *Classical porticoes were the principal decoration of townhouse facades. Here, outside doors lead to an identical pair inside, forming a vestibule between. The use of a house number emblazoned on the glass was a popular Victorian practice.* GE

④ *A beautifully grained interior door paired with a Victorian version of a classical doorcase. The elongated upper panels contribute to an impression of elegance. Corner blocks such as these would often feature roundels or other ornamentation.* HA

⑤ *Another interior doorway, featuring a lugged architrave and multiple mouldings on the overdoor. For a decorative finish, flat paint was the least expensive option, then graining (as used on this door); hardwood doors were costly.* BO

⑥ *Front doors from mid-century were often made with mouldings or raised panels reminiscent of Italian Renaissance models. Better houses would have carved door surrounds in Renaissance leaf or rope designs. This example has more abstract decoration.* GE

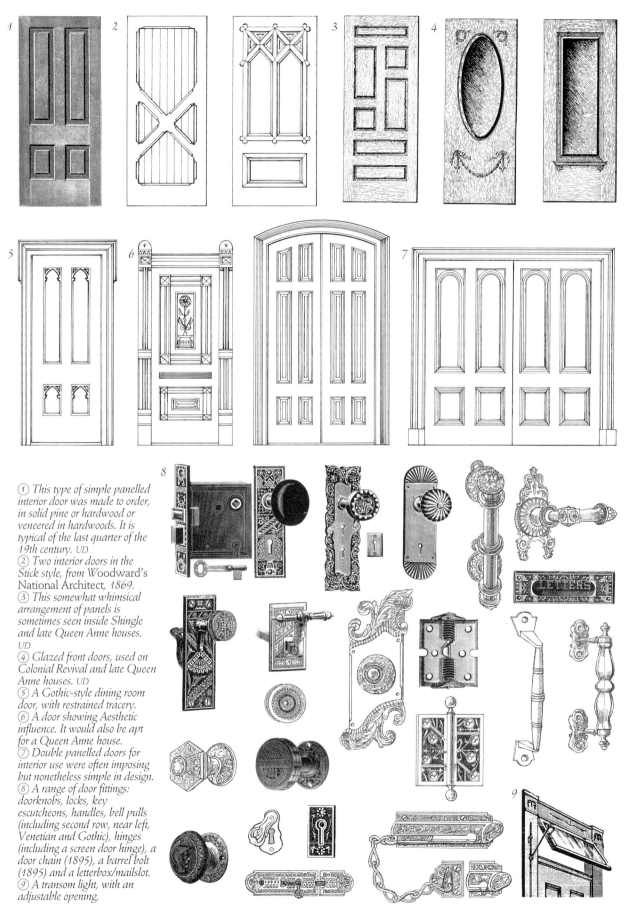

1 This type of simple panelled interior door was made to order, in solid pine or hardwood or veneered in hardwoods. It is typical of the last quarter of the 19th century. UD

2 Two interior doors in the Stick style, from Woodward's National Architect, 1869.

3 This somewhat whimsical arrangement of panels is sometimes seen inside Shingle and late Queen Anne houses. UD

4 Glazed front doors, used on Colonial Revival and late Queen Anne houses. UD

5 A Gothic-style dining room door, with restrained tracery.

6 A door showing Aesthetic influence. It would also be apt for a Queen Anne house.

7 Double panelled doors for interior use were often imposing but nonetheless simple in design.

8 A range of door fittings: doorknobs, locks, key escutcheons, handles, bell pulls (including second row, near left, Venetian and Gothic), hinges (including a screen door hinge), a door chain (1895), a barrel bolt (1895) and a letterbox/mailslot.

9 A transom light, with an adjustable opening.

Windows

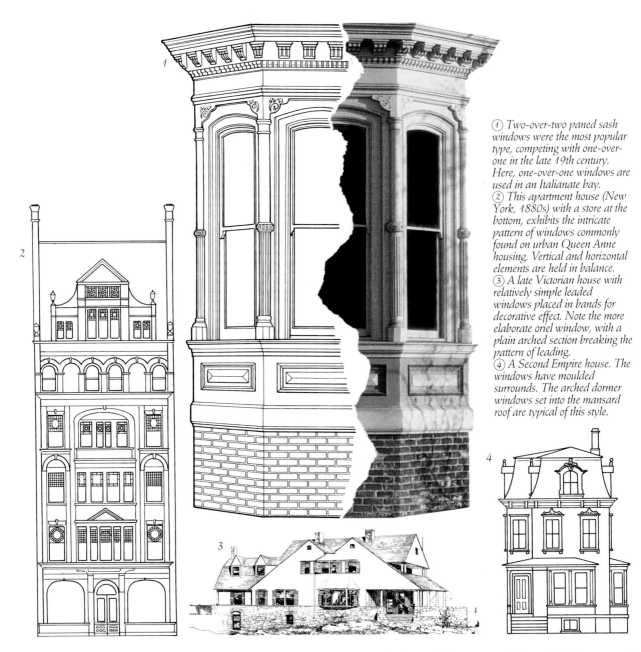

① *Two-over-two paned sash windows were the most popular type, competing with one-over-one in the late 19th century. Here, one-over-one windows are used in an Italianate bay.*
② *This apartment house (New York, 1880s) with a store at the bottom, exhibits the intricate pattern of windows commonly found on urban Queen Anne housing. Vertical and horizontal elements are held in balance.*
③ *A late Victorian house with relatively simple leaded windows placed in bands for decorative effect. Note the more elaborate oriel window, with a plain arched section breaking the pattern of leading.*
④ *A Second Empire house. The windows have moulded surrounds. The arched dormer windows set into the mansard roof are typical of this style.*

With the perfection of plate glass making, huge expanses of undivided glazing were now affordable. The use and design of glazing bars became a purely decorative decision, with few technical constraints. Thus, when the designers of Gothic Revival houses reintroduced diamond-paned windows, it was a design unaffected by any limitations on the size of the glass. Millwork catalogues offered vast assortments of windows. The simplest were plain, single-paned, double-hung types; the fanciest, with elaborately divided polygons of glazing, were for Queen Anne houses.

There was a renewed interest in stained glass. From the 1840s some houses featured windows with solid panes of coloured glass, particularly in the lights around front doors. In the 1850s leaded glass windows were introduced, continuing until the first decades of the 20th century. Elaborate leaded designs were popular on fireplace walls, in dining rooms, and on stair landings. Etched glass panels and glass decoration painted to simulate leaded glass also enjoyed a vogue.

In the second half of the 19th century, louvered or Venetian exterior shutters became standard, although canvas awnings or bonnet blinds were sometimes used instead. Many houses continued to have solid interior shutters. Wire mesh window screens for insect protection were introduced in the 1880s.

① *A Gothic casement window, with hood moulding, 1852.* SN
② *A mid-century Gothic sash.*
③ *Queen Anne sash windows, 1880s. The circle within a square is typical.*
④ *A sash window of 1878.*
⑤ *A sash window section in the Queen Anne style.* CK
⑥ *Two windows of 1869, one with a pediment, the other with a flat cornice and keystone.* WD
⑦ *Bay windows became common after c.1850, often used to update older houses.* CG

⑧ *An interior partial elevation, with cross-section above, of a window with inside shutters (shown half closed).* UD
⑨ *One of a pair of exterior shutters, with stationary slats above rolling slats.* UD
⑩ *Three examples of dormer windows, 1869. The first two are in the Second Empire manner, the third is typical Queen Anne. Dormers helped to elaborate the roof lines of even the simplest structures.* WD
⑪ *A semi-circular gable window (interior, left, exterior, right), dressed with stone in the context of a brick-built house.*
⑫ *Neo-classical window shapes gave Colonial Revival*

houses much of their style. UD
⑬ *A triple-fronted window with upper panes in leaded and coloured glass. It dates from the turn of the century.* UD
⑭ *This leaded and coloured glass design is from a Queen Anne-style house in San Francisco.*
⑮ *Designs for stained glass window sections in a loosely Aesthetic style.*
⑯ *A section of etched glass: various geometric designs were popular.* UD
⑰ *This sandblasted glass panel showing 17th-century pilgrims would have appealed to Colonial Revivalists. A turn-of-the-century design.* UD

① *Tall sash windows with exterior shutters. In this example, note the decorative use of shutters even where shade is provided by a deep veranda.* WT

② *Bay windows enjoyed great popularity in the Italianate style, and again in the Shingle and Colonial Revival styles. This is an Italianate example from Los Angeles.*

③ *A late Victorian upper-floor window set into a shingled facade. The upper pane of the sash is enlivened with a simple border of stained-glass panels. The paint colours in this example have been accurately restored.* HA

④ *Stained glass, Villa Montezuma, San Diego, 1887. The central panel depicts Sappho, the ancient Greek poetess who tutored girls in the Arts of music and poetry – apt for a room where music was played.* JBE

⑤ *Miscellaneous window fittings, late 19th century, including espagnolette bars for French doors (left), sash pull plates, sash lifts, and a shutter hinge (bottom right). Cast fittings with relief decoration were used from c.1860. Most designs were combinations of geometric and stylized decoration that are now termed "Eastlake".*

Walls

① *Fully panelled walls, often of American hardwood, were popular among the well-to-do in the late 19th century. This example, with a linenfold dado and star motifs above, dates from the 1880s.* SAL
② *A frieze beneath a papered ceiling. The design is made up of individual wallpaper strips: note how the flower sprigs overlap the strip below.* HA
③ *Floral wallpapers were popular: in some the botanical representation was highly naturalistic.* GE
④ *Papers with a dense all-over pattern were popular in the last decades of the 19th century. Typically, this example is restricted to the field of the wall, above a panelled dado with fine carved mouldings.* GW
⑤ *A William Morris wallpaper, in the "Chrysanthemum" pattern, above a panelled dado with echoing floral motifs. This wallpaper design was produced from 1877. Morris aimed to convey the vigour of plant growth without directly imitating nature.* HA

Almost every domestic room had a base moulding (skirting board/baseboard), and many had cornices (crown mouldings) of some type. After the 1860s wainscot and chair rails once more became regular features. In the 1870s, the dado frieze enjoyed a vogue.

It was recommended that walls be painted darker than the ceiling and that the trim work should be darker or lighter than the walls. Oil paints and distemper colours (calcimine) were both used. White or light-coloured walls were popular, although some writers argued for more adventurous choices. A. J. Downing felt that entrance halls should be painted in sober colours, or to resemble stone; parlours should be cheerful and bright.

After 1850, wallpaper was an affordable alternative to paint. Rococo Revival papers in the mid-century usually featured large leaf designs and architectural panels of scroll ornament, applied from skirting board/baseboard to ceiling. In the 1870s popular taste shifted to bands or friezes of paper above painted walls or wainscot. Lifelike organic designs were favoured.

In the late Victorian period hardwoods were recommended for trim moulding and wainscotting. Critics felt that native American wood species were most suitable, treated with a clear finish. However, pine grained or flat-painted remained the most common finish of wood for most late 19th-century house builders.

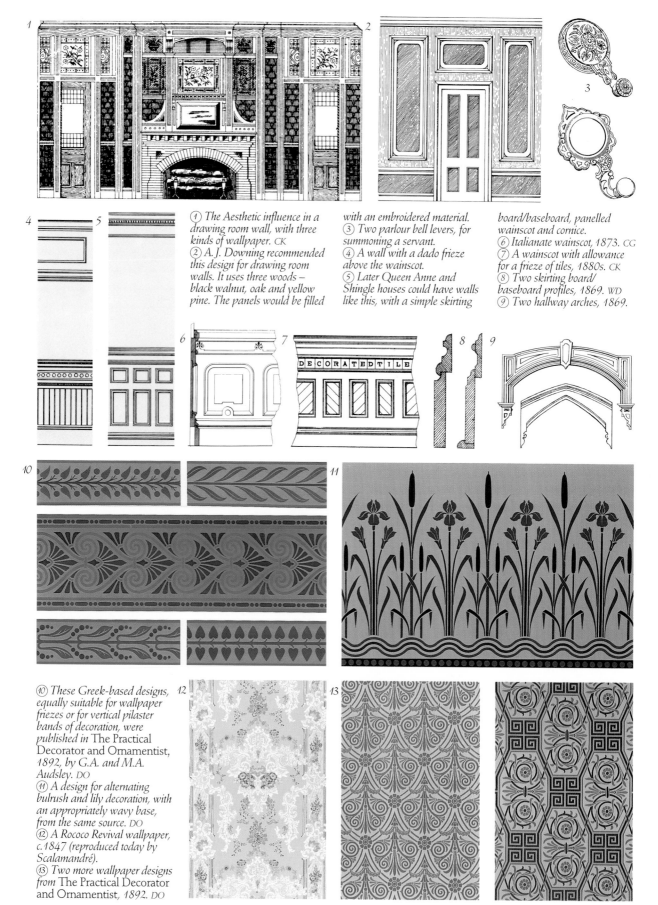

① The Aesthetic influence in a drawing room wall, with three kinds of wallpaper. CK
② A. J. Downing recommended this design for drawing room walls. It uses three woods – black walnut, oak and yellow pine. The panels would be filled with an embroidered material.
③ Two parlour bell levers, for summoning a servant.
④ A wall with a dado frieze above the wainscot.
⑤ Later Queen Anne and Shingle houses could have walls like this, with a simple skirting board/baseboard, panelled wainscot and cornice.
⑥ Italianate wainscot, 1873. CG
⑦ A wainscot with allowance for a frieze of tiles, 1880s. CK
⑧ Two skirting board/baseboard profiles, 1869. WD
⑨ Two hallway arches, 1869.

⑩ These Greek-based designs, equally suitable for wallpaper friezes or for vertical pilaster bands of decoration, were published in The Practical Decorator and Ornamentist, 1892, by G.A. and M.A. Audsley. DO
⑪ A design for alternating bulrush and lily decoration, with an appropriately wavy base, from the same source. DO
⑫ A Rococo Revival wallpaper, c.1847 (reproduced today by Scalamandré).
⑬ Two more wallpaper designs from The Practical Decorator and Ornamentist, 1892. DO

Ceilings

① *A grand Italianate stairwell skylight, with classical plaster mouldings, c.1847.* BO
② *Ceiling roses/medallions were carried on from the Federal*

period. This version would be appropriate to a Gothic or Italianate house. GE
③ *A panelled ceiling of c.1870, with wooden bosses. The use of*

stencilled stars to represent the night sky was a not uncommon conceit. NA
④ *Authors on design in c.1870 often focused on ceilings as an*

under-used vehicle for decoration. This example, combining stencilling with painted and gilded plaster, is especially exuberant. GW

Decorated ceilings were favoured in American Victorian houses. Taste-makers decreed that even the simplest rooms required cornices (crown mouldings); 14 inches (36cm) was held by some to be the ideal depth. Some critics advocated coloured or patterned ceilings, but plain white remained the habitual choice.

Plaster roses/medallions continued from the Neoclassical period, adapted to suit the various revival tastes. Thus, Rococo Revival roses/medallions gave way to Renaissance models later in the century. Other types of recommended plasterwork included panel mouldings, as well as, for the rich, various types of medievalized coffers and panels.

The post-Civil War period brought rich cycles of painted and papered ceiling decorations, ranging from cloud-borne cherubs to elaborate, interlocking geometric patterns and naturalistic borders. Less expensive papers, introduced after c.1850, were used to produce whole ceiling designs as well as borders and central panels. Stencilling was also used to decorate ceilings.

In the last decade of the century, some critics called for simpler ceiling design, using all-over papers in reticent patterns, with plain borders en suite with the designs on the walls below.

Ceilings could also be of tongue-and-groove boards, or of tin in secondary areas of the house.

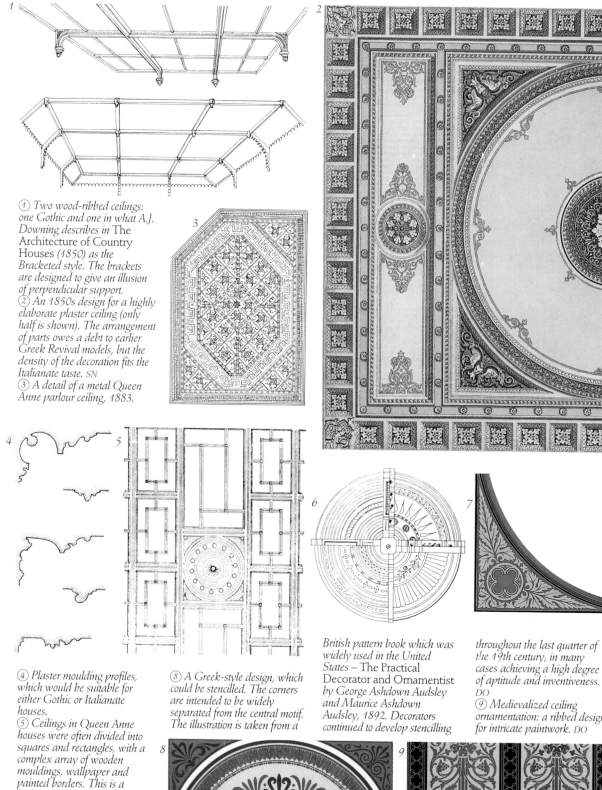

① *Two wood-ribbed ceilings: one Gothic and one in what A.J. Downing describes in* The Architecture of Country Houses *(1850) as the Bracketed style. The brackets are designed to give an illusion of perpendicular support.*

② *An 1850s design for a highly elaborate plaster ceiling (only half is shown). The arrangement of parts owes a debt to earlier Greek Revival models, but the density of the decoration fits the Italianate taste.* SN

③ *A detail of a metal Queen Anne parlour ceiling, 1883.*

④ *Plaster moulding profiles, which would be suitable for either Gothic or Italianate houses.*

⑤ *Ceilings in Queen Anne houses were often divided into squares and rectangles, with a complex array of wooden mouldings, wallpaper and painted borders. This is a high-style example of the 1880s.* PA

⑥ *Four alternative patterns for a central rose/medallion, 1880s.* PA

⑦ *An Aesthetic corner treatment, reminiscent of a Tudor doorway spandrel.* DO

⑧ *A Greek-style design, which could be stencilled. The corners are intended to be widely separated from the central motif. The illustration is taken from a* British pattern book which was widely used in the United States – The Practical Decorator and Ornamentist *by George Ashdown Audsley and Maurice Ashdown Audsley, 1892. Decorators continued to develop stencilling* throughout the last quarter of the 19th century, in many cases achieving a high degree of aptitude and inventiveness. DO

⑨ *Medievalized ceiling ornamentation: a ribbed design for intricate paintwork.* DO

Floors

A range of prefabricated parquet patterns, produced by a Philadelphia company, John W. Boughton (top). The wood blocks were sold ready-laid onto pieces of flexible cloth to make up the pattern. Parquet and "wood carpet" floors (bottom right) could also be bought in strips by the yard.

The most common floors throughout the 19th century were plain, unfinished, bleached pine boards. From the mid-century, darker stained and polished floors gained in popularity. As the century progressed, these softwood floors were often treated as sub-floors for decorative coverings, such as parquet.

Most home owners chose the flooring that best suited specific rooms. Thus, tiles were used for entrance halls because they were durable and decorative, while pile carpets were kept for the best rooms of a house.

Early in the period carpets in Rococo and stylized naturalistic designs were favoured. Oriental motifs were later preferred. Critics, however, argued for subtler designs that would set off walls and furniture, and by the end of the century pile carpets could be had in solid colours. Straw, coconut or cloth matting was used in most houses. Mats dressed up houses in summer, when rugs were taken up, and in more modest houses served all year round in place of carpets. They were used in bedrooms by all classes.

Floorcloths continued in use, especially in halls and kitchens. A newer option was linoleum (introduced c.1860) – a mixture of ground cork, ground wood and linseed oil laid on burlap or canvas backing. The well-to-do installed it in service areas, while poorer people used linoleum to imitate carpets and hardwoods.

① A fireplace hearth of glazed tiles, set into the plain boards that were standard for the Victorian house. Glazed tiles

with relief decoration were made in American factories from the 1870s. HA

② Durable encaustic tiles, of

inlaid earthenware, usually decorated with geometric designs based on their Romanesque prototypes, were

popular in all styles of houses. There were two major encaustic tile companies based at Zanesville, Ohio. GW

③ and ④ Two fine parquetry floors, in light and dark woods. NA

⑤ A square of patterned oilcloth, on which a stove would stand.

⑥ and ⑦ In 1839 Erastus B. Bigelow, based in Clinton, Massachusetts, patented power-driven looms for the manufacture of ingrain carpets, and during the 1850s he

developed similar technology for Brussels carpets. The centre of American carpet production shifted from Philadelphia to New England. Organic designs were most fashionable from the

1840s to the 1860s. Later, Oriental carpets enjoyed a vogue, and "Persians" were made by all the major American manufacturers of the 1880s.

⑥ An American Wilton carpet typifying the taste of the last quarter of the 19th century. (A reproduction by Scalamandré.) SCA

⑦ This detail of a naturalistic carpet owes much to the influence of French designs.

Fireplaces

Many late Victorian fireplaces had built-in cupboards, but this one, with its wealth of gilding and intricate carpentry, is exceptionally ornate. An effective feature of the design is the contrasting plain marble slip. Mary Gay Humphreys, the prolific writer on household taste, wrote: "The fireplace is really the domestic altar, the true rallying point of the household." SAL

Heating was an important issue for 19th-century Americans: surviving the winter in a wood house in a climate more severe than Europe's was a major conversational topic. Even after the fireplace was made technically obsolete by the widespread use of the stove and by central heating, it retained a symbolic and decorative importance. Stoves eliminated draughts, and thus made rooms seem stuffy, and therefore, to some critics, unhealthy. Moreover, an open fire was a sign of wealth, as it was more expensive to fuel than a stove, and implied servants to tend it. So the fireplace was not readily abandoned.

The most stylish fireplaces of the mid-century were Rococo Revival models in marble and Renaissance Revival designs with incised decoration on marble or wood. Later fireplaces followed Arts and Crafts models. Neo-classical types were reintroduced with Shingle-style houses.

Fireplaces held pride of place in the living halls of later Victorian houses, evoking the medieval spirit that architects tried so hard to foster. The seductive notion of the cosy hearth and the open fire was strengthened in some rooms by the addition of overmantels and robust combinations of display shelves, seats, decorative panels and works of art, making a complex ensemble that served as a focal point for the room.

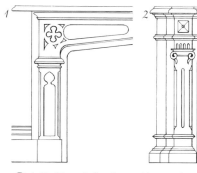

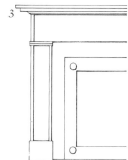

① A Gothic-style fireplace, with typical quatrefoil corners. The angle at which the arch is sloped is also characteristic.
② Three Renaissance Revival examples, with typical decorative details. The first is illustrated in Cummings' Architectural Details, published in New York in 1873. The second dates from 1869. The last of the

three, dating from the same period, is from a parlour in Batavia, New York.
③ Stone fireplaces of marble or slate were the first choice for the well-to-do. Simpler

houses could have plain stone surrounds of almost Neo-classical severity, like the example illustrated here, which is from a parlour of the 1860s.

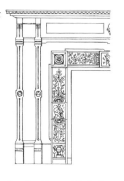

④ An elaborate slate fireplace, advertised by T.B. Stewart and Company of New York.
⑤ This fireplace features a slip of decorative tiles imported from the British firm Minton's.

⑥ A Queen Anne fireplace in pine featuring a pulvinated (convex) frieze.
⑦ A wooden chimneypiece from a late Victorian house. The tiles, in relief, depict hunting scenes. The grate has a cover for use in the summer. HA

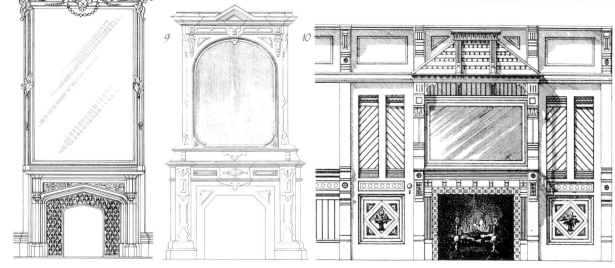

⑧ The pairing of a fireplace with an overmantel mirror was an 18th-century idea that became readily affordable after the 1850s. The combination of fireplace and mirror featured in every Victorian revival style except Shingle. This is a Gothic Revival

example of the 1850s; the mirror is framed by gilded wood.
⑨ An Italianate-style fireplace with overmantel mirror. From Woodward's National Architect, 1869. WD
⑩ An ambitious fireplace, with overmantel

mirror, designed for the hall of an opulent house in the Stick or Queen Anne style, 1880s. To the left is a closet door, to the right, a solid wood panel, matching the closet door in every detail except the handle and keyhole escutcheon plate. CK

① *Pattern books of the period illustrate richly bracketed overmantel fireplaces like this one. The vast mirror spread the lighting.* GW

② *Plain fireplaces, of almost Grecian simplicity, were produced throughout the period in wood, slate and marble. This is a marble example, dating from c.1850.* GE

③ *A grand overmantel fireplace, integral with wooden panelling of the room. Four small rectangular panels along the frieze illustrate polychrome scenes of chariots and other antiquarian motifs. Note the tiled hearth, in a checked pattern.* NA

④ *A Renaissance Revival fireplace with an overmantel mirror in a typical style. The flanking double columns and entablature*

produce an effect of grandeur. An unusual feature is the dogs' heads in the spandrels of the arched recess. NA

⑤ *Decorative tiles contrast with a wooden surround in this fireplace of the 1870s. On many such fireplaces the tiles would be pictorial, each one representing a different scene, as here. Fender benches like this were uncommon in 19th-century American houses.* GW

⑥ *An especially elaborate example of a Rococo Revival fireplace, suitable for an Italianate house. Simpler versions were more common: many were imported from Europe, although some were also made in the United States.* BO

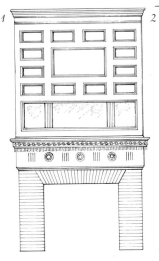

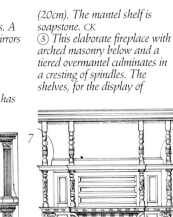

① *A typical Queen Anne fireplace of the 1870s or 80s. A wooden overmantel, with mirrors and a space for a picture, surmounts the glazed brick surround.*
② *Another Queen Anne fireplace, 1881. The alcove has a recess depth of 8 inches*
(20cm). *The mantel shelf is soapstone.* CK
③ *This elaborate fireplace with arched masonry below and a tiered overmantel culminates in a cresting of spindles. The shelves, for the display of* ornaments, *are a typical feature of the later Victorian period.*
④ *Reflecting the taste of the American Queen Anne style, this grand fireplace combines a glazed display cabinet, mirrors and shelves, with an elegant spindled gallery surmounting the composition.*

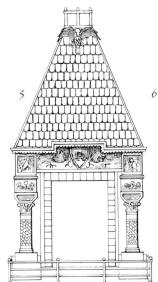

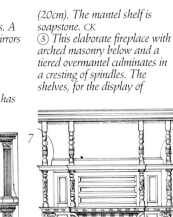

⑤ *Designed to dwarf the onlooker: a gargantuan fireplace dating from the 1870s. The Romanesque columns support an elaborate shingled hood.*
⑥ *A more refined fireplace of the 1870s or 80s, with Neo-classical swags, acanthus leaves and other motifs, and an urn above the overmantel mirror.*
⑦ *The generous display shelves on this example owe much to the Arts and Crafts movement.*
⑧ *A simpler, Arts and Crafts-inspired fireplace, 1881: a reinterpretation of earlier designs.*
⑨ *A fireplace heater of the 1880s. Its openwork domed top could be removed and replaced with a tin plate, upon which kettles could be boiled.*

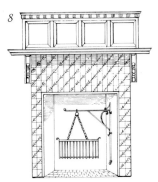

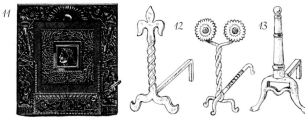

⑩ *Another fireplace heater, manufactured by Floyd, Wells and Company, Royersford, Pennsylvania, and illustrated in their catalogue of c.1900. It went under the trade name "Grand Social" and came in three sizes. As an alternative to the plain iron version, it was sold with nickel plates set in the sides and a nickel plate across the top. The sliding fire doors, when pushed back, convert the stove to an open grate.* FL
⑪ *An ornately ornamented fireplace heater, with a classical head design in the central cartouche.*
⑫ *Two designs for iron andirons, both dating from the 1880s, showing Arts and Crafts and Aesthetic influences.*
⑬ *A Colonial Revival-style andiron.*

Kitchen stoves

① *A built-in range, 1870s. Few survive in the United States, perhaps because they were more expensive to install and difficult to accommodate when buildings were modernized. Trade catalogues tend to show built-in and freestanding stoves in equal numbers.*

② *A sophisticated though cumbersome stove of the 1870s, used not only for cooking but also to heat water. The hood over the stove is a typical feature.*
③ *In 1902 Sears, Roebuck and Company offered this Acme American Range with the latest Rococo-style mouldings. Made of cast iron with nickel hinges and knobs, it has a tin-lined oven door and a porcelain-lined reservoir, or warming cabinet. It was suitable for burning hard or soft coal, or wood. By this period gas stoves were also very popular: they tended to be box-shaped, with two or four top burners. Some models had a tank for heating water.*
④ *Earlier Victorian stoves like this one of 1867 had less surface decoration, merely providing a flat cooking surface over a fire box.*

FIREPLACES

KITCHEN STOVES

By the mid-19th century the cooking range had been adopted into the American kitchen. Hearth cookery was becoming a lost art. However, acceptance of the cooking stove was hesitant, as the temperatures were at first difficult to gauge. Early Victorian designs followed early 19th-century prototypes: simple raised fire boxes with a flat cooking top next to a side oven. Mid-century improvements are documented in the 1869 edition of Beecher and Stowe's *American Woman's Home*, which describes a range that kept 17 gallons (64 litres) of water hot at all times, baked pies and puddings in a warm closet, heated flat irons under the back cover, boiled a tea-kettle and a pot under its front cover, baked

bread in the oven and cooked a turkey in the tin roaster, as well as providing a flat surface for cooking in pans.

By the 1880s gas stoves were being widely used. Together with oil stoves, they were recommended for hot weather cookery, as they needed to be lit only during the cooking period. Fuel costs made extended use of gas stoves expensive.

More decorative attention was given to stoves as the century progressed. Models began to mirror furniture design, featuring motifs such as Queen Anne legs and Rococo Revival cartouches. These decorations can be viewed as an attempt to make the new stove technology familiar to the homemaker.

Staircases

A grand panelled staircase from a Shingle-style house in Newport, Rhode Island. A sober design, with fine carpentry: much depends on the grain of the wood. SAL

Much was done, particularly late in the 19th century, to exploit the architectural and decorative value of stairs. Until the mid-century central stair halls were typical. This changed with the freedom in planning introduced with the Gothic and Italianate Revivals. Stairs were located asymmetrically near the front door and usually near the principal parlour. Gothic and Italianate stairs tend to be a single flight from floor to floor. The balusters were complex, round turnings and the newels were turned, faceted and chamfered. In simpler dwellings the newel could be the most elaborate piece of woodwork in the house.

With the adoption of combination living spaces and stair halls late in the period, stairs became the focus of further experiments, and more elaborate series of flights and landings were contrived. Often the principal landing between the entrance floor and the floor above featured a stained-glass window. The richest windows were pictorial, while the more modest ones were geometric. Stair halls were regularly lit by skylights, either with plain glazing or stair glass, sometimes with elaborate designs.

Carpet was the preferred stair covering, but floor cloths and matting were also used. Brass was a popular material for the stair rods, but iron and even, occasionally, silver are also found.

1 *A Gothic oak staircase of the mid-19th century. The solid chamfered newel and the tracery design of the balustrade are typical.*
2 *This staircase of the same period is in the Italianate style. Note the turned balusters and the more elaborate form of the newel post.*
3 *The newel in this example of the 1870s has a carved foliate design echoed in the balusters. The stair-ends have moulded decoration.*
4 *This staircase, in the Italianate style, dates from the 1870s.* BI
5 *An Italianate baluster-shaped newel, with ribbed base. The balusters themselves would echo the newel, in miniature. From Woodward's National Architect, 1869.* WD
6 *A staircase from a Shingle house, 1881.* CK
7 *Two newel designs, 1881, suitable for Queen Anne houses.*

8 *This Queen Anne design of the 1870s shows alternative treatments for cut-out designs.*
9 *Drops, or pendants, sometimes added interest to the underside of the staircase.* CK
10 *Exotic motifs, such as Islamic arches, were reserved for the grander houses.*
11 *A typical Italianate staircase with a single flight between stories, c.1870. The wainscotting that follows the line of the stair was sold in flexible strips.*
12 *Newel posts with a turned knob and facetted shaft were popular from the 1850s into the 1870s.* WT
13 *The Queen Anne staircase with stained glass in the landing window was a typical formula. Newel posts frequently featured a rosette motif.*

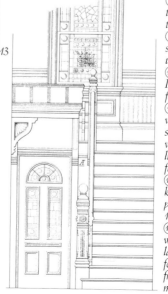

STAIRCASES

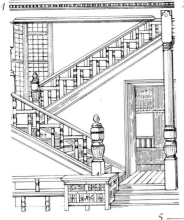

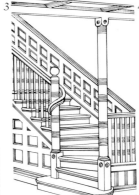

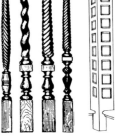

① *Architects of the Queen Anne, Richardsonian Romanesque and Shingle styles experimented with the length of flights and the number of landings. This example is from a combined staircase and living hall. The landing continues a little way to the left (not shown), forming a gallery from which to look down into the room or admire the view through the tall leaded windows.*

② *Another living hall staircase, with well-placed bench, 1880s. CK*

③ *This staircase, of the same period, turns to make room for a fireplace. CK*

④ *A staircase with carved Neo-classical decoration, including swags, festoons and scrolls.*

⑤ *A "woven" balustrade, Shingle style, c.1880.*

⑥ *Enormous drops (pendants)*

combine with a foliate balustrade in this carved Gothic stair.

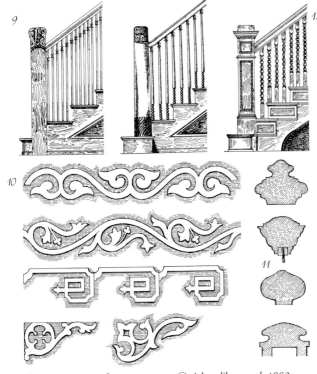

⑦ *Victorian manufacturers produced balusters based on 18th-century originals. These ones are c.1900. UD*

⑧ *A box-like newel, 1880s.*
⑨ *Three designs of 1903. UD*
⑩ *String decoration, 1903, showing the elaboration of the*

millworker's art. Available in yellow pine or oak. UD
⑪ *Typical handrail profiles, late 19th century.*

⑫ *Later Victorian stairs tend to have more square elements and to be heavier in scale. This example is from the 1880s. HA*

Built-in furniture

① A superbly panelled library from a house in the Queen Anne style. The glazed cabinets are inventively integrated into simple bookshelves. The gilded glazing bars, mouldings and pediments and the contrasting green painted woodwork are authentic. SAL
② This bookcase of the 1870s has Gothic carved detailing – for example, quatrefoils in the spandrels of the arches. The Gothic style was thought to be particularly appropriate for libraries. GW
③ This built-in pedimented china cabinet in the alcove formed between a fireplace and a wall has subtle gilding on the drawers and on the vertical mouldings at the sides. HA

Although freestanding furniture remained the more popular option, many Americans turned to built-in furniture in the last decades of the 19th century. Revival-style houses provided plenty of opportunities.

Closets became common in the 1870s, as people acquired more clothing than could be stored in chests and armoires. The number of books published in the United States also multiplied, and accordingly libraries with permanent shelves became common features in middle-class houses, while continuing to be built on an increasingly grand scale by the rich.

The introduction of the combined living and stair hall created ideal spaces for settles, below stairs and on landings. Also below stairs, or at the end of a range of public rooms, were Turkish or "cozy corners": luxuriously cushioned exotic spaces that played to the Victorian need for domestic sanctuary from the industrialized world. Benches and inglenooks were built to flank fireplaces. Window seats were popular in Shingle and Colonial Revival houses.

Most American kitchens housed only freestanding components, with the exception of some fixed sink enclosures. However, later in the century, built-in cabinets and appliances began to appear in kitchens, as well as in the pantries and sewing rooms of larger houses.

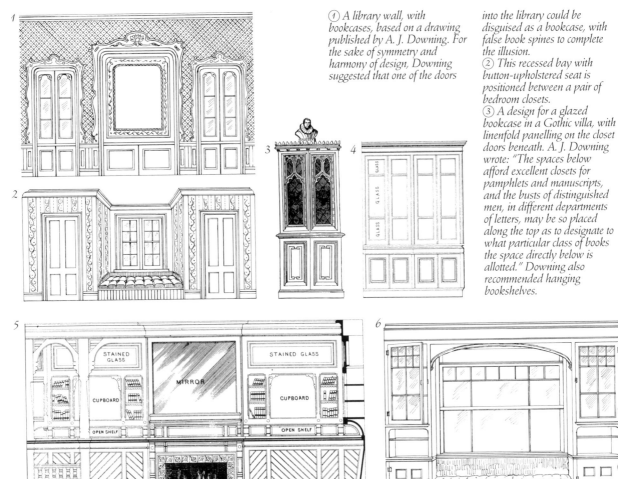

① *A library wall, with bookcases, based on a drawing published by A. J. Downing. For the sake of symmetry and harmony of design, Downing suggested that one of the doors* into the library could be disguised as a bookcase, with false book spines to complete the illusion.

② *This recessed bay with button-upholstered seat is positioned between a pair of bedroom closets.*

③ *A design for a glazed bookcase in a Gothic villa, with linenfold panelling on the closet doors beneath. A. J. Downing wrote: "The spaces below afford excellent closets for pamphlets and manuscripts, and the busts of distinguished men, in different departments of letters, may be so placed along the top as to designate to what particular class of books the space directly below is allotted." Downing also recommended hanging bookshelves.*

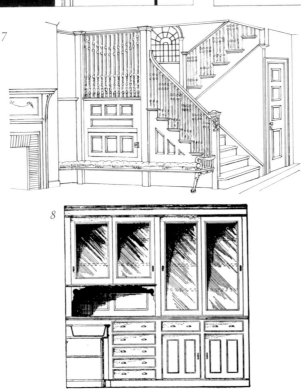

④ *A simple library bookcase. This could have been made any time between 1840 and 1900, but only for the well-to-do. Most Victorians kept books in freestanding furniture.* CK

⑤ *This Queen Anne wall design features an array of shelves and cupboards, all framing a fireplace overmantel. Intricacy of design was held to be a primary virtue.* CK

⑥ *A built-in settle with an arched canopy, and cupboards and shelving at either side. Suitable for a Shingle-style or Queen Anne house.*

⑦ *A staircase and built-in upholstered bench, with overtones of the Colonial Revival and Shingle styles. Note the typical window illuminating the landing at the turn in the stairs.*

⑧ *A built-in kitchen china closet, with an adjacent sink forming an L-shape. This example (1903) typifies late Victorian utility furniture with its simple panels and modest decorations.* RO

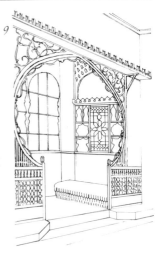

⑨ *An exotic, Moorish-type arch forms the entrance to a "cozy corner" with comfortable divans, on a half-stair landing. A hanging lamp and Oriental rugs were necessary parts of the overall effect. Such arrangements were a popular feature of the fashionable Victorian interior.*

Services

① *The early Victorian practice of enclosing plumbing fixtures in wooden cabinets built to match* the wainscot eventually acquired more fashionable overtones. *1888.* MOT

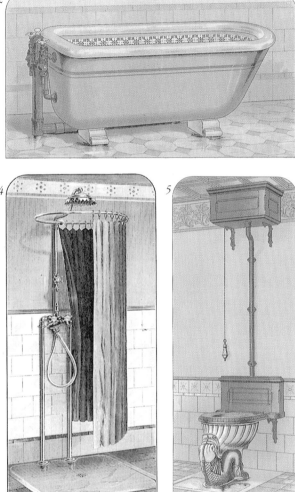

② *An Imperial porcelain bathtub with marble rim and legs, and inlaid around the rim with tiles. All-porcelain tubs were produced from the 1870s,* but they were expensive to transport and install. MOT
③ *A bathroom for those who preferred to dispense with cabinet work. It contains a* porcelain-lined bath and seat bath, and all-porcelain water closet. MOT
④ *Showers were introduced in the 1870s.* MOT

⑤ *Water closets could take on attractive forms such as this dolphin. The water tank above the seat was the standard design.* MOT

BUILT-IN FURNITURE

SERVICES

The first American bathrooms were installed in what had previously been storerooms or small bedrooms. Bathtubs, wash basins and water closets were not necessarily placed in the same room, or even close to each other. However, toward the turn of the century, architects began to designate specific spaces for bathrooms.

The first bathtubs affixed to the floor appeared at the time of the Civil War and were individually fabricated from sheet metal – lead, copper or zinc – encased in a wood frame. Painted iron baths stood several inches off the floor on feet cast in ball and claw shapes, or as scrolls with leaf patterns. The Mott Iron Works produced the first porcelain enamelled baths in 1873, and other manu-facturers such as Kohler followed suit. Porcelain had long been used for chamber pots, and was easily adapted for the fixed water closet, which at first was encased in a wooden box for concealment. From the 1830s inventors experimented with gravity-fed water systems which allowed for a sanitary flush. These devices were fully perfected in the 1890s, culminating in the self-washing bowl and siphon jet we use today.

The wooden roof gutters of the first half of the century were gradually replaced, first by cast iron and then by sheet-metal versions. Later Victorian house builders, following historic prototypes, sometimes used whimsical spouts and gargoyles to carry off rainwater.

① *An expensive washstand, in the "Eastlake" style, 1888. The marble top is set into a black* walnut, ash, cherry or ebonized cherry cabinet. MOT
② *An enamelled wash basin,* designed to fit into a corner, 1888. MOT
③ *A folding wash basin,* porcelain-lined, with bronzed, marbleized or painted exterior, 1888. MOT

④ *English ceramic basins with bands of decoration were imported. The less well-off used American-made versions in enamelled metal.* MOT
⑤ *The Victorian perfection of the metal tap/faucet made modern water systems possible.*
⑥ *A porcelain water closet with a self-raising seat.* MOT
⑦ *An all-porcelain bidet, 1888, in white or a subtle tint of ivory.* MOT
⑧ *Sinks with deep basins evolved from the wooden washtub.* MOT

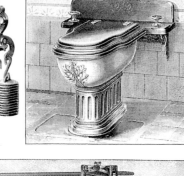

⑨ *The "Imperial" porcelain-lined washtub, with a wringer. The positioning of taps/faucets above the tub was an improvement on early designs, in which they were set inside.* MOT
⑩ *A slop sink, for emptying chamber pots, 1888.* MOT
⑪ *The "Rosemont" radiator (c.1898) (on the right), attached to an ornate heating stove.* FL
⑫ *The "pot belly" design became the classic 19th-century model for less formal rooms.* FL

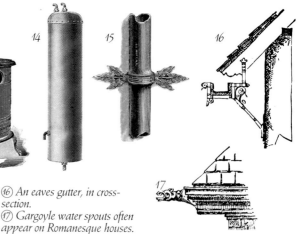

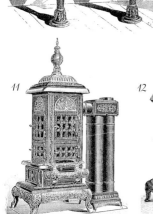

⑬ *A wood-burning stove, with side collar, c.1898.* FL
⑭ *A boiler, available in copper or galvanized iron.* MOT
⑮ *A detail of a cast-iron down pipe/downspout, with an ornamental bracket for fastening to the wall.* MOT
⑯ *An eaves gutter, in cross-section.*
⑰ *Gargoyle water spouts often appear on Romanesque houses.*

Lighting

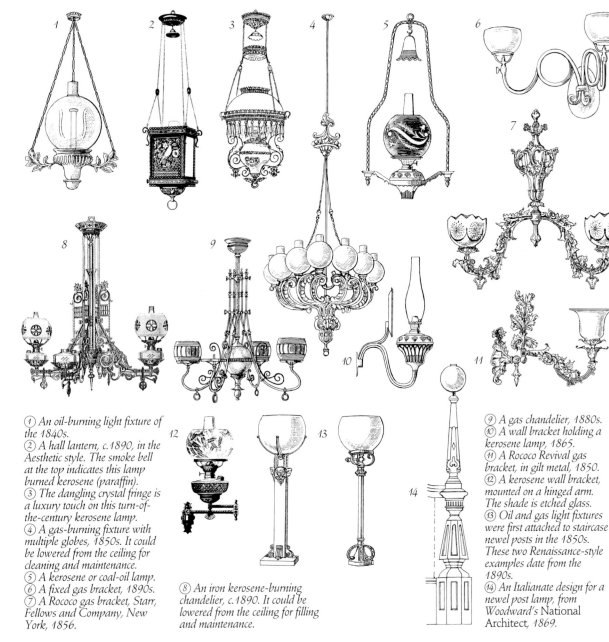

① An oil-burning light fixture of the 1840s.

② A hall lantern, c.1890, in the Aesthetic style. The smoke bell at the top indicates this lamp burned kerosene (paraffin).

③ The dangling crystal fringe is a luxury touch on this turn-of-the-century kerosene lamp.

④ A gas-burning fixture with multiple globes, 1850s. It could be lowered from the ceiling for cleaning and maintenance.

⑤ A kerosene or coal-oil lamp.

⑥ A fixed gas bracket, 1890s.

⑦ A Rococo gas bracket, Starr, Fellows and Company, New York, 1856.

⑧ An iron kerosene-burning chandelier, c.1890. It could be lowered from the ceiling for filling and maintenance.

⑨ A gas chandelier, 1880s.

⑩ A wall bracket holding a kerosene lamp, 1865.

⑪ A Rococo Revival gas bracket, in gilt metal, 1850.

⑫ A kerosene wall bracket, mounted on a hinged arm. The shade is etched glass.

⑬ Oil and gas light fixtures were first attached to staircase newel posts in the 1850s. These two Renaissance-style examples date from the 1890s.

⑭ An Italianate design for a newel post lamp, from Woodward's National Architect, 1869.

Between c.1850 and the century's end, life evolved dramatically from the sparing use of a modestly lit family room to a more general and constant form of illumination. This change was accomplished by combined use of candles, oil lamps, kerosene (paraffin) and, ultimately, electricity.

The most advanced lighting by 1850 was still gravity-fed oil and fluid-burning lamps. Popular in Gothic and Italianate interiors, they were improved by means of new burners and chimney designs. This type was superseded by gas light; shades and scrubbers made the light gentler and minimized the smell.

Kerosene, perfected in the 1850s, did not require installation of the complex and costly piping needed for gas. Also, kerosene fixtures could be moved for specific tasks. Gas, however, continued to be popular, as it did not require manual refilling of fixtures, and burned cleaner than kerosene. The use of kerosene with piped gas and, eventually, electricity provided a fail-safe for convenient but sometimes unreliable lighting systems.

The Edison system of electric lighting included an inexpensive carbon-filament lamp which gave a pleasant light and could be turned on and off like a gas jet. But as electricity became popular with the late Victorians, at the same time flattering candlelight gained renewed favour for evening entertainments.

SERVICES

LIGHTING

Metalwork

① A detail of an ironwork veranda-cresting, from the Hale House, Heritage Square, Los Angeles. HA
② This New York terraced/row house has especially fine cast-iron work, in the robust style that is typical of the period. The railings delineate a private area in front of the main facade. Cast iron often acquires a patina, which inhibits rust; it has a pleasing grainy quality, caused by the coarse sand employed in the mould, although this is often covered by successive repaintings. KT
③ A simple, functional cast-iron gate with spear-heads and spiked balls. A ubiquitous design. WT
④ Sheet-metal cornices, such as this one, are a common feature of Victorian facades in New York and other American cities. KT

Mass-produced metalwares were an everyday aspect of American Victorian life. Everything from nails to decorative finials could be made in factories by casting, and roller and extrusion processes, rather than at a hand forge. This factory-made metal-work was of high quality, richer in detail and in most cases less expensive than its early American prototypes.

By mid-century manufacturers had perfected the casting of hardware by the "lost wax" process. This was a boon to builders, as it meant that many pieces of door furniture/hardware that previously had to be handmade could now be cast with decorative designs. A range of metals was used, from inexpensive white metal to brass and bronze.

The increased use of decorative sheet metal is evidenced by sheet-metal cornices on town houses built in the second half of the 19th century. Sheet metal was also popular for weather vanes – one of the most inventive aspects of American building decoration. Designs ranged from simple directional arrows to cod fish and running deer.

At the end of the century, blacksmith work was revived as part of the nostalgia for Colonial designs. A particular highlight of the period is the decorative crestings used on Second Empire and Queen Anne houses.

① Decorative railings for balconies were made in an infinite variety of designs. They were used throughout the country, although iron balconies are most usually associated with the South. This example is from New York, and dates from the 1850s. The pendant ironwork decoration at the upper levels helps to unify the design.

② Cast-iron columns support a wire railing veranda. The wire used is of ¼-inch (0.6cm) thickness. The columns could be dispensed with, and brackets substituted, provided that the veranda did not extend too far from the exterior wall of the house. Verandas of this design could also be used at ground level, in which case the columns would not be necessary.

③ An ironwork stoop, from an 1857 catalogue. This example has a sober gravity, but more florid Rococo Revival designs were also popular at this period.

④ Cast-iron grilles like this were unusual on all but the fanciest Gothic-style Victorian houses. Cast-iron gates were more common.

⑤ Metal heating vents such as these became necessary when central heating was introduced in the 1830s. These designs date from the 1870s.

⑥ Metal urns and vases were used as garden ornaments, but could also be employed as finials to gate piers.

⑦ to ⑩ In the 1870s and 80s, wrought- and cast-iron garden railings grew in popularity.

⑪ A Gothic-style finial, suitable as roof decoration.

⑫ The motif of the galloping horse was a particularly popular weather vane design for the roofs of carriage houses and stables.

⑬ The complexity of Second Empire and Queen Anne houses was enhanced, at the roofline, by metal crestings and finials. The finial pictured here has a pennant at its tip, serving as a weather vane.

⑭ A profile and face-on view of a flower-shaped finial.

⑮ An iron finial with pennant, 1880s.

⑯ Iron roof crestings, from the 1870s. Second Empire houses often have such crestings arranged in a square on top of a tower with a steep mansard roof. The first of these two designs was produced by J.W. Fiske of New York, the second by the Phoenix Iron Works, San Francisco.

Woodwork

Woodwork was an essential medium for conveying the essence of a particular style, as demonstrated by all five examples on this page.
① *Octagonal houses were built in all the mid-century styles. Many have minimal ornamental detailing, but the encircling veranda could be ornate. This Oriental version was designed by the Philadelphia architect Samuel Sloan.*

② *A literal interpretation of the English half-timbered tradition which was very important to the American Victorian styles, particularly the Stick style. The last is characterized by patterns of vertical, horizontal and diagonal boards which make a highly decorative effect. Structural elements such as corner posts, brackets and railings tend to be large on Stick-style houses and without the elaborate ornamentation found on, for example, Queen Anne houses.* NA

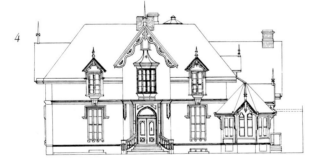

③ *Colonial Revival houses, like this one from Santa Monica, California, were built in great numbers from c.1890 to c.1910.*
④ *Wavy-edged bargeboards (vergeboards) on gables and dormers denote the Gothic Revival. Note how the finials complete the composition.*
⑤ *A variant of the Stick style, with wooden struts forming a decorative lattice beneath the deeply overhanging gabled eaves.*

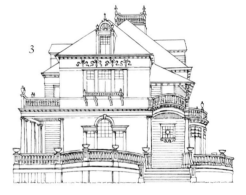

Many American houses in the period relied exclusively on woodwork for their rich decoration. Spectacular facades testify to an infinite number of decorative permutations. Most Gothic elements were carpenter-made. In the Queen Anne and Stick styles, millwork runs riot as a rich assortment of prefabricated items. Sometimes woodwork was patterned after European masonry prototypes.

Such elaboration was possible because of the abundance of wood in the United States and the development of specialized mills throughout the country. Firms offered scores of options, and there was infinite choice within the confines of the prevailing styles.

The role of decorative woodwork can be seen in the development of porches and verandas (piazzas). Because these were highly visible, appended features, their ornamentation was especially lavish. The posts could be elaborately turned or chamfered, there was space for repeated brackets, and the balustrade lent itself to further turnings or even pierced decorations, such as moon and stars motifs.

The richness of woodwork was highlighted by carefully conceived paint schemes. At least three colours were recommended for the exterior, and often many more (up to seven for Queen Anne). Shingle houses often used stained wood, with painted trim.

① In the Gothic Revival and Queen Anne styles, gables and dormer windows typically have bargeboards (vergeboards) and spire-like finials. Often finials continue to form a pendant.
② A gable ornament, 1873. CG
③ A Gothic bargeboard suitable for a porch gable on a cottage, 1873; also popular earlier. AJD
④ An array of different shingle shapes (6 inches/15cm wide). Often the shingles would be restricted to the upper levels of the house, with plain clapboarding below.
⑤ A wing-like sunburst bracket was a popular applied motif.

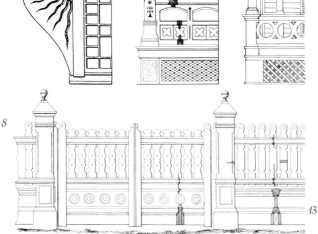

⑫ Spindles along the eaves of a rich veranda echo the balustrade of this 1880s house in New York. The architectural critic A.J. Downing wrote of verandas: "The unclouded splendor and fierce heat of our summer sun render this very general appendage a source of real comfort and enjoyment". JBE
⑬ An elaborate scrolled gable on a Queen Anne house, Los Angeles, 1894. Fanciful woodwork of this character is found on many West Coast Victorian houses. JBE

⑥ A piazza, or veranda, with incised, sawn and turned decoration, 1881. CK
⑦ Another piazza design, of about the same period.
⑧ An attractive double gate. In the Queen Anne style, the straight sawn boards and simple turnings of earlier idioms gave way to more complex designs. CK

⑨ A fence with relatively simple cut-out motifs. CK
⑩ Two decorative wooden door panels, 1881. CK
⑪ An example of interior woodwork: a screen used to make an arch in hallways, or to frame a "cozy corner", 1880-1910. Spindled and Moorish designs were also available.

ARTS AND CRAFTS

1860–1925

① *The Barn in Exmouth, Devon, England, c.1900, combines traditional materials – sandstone, pebbles, oak and thatch – with romanticized forms – the mighty chimneys and the welcoming "butterfly" wings.* S
② *The ground floor plan of a similar house.* HG
③ *The entrance floor plan of a typical American Craftsman house, 1907. Note the generous size of the main rooms, the built-in furniture and the inclusion of a porch (to encourage outdoor pursuits).*
④ *The Gamble House, Pasadena, California, 1908-9, is a masterpiece by Charles and Henry Greene.* GG

The Arts and Crafts movement sought, in the face of the grim industrialization of the 19th century, to create new and more beautiful environments in which people might live and delight in fine craftsmanship wrought with intrinsically attractive building materials.

The English critic John Ruskin (1819-1900) directed attention to the qualities of medieval architecture, holding up as models the members of craft guilds and the builders of the great cathedrals. A whole generation of artists and designers was influenced by Ruskin. Among them, William Morris (1834-96), who is most closely associated with the Arts and Crafts movement, took to heart Ruskin's pleas for honesty of materials and craftsmanship. The Red House, built for Morris in Bexleyheath, near London, in 1859, is the starting point of the new style. Its architect, Philip Webb (1831-1915), turned from the High Victorian Gothic style to a simpler vernacular architecture based on old English cottages and farmhouses. Webb built few houses, yet he influenced a whole group of younger architects working in the late 1890s.

By contrast, Webb's contemporary, Richard Norman Shaw (1831-1912), built many houses and created, almost single-handed, the influential British Queen Anne style, characterized by tile-hung facades, overhanging eaves and horizontal bands of leaded windows. He later called upon the work of Sir Christopher Wren and the detailing of 17th-century Flemish town houses to give his houses a more classical feeling. Shaw designed several small villas in the late 1870s for a new "artistic" suburb of west London called Bedford Park. The basic elements of red brick, white woodwork and features such as porches and oriel windows were rapidly adopted by commercial developers and used into the 1920s.

The Queen Anne style proved enormously influential in the United States, where it dominated architectural debate and practice from the 1870s. Shaw's style was given two very distinctive American features: an extensive use of wood, for shingle cladding, verandas and decorative facade details, and novel, informal planning. The latter is seen in the work of Henry Hobson Richardson (1838-86). Queen Anne features appear in Tuxedo Park, New York, built from 1885 and grander by far than Bedford Park.

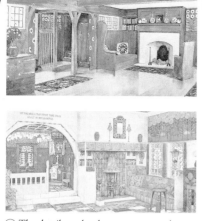

① *The details and palettes – one muted, one painted in light, limited colours – of these two room designs by M.H. Baillie Scott are typical of the best British Arts and Crafts interiors of the 1890s.* HG
② *The staircase in the Gamble House, Pasadena, California, 1908-9, epitomizes the beautiful crafted forms conceived by Charles and Henry Greene. Note the built-in settle, a popular feature of living halls.* GG

In general terms, the influence of early English prototypes on the masses and detailing of American Arts and Crafts houses was tempered by the impact of the traditional domestic building of Japan. The integrated interior spaces and the horizontality of Japanese houses strongly influenced Frank Lloyd Wright (1869-1959).

The tone of the Arts and Crafts interior was set by William Morris. In 1861 he founded Morris and Company which produced furniture, carpets, wallpapers and textiles. Everything was made to the highest standards and, where possible, using traditional methods and materials. For example, the original Morris wallpapers, with their floral and Gothicized designs, were printed from woodblocks, using natural dyes. (Confusingly, another, more commercialized firm called William Morris and Company also traded from London, owned by a namesake of the great designer and manufacturing Arts and Crafts metalwork.)

From the 1870s, Arts and Crafts interiors were increasingly influenced by the allied crusade in taste and decoration called the Aesthetic movement. Beauty and craftsmanship were central tenets, as they were to Arts and Crafts principles, but an interest in exotic styles and forms and the wealth of the patrons gave the Aesthetic movement a more sophisticated quality. There were two major phases to the movement. Interiors of the 1860s and 70s use rich soft colours and dense patterning which complement the contemporary Pre-Raphaelite school of painting. Oriental china, much in vogue among discriminating collectors, was displayed in abundance. By the 1880s this style had come to seem cluttered and a greater simplicity appears in the work of Shaw in England, and Sullivan and Stanford White (1853-1906) in the United States. White walls and ceilings give a sense of space to rooms which, especially in the United States, look to the East for inspiration.

The transition from the early to the later Arts and Crafts style may be seen in the work of the American architect Wilson Eyre (1858-1944), who favoured vernacular forms and open planning. He was much admired by the younger generation of British practitioners, such as C.F.A. Voysey (1857-1941) and M.H. Baillie Scott (1865-1945). Voysey's long low houses have simple forms, relieved by pleasing details such as his characteristic heart motif. British architects now worked for a new kind of client, the modest but prosperous businessman or professional who wanted something between the vaunting country house and the simple suburban houses of Bedford Park. Such patrons were encouraged in their tastes by the English periodical, *The Studio*, first published in 1893 and influential on both sides of the Atlantic.

The most important figure of the later British Arts and Crafts movement is Sir Edwin Lutyens (1869-1944), who could juggle with a few simple elements to achieve a strikingly original effect. His early houses rely upon half-timbering, but later he turned to the classical vocabulary, preferring the established traditions to the increasingly abstract experiments of his contemporaries. Late Arts and Crafts in the United States found a different path, one which referred back to first principles, but expressed them in a more modern idiom. Gustav Stickley, through his publication *The Craftsman* (1901-16), promoted a holistic view of living, whereby the house worked as a harmonious unit. Craftsmanship was used to reveal the qualities of natural materials. Charles and Henry Greene (1868-1957, 1870-1954), who worked as Greene and Greene in California, produced the finest Craftsman houses, employing beautiful woods and the best joinery in spacious houses. In their quest for the ideal living space, it is possible to trace a line from Richardson, to Greene and Greene and to the greatest American architect of the 20th century, Frank Lloyd Wright.

Doors

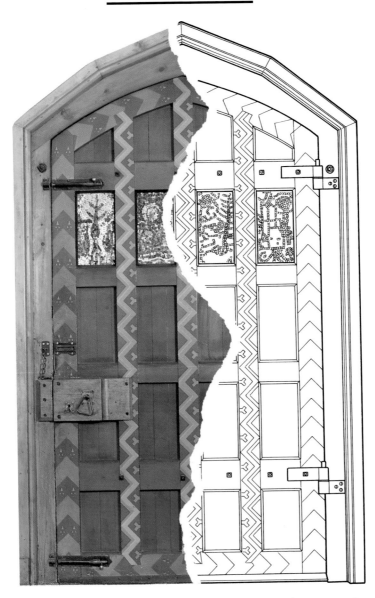

The inside of the front door of the Red House, Bexleyheath, near London, 1859. The house was the first commission of

Philip Webb, built for his close friend William Morris. The two men shared the ideals of fine, uncluttered craftsmanship,

based on historical and vernacular precedents. This sturdy door is reminiscent of medieval forms, but the

decorative chevrons and stylized stained glass are highly contemporary, striking embellishments. RH

The search for purer architectural forms drew designers to historical sources for their doors. Early Arts and Crafts doors, both external and internal, are often of plain plank construction, inspired by English medieval forms. These were usually fitted with elaborate iron hinges and a latch rather than a knob or handle. Another inspiration was the Georgian six-panelled door, although the proportions tend to be subtly altered.

As the entrance symbolized the welcome of the house, porches were an important feature of Arts and Crafts houses, particularly in later designs which look to vernacular precedents and often incorporate seats. C.F.A. Voysey, in Britain, developed an idiosyncratic form of

interior and outside door in the late 19th century in which three elongated panels are set beneath a glazed panel. This was much imitated and became the standard American Craftsman door of the early 20th century.

Grand Aesthetic Movement interior doorways of the 1880s had intricate carvings or painted door panels. The latter were very influential, and many standard Victorian four-panel doors were enhanced with painted or papered "Aesthetic" decoration: flowing floral and bird designs were most popular.

Leaded and stained glass were fashionable in both British and American doors. Some later designs show Art Nouveau influence, frowned upon by many architects.

① The plain plank door, with glazed panels above, derives from a design by C.F.A. Voysey. It became a typical feature of Arts and Crafts houses.

② A heavy carved front door that draws upon elements of Spanish design. London.

③ This doorway from the Henry Osborne Havemeyer house, New York, 1890-91, is sumptuously glazed with Tiffany glass. Such work is at the height of Arts and Crafts taste, in which Renaissance prototypes are as prevalent as traditional vernacular models.

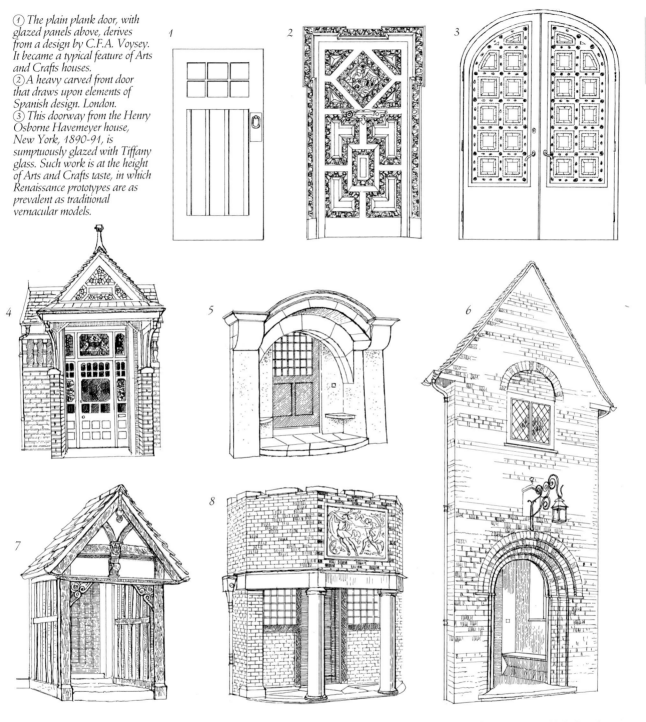

④ Glazed doors in the Queen Anne taste are typical of suburban houses throughout Britain. This porch displays the fancy white woodwork that is typical of the style, in both Britain and the United States.

⑤ This door by C.F.A. Voysey, c.1908, has a deeply recessed porch with built-in seating. The large simple forms are typical of the architect's style.

⑥ and ⑦ The influence of "Old English" models on Arts and Crafts architecture is seen in these two porches from large houses. The first incorporates a room above the entrance. It was designed by the architects Baillie Scott and Beresford for a house in Kent, 1927. The second, half-timbered example is from 1904.

⑧ This porch, published in The Studio in 1903, is an imposing feature on the facade of a large house. Built of brick, it incorporates a decorative stone relief and piers.

⑨ Elegant carved panels on and over doors are found in the most luxurious designs. This overdoor and door panel by Louis H. Sullivan feature spiked and curled foliate motifs, hallmarks of some of his best decorative work. Both details come from Chicago houses of the mid-1880s.

① *The front door of Olana, New York, the house of the artist Frederic Church, is enriched with a frame of Islamic decoration. Oriental influences were strong in Aesthetic movement taste. The window surmounting the doorcase creates a typically idiosyncratic composition, which aims to achieve an "artistic" effect.* O

② *The glazed upper panels of this front door in Bedford Park, west London, c.1880, are characteristic of the Queen Anne style introduced by Richard Norman Shaw.*

⑤ *The beautiful triple entrance doors at the Gamble House take stained and leaded glass to its ultimate expression: the sprawling oak tree encompasses the whole group and stretches into the transom lights. Charles Greene's design was executed in Tiffany Studios glass by Emile Lange.* GG

⑥ *These painted double doors are a fine example of Aesthetic work of the late 1880s.* O

⑦ *A false fanlight in Hampstead Garden Suburb, London, designed by Sir Edwin Lutyens, c.1910. The form is an imaginative interpretation of Queen Anne precedents.*

⑧ *A detail of a door in the East Parlour at Olana (1880s), showing the freehand and stencilled paintwork and the decorative door knob and escutcheon plate.* O

⑨ *A robust strap hinge of the 1860s. Medieval-type fittings were fashionable features of early Arts and Crafts doors.* CR

③ *This remarkable interior door from the Gamble House, California, 1908-9, makes great play of glass. It exhibits the traits of incipient Modernism in the dynamic balance of wide and narrow vertical elements.* GG

④ *This weighty door from The Debenham House, London, 1890s, shows a different, more traditional use of glass. The bright blue stained glass echoes the William de Morgan wall tiles. Note the great brass fingerplate/push plate.* DB

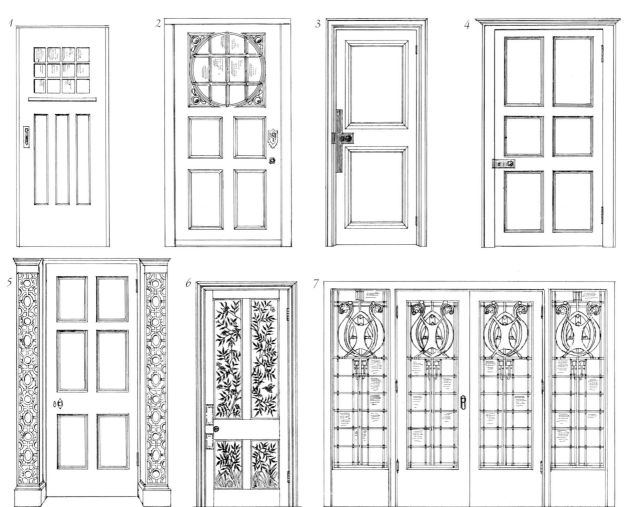

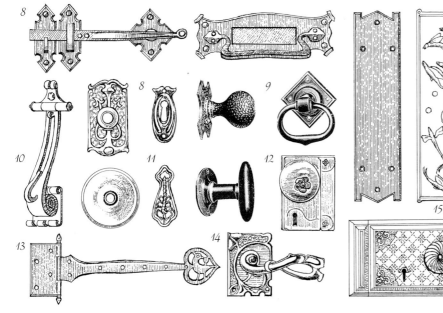

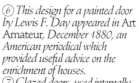

① and ② *Panelled and glazed doors. The first example recalls the designs of Voysey. The second, more elaborate design is from The Longcroft, Helensburgh, Scotland.*
③ *and* ④ *Two- and six-panelled doors were Queen Anne Revival*
forms. *The proportions of the second example, with the emphasis on width, identify it as a 19th-century fixture.*
⑤ *Surrounds could be richly carved, as in this doorway from Kensington Court, London, 1897.*
⑥ *This design for a painted door by Lewis F. Day appeared in* Art Amateur, *December 1880, an American periodical which provided useful advice on the enrichment of houses.*
⑦ *Glazed doors, used internally,*
gave additional light and a sense of space to a house. This stylish group of four glazed panels (a double door with side lights) is from the living room of a house in Riverside, Illinois.
⑧ *A wide variety of mass-produced items was available through builders' suppliers catalogues. Wrought-iron and cast-iron door furniture/hardware that resembled beaten work was popular.*
⑨ *These mass-produced items were sold under the name of Art Black Garden City Furniture. They reproduced wrought-iron work.* YM
⑩ *The* Studio *ran design competitions. This knocker was a prize-winner in the 1890s.*
⑪ *A copper escutcheon plate by Charles Emanuel, with an embossed scorpion.*
⑫ *An elegant door knob and lock by Charles and Henry Greene.*
⑬ *C.F.A. Voysey's characteristic heart-shaped metalwork was widely copied.*
⑭ *A brass handle from a Birmingham (England) foundry.*
⑮ *Thomas Elsley's chased lock and Emanuel's copper fingerplate/push plate are among the best examples of commercial door fittings.*

Windows

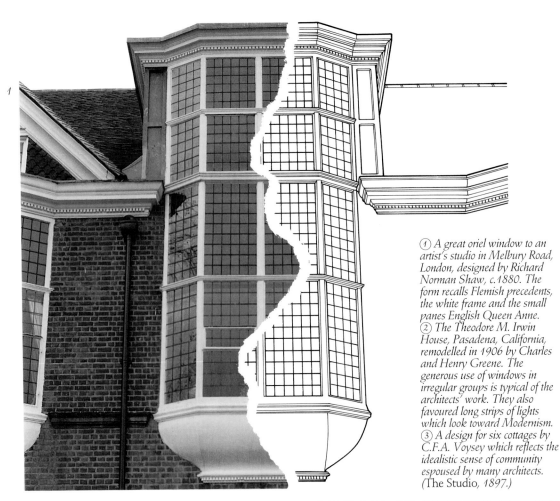

① A great oriel window to an artist's studio in Melbury Road, London, designed by Richard Norman Shaw, c.1880. The form recalls Flemish precedents, the white frame and the small panes English Queen Anne.
② The Theodore M. Irwin House, Pasadena, California, remodelled in 1906 by Charles and Henry Greene. The generous use of windows in irregular groups is typical of the architects' work. They also favoured long strips of lights which look toward Modernism.
③ A design for six cottages by C.F.A. Voysey which reflects the idealistic sense of community espoused by many architects. (The Studio, 1897.)

In the early years of the Arts and Crafts movement sash windows were associated with iniquitous, modern plate glass and vernacular wooden casement windows were considered the best models, with small panes of leaded glass. However, the advent of the Queen Anne style led to a new status for the sash from the 1870s onward. Richard Norman Shaw used sashes extensively and his tendency to elongate the proportions was highly influential. A popular arrangement in Britain and the United States was to pair an upper sash bearing small rectangular lights with a single paned lower sash.

The value placed on light and air is reflected in the large window areas on later Arts and Crafts houses. Bay and oriel windows were popular in Britain while uniform rows of windows were common on both sides of the Atlantic. In Britain the inspiration came from vernacular mullioned windows; the grandest houses had stone mullions but most had composition or terracotta, the latter being a notable feature of red brick Flemish-style town houses. In the United States arrays of windows often took a more modern form, with large panes topped by smaller panes: this was a trademark of Charles and Henry Greene. They also used random arrangements of windows, which broke up the masses of the facade. The Aesthetic taste favoured Islamic-style ogee arched windows and the use of stained glass.

① A typical American Craftsman window, with a shelf for flowers. Early 20th century.
② A narrow light by Charles Greene showing Spanish Colonial influence. 1923.
③ Window seats were very popular. This example is by Ernest Gimson. England, c.1910.
④ A detail of a "pair of cottages with common dining-room" and traditional casement windows. The Studio, 1901.
⑤ The oriel was often used in London, to circumvent regulations concerning property boundaries.
⑥ White-painted wooden frames are typical of Queen Anne houses. This Venetian window is from a summer house in New York State, late 1890s.

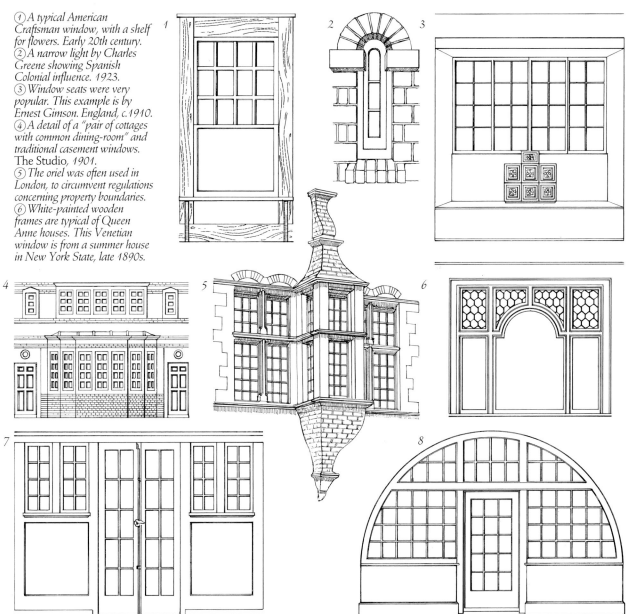

⑦ and ⑧ Designs combining windows and glazed doors were popular. The first group is from a Craftsman town house, c.1910. The second, English design is by C.F.A. Voysey, c.1904.
⑨ A tall window in Bedford Park, west London, 1880s, reminiscent of the great studio windows designed by Richard Norman Shaw for artists' houses in Kensington, London.
⑩ Two carved lintels, typical of the work of Louis H. Sullivan in Chicago, 1880s.
⑪ Leaded lights were used in commercial developments and show the influence of Aesthetic taste. New Jersey, c.1900.
⑫ Small windows are a feature of Arts and Crafts design. The first, c.1905, was sited above a row of built-in cupboards; the second, c.1899, allowed light into an inglenook.
⑬ Dormer windows were often used in groups. England, 1904.

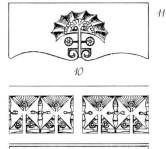

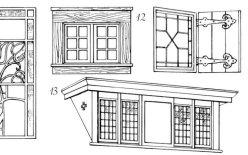

① and ② *Small dormer windows and other traditional vernacular forms were much used on smaller houses. These examples are from Hampstead Garden Suburb, London, c.1910. The first one has a small casement window set beneath a tile-hung gable above a deeply recessed porch. The second, symmetrical design on a semi-detached house, is enhanced by the graphic use of the pipes.* RS

③ *An elegant window divided into four narrow lights at the Gamble House, Pasadena, California, 1908-9.* GG

④ *British Arts and Crafts architects often attempted to unify the semi-detached house by symmetrical window groupings. Here, two windows belong to one house and the third to its neighbour.* RS

⑤ *Coloured glass was an important feature of many Arts and Crafts designs. The painted panes from William* Morris' house reflect his taste for motifs derived from nature. RH

⑥ *Frederic E. Church's studio in Olana, Hudson River Valley,* New York, 1880s, has an Oriental-style ventilation grille. It can be opened by means of pulleys. O

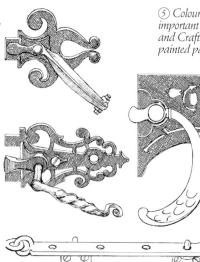

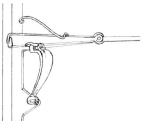

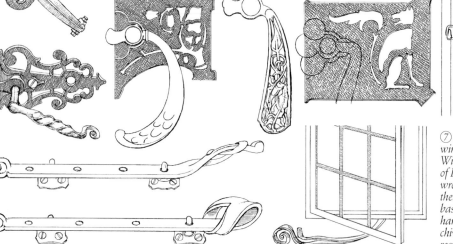

⑦ *Fancy fastenings and window plates were popular. William Morris and Company of London produced excellent wrought-iron items such as these (c.1920) on a commercial basis. The gryphon on the handle plate recalls medieval chivalry; the fixed casement restraint copies vernacular work.*

Walls

The rich reddish tones of the studio walls of Olana, built near the Hudson River, New York, in the 1870s and 80s, are typical of the broad tonal effects sought by "artistic" decorators and house owners. Stencilling was often used to outline the division of dado, field and frieze.

Pictures were hung close together in gilt frames, and formed part of a complete architectural composition, carefully calculated by designers to unify the room. The pointed form of the arch speaks of Islamic influence and is a motif found throughout this Moorish-style house. O

Although many Arts and Crafts interiors employ the tripartite division of the wall into dado, field and frieze, both British and American architects used taller dado panelling than the classic proportions dictated. Full panelling was also used on occasion, in the hall or dining room, but polished indigenous woods were limited to grander houses. Painted panelling is usually a flat or ivory white; sage green and olive green (derived from 18th-century practice) were popular Aesthetic colours. Stencilled friezes were also popular. Craftsman country houses often have structural log, stone or brick walls.

The fine wallpapers produced by Morris and Company of London from the 1870s rendered paper an acceptable wall covering, and William Morris designs were found in all classes of British houses and in better American houses. American firms such as Warren, Fuller and Company of New York were active from the 1880s. Early papers have floral and medievalized designs; Aesthetic papers of the 1880s show Japanese influence. Dado, field and frieze schemes were fashionable, but wallpaper borders were a less expensive alternative. Stamped papers reproduced the effect of old Spanish leather, used in the influential Peacock Room designed by Thomas Jeckyll and James Abbott McNeill Whistler for F.R. Leyland in London. Tapestry hangings were much used in late interiors.

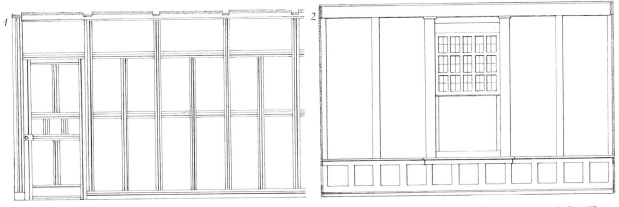

① Cottage-style houses for the middle classes often received an Arts and Crafts treatment. This illustration, originally published in the American periodical The Craftsman in 1905, shows a simple design for wainscotting.

② Another example from The Craftsman, 1907, showing partial wainscotting. Note the contraction of the dado and the consequent elongation of the field. The window forms a decorative panel.
③ This wall treatment was published in The Studio in the 1890s. It was designed by C.H.B. Quennell and features sinuous stencilled patterns within a panelled framework.
④ A wide variety of wainscotting was produced commercially. These three show high panelling with a frieze above. The first and last examples have plaster friezes, the second has a William Morris wallpaper frieze. Note the linenfold panelling, borrowed from Tudor originals. L

⑤ A wallpaper group for field and frieze, designed by Walter Crane in the 1890s. The frieze dominates the upper part of the wall, while the dado has been reduced to a residual skirting board/baseboard. The frieze narrowed during the 20th century.
⑥ Relief work and carving also enriched the Arts and Crafts interior. This plaster panel of piping shepherds, from a house in Colston Street, Bristol, is a delicate and charming detail.
⑦ Servants' bell levers were produced in an Arts and Crafts style. This brass fixture was designed by Thomas Elsley.
⑧ A handsome, abstract wood relief panel from the Barbe Residence in Chicago, designed by Louis H. Sullivan, 1884.
⑨ Frank Lloyd Wright, in his John Storer House, Los Angeles, of 1923, takes decorative abstraction to a logical modernist conclusion in these stone wall blocks.
⑩ A stone corbel taken from the Magpie and Stump, a house built on Chelsea Embankment, London, by C.R. Ashbee.

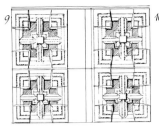

1

2

① *A British drawing-room, c.1901. The typical high dado panelling is surmounted by a shallow field hung with a silk tapestry; the frieze is stencilled.* S

② *This rosebush line of field, frieze and border wallpapers was produced by Jeffrey and Company, London, c.1909, who printed some of the best Arts and Crafts and Aesthetic papers, including designs by William Morris.* HHF

③ *These William de Morgan tiles include the blue glazes* which he created to simulate Isnik (Islamic-type) ceramics. The cypress and orange trees (top) are typical Islamic motifs. London, 1890s. DB

4

3

5

④ *William Morris designed 40 or more wallpapers, the first in 1862. Autumn Flowers (left) was first produced in 1888 and Larkspur (right) in 1874. Many papers are still printed today.*

⑤ *The crisp design of this panelling, 1908-9, is typical of Greene and Greene's work in California. The finish is of a high quality, down to the detailing on the small windows.* GG

Ceilings

The stencilled patterns of the ceilings at The Red House, Bexleyheath, near London, 1859, look back to medieval diaperwork in churches, a form of decoration which William

Morris advocated for both ceilings and walls. The effect has something of the intensity of a medieval manuscript illumination. RH

Ceilings in Arts and Crafts houses owe much to vernacular designs and materials. In the early phase of the movement, architects strove to remain as true as possible to late medieval forms. They used great chamfered beams, or designed plaster ceilings, complete with ribs, moulded pendants and bosses. Some Aesthetic movement ceilings show Oriental influence, with intricate coffering, painted and gilded. Inevitably these were costly finishes in terms of craftsmanship, and few could afford such luxuries. The movement in its maturity valued simplicity and utility, epitomized by the uniform lath and plaster ceilings found in American Craftsman houses of the early 20th century. Even the more ambi-

tious designs of Charles and Henry Greene in California tend to favour linear forms. They sometimes used wood stains, to highlight the geometrical shapes. Only their later work of the 1920s reveals a more decorative intent, with Spanish-style carved beams and embossed plasterwork. Barrel-vaulted ceilings were favoured in the grandest houses on both sides of the Atlantic, sometimes with musicians' galleries.

Painted stencilled decoration was desirable, but ceiling papers were far more common. These became acceptable in the wake of William Morris wallpapers. They were often embossed. In the early 20th century, intricate, prefabricated plasterwork became popular.

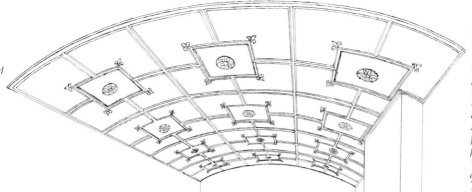

① *Plaster relief used on cornices and the main body of a ceiling usually derived from 16th-century and earlier English precedents. This curved living room ceiling from a ranch near San Antonio, Texas, was designed by the architects Adams and Adams. It was featured in the American periodical* The Architect *in 1917. The strapwork and quatrefoil leaves are true to Tudor workmanship.*

② *Barrel vaulting was desirable and usually consists of lath-and-plasterwork. The example from the Dana House, Illinois, by Frank Lloyd Wright, c.1903, shows incipient modernism. The second, traditional ceiling is by Philip Webb, 1859.* RH

③ *Exposed beams in English ceilings almost always refer to vernacular forms. These designs by M.H. Baillie Scott are for a living hall and a corridor, early 20th century.*
④ *The rich tradition of ceiling painting adapted by Aesthetic movement artists from the 1860s draws upon a number of sources. The first detail is in the Anglo-Japanese style (Vincent Stiepevich, New York, c.1875-85); the second is Islamic (P.B. White, New York, 1869); the third looks back to the Italian Renaissance (E.H. Blashfield, United States, c.1900).*
⑤ *By contrast, a geometric plaster ceiling panel by Louis H. Sullivan, late 19th century.*

Floors

① *This inlaid marble floor at Leighton House, London, is of Italian craftsmanship. It employs naturalistic forms in an Aesthetic manner. The soft pinks set within the black and white border make for a very sumptuous effect and create a striking contrast with the densely patterned staircase runner.* LG

② *This oak floor, inlaid with maple, appeared in* The Craftsman *in 1905. The border is based on an American Indian design and is typical of the simple decoration advocated by Gustav Stickley.*

③ *This long narrow rug with its restrained pattern complements the highly finished floorboards, laid in a chevron pattern.* GG

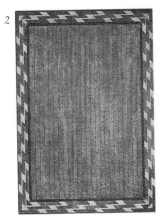

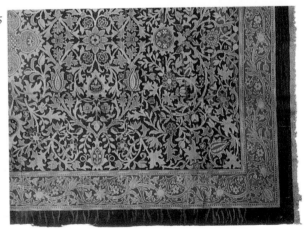

④ *A "Design for an Inlaid Floor, suitable for a City House" was published in* Decorator and Furnisher *in 1886. Shown here are the geometric framework of the design and a detail of the infilling pattern. The floor shows the influence of Near Eastern decoration.*

⑤ *A detail of an ingrain carpet by Morris and Company, early 1880s. Such rich symmetrical carpets were designed by William Morris and Christopher Dresser. They were prized in Britain but were more of a minority taste in the United States, where naturalistic or more austere designs held sway.* FR

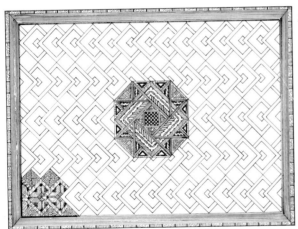

The only honest and acceptable forms of flooring for Arts and Crafts houses in both Britain and the United States are wood and stone. The finest wooden floors are cut from the full width of tree trunks and have a solidity which is unmatched. However, well-chosen planking was equally acceptable. Oak was the preferred wood in Britain, and its natural beauty would be enhanced by simple polishing. Craftsman designers favoured indigenous American woods, such as oak and maple, as well as exotic hardwoods. Gustav Stickley recommended that wooden floors should be at least as dark as the adjacent wall panelling. Staining was reserved for inferior pine flooring, to create the effect of a better timber, although in the early 1860s there was a short-lived vogue for painted floors such as deep blue or Indian red. These usually appeared only as borders to carpets. Stone flagging was particularly popular in country houses, for entrance halls, or living halls.

Carpets were widely employed. In Britain, William Morris and Christopher Dresser designed some very beautiful carpets, intricate and regular in their patterns. In the United States, authentic Turkish, Indian and Persian carpets, or simple matting, were favoured. However, most householders made do with machine-manufactured carpets: imitation Oriental in Britain, French-style floral or simple geometric in the United States.

Fireplaces

This chimneypiece, designed by Richard Norman Shaw for Cragside, Northumbria, England, in 1870, is a tour de force of Arts and Crafts work. The great carved corbels support the mantel shelf and frame the richly decorated recess, with its panels of ceramic tiles. The highly polished andirons were designed as part of the ensemble. CR

The Arts and Crafts search for the traditional values of hearth and home gave special importance to the fireplace. Inglenooks were the most significant manifestation of this preoccupation on both sides of the Atlantic; in grand architect-designed houses they could be massive. Simple chimneypieces of the 1880s have shelving for the display of blue-and-white china. The grandest resemble massive Renaissance chimney breasts; the most exotic are full-blown Islamic or Chinese set pieces. Plain stone or brick chimney breasts typify Craftsman designs of the early 20th century; more elaborate designs introduced carved overmantel plaques and deep metal hoods.

Tiling was very popular for fireplace slips. Some good designers collaborated with manufacturers on series of pictorial tiles. For example, Walter Crane tiles were made by Minton and Company of Stoke-on-Trent, Staffordshire, England, and the American Encaustic Tiling Company of Zanesville, Ohio. Kate Greenaway illustrations were also popular. More restrained tiles, often with relief decoration, were made by the likes of the Low Art Tile Works of Chelsea, Massachusetts. The English ceramist William de Morgan made exquisite and exclusive tiles, derived from Oriental patterns.

From the 1870s metal hob grates, dog grates and andirons were made, incorporating Aesthetic motifs.

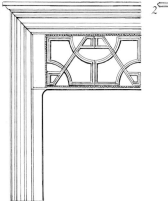

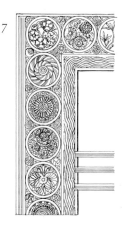

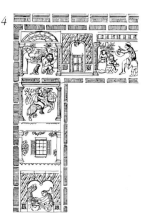

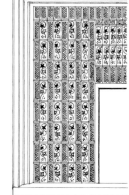

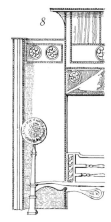

① and ② Designs in wood, typical of the Aesthetic taste.
③ A surround by H.L. and W.H. Fry, 1875. It was made in walnut, for a house in Cincinnati, Ohio.
④ Tiling was very popular. This American relief surround of 1896 is by H. C. Mercer.
⑤ Winslow Homer's "Pastoral" tiles, 1878, recall the work of Kate Greenaway.
⑥ This wood and tiled surround of 1924 shows Japanese influence.
⑦ This elaborate brass surround was made by Barnard, Bishop and Barnards of Norwich, England, c.1873.
⑧ The dog grate of this

fireplace by C.R. Ashbee derives from 18th-century models, but is enclosed in an Aesthetic surround.
⑨ An elegant tiled surround by C.F.A. Voysey, c.1903.
⑩ A Frank Lloyd Wright mosaic tiled design of 1904.
⑪ The use of brick and stone in later fireplaces shows a more stern and vernacular taste. This surround of 1906 is typical.
⑫ and ⑬ Limestone surrounds by W.B. Griffin for a house in Iowa, 1912. The second example has a granite panel.
⑭ T.E. Collcutt designed this glazed brick and tile surround for his house in London, 1898.

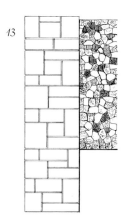

① *A simple brick chimney breast and hearth, designed by Philip Webb for the Red House in Bexleyheath, near London (1859). RH*
② *This handsome marble and tiled surround in Debenham House, London, was created by the architect Halsey Ricardo in the 1890s. DB*

③ *The inglenook in the living room of the Gamble House, Pasadena, California, 1908-9, is inspired by great 16th-century inglenooks. But the horizontal emphasis, the tiling and the strong, plain surfaces make the composition strikingly modern. The mahogany lanterns contain Tiffany glass. GG*
④ *A detail of a late 19th-century Aesthetic movement fireplace. The style of the inlay is derived from Italian Renaissance cabinets of pietra dura (inset slices of coloured marble*

and semi-precious stones). The wooden surround has been stained. LG
⑤ *A very dramatic compositon, featured in a special summer edition of* The Studio *in 1901. It was hand-wrought from "golden coloured metal" and the overmantel, which curves around the chimney breast, is supported by forged iron uprights. The embossed plaque reads "Wit Fancies Beauty, Beauty Raiseth Wit". The grate is of polished wrought iron. S*

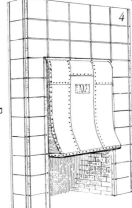

① and ② These examples are typical of vernacular stone chimneypieces in making a feature out of the whole chimney breast. Both were designed by Gustav Stickley.

③ This chimneypiece incorporates a copper hood and a chimney breast covered with matt, glazed tiles.
④ A more sophisticated, tiled surround. English.

⑤ Overmantels were an important feature of Arts and Crafts and Aesthetic interiors. Robert W. Edis' overmantel with cupboards and a mirror is topped with a classical motif.

⑥ M.H. Baillie Scott's small grate and surround from the late 19th century neatly incorporates the overmantel into the composition by means of tiered shelving.

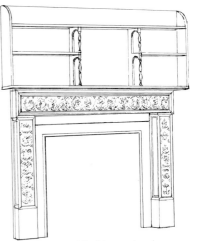

⑦ This chimneypiece of 1878 has a shelved overmantel above a tiled surround. China would have been displayed in profusion on the shelves.
⑧ Grander chimneypieces in the Aesthetic taste could be decorated with William DB

Morgan tiles as here.
⑨ This chimneypiece by George Jack dates from the 1890s and features a carved stone tablet of St George and the Dragon. Such subjects from myth and legend illustrate the close association between the

exponents of Arts and Craft principles and the Pre-Raphaelite Brotherhood of artists; both favoured subjects that recalled "Old England".
⑩ A dramatic ensemble by George H. Maher, made in 1904 for a house in Illinois. The

very wide chimneypiece has imposing, simplified pilasters and a marble overmantel with a central mirror.

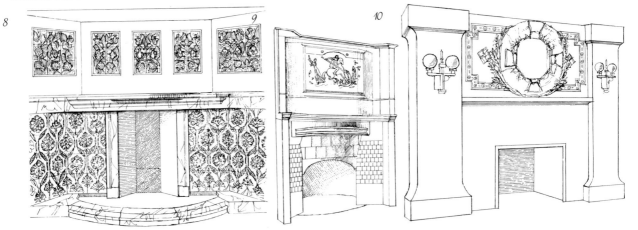

Tiled and relief decoration were hallmarks of chimneypieces.
①A relief panel for an overmantel. English, 1890s.
②A slip of tiles for the side of a grate. Minton and Co.
③A robust terracotta panel assembly by Louis H. Sullivan, 1884.

The grate and firedogs presented designers and metalworkers with an opportunity to demonstrate their "traditional" skills.
④ This grate by the Rathbone Fireplace Manufacturing Co., Michigan (1912), incorporates delicate leaf decoration and a sunburst motif.

⑤ This elaborate ensemble of 1882 comes from the J.L. Mott Iron Works of New York. The firedogs were designed en suite with the daisy-covered grate.

⑥An English austere wrought-iron grate with a hood in the later Arts and Crafts taste, by O. Ramsden and A.C.E. Carr. They followed medieval methods of construction and even included medieval-style jug-warmers in the design. The Studio, 1904.
⑦A dog grate by Gardiner, Sons and Co., of Bristol, England, 1929.
⑧ This dog grate by Nelson Dawson, forged in iron and brass, represents the highest quality of work produced on a commercial scale. It was featured in The Studio in 1903.

1

2

3

4

5

6

7

9

10

8

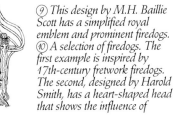

⑨ This design by M.H. Baillie Scott has a simplified royal emblem and prominent firedogs.
⑩ A selection of firedogs. The first example is inspired by 17th-century fretwork firedogs. The second, designed by Harold Smith, has a heart-shaped head that shows the influence of

C.F.A. Voysey. The simple wrought-iron firedog is the work of Gustav Stickley; it would have been used in a plain brick or stone fireplace. By contrast, the last example has a delicacy and inventiveness associated with the early decades of the Arts and Crafts movement.

Staircases

The staircase at the Red House, Bexleyheath, near London (1859), was designed by Philip Webb, who worked closely with William Morris, the owner of the house. It is boxed in to emulate medieval models. The newel posts, with their faceted pinnacles, also recall Gothic prototypes, the inspiration for much of Morris' early work. The natural materials and plain walls give a strong, almost monastic character to the staircase, recalling the work of G.E. Street, Philip Webb's master. RH

The staircase became a central feature of the entrance or living hall. The importance of its role in welcoming the visitor was recognized by critics, who praised those architects who provided both a gallery from which the hostess could be seen when a guest arrived, and an intermediary landing on which the actual greeting could take place. Most 19th-century staircases are of solid wood, either painted, if the wood is of inferior quality, or, ideally, polished. Balusters are often turned, like 17th- and 18th-century prototypes, and newel posts can be richly carved. The newels at Stanmore Hall, Middlesex, designed by Morris and Company in the 1880s, incorporated early electric lights.

In later Arts and Crafts taste the balusters are much simpler, with square profiles. They are frequently extended, to enclose the staircase within a cage of uprights, a system often used in Britain by C.F.A. Voysey. In the United States, the enhancement of the staircase within an open hall led to tours de force of craftsmanship, in highly finished woods, epitomized by the work of Charles and Henry Greene.

In Britain, wrought iron was used chiefly for stair railings, which could be sinuously elegant under Art Nouveau influence. In the United States, the Spanish Colonial and Mission styles were fashionable and entire staircases were made of elegant open ironwork.

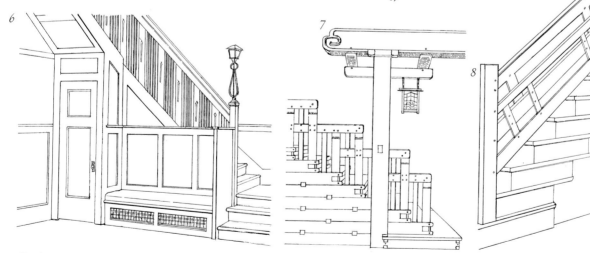

① Strong lines make this staircase by the American architects Spencer and Powers particularly effective. The uprights are equally spaced, even on the sharp bend, where the three uprights per step become two. The newel post is topped by a lamp. The Western Architect, April 1914.
② This staircase and landing was illustrated in The Studio in 1903. It utilizes the closed-string form; that is, the balusters are secured between the handrail and a diagonal brace which conceals the stair-ends.

Wooden staircases were preferred by most Arts and Crafts architects. The material lent itself to simple lines, enhanced by the natural decorative qualities of the grain.

③ These turned balusters from The Longcroft, Helensburgh, Scotland, are complemented on the half-landing by a fine newel post with a clasped orb. The designer has borrowed from Baroque staircase forms.
④ This elegant staircase couples a large, carved newel post with

thin uprights. Note the effective grouping of four uprights to each step. A cupboard has been built into the cavity beneath.
⑤ In sharp contrast is the elaborate surface decoration of the staircase at Stanmore Hall, Middlesex, by Morris and Company – typical of the best

work of William Morris' firm.
⑥ This staircase, published in the American periodical The Craftsman in January 1906, incorporates a settle and a built-in hall cupboard at the foot.
⑦ and ⑧ The staircase designs by Charles and Henry Greene have a distinctive Japanese

quality. The first example is from the Robert R. Blacker house at Pasadena, California, 1907. It is connected to the solid roof beams by a stout upright. The second staircase was constructed two years earlier for the Henry M. Robinson house, also in Pasadena.

① *William Morris and Company of London (no connection with the great designer) supplied wrought-iron and bronze balustrading. These examples, c.1920, show late Art Nouveau influences.*
② *A metal balustrade (c.1894) framed by arching columns.*
③ *Two refined wrought-iron designs: a Hispanic staircase by Charles Greene, c.1930, and twisted balusters of the 1870s.*
④ *The Moorish staircase at Olana, New York, 1870s. A detail is shown below the general view.* ○

⑤ *Newel posts received much attention from architects. Here, a typical plain example is flanked by a dramatic wrought-iron newel (4 feet/120cm high)*

by Louis H. Sullivan, c.1883, and the mighty newel post from the Edward C. Waller House, Illinois, designed by Frank Lloyd Wright in 1899.

The urn device appears in at least seven of Wright's houses.
⑥ *Enclosed staircases are typical of later Arts and Crafts work. The first, arched*

example, c.1900, is almost classical in feeling, when compared with the two rectilinear designs from The Craftsman, *1906.*

Built-in furniture

The library at Leighton House, Kensington, London, retains the built-in bookcases made when the room was built, 1879-81. The ebonized wood matches the richly incised doorcases in the room, and is relieved by a dust-baffling fringe of green stamped leather. The cornice profiles of these dwarf bookcases follow Renaissance precedents. The room served more as a study than a library, hence the limited shelving. LG

Built-in furniture appealed to the Arts and Crafts ethos of craftsmanship. A settle beside the inglenook, a window seat under a wide bay, or a bench and sideboard built against the wall of the dining room, all contributed to the sense of plain and traditional building. Built-in furniture was also practical, minimizing the clutter which late 19th-century designers saw as the besetting sin of mid-Victorian decoration.

William Morris set a precedent with the great settle in his Red House in Bexleyheath, near London (1859). Such early pieces were painted, and many items made for Pre-Raphaelite artists were enriched with panels of figurative work, often by the artists themselves. Such

weighty pieces remained popular until the end of the century in both Britain and the United States. However, the more sophisticated tastes of the Aesthetic movement of the 1870s and 80s appreciated extensive, beautifully finished blocks of shelving and cupboards, often designed around a fireplace with many shelves and alcoves in the overmantel.

Later fixtures are simply finished. The comprehensive built-in furnishings of early 20th-century Arts and Crafts houses – cupboards with solid doors and fine hinges and latches, glazed cupboards for books or china, peripheral seating in a living or dining room – are the precursors of modern furniture systems.

① *An impressive oak library from a house in Henley-on-Thames, Berkshire, England. A fine example of the medievalized aspect of Arts and Crafts design, it was carried out by William Morris and Company. The proprietor of this firm shared many of the aspirations of his famous namesake.* HHF
② *A typical glazed Craftsman bookcase, c.1909.*
③ *Wooden settles were popular Arts and Crafts features. This design, c.1908, includes a space for a writing table.*
④ *A detail of an inglenook by Charles and Henry Greene. The mahogany settle is punctuated by square ebony pegs which cover the screw heads. The adjoining cabinet has decorative, textured glass.* GG

⑤ *Kitchens could be practical without sacrificing the ideals of the Arts and Crafts movement, as seen in these well-proportioned units.* GG
⑥ *Rustic, medievalized cupboards from a bungalow kitchen, c.1905.*
⑦ *A recessed sideboard, published in* The Craftsman *in 1905, with dish cupboards and plain matt tiling. Leaded windows enhance the design.*
⑧ *A small built-in set of bedroom shelves, incorporating simple fretwork around the top. From a child's bedroom, c.1890.*

Services

① *A wash basin from Castle Drogo, Devon: a highly finished design by Sir Edwin Lutyens.*
② *William de Morgan tiles surround this original bath. More modest, mass-produced tiles were made by companies like Minton's and the American Encaustic Tiling Company.* DB

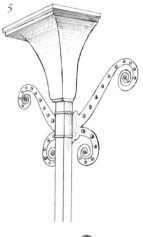

③ *A cast-iron stove with glazed tiles by Rathbone, Sard and Company of Albany, New York, 1885. Japanese-inspired Aesthetic taste strongly influenced commercial productions from the 1870s.*
④ *The simple kitchen sink from the Gamble House, Pasadena, California, 1908-9, contrasts with the refined detailing of the rest of the house. Its plainness reflects the*

Arts and Crafts preoccupation with utility. GG
⑤ *A down pipe/downspout from the Howard Longley House, Pasadena, California, (Greene and Greene, 1897). The rectangular profile and the scrolled brackets have a Gothic quality.*
⑥ *and* ⑦ *Guttering and a rainwater head from a commercial catalogue.* GPD

The servicing of an Arts and Crafts house was in essence little different from that of any house of the period. However, in Britain, the "Old English" and "Queen Anne" styles did make special demands upon craftsmen. The exteriors required leadwork of a very high standard, and architects paid particular attention to down pipes/downspouts and to their hopper heads/ leader heads. These are often beautifully wrought and decorated with patterning, or with initials and the date of the house. In this they reflect the English vernacular tradition. American Craftsman houses tended to have simple, unobtrusive guttering, although Charles and Henry Greene designed capacious rainwater heads with

decorative brackets for their houses in California.

Aesthetic and artistic motifs were often incorporated into the productions of commercial companies. American manufacturers added relief-work to the casings of heating stoves, as well as ceramic tiles by the likes of the J. and J.G. Low Art Tile Works of Chelsea, Massachusetts. Such stoves were frowned upon by purists, who found the less obtrusive, new central heating more acceptable. This was used increasingly after the 1880s.

Architect-designed fixtures remain true to the aesthetic: the basins at Castle Drogo, Devon, by Sir Edwin Lutyens (1910-30), are set within handsome oak casings, with turned balusters concealing the piping.

BUILT-IN FURNITURE

SERVICES

Lighting

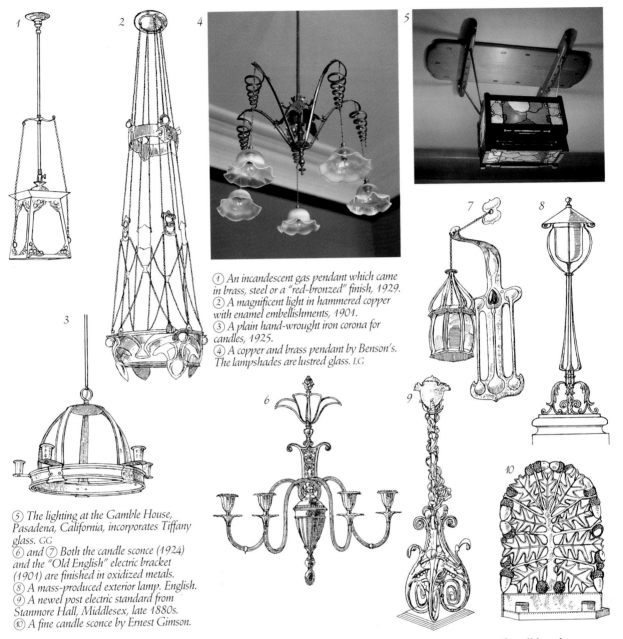

① *An incandescent gas pendant which came in brass, steel or a "red-bronzed" finish, 1929.*
② *A magnificent light in hammered copper with enamel embellishments, 1901.*
③ *A plain hand-wrought iron corona for candles, 1925.*
④ *A copper and brass pendant by Benson's. The lampshades are lustred glass.* LG

⑤ *The lighting at the Gamble House, Pasadena, California, incorporates Tiffany glass.* GG
⑥ *and* ⑦ *Both the candle sconce (1924) and the "Old English" electric bracket (1901) are finished in oxidized metals.*
⑧ *A mass-produced exterior lamp. English.*
⑨ *A newel post electric standard from Stanmore Hall, Middlesex, late 1880s.*
⑩ *A fine candle sconce by Ernest Gimson.*

The heyday of the Arts and Crafts movement in the 1880s coincided with the provision of the first satisfactory domestic electric lighting. In Britain, electricity was initially considered unaesthetic because of its glaring brilliance, unflattering to ladies. However, some rich patrons liked the novelty, and Richard Norman Shaw, for one, worked with it from the first.

The principal British supplier of electric lighting was Benson's, who were producing a wide range of lamps by the mid-1890s. In the United States, I.P. Frink of New York was one of the biggest manufacturers, supplying electric (as well as oil and gas) lights throughout the country by the 1880s. Either a central "electrolier" (electric chandelier) was used, or a series of wall brackets were fixed at frieze height. Copper and brass were favoured, and many designs are closely related to Art Nouveau forms, with delicate wrought ironwork and elaborate twisted metal decoration. In the United States, Renaissance Revival gas chandeliers were fashionable in the 1860s and 70s and simpler Japanese styles were added in the 1880s. Early electric light bulbs were small, spherical and of clear glass, but by 1900 flowers and flames had appeared; they were often used without shades.

Vernacular-style branched lights and sconces were made in wrought iron, and the demand for candle sconces continued anachronistically into the 1920s and 30s.

Metalwork

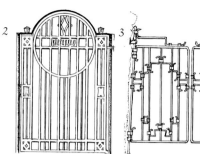

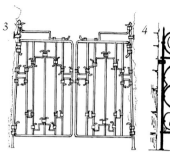

① to ④ Handsome wrought-iron double gates, made by the Birmingham Guild of Handicraft of England; a stylish entrance gate, c.1920; a design by Greene and Greene, c.1905; a dynamic fence and gate group by Alfred A. Newman, London, 1884.
⑤ Elaborate wrought-iron gates, forged, "in the 13th century manner". S

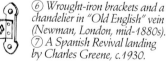

⑥ Wrought-iron brackets and a chandelier in "Old English" vein (Newman, London, mid-1880s).
⑦ A Spanish Revival landing by Charles Greene, c.1930.
⑧ "The Soul of the Sunflower" fireback by Elihu Vedder (United States, 1882).
⑨ A sinuous stove-grate panel.
⑩ A rugged bootscraper.

Every detail of the Arts and Crafts house had to be of the highest quality. In many architect-designed houses every last latch was conceived by the designer. However, as Arts and Crafts and Aesthetic taste became popular a wide variety of commercially produced metalwork became available, including panels and grilles as well as railings and gates. The United States took the lead from Britain. Wrought iron, brass and, for the best commissions, bronze were used.

Ironwork gates and railings can be quite simple, incorporating a plain square upright, topped with a decorative finial, although Gothic-style interlaced and foliate designs were extremely popular. Specially commissioned work was often elegantly geometric or florid, in the spirit of 17th-century masters like Jean Tijou.

The sunflower motif was very popular in Aesthetic tastes. It was prominently displayed in the iron pavilion designed by Thomas Jeckyll and made by Barnard, Bishop and Barnards of Norwich, England, for the American Centennial Exposition in Philadelphia, 1876. Firms like the J.B. Cornell Foundry of New York used the emblem commercially.

Increasingly in the early 20th century metalwork took on an abstract elegance, and in the United States architects like Charles and Henry Greene pushed the boundaries of Arts and Crafts taste toward a modernist aesthetic.

Woodwork

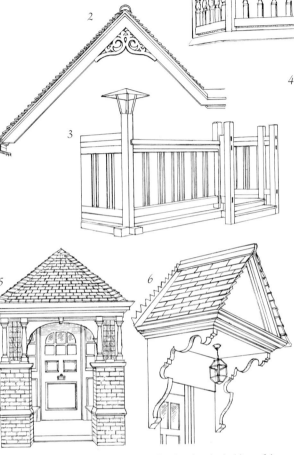

① *A balcony, set above a deep bay window, c.1880. The turned balusters recall Baroque models.*

② *Bargeboards, with fretwork or carved decoration, reflect the early Arts and Crafts interest in British vernacular details.*
③ *This porch from California, 1906, is a fine example of the refined designs of late Arts and Crafts. The post caps have a Japanese quality.*

④ *The shingle cladding of the Gamble House, Pasadena, California, 1908-9, recalls an early development in American architecture, where shingles of wood sometimes replaced the tile hangings of English cottages. More immediately, it is related to the widespread use of shingles*

on American Victorian and Beaux Arts houses. The overhanging eaves are fundamental to many designs by Charles and Henry Greene. GG
⑤ *to* ⑧ *Porches and hoods from Bedford Park, west London, constructed in the 1880s. Some houses have full projecting*

structures with built-in seats, others have variously shaped hoods with carved wooden brackets. The shell-head and the double ogee-shaped pediment on the right are true to authentic Queen Anne forms, as used in England in the early 18th century.

The refined and skilful use of woodwork is at the heart of Arts and Crafts principles. The return to the esteemed values of craftsmanship and beauty is seen throughout Arts and Crafts and Aesthetic houses. It is also displayed in "traditional" wooden features: fences, gates, porches, balconies and verandas.

The importance of the home, and the equally important notion of hospitality, meant that property boundaries were carefully considered. Most fences have great purity of line, with series of square-profile balusters. Turned balusters are also found, inspired by 17th-century forms, and in the Aesthetic taste more exotic, Oriental forms are adopted. Proportions were also

important, fences and gates tending to be quite elongated. Gates often incorporate pergolas or trellis.

The British Queen Anne style was widely adopted by Arts and Crafts architects. Bedford Park, London, the first garden suburb (mostly designed by Richard Norman Shaw in the late 1870s), has a wealth of Queen Anne porches and hoods, also bargeboards; the woodwork is painted white, characteristic of the style.

Porches, more homely than imposing, were important to American Craftsman architects. So too were verandas, used to encourage people to spend time outside. These could be supported by whole tree trunks in country or mountain houses – truly rustic interpretations.

① *A characteristic form of Arts and Crafts fencing is a repeated group of three short and two tall members with a cross-piece.*
ACG

② to ⑤ *Four distinctive gates. The first is a very narrow garden gate with fretwork panels, by Charles and Henry Greene. It featured in the American periodical* The Architect *in 1915. The next is from Bristol, England. Here, the fretwork reproduces Tudor strapwork. Note the secondary status of the gate. The third example, with its pleasing frame, was awarded an "honourable mention" in* The Studio, *c.1900. The last is from a house in Berkeley, California (Greene and Greene, 1909); it has a modern flavour.*

⑥ *A typical fence, c.1902, with plain uprights, subtle angles and sparing fretwork.*

⑦ *A wide entrance gate with characteristic post capping.*

⑧ *Double gates by Greene and Greene. The flanking fencing repeated the chevron pattern.*

⑨ to ⑪ *Internal landing rails. The first example is a late flowering of Gothicized forms (English, c.1920). The second is by Frank Lloyd Wright, from a house in River Forest, Illinois, 1899. The circular motif is picked up in the newel post (see page 328). The last rail is a good example of understated Craftsman design, c.1906.*

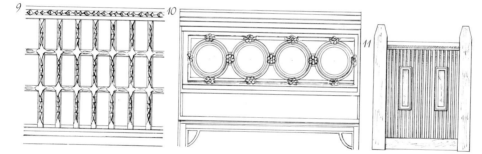

⑫ *A band of carving: a modern interpretation of interlaced Gothic work. This detail was praised by Walter Crane in his* Ideals in Art, *1905.*

⑬ *A ceiling screen from a Chicago house by Louis H. Sullivan, c.1885; an original use of spindles, much favoured in American screen designs.*

⑭ *Aesthetics overcoming utility: this settle with Celtic-style vents hides a radiator. (New York, 1914.)*

⑮ *The wooden veranda of Olana in the Hudson River Valley, New York, dating from the 1880s, is set against a wall of undressed and unequal stones. The contrast between the exotic Orientalism and the pragmatic settler-style walling is a feature unique to the American Arts and Crafts movement.* O

ART NOUVEAU

1888–1905

③ *Frank Lloyd Wright's Robie House, Chicago, 1909 – a classic design of the Prairie School. The long, low form of the house bears a sympathetic relationship to the flatlands of the American Midwest. Wright's genius defies categorization, but to claim his Prairie Houses for Art Nouveau brings out some illuminating counterpoints with Mackintosh.*

① *and* ② *Charles Rennie Mackintosh was the leading Art Nouveau architect and designer in Britain – although his work, in its geometric purity, has little in common with the swirling forms fashionable in Continental Europe. Shown here are two views of The Hill House, Helensburgh, Scotland, 1902-03, a substantial villa which he designed for the publisher W.W. Blackie. The severity of the exterior owes much to the Scottish vernacular tradition – the simple houses built for Scottish barons in the 17th century, with their conical-capped angle towers, small windows, massive double-pitch roofs and huge chimneys. Mackintosh has given the house an intriguing profile, with ingenious interplay of volumes. The internal layout, too, shows great ingenuity in the handling of space. HL*

The exuberant, curvilinear Art Nouveau style which wound its tendrils around France, Belgium and Germany between 1890 and 1910 was never fully developed in Britain or the United States: these countries merely "sampled" it, often in the form of Art Nouveau detailing added to dwellings that are otherwise quite traditional. The makers of fixtures and fittings added the new style to their catalogues, usually under the heading "artistic". But the number of people willing to commit themselves to the radical Continental approach, transforming a whole interior including fabrics and tablewares into a composition of tense and curving organic lines, was relatively small. To be pleasantly "modern", it was enough to choose a few daring details.

Liberty's store in London's Regent Street, a major outlet for Arts and Crafts designs, also marketed a range of wallpapers, textiles and decorative objects which have all the characteristics of Art Nouveau. In the catalogues these objects are depicted in settings that blend Arts and Crafts with the new, more flamboyantly decorative manner. Although most Liberty designers disowned the Art Nouveau label, the phenomenon was so intimately connected with the store that in Italy it was called the "Stile Liberty".

In the United States a few practitioners worked in an idiom closely related to French Art Nouveau. One was Louis Comfort Tiffany, whose glasswares, stained glass panels and lamps were exhibited in Paris (Salon 1895) and sold there at the store owned by Samuel Bing. Tiffany also designed interiors, with plant-like, often asymmetrical forms executed in rich materials.

Whereas Art Nouveau designers in Continental Europe developed the concept of unified design in a way that was organic and highly decorative, Britain and the United States stayed closer to the core ideas of Arts and Crafts. The two most important and innovative practitioners of unified design were Charles Rennie Mackintosh (1868-1928) in Glasgow and Frank Lloyd Wright (1869-1959) in Chicago. Both based their work on geometric discipline rather than curvilinear organic form.

By the beginning of the 20th century, Mackintosh (with his collaborator and wife Margaret MacDonald) had developed a style of which his English contemporaries were deeply suspicious, referring to it as the "Spook Style" on account of its elongated forms and pale colours. Essentially, the Glasgow interior is characterized by simple forms exploited for their sculptural qualities, with windows and doors unframed and recessed into the walls to emphasize their solidity and mass; by cool pastel colours; by furniture (built-in and freestanding), surface decoration, textiles and metal fittings all corresponding to a system of repeating

The hall of The Hill House, Helensburgh, Scotland, by C.R. Mackintosh exemplifies his characteristic use of grid patterns (for example, in the carpet), soft colours contrasting with brighter colour accents, and openwork screens to divide the space. Woodwork could be in harmonizing dark tones, or black, or sometimes painted ivory white. HL.

patterns; by slightly curving vertical lines suggesting, but not imitating, plant forms; and by grids and formalized rose shapes offset by occasional springing curves. Such rooms, in their clean, sparse beauty, have much in common with Japanese design. Mackintosh's influence was felt in the United States, where it was known through publications like *The Studio*.

Frank Lloyd Wright, who denied the influence of any master or movement, produced a series of domestic buildings between the mid-1890s and 1910 which were startling in their innovative treatment of form and interior space. In contrast to Mackintosh, his ideas were well received in his own country. The period of his career when he was designing houses for the suburb of Oak Park, Illinois, 1901-1909, is one of his busiest. In Wright's

hands the sweeping horizontals of roof lines, mouldings and extended interior spaces, balanced by stressed verticals in the brick or stone chimney, coloured window glass and internal pillars, become abstract patterns while still retaining domestic character and comfort.

Wright's low-slung houses of the Midwest, and similar houses by some talented contemporaries, constitute a distinctive "Prairie Style", whose notable features include deeply projecting eaves, stucco-covered exterior walls, bands of casement windows, and a large, low chimney that forms the hub of the house. To extend Art Nouveau to embrace such ideas might seem to be stretching the style's definition; but to do so is instructive, as it highlights some interesting parallels and contrasts, especially with the work of Mackintosh.

Doors

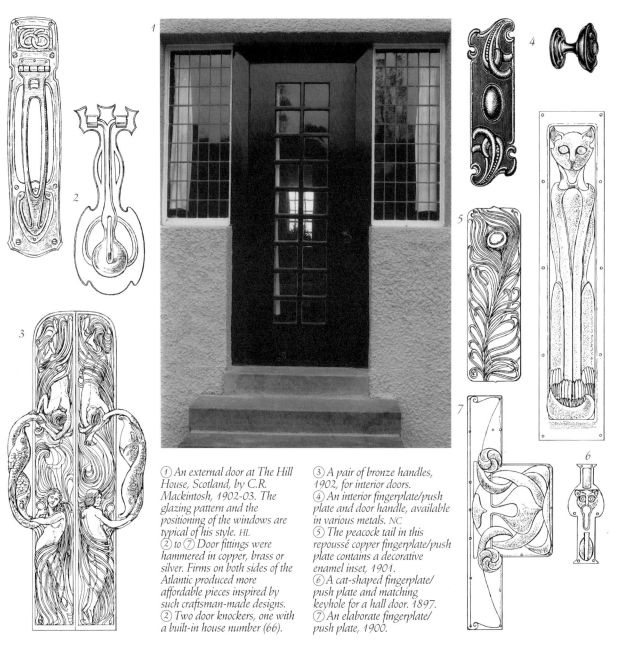

① *An external door at The Hill House, Scotland, by C.R. Mackintosh, 1902-03. The glazing pattern and the positioning of the windows are typical of his style.* HL
② *to* ⑦ *Door fittings were hammered in copper, brass or silver. Firms on both sides of the Atlantic produced more affordable pieces inspired by such craftsman-made designs.*
② *Two door knockers, one with a built-in house number (66).*

③ *A pair of bronze handles, 1902, for interior doors.*
④ *An interior fingerplate/push plate and door handle, available in various metals.* NC
⑤ *The peacock tail in this repoussé copper fingerplate/push plate contains a decorative enamel inset, 1901.*
⑥ *A cat-shaped fingerplate/ push plate and matching keyhole for a hall door. 1897.*
⑦ *An elaborate fingerplate/ push plate, 1900.*

In Britain and the United States it is not unusual to find doors with Art Nouveau styling in an otherwise orthodox building. Even more commonly, a standard door, panelled in the traditional manner, can be dressed with knobs, escutcheons, letterboxes/mailslots and hinges in the new style – for example, peacock feather or heart-shaped leaf motifs.

Surrounds, where they show organic, sweeping lines at all, do so in a conservative manner. The traditional classical references – pillars, pilasters, architraves, pediments – are not supplanted, but their geometry is modified by the introduction of curves. In a typical treatment, outwardly sweeping lines, in place of a

capital, could link the upright elements of the frame to the architrave. Similarly, on an exterior door, the semi-circular pediment could be extended outward in an organic curve from the columns to form a hood.

Coloured glass is important in exterior doors. Often there are two or three vertical lights decorated with for-malized plant forms or vertically stressed abstract patterns in the manner of C. R. Mackintosh or Frank Lloyd Wright. The decoration of the glass is often echoed in the coloured ceramic tiles used to dress interior walls of porches: such tiles can create a repeated pattern, one large motif, or even a pictorial scene. Both glass and tiles were mass-produced in Art Nouveau styles.

DOORS

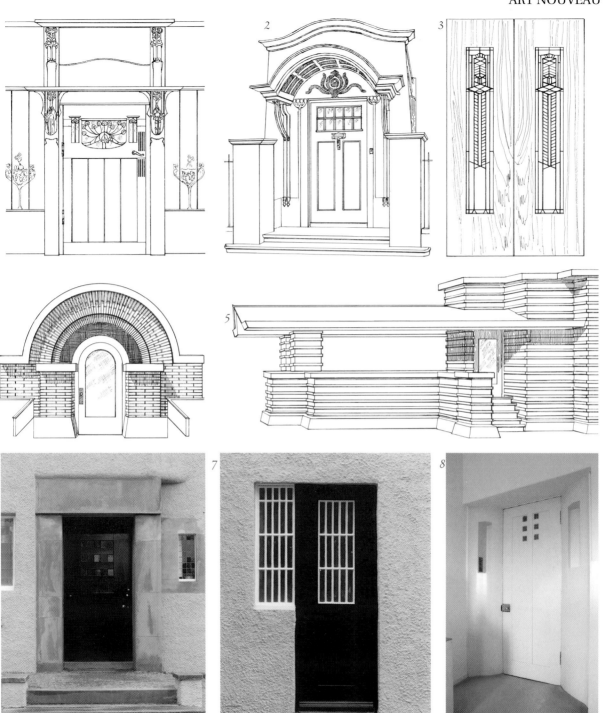

① A design of 1899 for an
internal door with a stylized
floral stained glass panel. Plant
motifs provide a visual link
between the upper decorative
panel and the "capitals" of the
doorcase. This organic design is
quintessential Art Nouveau.
② This doorway of 1904 is a
type found on larger houses and
apartment blocks in Britain and
the United States after the turn
of the century. Brackets of
decorative metalwork provide a

foil to the arched hood.
③ Double glazed doors from
Frank Lloyd Wright's Robie
House, Chicago, 1909. The
upward, vertical form of the
leading motifs contrast with the
strongly horizontal emphasis of
the house itself.
④ The entrance porch of Frank
Lloyd Wright's Dana House,
Springfield, Illinois, 1903, has a
roof of stained glass and a
narrow arch of glass crowning
the arched door.

⑤ A characteristic device of
Frank Lloyd Wright is to extend
the porch in a long horizontal
sweep emphasized by the design
of the brickwork. The door itself
is given minimal emphasis, but
serves as a vertical "anchor" to
the composition.
⑥ The main entrance at The
Hill House, Helensburgh,
Scotland, by Charles Rennie
Mackintosh, 1902-03. The
dressed stone architraves and
lintel indicate the doorway's

importance: this is necessary, as
the entrance is on a side elevation
rather than a main facade. HL
⑦ On this side door from the
same house, the simple grid of
door and adjacent window
create a lighter mood. HL
⑧ The main bedroom door at
The Hill House, with vertical
niches echoing the shapes of the
door panels. HL

Windows

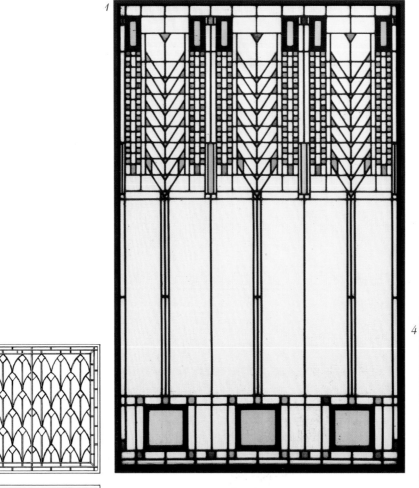

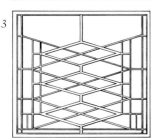

The first three windows here are by Frank Lloyd Wright. By using "leading" made of copper electroplated with zinc, he was able to make the supports stronger and therefore thinner.
① A version of the Tree of Life, Buffalo, New York, c.1903-05. It measures 41 x 26 inches (105 x 67cm). CNY

② An earlier window design for the architect's own house at Oak Park, Illinois, 1895.
③ From the billiard room of Wright's Robie House, Chicago. Very thin "leading" is combined with the usual thickness.
④ An anonymous Prairie School design of c.1910, for a lightly frosted window with tulips.

The asymmetrical, curving windows of Art Nouveau architecture in Continental Europe were seldom used in domestic buildings in Britain or the United States. More typical is a treatment found in the work of both Charles Rennie Mackintosh and Frank Lloyd Wright where the window, usually a casement, is deprived of its traditional exterior surround and is either set flush with the wall surface or recessed to stress the volume of the architecture.

Decorative glass was popular, and was used to "update" windows which were traditional in form. Treatments vary from patterned panels set around the edges of sash windows to all-over coloured glazing in casements and even French doors, particularly those leading into a conservatory. The most elaborate examples depict stylized scenes, landscapes, or compositions of birds or plants. Others depict abstract designs based on plant or geometric forms. In the United States the opalescent glass developed by John La Farge was widely imitated, as were the window designs of Tiffany.

Window fittings, like door hardware, favour elongated shapes. A tapering line terminating in a heart-shaped honesty leaf was particularly popular for hasps and hinges. Iron was a favourite material as it harmonized with the leading of the glass, but examples of iron combined with brass are also widely found.

WINDOWS

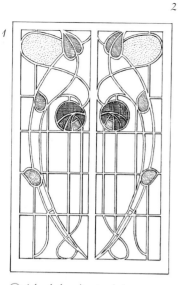

1

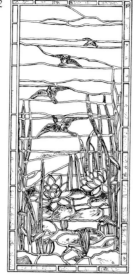

2

3

4

① *A leaded and stained glass panel with rose and foliage motifs by George Walton, after a design by C.R. Mackintosh. Height 52 inches (130cm).*
② *A leaded landscape window, showing birds rising from a marshy pond with lotus blossoms and grasses, early 20th*

century. Height 47 inches (118cm).
③ *One of three panels making up an elaborate grape trellis window by Tiffany Studios, New York. The clear lattice sections are offset by a colourful naturalistic framework above.*
④ *A few of the windows*

published in the general catalogue of E.L. Roberts and Co., Chicago, 1903, are distinctly Art Nouveau in style.
⑤ *A stained glass fanlight window attributed to Tiffany Studios, New York, c.1885. The design was carried out in shades of deep mauve, turquoise, olive*

green, red, ochre, blue and mustard, with moulded details. Length 49 inches (123cm).
⑥ *A bedroom window of Mackintosh's Hill House, Helensburgh, Scotland. The window and even the shutters are curved to follow the curve of the bay. HL*

5

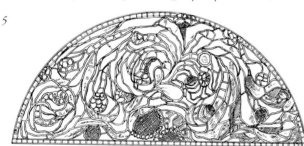

6

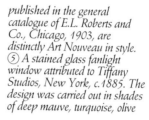

⑦ *The main window of the drawing room of The Hill House by Mackintosh. On either side of the window seat are built-in book and magazine racks. The two "columns" flanking these*

have no structural purpose, but are designed to balance the horizontality of the window. HL
⑧ *The staircase window of The Hill House. Its vertical form echoes the staircase itself. HL*

7

8

Walls

The hall of The Hill House, Helensburgh, Scotland, by C.R. Mackintosh has straps of dark-stained pine, between which are stencilled motifs based on organic forms. The rhythm of the panels along the wall is typical of Mackintosh. HL

Of the variety of wall treatments associated with Art Nouveau, one of the most important, simply because it was readily available, was wallpaper. It was marketed by many firms such as the York Wallpaper Company and M.H. Birge and Sons in the United States, and Liberty and the Silver Studio in Britain. The muted colours and flat patterns of rhythmic, curving forms are a complete contrast with the naturalistic, brightly coloured designs of the mid-19th century. A notable British designer was Arthur Heygate Mackmurdo, who favoured undulant sea plant motifs. Wallpaper firms also produced friezes to be used in conjunction with a paper or to trim a plain wall. Occasionally, paper was used with a frieze of moulded plaster.

Colour-washed walls were used in more "artistic" homes. Charles Rennie Mackintosh favoured pastels or white, set off by a stencilled pattern at the top of the wall or accentuating a feature such as a fireplace or window.

Frank Lloyd Wright, Mackintosh and other important designers employed wood panelling, and there are many examples illustrated in *The Studio* and, in the United States, *The Craftsman*: in all cases the traditional forms have given way to a strongly vertical emphasis with minimal horizontal division. Decorative tiling was employed, but, excepting large and stylish interiors, it tended to be confined to the bathroom.

1

2

3

① *Wallpaper offered an easy opportunity to update a room in the new style. Favourite motifs include stylized flowers, sea plants, birds and the ubiquitous peacock feather, printed in rich colours. This example is a design by C.F.A. Voysey, c.1897, used in Britain and the United States.* PR

② *Bold wallpapers such as this would normally be used as a field above a panelled dado.*

③ *Stencilling could be used as a frieze, or sometimes to decorate the entire surface. This is a wall from the drawing room of The Hill House, by C.R. Mackintosh. Within a geometric, trellis-like frame, stylized roses, echoed in the light fixture, provide a softening effect.* HL

④ *Tiling was used in halls, porches and occasionally on staircase walls. This tiled frieze shows a complex pattern of birds and entwined serpents between white borders.* DB

4

5

6

⑤ *Another Art Nouveau wallpaper, c.1890, with typical plant motifs making a sinuous pattern.* PR

⑥ *A simple wood-panelled dado, with an alcove for a chair. The Hill House, Helensburgh, by C.R. Mackintosh.* HL

Ceilings

① *Stencilled ceiling motifs like this one were occasionally used in the corners, or sometimes created a swirling border.*
② *Frank Lloyd Wright's Prairie House ceilings normally make use of dark wood beams against light plaster. This ceiling for the playroom in his own house at Oak Park, Illinois, 1895, is* exceptional. The central ceiling light is the first use of enclosed, indirect electric lighting. HABS
③ *A ceiling paper design of c.1895. The pale colours are typical of ceilings generally: stronger colours were reserved for the walls. PR*

In accord with the Art Nouveau emphasis on integrated design, ceilings in the interiors of the pioneering designers are often treated in the same way as the walls. Charles Rennie Mackintosh, for example, continues his controlled pastel planes without a break from wall to ceiling, while Frank Lloyd Wright sometimes uses the same materials for both, or carries over a motif from the vertical to the horizontal.

In both Britain and the United States the influence of the Arts and Crafts movement was such that a simple, beamed ceiling often appears in rooms which are Art Nouveau in almost every other detail.

However, in most houses of the period, ceilings were fairly traditional, still following the formula of central rose/medallion plus mouldings, and this is true even of houses constructed with a considerable amount of Art Nouveau detailing. One approach in such houses was to modernize the interior by means of ceiling papers moulded with swirling Art Nouveau patterns: these could be painted to co-ordinate with the walls. An alternative treatment was simply to colour-wash both ceiling and frieze entirely.

White ceilings during this period were denounced as cold by writers on household taste. If decoration was to be absent, at least a tint would be used – for example, cream or grey-blue.

Floors

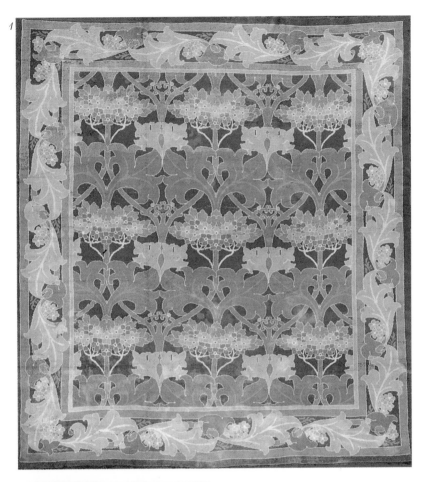

① A carpet with repeating flower motifs by C.F.A. Voysey, c.1890-1900, made by Morton and Company in Co. Donegal, Ireland. The colours are typical of the period. One hallmark of Voysey's work is his ability to stylize while keeping faith with natural forms. FR
② A detail of the hall carpet at The Hill House, Helensburgh, Scotland, by C.R. Mackintosh. The precise positioning of the chair over the gridlike motif, and the matching design of the chair back, are characteristic of Mackintosh's attention to detail. HL

The polished wood floor – either parquet or carefully laid boards – was an important element of the Art Nouveau interior, as it formed a perfect background to the carpets and rugs which were such prominent features of a room. It was also, of course, a rich, warm surface in itself.

Embroidered textiles were a more important medium for the sinuous, French-influenced version of Art Nouveau design than carpets were. However, Gavin Morton of Scotland created some patterns which interpreted the abstract floral (especially rosebud) repeats of the Glasgow School for machine-made or hand-woven carpets. More common, however, was a naturalistic floral style carried over from the Arts and Crafts movement. Oriental rugs were also a standard accompaniment to the Art Nouveau manner.

Charles Rennie Mackintosh's carpet designs were few (although he took to textile design in the latter phase of his career). They were mostly simple, undemonstrative, in pale colours, often with square motifs echoing other aspects of the room. In some Art Nouveau interiors carpets are totally plain.

Tiles were used most often in hallways or, more especially, conservatories, where an element of colourful exuberance would be permissible even to those of relatively conservative tastes.

Fireplaces

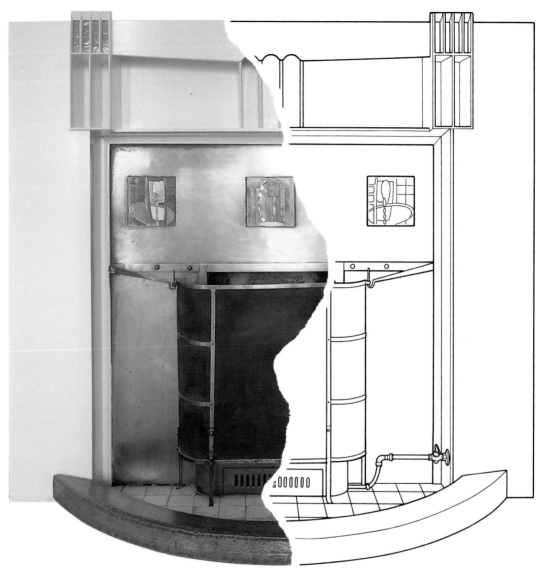

The main bedroom fireplace at The Hill House, Helensburgh, Scotland, by C.R. Mackintosh, 1902-03. The *organic motifs in a palette of pinks are subtly balanced, and contrast well with the cast iron. Note the hook-on firescreen.* HL

The fireplace was a feature in which the Art Nouveau style could be announced emphatically, even in mass-produced housing. In the work of the leading designers it often becomes extended, with shelving and cupboards incorporated into the surround.

C.R. Mackintosh's fireplaces tend to repeat the forms of his built-in furniture, and coloured glass mosaics around the grate often set off the colours used elsewhere in the room. Frank Lloyd Wright's designs are abstract compositions often extending across the whole wall in a series of horizontal bands. In the typical Prairie Style interior the fireplace is treated as a massive form at the symbolic heart of the house.

Wooden surrounds are used in many interiors, painted or simply stained, and incorporating elongated forms and stylized plant shapes. Marble or fake marble was generally used in a more exuberant way with strong curves: there are some very elaborate examples featuring sculpted caryatids with flowing hair. But undoubtedly the most organic forms occur on cast-iron surrounds, which were intended to be black-leaded. Common to wood and cast-iron fireplaces were the ceramic tiles produced in a huge range of designs – by Pilkington, Doulton and others in Britain and by The American Encaustic Tiling Company and other manufacturers in the United States.

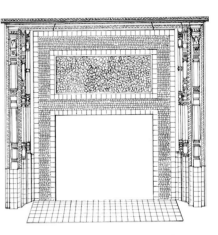

① A drawing room fireplace by E.A. Templar, of the Glasgow School, showing a distinct Mackintosh influence.
② A less disciplined design of 1902. The canopy is treated as a pastoral landscape, with a sunrise and trees. Note the built-in clock, whose surround picks up the landscape theme.
③ This flat-fronted Tiffany fireplace, encrusted with mosaic, shows a love of gorgeous materials and colour.
④ Made in beaten lead, this piece is by Charles Rennie Mackintosh. The extreme simplicity of the grate is characteristic of his work.
⑤ A 1903 design, with bird motifs and the usual flowers.
⑥ This simple design, shown with wall frieze and side panels, dates from c.1895.

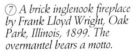

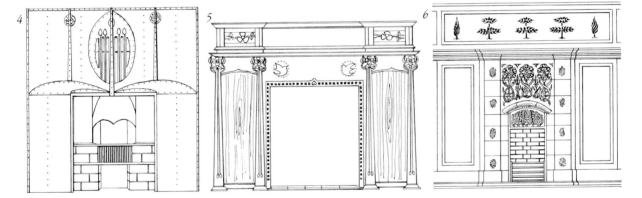

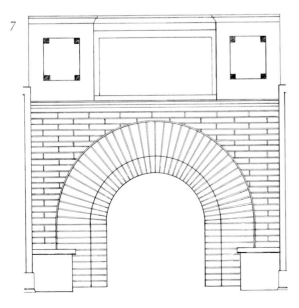

⑦ A brick inglenook fireplace by Frank Lloyd Wright, Oak Park, Illinois, 1899. The overmantel bears a motto.
⑧ Another Wright fireplace, Chicago, 1909. Austere brickwork is combined with stone blocks and a lintel.

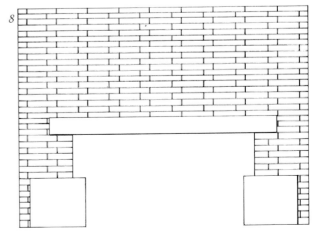

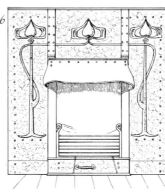

① *A cast-iron Art Nouveau fireplace, painted white. This type was mass-produced, and fitted into a conventional interior without being too incongruous.* BR

② *This example, from the same house, is more sculptural. The plant forms are accompanied by owls perched in the upper outer corners.* BR

③ *A typical beaten copper fireplace by the Scottish designer George Walton, made in 1904. The grate is by C.F.A. Voysey.*

④ *The drawing room fireplace at The Hill House, Helensburgh, Scotland, by C. R. Mackintosh, 1902-03. Five ovals of coloured and mirror glass are set in a mosaic surround. Fire irons hang from bright steel hooks.* HL

⑤ *The grate gave ample opportunity for decoration. This one with doors dates from 1901.*

⑥ *A craftsman-made piece in wrought copper, 1901.*

⑦ *The gas fire with artificial coals was made in both Britain and the United States. This is the English "Derby", from 1901-02.* DG

⑧ *A strongly horizontal grate by Frank Lloyd Wright, Riverside, Illinois. The logs, held straight, become part of the composition.*

⑨ *Made in wrought iron, a British Art Nouveau basket grate of 1903.*

⑩ *This firedog in polished bronze is decorated in typical Art Nouveau style with translucent enamel bosses, 1904.*

⑪ *One of a pair of firedogs from Frank Lloyd Wright's Robie House, Chicago – angular and austere.*

Staircases

① Charles Rennie Mackintosh's staircase at The Hill House, Helensburgh, Scotland, shows his sensitive handling of space. The balusters are close together, creating a lively rhythm, yet without closing off the stairs from the hall. HL.
② Mass-produced iron balusters and balustrades
supplied to the building trade could be used to update an existing staircase. These examples present a contrast: one interpretation is organic, the other more geometric in form.
③ An American staircase with the subtlest Art Nouveau detailing exhibited on the newel post, c.1903.

Whereas Continental European staircases in the Art Nouveau style tended to be elaborate curvilinear forms whose iron balustrades echoed the forms of water plants or root systems, the more rectilinear style characteristic of Britain and the United States called for a less ostentatious treatment. Wood remained the favourite material.

In most houses novelties are found only in the detailing. Piercing of balusters with simple shapes was adopted by many manufacturers. Stair carpets, which seldom reflected the Art Nouveau style, were often used with decorative metal rods tapering at each end to a heart-shaped finial.

Staircase windows contributed to the overall effect, as they were often distinctively patterned, and often tall so that they emphasized the vertical movement that a staircase implies.

Sometimes, in the Arts and Crafts manner, plain square-section balusters were placed so close together that they formed a kind of screen, the lower part of which could be filled in to form a rectangle of solid wooden panelling. The plain newel post could be extended right to the ceiling. If there was space on the landing this could be used to display a striking piece of furniture, such as a tall-backed chair, perhaps harmonizing with a striking lighting pendant.

Built-in furniture

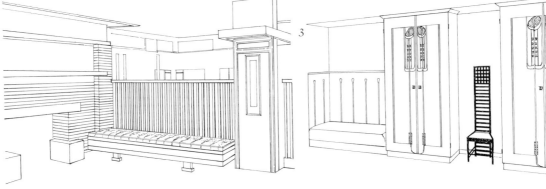

① *In the library-study at The Hill House, by C.R. Mackintosh, stylized organic decoration above the bookshelves and on the* adjacent cupboard/closet *enlivens rectangular forms.* HL
② *A fireplace settle by William E. Drummond, built for a house* in River Forest, Illinois, 1910. *The low bench seat is typical of the Prairie Style and Art Nouveau.*

③ *A bedroom wall, The Hill House. The chair plays a key part in the effect. Pink glass insets ornament the wardrobes.* HL

Although built-in furniture had existed before the 1890s, the Art Nouveau style produced new, imaginative interpretations. A reassessment of the elements that make up an interior led to greater flexibility in design. A cupboard/closet, for example, could be part of the overall composition of a room, instead of a separate entity; it could also be an extension of the bookcase. A fireplace could serve as a display unit, with shelving.

Charles Rennie Mackintosh's cupboards, decorated with mouldings and paintwork which echo the vertical emphasis of the wall motifs and freestanding furniture, form niches containing built-in seating. His fireplaces spread up and across to incorporate display shelves.

Simple boxy shapes with decorative relief provided by glass or metal inlays are a hallmark of the Mackintosh style. His combination of white painted wood with purple glass and stencilled roses is well known, but his built-in furniture could equally be ebonized, or stained dark and waxed. Handles are usually recessed. Inglenook seating is found, but without any cosy vernacular overtones.

Frank Lloyd Wright exploited the sculptural possibilities of built-in furniture. Even in smaller houses, where the purpose was often mainly to save space, the concept of unified decoration was followed, with built-in furniture linked to fireplaces or windows by the use of repeated decoration.

Services

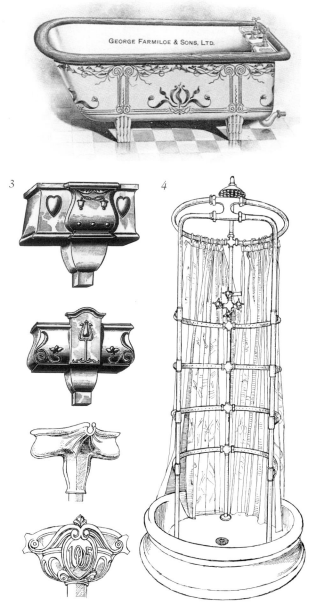

① *Ornate ironwork, tiles and a sinuously curving mirror surround bring Art Nouveau styling to a commercially produced wash basin, c.1910.* FO
② *The painted decoration on this bathtub nods towards Art Nouveau, but the taps/faucets are conservative in style.* GFB
③ *Rainwater hopper heads/ leader heads of the early 20th century are often modishly styled, as in these examples.* MCA
④ *A shower of c.1900, with elegantly curving pipework for side jets.*

Domestic technology was advancing fairly swiftly in the 1890s, and the Art Nouveau style was used for some fixtures which were themselves new in concept. Showers were being incorporated into bathrooms, sometimes as part of the bath, sometimes as a separate unit: often the water theme is aptly expressed in aquatic plant motifs and in the overall shape of the plumbing and the shower head. Baths themselves, while retaining their traditional shape, were designed with legs which echo the curving forms of the new style. Although wood was still used to panel more opulent bathrooms, decorative tiles were becoming important, used behind the bath and shower. The motifs on such tiles could be repeated on the water closet bowl and the wash basin.

The makers of iron cisterns, no less than the manufacturers of porcelain fixtures, decorated their wares with Art Nouveau ornament; they also provided decorative brackets to match. However, the decorative aspects of the relatively new gas water heater were usually confined to the supporting ironwork.

The late 19th century saw an increasing sophistication in the design of kitchen ranges, and some of these had Art Nouveau styling. Although C.R. Mackintosh applied as much energy to kitchen design as to his other rooms, kitchens were still the province of servants, and on the whole received little attention to decorative detail.

BUILT-IN FURNITURE

SERVICES

Lighting

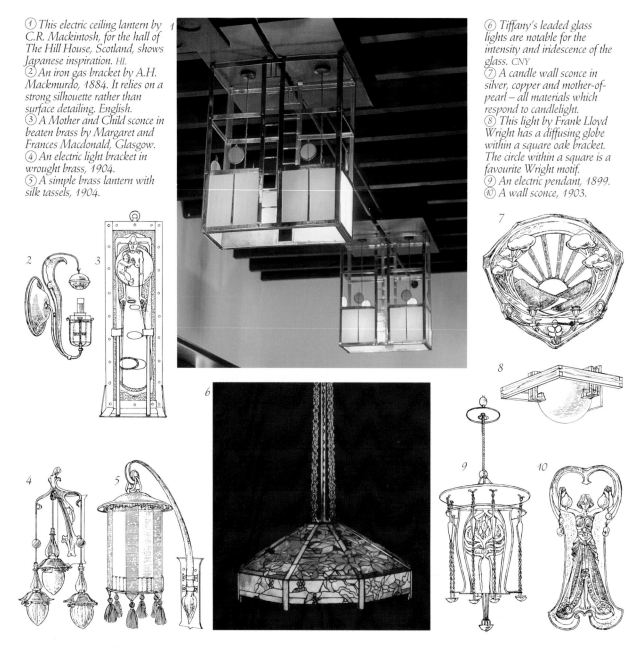

① *This electric ceiling lantern by C.R. Mackintosh, for the hall of The Hill House, Scotland, shows Japanese inspiration.* HL
② *An iron gas bracket by A.H. Mackmurdo, 1884. It relies on a strong silhouette rather than surface detailing. English.*
③ *A Mother and Child sconce in beaten brass by Margaret and Frances Macdonald, Glasgow.*
④ *An electric light bracket in wrought brass, 1904.*
⑤ *A simple brass lantern with silk tassels, 1904.*

⑥ *Tiffany's leaded glass lights are notable for the intensity and iridescence of the glass.* CNY
⑦ *A candle wall sconce in silver, copper and mother-of-pearl – all materials which respond to candlelight.*
⑧ *This light by Frank Lloyd Wright has a diffusing globe within a square oak bracket. The circle within a square is a favourite Wright motif.*
⑨ *An electric pendant, 1899.*
⑩ *A wall sconce, 1903.*

By the 1890s electricity was available to at least some houses in England and the United States. Its immediate use was in lighting, although gas fixtures were still being installed, and would be for another twenty-five years. Both gas and electric lighting gave much greater scope to designers than ever before. For the designer-architects this flexibility was highly attractive.

For people who were "dressing" an interior a range of options was available. Louis Comfort Tiffany first offered his leaded glass shades to the public in 1895, and these were mass-produced at a more accessible price by Handel and Company. (United States). By 1904 numerous companies were making richly coloured shades based on plant forms and influenced by Tiffany; intended for electric lighting, they were marketed with chains for fixing to the ceiling.

Other options included pendant fixtures in metal. Copper and pewter were particular favourites. A decorative metal "cage" would support and protect a glass globe which housed the bulb. There was a vogue for multiple lights supported by metal arms fashioned in the shape of plant stems and suspended from the ceiling by a single "root". Some wall sconces were suitable for both gas and electricity. The pewter or copper could be enriched with enamelling, and the plaque or reflector played an important decorative role.

Metalwork

① *C.R. Mackintosh's simple wrought-iron gate at The Hill House, Helensburgh, Scotland. Replacing the traditional spikes are small disc-shaped finials, each of which rises from a cluster of verticals with swirling lacework at the top. HL*

② *Weather vanes were very popular in the period. This example won a prize in a competition run by The Studio magazine in 1903.*
③ *Another prize-winner from the same competition .*
④ *and* ⑤ *Iron verandas with Art Nouveau flourishes. NC*

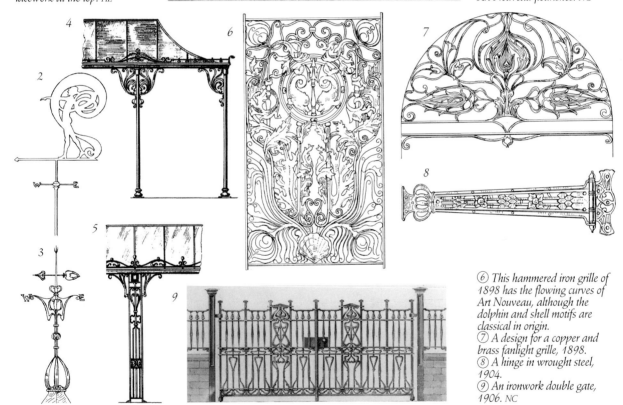

⑥ *This hammered iron grille of 1898 has the flowing curves of Art Nouveau, although the dolphin and shell motifs are classical in origin.*
⑦ *A design for a copper and brass fanlight grille, 1898.*
⑧ *A hinge in wrought steel, 1904.*
⑨ *An ironwork double gate, 1906. NC*

Iron is a material that lends itself well to Art Nouveau forms. Both cast and wrought iron were used in the manufacture of accessories for the house. The architect-designers of the period considered fences, gates and the like as part of the house as a whole, so that Frank Lloyd Wright, for example, in his Oak Park houses, uses the same motifs on the gates as in the leading of the windows.

Manufacturers' catalogues and design magazines show items that are intended as stylish additions, rather than as components of a unified design. One example is Art Nouveau fanlight/transom light grilles: these display sinuous plant-like forms with an almost Continental European exuberance, yet are shaped to fit the geometric fanlight/transom light of a standard Victorian house. A similar point could be made about conservatories, where plant forms were arguably more appropriate, and verandas.

Town house railings gave ample scope to a curving line in the Celtic style made popular by Liberty. In the 1890s there was a revival of "quaint" accessories such as weather vanes, and these too reflect Art Nouveau influence. In more utilitarian aspects of design this influence was less marked: for example, there are ornamental down pipes/downspouts, but the decoration tends to be confined to the rainwater heads.

EDWARDIAN

1901–1914

Elevation.   Attic Plan.

Ground Plan.   Chamber Plan.

NORTH   ELEVATIONS   SOUTH

GROUND FLOOR   PLANS   FIRST FLOOR

SCALE of FEET

Fig. 23.—Pair of Six-roomed Cottages.

FIRST FLOOR PLAN

FIG. 127.—FLATS AT EARL'S COURT SQUARE.

R. A. Briggs, Architect.

① *The "double-fronted" terraced/row house, with central front door and staircase, increased in popularity during the Edwardian period. A generous bathroom with separate water closet is provided in this three-bedroomed example. Roughcast, or pebbledash, rendering was a means of finishing the facade when cheap bricks were used – as on the upper story here.* MID
② *Semi-detached houses were generally less*

expensive than detached houses, as they shared a wall. This example is in the cottage style, popular in new garden cities and suburbs. The plan shows both ground and upper floors. There is only an outside water closet and no bathroom: the bathtub may be a tip-up type in the kitchen. SUT
③ *Mansion block apartments became popular during the 1890s. The drawing rooms and dining rooms in this Queen Anne-style London block are light and airy, with balconies and bay windows on the front: the services and servants are at the rear.* PE

A new century, and a new reign: for the historian of architecture, the timing is all too temptingly convenient. However, Victorian values and traditions did not come to a halt with the Queen's death in 1901, but continued into the Edwardian era, with subtle variations, until the watershed of World War I.

Just as Victoria's reign saw the evolution of the railways, Edward VII's was the age of the motor vehicle. At first the motor car was a novelty for the very rich, but gradually it made room for itself in the coach house, and stables became superfluous.

Until the late 19th century, Londoners and other English city-dwellers usually preferred to live in houses, however tall and narrow, whereas in Paris and other Continental cities apartments had been commonplace for years. The Edwardian period saw the introduction of the "mansion block" (apartment building) in London on a large scale. Perhaps the main incentive for this was the invention of the electric lift/elevator, or "ascending carriage". Improvements to plumbing and drainage also made a big difference: apartments could now have central heating and a 24-hour supply of hot water, and could be hygienically linked to the sewerage system.

Apartments were soon perceived as offering a conven-

ient, secure and economical way to live. Many better-off families had second homes in the country, and spent more time on travels abroad. It was far more convenient to close up an apartment temporarily than a house. The porter was always available to take deliveries and messages. Many of the better blocks included self-contained apartments, served by communal lounges and dining rooms, as in a grand hotel. "Bachelor flats" of this nature were much in demand.

In central London there was a building boom, coinciding with the expiry of many of the leases granted in the Georgian period. Much of the Duke of Westminster's estate in Mayfair was redeveloped, as were the Portman and Portland estates in the Marylebone area.

By 1900 the battle of the styles was more or less over, and there was a general acceptance of eclecticism. Luxury and comfort were higher priorities than the championship of one style or another. The favoured mode for domestic architecture in towns tended to be a debased Baroque – a cross between "Dutch" and "Queen Anne", with red bricks and white stone dressings. There was also a vogue for the French "Louis" styles (XIV, XV and XVI), especially for the interiors of apartments, where Parisian precedents were followed. This trend was

① *A modest sitting room, "more used by men than women", c.1910. Browns and greens were popular. The walls were often divided into panels: here, the dado "panelling" is carried out in Lincrusta or Anaglypta wallpapers. The fireplace is typical.* BF
② *A grander drawing room, showing the influence of the Arts and Crafts movement.* BB

encouraged by Ogden Codman and Edith Wharton, two influential writers who expressed their Francophile views in the book *The Decoration of Houses*, published in England and the United States in 1898.

In the country, mock Tudor maintained its popularity, with leaded windows and half-timbering. The vernacular tradition provided a rich source of ideas. Other powerful currents permeated into the mainstream of design. The influences of Art Nouveau, Japanese styles and the Arts and Crafts movement could all be seen in watered-down, commercial forms.

In 1911 Ernest Willmott, in *English House Design*, maintained that the best work in domestic architecture had been done in the previous decade. He based his chief principles of house design on a series of objectives: repose, proportion, scale, rhythm, colour, harmony and texture. The very best Edwardian houses excel in all these aspects. Another widely read author on the architecture and taste of the period was Walter Shaw Sparrow, who, in *Our Homes and How to Make the Best of Them* (1909), suggested that architects should have three primary aims:

"1. To treat with commonsense and a just freedom the best traditions, both Gothic and Classic.

"2. To break away from that intricate planning which from the 16th century to the 18th gradually separated household comforts into so many rooms that they became expensive discomforts.

"3. To arrive at moderation and economy without loss of essential comfort and privacy."

The average, moderately sized Edwardian house was planned in a manner that reflected the social preoccupations of the time. If the house was large enough to provide for servants, they were usually tucked away beyond the kitchen or up in the attic. The family rooms would consist of a drawing room in which to receive guests, and a dining room (often oak-panelled), with the possible addition of a billiards room and conservatory. The library, study and smoking room would often be amalgamated into a single all-purpose male room. Upstairs a bathroom or two was standard.

The large household furnishers, such as Hamptons, Waring and Gillow, Maples, or Trollope and Sons, were entrusted with the creation of entire interiors. Some of these companies later developed into department stores, others into building contractors or estate agents.

For the less well-off there were municipal and private projects for flats, tenement houses and model cottages and villages. In 1898 Ebenezer Howard published a far-seeing utopian vision which later appeared as *Garden Cities of Tomorrow*. This little book had an immense and beneficial influence in promoting inexpensive housing for the poor. Another key figure was J. St Loe Strachey, the publisher of *The Country Gentleman Magazine*, who argued that the problem of rural depopulation could only be solved by the £150 cottage; this was considered the maximum capital cost that an agricultural worker could pay back from his wage.

In pursuance of Howard's and Strachey's ideas, a Garden City Company was incorporated, and acquired a site at Letchworth, Hertfordshire. The architects Parker and Unwin laid it out, and there was a competition to build the best £150 cottage. Most of the nearly 100 entries survive to this day, ranging from a circular concrete design by Cubitts Reinforced Concrete to rural weatherboarded cottages by Oswald P. Milne. Letchworth became the model for Hampstead Garden Suburb, which soon followed. The Garden City ideal was imitated by canny speculators, and made a distinctive contribution to the English suburban landscape.

Doys

An excellent example of a doorway to an Edwardian town house. The style is based on early Georgian forms, coupled with a checked tile pavement which is very much a

late Victorian or Edwardian feature. The modern decoration is appropriate, as duo-tone schemes were popular (although the contrast here may be a little too pronounced).

Less formal than its Victorian predecessor, the Edwardian front door can reflect the strong influence of the Queen Anne Revival or Art Nouveau styles. In a grand house it will have been constructed to the specifications of the architect and will generally be made of teak or untreated oak, with a dressed stone or terracotta surround. Front doors to more modest houses are made of mass-produced softwood which would have been painted. The range of paint colours extended beyond the green favoured by the Victorians, and the door panels and frames were often decorated in contrasting shades.

The front door to a suburban house frequently has a glazed top panel to allow light into the hallway. In a

Queen Anne-style door, this panel will have plain or bevelled rectangular panes of glass, while the Art Nouveau door has coloured leaded lights, often arranged to form an abstract design. Electric doorbells are a regular feature, but knockers continue to be fitted.

Terraced/row houses are characterized by their wooden porches with turned spindles, brackets and fretwork, available from joinery manufacturers; dressed stone porches are a feature of some larger houses.

Internal doors remain more traditional in style. They may be in a polished hardwood such as teak or mahogany with ornate metal fittings, or in less expensive softwood which would have been painted.

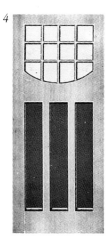

① to ⑤ *Typical Edwardian
suburban front doors from the
London builders' merchant
Young and Marten. They all
have glazed panels to allow light
into the hall. The two doors with
glazing bars show a strong
Queen Anne influence.* YM

⑥ *Extra light could be provided
by the addition of side windows
and fanlights/transom lights.* YM
⑦ *Doorways are still often
dressed in a terracotta surround,
as in the Victorian period.* HP

⑧ *The Edwardians painted
their front doors in a variety of
colours, and it was fashionable
to paint the panels in a lighter
shade.* TP

⑨ *A Tudor-styled dressed stone
porch with bracketed canopy.*
⑩ *and* ⑪ *Prefabricated
wooden porches in a variety of
styles could be purchased direct
from joinery manufacturers.*

① The entrance to a mansion block of apartments in the Queen Anne style. The glazed door and the green paintwork are typically Edwardian.
② This part-glazed front door has a side window and a transom light to increase illumination in the hall. The electric bell (a standard feature by this period) may be original.
③ This glazed porch has been added within a Queen Anne style canopy. The Art Nouveau side-lights, white woodwork and checked paving are characteristic of the period.
④ Glazed panels for doorways. The designs are simpler and more free-flowing than those of the Victorian period. GFB

⑤ Simple four-panelled doors remained popular for modest houses and less important rooms of grander houses. Here, the architrave is quite elaborate and has plinth blocks. EL
⑥ Polished hardwood doors enhanced rich furniture. This six-panelled example has a Georgian character. EL
⑦ Elegant door plates were typical of grander houses. French-style sets like this were popular from the late 19th century. BR
⑧ A sprung door closer, on a door separating the servants' quarters from the rest of the house. EL
⑨ A stylish handle, en suite with the escutcheon plate. EL

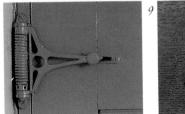

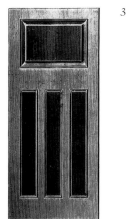

① to ④ *A selection of internal doors from Young and Marten's wide range. They would have been supplied in yellow deal prepared for painting. The panel mouldings were usually of simple circular section. Doors are often three panels in width.* YM

⑤ *A framed, ledged and braced door with tongued-and-grooved V-jointed boarding. Less expensive to produce, such doors were used in kitchen and service areas.* YM

⑥ *and* ⑦ *Two illustrations from paint manufacturers Thomas Parsons and Sons' Ornamental Decoration, 1909. The first shows an Adam-style drawing room door, picked out in the newly invented "silver aluminium" paint; the second is japanned and picked out in "Endelline" flat enamels with finishing touches in aluminium paint.* TP

⑧ *By 1900 the electric bell was a standard feature. These are four brass examples from Nicholls and Clarke.* NC

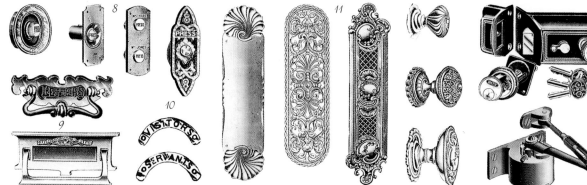

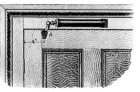

⑨ *Two brass letterboxes/mail slots. The top one shows a marked Art Nouveau influence and incorporates a door knocker; the lower example has a handle.* YM

⑩ *In town houses with only one* main door there would be two bells, one for house guests and the other for servants and tradesmen. NC

⑪ *Brass fingerplates/push plates and knobs for interior doors, c.1900.* NC

⑫ *Cylinder locks to front doors were introduced in the late 19th century. This cylinder is bronze. Keys were finished in copper or brass.* YMA

⑬ *Spring-action door checks were a popular feature.* NC

Windows

① *A fine bow window on two stories. The use of tiles and red brick derive from Queen Anne architecture, but the proportions and details are entirely Edwardian. The casements are standard metal windows, inserted into wooden frames, a popular arrangement that has continued throughout the 20th century.*

② *Planning laws barely existed in Britain in the early 20th century. Bungalows proliferated; they were mass-produced in prefabricated form and sprung up all over the countryside and coastline. This very typical example was manufactured by David Rowell and Company of Westminster, London. The construction was light and inexpensive, primarily of wood, with asbestos tiling. DR*

③ *Generally, Edwardian houses have a lighter appearance than Victorian ones, with more space given to windows. The bay window was still popular and was often divided into a greater number of segments than in the 19th century. In the case of this semi-detached suburban house, the top lights are typically divided into smaller panes. White became a popular choice for woodwork, instead of shades of green.*

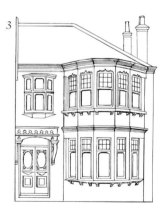

New methods of production enabled steel-framed windows to compete with those made from wood. Standard steel profiles for casements were mass-produced. The frames could be inserted straight into prepared brick or stone openings, or into wood subframes. For the most expensive houses, windows made from gunmetal or bronze were favoured: it was not necessary to paint them and therefore they were considered to be maintenance free.

Although metal frames encouraged to some extent a departure from the sliding sash window, speculative builders continued to install wood-framed sashes. In the Queen Anne style, the top sash will often have small panes of glass divided by a number of thick glazing bars, with a single sheet making up the lower half. Bay windows continue to be a characteristic feature of terraced/row houses.

Stained glass was popular for staircase and landing windows particularly when these were overlooked by neighbours. Art Nouveau influence is often seen in the designs.

The exterior paintwork of sash or casement frames was usually in a contrasting colour to the sill and subframe. Green and cream was a favourite combination, but cream would also be used with other colours as the range of available paints increased.

WINDOWS

① A sliding sash window. The top sash is divided into small panes, a popular style retained from the Queen Anne Revival. EL.

② This stone-dressed window with four-centred arches and indented spandrels is of a simplified Tudor character. EL.

③ A dormer window in the steep pitch of a mansard roof. The shallow curved hood, designed to throw off rain, has a rather classical appearance. BB

④ A triple sash window with a cornice and broken curved pediment. The external sash pull handles gave a better grip when opening the top sash. A Queen Anne influence is evident in the top lights which are decorated with small leaded panes. BB

⑤ Delicately tinted glass and patterned leading decorate this attractive bay window. BB

⑥ The same window, seen from the exterior, contributes to an interesting elevation. Each of the four leaded windows is distinctly Edwardian in character while paying respect to the Arts and Crafts movement. BB

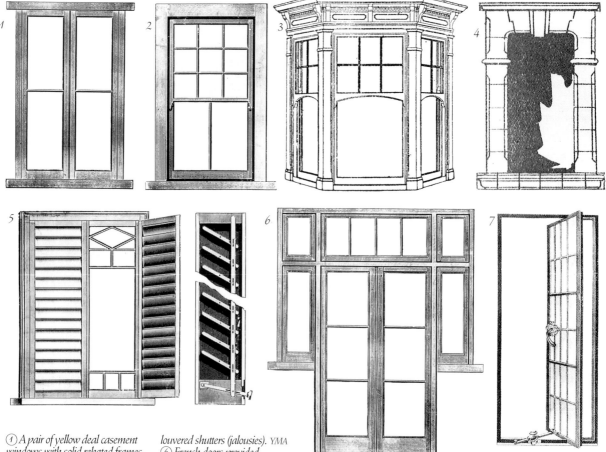

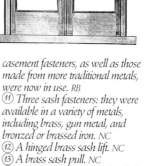

① A pair of yellow deal casement windows with solid rebated frames, supplied ready for painting. YMA
② This double-hung sash window with iron pulleys has characteristic smaller top panes with a simple divided lower sash. YMA
③ A double-cased bay window with moulded brackets; again there are smaller panes at the top. CJ
④ A basic pattern for the still-popular terracotta surround. HP
⑤ Continental holidays encouraged a taste for wooden louvered shutters (jalousies). YMA
⑥ French doors provided convenient access to the garden; this example includes side windows. YMA
⑦ A metal casement window with an unusual hinge which exposes both sides of the window for easy cleaning. GS
⑧ and ⑨ Two iron casement fasteners. The wrought-iron scroll handle on the left was particularly popular. NC
⑩ Chromium-plated window casement fasteners, as well as those made from more traditional metals, were now in use. RB
⑪ Three sash fasteners: they were available in a variety of metals, including brass, gun metal, and bronzed or brassed iron. NC
⑫ A hinged brass sash lift. NC
⑬ A brass sash pull. NC
⑭ A sturdy brass espagnolette bolt, used for closing French doors. EB
⑮ Two angular copper-finished casement stays. RB
⑯ Two brass casement stays; the top one is a wedge stay secured by a screw. NC

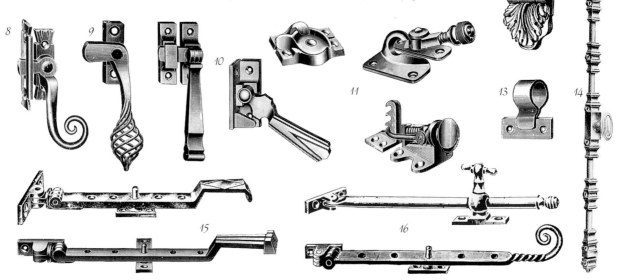

Walls

① *This idea for an entrance hall was published in 1909 by Thomas Parsons and Sons to advertise their ready-mixed "Endelflat" enamel paints. The walls are painted in the* *traditional divisions for panelling: dado, filling and frieze. The Adamesque swags are stencilled. Note how the floor design blends in with the overall design.* TP

② *The Tynecastle Company developed its embossed "vellum" to reproduce moulded panelling. It was made in room-height sections and could be "grained" or* *painted in "any shade of oak", according to the manufacturers. The linenfold panels at the base of the section are a fashionable Tudorbethan touch.* TC

Edwardian walls often display an extraordinary mixture of historical styles. Georgian forms are the most popular, and delicate Adamesque swags might accompany rugged early Georgian mouldings, finished off with a Regency Stripe wallpaper. The French classical styles were popular with the wealthy, and with the owners of apartments who wanted to create a grand impression in a limited space.

With the introduction of quick-setting plasters, such as Keenes and Parian Cement, and a great number of affordable ready-mixed paints, it was easier than ever before for the amateur to do his own decorating. The quality of wallpapers improved and new ranges were brought out each season. Wallpaper friezes enjoyed a vogue. Embossed papers such as Tynecastle, Anaglypta and Lincrusta-Walton were extremely popular. These were inexpensive and some could be painted. Different materials were often combined: an Anaglypta frieze might surmount a canvas covering, framed by white painted deal (pine or fir) bands.

The Tynecastle Company developed facsimile wood panelling in embossed "vellum". Made from compressed paper on a canvas backing, it could be cut to size and painted or stained. Oak or walnut panelling is found in the better houses; Tudorbethan or Georgian patterns were the most popular.

① *A charming panel from a house in Yorkshire which shows the personification of Architecture holding up a model of the house itself. This romantic notion is typical of the period, when the home was appreciated as an important element of English life.* BB
② *An extravagant console bracket used to form the springing of an archway across the hall of a modest town house. This sort of feature tended to be used indiscriminately by speculative builders from the late 19th century until World War I. Similar brackets in fibrous plaster could be readily purchased from most builders' suppliers.* BR
③ *From the same house, an elaborate bracketed cornice is superimposed above a deep scroll frieze over the picture rail. Although impure in detail, the whole produces a rich classical effect.* BR
④ *This is a more elegant and sophisticated treatment of the frieze and cornice. The frieze is in Anaglypta, whereas the cornice above is plaster. The swags in this example are derived from the "Adam" period. The overall effect is characteristically Edwardian.*

⑤ *A plaster dado infill panel. It is unusual to find this degree of elaborate detail in Edwardian plasterwork.* EL

⑥ *The use of polished oak or hardwood for raised features, such as dados and skirting boards/baseboards, became very popular.* EL

⑦ *The space under the stairs was often framed and panelled in wood. A cupboard might be introduced for storage.* EL

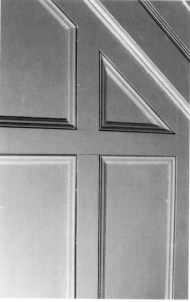

1 No. 565   No. 623   No. 567

Scale 1″ to a foot.

1911

2

① *Minton produced an enormous range of wall tiles. Tiles were used in porches, passageways and bathrooms. Art Nouveau and particularly Arts and Crafts designs were popular on the more delicately coloured tiles, such as the three examples here. The border bands and designs at the skirting board/baseboard and frieze levels enhance the overall appearance.*
② *Electric bell and indicator boards were located on walls in or near the kitchen. A light would show the maid which room to go to. Even quite small apartments would have such a board. YM*

3

③ *The Tynecastle Company was well known for its very popular plaster-like embossed canvas friezes and enrichments. Georgian designs were particular favourites. TC*
④ *Fibrous plaster brackets such as these were used to embellish interior archways and were often a feature in halls.*
⑤ *Examples of Anaglypta. There were many patented textured materials which were very durable and commonly used on the dado of hall and staircase walls. Designs resembling panelling, like the second example here, were popular. RL*

4   *5*

⑥ *Wallpapers with simulated fabric finishes were much in demand. This pink moiré striped paper from 1914 would be suitable for a drawing room or bedroom. CBA*
⑦ *A "chintz" wallpaper and frieze, very popular for bedrooms. Some elaborate scenic friezes had 13-foot (4m) repeats. CBA*

6   *7*

Ceilings

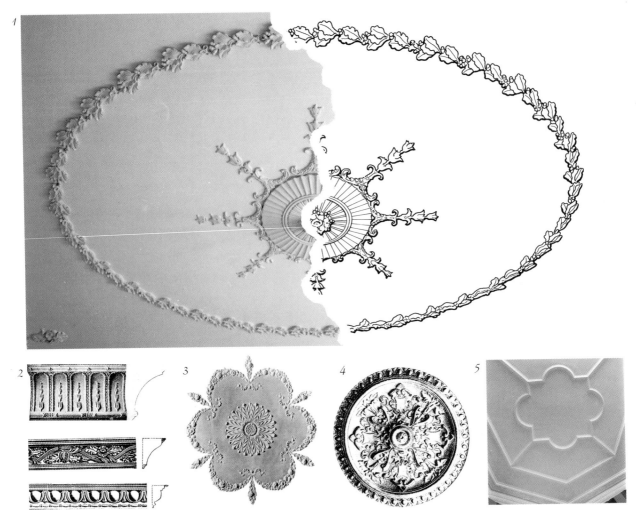

① *Typically eclectic elements from the ceiling of a London house. The fluted central rose/medallion with radiating palmettes reflects late 18th-century "Adamesque" classicism; the outer ring is earlier 18th century in character. BR*
② *Three cove and cornice mouldings. The top one is embossed steel which was supplied in 8-foot (240cm) lengths that could be cut to size and nailed onto wooden battens. The others are "paper-stucco" mouldings. Such details, made from composition, embossed paper and derivatives of papier mâché, were widely produced as an alternative to plasterwork. YM*
③ *An Anaglypta ceiling rose/medallion in a debased Georgian style. It would have been pasted directly onto a flat plaster ceiling. AC*
④ *This "paper-stucco" rose/medallion is just over 2 feet (60cm) in diameter. YM*
⑤ *Plaster ribbing on the ceiling was a popular treatment. The ribs could also be made of wood, Anaglypta or other moulded materials. EL*

Ceilings tend to be lower and on the whole much plainer than in the Victorian period. This was in keeping with the vernacular revival. For example, cornices are no longer regarded as essential.

The fashion for Tudor architecture is seen in exposed oak beams with plaster infill, and in stuccoed ceilings in low relief. Pre-cast fibrous plaster was popular; it was modelled in sections and could achieve a very high standard of finish. G.P. Bankart supplied many designs, including some in the Adam style.

Numerous inexpensive materials catered for the mass market. Applied decorative motifs were made in composition (an amalgam usually based on wood pulp or paper). Compressed paper and canvas materials such as Cordelora, Anaglypta and Tynecastle Tapestry reached their heyday: Tudor strapwork and various Georgian styles including "Adams" were popular. Polished oak bolection mouldings were often applied in large panels on a plain plaster ceiling. Ceiling papers in pale silvery-grey patterns on white were thought stylish; the patterns tended to have flowing designs with a regular repeat in each direction. Clean electric lighting ended the need for frequent redecoration.

Stamped steel ceilings, introduced from the United States, sometimes imitated historical plaster designs. Large sheets could be applied over an existing ceiling.

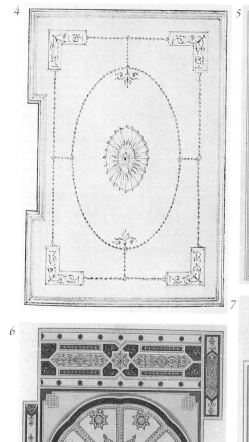

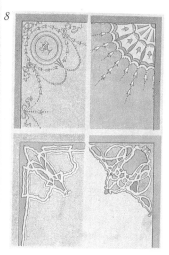

① Embossed steel ceiling panels were sold on the basis of safety and convenience: they were fire-resistant and a ready-made alternative to plaster. They were also said to be "non-absorbent and free from microbes and bacteria". These "Yemart" panels (c.1910) imitate Tudor designs. YM

② Anaglypta could be supplied in large panels, which were pasted onto plasterwork. The first example imitates an Adam ceiling, while the second has a ring of Tudor about it. AC

③ A typical lightweight ceiling paper, c.1914. Thin papers printed in shiny pale grey ink had an attractive sheen. The reflected light gave animation to the ceiling. CBA

④ A ceiling for a bedroom or drawing room with an Adamesque design in "fibrous plaster", by H.E. Gaze Ltd, an established London company. HEG

⑤ to ⑦ These drawing room ceilings are from the Thomas Parsons and Sons book, Ornamental Decoration, 1909. Parsons were paint manufacturers, so it was in their interest to promote colourful painted designs. The first example is painted in flat enamels with silver aluminium-based highlights. Aluminium paint was a great novelty in Edwardian England. The second is an exotic design, in the Moorish style. The last design is in warmer colours. TP

⑧ Corner designs were often painted. The bottom two have an Art Nouveau quality. TP

Floors

Special Books of actual Samples post free

No. 4980—3/10 per yard.

Parquetry. No. 1/1106—3/9 per yard.

Staines' Inlaid Linoleum. No. 3292—2/7 per yard.

Parquetry. No. 1/1124—4/6 per yard.

No. 4940—3/10 per yard.

Staines' Inlaid Linoleum. No. 3205—2/7 per yard.

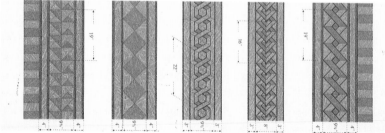

① *Six inlaid linoleum samples from Harrods of Knightsbridge, London, 1910. It was still the fashion for lino to simulate more expensive floor finishes such as parquet or carpeting.* H

② *Parquet was hugely popular. Parquet borders were often laid around the edge of a softwood floor, which was then covered with a carpet. This is part of the range of ready-joined parquet made by Bennett's "Tungit" Wood Flooring Company of Stratford, East London.* BT

Tongued-and-grooved floorboards are the most popular form of domestic flooring. Waxed or polished oak or teak boards are found in grander houses, but pine boards are far more common. These would be varnish-stained around the edges, to frame a carpet (wall-to-wall carpets are reserved for the principal rooms of better houses). Parquet borders were also popular in the principal rooms. Good parquet was laid using one-inch (2.5cm) thick blocks. However, the type used in suburban villas was much thinner and came in ready-assembled panels fixed to a cloth backing and was laid directly onto the existing floorboards. Wood-block floors were laid on a cement base covered

in bitumen, without any joinery. A herringbone pattern was most common, stained or polished. Such floors are found in kitchens and passageways and in the living rooms of suburban houses.

Entrance halls usually had red quarry tiles; fancy shapes, such as hexagons, were popular. Six-inch (15cm) square quarry tiles are found in kitchens. Bathroom floors tend to be tiled in black and white checked patterns, although linoleum was a warmer and less expensive alternative. Linoleum was extremely popular for service corridors. Many new cement-based surfaces imitated mosaic, marble or stone; real marble was reserved for the grandest houses.

1

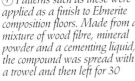

A

B

C

J

K

L

No. 1819   No. 1820   No. 1821

No. 1823   No. 1822   No. 1828

No. 1829

No. 1824

No. 1825   No. 1826   No. 1830   No. 1831

No. 1827   No. 1832

No. 1833   No. 1834   No. 1835

SCALE—FOR ¾ INCH HEXAGONS, ¾ INCH TO A FOOT.
SCALE—FOR 1 INCH HEXAGONS, ½ INCH TO A FOOT.

① *Patterns such as these were applied as a finish to Ebnerite composition floors. Made from a mixture of wood fibre, mineral powder and a cementing liquid, the compound was spread with a trowel and then left for 30* hours to dry. Once painted and polished, it was waterproof, slip-resistant and durable. BT
② *A popular floor for halls and bathrooms was "Tesella Uniforma" mosaic, which came in ready-assembled panels. GH*

3

648   649   650

651   652   653

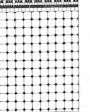

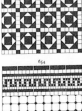

654   655   656

SCALE: ⅛ INCH TO ONE FOOT.

4

③ *Baked clay tiles were the commonest form of paving. Geometric patterns made up from small black and white tiles were popular for bathrooms and conservatories. A terracotta finish was popular for passageways. GH*
④ *Carpets were preferred for the principal rooms of larger houses.*

Most households still used loose carpets but wall-to-wall carpets were available. These Axminster and Moquette samples (based on old French and Persian designs respectively) are from Waring and Gillow, London. A black background was particularly popular. Borders to these carpets were bought separately. WG

Fireplaces

This Edwardian fireplace has been placed in a "Tudor" panelled setting. Victorian dark oak has given way to the subtle tones of stained and polished pine. The marble architrave frames tiled cheeks, which would have helped to throw heat into the room. Dog grates such as the one shown here would often be found in the hall or dining room of grander houses. BB

The main preoccupation of the period, so far as fireplaces were concerned, was to achieve greater efficiency with less fuel consumption. Slow combustion techniques were constantly being improved. The cheeks of the fireplace would be made from fire-brick, and splayed at the sides, with the back sloping forward, so as to project more heat into the room. The splayed sides also had the effect of reducing the size of the grate, so that less fuel was used. Often the grate was ventilated directly from outdoors so that the fire did not draw a cold draught from across the room.

In rural, woodburning areas and when the Baronial or Tudor look was desired (for example in entrance halls)

dog grates were still popular, allowing large logs to be accommodated. The inglenook was a popular and cosy way of forming draught-free seats around the fireplace.

Chimneypieces take many forms. There is now a greater use of glazed tiles, and these tend to be more elegant than in the Victorian period. They were popular in simple plain colours with metallic glazes. Small shelves are often incorporated in the chimneypiece for ornaments or for books. There was great freedom in those designs that derived from Art Nouveau models, and rigorous copyism in those based on the Queen Anne and Georgian styles. Classical wood fireplaces were frequently pine painted in gloss white or matt Georgian green.

① The "Hue" fireplace from a Young and Marten catalogue. The surround and the semi-circular curb are in plain glazed faïence (tin-glazed earthenware); the hearth is in matt glazed tiles. YM
② A "Devon" fire (1907), with a loosely Neo-Georgian surround. Designed by Edwin Lutyens, this fireplace was tiled with either an eggshell or a majolica glaze. PW
③ An "artistic" tile fireplace from Young and Marten. This model would have been thought suitable for a bedroom. It had an adjustable canopy that could be closed to reduce the draught. YM

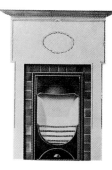

④ This simple cast-iron fireplace with a tall overmantel shows Arts and Crafts influence. CA
⑤ The Tudor look, with glazed

"briquettes", was thought appropriate for a dining room, billiard room or library. The curb could be faïence, copper, brass or

iron. The overmantel came in pine (painted), oak (fumed and wax-polished) or walnut or mahoghany (polished). PW

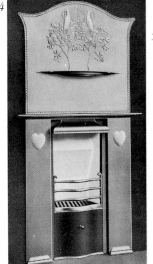

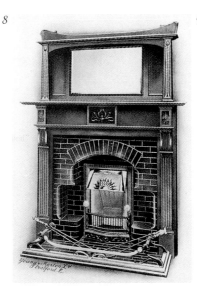

⑥ The Edwardian fireplace would often take on an Adamesque appearance, which was popular in the drawing room. The surround and overmantel here are in white painted pine, with an inset mirror. The brass canopy has an Adamesque repoussé motif. PW
⑦ Enamelled slate chimneypieces were still available in the Edwardian period, and were decked out to look like inlaid marble. Various permutations of colours were available. This model was available from Gardiner and

Sons Ltd of Bristol. GS
⑧ A slightly retrogressive design, the "New Richmond", from Young and Marten. The tiled surround is set into a mantel of pine, supplied ready for painting.

The overmantel, with mirror, could be painted pine or polished walnut. YM
⑨ This design (1906) for a pine fireplace surround (shown here before painting) is highly

eccentric: it incorporates a small glazed ornament cupboard and two mirrors. Ornaments were intended to be displayed in a row on the top shelf as well as the mantel shelf. NC

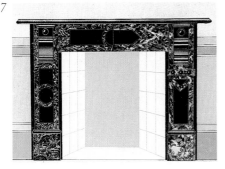

FIREPLACES

① *In less expensive fireplaces cast iron was often used instead of wood: the enrichments could be easily and repeatedly cast. In this example, painted white, the "Tudor" lining and tiled hearth are likely to be a later addition.* BR

③ *This Edwardian 18th-century interpretation was included in the Carron Company's selection of "Artistic" firegrates. It is a relatively free treatment of period detail: pendant drops decorate the pilaster panels under squat acanthus scroll brackets, with floral swags of a different character on the lintel. There is a marble slip between the register grate and the wooden surround. The pierced steel fender and the fire-irons are characteristic of the period.* CA

② *This Georgian-style fireplace surround is carefully detailed in the "Adam" manner. The treatment of the plain glazed tiling with an enriched border is typically Edwardian. The integral grate is lined with firebricks.* CA

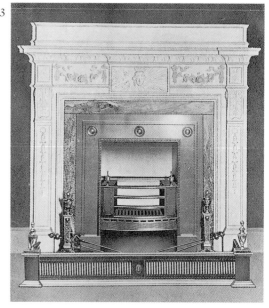

④ *A white-painted cast-iron bedroom fireplace. The attractive tiled cheeks show an Arts and Crafts influence.* EL

⑤ *Another bedroom fireplace, in this case with a characteristically deep frieze containing a central swag-decorated label panel. The depth of the frieze compensates for the shallowness of the fireplace opening.* EL

FIREPLACES

1

2

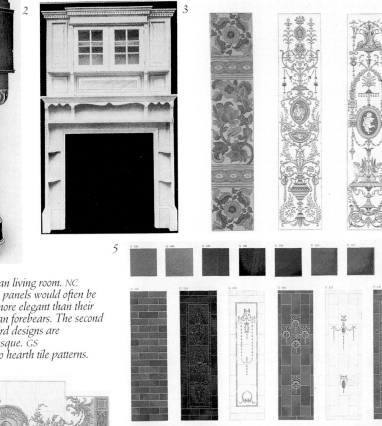

3

① *An extraordinary Gothic fireplace. The surround is fumed oak with marble slips,* Dutch green tiles and a hammered copper canopy. The curb is also copper. MI

5

② *A distinct "Queen Anne" influence is evident in this chimneypiece of 1906. With its little shelves and glazed cupboard for china ornaments, it could only be Edwardian. It would be suitable for a* suburban living room. NC
③ *Tile panels would often be much more elegant than their Victorian forebears. The second and third designs are Adamesque. GS*
④ *Two hearth tile patterns.*

4

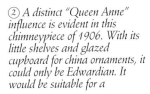

No. 643. Hearth, 48×12 inches, consisting of 26 Tiles including border, price 30/-

No. 944. Hearth 54×12 inches, consisting of 29 Tiles including border, price 50/-

6

7

8

9

10

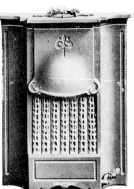

11

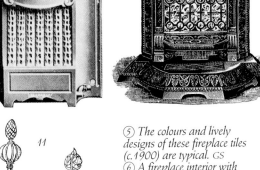

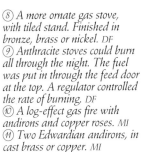

⑤ *The colours and lively designs of these fireplace tiles (c.1900) are typical. GS*
⑥ *A fireplace interior with copper repoussé canopy. Note the simple daisy motif. MI*
⑦ *Gas fires were becoming simpler in design and more efficient. A big advance was the use of clay elements. This model has a boiling ring on top for a kettle. WG*

⑧ *A more ornate gas stove, with tiled stand. Finished in bronze, brass or nickel. DF*
⑨ *Anthracite stoves could burn all through the night. The fuel was put in through the feed door at the top. A regulator controlled the rate of burning. DF*
⑩ *A log-effect gas fire with andirons and copper roses. MI*
⑪ *Two Edwardian andirons, in cast brass or copper. MI*

Kitchen stoves

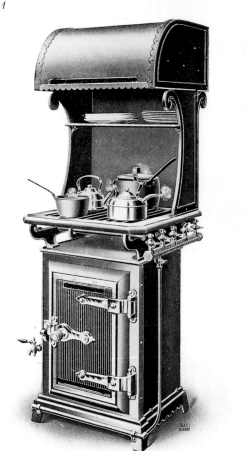

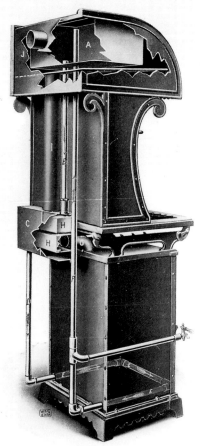

① *Gas cooking became increasingly popular during the Edwardian period. This is the Imperial Gas Cooking Stove, which was the last word in technology when shown in Nicholls and Clarke's catalogue for 1906. It circulated hot water, and thus competed directly with the coal-fired range. The water* in the tank above the hood was heated by the oven. NC
② *A more modest gas store, "The Favourite", c.1910. This had two boiling burners and a grill, as well as an oven, and was made by O'Brien Thomas and Co.* OB
③ *The "Beeton" stove was the General Electric Company's latest model in 1910. The finish was* black enamel, easy to clean, though derived from the "black lead" tradition. The stove was provided with its own heavy solid tin or copper pans. GEC
④ *The optional switchboard for the Beeton stove. The alternative was to buy the more expensive version of the stove (shown) with rotary switches on the side.* GEC

Traditional coal ranges had already achieved a high standard of efficiency in the Victorian period. There were not many more improvements that could be made to them, although ease of maintenance was one. In Edwardian times the stoves were increasingly set in tiles and provided with tiled backs, and there was a gradual introduction of enamelled finishes: all these improvements helped to make cleaning easier. However, most ranges still needed regular blackleading, an unpleasant job that was relegated to the housemaid, where one was available.

Gas stoves were constantly being improved. They could be hired on a quarterly basis from local gas companies. Their form was compact, with the grill under the hotplates and the oven at the bottom, very much like the standard design today. Makers paid careful attention to ease of cleaning, and also to making the gas taps/faucets as safe as possible. The early gas stoves were immensely heavy as they were made of iron and the ovens were lined with firebrick. A notable early manufacturer was the Carron Company.

The two problems associated with early electric stoves were their expense and the time the hotplates took to warm up. Although electric stoves achieved some popularity, the early models never seriously competed with gas.

Staircases

An Edwardian open-string stair, with an unusual and imposing square-turned newel post. The popular square-cut balusters continue the form: they would have needed sophisticated machinery as they could not be rotated on a lathe in the traditional way. EL

Perhaps the main departure from Victorian precedent was the wish for a proper stair hall in even comparatively modest houses. Mrs Peel in her book *The New Home*, published in 1903, recommends making an archway between the hall passage and the front living room of a small terraced/row house. The space thus gained was seen as appropriate for entertaining, and could double up as a dining room. A screen could be placed across the corner to obscure the front door. In larger houses an effort was made to accommodate the stairs in a generous entrance hall, usually with a grand chimneypiece, or cosy inglenook.

In the average house the actual joinery details of the staircase differed little from those of the late Victorian period. "Georgian" and "Adam" ornamentation might be found in the grander balustrade, but many houses, influenced by Arts and Crafts styles, favoured a simple staircase with thin undecorated balusters placed close together.

In middle-class houses it was now commonplace for housewives to do their own dusting, and this had some subtle design implications. Stair rods, which had hitherto been almost always brass and needed polishing once a week, were now made in oak and were virtually maintenance-free. The deep-cut mouldings of the Victorian staircase were softened to make cleaning easier.

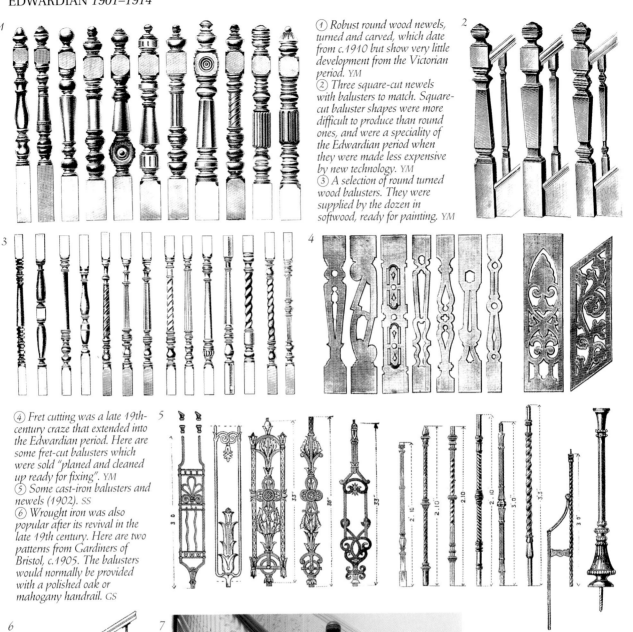

① *Robust round wood newels, turned and carved, which date from c.1910 but show very little development from the Victorian period.* YM

② *Three square-cut newels with balusters to match. Square-cut baluster shapes were more difficult to produce than round ones, and were a speciality of the Edwardian period when they were made less expensive by new technology.* YM

③ *A selection of round turned wood balusters. They were supplied by the dozen in softwood, ready for painting.* YM

④ *Fret cutting was a late 19th-century craze that extended into the Edwardian period. Here are some fret-cut balusters which were sold "planed and cleaned up ready for fixing".* YM

⑤ *Some cast-iron balusters and newels (1902).* SS

⑥ *Wrought iron was also popular after its revival in the late 19th century. Here are two patterns from Gardiners of Bristol, c.1905. The balusters would normally be provided with a polished oak or mahogany handrail.* GS

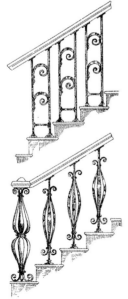

⑦ *A typical turned newel post with polished hardwood handrail. The square turned balusters are in painted softwood.* BR

⑧ *A small selection of typical Edwardian stair rods and clips, which were popular in polished and lacquered brass.* NC

Built-in furniture

① *This fireplace doubles as an "inglenook" and a "cozy corner". The glazed wooden cupboards are very typical of the period. The entire unit is a good example of the commercialization of the Arts and Crafts ideals.* OH

② *A neat built-in bookcase, with cupboards below and adjustable open shelves above.* BB

③ *Built-in window seats were popular and were particularly well suited to bays which offered an attractive outdoor view. The bases also frequently served as a radiator casing or as a useful storage compartment.* BB

④ *This floor-to-ceiling built-in bedroom unit includes a chest of drawers, a closet for shoes, with a wardrobe alongside. The flat surface could be used as a washstand: even in Edwardian times not everybody would have approved of having plumbing in the bedroom. The unit has a painted finish which would have been integrated with the decoration of the room.* MH

Built-in furniture was especially popular in apartments for its economical use of space. In bedrooms and dressing rooms of both apartments and houses, built-in wardrobes were installed on a wider scale than before. Where ceilings were low, the wardrobes might be full-height to avoid a dust trap on top. However, in rooms with high ceilings it was usually decided not to take the wardrobe up to the ceiling, as the upper shelves would be rarely used, and might become a home for vermin: shoulder height was a common choice. Chests of drawers could be built in too, often with a cupboard above, the whole ensemble matching wood panelling around the walls. Built-in dressing rooms were the preferred choice,

as it was thought unhealthy to sleep in a room where clothes and shoes were stored. Cupboards might be punctuated by a few open ornament shelves. Small apartment bedrooms sometimes had a unit combining dressing table, clothes drawers and washstand.

Libraries were often equipped with adjustable shelves covered by glazed doors. In dining and drawing rooms the wall recesses at each side of the fireplace were frequently busy with built-in cupboards or open shelves for ornaments – or even, in apartments, a linen press.

Kitchen dressers of the period tend to have enclosed panelled cupboards below the open worktop, and shallower glazed cupboards above.

STAIRCASES

BUILT-IN FURNITURE

Services

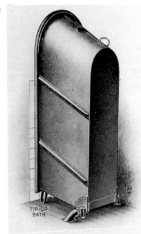

① *A patent tip-up bath (1909) in sheet steel for use where space was limited. The bath pivoted on its waste pipe. TW*
② *Another space-saving idea was to combine the bath with the* basin. *The same set of taps/faucets served both, by adjusting a lever as on a modern shower fixture. The manufacturers (George Farmiloe and Sons) stressed that the water* from the basin did not pass out into or through the bath. GFB
③ *A Doulton's cast-iron "sitz" bath with white vitreous enamel finish, 1904. This type saved on both space and water. DA*

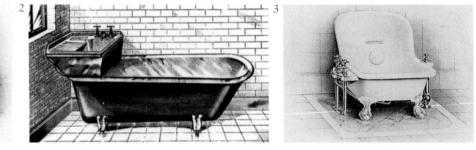

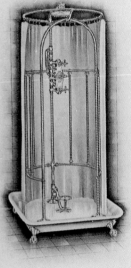

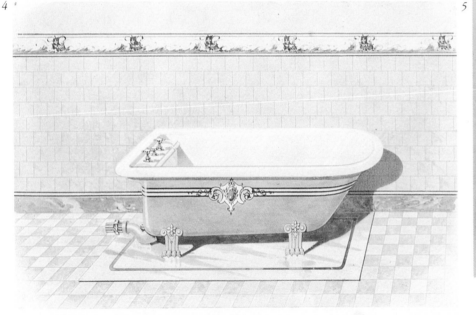

④ *This cast-iron bath is from the Macfarlane's Castings catalogue, 1907. The finish may be either* vitreous enamel or white porcelain, with a painted design on the outside. Compared with the *Victorian period, the decoration is more delicate and elegant; the wall frieze enhances this effect. MCA*

⑤ *A shower unit, with copper spray pipes and waterproof curtains, 1904. DA*

By the start of the 20th century, bathrooms, or at least baths, were provided in virtually all new houses. In working-class dwellings the bath was often located in the kitchen or scullery near the boiler – sometimes concealed beneath the floor, and revealed by lifting a trap door; in other cases it was stored and secured on end inside a cupboard and pulled down when needed. Most middle-class houses had a proper bathroom, and a separate water closet, off the staircase landing.

Hot water systems improved during the period. An independent domestic boiler would supply enough hot water for a storage cylinder for the bath and for general household use; sometimes a heated towel rail, or else a radiator in the hall, was also included on the circuit. The old-fashioned and unreliable geysers fell out of favour, although they lingered on in builder's catalogues.

Much thought was given to hygiene. It was no longer believed healthy to encase baths in wood panelling. Ceramic baths were highly regarded, but were heavy and expensive. Cast-iron baths stood on legs (often with claw feet) to make them easy to clean underneath. Bathroom curtains and soft furnishings were frowned upon as harbourers of dirt and microbes, so the windows were fitted with obscured glass. Usually, the fixtures themselves were more streamlined, with fewer dust traps, than those of the previous period.

1

2

① An elegant wash basin, with the decoration under the glaze. This style was also produced in five-sided versions, angled to fit into a corner. GFB
② A pedestal water closet from George Farmiloe and Sons Ltd, c.1909. Floral decoration on the bowl was losing popularity, and the profile was becoming much smoother for the sake of cleanliness. The seat was birch on cast-iron brackets. GFB
③ A shower fixture for use above a bath, with china handle and brass chain. NC

3

4

5

④ The top tap/faucet here is of the quick-turn type, available in gun-metal or nickel-plated, with an ebony handle. The lower example is a combination tap/faucet for a bath, with a lift-up waste knob. NC
⑤ A standard bidet, with a valve for mixing hot and cold water, 1904. The lever operates a rising spray. DA
⑥ A combined bath and shower, from a house built in 1902. Note the decorative hinges on the door that gives access to the plumbing. MM
⑦ The "Acme" patent geyser (water heater) could serve both a bath and a basin. It ran very economically off gas, and would take about 20 minutes to fill a hot bathtub. The geyser was supplied in a polished copper finish or, at extra cost, nickel-plated. By this period the geyser was quite old-fashioned. GFB
⑧ A heated towel rail. DA
⑨ Water and steam heating were increasingly popular in grander houses. This dining room radiator (1904) has a double-doored oven, containing shelves, where food could be kept warm. AR
⑩ An "artistic" cast-iron rainwater head. YM
⑪ These rainwater pipes hark back in style to the late Victorian period. MCA

6

7

8

9

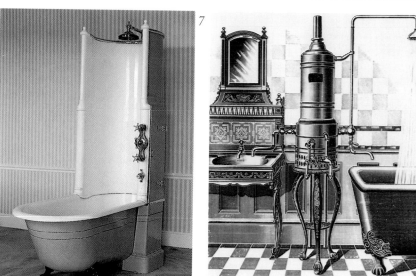

10

11

Lighting

① By 1911 the General Electric Company catalogue ran into three large volumes, one of which was almost entirely devoted to light fixtures. This G.E.C. ceiling light or "electrolier" – the "Cowbridge" – is in gilt-coloured polished brass. It would be suitable for a large drawing room or a ballroom. The bowls may be cut glass or satin finish. GEC
② The invention of the inverted gas burner made possible the downlighting gas pendant. This one is typical (Young and Marten, 1910). YM

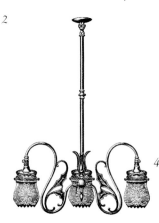

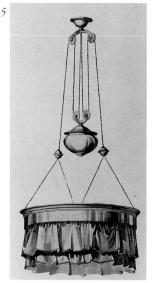

③ A polished brass wall bracket with opal glass shades. Wall brackets were very popular. In smaller rooms all the fixed lights might be wall-mounted, with supplementary standard lamps for reading or sewing. GEC
④ A French-style ormolu (gilt bronze) wall fixture with twisting ribbonwork. N. Burst and Co. (Wardour Street, London). Such brackets were also available in Neo-classical styles, with urn finials. NB
⑤ Silk-skirted lamps, with counterbalanced weights so that they could be raised and lowered, were popular over dining room tables. This is the G.E.C. Penistone model. GEC
⑥ Modestly styled pendant electric lights such as these would have been used primarily on landings and in corridors. GEC
⑦ Two characteristic wall switches. Covers could be fluted brass or plain china. Such switches have become popular again today. GEC

Electric lighting increased in popularity throughout the Edwardian age. Even so, by 1910 less than 5 per cent of households had electricity. Public supplies were available in all large cities and towns, but the cost varied from place to place. In most poorer households and in rural areas, candles and oil lamps were still the main source of light. Coal gas lighting was provided in towns: it was dirty and unhealthy because of the fumes.

Large country houses had their own private generators, normally run on petrol or oil. Acetylene gas lighting was promoted by the Imperial Light Company.

Electricity allowed a new freedom in the design of light fixtures. Many original designs were produced by W.A.S. Benson of Bond Street, London, whose work was widely copied. However, these Arts and Crafts ideas were popular only with a select market. Most people preferred their light fixtures to mimic the chandeliers and brackets of the candlelit era. Candlelight was often the chosen ambience for dinner. It was made easier by the invention of "Arctic Light": a cylinder which contained the candle on a spring and pushed it up as it burnt, so that the shades never needed adjusting.

In bedrooms and corridors small pendant lights with cut-glass shades were most popular. Chandeliers, elaborate sconces and standard lamps were used for drawing rooms, smoking rooms and libraries.

Metalwork

By the Edwardian period wrought iron had enjoyed a revival and was as popular as cast iron. This very elaborate scrolled work in the classical

revival style, from Berkeley Square, London, is an excellent example. The leaves are so modelled that they do not collect water.

The home and export markets for cast iron flourished during the Edwardian period. The railway network, and powerful traction engines on the roads, enabled large castings to be conveyed all over the country. The foundries kept their old moulds in their extensive storage yards, so the range of patterns they could produce at short notice increased by the day, and their pattern books reflect this diversity.

The tight formality of late Victorian cast iron gave way to freer designs influenced by the French Louis XV and XVI styles and by Art Nouveau. At the same time many ironwork designs reflected the revival of interest in the Georgian era. Work of the 18th and early 19th centuries recorded in L.N. Cottingham's *Smith and Founder's Director* of 1824 began to be recopied. Cottingham-derived designs include simple spearhead railings, and balcony fronts for the new mansion blocks of apartments – which often featured a honeysuckle or Greek key motif.

Cast iron was by now almost universally used for rainwater down pipes/downspouts and hopper heads/ leader heads, and for drain covers.

Much of the elaborately detailed cast iron of the Edwardian period was removed in the 1940s to "help the war effort" – although most of it was melted down only after the war was over.

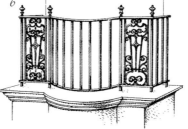

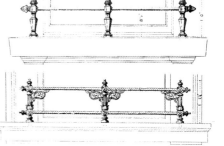

① and ② Cast-iron porch canopies, with glazed roofs, were much more widely used than their scarcity today suggests. The lower example is for a double doorway in a terrace. Both were made by Young and Marten of London. YM
③ Wirework porches, popular for cottages, were a legacy from the Regency period. This example (1905) has a zinc roof. GS
④ Glazed porches kept out draughts and could be attractive when filled with potted plants. This one is from c.1910. MC
⑤ and ⑥ Two wrought-iron balcony designs. The bracketed one would probably have acted as a porch to a doorway . GS

⑦ Ironwork guards to protect window boxes are very similar to Victorian designs. MCA
⑧ and ⑨ A selection of typical wrought-iron front entrance gates and railings from Gardiners' range, c.1900-05. The last gate shows Art Nouveau influence. GS

⑩ A pair of wrought-iron carriage gates. The finials were solid forged. GS
⑪ From the same manufacturer, a delicate wrought-iron garden gate. GS
⑫ Bootscrapers were available in a range of designs. In addition to those shown here there was a type with six scraper bars arranged in a row. Some

scrapers had a long spike for fixing into the ground. MCA
⑬ Weather vanes were popular on rooftops or surmounting ventilators. This design by Maxwell Ayrton nostalgically harks back to coaching days. Golfing scenes were popular.

Woodwork

① *A picturesque bark-encrusted trellis fence in English larch.* WW
② *A wood-framed conservatory by Messenger and Company, c.1905. The simple dentil cornice and pedimented doorway reflect the classical revival. The small panes of glass beneath the roof are a very typical turn-of-the century feature.* ME
③ *A room lined with* treillage *– complex trelliswork based on French precedents and used inside and outside the house. The leading manufacturer was J.P. White and Company.* GR
④ *Entrance gates for a house drive, supplied in oak or pine.*
⑤ *An ornamental garden gate with a square aperture that gives access to the latch. The same company produced gates with small pierced heart motifs, or balusters, or rectangular fretwork.* YM

⑥ *A modest garden gate, in oak or pine. If in pine, it would be painted to match the house.* WW

⑦ *This ornamental fretwork arch was designed to make a feature in the hall or in a passageway.* AOH

⑧ *A typical porch canopy bracket with turned balusters in the late Queen Anne Revival style.* YM

⑨ *A substantial gateway for the driveway to the motor house (garage) or stables.* CM

Privacy was appreciated more than ever before in the modest gardens of the Edwardian suburbs, and fencing accordingly became an important commodity. Pine was often used as a economical material: with pressure treatment and the use of constantly improving preservatives, it could now be made to last longer without repainting.

An important use of woodwork was in the conservatory and the greenhouse. The firm of William Cooper Ltd, one of the largest joinery manufacturers in London, sold nearly 10,000 conservatories and greenhouses a year throughout the Edwardian period.

Treillage, or decorative trelliswork, became fashionable both in the conservatory and in the town garden. A notable manufacturer was the garden specialist J.P. White of Bedford, whose products included screens for blank walls and niches, as well as trellis temples and obelisks.

The revival of Tudor styles in suburbia was manifested in the use of fake timbered gables – dark wood beams with rendered panels in between. Wooden balconies, porches, eaves brackets and bargeboards often show great individuality.

An alternative gable treatment was the application of wavy-edged boarding in oak or elm, which lent a rustic look to summerhouses, garages and garden buildings.

METALWORK

WOODWORK

AMERICAN BEAUX ARTS

1870–1920

① *The Isaac Fletcher House, New York, by C.P.H. Gilbert, 1899, illustrates the François Premier style, characterized by steeply pitched roofs, dormer windows and limestone facades encrusted with carving.* UI
② *The Andrew Carnegie Mansion, New York, 1903: the architects, Babb, Cook and Willard, mixed elements of Georgian and French Renaissance styles.* CW
③ *A moderately sized Beaux Arts house, Forest Hills, Queens, New York, with Colonial detail, c.1920.* FH
④ *This 1886 floor plan for a resort cottage shows the Beaux Arts emphasis on symmetry.*

The American Beaux Arts movement flourished between 1876 and 1930, and encompassed a variety of architectural styles which were derived from historic precedents.

In the post-Civil War period the nation's economy grew rapidly until in the last quarter of the 19th century it came to rival that of Europe. Political and financial leaders, acutely conscious of the nation's new status, commissioned public architecture which reflected American power. At the same time, many private fortunes were being made, and hundreds of wealthy citizens were building lavish town houses and country estates in which specific motifs were borrowed from historic European styles. The splendid new mansions were reminiscent of French chateaux, Italian palazzi and Elizabethan manor houses, and their owners may have perceived themselves as modern equivalents of Renaissance princes.

To serve the demand for lavish domestic architecture, there was now, for the first time, a convenient supply of young, academically trained architects. Architects replaced builders' handbooks as the chief arbiters of style. Architecture as a profession had developed only in the 19th century, and the most prestigious architectural school was the Ecole des Beaux Arts in Paris. The first American to graduate from the Ecole's rigorous five-year course was Richard Morris Hunt (1827-1895), who after leaving the school travelled in Europe and Egypt and worked briefly in Paris; he returned to the United States in 1855. Many other American graduates of the Ecole followed a similar pattern. Newly founded architectural schools in the United States adopted Beaux Arts practices and were often staffed by Beaux Arts alumni. Parisian influence shaped American design through these channels.

Ecole teaching during the 19th century stressed the importance of a clearly articulated floor plan. Fenestration and the disposition of wings were often symmetrical, and responded to the plan. The Ecole pro-

1

① *Shingle-style houses such as this one in Newport, Rhode Island, incorporated Queen Anne and Colonial Revival motifs; all exterior surfaces were covered with shingles in contrasting patterns.*

② *In this country house in Great Barrington, Massachusetts, by McKim, Mead and White, 1884, the unlikely plan of a French château has been worked into an intricate grid of rooms.*

2

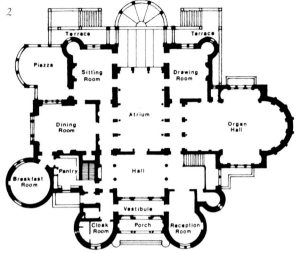

moted the use of advanced technology, and Beaux Arts architects perceived no conflict between the modern functions of buildings and the exploitation of historically derived detail. Architects incorporated complex electrical systems, elevators, mechanical communication devices and sophisticated bathroom and kitchen equipment into their houses. And, just as they enriched the exterior features with period detail, they also embellished the equipment inside: acanthus leaves curled around the corners of brass switch plates, cast-iron dolphins were applied to the feet of stoves and bathtubs. Often, these details related to a single architectural theme, uniting interior and exterior treatments.

Beaux Arts architects commonly incorporated the work of other artists – for example, exquisite stained or coloured glass windows and screens by John La Farge (1835-1910) and Louis Comfort Tiffany (1848-1933), or sculpted fireplace surrounds, pediments or entrances by Augustus Saint-Gaudens (1848-1907) and Karl Bitter (1867-1915). Cabinetmakers, too, such as Gustav and Christian Herter (1830-1898, 1840-1883), worked in concert with architects, making magnificent suites of furniture which related to the treatment of the interior. Garden plans, similarly, reflected the symmetrical rhythms of the house plan. In short, Beaux Arts design emphasized unity, in contrast to the competing patterns, textures and styles of the Victorian aesthetic.

Architects tended to specialize in one or two particular styles. Richard Morris Hunt initiated the trend by designing a series of limestone mansions modelled upon French Renaissance chateaux for the Vanderbilt family and other millionaires. He popularized the "François Premier" style, characterized by steeply pitched slate roofs with elaborate crest railings, rows of dormer windows enriched with crockets and finials, square towers, turrets, tall chimney stacks, ornately carved

balustrades, gargoyles and massive arched entrances. Interiors often had vaulted banquet halls lined with tapestries and enormous hooded stone fireplaces.

Another version of the French Renaissance style was practised by the partnership of John M. Carrere (1858-1911) and Thomas Hastings (1860-1929), whose work drew largely on 17th- and 18th-century prototypes by architects such as Jacques-Ange Gabriel or Claude Perrault. Houses in this style have low-pitched roofs behind a balustrade, colossal pilasters, arched windows and doors, and rusticated bases. Varying amounts of carved limestone decoration – scrolls, console brackets, fascias, garlands and cartouches – surround windows and doors. The firm also designed houses in a French provincial style which featured high-hipped roofs punctuated with small dormers, and brick elevations enlivened with limestone quoins.

The firm of William A. Delano (1874-1960) and Chester H. Aldrich (1871-1940) specialized in Georgian Revival or English Regency Revival styles. Elevations (of both town and country houses) featured broad red-brick walls with crisp symmetrical arrangements of wooden sash windows with black or dark green shutters. Thin strips of white marble trim ornamented window sills and door surrounds. Interiors incorporated round and oval forms, saucer domes, niches and blind arches, recalling the work of English architects such as John Soane or Henry Holland.

Addison Mizner (1872-1933), working primarily in Palm Beach and south Florida, created exotic Spanish or Mediterranean Revival winter homes, which featured stuccoed walls, tile roofs, loggias, open courtyards, and elegant ironwork.

Variants of English Gothic Revival houses were common throughout the period, particularly after 1900. Called the Tudor Style by Americans, the idiom really

A French Renaissance Revival room. Panelling, moulding and other details were designed to create an impression of period magnificence. Even modern fixtures such as the electric chandelier have been modelled on period prototypes. ES

incorporated elements of English Tudor, Elizabethan and Jacobean architecture. Examples ranged from enormous stone mansions modelled on Jacobean manor houses to half-timbered cottages. Most were asymmetrical in plan, many-gabled, with mullioned windows and tall chimneys. Inside, heavily carved oak panelling, ornate oak stair balusters, iron sconces and chandeliers contributed to the Late Gothic mood. The Tudor style was popular in scaled-down form in suburban districts.

Of all these historically derivative styles, the most pervasive was the American Colonial Revival, which in part owed its strength to the 1876 Centennial of the American Revolution. As early as 1874 the architects Charles F. McKim (1847-1909) and Stanford White (1853-1906)

began to graft Colonial details such as porticoes and Palladian windows onto their Shingle-style houses, but the first full-blown examples of the Colonial Revival date from the 1880s. Gradually, architects grew bolder and historically more accurate in their use of Colonial and Federal features. Later regional developments include Spanish Colonial and Southern Colonial. Colonial houses are still constructed in great numbers today.

Although Beaux Arts architects worked in a range of revival styles, they did not replicate historic houses. Instead, they used historic detail to embellish houses that incorporated new domestic technology, ample service space and modern floor plans. While these houses borrowed from history, they were designed for contemporary living.

Doors

Renaissance Revival doors, richly ornamented but restrained. All the mouldings, and the door plates and handles with intricate Renaissance tracery, share a flat quality: ornament is kept close to the surface. ES

The doorway of a Beaux Arts house announces, with a flourish, the selected period style: oak-plank doors with leaded glass panes and hoodmoulds (stucco or stone) for Tudor; raised panels, fanlights/transom lights, side lights and carved classical details for Colonial; carved limestone swags, garlands, cartouches and rusticated masonry for French Classical. Bronze door frames holding huge panels of plate glass were common, with a variety of surrounds. Such grand entrance doors superseded the deep porches of the Victorian era.

Service or secondary doors are numerous – to the back terrace/row, the garden path, the kitchen, the coal chute and cellar, the servants' quarters. In later, smaller, sub-urban houses there were also doors to the garage. Handsome catalogues of the era illustrate "François Premier" door knobs and latches, Italian Renaissance knob plates or bolts, or plain round, brass knobs, suitable for Colonial or Georgian treatments.

Inside a grand Beaux Arts house, wide, open archways link halls and main living spaces. Wooden doors in historical styles (often mahogany) separate bedrooms and more private living areas. Many doors lead to specialized storage rooms, such as linen, hall and telephone closets. In lavish French-inspired interiors the door panels could be painted with floral decorations, trophies or romantic landscapes.

① *A Romanesque Revival door with rusticated masonry surround, c.1889. The arched head is formed by voussoirs. The door is embellished by elaborate iron hinges and grillwork containing a cartouche.*

② *Three front doors from the E.L. Roberts and Co. catalogue, Chicago, 1903. The second example has a cut-glass panel. The last one combines a carved garland with "art" glass.* RO

③ *This doorway from a town house of c.1900 is surmounted by a delicate iron balcony. The surround draws on a variety of architectural sources, including French Classical and Georgian. Small side windows, covered by grilles, light the entrance hall.*
④ *A magnificent Beaux Arts doorway modelled on French Renaissance prototypes. A broken, scrolled pediment holds garlands and a cartouche. Tall rusticated columns frame elaborate double doors and a transom light. Mckim, Mead and White, 1902.*
⑤ *Another McKim, Mead and White design, in the Italian Renaissance style. The carved surround features figures on the console brackets and a variety of foliate motifs. The doors themselves incorporate metal grilles.*
⑥ *A Colonial Revival door of six panels, set into a portico derived from Palladian designs.*
⑦ *This Colonial Revival doorway is typical of suburban houses. A swan's-neck pediment frames a fluted urn, and fluted columns flank the door with six raised panels.*

⑧ *The Neo-classical Revival: the porch is supported by columns with Corinthian capitals, and the door is surrounded by side lights and an elliptical fanlight.*
⑨ *Plain surfaces and simple mouldings achieve a Neo-classical effect more economically.*
⑩ *Another version of a Colonial Revival doorway for a suburban house. The "fanlight" is composed of wedge-shaped pieces of wood.*

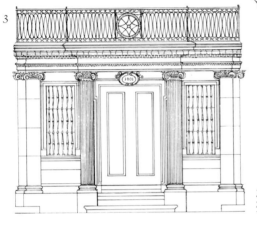

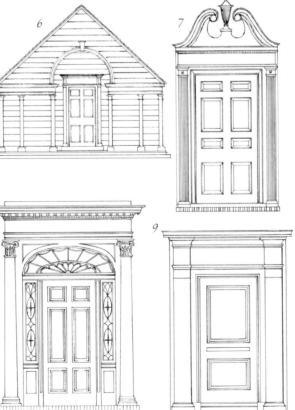

① This extravagant Tudor Revival doorway features mullioned and transomed windows and a stone surround with quoins and a four-centred arch. The door itself is composed of thick planks and has long strap hinges. The arrangement of the door and its two sidelights, however, is based on Colonial rather than Tudor designs. FH

② A bubble-like canopy of bronze and glass shields the front entrance of a New York mansion. This type of canopy had no historic precedent but is typical of late 19th-century Parisian architecture. CW

③ A pair of doors with glazed panels, beneath a stained-glass fanlight that incorporates garlands and a circular cartouche. CW

④ The Georgian Revival style: a mahogany door with eight panels, set within thin pilasters and an entablature with a projecting cornice. UI

⑤ An interpretation of linenfold panelling, with royal portraits on the upper panels, makes explicit reference to the Tudor style. FH

⑥ A gilded doorplate and handle in French Renaissance style, with delicate scrolled decoration. ES

⑦ An elegant arched door surround from The Elms, Rhode Island. A band of fasces (bundle of rods) encloses the arch, which frames a trophy, a panel enriched with wave motifs, and various mouldings: details drawn from French Classical or French Empire sources. ES

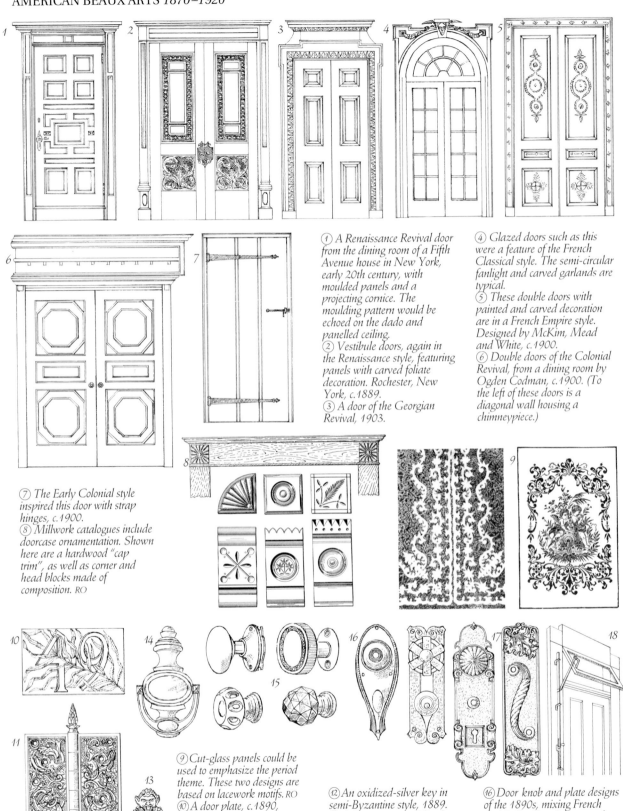

① A Renaissance Revival door from the dining room of a Fifth Avenue house in New York, early 20th century, with moulded panels and a projecting cornice. The moulding pattern would be echoed on the dado and panelled ceiling.
② Vestibule doors, again in the Renaissance style, featuring panels with carved foliate decoration. Rochester, New York, c.1889.
③ A door of the Georgian Revival, 1903.

④ Glazed doors such as this were a feature of the French Classical style. The semi-circular fanlight and carved garlands are typical.
⑤ These double doors with painted and carved decoration are in a French Empire style. Designed by McKim, Mead and White, c.1900.
⑥ Double doors of the Colonial Revival, from a dining room by Ogden Codman, c.1900. (To the left of these doors is a diagonal wall housing a chimneypiece.)

⑦ The Early Colonial style inspired this door with strap hinges, c.1900.
⑧ Millwork catalogues include doorcase ornamentation. Shown here are a hardwood "cap trim", as well as corner and head blocks made of composition. *RO*

⑨ Cut-glass panels could be used to emphasize the period theme. These two designs are based on lacework motifs. *RO*
⑩ A door plate, c.1890, showing Art Nouveau influence.
⑪ This Renaissance-style hinge was made in brass, by Hopkins and Dickinson, 1889. It has engraved surfaces and attenuated hinge finials.

⑫ An oxidized-silver key in semi-Byzantine style, 1889.
⑬ A Renaissance oxidized-silver escutcheon, 1889, cast with mask and foliate motifs.
⑭ A brass Colonial Revival door knocker, c.1920.
⑮ Four door knobs, not in any specific historic style. The bottom two are pressed glass.

⑯ Door knob and plate designs of the 1890s, mixing French and Italian Renaissance and Byzantine themes.
⑰ A door handle, showing Art Nouveau influence.
⑱ The transom lift was intended to improve ventilation. American Manufacturing Company, 1880s.

Windows

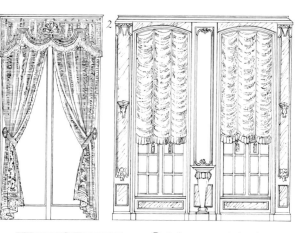

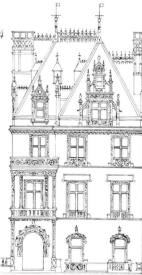

③ This sliding blind/shade
operates on the sash principle.
The cross-section shows how
the three parts of the blind fit
inside the two sashes. RO
④ The window features of this
François Premier-style house
by McKim, Mead and White
include: limestone hood moulds
with crocket finials; carved
stone balconies on the upper
floors; and elaborate dormer
windows with stone pinnacles.
Such surrounds often held
large sheets of plate glass,
rather than the smaller panes
which were actually used in the
French Renaissance.
⑤ A variation of the Colonial
Revival style, with six-over-
six sash windows and
shutters.

① A three-part window bay
and balcony on the Andrew
Carnegie Mansion, New York,
by Babb, Cook and Willard,
1903. The heavily carved
limestone surround features
scrolls and a cartouche, and the
balcony beneath rests on console
brackets. All these details are
drawn from the vocabulary of
French Classical design. CW
② Elaborate Beaux Arts
window treatments. On the left
is a window with fringed
pelmet/valance and swags. On
the right, casement windows
with arched heads flank a
narrow pier mirror and console
pedestal. These windows are
dressed with festoon blinds/
Austrian shades.

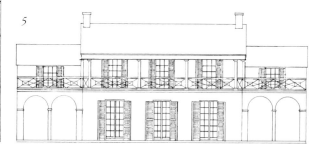

Windows and window surrounds conform closely to
period themes. The Colonial Revival style features
six-over-six paned sashes often with taller triple sash
windows on the main floor; sometimes their wooden
surrounds contain carved garlands or a Greek key pattern.
The French Classical style windows have arched or semi-
circular heads and are frequently framed with carved
stone garlands, bands of guilloche or rusticated masonry.
The François Premier style, popularized by Richard Morris
Hunt, is notable for heavily carved hoodmoulds on principal windows and busily crocketed dormer windows.
Italian Renaissance style windows are grandly restrained,
with either aedicule surrounds or pedimented heads.

Spanish Revival windows often have ornamental iron
grilles and sometimes florid Baroque decoration embel-
lishes windows over the front door. Tudor Revival windows are characterized by small panes and stone mullions.

Not all Beaux Arts window treatments followed period
prototypes. For example, many large houses had conservatories, and architects usually laced the iron supporting
structure with invented decoration or period motifs.

Beautifully tooled brass or gilded bolts and latches,
forged by firms such as Caldwell and Company or P. E.
Guerin, ornamented French and Italian style windows.
Cruder iron hardware was applied to Tudor and Spanish
style window frames.

① *The use of a small-paned upper sash with a single pane on the lower sash, as in the central dormer window here (1895), was common in Shingle-style houses. The gable decoration is unusual.*
② *The details on this facade, including windows with crocket finials and a limestone balcony carved with dolphins, leaves and figures, are taken directly from François Premier sources. New York, 1899. UI*
③ *This upper-floor window* (1903) *has a muscular character. The console brackets, as well as specific motifs on the balcony, derive from French Classical houses. CW*
④ *This window, with a carved arched surround, is from the library of the Andrew Carnegie Mansion, New York, 1903. CW*
⑤ *The height, the slender proportions and the curved glazing bars all contribute to the elegance of these French doors, 1895. ES*

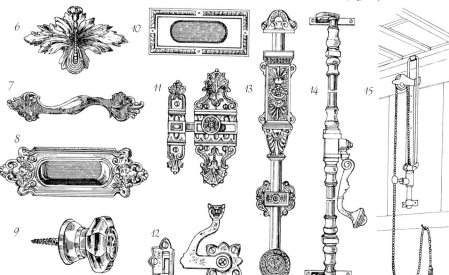

Firms such as P.E. Guerin of New York specialized in superbly wrought hardware in brass, bronze and other metals.
⑥ *A Louis XIV sash lift.*
⑦ *A Rococo bar sash lift.*
⑧ *A flush sash lift, 1914.*
⑨ *A cut-glass shutter knob.*
⑩ *A flush sash lift.*
⑪ *A sliding window bolt.*
⑫ *A Louis XIV shutter latch.*
⑬ *A sliding surface bolt.*
⑭ *An espagnolette bolt, for French doors, 1905.*
⑮ *A skylight lift, 1889.*

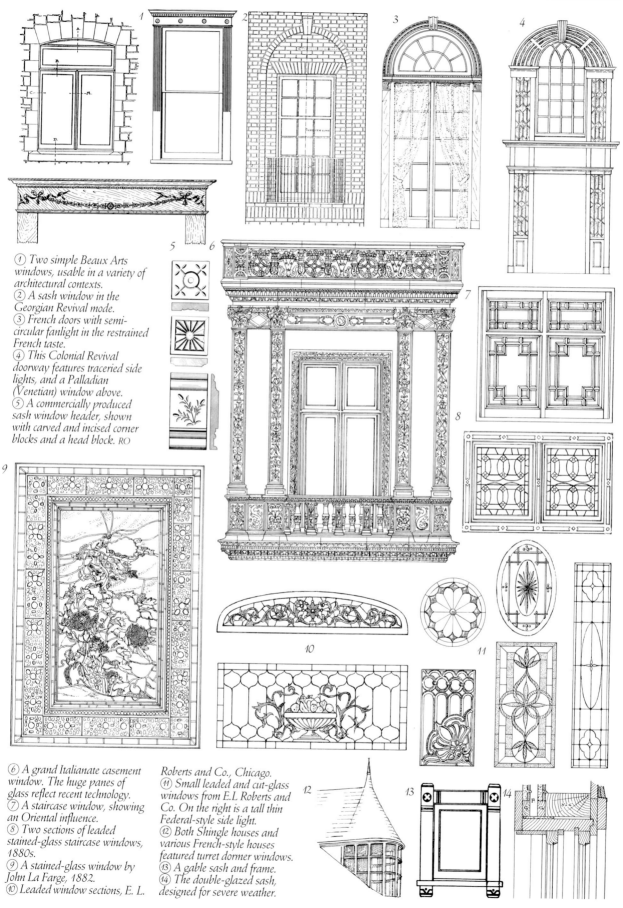

WINDOWS

① Two simple Beaux Arts windows, usable in a variety of architectural contexts.
② A sash window in the Georgian Revival mode.
③ French doors with semi-circular fanlight in the restrained French taste.
④ This Colonial Revival doorway features traceried side lights, and a Palladian (Venetian) window above.
⑤ A commercially produced sash window header, shown with carved and incised corner blocks and a head block. RO

⑥ A grand Italianate casement window. The huge panes of glass reflect recent technology.
⑦ A staircase window, showing an Oriental influence.
⑧ Two sections of leaded stained-glass staircase windows, 1880s.
⑨ A stained-glass window by John La Farge, 1882.
⑩ Leaded window sections, E. L. Roberts and Co., Chicago.
⑪ Small leaded and cut-glass windows from E.L Roberts and Co. On the right is a tall thin Federal-style side light.
⑫ Both Shingle houses and various French-style houses featured turret dormer windows.
⑬ A gable sash and frame.
⑭ The double-glazed sash, designed for severe weather.

Walls

① A treatment of a large curtained opening between two rooms, with Islamic influence in the complex woodwork.
② This wainscot features a beautifully inlaid panel beneath the chair rail. The wall above is covered with red damask, a popular period treatment. *ES*
③ and ④ Panelled wainscotting of plain design was available from a number of commercial suppliers. The first example is oak; the second has white pine stiles and rails and yellow pine panels. *RO*
⑤ Wooden mouldings, factory-made in pressed pine, poplar or cypress, and purchased by the foot. *RO*

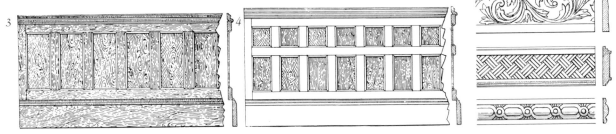

High-style French Classical drawing room, dining room and library walls usually had carved wooden panels (boiseries), sometimes with shallow-relief ornament (trophies, festoons). The ground might be painted white, green or blue, while the mouldings and carved ornament were picked out in gold.

Stained oak panels typify the Tudor and Jacobean Revival styles. These could be carved in linenfold designs, or employed intricate patterns of intersecting squares, rectangles and lozenge shapes. Strapwork carving enriched corners or chimney breasts.

Georgian Revival panelling was much plainer, with carving or moulded decoration reserved for the chair rail, cornice and chimney breast or the edges of stiles and rails. Colonial Revival interiors relied on a combination of panelled surfaces and smooth plaster. Many plaster walls were interrupted only by a chair rail, which could be symmetrical or "pedestal" (flat on top with a series of narrower mouldings beneath). Colonial Revival panelling resembled Georgian prototypes, or was constructed of plain, beaded boards.

Panelled dados (with painted plaster or wallpaper above) were especially popular in halls and dining rooms. Thin marble slabs covered walls in the grandest French or Italianate mansions. Marble or limestone walls might be used as a foil for brilliant tapestries.

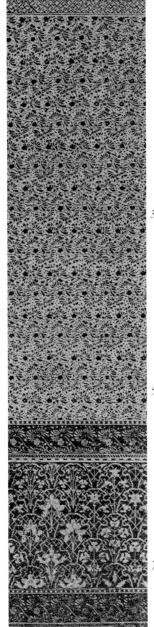

① A three-part wallpaper design by Samuel Codman, c.1880.
② A dining room design. The narrow display shelving above the chair rail was a common Beaux Arts device. The stencilled pattern in the shallow field shows Art Nouveau influence. SK
③ A panelled foyer wall, 1888. The wooden grid of recessed and moulded panels with lozenge-shaped panels at the top was typical of Renaissance Revival interiors of the 1880s.
④ The popularity of spindle screens reached its height in the Beaux Arts era. This one (half is shown) screened the top of a bay window.
⑤ The cornice details, chimney breast panelling and skirting board/baseboard here are all typical of early 20th-century Colonial Revival interiors.

⑥ A robust combination of French Rococo and Neo-classical carving and plasterwork, featuring paired columns flanking a pier glass and medallions of plaster with bow-knots at the top. By Ogden Codman, 1904.

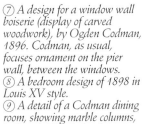

⑦ A design for a window wall boiserie (display of carved woodwork), by Ogden Codman, 1896. Codman, as usual, focuses ornament on the pier wall, between the windows.
⑧ A bedroom design of 1898 in Louis XV style.
⑨ A detail of a Codman dining room, showing marble columns, in French Classical style.

① The Beaux Arts interest in exotic Oriental design is obvious in the Japanese-influenced wall treatment of this house in Forest Hills, Queens, New York. Panels beneath the windows feature a gilded ground overpainted with dragonflies and vegetation. Note how the reed motifs continue onto the mirrors above. FH

② A plaster frieze, just below ceiling level, above wooden panelling in Tudor Revival style. Vine and leaf motifs are framed by two rope mouldings. The owl is one of a series of motifs, including fleur-de-lys, all the way around the room. FH

③ Glazed tiles were used to cover the walls of bathrooms and kitchens in the Beaux Arts era. This example, from the bathroom of The Elms, Newport, Rhode Island, features a row of tiles with a raised pattern of delicate festoons containing garlands of flowers, ribbons and bows. The design has obvious period connotations. ES

④ Wooden or plaster mouldings that divided walls into sections are typical of Beaux Arts interiors. Sometimes these mouldings were further enriched with carved or moulded ornament. This French- or Italian-style treatment features roundels at the re-entrant corners of the inner moulding, and scrolls and acanthus leaves flanking a cartouche at the top of the outer moulding: these details are gilded to match the frieze above. FH

⑤ A fairly plain wall treatment. The raised, panelled skirting board/baseboard serves as a pedestal for pilasters on the corners and door surrounds. The flat sides of the pilasters are ornamented with raised mouldings. UI

Ceilings

① *A beamed ceiling with carved leaf motifs on the beam-ends. Note the use of small-scale carving to punctuate the timbers.* UI

② *This magnificent wooden ceiling, with its Gothic pattern of mouldings and its intricately carved bosses, is in an Old English style.* UI

③ *The juncture of wall and ceiling can be ornamented with lavish plasterwork – here including reeded and egg-and-dart mouldings.* UI

④ *An extremely elaborate variant of a coffered ceiling, with Renaissance-style carving on the rafters and gilded dragons in between.* ES

Most ceilings in the Colonial or Georgian styles are coated with smooth white plaster. In some imitations of 17th-century rooms, exposed unpainted beams frame strips of white plaster on laths of wood. Other Colonial style ceilings have plaster decoration – usually beaded mouldings around the perimeter or leaf motifs encircling the base of a chandelier. Plaster cornice mouldings, loosely classical, mark the intersection of ceiling and wall. Most of the moulding was applied to the wall, but sometimes half-round plaster beads would also be applied to the adjacent ceiling.

Classical ceilings are also plastered, but often feature painted scenes with clouds, cherubs and mythical fig-ures. Raised wood or plaster mouldings, richly carved or gilded, divide the surface into panels. Italian Renaissance Revival ceilings are of wood, featuring a grid of deep coffers, with rosettes at the centre, and bright reds, blues and gold enlivening the carvings. Spanish Revival ceilings are similar, but usually not so heavily ornamented; they are often dark-stained.

Houses in the English Tudor or François Premier styles often have great halls with huge timbered ceilings. Exposed beam ends may be carved, as may the corbel stones supporting the beams. The beams do not necessarily support the roof, as steel or other modern materials could carry the load.

① *A coffered ceiling in the Renaissance style, from a New York dining room of 1887, by Alfred Zucker and Company.*
② *The ceiling of a drawing room in a house in Boston, Massachusetts, 1880 (architects: Sturgis and Brigham). The interlacing circular and square patterns are reminiscent of the intricate ceilings of the Aesthetic movement.*
③ *A domed ceiling from a hallway decorated in the Persian style, 1880s. The richly patterned surface features carved, painted and moulded plaster detail.*

④ *A section of a stamped steel ceiling, manufactured by H.S. Northrop, New York, c.1885. The scrolled foliate decoration, pressed from the back, is fairly typical. Ceilings of this type, which were installed in sections, were used more commonly in commercial buildings, although there was also some residential use.*
⑤ *A ceiling design with moulded plaster decoration in the Renaissance taste, c.1885.*

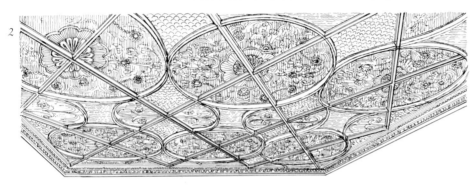

⑥ *A stucco-like composition ceiling in the Empire style, c.1890, from the Stereo-Relief Decorative Company, New York. It was claimed that the patented process produced exceptionally dense relief patterns, and was fireproof.*
⑦ *Profiles of cornice mouldings, made by E.L. Roberts, Chicago, 1903. RO*

Floors

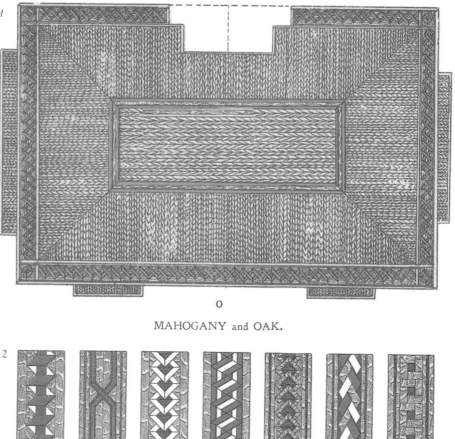

MAHOGANY and OAK.

① *A parquet design, c.1900. Some firms produced instant parquet composed of wood blocks glued onto cloth.* UD

② *Parquet borders, combining various woods (oak, maple, cherry, walnut, mahoghany), 1895.* UD

The most common flooring material is wood, especially oak parquet, which in drawing rooms, dining rooms and libraries of elegant French or Italian Renaissance houses often has a herringbone or basketweave pattern in the centre with a complex border in various hardwoods such as cherry or mahogany. Border motifs often derive from period sources. Minor rooms also have parquet, usually without elaborate borders.

Colonial Revival houses tend to have straight board floors, rather than parquet. Instead of the wide or randomly sized planks of pine or local hardwoods that would usually be found in an authentic Colonial house, most Colonial Revival floors are of uniform oak boards,

two to three inches (5–7.5 cm) wide. This thin oak strip flooring, with inlaid borders at the margins, is also found in Tudor Revival houses. It became the standard floor finish for later, smaller houses in the Beaux Arts manner.

Marble foyer or hallway floors in alternating black and white squares or lozenges are common in a range of revival styles – Renaissance, Georgian or Colonial. The grandest houses have entrance floors of exotic, highly coloured marbles. Terrazzo was occasionally used for halls, foyers or conservatories. Unglazed terracotta, practical for summer residences or houses in warmer climates, often covers floors in a Spanish Revival or Spanish Colonial Revival setting.

CEILINGS

FLOORS

① Long, slim oak boards form a chevron parquetry pattern, with three running boards making a subtle border. ES
② This parquetry floor features a checked pattern, with a curved border easing the transition between the door threshold and the main floor space of the room. UI

③ A detail from a Sears, Roebuck and Company (Chicago) advertisement for "Royal Acme High-Grade Hardwood Flooring", 1910. Tongued-and-grooved maple boards interlocked at the ends as well as down the sides, as this illustration shows. Maple was a hard-wearing surface and

hence it was suitable for a kitchen or hallway; it was also easy to clean and could take an attractive oil finish. When the aim was a beautiful appearance, plain oak was used instead. Quarter-sawn red oak offered a useful compromise between practical and aesthetic needs.

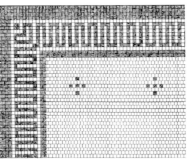

④ A ceramic mosaic tile floor, delivered in pre-laid sheets two feet (60cm) square. It was suitable for bathrooms, kitchens and service areas. From Sears, Roebuck and Co., Chicago.
⑤ A black and white tiled floor was most commonly used in hallways, but sometimes in

dining rooms too. It was also suitable for garden rooms and conservatories.
⑥ A detail from an American Brussels (looped-pile) luxury carpet of 1870. From the Lowell Manufacturing Company.
⑦ A detail from an American ingrain (non-

pile, reversible) carpet of the same date.
⑧ American carpet manufacturers in the Beaux Arts period all made Oriental-style rugs, but genuine Eastern rugs were also very popular. This is an Islamic prayer rug, used at the Biltmore House, North Carolina. BIL

Fireplaces

A broad, low, wooden fireplace of unusual proportions adorns a François Premier-style salon in the Isaac Fletcher House, New York (now the Ukrainian Institute). The wide pointed arch surround that frames the marble facing is a late Gothic device. However, the relatively correct Corinthian columns flanking the fireplace reflect the influence of the Italian Renaissance. The carvings in the spandrels of the arch are also in the Renaissance taste. The architect of the house, C.P.H. Gilbert, understood that François Premier was a transitional style, linking French Gothic traditions with innovations of the Renaissance. The plated four-centred frame around the hearth, which is fronted by an amber-coloured marble slab laid flush with a parquet floor, also bears Gothic-style tracery. UI

By the end of the 19th century, most houses of any size had central heating systems. Thus, fireplaces in the Beaux Arts period were freed from function. They could be used on winter evenings but their main purpose was ornamental and symbolic. The magnificent fireplaces in entrance halls announced the style of the house to anyone who came in through the front door.

The enormous halls or galleries of mansions in the François Premier style featured fireplaces tall enough to walk into, with huge limestone hoods tapering back toward the wall as they climbed to the ceiling. Italian Renaissance Revival types are also very tall, but do not have such large hoods and are framed by stone or marble surrounds with classical carving. Spanish Revival fireplaces often adopt similar forms, with rows of stone or wood carvings on the chimney breast. Fireplaces of the French Classical Revival styles are smaller – frequently comprising a wooden frame of delicate Rococo leaf carving, or a shallow marble mantel shelf with Louis XVI columnar supports.

The Georgian Revival manner is marked by elements of a single classical Order in wood or marble, with reeded or plain columns. Overmantel panels tend to have shoulders (croisettes) or a broken pediment at the top. The Federal style uses similar devices, but incorporates Adamesque detail.

① Abstract Moorish and Oriental elements are mixed in this fireplace of 1882-3.
② The exotic columns and central lyre ornament are redolent of the Empire style.
③ A Renaissance Revival fireplace carved in stone, with classical busts in the frieze.
④ A panelled wooden surround frames this fireplace of c.1890, with overmantel mirror. The Renaissance-style brackets and garlands are arranged in a distinctively 19th-century manner.
⑤ Here, the panelling above the mantel shelf has Tudor connotations, but the columns and the tiled surround do not relate to the same period theme. The frame of full-height columns was popular from c.1880 to c.1920.
⑥ Although elliptical or circular mirrors were the focal point of decoration in many French and English 18th-century overmantel designs, this treatment of 1880 had no historic precedent. The mantel shelf, with thick reeding underneath, is also highly inventive.
⑦ All the details of this fireplace and overmantel are academically correct and relate directly to French Renaissance models. It dates from 1910.
⑧ This low fireplace resting on acanthus leaf consoles, with a tall mirror above, is copied precisely from 18th-century French models.
⑨ Certain motifs here, such as the carved strapwork on either side of the mirror, are drawn from historic sources, but the amount of carving and the distinctive combination of details reflect late 19th-century taste.

① *The four-centred arch and carved spandrels of the stone surround and the linenfold panelling above contribute to the Tudor character of this design.* FH

② *Coloured marbles within a tabernacle of carved mahogany. The architectural devices and motifs derive from French and Italian Renaissance sources.* ES

③ *Attenuated columns, quatrefoil patterns and floral and foliate motifs adorn this Tudor Revival fireplace.* FH
④ *Console brackets support* the mantel shelf of a marble fireplace in the French Classical style. UI
⑤ *Plain brickwork contrasts with finely carved wooden* columns topped with composition capitals. CW
⑥ *Beaux Arts architects often incorporated antique architectural artefacts into* interiors. This is a Regency marble fireplace, c.1810. UI
⑦ *A fireplace detail, showing marble slip, carved acanthus leaf and dentil mouldings.* CW

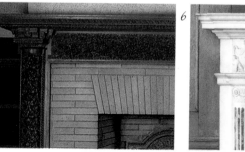

① An Italian Renaissance-style fireplace of c.1890 flanked by stone Corinthian columns, with a carved frieze.
② Another design in a loosely Italian Renaissance style, with mirrored overmantel, 1883.
③ This massive fireplace with marble and mosaic decoration was designed for the Cornelius Vanderbilt II house in New York by Augustus Saint-

Gaudens and John La Farge.
④ The hood on this chimneypiece was made in antique brass. The panels in the overmantel symbolize night and morning. New York, 1880s.
⑤ A drawing room chimneypiece in opulent French style, with mirrored overmantel.
⑥ Onyx with a surround of painted wooden panelling: a grand Renaissance-style

fireplace, with Oriental overtones, from the Henry Villard House, New York, 1880s.
⑦ Grates often came with a decorative "summer piece", which was put in place when the fire was not in use. For lightness, these could be in steel rather than cast iron. RO
⑧ A grate without the summer piece in place. The handle connects to a shaking and

dumping attachment, used to separate the ashes and dead cinders from live coals. RO
⑨ A gas grate for a fireplace with a wooden surround, shown in the closed position. For use, the upper part of the screen was removed, but the decorative grille remained fixed.
⑩ Three andirons: wrought iron; brass and iron; and another wrought-iron example.

Kitchen stoves

① *A cast-iron range by Abendroth Brothers, New York. The mouldings are heavy but not excessively ornate.* OM
② *The "Acme Regal Steel Range", advertised in the Sears, Roebuck and Company catalogue, c.1902. The cast-iron range featured an upper grill/ broiler and nickel-plated decoration incorporating familiar* motifs – cartouches, C-scrolls *and foliate decoration.*
③ *A gas range of 1889 manufactured by George M.* Clark of Chicago. Gas ranges *were slowly gaining in popularity. This model has a grill/broiler at the base. As stove* technology progressed, ornament *became sparser.*
④ *A General Electric range, 1913. The design of early electric stoves (1890-1910) was based on gas stoves. Both types of heating source took up less space than previous fuel types. After c.1900, gas and electric stoves were mounted on iron legs.*

FIREPLACES

KITCHEN STOVES

During the Beaux Arts era wood-burning stoves were supplanted by coal-burning ones; gas models followed. Cast iron was used consistently throughout the period. The High Victorian round- or pot-bellied designs were replaced by square, low, cast stoves with symmetrical arrangements of four to eight burners. Underneath, two hinged doors opened to the fire. The cast iron was moulded into intricate patterns of lattice, grape vines, and Neo-classical detail. Often, nickel mounts, hinges and door panels provide further embellishment. The flue consists of a tin pipe elbowing out of the back and into the wall. In front of the flue and above the burners are elevated boilers or racks for warming food. The upper portion of the stove is typically covered with leaf decoration or ornamented with Renaissance-style mounts.

By 1900 electric and gas stoves had been introduced with great success. The new stoves were smaller, and stood on four legs a foot or so off the floor. The design of gas stoves parallelled sanitary fixtures by incorporating enamelled surfaces. Plated metal mounts or hinges often appear on the early gas stoves, but there was not nearly as much decorative metalwork as on the earlier wood- or coal-burning types. By the end of the period, the most up-to-date examples were ornamented only with round plastic knobs and perhaps chrome-plated handles and strips.

Staircases

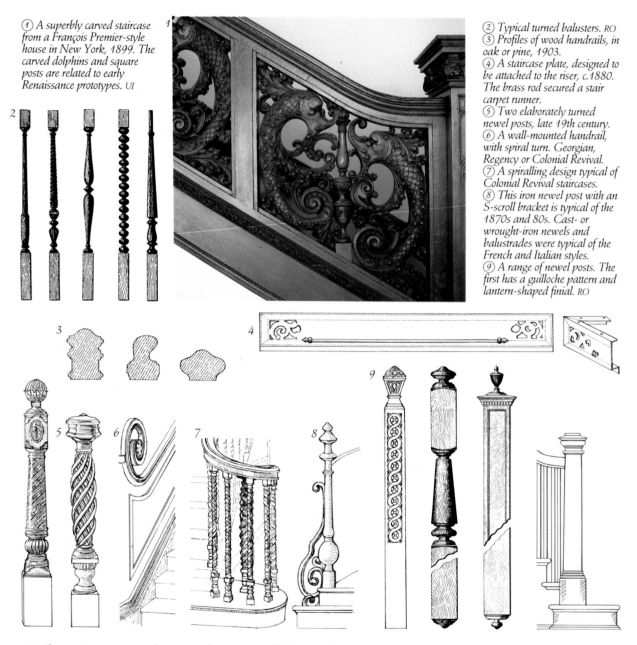

① *A superbly carved staircase from a François Premier-style house in New York, 1899. The carved dolphins and square posts are related to early Renaissance prototypes.* UI

② *Typical turned balusters.* RO
③ *Profiles of wood handrails, in oak or pine, 1903.*
④ *A staircase plate, designed to be attached to the riser, c.1880. The brass rod secured a stair carpet runner.*
⑤ *Two elaborately turned newel posts, late 19th century.*
⑥ *A wall-mounted handrail, with spiral turn. Georgian, Regency or Colonial Revival.*
⑦ *A spiralling design typical of Colonial Revival staircases.*
⑧ *This iron newel post with an S-scroll bracket is typical of the 1870s and 80s. Cast- or wrought-iron newels and balustrades were typical of the French and Italian styles.*
⑨ *A range of newel posts. The first has a guilloche pattern and lantern-shaped finial.* RO

The staircase was a dominant feature, establishing the tone of a Beaux Arts interior even if it was placed on one side rather than centrally.

At the outset of the era, the most popular type was a version of Italian Renaissance design in wood. Three turned balusters rested on each tread. The newel posts were huge, often square, with turned sections and carved panels; they could be capped with finials or electric torchères (often in the form of bronze figures).

Tudor or Jacobean Revival staircases, also wooden, had thicker balusters. In some Tudor and early French Renaissance Revival examples, the handrail was supported by wooden arches that stood on the string board. But the most elaborate wooden balustrades (Italianate, Tudor or early French Renaissance) are those with sections of pierced and carved decoration framed by square posts, as in the photograph above.

Georgian and Colonial Revival staircases are more delicate, with turned, columnar or vase-shaped balusters, and spiral-turned or fluted newel posts. The handrail often ends in a spiral around the post. Often the stairs and balusters would be painted white, while the handrail was stained or painted brown.

Shingle-style staircases tend to be screened by rows of spindles, drawing upon an eclectic array of sources, including Persian, Japanese and Queen Anne motifs.

① *A superbly carved Renaissance Revival stair. The silhouette of the reeded balusters and the festoons on the huge newel are distinctive.*

② *Another Renaissance Revival staircase, 1880s. The balustrade is more closely modelled on period prototypes than in the previous example, although the rather spare spacing of turned balusters and posts is unusual.*
③ *A simple Colonial staircase, c.1910. The treads and handrail could be mahogany, the rest of the woodwork painted white.*

④ *A versatile design of the early 20th century, available commercially.* RO
⑤ *A cast- and wrought-iron stair, 1880s. This relatively unornamented form, with bolted cast-iron supports, was* especially recommended for service areas.
⑥ *This Colonial Revival balustrade is from a house in Forest Hills, Queens, New York, c.1915. The fairly simple, bold treatment would be* suitable for a modestly sized house. Bold spiral-twist balusters support a ramped handrail. FH
⑦ *This Renaissance Revival newel post (1903) is relatively small: the glory of the staircase is* in its magnificent carving. CW
⑧ *Lacy wrought-iron balustrades were typically used for grand houses in French classical styles. This example is from The Elms, Newport, Rhode Island, 1895.* ES

① *Typical carved decoration on the stair-ends of a Colonial Revival staircase.* FH
② *A stair and screen, Newport, Rhode Island (McKim, Mead and White, 1880-82), with Oriental and Colonial motifs.*
③ *A spindle and lattice screen, by Henry H. Richardson, 1881.*
④ *The elaborately spindled staircase of the J. Piermont Morgan House, New York. In the arch's spandrels, small pieces of stained glass were set between gilt wires in squares of oak.*
⑤ *Renaissance Revival grandeur, Boston, Massachussetts (Peabody and Stearns, 1877-9).*
⑥ *This section of a spindle screen relates to classical rather than Oriental precedents.*
⑦ *A Moorish design, early 20th century.* RO

Built-in furniture

① A bar in a Beaux Arts residence in Forest Hills, Queens, New York. An ingenious and very free interpretation of the Tudor style, with dark-stained wood panelling and carvings that resemble ship's figureheads. The right-hand section of the bar is hinged for access. FH

② From the same house, another feature in panelled Tudor style – shelves and cupboards alongside a fireplace – but with distinctively Beaux Arts features, such as the spindled section in the centre, above the display shelf. The linenfold panelling is typical of the style. FH

STAIRCASES

BUILT-IN FURNITURE

During this period there was a heightened interest in service and storage. Kitchen and pantry areas featured walls of cabinets in two tiers: glazed above, solid underneath. Pantries accommodated warming shelves and countertops. Bedrooms, too, were equipped with huge walls of panelled closets. Telephone rooms tucked underneath the stairs were furnished with a chair, a built-in shelf and possibly a door with a glazed panel, for privacy. All of these cabinets and closets were enriched with mouldings, panels, glazing bars and hardware in the relevant historical style.

For a Tudor or Gothic Revival interior, the appropriate choice was wide oak panelling and carved oak trim with ogee arches, quatrefoil and trefoil motifs. French-style cabinets and doors featured painted wooden panels with gilt hardware. Many Oriental schemes included ebonized cabinetry. Sometimes a system of low cabinets around all or most of the dining room also carried the architectural theme. Ebonized cabinets often served as shelves for Oriental porcelain.

Deep window seats were standard in Colonial and Georgian Revival houses. They were most often in a bay window or across the bottom of a large hall or stairwell window; the hinged seat would open for storage. Tudor and Gothic Revival interiors had inglenooks – a feature also of Mission Style houses of the same period.

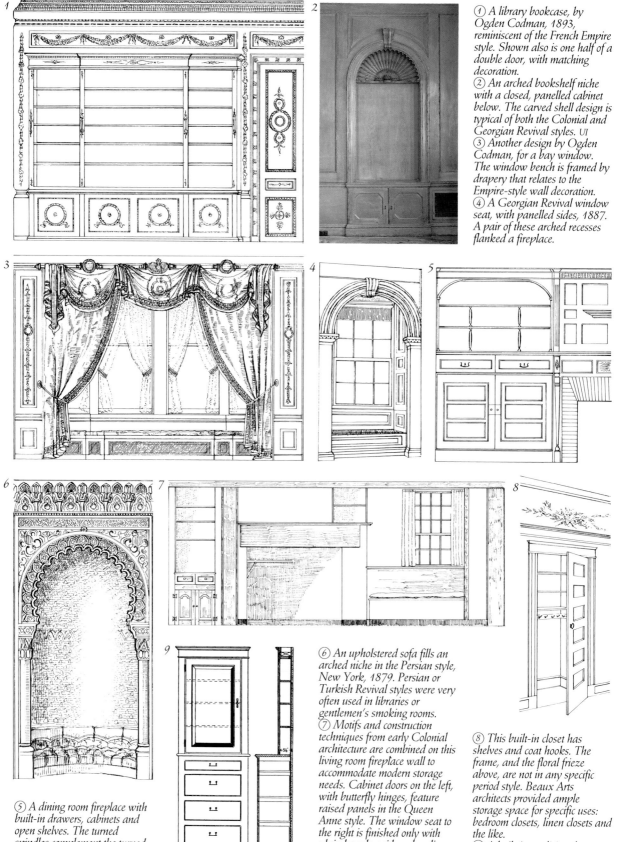

① A library bookcase, by Ogden Codman, 1893, reminiscent of the French Empire style. Shown also is one half of a double door, with matching decoration.
② An arched bookshelf niche with a closed, panelled cabinet below. The carved shell design is typical of both the Colonial and Georgian Revival styles. UI
③ Another design by Ogden Codman, for a bay window. The window bench is framed by drapery that relates to the Empire-style wall decoration.
④ A Georgian Revival window seat, with panelled sides, 1887. A pair of these arched recesses flanked a fireplace.

⑤ A dining room fireplace with built-in drawers, cabinets and open shelves. The turned spindles complement the turned column of the fireplace surround. Typical of a modest, suburban Beaux Arts interior.

⑥ An upholstered sofa fills an arched niche in the Persian style, New York, 1879. Persian or Turkish Revival styles were very often used in libraries or gentlemen's smoking rooms.
⑦ Motifs and construction techniques from early Colonial architecture are combined on this living room fireplace wall to accommodate modern storage needs. Cabinet doors on the left, with butterfly hinges, feature raised panels in the Queen Anne style. The window seat to the right is finished only with plain boards, with no beading or applied moulding. The intention is to create an appearance of simplicity.

⑧ This built-in closet has shelves and coat hooks. The frame, and the floral frieze above, are not in any specific period style. Beaux Arts architects provided ample storage space for specific uses: bedroom closets, linen closets and the like.
⑨ A built-in medicine chest (with mirror) and towel drawers, 1903. A side-view cross-section is shown alongside. RO

Services

① *This water closet unites up-to-date technology with finely crafted, historically derived ornament. It is disguised as a Louis XVI side chair with a caned skirt, seat and back. Even the handle of the water* tank chain is beautifully ornamented. ES
② *The bathroom of the Esakoff House, Forest Hills, New York, is treated as if it were an ornamental pavilion. The domed ceiling is covered with* gold leaf and painted decoration. The porcelain sink is supported on delicate cabriole legs. FH
③ *A heavy porcelain bathtub with rich ornamentation. From The Elms, Newport, Rhode Island.* ES
④ *A radiator grille from the Andrew Carnegie Mansion, New York, 1901, by Babb, Cook and Willard. Carnegie insisted on the most modern and sophisticated heating equipment.* CW

BUILT-IN FURNITURE

SERVICES

In the mid-1870s well-equipped bathrooms were exceptional. By 1917 they were commonplace.

The standard bathtub had feet and was made of porcelain-coated iron, often featuring a painted exterior. Horizontal bands of colour, Greek key or other classical motifs encircled the top. By 1920, this type was being eclipsed by the built-in porcelain enamelled bathtub, extending to the floor.

Porcelain water closets developed similarly. Initially, all the individual elements were decorated: the metal handle of the raised tank cabin could be elegantly cast, the wooden seat could be painted with flowers or trees, even the porcelain bowl sometimes featured a decora-tive glaze. Later in the period the housing became less elaborate. The bowl was freestanding, the water tank was placed directly behind it, and the porcelain surfaces were left plain. White was the usual finish.

Wash basins were enclosed with wooden cabinets or set into metal stands, or featured four porcelain legs or a single porcelain pedestal. The metal frames could be ornamented with nickel- or brass-plated ornaments at the corners and feet. Often a porcelain pedestal took the form of a fluted column on a plinth. Taps/faucets, stopper tops, hot and cold water levers were modelled on historic hardware in the French or Italian taste, or in some other revivalist style.

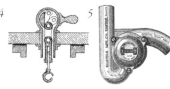

① The "Renaissance" siphon jet water closet, 1897 (J.L. Mott Iron Works, New York).
② A late 19th-century water closet with acanthus leaf decoration (Sanitas, Boston).
③ The "Manhattan" porcelain lined roll-rim bath, with eagle's-feet supports (Henry Shane Manufacturing Co., New York).
④ On the Sanitas wash basin (1880s), a lever was used to open or close the outlet – an innovation of the time.
⑤ A trap for a Sanitas wash basin, described in 1887 as "the only self-scouring, simple water-seal trap ever invented".

⑥ A Sanitas wash basin, with floral decoration, 1887.
⑦ A double wash basin, 1880s.
⑧ Washtubs could be galvanized iron with a porcelain lining, or brown glazed earthenware. The use of Beaux Arts detailing on such a utilitarian object says much about the times.

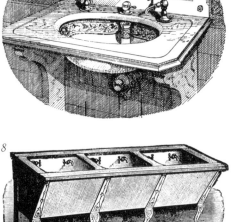

⑨ A boiler, made in copper, c.1900 by Randolph and Clowes, Waterbury, Connecticut. Central heating and hot water were preoccupations of the age.

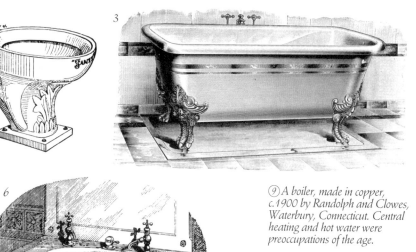

⑩ A "side-feed" boiler, by Gorton and Lidgerwood Co., New York, 1898. This would be housed in a utility room, and operated by a servant.
⑪ A radiator, c.1890, made by Gillis and Geoghegan, New York.
⑫ A radiator of 1904, made by the American Radiator company. It could be dismantled into halves, and was designed to fit around a pillar or column. AR
⑬ Sewage disposal in country and suburban regions remained less sophisticated than town systems. This cross-section shows a septic tank with filter bed. In the house, note the washtubs in the basement, the kitchen sink and range on the entrance floor and the sanitary fixtures above.

Lighting

① *An electric chandelier in "modern French" style.* ES
② *A three-branched sconce in Rococo taste, 1891.*
③ *A Renaissance Revival chandelier, 1888.*
④ *A Persian lantern, 1882.*
⑤ *An exterior lantern set in a Colonial Revival fanlight.*

⑥ *A gas-burning torchère on a newel post, 1875.*
⑦ *A gas chandelier, c.1880, conservative for its date.*
⑧ *A plain gas-burning sconce of brass and glass, 1880s.*
⑨ *A wrought-iron lantern on scrolled bracket, c.1900.*
⑩ *An elaborate open-worked wrought-iron lantern finial.*
⑪ *A wrought-iron gate overthrow, Georgian style, with a more current hanging lantern.*

Gas-burning fixtures were the most common lighting source at the beginning of the Beaux Arts period, but by 1900 electric fixtures were equally prevalent. Chandeliers and sconces were especially popular. There was a burgeoning interest in authentic period lighting fixtures, rewired for electricity.

Contemporary "French"-style chandeliers were made of gilded metal with tiers of crystal prisms. Some featured twisted branches with candle sockets in the Rococo taste, others a bronze oil-burning font with gilded mounts in the Empire style. Spanish Revival chandeliers, torchères, sconces and lamps were typically of wrought iron. Wheel-like chandeliers comprised thin radiating iron rods joined at the middle with a finial; simple iron sockets were placed around the rim. Addison Mizner, who designed Mediterranean style villas in Palm Beach, Florida, produced wrought-iron and wood furnishings in the Spanish style, including lighting fixtures.

Colonial Revival houses usually contained an array of branched glass chandeliers, either authentic or reproduction. Reproduction "Queen Anne" chandeliers, featuring a brass globe and ornate branches with strapwork, were also popular. In the first half of the period, huge bronze or gilded metal chandeliers in the Italian Renaissance style were much in vogue.

Metalwork

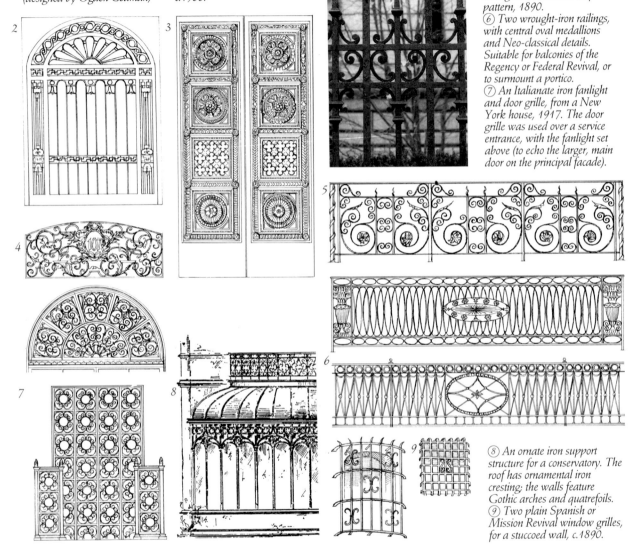

① A detail of spear and scroll motifs from a garden wall iron railing. CW
② Arched wrought-iron and glass doors such as this (designed by Ogden Codman, New York, 1912) are typical of grander houses in French Classical or Italian styles.
③ Cast-bronze doors, with typical Italianate details, c.1900.

④ An iron grille for a transom light, with a street number in the cartouche (McKim, Mead and White, 1898).
⑤ A typical balcony or porch railing with scroll and leaf pattern, 1890.
⑥ Two wrought-iron railings, with central oval medallions and Neo-classical details. Suitable for balconies of the Regency or Federal Revival, or to surmount a portico.
⑦ An Italianate iron fanlight and door grille, from a New York house, 1917. The door grille was used over a service entrance, with the fanlight set above (to echo the larger, main door on the principal facade).

⑧ An ornate iron support structure for a conservatory. The roof has ornamental iron cresting; the walls feature Gothic arches and quatrefoils.
⑨ Two plain Spanish or Mission Revival window grilles, for a stuccoed wall, c.1890.

Many Beaux Arts houses in French Classical or Italian styles had walled gardens, and even small urban residences had walled yards: the walls would be topped with wrought iron railings, and would often incorporate iron gates or sections of iron grillwork. French Classical-style houses often had elaborate iron fanlights/ transom lights surmounting their front doors, with cartouche, scroll and guilloche motifs; in towns and cities the street number was frequently cast in the cartouche. On French-style houses the principal floor casements often opened onto a wrought iron railing or balcony. François Premier residences, popularized by Richard Morris Hunt, featured delicate iron crest rails on the rooftops. Conservatories, very popular at this period, comprised glass panels set into an iron frame encrusted with foliate and flower motifs, or with Neo-classical detail, with a decorative roof crest.

Spanish-style houses feature only modest exterior ironwork, such as thin window grilles, but inside there was a wealth of ironwork on display – light fixtures, room dividers, wall plaques, and the like.

Other interior ironwork was occasioned by new technology: for example, elevators might have ornamented iron gates on each landing, or solid elevator doors combining bronze and iron decoration. Radiator covers were also treated decoratively.

Woodwork

① *A Colonial Revival fence post with lemon finial, c.1915.*
② *Colonial Revival gates with curvilinear crest rails, c.1915.*
③ *A wooden balustrade on the stair landing of the G.B. Bowler House, Bar Harbor, Maine (architects Rotch and Tilden), 1882. Typical of elaborate stairs in living halls.*
④ *A selection of turned wooden porch balusters, c.1910. RO*
⑤ *The turret of a Shingle-style house in Newport, Rhode Island, with flush-boarded cornice and contrasting sections of different types of shingles.*

⑥ *This wooden spindle screen shows both Islamic and Queen Anne influences. These screens were composed of both turned spindles and sections of fretwork. They were mounted above posts in a running frieze on exterior porches, or mounted in sections around interior staircases. This example, from a staircase, dates from 1879.*
⑦ *A Colonial Revival house, with recessed columned porch, dormers and a steep gable roof.*
⑧ *An eclectic Beaux Arts house with loggia and side porches. It combines elements of Colonial and Italianate styles.*

The exuberant style of woodwork that embellished Victorian eaves, porches, dormer windows, gables and door surrounds was not as popular in Beaux Arts houses. Heavily carved bargeboards (vergeboards) went out of style, but wooden decoration did enliven porches, verandas, cornices and windows.

Shingle-style houses are particularly inventive in their exterior woodwork. Heavy cornices, often composed of a flush-boarded "frieze" and flanking rows of ogee or half-round mouldings, are typical. Porches generally feature plain columns with smooth shafts, and many incorporate sections of trellis, loosely modelled on Far Eastern and Islamic prototypes. The shingles themselves can be combined on the exterior in different shapes, creating contrasting textures.

A hallmark of the Tudor Revival is half-timbering. Square timbers, with thick corner braces, support porch or canopy roofs. Exposed beam-ends terminate in carved finials, and the brackets beneath these beams may have carved foliate or animal motifs.

In Colonial Revival houses the small porches or porticoes have columns, capitals and cornices derived from classical sources. Italianate Beaux Arts houses often have deep overhanging eaves, held by long wooden brackets. Attached pergolas are a common feature of the Colonial Revival and Italianate styles.

METALWORK

WOODWORK

TWENTIES AND THIRTIES

① *One architectural theme of the period, as much apparent in American Art Deco houses as in English suburbia, is the rounding of corners and the reinterpretation of traditional features such as the porch. This is an English example, c.1930, from Dorset. The white-rendered facade is typical.* SP

② *La Casa Nueva, near Los Angeles, 1924-5: a house in the Spanish Colonial Revival style, which from c.1920 to the early 30s was virtually the norm in southern California. Key features are clay tiled roofs, roughly plastered walls, arched doorways and wrought-iron window grilles.* CN
③ *Apartment blocks of the 1930s show Modernist influence in their clean lines and absence of ornament.* AG
④ *Weekend homes were built in prefabricated form. This bungalow (with plan alongside) dates from 1937.* TI

The Art Deco style, named after the Paris exhibition of 1925, the Exposition Internationale des Arts Décoratifs et Industriels, has come to be seen as the quintessential style of the 1920s and 30s. Certainly, the works shown at this exhibition were innovative and influential. However, Art Deco is far from being the only important style of the period. In 1925 many designers were adapting historical forms to a modern sensibility, along with various exotic and "primitive" influences. A little later came the influence of Modernism: indeed, it is this that characterizes the Art Deco of the 30s, with its streamlined forms, and its predilection for chrome and synthetic materials.

Although the Exposition was international, the United States did not have a pavilion because, as designer Paul Frankl remarked, there was nothing worth sending, except for architecture. He meant skyscrapers, not domestic buildings, which brings us to one of the paradoxes of American design during the 20s. Technologically, the United States was the most advanced country in the world, and this technology was bravely displayed

in public buildings. Domestic architecture and interior design were much more conservative. There were exceptions. Architect-designers such as Frank Lloyd Wright were producing some startling houses in the 20s – for example, Wright's "textile block" buildings in California, constructed from patterned concrete blocks. Typical of the period, however, is the fashion for past styles. The most popular revivals were the English and Spanish Colonial styles, along with adaptations of European historical types. A design company such as Mellor, Meigs and Howe could produce an interior on almost any theme: particularly successful was a kind of romanticized medieval mode.

By the second half of the 1920s it is possible to discern a design idiom emerging that was peculiarly American and which made full use of technology. Architects such as Eliel Saarinen and Raymond Hood, and furniture and interior designers such as Paul Nelson, Kem Webber, Ascherman, Joseph Urban and Paul Frankl, began to work in a style in which simplified, geometric forms, inspired in part by European Modernism, were

① *A detail of the kitchen of La Casa Nueva, near Los Angeles – a Spanish Colonial Revival house of 1924-5. The colourful tiles are a typical feature of this style.* CN
② *A 30s bathroom, showing marked Art Deco influence in the graphic decoration and distinctive colour scheme.* BS

rendered luxurious by rich textures and new materials. Interestingly, the forward-thinking architects and designers were those experienced in designing for the film industry. Perhaps the American sensitivity to textural and tonal contrasts in interiors, and to dramatic massing of form in exteriors, is related to the discipline of designing for a black and white medium.

During the 1930s this style became, with variations, a language used and understood across the United States, although the revivalist taste remained strong. Despite the Depression, Modernist Art Deco interiors remained exuberant. The most extreme examples of this style are to be found on the West Coast and in Florida (especially Miami Beach). Modern materials – chrome, plastics, new types of glass – were used in conjunction with concealed lighting to create rooms of extraordinary inventiveness. These ideas were copied freely by commercial companies who were finally persuaded that the new style was here to stay.

Toward the end of the 1930s, many fashionable interiors were being dressed in a Neo-Baroque style with curving forms and plentiful use of drapery. At its best, this style is witty, and not slavishly revivalist.

Unlike the United States, Britain did exhibit at the 1925 Exposition, but the British pavilion was badly received: the objects on show were thought to be drab, old-fashioned re-workings of Arts and Crafts styles. In many ways, the situation in Britain was similar to that in the United States: manufacturers were unwilling to produce objects in a new style which they failed to understand.

The impact of new ideas from Continental Europe was first seen in public architecture: domestic building lagged behind. Houses of all types and at all levels of expense were being built in a revivalist manner best described as "Tudorbethan" (from "Tudor" and "Elizabethan"). Many of the suburbs developed by specula-

tive builders around the large cities are in this style, but so too are larger, more exclusive houses. The architecture is characterized by deliberate "period" detailing, including timbering, gables, porches, stained glass and so on. A small suburban house would have almost no period referencing inside – except for that installed by the owner. However, a more opulent house of the type generally referred to as "Stockbroker's Tudor" would undoubtedly have panelling, beams and a grand staircase with richly carved newels. This term is also an apt description of many American houses of the 20s.

The Modernist influence becomes apparent in domestic architecture only at the end of the 1920s. Britain had a number of good architect-designers working in the Modernist manner. Descriptions of modern interiors were featured in Duncan Miller's influential book, *More Colour Schemes for the Modern Home* of 1938, which depicts a variety of 1930s trends, from disciplined Modernism, through a de luxe version (which has affinities to American interiors of the period), to witty plays on period styles in the manner of Syrie Maugham and Oliver Hill. Some of these ideas caught the public imagination – for example, the use of white or near-white to dress walls and floors had become a fashionable cliché by the end of the 30s. Mirrored walls, successfully used by Oliver Hill, came into vogue and remained there for several decades. The abstract patterned carpets and rugs first produced by E. McKnight Kauffer and Marion Dorn spawned a thousand imitations. The murals painted by Rex Whistler and Allan Walton inspired scenic wallpapers.

By the late 1930s even suburban houses were beginning to have some modern features, such as metal windows (sometimes with rounded corners in the "suntrap" style). Manufacturers' catalogues reflect, sometimes with amusing results, a demand for modern fixtures alongside the continued popularity of revivalism.

Doors

The use of a brick entrance surround to contrast with a plain rendered wall surface is common in English suburban houses of the 1930s. In many examples the main surface is pebbledashed – an all-over covering of small pebbles. SP

There is no standard Art Deco door, but some decorative elements recur, particularly in the late 20s and the 1930s. The combination of metal and glass is important – often within a stepped surround, which may include a window or sculpted panel. The door itself might be heavy glass, reinforced with iron or bronze worked into stylized natural forms or abstract patterns. In British suburban houses, instead of metal, wood might be used, radiating in a sunburst pattern. The influence of Modernism encouraged flush doors with no moulding, and with minimal door fittings. Metallic finishes are sometimes used inside the house, or metal sheet cladding on exterior doors. In Britain, a backward-

looking type was the panelled wooden door with stained glass. Some wooden doors had small windows in "arty" shapes, such as diamonds or hearts. Heavy panelling in dark wood with carving and decorative metalwork typify the American West Coast Spanish Revival style.

In the 1930s porches become a feature of many houses. In Modernist-influenced houses they may be formed by a cantilevered upper story. Elsewhere they vary from simple gabled constructions to elaborate affairs with columns, sometimes incorporating seats. The more traditional doors were still dressed with fingerplates/push plates, lock escutcheons and handles, which by the 30s were available in Bakelite as well as various metal finishes.

① *The sunray motif was used on doors of all kinds. This example, in wood and glass, is from Miami Beach, 1939.*
② *to* ④ *These doors are all solidly made, in Swedish redwood and oak, and show the lingering influence of the Arts and Crafts movement. The last example would fit beneath a porch.*

⑤ *Here, in a Modern house in Northampton, England, 1927, the door forms a composition with the cantilevered porch and staircase window above.*
⑥ *A design of 1929; the door was executed in chased metal.*
⑦ *This 30s porch in Miami Beach is typical in its slender pole and zigzag iron balustrade.*

⑧ *Spiralling pillars of tiles add novelty to a conventional 30s English suburban house.*
⑨ *The influence of French Art Deco shows strongly in this Miami Beach stepped door surround (Norden and Nadel, 1937) with stylized relief and metal lighting fixtures at either side.*

⑩ *Another Miami Beach design (1939), using glass tiles. These tiles were marketed under trade-names such as Vitrolyte and Carrara.*

⑪ *Key features here are a convex pediment, wavy border (reflected in the door itself) and conical lighting fixture. (Miami Beach, 1939.)*

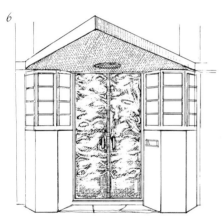
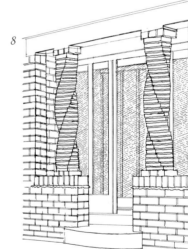

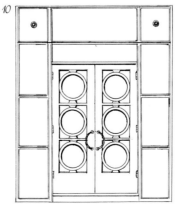

① A simple glazed door in a recessed porch, 1930s. The simple brick pattern edging the hood adds a touch of modernity, whereas the stone-dressed windows carry nostalgic evocations of the past. SA

② The leading pattern here is distinctly but not obtrusively modern. The juxtaposition of dark and light paintwork makes a graphic composition within the brickwork surround. SM

③ Elaborate Baroque plasterwork contrasts with the plain white wall of a Spanish Colonial Revival house. The door is oak, with a typical interlaced design. CN

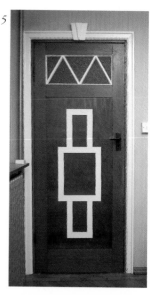

④ An Art Deco doorway in Miami, Florida. The asymmetrically patterned door in a strong design is set centrally in a relief panel of great complexity, evoking tropical luxuriance. PO

⑤ Graphic patterns formed by inlays are a feature of some 1930s doors. This one relies on the contrast of stained and white-painted pine. The handle is Bakelite. SM

⑥ A stylized, simplified version of linenfold panelling in a Tudorbethan house of the 1930s. SA

⑦ In these luxurious double doors from the same house, the linenfold panelling is more elaborate and rendered to

imitate the historic design. The arched panels and elaborate surround reinforce the theme of baronial grandeur. SA

⑧ An interior door of the Spanish Colonial Revival, Los Angeles. The two leather panels are held in place by patterns of

nickel-silver bosses which mimic saddle and spur decorations. Note the decorative door handle. CN

① and ② Examples of mass-produced interior doors fitted to smaller houses in the 20s and 30s. They were made in Columbian pine.
③ This interior door, with stylized pediment and simplified moulding, is typical of the playful treatment of historical styles in 30s interiors.
④ Custom-made for a medievalized interior, this door has heavy ironwork hinges.

⑤ A pair of doors covered in strips of lizard skin, dating from c.1930.
⑥ A pair of flush doors of the 20s showing the influence of French Art Deco metalwork (although the design could equally well be painted or inlaid).

⑦ A glazed door design of 1929. The glazing bars might be wood or even chrome.
⑧ A Spanish Revival door showing typical interlaced wooden moulding.
⑨ A wooden door of the early 1920s, Palm Beach, California.
⑩ An archaic-style knocker made by P. and F. Corbin of New Britain, Connecticut (1929).
⑪ A 1920s lockplate and knob (Yale, United States).
⑫ to ⑯ A range of lock sets. The first example was made in Bakelite with a marbled finish.
⑰ This "Tulip" set of handle and key escutcheon was also available in a "Pear" design.
⑱ An Art Deco letterbox/mailslot from Indianapolis.
⑲ A letterbox/mailslot with knocker, by Rowe Bros. English.
⑳ This set of knob, letterbox/mailslot and door bell/bellpush in a 30s Art Deco style was available in brass, stainless steel or chromium plate.

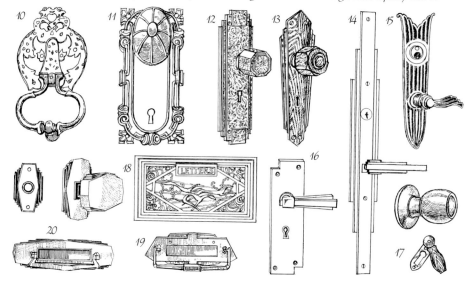

Windows

① *An elaborate gable in the half-timbered Tudorbethan manner above a leaded window.* SA
② *Metal-framed windows in the "suntrap" style, with rounded glass on the bays, are a feature of these flat-roofed English suburban houses.* AA
③ *Sash windows, with decorative shutters, in an American house in the Colonial Revival style, 1927.*

The French technique of using panes of glass of different sizes to create a rectilinear composition, and the idea of building a wall out of glass bricks, were both adopted in Britain and the United States. Metal framing was much favoured in the 1930s, and the glass at the corners of windows could be rounded in the "suntrap" style. Small circular "portholes" occur, especially in Modernist-inspired buildings: they are metal-framed and open on a central pivot. It is not unusual to find traditional window types updated with metal framing, squared bays, glass louvers and the like. Glass with decorative frosting was popular on both sides of the Atlantic, with patterns ranging from simple geo-

metric borders to stylized plant and animal motifs.

Traditional features include dormers, leaded lights and, in Queen Anne style houses, wood-framed sash windows with simple stone surrounds. In English suburbia coloured glass might feature sunray, galleon or bird motifs. An alternative was clear glass divided into rectangular panels with a central small casement.

By the 1930s it was possible to find, in the same catalogue of window fixtures, simple geometric types, elaborate items inspired by French Art Deco metalwork, and historical pieces suitable for small-paned and lead-lighted windows. The Arts and Crafts influence is still evident well into the 1930s.

① *A metal casement window from a Hope's catalogue of 1934 (viewed from inside). The central panes are fixed, and the casement stays have locking screws.*

This is the most common type in English modern houses of the 30s. ② *Also from Hope's, this window is double-glazed. It was available in a bronzed finish.*

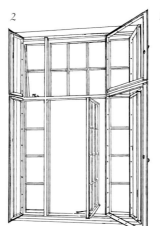

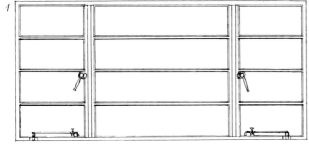

③ *A standard wood casement frame of the 30s, available from Austins (England) in two different heights and four widths. At extra cost, it was sold with an oak sill.*

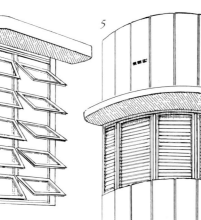

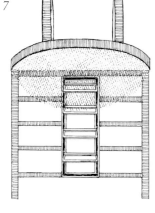

④ *Louvered windows in a 30s Art Deco apartment in Miami Beach, Florida.*
⑤ *Another Art Deco type is the use of flat windows arranged in series around a curved bay.*

⑥ *An English suburban version of the wooden bay window, made by Austins. Coloured glass was often fitted in the small panes at the top. "Leaded lights" are also common in windows of this type.*

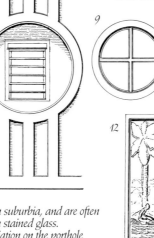

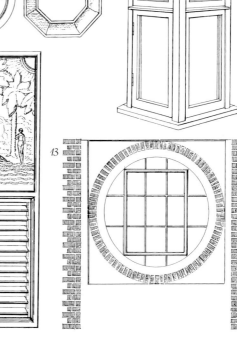

⑦ *Hoods sometimes feature in Art Deco windows as part of a geometric composition. The hood edge, together with any decorative detailing on the wall, would be in a strong colour to contrast with a largely white exterior. This is a design from Miami Beach.*
⑧ *Again, this window – a rectangle framed by coloured mouldings – shows the Art Deco fascination with simple shapes.*
⑨ *Wooden-framed circular windows were sometimes known as "bullseyes". They are common*

in English suburbia, and are often filled with stained glass.
⑩ *A variation on the porthole theme common in Art Deco seaside building, for example on the American West Coast.*
⑪ *Angled windows were mass-produced for suburbia.*
⑫ *The pairing of a window with a decorative relief panel was not unusual.*
⑬ *A circular window containing a square casement, and surrounded by decorative brickwork. This style appears in English Queen Anne Revival houses.*

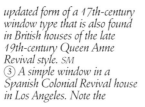

① A simple hallway casement window, set into a round-headed niche. The leaded glazing carries traditional overtones, but the overall effect is modern. The house dates from the 1930s. SM
② From the same house, an updated form of a 17th-century window type that is also found in British houses of the late 19th-century Queen Anne Revival style. SM
③ A simple window in a Spanish Colonial Revival house in Los Angeles. Note the deliberate irregularities in the leading. The Mexican tiles of the window seat are typically exuberant in pattern and colour. The window has a central hinge for opening and closing. CN
④ The wrap-around styling of these windows in a bay above an entrance porch is typical of the 1930s. AA
⑤ A stained-glass window of high quality, with a fine heraldic window catch. Armorial glass is a common feature of grander houses in the Tudorbethan style. SA

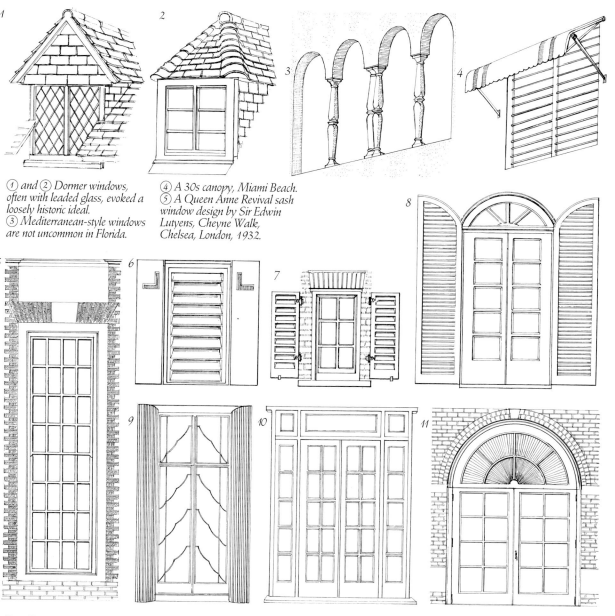

1 and 2 Dormer windows, often with leaded glass, evoked a loosely historic ideal.
3 Mediterranean-style windows are not uncommon in Florida.

4 A 30s canopy, Miami Beach.
5 A Queen Anne Revival sash window design by Sir Edwin Lutyens, Cheyne Walk, Chelsea, London, 1932.

6 to 8 Shutters may give scope for Modernist decorative detailing, or are slatted to create bands of shade. These are 30s examples.
9 Decorative etching is a typical Art Deco window feature.

10 to 11 French doors were important. The first is a standardized unit. The second, custom-made for a New York residence, has Regency overtones.
12 A latch detail from a Tudor-
style casement with leaded glass.
13 A sash fastener of the "Brighton" pattern, made by Louis G. Ford of Eastbourne, England. Available in chrome or brass.
14 to 17 Range of modern window
handles from various makers.
18 to 20 Casement stays could be plain or have Art Deco or other contemporary detailing on the splayed end – for example, a stylized shell pattern.

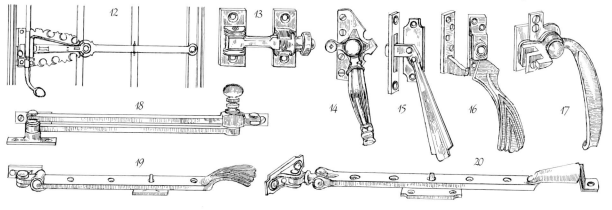

Walls

① *Trompe l'oeil murals give a spacious feel to an entrance hall in a late 30s design. CS*
② *and* ③ *Witty borrowings from history were common. The "bamboo" pilasters (1939) were used with a plain wall. The fluted pilasters would contrast with a strongly coloured wall.*
④ *Wood panels were sometimes dyed for a striking effect. This 1932 catalogue page shows*

some of the effects available. Virtually any grain could be imitated by a good painter or decorator, to simulate the more expensive woods. Grained papers were also produced. JS
⑤ *Strong geometric shapes give this contoured wall of 1924 the appearance of a folding screen.*
⑥ *A detail of a bracket. Stepped curves frame an alcove (New York, 1936).*

In the 1920s wallpaper in fashionable homes fell out of favour, giving way to plain or textured colour-washed surfaces, or sometimes geometrical patterns, executed in panels of contrasting woods, lacquer or simply in painted mouldings. At the end of the decade there was a vogue for metallic wall finishes (a particular favourite was silver). In the 1930s the "all-white" interior enjoyed great popularity: actually, the walls were usually off-white, and were often slightly textured.

Decorative panels of moulded plaster are found over fireplaces or doors or as a central feature of a wall; or the wall itself can be treated sculpturally.

Mural painting enjoyed a revival: a whole wall could be transformed into a trompe l'oeil landscape or an abstract composition. Mirrored wall surfaces became increasingly important as manufacturers began to provide a vast range of coloured and patterned glass and the necessary adhesives.

The suburban interior retained many of the features that were being rejected elsewhere, notably skirting boards/baseboards and picture rails. Wallpaper now often took the form of decorative borders and self-contained panels (or even imitation murals). Wood panelling was stripped and waxed rather than painted and varnished: an alternative was moulded papers which could be "grained" in imitation of exotic woods.

WALLS

1. Glass was used in various ways, from simple panels, often tinted, to mirror glass strips which give an effect of broken reflections, as in this 30s example. CS
2. Plaster or stucco wall panels could be purely abstract, or depict stylized natural forms. Decorative plaques in the 20s were brightly coloured; 30s decorators favoured cream or white.
3. A detail of a tile pattern for a half-tiled bathroom, with checked border and moulded lip.
4. Pictorial tiles might appear as features in a plain tiled wall, or in a framed plaque. CF
5. Decorative tile borders were sold to use with wall tiles or fireplace surrounds. These are handpainted. CF
6. Wallpapers might be deeply traditional, as in this floral example of 1932, or whimsical, or sometimes abstract. Wallpaper borders beneath the picture rail are a feature of the period. KW
7. Wallpaper cutouts are a feature of the 30s. This page from a pattern book shows a decorative cutout for a corner: it would be fixed over the main paper. KW

Ceilings

① *A Spanish Colonial Revival timber-beamed ceiling from a 1920s southern California house by George Washington Smith (1876-1930), who was based in Santa Barbara. Timber beams,* in one form or another, are a commonplace of the period. Here they are finely carpentered, with green-painted chamfered corners along the main timbers. ② *A painted drawing room in* gold and black, Port Lympne, Kent, England, dating from the early 1920s. ③ *In modern houses that did not reflect the timber tradition, ceilings of the 1920s and 30s were often* plain, sometimes coated in gloss paint. The pendant light fixture frequently provided the only ornamentation. Ceiling roses/medallions are found only on conscious historic revivals.

In fashionable interiors from the 1920s onward, a popular treatment was to cove the wall into the ceiling: the coving was treated as part of the ceiling and was often painted the same colour, its lower edge defined by a decorative border. Coloured ceilings were a feature of the 20s: they were sometimes painted to match the walls, sometimes in a powerful contrast. Mouldings, when used, are simple outlines, which are often picked out in a different colour.

Coving remained popular in the 1930s, but now was used with simple geometric mouldings on the ceiling itself, to produce a sculpted effect consistent with the wall treatment. Strong colour on the ceiling was no longer fashionable by the 1930s. Mouldings and coving were painted in white or a very pale tint, often to match the walls. Prefabricated mouldings of a more elaborate type suited rooms in a whimsically traditional style.

In the Tudorbethan suburban house there was at least a vestigial reference to traditional timbering, in the mouldings that divided the ceiling area into rectangles. Moulded papers could create a plasterwork effect. In the more expensive type of Tudorbethan house, wood beaming was employed as pure embellishment, without any structural purpose. Beams were also a feature of the Spanish Colonial Revival; another approach was to cover the ceiling with painted or carved wood panels.

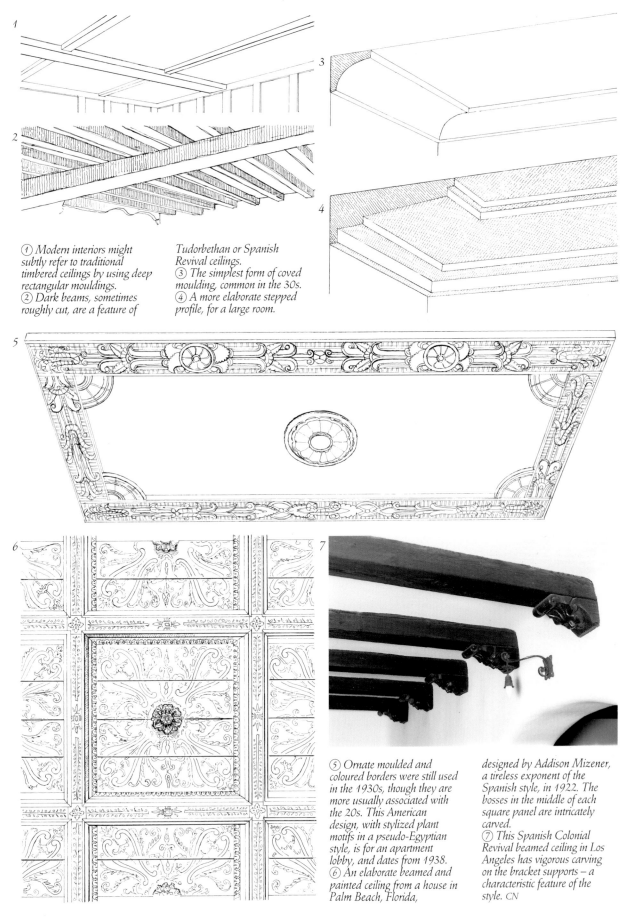

① Modern interiors might subtly refer to traditional timbered ceilings by using deep rectangular mouldings.
② Dark beams, sometimes roughly cut, are a feature of Tudorbethan or Spanish Revival ceilings.
③ The simplest form of coved moulding, common in the 30s.
④ A more elaborate stepped profile, for a large room.

⑤ Ornate moulded and coloured borders were still used in the 1930s, though they are more usually associated with the 20s. This American design, with stylized plant motifs in a pseudo-Egyptian style, is for an apartment lobby, and dates from 1938.
⑥ An elaborate beamed and painted ceiling from a house in Palm Beach, Florida, designed by Addison Mizener, a tireless exponent of the Spanish style, in 1922. The bosses in the middle of each square panel are intricately carved.
⑦ This Spanish Colonial Revival beamed ceiling in Los Angeles has vigorous carving on the bracket supports – a characteristic feature of the style. *CN*

Floors

Simple geometry, with circles intersected by straight lines, is characteristic of Art Deco floor patterning. This terrazzo floor is in a 30s house in Miami Beach, Florida. The juxtaposition of brown and black is also typical. PO

I n fashion-conscious houses, rugs and square carpets with stylized floral or geometric patterns were used to coordinate with walls and furniture. Wall-to-wall carpets tend to appear only in the most exclusive interiors. A standard treatment is parquet flooring, constructed in different patterns ranging from simple herringbone to some complex geometric arrangements. On the whole, lighter woods were preferred in the 30s. In less smart houses, an alternative to parquet was boarding which could be stained and varnished.

The patterned floor becomes increasingly important in the later 20s and the 30s. Linoleum by this time, on both sides of the Atlantic, had been elevated to a high-

fashion item. Inlaid linoleums could be made to order; alternatively, lino tiles were available in various finishes, including fake marble, and all these of course could be laid in different patterns. The simple check was popular, as was an overall colour with a contrasting border or a "frame" for the carpet. Printed lino, a favourite in suburban homes, was produced in a vast range of patterns and some textures. Mostly, it was used with rugs or carpet squares.

Ceramic tiles were not much used in Britain, but were an important feature on the West Coast of America: in particular, houses in the Spanish Colonial Revival style had floors of small terracotta tiles.

FLOORS

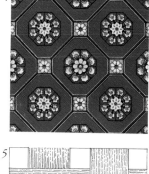

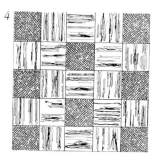

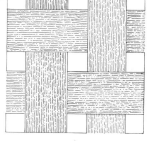

① to ⑥ *Durable floor surfaces of the period included cork linoleum in geometric patterns that loosely imitated encaustic tiles, parquet or woven matting. Linoleum was sold in tiles or strips and was used in suburban houses in conjunction with a central carpet or with rugs. It was often grained to imitate marble.* CC

⑦ to ⑩ *Parquet retained its popularity. Elaborate patterns such as these would be laid with a plain border at the wall. The first two examples are traditional French designs. The third is the familiar herringbone design. All four were published in* The House Beautiful Furnishing Annual *of 1926. Most modern designers preferred lighter coloured woods.*

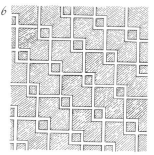

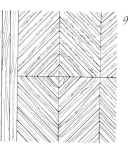

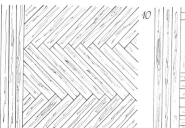

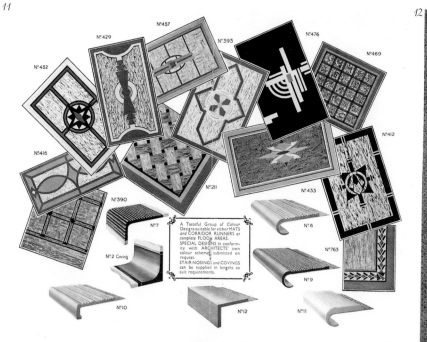

⑪ *Some rubber flooring manufacturers produced mats, runners and special strips of flooring for staircases, including some pieces that gave* protection to the noses of the treads. These examples (Warne's, Essex, English, c.1937) include some striking Art Deco designs. WA

⑫ *A corner detail of an Art Deco woollen carpet. (The colours are grey-green and dark brown on a salmon and white background.)* CI

Fireplaces

The mellow warmth of brick and tile appealed to nostalgic yearnings in the 20s and 30s. This British example (1929), with glazed cabinets, combines modern and traditional ideas. The English style was much liked in the United States. OE

Fireplaces retained their importance in a period when they were no longer strictly necessary. It was normal even for centrally heated houses to have them, and for imposing surrounds to frame electric fires. Gas fires were less popular, because they were obtrusive in appearance.

By the 30s the fireplace is often reduced to a simple rectangular opening emphasized by nothing more than a chromed edging, while the surround becomes almost a sculptural element. The hearth may be a simple slab of polished stone. Any fireplace furniture will often be chrome or steel, and elegantly simple in form.

Stone and brick hearths and chimney breasts are often found, usually without ornamentation. Furniture for fire-places of this type include a decorative firebasket or fire dogs, usually of iron.

A number of period styles continued in use, although these were usually simplified: it is not unusual to find an updated Adam-style fireplace in an interior that is not otherwise revivalist. Houses of the Tudorbethan type sometimes had inglenooks. The Arts and Crafts influence still shows in beaten brass and pewter curbs, poker and brush sets, and coal boxes.

Tiled surrounds are a commonplace of the English suburban style. They are usually of a beige or buff colour, and pay a passing homage to the "modern" styles in being stepped or, less frequently, asymmetrical.

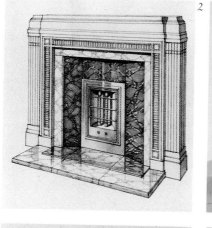

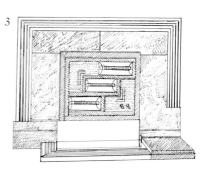

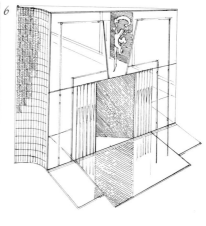

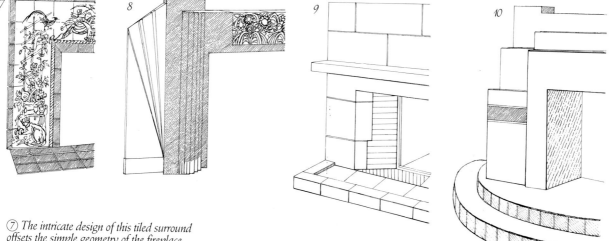

① *The style here is understated classical, with a marbled infill. Electric fires were available before the 20s, but did not have custom-made wall surrounds until the 30s.* GJ
② *An electric fire in a more modern, streamlined surround, in beige marble with a black top (Berry's, London).* BE

③ *Stepped asymmetry gives a modern look. The reflectors are bright metal, the surround matt-black, and the infill green marble.*
④ *Berry's electric "Magicoal" fires were*

operated by foot switches. Coal-effect fires were introduced in 1921, by Belling. BE
⑤ *A beige-tiled fireplace with traditional hearth and grate, c.1935.* LF
⑥ *An opulent fireplace design in rose-tinted mirror glass with an acid-embossed motif and fluted decoration at the sides.*

⑦ *The intricate design of this tiled surround offsets the simple geometry of the fireplace itself. In lieu of a mantelshelf there might be a separate shelf on the wall above.*
⑧ *A wood and silver fireplace, with ornate decorative fascia and Art Deco-style banded side wings.*

⑨ *A fireplace in biscuit faïence by Peter Behrens, with a Devon clay firebowl. A low cornice harmonizes with the curb. This British design, of 1934, is on the borderline between modern and traditional.*

⑩ *The stepped design here provides shelves at different levels. The curved hearth with tiled edges is distinctive.*

① The styling of this fireplace, with its asymmetrical stepping, mottled tiles and wood framing, appears with many variations in the 30s. The illuminated niche in the chimney breast is also characteristic. SM

② High styling of c.1936 in Miami, Florida. Fireplaces of this type are uncommon in Britain, where Art Deco was more constrained by references to the past. PO
③ The weighty baronial style, with Romanesque columns and a carved beam as a lintel. SA
④ A brick and tile fireplace, in a simplified version of the Tudorbethan style. SA
⑤ The basic inspiration here is the 18th century, but the simplification and the stepped form of the mirror with its wavy borders are 30s. CS
⑥ An American Spanish Colonial Revival fireplace of the 1920s with a typical tiled surround and hand-modelled frieze. The wrought-iron fireplace furniture is characteristic. CN

① A modern treatment, in brick, of the medieval hooded fireplace, designed for a sloping ceiling.
② Fireplaces would occasionally incorporate a clock. This one is shown with a portable electric fire with decorative backplate.
③ The asymmetrical design of this early 1930s fireplace is emphasized by chrome edging and by built-in striplights.
④ This design was shown in American House and Garden, 1929. Fireplace: brass and bronze.
⑤ A Spanish-style adobe fireplace for a New Mexico living room, designed in 1935. It sits in the corner of a room.
⑥ This fireplace (1929) – a fantasy on a historical theme – was designed for a large inglenook. The design on the overmantel is painted.
⑦ A frameless circular overmantel mirror dominates this simple fireplace with decorative metal guard bars.
⑧ A 30s andiron of shiny steel in an unusual design.
⑨ This andiron was made in steel with brass ornamentation.
⑩ A cockerel andiron of the 30s.
⑪ These andirons in chromium plate and wrought iron came with matching fire basket and poker, tongs and shovel set.
⑫ In contrast to the previous example, this is a thoroughly historicized design, with urn finials and scroll feet.

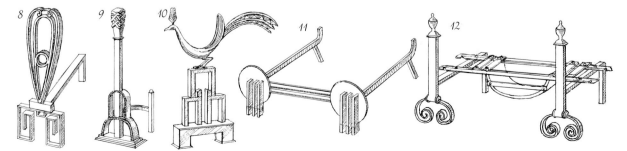

Kitchen stoves

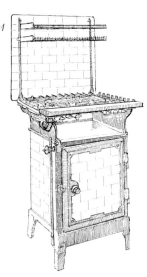

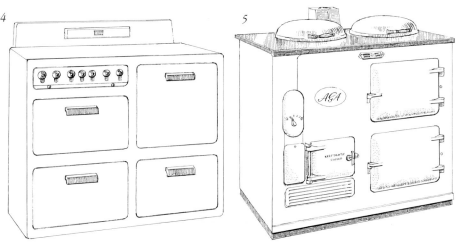

① *The Radiation "New World N 16" gas stove. This stove, of 1923, was the first to incorporate thermostatic oven control. The gas burners are raised above the oven, which is on legs to facilitate cleaning. The splash-back and plate rack became standard during the 1920s.*
② *The Eagle combination grate of c.1935 was a modern version of the old-fashioned Dutch oven. Combination grates combined, within a single unit, a fireplace with a back boiler and a number of ovens for cooking. A tiled surround was usual. EC*
③ *A two-oven temperature-controlled gas range with large boiling and grilling hotplate and overhead plate rack. JW*
④ *This stove was designed by Norman Bel Geddes for the Standard Gas Equipment Corporation, United States, 1933. The white finish and the*

skirt extending to the floor were influential on both sides of the Atlantic.
⑤ *A 1939 model of the AGA*

designed by Dr Gustav Dalen in the 20s. The early models had legs. AGAs worked on the principle of heat conservation:

hence, the domed lids over the hobs. The AGA also provided a supply of hot water for the household, from its back boiler.

Gas and electric stoves had been available in various forms since the 19th century, but it was only after 1918 that they began to gain widely in popularity and come down in price.

In the 1920s and early 30s stoves were finished in a mottled enamel or tile, usually with a white door which fastened rather like a cupboard with a latch (this was eventually superseded by a Bakelite handle). Such stoves were utilitarian in appearance, raised from the floor on legs, with gas burners supported by their feed pipes above the body of the stove. Electricity was relatively expensive, electric ovens took longer to heat up than gas, and the heat was less easy to control: for

this reason gas stoves remained more usual in Britain, and it was for gas that the first thermostatic oven control was developed in 1923. The basic design of the stove changed little during the period, except for the addition of features such as splash-backs.

The United States was more advanced in the design of kitchen equipment. American manufacturers were producing compact streamlined stoves early in the 30s. These are characterized by a "skirt" that extends to the floor and by the incorporation of burners into the body of the stove, to make the lines smoother. Instead of the mottled enamels of earlier models, the new designs were finished in white with minimal trim.

Staircases

① *An Art Deco example from Miami, Florida. The contrasting tones, half-round mouldings, and the stepped dividing wall, are all typical.* PO
② *This Spanish Colonial Revival staircase shows the characteristic use of Mexican tiles and wrought-iron balustrades.* CN
③ *A Tudorbethan staircase, with Gothic carvings. The typical enclosed balustrade alternates with open balusters on the landings.* SA
④ *The newel post, by the addition of stepped moulding, becomes reminiscent of a skyscraper. Note the landing light built into the newel – a feature of many Art Deco interiors, first found in hotels and cinemas.* SM

Smart houses in the late 1920s and through the 30s were often conceived as a flow of space rather than a series of closed boxes: hence, the staircase is often visible from the principal rooms. Cantilevering allowed the stairs to follow the line of a curved or flat wall with no support on the sides. The visual lightness of such staircases was emphasized by open treads.

In the 1930s chromed banisters were in vogue. Types range from the simple tubular bar to more elaborate arrangements of tubular and ribbon forms. An alternative to chrome was plywood, which could be shaped to follow the line of a curved staircase.

Wooden stairs rising from a main room are a feature of the Spanish Colonial Revival style, but the treads are closed and the stairs are usually screened with wood panelling on the room-facing side.

A staircase leading to a gallery may be found in the more sizeable Tudorbethan house. The grand staircase also occurs in miniaturized form in smaller suburban houses, often with a small half-landing, the whole thing constructed in mass-produced wooden components, stained in a dark oak colour and varnished.

The use of staircarpets necessitated metal rods to hold the carpet in place. These were available in several types, as simple metal rods with plain socket fixtures, or with a variety of decorative finials.

KITCHEN STOVES

STAIRCASES

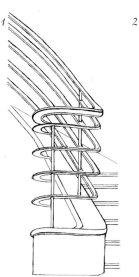

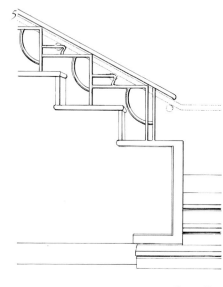

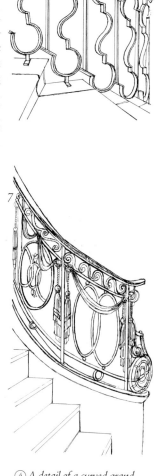

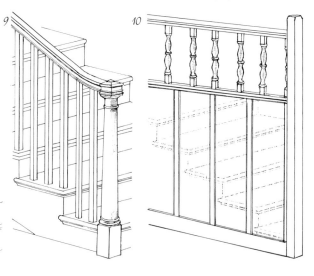

① and ② Chromed metal or tubular steel was an ideal material for stairs, and could be combined with a waxed oak handrail. These designs of the mid-30s show how the rails might be coiled to make the newel post.

③ A 1930 design, with broad ribbons that interweave through the tubular uprights.

④ A detail of a curved grand revivalist staircase with a wooden handrail, designed by Sir Edwin Lutyens in 1932.

⑤ This design (1929) has more solidity, the delicate ironwork contrasting with a massive stepped balustrade in marble.

⑥ A typically 30s treatment, of pale laminated wood in a tubular metal framework.

⑦ The ultimate in revivalism. The metalwork is wrought iron and bronze, with the rope and tassel ornaments gilded in leaf.

⑧ Six bars of bleached mahogany are held in place by tubular chromium uprights. (California, 1939.)

⑨ A standard American suburban staircase, 1925.

⑩ Short flights of steps could be enclosed with panelling, with a horizontal balustrade on top. This example borrows from old English styles, but actually comes from a New York apartment.

Built-in furniture

Built-in furniture in a complicated configuration around adjacent walls is a common feature of Art Deco-inspired interiors. In this example a desk is cleverly integrated with bookshelves, a cupboard and a wall-mounted electric fire. CS

Space-saving built-in furniture was a feature of housing in the inter-war years. This was prompted in part by the smaller size of houses and apartments, but by the 1920s built-in furniture had become chic, and appeared even in dwellings where space was not critical. Existing interiors were often remodelled by interior designers to achieve the built-in look. Possibly the most popular built-in items were bookcases (sometimes with cupboards below) which were built into the recesses at either side of the chimney breast. Laminated wood gave scope for fitting walls from floor to ceiling with niches to contain bookshelves, display shelves or concealed cupboards. In bedrooms such false walling was employed to disguise

wardrobes: a typical arrangement is two wardrobes with central built-in vanity unit.

Laminated wood was also used to create units that projected from the wall. Some fashionable interiors of the 1930s feature constructions that incorporate enclosed seating on one side and a combined record player and radio on the other. Cocktail bars could also be built in as apparent extensions of the wall.

In some modern-styled houses or apartments put up in the 1930s, built-in furniture was standard: the amalgamation of eating space with cooking or living space heralded the appearance of the built-in breakfast niche with benches and fixed table.

① *A sofa, convertible into a bed, framed by a veneered wooden wall unit. The upholstery is in contrasting tones. Above the sofa is a stand with recessed compartments for books and the like, with a lighting fixture at either end. The design dates from 1937.*

② *A sofa-bed designed for a children's room. The built-in toy cupboard in white waxed oak at the head of the bed has a circular night light.*

③ *Wall-mounted console tables are a Neo-classical feature, here seen in a marblized modern version designed by the English interior decorator Syrie Maugham. It was intended to be surmounted by a mirror, in a dining room.*

④ *A built-in desk with uplight support, dating from 1936.*

⑤ *This fixed dining table (1934) is designed to occupy a corner of a living room. The surface is waxed mahogany.*

⑥ *Designed by Joseph Urban and shown at a Metropolitan Museum, New York, exhibition in 1929, this desk and bookshelf unit for a "man's den" makes interesting use of a wall recess. The freestanding desk fits snugly in the alcove.*

⑦ *Built-in furniture for a London nursery (architects Pakington and Enthoven, 1936). The cupboards and shelves are designed to be in pine, painted cream to match the walls, with scarlet handles and drawer pulls.*

⑧ *A bookshelf and cupboard unit of 1936, with interesting uprights on the corners: these may serve a purely decorative purpose, or alternatively can act as book-ends.*

⑨ *A built-in bookcase with a clerestory window above. This is in the living room of a Frank Lloyd Wright house in Okemos, Michigan, 1939.*

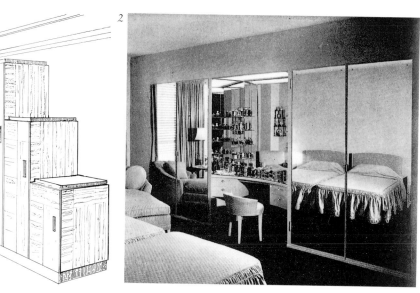

① *Built-in stepped units are typical of the period. This trio of cupboards (1933) was intended to stand at one end of a wall with the taller unit fitting into the corner.*
② *A bedroom with an unusual recessed dressing table and mirrored wardrobe doors, all built-in, designed by James F. Eppenstein of Chicago.* CS
③ *A dressing table arrangement by Paul Nelson, Chicago, c.1929, designed for an alcove. Alongside the mirror are light-diffusing panels with lamps behind.*
④ *Resembling a wardrobe when the door is closed, this is actually a concealed wash basin with mirror (1933). Such disguises are a commonplace of the period, especially in classicized interiors.*

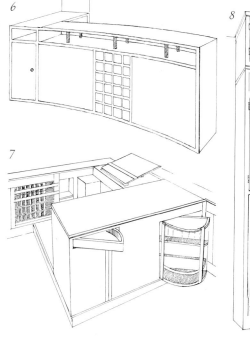

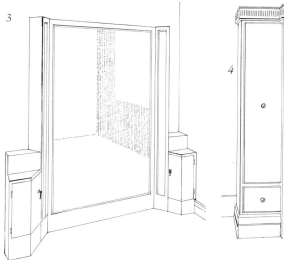

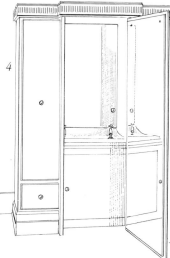

⑤ *A traditional glazed display cabinet for a dining alcove.*
⑥ *This built-in cabinet for a living room incorporates a record player, radio, drinks cabinet and other storage space. It was finished in Japanese ash of a fine figured veneer.*
⑦ *An L-shaped built-in desk, with concealed liquor cabinet and telephone shelf – both features revolve into the desk when not in use, presenting a plain surface. Henry Dreyfuss, New York, 1933.*
⑧ *In the kitchen, a refrigerator could be combined in various ways with built-in furniture. This is an idea from Electrolux (London) for using a refrigerator as the base unit in a stack of cupboards reaching from floor to ceiling (1936).*
⑨ *A detail of a built-in kitchen (1936). The woodwork was designed to be painted white with blue edges, and the ledges covered in blue linoleum.*

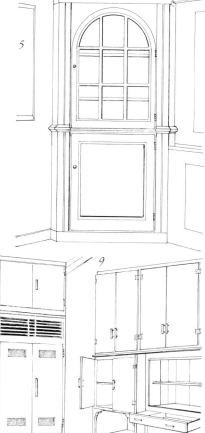

BUILT-IN
FURNITURE

Services

The square Neo-Angle bath by the American Radiator and Standard Corporation, New York. The diagonal recess is as large as that of a conventional 5½-foot (165cm) bath. The shower seat at the rear doubles conveniently as an accessories shelf. CS

Baths in the 1920s were cast-iron and retained their legs. Washbasins were usually supported on a metal frame or brackets, with a rail for towels. Water closets were still being made with a separate cistern and a chain flush. Luxurious bathrooms might be decorated with a mural and equipped with a vanity unit and perhaps a bath in a historical fantasy style.

In the 1930s bathrooms became more compact. A common feature was a built-in bath set into a recess, possibly next to a cupboard. Such a bath would often have a shower attachment: separate shower cabinets with glass panels were restricted to more expensive interiors. The tub on legs was giving way to a boxed unit,

the panels of which could be moulded or tiled. Bath fixtures were now available in clean, modern shapes, in chromium, and mixer taps/faucets became more common. Pedestal wash basins were available in a variety of shapes. Water closets were made with a lower cistern.

Despite the appearance of new appliances, it was not until the 30s that kitchens acquired a more modern look. The United States was rather more advanced than Britain, and in the early 30s already had heating stoves and water heaters in clean, modern designs, and stainless steel sinks. In Britain the typical sink of the 30s was the "Belfast" type – deep, white-glazed, flanked by a wooden draining board, with an adjacent space for a boiler.

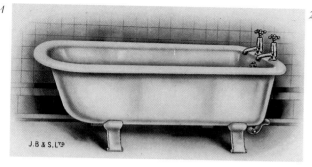

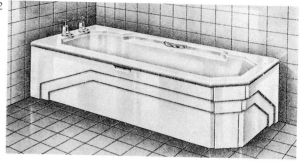

① A cast-iron rolled-edge bath, with white porcelain enamel on the inside and over the roll. The fixtures are chrome-plated. BS
② A typical modern design of the mid-30s. Streamlined details include a recessed hand-grip. BS
③ A deep oval bath by the British architect Oliver Hill, mosaic-tiled on the inside.
④ The "Viceroy" bath and shower by the Kohler Company, Kohler, Wisconsin, 1927. The

bath is equipped with a rubber hose and shower spray.
⑤ This American shower of 1939 shows the fascination with new materials: the screen is in Blue Ridge Flutex, a patterned glass, bent to make a rounded corner.
⑥ A metal-framed plate glass door, with ventilating panel above, was a neater alternative to the shower curtain. This example has a shower base of Sicilian marble. BS

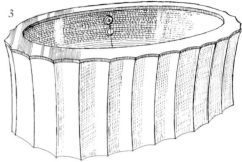

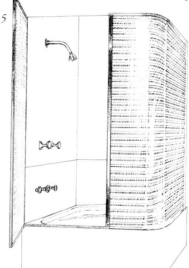

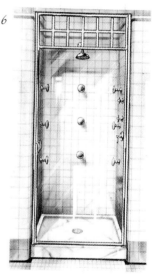

⑦ This English design of 1935 was available in white, black, ivory, blue, pink and green. LF
⑧ Water closet flushers in earthenware, wood and rubber. Chains could be brass, nickel-plated or nickel-chrome. BS
⑨ A white-glazed toilet roll

holder with wood roller.
⑩ A recessed soap holder.
⑪ A bidet by Shanks, Bristol, England. 1938.
⑫ Hot-water towel rails were chromium-plated. Sometimes the central horizontal tubes were linked by an inset radiator.

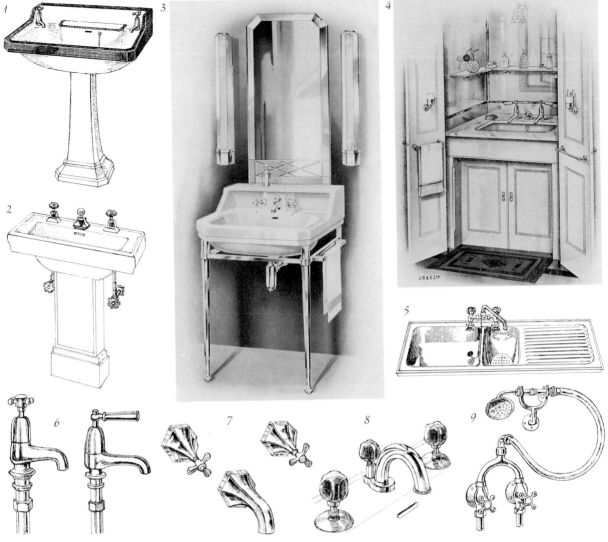

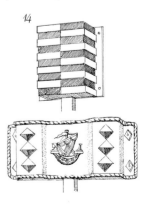

① This wash basin has a black trim, and would perhaps be used with black and white tiles.
② A wash basin of 1936 (Standard Sanitary Manufacturing Co., New York).
③ Some basins incorporated a towel rail, joint-flow tap/faucet and brilliant-cut and bevelled mirror. 1933. BS
④ Bedroom wash basins were often hidden within cupboards. RB

⑤ A kitchen sink of 1935.
⑥ Taps/faucets could be porcelain-enamelled, chromium-plated, nickel-silver or yellow metal. The first of these pillar types is the standard spoke-top; the second is lever-operated.
⑦ Hexagonal bath taps/faucets were one variation on the norm.
⑧ Modern bathtub hardware by George Sakier, New York, 1932.

⑨ Shampoo units, nickel- or chromium-plated, came with a wall hook. The tube was rubber.
⑩ This corner boiler has sliding firedoors and ashpit doors. It would be used in Britain for boiling laundry.
⑪ A portable water softener, attached to any tap/faucet by a rubber tube. Soft water was believed to be better for food, the complexion and health.

⑫ and ⑬ Two items showing how one maker could offer both conservative and modern styles – a gas-heated radiator and a wall-mounted gas panel heater.
⑭ Rainwater heads gave a chance for decoration. The modern design is in cast iron (30s) and the traditional design is lead (1927). Art Deco forms include stepped diagonals and stylized ears of wheat.

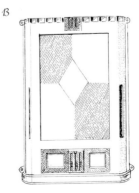

Lighting

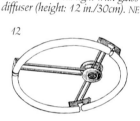

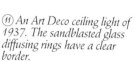

① *A 30s tubular ceiling light, in bronze, silvered, chromium or antique brass finishes.*
② *A pendant by Lightolier, New York, 1930s.*
③ *A wrought-iron pendant.* NE
④ *The shade here is pleated silk, with an opal glass bowl beneath.*

⑤ *A light of the "fancy open unit type", satin-finished shade.* NE
⑥ *A lead crystal bowl, heavily hand-cut.* NE
⑦ *Incorporating shells, this 30s pendant was designed for a hall.*
⑧ *A "shell" wall light with glass diffuser (height: 12 in./30cm).* NE

⑨ *A ship finial tops this wall light in wrought iron, United States, 1926.*
⑩ *For outdoors, an iron light fixture (height: 23 in./58cm).*

⑪ *An Art Deco ceiling light of 1937. The sandblasted glass diffusing rings have a clear border.*
⑫ *This ceiling light in the Art*

Deco style uses three curved electric lamps (Tucker and Edgar, United States).
⑬ *Bed lights could be wall-mounted, or hung over the bed*

head with weighted tags.
⑭ *Spotlights were surprisingly modern-looking in appearance.*
⑮ *Ceiling plates for bowl-type pendants were available in brass, copper and silver finishes. The chains were sold separately.* MAA
⑯ *Switches were available in Bakelite. Popular colours were brown, white, and brown on white. Note the subtle Art Deco detailing in the third of these examples.* MA

The central pendant ceiling light, sometimes supplemented by wall sconces, was the most usual form of fixed lighting in the period. Examples of the 20s are by definition luxurious, as electricity was expensive and not yet widely available, particularly in Britain.

In the United States concealed lighting was in use by the end of the 1920s. Tubular lamps were hidden behind mouldings at the edge of the ceiling to give a diffused glow and to highlight architectural detailing. Such lighting could also be found in the more luxurious interiors in Britain by the mid-1930s.

Many catalogues of the early 1930s show a range of pendants and other lights in tinted or marbled glass, usually in the form of an inverted bowl with chains to attach it to a metal ceiling rose/medallion. Modern variations on the chandelier pattern also remained popular. Wall sconces, also in glass, were often fan- or shell-shaped. Less expensive fixtures were made from synthetic parchments and vellums; some were intended for bed heads or dressing tables.

The modern interior could be lit by ceiling fixtures of chrome or glass in appropriately modernist shapes, including globes attached to chrome ceiling plates.

For revivalist interiors various historical styles were available, and special candle-shaped bulbs were made, as well as a range of small parchment shades.

SERVICES

LIGHTING

Metalwork

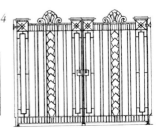

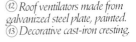

① *A wrought-iron life-size wall figure, for a garden room (1938). At night a shadow is thrown.*
② *Railings for a 30s mansion.*
③ *An iron balcony, Miami Beach.*
④ *Gates with a hint of Art Deco.*
⑤ *A radiator grille of c.1930.*
⑥ *A bronzed floor grille made by Tuttle and Bailey, New York, 1929.*

⑦ *A radiator grille in wrought iron, by Edgar Brandt, 1920s.*
⑧ *A metal screen door: flamingoes are typical of Miami Beach styles.*

⑨ *Metalwork entrance doors for a New York apartment block, c.1928.*
⑩ *A cast-iron finial.*

⑪ *A dragon weather vane of 1937: the height is 5 feet/1.50m.*

⑫ *Roof ventilators made from galvanized steel plate, painted.*
⑬ *Decorative cast-iron cresting.*

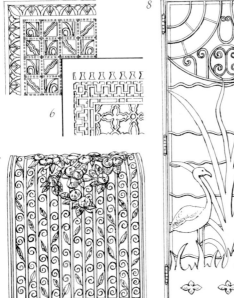

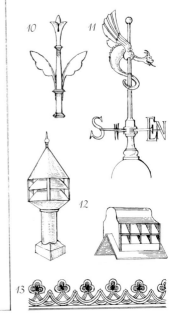

Many architects incorporated ornamental metalwork in their buildings, and it was also common to commission ironwork as a way to "update" an existing house. The influence of Edgar Brandt's Art Deco motifs for door, window and radiator grilles was felt in Britain and the United States, and Brandt-influenced motifs also occur in the 1920s on rainwater hopper heads/leader heads. Most popular was the stepped fan shape of head which persisted throughout the 30s.

Window grilles perform the double function of decoration and security. Examples of the 20s often feature stylized plant and animal forms, while 30s types tend to be more abstract, linear compositions. Glazed front doors were given decorative, protective gates.

In Britain, but even more so in the United States, balconies and railed terraces were a feature of luxurious, fashionable 30s architecture. There were simple streamlined shapes influenced by the metalwork on ocean liners, as well as more decorative curvilinear forms.

Ornate grilles, balcony rails and gates feature in the American Spanish tradition, but here the ironwork is heavily wrought in a style incorporating Baroque motifs.

Metal fixtures were made for houses in the Tudorbethan style. Rainwater heads were ornamented with motifs including coats of arms. Pseudo period details such as weather vanes enjoyed great popularity.

Woodwork

① *A sunburst gate, typical of 20s and 30s English suburban houses. This is an early example.*
② *Garage doors, with a sliding mechanism. Garages were built into larger houses by the late 30s. MA*
③ *Cedar cladding gave a rustic appearance to some 30s houses. This design dates from 1934.*
④ *An all-wood weekend house, with a detail of the window design. FP*

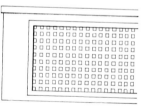

⑤ *A wooden radiator covering with turned legs and iron grille.*
⑥ *Two latticed radiator covers of the 1920s.*
⑦ *Combined gates for the house and the drive were common in English suburbia. MAA*
⑧ *Garden gates show considerable ingenuity in the design of struts and apertures, though they are never complicated. MAA*

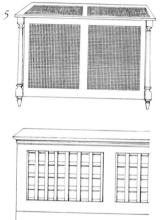

Wood was used prominently as an exterior trim on Tudorbethan-style houses. On the smaller suburban dwellings, such trim was often confined to gables or to porch detailing. Larger and more expensive houses could be fully "timbered" : this treatment was purely ornamental, having nothing to do with the actual structure. Exterior wood trim was also a feature of Vernacular Revival houses in Britain and the United States.

Gardens were a feature of suburban development, and most houses came complete with a simple fence and a gate. Catalogues offered a variety of styles for those in search of an individual touch. The options included woven fences, fences scalloped between the posts, and solid fences with an openwork top. A range of decorative fence posts was also available. Garages were being made by the late 20s, in standardized sections for on-site assembly. The same manufacturers also produced chalet-type bungalows intended for weekend use at the seaside. Usually very basic inside, they often had interesting detailing on the exterior, such as turned crockets on the gables, decorative porch rails and the like.

The radiators available in this period were not particularly attractive. A typical solution was a lattice-fronted box, which could be left as natural wood and polished, or painted to match the colours of the room.

WOODWORK   METALWORK

THE MODERN MOVEMENT

1920–1950

① *The English architect Oliver Hill built Landfall at Poole, Dorset, in 1938. The roof terrace has views of Poole Harbour, a famous yachting location, and the streamlined style of the house, with porthole windows and railings to the exterior staircase, reflects the nautical imagery associated with Modernism.* OL
② *The ground floor plan of Landfall, Poole, Dorset, 1938. The paved terrace area reflects the outline of the house.*

1

③ *Walter Gropius's own house at Lincoln, Massachusetts (1938), features a projecting mesh porch and metal framing; it is a continuation of the white cubic architecture of the 1920s, but blends more subtly into the landscape. Gropius, former director of the Bauhaus school, had left Germany for England in 1934 where he entered into partnership with E. Maxwell Fry; in 1937 he was invited to become Professor of Architecture at Harvard.* PO

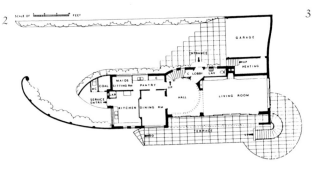

2

3

Part visionary, part practical, part elitist and part socialist, the Modern Movement was a self-conscious style that refused to acknowledge that it was a style. It was created by architects and theorists who wished to break with the past and express the spirit of the machine age, but they could also invoke the past in support of their revolution. In its aim to change society's attitude to design by telling the public what was good for them it was not universally popular; most Modern Movement houses in Britain and the United States before 1950 tended to be architect-designed residences, and few developers were prepared to risk speculative building in an uncommercial style. After 1950 a more popular form of Modernism emerged, although architects have continued to build experimental houses that are intended to carry forward Modernism's belief in constant change.

In the early 1900s leading German and Austrian designers reacted against the excessive and undisciplined ornament of Art Nouveau and laid the foundations for an architecture reliant on space, proportion and smooth surfaces. The Austrian architect Adolf Loos (1870-1933) spent three years in the United States from 1893 to 1896 and studied the buildings of Louis Sullivan (1856-1924) in Chicago which combined clear structure with original non-historic ornament. Loos's essay *Ornament and Crime* (1908) rejected ornamentation as degenerate. Sullivan's disciple Frank Lloyd Wright (1867-1959) designed buildings after 1900 that

gradually shed ornament and relied on space and pure architectural form. These were initially more influential in Europe than in the United States, and their demonstratio of a new expressive power of space and form made a deep impression on architects such as Walter Gropius (1883-1969) and Ludwig Mies van der Rohe (1886-1969) both of whom consolidated and defined a doctrine of Modernism in the 1920s.

In the 1920s Modernism in architecture became the vehicle for many ideas about art and society, from the mystical to the materialist. Movements such as the Dutch De Stijl and Parisian Purism, led by Le Corbusier (1887-1965), produced manifestos and a small number of buildings, nearly all houses, to demonstrate the revolutionary nature of their methods. Le Corbusier's book *Vers une Architecture* (1924; translated into English in 1927), outlined his "Five Points for a New Architecture": *piloti* (houses on pillars), horizontal windows, free plan, free facades and flat roofs for roof gardens. These aesthetic definitions were demonstrated at the Weissenhofsiedlung in Stuttgart, a "live" housing exhibition organized by Mies van der Rohe for the Deutsche Werkbund in 1927. All the buildings there were white-walled (apart from some startling blue ones by the Dutch architect Mart Stam) and had flat roofs. These became distinguishing marks of the style, whether they were used as part of a radical architectural programme or as a decorative novelty.

① *The axonometric drawing for a 1930s Californian house by Richard Neutra, based on a lightweight steel frame. The large windows provide an extensive view of the surrounding landscape. One of several émigré architects from Austria, Neutra found clients willing to experiment with informal open-plan living.*
② *The living area of Austrian-born Rudolph Schindler's West Hollywood house, California, 1921-2. Modernism was an international style created in Europe on foundations laid in part by Frank Lloyd Wright, then reintroduced to the United States in the 1920s and 30s. The interior of this house reflects some of Wright's style, but Schindler simplifies the surfaces and use of space. SR*

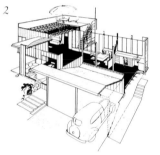

In England these ideas were viewed with some suspicion although from 1927 onwards aspects of Continental modernism were gradually introduced. In the first flush of enthusiasm for Modern architecture in the early 1930s certain English architects felt it a matter of pride to build houses with thin concrete walls to make the barrier between inside and outside as thin as possible. The interstitial spaces that played such an important role in the climatic adaptation of traditional structures were all-but abolished as being a shameful hidden secret. Pure concrete walls, however, were soon found to be cold and harsh since they were given little insulation. Metal windows with large panes acted as cold bridges and ran with condensation.

By the end of the 1930s timber, brick and stone were used for whole or part of the construction even by architects previously devoted to concrete. In the process, it was possible to achieve a closer assimilation to the regional styles of different parts of the country, since the white architecture was unpopular for its alien appearance. Not all the "white" houses were actually white. Pink was a popular colour while sometimes the cubic shapes of the composition were differentiated by colour. The recent restoration of High Cross House, Dartington, Devon, designed in 1932 by the Swiss-American architect William Lescaze for the headmaster of a progressive boarding school, has reinstated a bright blue colour to part of the exterior. Timber window frames often replaced metal by the late 1930s although they always had a thin profile. Monopitch roofs with overhanging eaves were copied from Scandinavia. These designs prefigured the more varied Modernism of the post-war period.

Only a small number of Modern houses was built in England in the 1930s, and few were of any great size. The new style was promoted on the basis that it was healthy, hygienic and efficient, offering rational solutions to modern problems. It was also claimed to be more honest than any replication of older styles or addition of art deco style ornament. These claims were probably exaggerated and the solutions created new problems of their own when new techniques and materials were used, but the designs were inspired by an aesthetic delight in space, colour and light that traditional styles could not offer. Although elaborate craftsmanship was no longer wanted, the high quality of joinery was carried over from traditional construction and fine timbers were used. Clean-lined furniture, textiles and tableware were available to enhance the Modern look and the cheap bent plywood designs of the Finnish architect Alvar Aalto were particularly popular.

Although the free plan was a Modernist aim, flat roof houses were not much more open than those in more traditional styles. Since most of these houses were designed to have living-in servants, there was limited scope for revolutionary planning. Techniques of central

① *The American architect William Lescaze built High Cross House, Dartington, Devon in 1932 for the headmaster of England's leading progressive school.* MOU

② *Glass brick walls gave dramatic effects at night, seen here at the Herbert Bruning House, Wilmette, Illinois, 1936, by George Fred Keck.* CHS/B

③ *Contemporaries recognized the classic quality of Bentley Wood, East Sussex, designed for himself by Serge Chermayeff in 1938. The timber house is poised in an open landscape with a famous early stone sculpture by Henry Moore commanding the view from the end of the projecting terrace. Timber returned to favour at the end of the 1930s and was used for several houses built by Chermayeff in the United States after his emigration in 1940.* APR

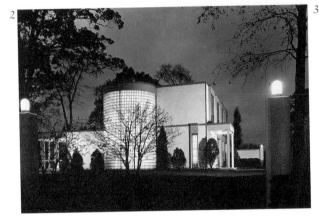

heating were still poorly developed and the Modernist insistence on clean uncluttered spaces caused heating pipes and electric wiring to be buried in the structure and almost impossible to replace, although houses became much easier to clean. A more practical aspect of the same concern with neatness was the increased use of built-in furniture which responded to the detailed and highly specific provision of spaces for particular activities. Some houses were equipped with the thoroughness of yachts with built-in cocktail cabinets, sound systems, clocks, wardrobes and drawers under built-in beds.

Although no longer an essential, the fireplace tended to survive to give focus to the living room. A few houses and flats had a double-height living room to create the interesting spaces that were intended to replace the interest provided by ornament and decoration. While flat roofs and balconies were intended for sun-bathing, they were not, it seems, used very often. Some occupants of these houses took advantage of the large sliding windows to develop a closer relationship with the garden as well as enjoying the sunlight, which was then seen as unequivocally health-giving.

The majority of Modern houses were free-standing in country or suburban settings. A few notable examples of town houses were built, in which the organization of the Georgian terrace house was reconsidered and improved with the advantage of new construction and the flat roof. In Ernö Goldfinger's terrace of houses in Willow Road, London, the concrete enclosure of the spiral staircase becomes a structural element and takes up

less of the living space. Bathrooms with skylights in the flat roof leave good views from the bedrooms while the concrete frame allows for split-level rooms.

In the United States, Modernism was consciously promoted in the 1930s, as in England, since there was little continuity from the early works of Frank Lloyd Wright. Fallingwater, at Bear Run, Pennsylvania, which Wright designed in 1935 for Edgar Kaufmann, helped to revive a fashion for rough natural materials. Wright's "Usonian" houses, built from 1937 onwards, were intended for cheap construction and employed a simplified style with interlocking volumes and projecting flat roof planes. In the 1920s and 30s Rudolph Schindler and Richard Neutra, both from Vienna, built remarkable houses in the Los Angeles area, benefiting from the warm climate by reducing the mass of the building and stressing the continuity of indoor and outdoor space. The emphasis on airy lightness was continued in the famous series of Case Study houses after World War II.

Technical innovation was a selling point for Modernism in the 1930s with examples like the lightweight metal Aluminaire House built for an exhibition in 1931; re-erected on Long Island, it is now in the process of being restored as a museum exhibit. This prototype was never developed, and Buckminster Fuller's famous hexagonal Dymaxion House, designed in 1929 to be supported on cables from a mast, was never even built. Most American Modernist houses of the 1930s were in the European flat-roofed, streamlined style, only larger and more fully equipped. Among the advanced features of the Earl Butler house (1935-7) at

① *Mossberg House, South Bend, Indiana, by Frank Lloyd Wright, 1946. The United States' greatest twentieth-century architect built many smaller houses in the later phase of his career for clients of relatively modest means.* HEI

② *The interior of Earl Butler House, Des Moines, Iowa, by Kraetsch & Kraetsch, 1935-7, was equipped for streamlined modern living in an open-plan space. American designers were fascinated by a vision of a mechanized future, typified in the New York World's Fair of 1939.* CHS/H

Des Moines, Iowa, were a central ramp, air condition-ing, dishwasher and waste-disposal unit, an electric eye to operate the garage doors, high-capacity freezers and an internal telephone system, all of which (except per-haps the latter) have become standard equipment.

The book *Tomorrow's House*, produced by *Architectural Forum* magazine in 1945, appealed to practical common-sense needs like storage and adaptable living spaces while admitting that it would take a considerable effort to shift ordinary house builders and lending institutions away from the familiar revival styles of Colonial and Spanish. The American entry into World War II in 1941 introduced a new climate of austerity and directed Federal resources into housing for war workers. Rational planning and economy were combined with a high standard of mechanical servicing in housing pro-jects where the designers were at last more concerned with how the building performed than whether it looked modern. The same considerations influenced the design of prefabricated emergency housing in Britain at the end of the war, resulting in dwellings that have remained popular while long outlasting their pre-dicted short lifespan. When Modernism became more popular in the 1950s, it was partly because it found more ways of substituting for the lost architectural interest of decorative detail. As at the outset of Modernist influ-ence in Britain and the United States, much of the

inspiration came from Le Corbusier who abandoned his pure white style around 1930 and continued making brilliant experiments until his death in 1965.

The Modern Movement cannot be said to have had a clear historical end. It always existed concurrently with other ways of designing. Its claim not to be a style but to be based on eternal truths and at the same time to be the style of the age was inherently contradictory. Intentionally or not, it became a style because the mate-rial and emotional conditions of succeeding decades left their mark on architects and designers notwithstanding their powerful taboos against decoration.

Its later history is considered in the next section. After a period of unpopularity, Modernist houses are now attracting interest, not so much as the forerunners of the future they once seemed, but as the rare relics of a specific moment in history. In England, Goldfinger's 2 Willow Road, London, and Lescaze's High Cross House, Dartington, are open to the public and several other houses of the period are being restored with the care normally given to older buildings. In the United States, Walter Gropius's house at Lincoln, Massachusetts, several works by Frank Lloyd Wright and the Schindler-Chase houses in Hollywood, California, are among a growing number of buildings whose interest has extended outside the narrow con-stituency of architects to embrace a wider public.

Dong

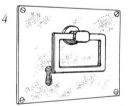

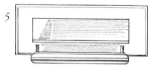

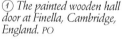

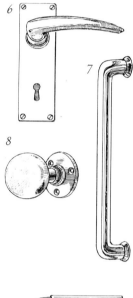

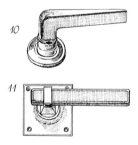

① *The painted wooden hall door at Finella, Cambridge, England.* PO

From the 1930s, metal lever handles were considered to be more functional than knobs.
② *and* ③ *Designs that combined locks and handles were popular.*
④ *A polished steel square handle with lock designed by Lord Snowdon in the 1960s.*

⑤ *A combined letterbox/mailslot and grip handle.*
⑥ *A sprung lever handle and lock.*
⑦ *"D" handles were an elegant and popular form.*
⑧ *A plain functional metal knob handle.*
⑨ *A lever handle with tubular grip.*
⑩ *A tapering flat handle.*
⑪ *An unusual 1930s plastic handle.*

The Modern Movement sought to eliminate superfluous detail and to achieve broad unified surfaces. This desire coincided with the popularization of plywood, which revolutionized the door. The thin layers of wood, which were bonded together under pressure, produced flush doors with no panels or mouldings; and the layers could be built up so that their total weight was equal to that of a solid wood traditional door. Plywood was used for both external and internal doors. Internal sliding doors were popular in the United States. In Britain in the 1920s a metal-faced plywood was developed by the Venesta Company.

Glazed doors also became popular, as front doors and as garden doors: in apartments they were used to integrate living spaces with balconies. Doors leading to outdoor areas were often metal-framed with wire-reinforced glass panes: in Britain this was known as "Georgian" wired glass (surely one of the most inappropriate product descriptions in history).

By the late 30s, hardwood-framed front doors with large glazed panels were popular. It became fashionable for doors to have "radiussed" curved corners; this type of door continued to be produced during the postwar period. Door fittings were kept to the minimum and the letterbox/mailslot was often set into a panel flanking the door to preserve the unity of the surface.

① *Modernism with a touch of glamour: the polished metal front door has a stepped frame. Hollywood, California, mid-1930s.*

② *A glass front door with radiussed corners and a long "D"-handle, designed by Denys Lasdun for a house in Paddington, London, 1939. The letterbox/mailslot is let into one of the adjoining floor-to-ceiling side windows.*

③ *An unusual reinforced concrete porch over an arch-headed door, designed by Lubetkin and Tecton, Haywards Heath, Sussex, 1936.*

④ *A glazed entrance door with a deep projecting wooden canopy. The porch, which is supported by joists, is complemented by the paved area beneath, designed to the same dimensions.*

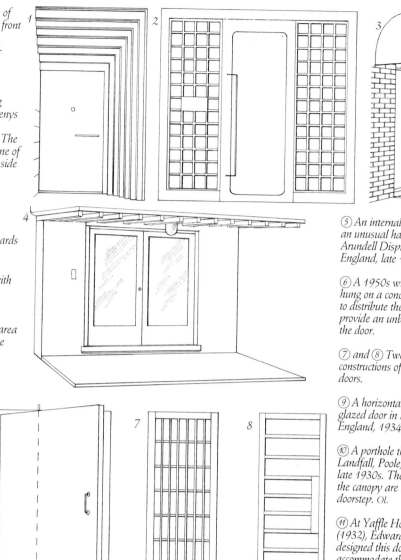

⑤ *An internal metal door with an unusual handle. By the Arundell Display Company, England, late 1920s.*

⑥ *A 1950s wide wooden door hung on a concealed pivot hinge to distribute the weight and provide an unbroken surface to the door.*

⑦ *and* ⑧ *Two typical frame constructions of 1930s flush doors.*

⑨ *A horizontally banded glazed door in Somerset, England, 1934.* PO

⑩ *A porthole theme is used at Landfall, Poole, Dorset, from the late 1930s. The curved forms of the canopy are repeated in the doorstep.* OL

⑪ *At Yaffle House, Dorset (1932), Edward Maufe designed this door to accommodate the slope of the ceiling. The stepped moulding of the frame emphasizes the door's form.* YH

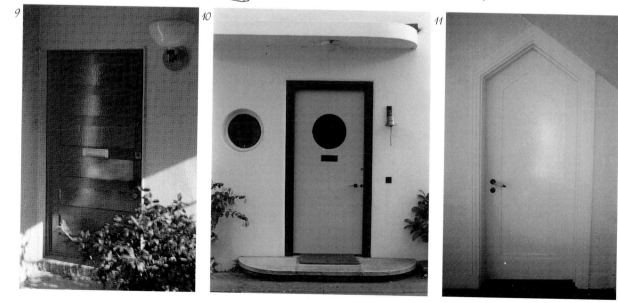

Windows

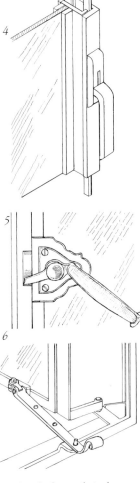

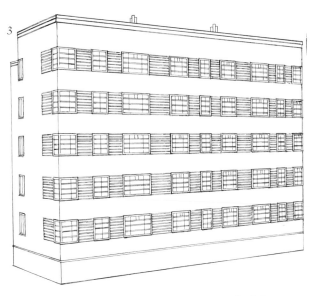

① *Dramatic use of glass bricks as an alternative to a solid wall in a Manhattan house designed by William Lesacaze in 1934, the first Modernist town house in the United States.*
② *A simple steel-framed window with carefully proportioned panes and a mesh balcony, designed by Ernö Goldfinger, London, 1939.*
③ *Council-owned apartment block in Liverpool, England, designed by Lancelot Keay in 1934. The elevations were designed around the horizontal divisions of the windows: the corner window was a Modernist device which became a cliché.*
④ *A specially designed handle for Highpoint Flats, the London apartment block designed by Lubetkin and Tecton in 1935.*

The handle fits neatly in the frame and was easy to clean.
⑤ *An elegant handle with curved plate at Yaffle House, Poole, Dorset, 1932, manufactured by Crittall's.*
⑥ *This projecting hinge made cleaning the outside of the window easy.*

Fresh air and maximum sunlight were Modernist prerequisites. Architects designed large windows which ideally formed a continuous element with an outside wall. Living areas had windows, some on sliding runners, that rose from ground to ceiling level. Picture windows were introduced to "frame" views. Some windows could fold away completely like a concertina, others were able to be wound down into the sill.

Frames were generally made of steel but wood became acceptable in the late 30s. In England this was due to a Scandinavian influence. In the United States, Walter Gropius was also using wood and experimenting by recessing the window so that the overhanging lintel controlled the amount of absorbed sunshine. In England, Ernö Goldfinger's "photobolic screen" introduced more daylight into a room by having what was in effect two windows on top of one another. The smaller top one was recessed so that a ledge was created over the lower window. The ledge was painted white and reflected more light into the room. Mass-produced windows were manufactured in England by Crittall's. The panes were horizontal rectangles, opening as side-hung or top-hung casements. A small degree of decoration was provided with "V"-shaped glazing bars. Curved corner windows became a symbol of the speculative builder's interpretation of Modernism.

WINDOWS

① The popular range of Crittall's windows was based on multiples of standard sizes.
② The concertina windows at the Highpoint apartment block in London could be folded back to allow virtually the whole living room wall to be open.

③ Louvered windows provided ample ventilation.
④ This metal-framed window is fitted with projecting hinges to allow the casement to open back against the wall. It also has sub-lights below: these were designed to protect furniture and ornaments from wind and rain when the casement was opened. The window was supplied with a rolled steel sill.
⑤ These French doors were designed to fold back and to run on tracks top and bottom.
⑥ A boxed-out glazed balcony with opening side windows, designed to catch the sun. Bristol, England, c.1960.
⑦ A stair tower with wood-framed circular windows designed by Tayler and Green. TG
⑧ An uninterrupted flow of space is created by these windows which effectively become a wall of glass in this vaulted Washington DC house, c.1964.
⑨ A black tiled sill and Crittall's casement fastener, from Yaffle House, 1932, designed by Edward Maufe. YH
⑩ The porch which extends from the Gropius House at Lincoln, Massachusetts, has floor-to-ceiling screens of mosquito mesh. 1938. PO

Walls

① *Ernö Goldfinger achieved a smooth unified treatment of walls and door by using a fine plywood. London, 1939. EG*
② *The rough-finished plaster walls at the Schindler House, West Hollywood, California, are interrupted by slit windows. 1921-22. SR*

③ *A trompe l'oeil surrealist mural breaks into a late 1930s living room. PO*
④ *A white-painted plaster relief of "Mr Funshine", in a private apartment at Blackpool Casino, in the north of England, 1939. PO*

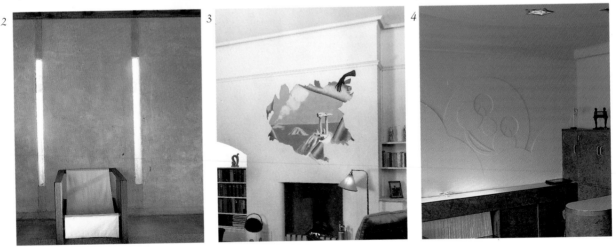

One of the identifying characteristics of the first phase of Modernism was the elimination of pattern and texture in walls: smooth plaster was *de rigueur*. The main modification was the use of plywood linings in dining rooms and studies. Occasionally murals appeared, painted in vignette style. Glass bricks were used by some architects to admit more light. Room dividers were popular in apartments with open-plan layouts.

In the United States, Frank Lloyd Wright continued to use rough stone and brick textures, even in his most "modern" house, Falling Water, Pennsylvania, 1935. The Modern Movement's appreciation of texture was changed by the innovative use of contrasting plaster with rough brick and rubble stonework, a theme developed initially by Le Corbusier.

The effect of this change in style was barely perceptible in England where, even in the l950s, rubble work was considered to be too folksy; regular materials like brick and concrete blocks were preferred, although the bricks might be roughly laid with deep mortar joints. Pine tongue-and-groove boarding replaced plywood panelling. There was a striking revival in wallpaper design. Different related patterns were mixed in one room, often with black linear designs on pastel backgrounds in living areas, and culinary designs in the kitchen. In the 1960s, hessian became popular.

Ceilings

① *A wooden ceiling of Japanese simplicity at the Schindler House in West Hollywood, California, 1921-2. SR*
② *An etched-glass ceiling dome by Raymond McGrath at Finella, Cambridge, England,* with *"Pictavian" Scottish symbols, 1929. PO*
③ *Berthold Lubetkin designed this penthouse in Highgate, London, in 1938, developing the decorative qualities of modern architecture through colours, textures and curved forms. APR*

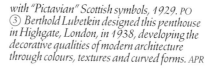

The ceiling is perhaps the most unpromising area of the Modernist house. The very presence of a cornice or ceiling rose/medallion could be enough to disqualify the whole house from the category. Ceilings were sometimes painted in white gloss paint to add reflection; some incorporated electric ceiling heating, an innovation aimed at removing all visible evidence of appliances, but which was found to be ineffective and uncomfortable.

The doctrinaire discipline of Modernism discouraged any ceiling decoration. However, in 1929 at the very beginning of the English Movement, Raymond McGrath broke the rules at Finella, his conversion of a Victorian house in Cambridge. It has a three-sided "vault" of glass in the hall, leading to a groin vault in plywood originally covered in silver leaf and an etched glass dome in the dining room.

Post-war Modernism introduced a more organic style of architecture, and ceilings were allowed to follow a less rigid line. In the United States, wooden boarded ceilings became popular, often as a continuation of the wall surface. Varnished pine was frequently used. Generally, there was a more sculptural approach, and Philip Johnson's Guest House at New Canaan, Connecticut, with its twin shallow vaults supported by slender columns, foreshadows Post-Modernism.

Floors

① A tile mosaic in the hall at Yaffle House, Poole, Dorset, England, 1932, showing the house itself designed by Edward Maufe for tile manufacturer Cyril Carter. YH

② Jointed blocks of travertine laid in such a way that they emphasize the octagonal shape of the room. YH
③ Fine quality hardwood floors with

modern rugs were popular. 1938. OH
④ A stainless steel insert is used to create a bold statement in this detail of a 30s travertine block floor. YH

The Modernist attitude to patterned surfaces is reflected in the design and treatment of floors: stark elegance could only be achieved with the minimum of decorative distraction. Wood is the most commonly used material. Floors are generally of dark polished hardwood, laid as boards or parquet. There would often be a rug with a bold abstract design and the wooden floor would be seen as a border. Wall-to-wall carpets were an expensive luxury and tended to be confined to the principal rooms of grand houses; even then they made little impact until the period was well advanced. For economy, plain linoleum laid on a cement screed or on plywood was generally used. In Britain, an exception to the deliberately unpatterned approach can be seen at Finella, the Victorian house in Cambridge refurbished by the architect/designer Raymond McGrath in 1929, where the hall and dining room were experiments in inlaid "Induroleum", a rubber flooring material thought to be superior to linoleum.

For kitchens and halls, quarry tiles are common; cork tiles or linoleum are found in bathrooms or, very occasionally, mosaic. In a few Modernist houses, cork tiles were used throughout. Stone floors, laid in blocks or as random "crazy paving", were an option most often explored in the United States. In the later Modernist period in Britain, brick floors are seen.

Fireplaces

A majestic but simple fireplace with copper canopy designed by Rudolph Schindler, California, 1922. Rich materials used in this way reflect the work of Adolf Loos in pre-1914 Vienna, where Schindler's career began. SR

In spite of the availability of alternative forms of heating, fireplaces remained popular. W.H. Auden wrote in *Letter to Lord Byron* (1937): "Preserve me above all from central heating/It may be D.H. Lawrence hocus-pocus/But I prefer a room that's got a focus". Even Modernist architects agreed. However, the architectural form of the fireplace was greatly simplified. A plain stone surround set flush with the wall was common in the 1930s, sometimes with a tile infill. Rougher surfaces for the infill section, such as flint or stone, became popular in the later 30s. Sometimes panels of stone or metal were set into the chimney breast in an asymmetrical composition, and built-in bookcases were lined up with the fireplace. A recessed space for the storage of wood was often provided.

The United States was the real home of the Modernist hearth, and a mythology was created through the work of Frank Lloyd Wright, Marcel Breuer and others. Taking up the entire wall of a room, the fireplace became a focal point, built of rugged stonework.

Where solid fuel was no longer used, electric fires were often installed in the wall. Stylish surrounds were made from coloured opaque glass or stainless steel.

In the 1950s a freestanding fire with its fluepipe connected directly to the chimney became a possibility. This heat-saving device was popular in smaller houses.

① A two-unit gas fire with bronze-lustred finish, set into an onyx surround. Bratt Colbran and Company, 1934.
② A late 30s fireplace. The hearth is recessed well above floor level and small square tiles form the surround.
③ A late 1930s British fireplace surround, simply moulded, designed to take a standard fire. The detail shows a typical grate with front rail, raised for ventilation from below.
④ An off-centre fireplace, designed as part of a built-in bookcase and shelf, with plywood facing, 1938.
⑤ At Frank Lloyd Wright's Fallingwater, Bear Run,

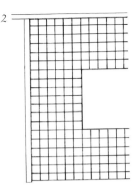

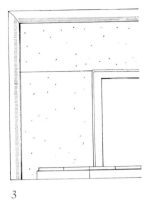

Pennsylvania (1935), the stone chimney and hearth are built like an external wall.
⑥ The open living area of a house in California designed

by Richard Neutra is divided by this fireplace which features "crazy paving", typical of the "Contemporary" style of the 1950s.

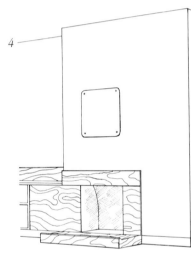

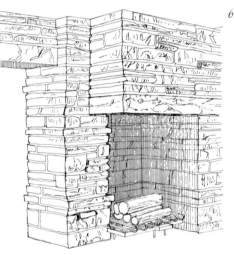

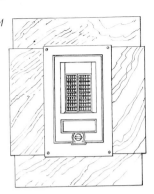

⑦ Copper louvered vents are used as an architectural expression of electricity, and successfully conceal the

appliance behind. Designed by Russell Wright in the United States, it is an example of the Modernist use of metal as a

decorative feature. CS
⑧ Stainless steel is used to form the surround and hearth of the fireplace at Yaffle House, Poole,

Dorset, 1932. YH
⑨ Ernö Goldfinger set this raised fireplace into a concave chimney breast, 1939. EG

Kitchen stoves

① *The British "Minette" stove still has legs. It is fitted with a hinged hob/cook-top cover that forms a splashback and shelf when open. 1935.*
② *The lid to the boxed-in "Kabineat" gas stove had an automatic self-locking plate rack. Britain, 1935.*
③ *The legs of this twin-hob/*

cook-top American electric stove have virtually disappeared. The neat bar handles give it a streamlined appearance.
④ *A British gas stove designed*

to be fitted into a constricted space. 1935.
⑤ *A pioneering American electric island unit with cupboards in its curved ends. 1937.*

The Modern Movement's concept of the kitchen as an integral open-plan part of the living area brought about a rapid change in the appearance of kitchen stoves.

In the United States, which was in advance of Britain, gas stoves had become more streamlined by the end of the 30s. They had lost their utilitarian look: the grey speckled enamel had been replaced by a white finish with chromium trim, and manufacturers had dispensed with the need to raise the oven on legs. Both gas and electric stoves became modular units in the newly fashionable fitted kitchen, and they could be installed in awkward corner spaces to create efficient work areas. The hob/cook-top was aligned with laminated counter-tops to form a continuous work surface. Oven insulation was improved by the addition of interior glass doors; and safety, in the case of gas stoves, by the introduction of pilot lights. Automatic timers – often displayed with the dials on the splashback – were another feature common to both types of stove.

The most revolutionary development in stove design was the "island" unit, a precursor of the customized arrangements in many modern kitchens where hobs/cook-tops and ovens are independent of each other and may have different fuel sources. The island was formed in the middle of larger kitchens, with a brick base and a hood fitted with an air extractor fan.

Staircases

① *The spiral stair with cantilevered wooden treads at Ernö Goldfinger's London house, 1939. The polished handrail and laced string balustrade emphasize the elegant curve. EG*
② *An impressive display of architectural skill and bravura is shown in this reinforced concrete exterior stair with tubular handrail. The house, Landfall, at Poole in Dorset, England, was designed by Oliver Hill in 1938. OL*

③ *The wooden staircase at the Schindler House in West Hollywood, California, 1921-22. SR*
④ *This spiral concrete stair winds its way around the broad central pillar at The Studio designed by Tayler and Green, London, 1939. The metal handrail is shaped to take the form of the pillar. TG*

Staircase design played a major role in the Modern Movement's opening up of internal space. Even in houses of conventional plan, the hallway would be lightened by a large window. As a transitional phase of design, a solid balustrade was made of plywood, and the same treatment was also given to older staircases to "modernize" them. More commonly, the Modernist balustrade would be of metal, with exaggerated sloped and horizontal elements following the rise of the staircase and giving a streamlined look. Close followers of Le Corbusier would have reinforced concrete stairs, with solid balustrades, rising from the main double-height room of the house. Art Deco influences would curve the stair and finish the balustrade off with a rounded newel.

Spiral stairs were used to save space, often in reinforced concrete. Walter Gropius put an external iron spiral stair on his house at Lincoln, Massachusetts, while in England, Oliver Hill's external stair at Landfall, Poole, 1938, adds a touch of architectural panache. The same house has a beautiful curving wooden ladder stair leading from the floor above the entrance level to the roof. Many Modernist houses had a nautical-style ladder for access to an upper sunbathing level.

The wooden open-tread stair became standard in the 1940s and 1950s, and often rose from the main room.

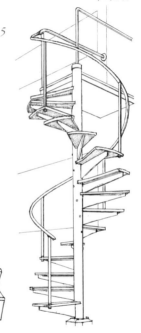

① *A fine curving stair at Shrub's Wood, Chalfont St Giles, Buckinghamshire, by Mendelsohn and Chermayeff, 1935.* PO

② *At The Homewood, Esher, Surrey, by Patrick Gwynne, 1938, the spiral stair emerges onto a broad landing.* PO

③ *A mysterious ascent to the roof of St Ann's Hill, Chertsey, Surrey, a circular house by Raymond McGrath, 1936.* PO

④ *An elegant use of concrete is displayed in this gently curved unsupported staircase with undercut risers. The staircase has a tubular metal handrail.*

⑤ *This external iron spiral staircase was designed by Walter Gropius for his house at Lincoln, Massachusetts, 1938.*

⑥ *An internal reinforced concrete stair with a bedded-in tubular handrail, 1934.*
⑦ *The return of traditional materials: oak is used for this late-30s stair and handrail, but with typical Modernist metal mesh balustrade panels.*
⑧ *A straight-flight stair with closed string, New York, 1935. The handrail is aluminium.*
⑨ *Flowing lines are characteristic of the Modernist period. Here regular loops of steel are arranged up the staircase: the treads and a chromium rail on the upper floor provide the points of contact. A brass handrail accentuates the staircase's form, 1938.*

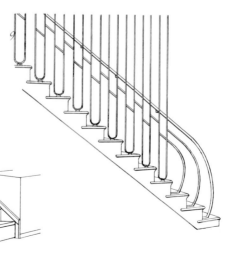

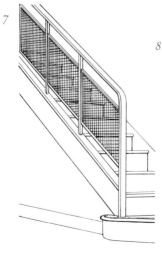

STAIRCASES

Built-in furniture

① *A 30s built-in sideboard/ room divider. The dumb waiter connecting with the kitchen two floors below rises out of the counter top. There is a crisp decorative contrast of painted and natural wood.* TG

② *A wooden cabin-style child's bed with drawers beneath, 1939.* OH
③ *A built-in sideboard and refectory table with matching stool by Rudolph Schindler, California, 1922.* SR

While Modernism exercised an inhibiting influence on many aspects of domestic design, built-in furniture was a positive contribution. The aim was to leave living space as uncluttered as possible, and to revive the Neo-classical ideal of a completely coordinated room. The Movement coincided with a more flexible attitude to the family as a social unit, and with it a desire to simplify life and to minimize household chores.

Almost every item of furniture could be included in this category. A Modernist house would have built-in bookshelves, seats and benches (all could be used as room dividers), cupboards in bedrooms, bathrooms and kitchens, even toy-cupboards in nurseries; cocktail cabi-

nets and spaces for radios and record players were also featured in some houses. Doors were hinged or sliding. Built-in beds, with shelves beneath as in a ship's cabin, were popular for small bedrooms. Fixed seating could be arranged around the hearth. Forms were simple and would have been finished in white paint or veneer, unless made of solid hardwood. An extension of built-in furniture was the development of ranges of furniture with modular coordination which could be assembled together. The 1930s attachment to ship-like fitted interiors cooled during the post-war period but it left a legacy, particularly in kitchens and bathrooms, which became a selling point.

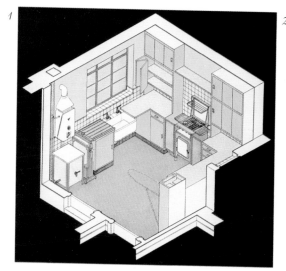

① A 1930s built-in kitchen. The advantage of built-in cupboards, with devices such as the concertina door shown here, convinced even those who rejected Modernism as a total style. British. AG
② Smaller apartments in particular could profit from the space-saving benefits of built-in furniture. This example is a typical 30s dado-level unit made up of cupboards and bookshelves in ash and walnut with an electric fire. CS

③ The sofa at 2 South Parade, Chiswick, London, folds out to become a double bed, complete with lights and bedside tables; by Dugdale and Ruhemann, 1937. APR
④ A 1930s built-in glass shelf unit supported on slender chromium legs. British.
⑤ A seating corner: the armrests contain bookshelves and have mirror-glass tops. Paul Frankl, New York, c.1935.

⑥ At Bentley Wood, East Sussex, by Serge Chermayeff, 1938, built-in cupboards made a tidy wall with recesses for objects. APR

⑦ A practical and elegant fitting from the hall at Shrub's Wood, 1935, giving storage and a convenient ledge. PO

BUILT-IN FURNITURE

Services

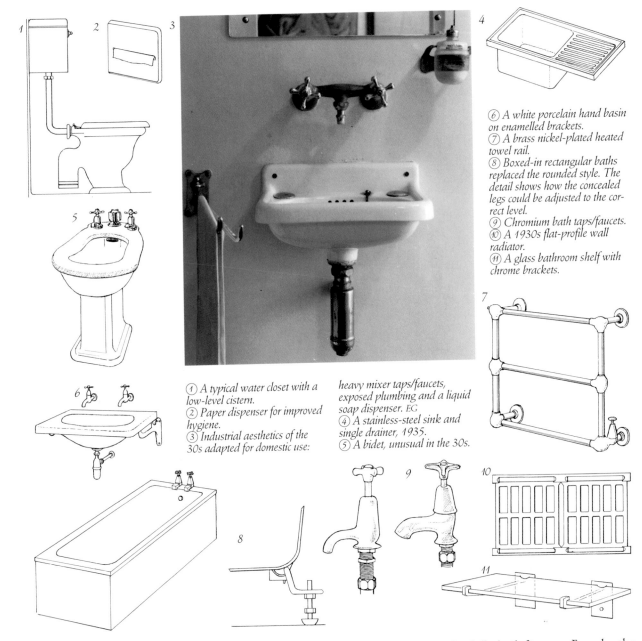

⑥ *A white porcelain hand basin on enamelled brackets.*
⑦ *A brass nickel-plated heated towel rail.*
⑧ *Boxed-in rectangular baths replaced the rounded style. The detail shows how the concealed legs could be adjusted to the correct level.*
⑨ *Chromium bath taps/faucets.*
⑩ *A 1930s flat-profile wall radiator.*
⑪ *A glass bathroom shelf with chrome brackets.*

① *A typical water closet with a low-level cistern.*
② *Paper dispenser for improved hygiene.*
③ *Industrial aesthetics of the 30s adapted for domestic use:* heavy mixer taps/faucets, *exposed plumbing and a liquid soap dispenser.* EG
④ *A stainless-steel sink and single drainer, 1935.*
⑤ *A bidet, unusual in the 30s.*

The design of bathrooms and other services developed through the 1920s and 30s without reflecting the debates about acceptable style: a Modernist bathroom would scarcely differ from one found in an Art Deco or Neo-Tudor house. But there was an emphasis on health and hygiene, and the bathroom assumed greater importance: Le Corbusier integrated the bathroom with the main living space in one of his houses.

Bathroom fixtures tended to be enclosed: baths were boxed in, and the low-level water closet cistern was often concealed behind panelling. In the United States particularly, the bathroom was the last word in comfort and luxury, with extensive use of tiling, coloured vitrolite cladding and solidly built fixtures. Even by the 30s there was a preference for showers over baths, whereas in Britain these were an acquired taste. The bidet was still a rather daring Continental European luxury.

A standard piece of equipment was the heated towel rail. Usually made from chrome, there was also a glass-tubed model with chrome supports. Taps/faucets were influenced by industrial design and the cross-shaped capstan top was phased out in favour of other styles.

Various methods of central heating were employed: under-floor electric heating, because it best achieved the aim of invisibility, became fashionable when it was introduced in the 1950s.

Lighting

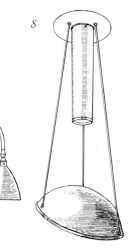

① *An external uplighter at The Homewood, Esher, Surrey, becomes an abstract form.* PO
② *A British version of the standard globe ceiling light, associated with the Bauhaus, 1934.*
③ *An amusingly designed paper shade in handkerchief style for a pendant light at the*
Schindler House in West Hollywood, California. SR
④ *A wall light with upturned fluted reflector.*
⑤ *The wall-mounted articulated Bestlite, a classic British product of the early 30s.*
⑥ *A chrome swan-neck globe wall light. Globes were particularly popular in the 1930s.* TG

⑦ *A hanging globe from New Farm, Great Dunmow, 1934, the home of F. W. Crittall whose company made steel windows for modern houses.* PO
⑧ *An artist's studio ceiling light, fitted with a large bowl reflector, 1934.*

The early period of Modernism concerned itself intermittently with built-in electric light fixtures. In the evolution from Art Deco, some entertaining geometric centre lights were found in Modernist interiors. Few ceiling fittings were allowed to interrupt the "purity" of the room: when they were present they were usually hemispherical globes mounted against the ceiling or occasionally adjustable pendant lights would be used over dining room tables. Wall-mounted lights, either in the form of upturned bowls or globes on stems, were a popular alternative. A wall-mounted articulated light on a chrome stem with a curved cone shade became available for reading or desk work. Architects would often specify their own requirements for designs, such as special ceiling tracks for work areas and concealed lighting, which became fashionable and more available generally in the post-war period.

This was the time that the design of light fixtures became more varied, with a greater use of plastics and much influence from Scandinavia in the profiles of lampshades. By the 1940s, fluorescent tube lighting became common in kitchens and bathrooms. This was favoured in the United States because it produced much less heat than ordinary bulbs. By the 1960s, spotlight tracks became more widely available, introducing a great diversity of light sources within a single unit.

Metalwork

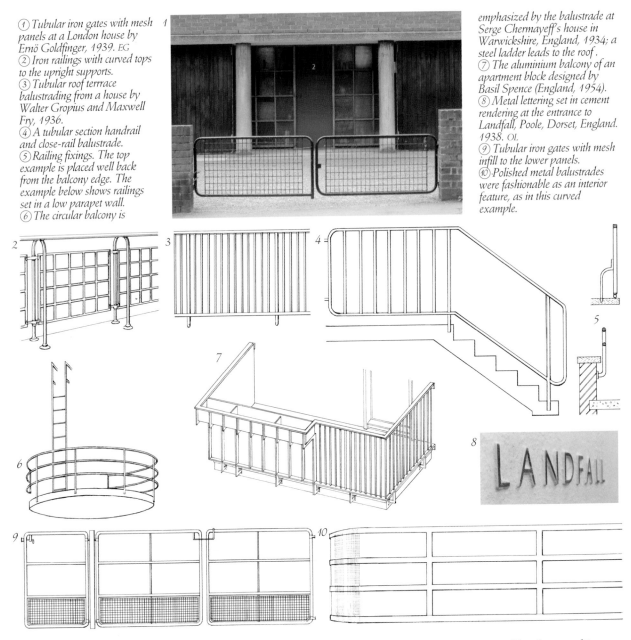

① *Tubular iron gates with mesh panels at a London house by Ernö Goldfinger, 1939. EG*
② *Iron railings with curved tops to the upright supports.*
③ *Tubular roof terrace balustrading from a house by Walter Gropius and Maxwell Fry, 1936.*
④ *A tubular section handrail and close-rail balustrade.*
⑤ *Railing fixings. The top example is placed well back from the balcony edge. The example below shows railings set in a low parapet wall.*
⑥ *The circular balcony is*

emphasized by the balustrade at Serge Chermayeff's house in Warwickshire, England, 1934; a steel ladder leads to the roof .
⑦ *The aluminium balcony of an apartment block designed by Basil Spence (England, 1954).*
⑧ *Metal lettering set in cement rendering at the entrance to Landfall, Poole, Dorset, England. 1938. OL*
⑨ *Tubular iron gates with mesh infill to the lower panels.*
⑩ *Polished metal balustrades were fashionable as an interior feature, as in this curved example.*

For public and industrial buildings, Modernism was often seen as a style of metal and glass. On the domestic level, more solid and conventional materials prevailed, but still allowed for interesting metal detailing. Balconies and handrails tended to be made of tubular iron. Where panels were needed in balconies or gates, the standard way of filling them, borrowed from Continental European examples, was with a woven mesh of thick wire, framed in a panel with curved corners; although this is rather utilitarian, it is an essential part of the Modernist look. Tubular balconies could be bent to form the curves that were the relieving features of Modernist houses. The visual weight

and spacing of the balusters was of fundamental importance. Sometimes they were round in section, sometimes thin square-sectioned bars.

Iron columns were used as structural supports: they were usually made as thin as possible to create the effect of weightless architecture. They were normally round in section, but occasionally "I"-section columns were substituted.

Although Modernist metalwork remained very simple, such detailing as there was could be very fine. During the period of post-war shortages, prefabricated-steel houses were made in Britain; they offered many built-in metal details, including light switches in door frames.

Woodwork

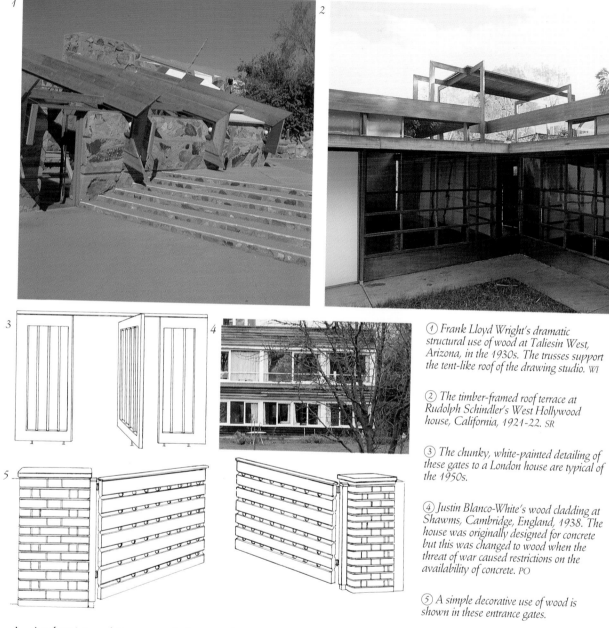

① *Frank Lloyd Wright's dramatic structural use of wood at Taliesin West, Arizona, in the 1930s. The trusses support the tent-like roof of the drawing studio.* WI

② *The timber-framed roof terrace at Rudolph Schindler's West Hollywood house, California, 1921-22.* SR

③ *The chunky, white-painted detailing of these gates to a London house are typical of the 1950s.*

④ *Justin Blanco-White's wood cladding at Shawms, Cambridge, England, 1938. The house was originally designed for concrete but this was changed to wood when the threat of war caused restrictions on the availability of concrete.* PO

⑤ *A simple decorative use of wood is shown in these entrance gates.*

Modernist architects tended to prefer inorganic materials, as befitting the machine age; but wood played an interesting and significant role in the history of the movement. Frank Lloyd Wright, notably, used wood as it came, straight from the sawmill, enjoying the crudeness of finish.

In Britain, smooth wood was used for internal details until the later 1930s; then a feeling for organic architecture, inspired partly by Wright and partly by Scandinavian architects like Alvar Aalto, introduced houses made entirely from wood. Mostly, it was used in plain sawn sections and standard widths, without any ornamental treatment. In the post-war period, architects of a younger generation liked the massive quality of wood, in contrast to the spindly Festival of Britain style, which had arisen at a time of severely restricted timber imports. They made imaginative use of wood fences and screens, usually of white-painted deal (fir or pine).

Wood is fundamental to the American way of building, but many Modernists neglected it in order to prove their credentials. Walter Gropius and Marcel Breuer, coming from Europe, exploited the wood tradition with vertical cladding, pergolas and external stairs, all still very simply conceived. Timber-framed houses, some demountable or factory-made, were widely used to provide for wartime housing needs in the United States.

METALWORK

WOODWORK

BEYOND MODERN

1950–1996

① Lightweight industrial products give freedom and openness at Pierre Koenig's Case Study House 21, Los Angeles, California, 1958. SHU

② More collector's object than practical dwelling, the Farnsworth House at Plano, Illinois, 1946-51, by Mies van der Rohe is the ultimate in ethereal living. HB

As the twentieth century nears its end, the Modernism of its middle years begins to look more like the exception than the norm it supposed itself to be. While the technical advances of modernity brought advantages to all, the aesthetic of Modernism, intended as a liberation, often seemed like a straitjacket.

In the years after 1950, this was hardly apparent. Many of the original generation of European Modernists were working in the United States and their work became widely publicized. The designs of Marcel Breuer, a Hungarian who had worked in Germany, Switzerland and England, were influenced by the naturalism of Frank Lloyd Wright and the relaxed American lifestyle. In 1949 he exhibited a show house at the Museum of Modern Art in New York with timber-lined walls, a stone feature fireplace and a single big sloping roof, elements of which were replicated in millions of American ranch houses. Breuer worked to fit each of his houses to the client's needs, recreating from different resources something of the ideal world of calm and unity found in the Arts and Crafts period. He wrote in *Sun and Shadow: The Philosophy of an Architect* (1956; p.34), "transparency needs also solidity… because total transparency leaves out such considerations as privacy, reflecting surfaces, transition from disorder to order, furnishings, a background for you, for your everyday life."

He may have been thinking of the Farnsworth House (1946-51), Plano, Illinois, by Ludwig Mies van der Rohe, floating off the ground in pure white painted steel and glass but impossible to live in. It provoked a famous quarrel between architect and client and inspired other glass houses like the Glass House by Philip Johnson at New Canaan, Connecticut, but it was never intended as a solution to housing ordinary people. The Case Study houses in California pursued steel and glass construction through the 1950s in the hope of creating new standard patterns. The most famous of these, the Charles and Ray Eames House (1949) at Santa Monica, California, introduced colour and variety among the industrially-produced steel components of which it was built and was another version of the Contemporary style.

In the United States and Britain (where the term acquired a pejorative tone), Contemporary was both a contin-uation and revision of Modernism, introducing a decorative playfulness and a spatial freedom that had been lacking between the wars. American houses are full of optimism for a new way of life. Solid elements appear weightless, as if the conquest of space had defeated earthly gravity. After the war, living-in servants disappeared almost completely from middle-class life and the result was a considerable liberation in space, allowing the kitchen to be placed closer to the heart of

*An ideal of American easy living at the Mirman
House by Buff, Straub and Hensman, 1958-9.
Inside and outside are merged in the Californian
climate, and built-in furniture reduces clutter
to a minimum. The bright 1950's look carried
through fabric colours and domestic objects. SHU*

the house. Kitchens and bathrooms were smaller than they would be today, since small size denoted efficiency. Several uses were often combined in one large room, often with varied ceiling heights and sometimes with a sunken seating area or "conversation pit". Children were given a larger place in the house than before, although sometimes cunningly segregated from their parents. As the English revue entertainers Flanders and Swann sang in 1958: "Our boudoir on the open plan has been a huge success. Now everywhere's so open that there's nowhere safe to dress." This demonstrated how liberation can have its drawbacks. As teenage culture emerged at the end of the 1950s with transistor radios and record players, there was a reaction in favour of separate rooms.

British houses of the 1950s tended to be smaller and more cheaply built than their American counterparts but their ingenious use of space included bringing the staircase into the main living room as a ladder stair and virtually abolishing hallways and corridors. A freestanding pavilion plan was generally favoured with numerous ways out into the garden. The claim of interwar modernists to design houses based on the logic of the plan rather than on a pre-conceived image of the exterior was more fully realized in the 1950s and the exteriors can seem unimpressive compared with the pleasing quality of the internal spaces. Economy in materials was combined with a problem in getting good craftsmanship after the war. Unlike traditional styles in which applied mouldings can cover difficult transitions from one surface to another, Modernism is unforgiving in its standards of finish. The recessed joint or "flashgap" was a popular detail of the period. Brick was widely used and there was no return to the smooth concrete (or pseudoconcrete) forms of the 1930s. Inside, wood veneers were a popular finish, combined with areas of

The Thematic House. London, by Charles Jencks, 1982-5. The eclectic furnishings and the cheerful colouring show how Post-Modernism can succeed as a popular, adaptable style, regardless of any symbolic messages that are being carried. JE

exposed brickwork. Interiors might contain a mixture of figured synthetic and natural materials. Peter Wormersley's house at Farnley Hey, Yorkshire, 1954, is an example of the use of varied materials and open planning that was publicized in its time and stands comparison with Breuer's designs. In England it was a highly productive period for small houses, many built by architects for themselves and incorporating a number of original ideas and prototypes.

In the 1960s houses became more inward-looking and the thin lines and sharp colours of the 1950s gave way to more solid earth-bound textured surfaces of timber, brick and concrete with a distinctive palette of browns, greens, oranges and purples. The courtyard house was a favourite type and was urged (without much success) by theorists in the United States as an antidote to the land-hungry suburban tracts where each house stood in its own patch of ground. In England its introversion suited the national temperament and the crowded conditions for building. The 1960s brought fantasy visions of underground dwellings, tent structures and a renewed interest in steel construction, increasingly in the lightweight version known as High-tech which sees itself as a continuation of Modernism although the use of technology is often decorative.

Classical architecture conducted a rear-guard action against the dominance of Modernism. Architects whose careers began before World War I such as Philip

① *John Outram designed this house in Sussex, England, 1985. The design is notable for its complex symbolism, but also for the fine craftsmanship and materials employed. In the refined surface decoration there are reminiscences of the English Neo-classical architect Sir John Soane (1753-1837), as well as of 1930s styles.* OU

② *The Pavilion, Little Horkesley, Essex, by Raymond Erith, 1970. A small country house by Britain's best-known classical revivalist of the post-war period. The client wanted a French feeling, which Erith provided, departing here from his preference for Italian forms. The plan is one room deep, without corridors.* PO

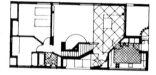

③ *The house in Chestnut Hill, Philadelphia, 1962, designed by Robert Venturi and John Rauch: one of the starting points of the revolt against Modernism. The gabled entrance front suggests formal symmetry, but sets up a game of hide and seek: behind this facade, symmetry is playfully overturned, as the two plans and cross-section alongside show. This small house is packed with inventive ideas, yet is easier to live in than many Modernist "diagrams".* PO

Trammel Schutze in Georgia and Sir Albert Richardson in England were still active in the 1960s and continued to build classical, colonial and neo-Georgian houses, showing that good craftsmen were in fact still available. Small numbers of younger traditionalists carried forward this smouldering torch, largely ignored by other architects. When Raymond Erith and his partner Quinlan Terry built Kingswaldenbury, a large neo-Palladian country house in Hertfordshire, between 1969 and 1972, they thought it would be the last of its type. Time has proved otherwise, and the 1980s brought a series of house commissions for architects in a classical style. Some, like Terry, have an evangelical belief in their chosen style, others have adapted to the fashion of the moment. Classicism has a popular appeal and Georgian features are found in many speculative houses, although on this level they are seldom finely crafted or integrated into the architecture.

Other architects who rejected the mechanistic forms of Modernism turned instead to vernacular prototypes. The theme of constructional honesty and truth to materials interweaves with Modernism. It provided an escape route that did not imply an ideological about-turn in the houses of Peter Aldington and David Lea in England or the San Francisco cottage revival of Donald MacDonald. Neo-vernacular has won a broad consensus and forms the basis for experiments in applying urban design codes in the Florida resort developments by Andreas Duany and Elizabeth Plater-Zybeck and the Duchy of Cornwall village development at Poundbury, Dorset, promoted by the Prince of Wales. In England, the products of speculative builders tend towards Tudor or Georgian, although neither style is much apparent internally. Local character is copied in "heritage" areas and it is now virtually illegal to build a modern-looking house in a conservation area. Architects committed to Modernism find opportunities where they can.

In 1962 the architect Robert Venturi built a house for his mother in Chestnut Hill, a suburb of Philadelphia, that may have started a revolution. Modest though it seems, this house with its symbolic gable and applied arch moulding was the beginning of a new emphasis on the meaning of architecture that Modernism had deliberately ignored in its search for technical perfection and aesthetic abstraction. While Mies van der Rohe said "Less is more", Venturi answered "Less is a bore". The Post-Modern movement which stemmed from Venturi's appeal for complexity and layers of meaning in architecture became widely popular in the 1980s. Its superficiality and smartness seemed to suit the spirit of

① *Honeymoon Cottages at Seaside, Florida, by Scott Merrill, 1988-90. Their design is controlled by a detailed building code.* MOR

② *A house in Islington, London, by Future Systems, 1994. The sloping glass continues the ideals of the early modernists and is visually striking.* DAV

③ *European neo-classicism of the 1810s is recalled in Michael Graves's own house at Princeton, New Jersey, 1993. Light falls to the entrance below the temple-like balustrade.* ROC

④ *Kingswaldenbury, by Raymond Erith and Quinlan Terry, 1972, is shown here in Terry's linocut print.* PO

the decade, but it also provided much needed entertainment and relaxation from the formality prevailing in the architectural debate. In contrast to the depersonalized purity of Modernism, it allowed for individuality from the architect and the client. As in the 1920s in Europe, private houses for wealthy clients became an important architectural laboratory and the experiments ranged from the houses of Peter Eisenmann in upstate New York, built to resemble complicated intellectual diagrams, to the luxurious and popular designs of Robert Stern. Post-Modernism had its main opportunities as domestic architecture in the United States, although John Outram's house in Sussex, built for Austrian clients, is a notable exception. In the mid 1990s, Post-Modernism has lost its novelty and appeal although it undoubtedly acted as a liberating force.

With Post-Modernism came an increasing interest in interior decoration. Social aspiration was fed with books and magazines, and a person's identity became defined by the decorative background of their life as never before. Forgotten painting techniques of marbling, graining and dragging were revived to give frantic interest to every surface. Authenticity, to which this book itself is a testimony, became a filter through which creativity had to pass in a self-conscious awareness of period style, although the treatment of kitchens and bathrooms required some inventive adaptation bordering on fantasy or fake. While much genuine knowledge

was recovered and displayed in the restoration of historic houses, time appeared to stand still without the call for innovation in contemporary work.

Such a condition of stasis could not last indefinitely. Even in the economic recession of the early 1990s new furniture and decorative art has begun to flourish and find a wider clientele. No stylistic label has yet emerged for the style which reverts to the wilder aspects of the 1950s, mixing classic Modern furniture and colourful pots, automata or screen-printed fabrics composed of jumbled and collaged images. The old antagonism between Modernism and all other styles seems to have been overtaken by a new ornamentalism, although this is not so much expressed in the enrichment of the permanent and fixed parts of the house as in the accumulation of movable items. A puritanical country look has helped the recession-bound 1990s to find its identity through mass-produced versions of Shaker chairs and candlesticks. On a more serious level, theorists such as Christopher Alexander have analyzed what qualities of traditional building – plan, space and ornament – combine to make it so much more satisfying than later work. It remains to be seen whether designers will discover how to give these elements the visual strength and vitality they possessed in the pre-Modernist past, or whether they will take the easier road of recycling superficial variants of earlier styles like the sampling and remixing of their contemporaries in the music business.

Doors

① *This strongly axial design uses brickwork inventively. Robert Adam, Crooked Pightle, Hampshire, England.* AD
② *Classicism is complicated by added references in this entranceway by John Outram, Sussex, England. The doors lead to a conservatory, which makes the use of latticework – suggestive of a garden trellis – especially appropriate.* OU
③ *The entrance to a house in Stony Creek, Connecticut, by Venturi, Scott Brown and Associates, 1983. The large "rose window" ship's wheel is a reference to the waterfront site and the nautical traditions of the region. The use of mirrors in place of windows is a wry touch.* VE
④ *An internal door in the hall of the Sussex house by John Outram. The trelliswork effect is made from grey-stained sycamore veneers.* OU

With the return to symbolic meaning in architecture after the denials of Modernism, doors resumed their ritual function. This could be expressed ironically (a small house entered through a miniature temple); or, more sympathetically, the door could be ornamented to celebrate the act of arrival and the idea of ownership. Modernist glass doors revealing the inside of the house fell prey to fears about security: stronger, more solid doors were now desirable.

Builders' supply merchants developed a range of hardwood doors which enjoyed great popularity. Often these would have an integral fanlight of vaguely Georgian character in the door itself – a practical but unsightly device. Although the plywood flush door remains supreme for internal use on grounds of economy, it is no longer made to pre-war standards of quality: attempts are often made to disguise this by the use of additional mouldings. Door surrounds have been adapted from Georgian models, which sometimes influence the design of the room. The Georgian six-panelled door is a standard catalogue item. High-tech doors use colour and manufactured materials (metal, plastic) but remain a minority taste.

In door furniture many "period" forms have been revived. Other fittings have continued the Modernist machine aesthetic.

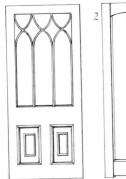

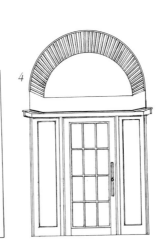

① ② and ③ *Three catalogue doors (exterior): Gothic Ogee, a mahogany-faced door with* imitation planking, and Tudor. All three of these doors date from the 1980s. British.

④ *This example of freely adapted classicism is the entrance porch to a limestone house in Austin, Texas, designed by Hal Box, 1980s.*

⑤ *A Georgian-style surround, which may be used in a Post-Modern context or alternatively as pure kitsch.*

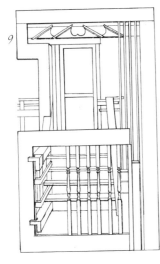

⑥ *A bizarre, bug-eyed manifestation of Post-Modernism: an entrance flanked by twin garages, designed by the Connecticut architects BumpZoid.*

⑦ *A Neo-Stick-style entrance to a riverfront apartment block in New Haven, Connecticut, 1980s.*

⑧ *Not so much the door, more the entrance experience at Future Systems' house in Islington. It is shown here to dramatic effect at night.* DAV
⑨ *A complex layering of catalogued products: Charles Jenks's Garagia Rotunda, Wellfleet, Cape Cod, 1977. The entrance door is announced by a double broken pediment.*
⑩ *A joke door surround to a re-modelled Los Angeles bungalow, dating from the 1970s.*
⑪ *A Georgian-style doorcase by Robert Adam, Hampshire, England, 1986. The brackets were cut from a template.*

Interior doors:
① *A catalogue door with "Stopped Chamfer" mouldings, available in European redwood, 1980s. Britain.*
② *A glazed interior door, available in Brazilian mahogany, in three sizes.*
③ *Imitation Wild West saloon doors – a typical example of a lighthearted cultural allusion. They might be used to separate a kitchen from a dining area. Britain.*
④ *A restaurant-style metal door adapted to domestic use, with a mirror instead of a window.*
⑤ *A planked hardwood door, with three glazed strips.*

⑥ *A classical door with carved architrave by Francis Johnson, 1960s. Johnson is one of the best-known British exponents of*
pure classical revivalism.
⑦ *This door surround is influenced by the Neo-classical forms of Sir John Soane.*

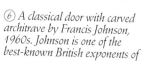

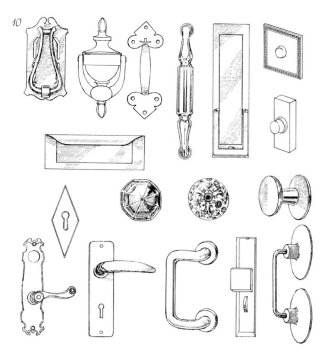

⑧ *A monumental Classical Revival door surround.*
⑨ *This door has a swirling Neo-Rococo surround.*
⑩ *Door fittings display stylistic pluralism. The examples here include period revivals (Tudor, Georgian). Some handles (top row, 4) are used with a ball catch, so that the door clicks*
into place. The upright letterbox/ mailslot (top, 5) has a built-in knocker.
⑪ *An inventive use of stained-glass panels in Robert Adam's house at Crooked Pightle, Hampshire, England. The design carries through the theme of classicized symmetry used elsewhere in the house. AD*

Windows

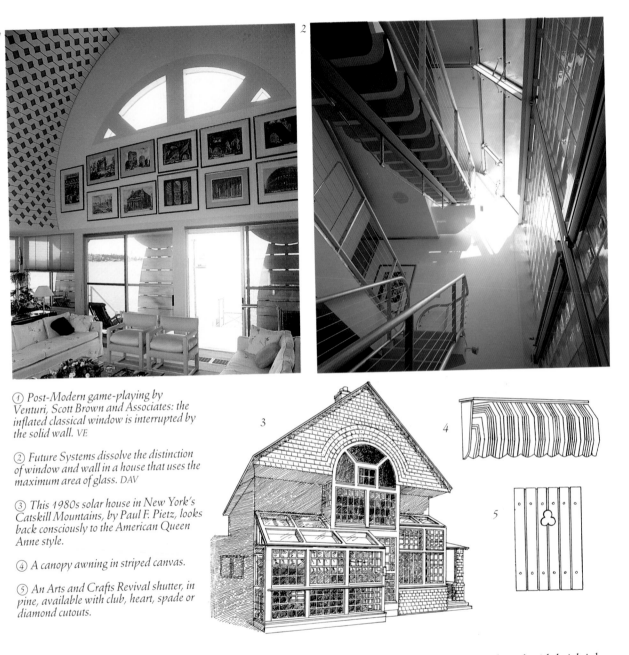

① *Post-Modern game-playing by Venturi, Scott Brown and Associates: the inflated classical window is interrupted by the solid wall.* VE

② *Future Systems dissolve the distinction of window and wall in a house that uses the maximum area of glass.* DAV

③ *This 1980s solar house in New York's Catskill Mountains, by Paul F. Pietz, looks back consciously to the American Queen Anne style.*

④ *A canopy awning in striped canvas.*

⑤ *An Arts and Crafts Revival shutter, in pine, available with club, heart, spade or diamond cutouts.*

For Modernist architects the window was ideally a transparent and invisible screen between inside and outside. For Post-Modernists it could be reinterpreted as part of an architectural code, relating to the composition of the facade as a whole, jokily suggesting a period reference, or perhaps some subtle ambiguity. The result of these approaches was to introduce a much greater variety of window forms.

In the houses of classical revivalists, the Georgian sash window naturally dominates, and has become a standard production item available for restoration work. For new speculative building, varnished hardwood is preferred to painted softwood as it is supposedly main-tenance-free, although when combined with brick it has an unpleasant visual effect. Replacement double-glazed windows, with aluminium or, latterly, plastic-coated metal (UPVC) frames, have been promoted. These have been given crude "Georgian" or "Tudor" styling, and have wrecked the appearance of many otherwise pleasing cottages and small houses.

Window catches and fittings in this period are usually standard modern or Georgian-style items, as the architectural ironmongery industry has not re-tooled to meet rapidly changing architectural fashions. The use of such details, even where incongruous, has usually been relatively inoffensive.

WINDOWS

① Criss-crossing tension wires offset by the horizontal lines of a Venetian blind.
② Screened sash windows and a void in the wall: a joke face. Charles Jenks.
③ A small balcony supporting oversailing eaves above. Seabridge Villas, California.
④ Decorative glazing bars combine with a full Palladian architrave and consoled cornice. Quinlan Terry, England, 1981.
⑤ Frank Lloyd Wright Revival corner window on a house by D. MacDonald, United States.
⑥ The metal-framed Velux rooflight is a standard British unit for attic/loft conversions.
⑦ A round-headed window with iron grille, from a modern interpretation of the Spanish Colonial Revival style, California.

⑧ Window hardware tends to be less inventive than door accessories, despite some historical revivals. This is a selection of catches and casement stays of the period.

⑨ A round-headed window with unusual terracotta paterae, by Robert Adam, from his own house at Crooked Pightle, Hampshire, England, 1989. AD
⑩ Mock windows are part of the Post-Modern repertoire. This example in lead and granite is from Graham Ovenden's house, Barley Splatt, Cornwall, England. The shape represents a crossbow. OV

⑪ Set into the main facade of a house by John Outram in Sussex, England, this T-shaped wood-framed window is part of a complex composition of squares and rectangles. OU

Walls

① *A wall by John Outram, in the entrance hall of a house in Sussex, England, 1985. Polished dark red stucco contrasts with bands of burr elm veneer edged with aluminium. The stucco has been polished with a hot iron to give it a shiny, marble-like surface. The style recalls the "moderne" designs of the 1930s. OU*

② *A mural with collage and painting under glass by Alan Powers, 1992, is a deliberately festive form of decoration, with Hawksmoor steeples and the dome of St Paul's flanked by the lion and the unicorn. This is a celebration of the spirit of London. CN/A*

③ *Instant history in a mural by Alan Powers, 1984, evoking Neo-classical Germany. The painting is confined within a painted border to enhance the architecture of the room. PO*

The rediscovery of ornament has created opportunities for various enrichments of the wall surface. Classical features which might have been out of place on the exterior of a house were often used inside instead; and with apartments, of course, this was the only place to put them. Columns, pilasters, rustication and other classical details gave a set of forms with overtones of cultural status and a recognized set of rules, to be observed or departed from as required. Simple devices like the moulded wooden chair rail have returned to favour as a way to modulate the surface. Plaster arches, niches and recesses have been revived.

Probably the most pervasive wall treatment has been decorative painting, ranging from trompe l'oeil murals to textured surfaces. The rage for faux finishes has dominated both sides of the Atlantic, but also simpler ragged and broken paint effects have had a revival since their last phase of popularity in the 1920s.

The purity of the Modernist aesthetic was already compromised in the 1950s by strongly patterned tiles and wallpapers, and these have remained popular ever since. Where the means were available, texture could be brought into a room by the use of real materials – different kinds of stone, exposed brick and mosaic. This is an idea that originated with High Modernism in the 1930s and soon made its way to a popular level.

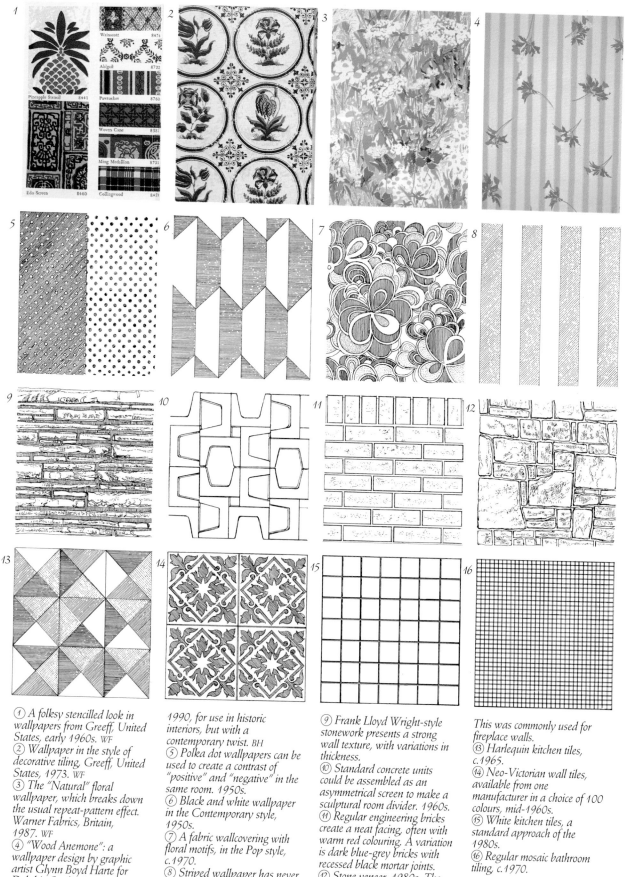

① A folksy stencilled look in
wallpapers from Greeff, United
States, early 1960s. WF
② Wallpaper in the style of
decorative tiling, Greeff, United
States, 1973. WF
③ The "Natural" floral
wallpaper, which breaks down
the usual repeat-pattern effect.
Warner Fabrics, Britain,
1987. WF
④ "Wood Anemone": a
wallpaper design by graphic
artist Glynn Boyd Harte for
Dolphin Studio, London,

1990, for use in historic
interiors, but with a
contemporary twist. BH
⑤ Polka dot wallpapers can be
used to create a contrast of
"positive" and "negative" in the
same room. 1950s.
⑥ Black and white wallpaper
in the Contemporary style,
1950s.
⑦ A fabric wallcovering with
floral motifs, in the Pop style,
c.1970.
⑧ Striped wallpaper has never
been long out of fashion.

⑨ Frank Lloyd Wright-style
stonework presents a strong
wall texture, with variations in
thickness.
⑩ Standard concrete units
could be assembled as an
asymmetrical screen to make a
sculptural room divider. 1960s.
⑪ Regular engineering bricks
create a neat facing, often with
warm red colouring. A variation
is dark blue-grey bricks with
recessed black mortar joints.
⑫ Stone veneer, 1980s. The
thickness is 4 inches (10cm).

This was commonly used for
fireplace walls.
⑬ Harlequin kitchen tiles,
c.1965.
⑭ Neo-Victorian wall tiles,
available from one
manufacturer in a choice of 100
colours, mid-1960s.
⑮ White kitchen tiles, a
standard approach of the
1980s.
⑯ Regular mosaic bathroom
tiling, c.1970.

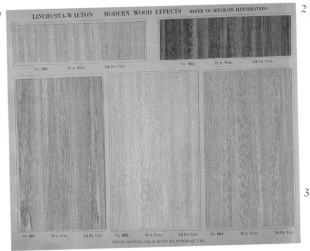

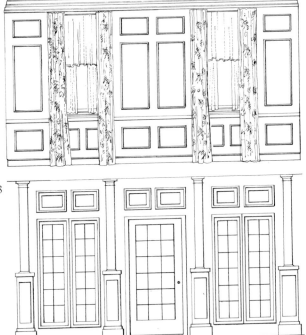

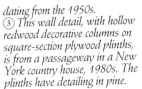

① A range of wood-effect wallpapers, 1952-3. WN
② Plain moulded panelling, with a ceiling cornice – a conservative treatment, shown here with floral curtains framing sheer drapes. United States, dating from the 1950s.
③ This wall detail, with hollow redwood decorative columns on square-section plywood plinths, is from a passageway in a New York country house, 1980s. The plinths have detailing in pine.

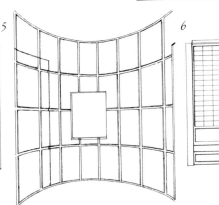

④ An ash wood grid screen in a New York apartment, with glazed squares, 1980s (Peter L. Gluck and Partners).
⑤ A curved panelled wall, with a window through into a living room – part of a circular "rotunda" hugging the foyer of a New York apartment, 1980s.

⑥ A translucent Japanese-style wall screen, with sliding components. The Japanese style is an influential variant of the woodworking tradition. Fine woods are a key ingredient.

⑦ The distressed look became fashionable in the late 1980s. Here, real holes (for ornaments) through from bedroom to living room combine with painted effects of Romantic decay.

⑧ Columns are an important element of the Post-Modern architectural vocabulary. Here, Doric columns in pairs between windows evoke ancient Athens. The deep frieze conceals air-conditioning ducts – a clever use of disguise. Designed by David Hicks, 1970s.
⑨ A detail of a rusticated surround in a generously sized basement swimming pool area by Robert Stern, New Jersey, 1980s. The column supports were inspired by the palm tree columns of the Brighton Pavilion, England – one of the jewels of Regency architecture. Stern has deployed glistening tiles, glass and metal surfaces to create a grotto-like character. Note also the false masonry pilasters.

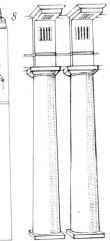

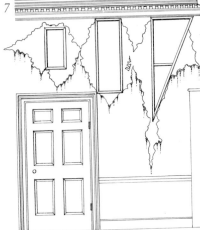

Ceilings

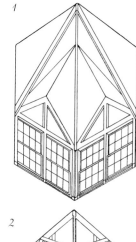

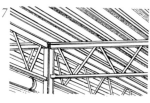

① *A pyramid space with ribs in a square garden room, Pennsylvania.*

② *Exposed roof trusses are a theme of the period. William Turnbull, California.*

③ *A groin-vaulted passageway in plaster by British architect Francis Johnson.*

④ *A ceiling by Charles Jencks, London, with shiny surfaces and directional lighting.* JE

⑤ *A house on the Marsh Estate, East Coast, United States, by Centrebrook, 1993. Gothic architecture was once believed to have originated from groves of trees.* MCG

⑥ *A passageway ceiling with skylights.*

⑦ *High-tech industrial ribbed steel, 1970s.*

⑧ *A shallow barrel-vaulted ceiling, in Maryland, with cedar slats on laminated curved beams. Don A. Hawkins.*

The virtual elimination of the ceiling as an area of interest during the Modernist period was gradually replaced by a new range of decorative possibilities. Some of these relied on revealing or enhancing the structure of the roof, whether metal or timber. The return to pitched roofs allowed architects to explore the visual drama of skeletal internal roof structures. Another option was to create new architectural forms within the envelope of an existing building, often incorporating lighting. The early 19th-century Neo-classcial interiors of Sir John Soane, particularly the Breakfast Room of his home in Lincoln's Inn Fields, London, a famous "room within a room" (see page 183), were influential as examples of intricate structure on a small scale.

The potential of painted decoration, either simple cloudscapes or more elaborate painting, was rediscovered after many years of neglect. The symbolism of ceilings representing the sky or cosmos was a natural avenue of exploration for Post-Modernists.

Among neo-traditional architects, ceiling embellishment was often confined to a classical cornice, although more elaborate moulded ornament was frequently attempted. Careful restoration projects, and the division of houses into high-class apartments, has kept the suppliers of fibrous plaster cornices and ceiling roses/medallions in business.

Floors

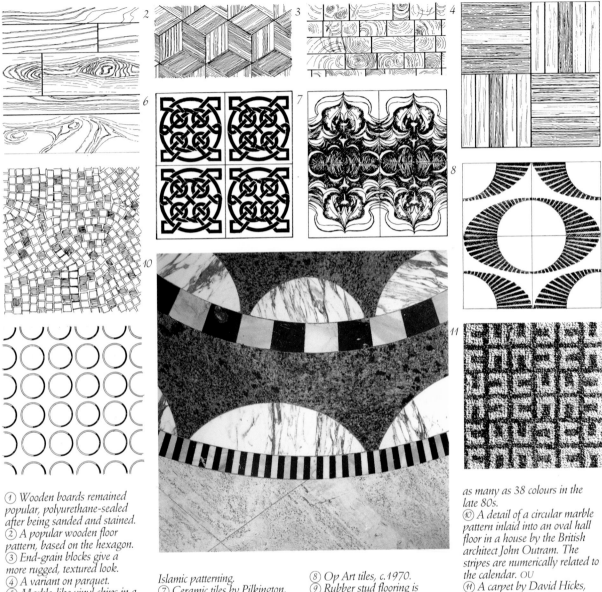

① *Wooden boards remained popular, polyurethane-sealed after being sanded and stained.*
② *A popular wooden floor pattern, based on the hexagon.*
③ *End-grain blocks give a more rugged, textured look.*
④ *A variant on parquet.*
⑤ *Marble-like vinyl chips in a bed of clear vinyl, mid-60s.*
⑥ *Ceramic floor tiles with*

Islamic patterning.
⑦ *Ceramic tiles by Pilkington, England, mid-60s. The style is Art Nouveau Revival.*

⑧ *Op Art tiles, c.1970.*
⑨ *Rubber stud flooring is usually available as tiles. One English company was offering*

as many as 38 colours in the late 80s.
⑩ *A detail of a circular marble pattern inlaid into an oval hall floor in a house by the British architect John Outram. The stripes are numerically related to the calendar.* OU
⑪ *A carpet by David Hicks, England – a bridge between "period" and modern.*

Certain tastes from the Modern Movement, such as hardwood block and strip flooring and quarry tiles, remained popular among architects in the second half of the 20th century. However, a great range of additional flooring materials was added, including mosaic, tiles with printed or relief patterns, cut and inlaid linoleum, and decorative wood. Marble remained in favour for luxurious, simple effects.

The patterns produced in these newly re-discovered materials tended to be rectilinear and geometric. The classical taste encouraged evocations of Italy and Ancient Rome in marble, mosaic or linoleum, with various forms of historically based repeating pattern. The need for

economy often meant that the scale of the original pattern was enlarged, so that fewer individual pieces would need to be cut and laid. Patterns with a trompe l'oeil quality tended to suffer in the transformation.

Other decorative languages of the world were pillaged for patterns in the 1950s and 60s, including those of the Middle East and Africa. More recent designs from Art Nouveau and the early Modern Movement were also used. For the high-tech look, rubber stud flooring or patternless carpet were favoured. A wide range of carpet patterns appeared, some with a historical flavour, others based on forms from graphic design. Painted floor decoration was also revived as a period style.

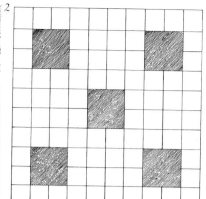

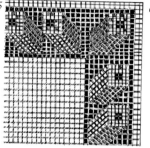

① Linoleum partially painted in a zigzag design to resemble a colourful rug, mid-1970s.

② Black and white tiles were a stylish option for a living room in the 1950s and early 60s, a period when strong patterns and bold contrasts were enjoyed on both sides of the Atlantic.

③ Grained wood-effect linoleum was another very popular 1950s floor choice.

④ Kitchen floor tiles. These again exemplify the penchant for strong patterning shown in the early 1960s.

⑤ Romano-British floor patterns have inspired a recent range of ceramic mosaics (Paris Ceramics, London, 1990). This border pattern is the Ishar. Other options are the Guilloche, Greek Key and Vitruvian Scroll.

⑥ This elaborate floor pattern from the entry hall of a Chicago house uses contrasting marbles and granites. Designed by the architects Rudolph and Associates. The floor was store-assembled in three large segments, which were transported to the site and laid in a mud setting bed on a concrete subfloor. The pattern has overtones of Frank Lloyd Wright and the Prairie School.

⑦ A painted marble-effect wooden floor, based on a design from the royal palace, Caserta, Naples, late 1980s.

⑧ For the Cambridge house of lettercutters David and Linda Kindersley, Maggie Angus Berkowitz made a personalized floor of painted tiles in the 1980s. The floor is on a well-lit landing which forms a sitting place. MAB

Fireplaces

① *The form of this rounded chimney breast is highlighted by blue trim at ceiling level. A monumental treatment by*

Venturi, Scott Brown and Associates, Connecticut, 1984. VE
② *In a Neo-Renaissance hooded fireplace by Robert*

Adam, moulded consoles with lions' feet revive a forgotten classical form. Crooked Pightle, Hampshire. AD

③ *An imposing fireplace with engaged columns by John Outram, in the library of a house in Sussex, England, 1980s.* OU

The decorative fireplace has returned to favour in the Post-Modern period. It represents some primal need for warmth and light, and for a hierarchical arrangement of the main living space around the hearth.

The range of forms is very extensive, from straightforward classical reproduction to Mannerist invention on classical themes. Fireplaces have been the occasion for many displays of Post-Modern wit and symbolic treatment. Some of the Modern Movement's innovations – freestanding island fireplaces, and fires with hoods and stovepipes – have continued in use. The Contemporary Style of the 1950s also added its contribution in the form of decorative materials, – stone,

mosaic, rough slate and so on – treated as a fire surround or as an entire hearth wall.

This period has seen an increased demand for historical fireplaces (stimulated, in Britain, by the development of convincing imitation coal fires, fuelled by gas). In no other area has the architectural salvage trade been so active: many of the fireplaces torn out in the previous fifty years have been conscientiously replaced. When the supply of originals faltered, reproductions began to be made in white statuary marble which differed from the originals only in looking too new. An alternative approach is to have a wood surround painted in a faux finish imitating the marble of the owner's choice.

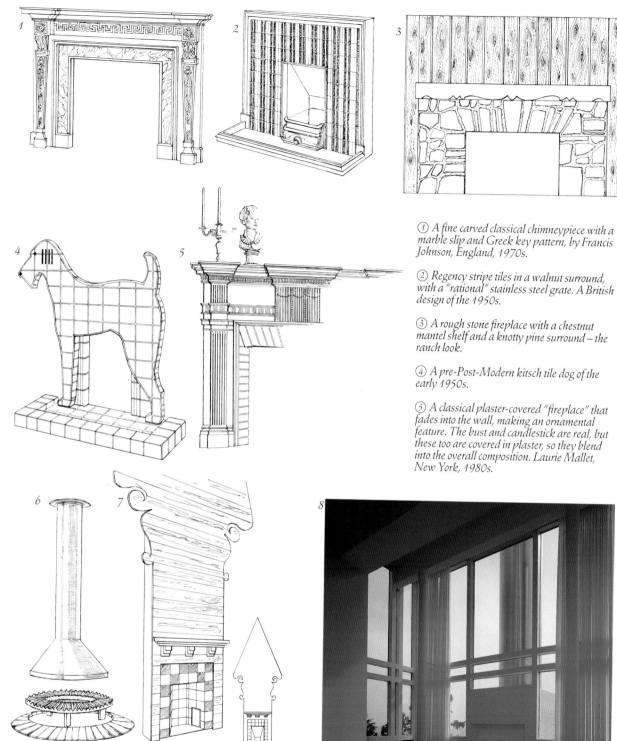

① A fine carved classical chimneypiece with a marble slip and Greek key pattern, by Francis Johnson, England, 1970s.

② Regency stripe tiles in a walnut surround, with a "rational" stainless steel grate. A British design of the 1950s.

③ A rough stone fireplace with a chestnut mantel shelf and a knotty pine surround – the ranch look.

④ A pre-Post-Modern kitsch tile dog of the early 1950s.

⑤ A classical plaster-covered "fireplace" that fades into the wall, making an ornamental feature. The bust and candlestick are real, but these too are covered in plaster, so they blend into the overall composition. Laurie Mallet, New York, 1980s.

⑥ A floor-level hearth (an old gearwheel) with hood.

⑦ A Post-Modern Baroque overmantel in a Pennsylvania library – cut from a template in popular boarding. Soapstone tiles form a slip. The diagram shows how the profile becomes triangular in the roof space. Jeff Riley, Centrebrook Architects.

⑧ A discreet fireplace permitting both a focus and a distant view at Richard Meier's Douglas House, Lake Michigan, 1971-3. ROC

FIREPLACES

Kitchen stoves

① *A gas stove of the early 1950s, incorporating eye-level foldaway grill and warming cupboard beneath the oven.*
② *A Belling electric stove, British, 1958: a simple standard unit in white enamel. BG*
③ *A clean-lined model by McClary, United States, 1965. American stoves outstripped British ones at this period.*

④ *An Anglo-American stove, with rotisserie, pull-out hot-plate and high childproof control. Thompson-Tappan, 1961.*
⑤ *A twin-burner stove by Jenn-Air, late 1970s. This American company pioneered the down-draught extractor, allowing barbecue-style cooking indoors.*
⑥ *The minimalist style: a ceramic hob/cook-top set in a worktop. Early 1980s.*

Although the kitchen has become one of the most expensive and important rooms in post-war years, stoves tend to be self-effacing. Usually they line up with the work surfaces of the built-in kitchen, the oven door looking much like a cupboard. Stoves set into island work counters continue to be popular.

Efforts to vary the design of the stove, with separated hobs and ovens mounted into the wall, follow the same rule of visual unobtrusiveness. Today there is little choice available. Even when the kitchen is executed in a fantasy period style, the stove tends to be clean-lined and minimalist.

The main variation is the Aga, or some equivalent archaic form of heavy iron stove. These have their devotees for cooking, and have also become established as designer cult objects. Manufacturers have cleverly introduced a range of bright colours in addition to the conventional cream. Designers of other forms of modern stove would do well to follow this lead. Stoves of the 1950s and 60s also have their champions.

Gas stoves have not advanced in design as rapidly as electric stoves, largely because they do not have the same potential for compactness and electronic controls. The combined use of gas and electricity in one unit reflects the continuing quest for maximum efficiency and convenience.

① *Bringing home the industrial look in the 1990s by Britannia Domestic Appliances.* BRI
② *A simple but efficient kitchen in a house near Carlisle by Ryder & Yates, 1958.* CN/B
③ *Progressive architectural living and economy of space at the Cullinan House, London, 1965, where the kitchen forms an island in an open plan upper floor.* PO
④ *General Electric provided a combined dishwasher, cooker and sink unit for Pierre Koenig's Case Study House 21 in 1958. With pristine surfaces like these, the kitchen was allowed back into the body of the house after a 500-year banishment.* SHU
⑤ *The kitchen as performance space, dramatized here beneath the mezzanine of the Future Systems house in Islington. The stainless steel island unit becomes a sculptural object.* DAV

⑥ *Fitted kitchens combine images of efficiency and security with warm colours and surfaces. They represent modernism's most effective penetration of daily life. Kitchen by Bulthaup, 1988.* BUL

Staircases

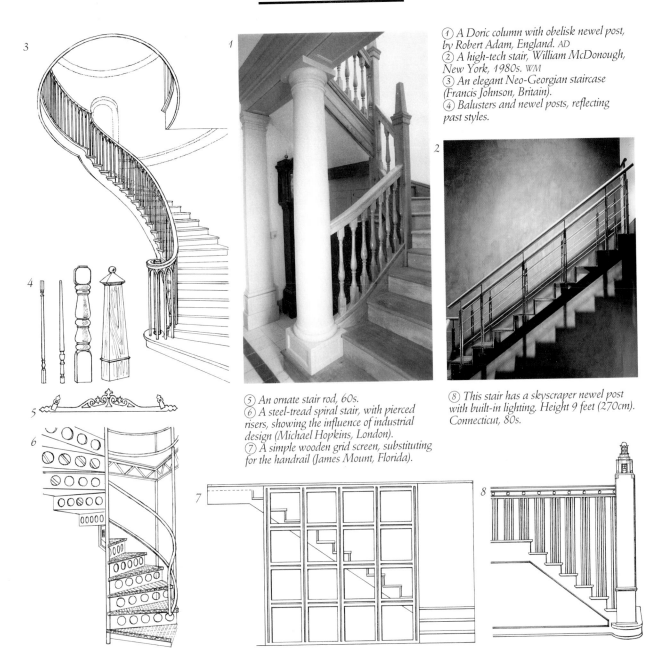

① *A Doric column with obelisk newel post, by Robert Adam, England.* AD
② *A high-tech stair, William McDonough, New York, 1980s.* WM
③ *An elegant Neo-Georgian staircase (Francis Johnson, Britain).*
④ *Balusters and newel posts, reflecting past styles.*

⑤ *An ornate stair rod, 60s.*
⑥ *A steel-tread spiral stair, with pierced risers, showing the influence of industrial design (Michael Hopkins, London).*
⑦ *A simple wooden grid screen, substituting for the handrail (James Mount, Florida).*

⑧ *This stair has a skyscraper newel post with built-in lighting. Height 9 feet (270cm). Connecticut, 80s.*

The opportunity that staircases present for architectural statement or decorative display has produced a wide variety of results in recent decades.

In Post-Modern houses the stairs will tend to be subdivided into short flights, turning at right angles at each half-landing in order to enhance our appreciation of the house's spatial qualities. Uncarpeted wooden treads are usual. The woodworking traditions on both sides of the Atlantic have been reactivated to provide a variety of balusters and newel posts, often incorporating Victorian or Arts and Crafts reminiscences. Sometimes – especially in the United States, in California – an upper walkway linking a staircase landing to the bedrooms will run dramatically over the living room.

High-tech staircases have exploited the language of metal components, including pierced treads and risers and tensioned wire balustrades.

Classical Revival staircases can be surprisingly plain, with little variation on 18th-century models. Occasionally an imperial staircase, or a simpler cantilevered curve, can create a majestic effect. Plain square-section wooden balusters are commonly found. Wrought iron is sometimes installed as a form of decorative tracery. Mass-produced turned balusters are also part of the architectural repertoire, although they have seldom been made to very good patterns.

① A staircase in Louis Kahn's Korman House, Pennsylvania, 1971-3. ROC
② A concrete and stainless steel staircase by Carlos Zapata Design Studio and Una Idea Architects, Florida, 1994. EST
③ High-tech staircase by John Young, a partner of Richard Rogers, in his apartment in Hammersmith, London. ARC
④ Classical design skills were used at Ashfold House, Sussex, by John Simpson. SI
⑤ Staircase to heaven at Richard Meier's Douglas House, Lake Michigan. ROC
⑥ The glitter of hard surfaces at this Future Systems house. DAV

⑦ An elaborate entry gives access to Sir Basil Spence's house in Hampshire, 1962. APR
⑧ A classic ladder stair of 1955 at Farnley Hey, Yorkshire. PO
⑨ Oak staircase in a Suffolk cottage extension by Shawn Kholucy, 1990. PO
⑩ An open-tread cantilevered concrete staircase with a shaped tubular handrail, London, 1954.
⑪ Here, open mahogany treads create a feeling of spaciousness; the wooden handrail and panel are supported by metal rods. 1960s.
⑫ A simple softwood ladder stair: the lower rail is of the same wood while the handrail is of hardwood to provide a contrast. Early 1960s.

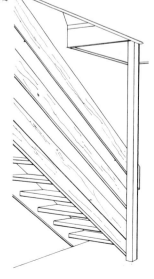

STAIRCASES

Built-in furniture

① *A witty working space by Charles Jencks, making use of tiered pigeonholes. Note the freestanding slide cabinet.* JE

② *A passageway display case with natural light, by John Outram, Sussex, England, 1985: an old idea reinterpreted.* OU

③ *The tradition of conspicuous storage: closets and a plans chest in a design by Venturi, Scott Brown and Associates.* VE

④ *A free-floating cabinet held by steel columns in a house by Patrick Gwynne at Henley-on-Thames, Oxfordshire, 1959.* PO

The popularity of built-in furniture as a solution to the problem of living in small spaces without clutter is immune to vagaries of style or ideology. In the rejection of Modernism as an aesthetic, the diversity of built-in elements has been given a greater variety of expression. Classical details have been favoured for the more architectural features, such as bookcases. Wood detailing is either painted in a flat colour or given a faux finish. Post-Modern bookcases may take on architectural forms relating to the design of the house. High-tech bookcases may be entirely of metal, finished in grey or black, with glass display shelves.

Kitchens have become a major industry in themselves,

with a variety of styles, including Country Pine, Georgian, Art Nouveau and other hybrids. Cupboards in these styles bear no relation to any historic precedents their labels might be intended to evoke. "Modern" has always been available as an alternative to putting panel mouldings on the refrigerator door.

Built-in seating has mostly been rejected as too inflexible, although the fashion for sunken seating areas has been carried through from Modernism. Built-in bedrooms tend to be less stylistically ambitious than their equivalents in living rooms or kitchens. The louvered door for wardrobes was one of the most popular innovations of the 1960s.

① A "sound wall" of c.1952, housing a radio, television, record player and tape recorder. The middle section holds the speaker and storage shelves behind lattice doors.
② Shoe racks on the back of a built-in wardrobe's pivoted door provide useful storage.
③ Louvered wardrobe doors, painted white, are a typical style of the late 1960s.
④ A full-bodied classical library, by Roderick Gradidge, Easton Neston, Northamptonshire, England, 1970s.

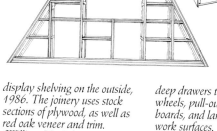

⑤ These angular room dividers with simplified columns enclose an intimate seating area. American, 1980s.
⑥ A sunken conversation area, with sofas upholstered in black leather, c.1970.
⑦ Integral with this curved bed is a drawer unit with a dressing table knee-hole, a space for bedtime reading and a built-in bedside table, c.1975.
⑧ Conran pine kitchen units, with thumb holes in the drawers, Britain, early 1970s. Terence Conran specialized in low-cost, basic, stylish furniture and accessories, in reaction to the mediocrity of post-war design. His highly influential London store Habitat opened in 1964.
⑨ A detail of a highly styled kitchen of the 1980s. The cabinets are covered in corrugated white laminate. (Eric Owen Moss, California.)
⑩ Kitchen units with gridded glass doors, like top cupboards here, evoke Vienna Secession designs. The tiny squares are contrasting plugs of maple. (Shope Reno Wharton, Connecticut, 1986.)
⑪ An island kitchen, with display shelving on the outside, 1986. The joinery uses stock sections of plywood, as well as red oak veneer and trim. (William M. Cohen, New York.)
⑫ This kitchen of c.1960 has deep drawers that pull out on wheels, pull-out chopping-boards, and laminated plastic work surfaces.
⑬ Display shelving in an attic space, around a gable window.

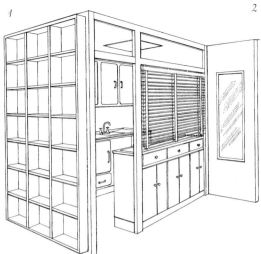

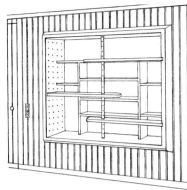

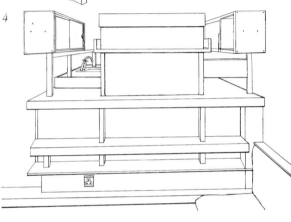

① *Living space partitioned by room dividers: in this 1950s example the drawers could slide two ways for access from both the kitchen and dining area.*
② *A framed bookcase unit set into a wood-boarded wall. The shelves are adjustable. British.*
③ *Built-in bedroom in a California condominium, by Moore, Lydon, Turnbull & Whitaker, 1964-5.* FRE
④ *This 1950s shelved room divider separates the kitchen from the sunken living area.*
⑤ *David Lea's comfortable studio in Somerset, 1988.* JO

⑥ *This Buckinghamshire house by Peter Aldington, 1963, adapts vernacular ideas with an intimate space demarcated by a fireplace.* PO
⑦ *At Farnley Hey, by Peter Wormersely, 1955, the space was elegantly screened with built-in fittings.* PO
⑧ *John Simpson's Ashfold House, 1984-90, has elaborate built-in fittings to give unity to the neo-classical rooms.* SI
⑨ *This 1960 Liverpool house has such original features as this display shelf in the dining room, meant for serving cocktails.* PO

Services

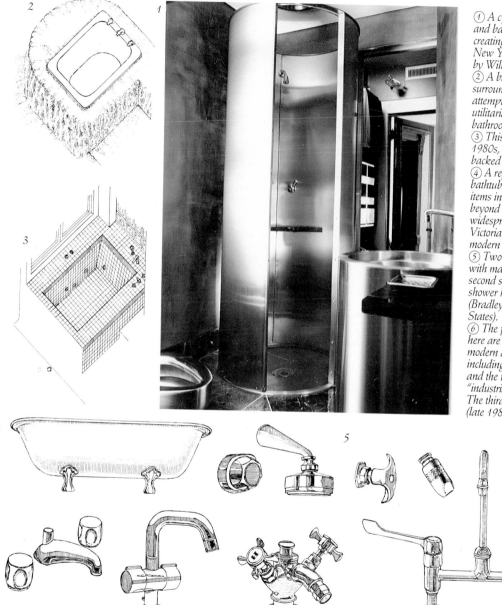

1 A cylindrical shower cabinet and basin pedestal in steel, creating a Futurist fantasy in a New York residence designed by William McDonough. WM
2 A bath with carpeted surround, 1975 – part of the attempt to disguise the utilitarian nature of the bathroom.
3 This custom-made jacuzzi, 1980s, has a tiled surround. It is backed by frosted glass blocks.
4 A reproduction Victorian bathtub. The popularity of such items in the 1970s, 80s and beyond testifies to the widespread interest in Victoriana as an antidote to modern uniformity.
5 Two sets of shower heads with matching taps/faucets. The second set is from a multiple shower head, for large families (Bradley Corporation, United States).
6 The four mixer taps/faucets here are variations on both modern and traditional themes, including minimalist modern and the type with an "industrial" long-lever handle. The third example is for a bidet (late 1980s).

The bathroom, no less than the kitchen, has assumed an unprecedented importance in the changing lifestyles of the last twenty years. It is now seen by many as a place for relaxation, even fun, as expressed in special forms of bath, such as the jacuzzi, and in the more adventurous use of colour, pattern and other aspects of decoration. At the same time, partly out of nostalgia and partly as a way to make the bathroom more like another living room, the Victorian cast-iron roll-top bath on moulded feet has returned to favour, either as a salvaged item or in new castings. The standard complement for it is a salvaged or reproduction mixer tap/faucet and shower head.

Other bathroom fixtures reflect great efforts to avoid the streamlined reticence of Modernism, although manufacturers of sanitary wares always take a long time to catch up with fashion. More depends on the tiling and choice of accessories than on the shape of the fixtures themselves. The high-tech use of bright colours has influenced the design of plastic and enamelled taps/faucets.

Heating appliances have not, on the whole, risen above a mediocre level of design. Studio stoves and wood-burning stoves have become valued supplements to central heating. Decorated cast-iron stoves on the Scandinavian model have proved popular.

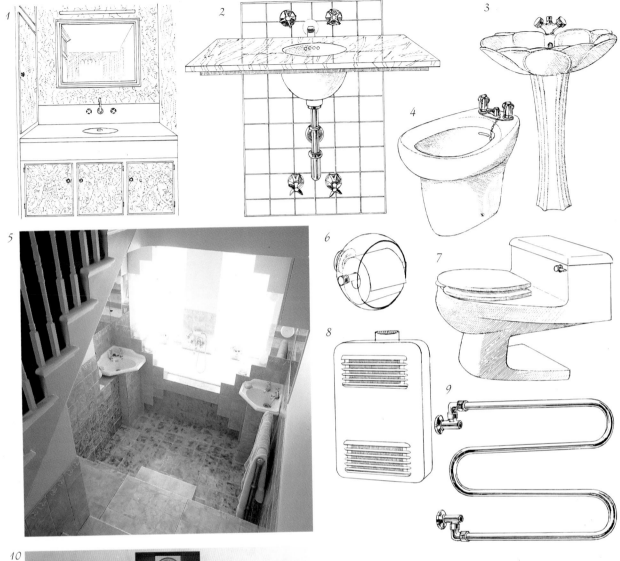

① A 1960s marble-top wash basin, with gilded taps/faucets set into the wall. Patterned wallpaper helps the unit blend into the bedroom.

② An elegant modern wash basin surround, with marble counter top and exposed pipework below. The basin is steel. Morphosis, California.

③ The Orchidee wash basin, 1980s, in a so-called "pure Art Nouveau" style. Aquaware, Duravit, Britain.

④ The Curzon bidet by Shanks, England, 1960s.

⑤ A formally arranged bathroom, with Art Deco-style framing to the bath recess. Charles Jencks, London. JE

⑥ A tinted glass globe toilet roll holder by Adamsez. Britain.

⑦ A sleek toilet design by American Olean.

⑧ A bronzed gas convector heater, early 1950s.

⑨ An "S"-bend heated towel rail.

⑩ In the 1990s the Danish firm Bang & Olufsen made its mark with compact wall-mounted CD and cassette players, operated by the wave of a hand through a light beam. BAN

Lighting

① Suitable for use over a dining table, this wicker lampshade is controlled by a pulley, 1953.
② Compressed fibreglass is the material of this inexpensive Sheerlite cylinder shade, Britain, 1965.
③ Nostalgic evocations in a deliberately rusted iron chandelier, 1987.
④ A pierced multi-coloured cardboard shade with wooden rings, English, 1954.
⑤ A metal hanging light, with enamelled coloured finish.
⑥ Bulkhead lights are intended for outdoor use, but some designers have employed them indoors.
⑦ This heavy-duty steel wire guard is intended to dress a bare bulb. (Daniel Woodhead, United States.)
⑧ Tiffany-style lights reflect the continuing interest in Art Nouveau designs, on both sides of the Atlantic.
⑨ A Quarto bowl uplighter – a classic from the Italian company Flos, designed by Tobia Scarpa, 1973.
⑩ A five-candle wall sconce, for the dining room.
⑪ This pendant, the Frisbi, manufactured by Flos, has a diffusing disc which catches the light. Designed by Achille Castiglioni, 1978.
⑫ The paper globe with wire rings: the least expensive type of pendant, inspired by the Japanese paper lantern.
⑬ A track-mounted square spotlight, c.1970, especially suitable for a kitchen.
⑭ A spotlight on a vertical rod, by the Italian company Arteluce, 1980s. This would be suitable for lighting works of art. It is designed to take a quartz-halogen bulb.

From the attempts in the 1950s to make light fixtures more decorative in themselves, there has been a development toward minimalism. Halogen lights have made large fixtures unnecessary. Spotlights and tracks can now be virtually hidden. Thus, a room may have two lighting systems, one based on decorative fixtures of limited utility, such as chandeliers, and another, invisible system that does the work of lighting the room. Handled well, the result can be better lighting for atmosphere, and a greater freedom in the development of fantasy light fixtures.

The 1950s Contemporary Style produced some amusing light fixtures, often with paper or metal shades in black or primary colours, pierced with small circular openings. The occasional use of straw gave a Mediterranean slant. The low-cost paper globe shade followed, and proved to be one of the most successful designs of recent times. High-tech imagery appears in the use of marine light fittings, especially bulkhead lights with wire cages. Post-Modern nostalgia for Art Deco has brought back the quarter-sphere bowl uplighter as a wall fixture, and led to a variety of inventive fixtures, particularly from European companies such as Arteluce and Flos. Neo-classical leanings have lately been responsible for the widespread use of real candles, in chandeliers and wall sconces.

SERVICES

LIGHTING

① *Holger Strom of Kilkenny Workshops designed this plastic lampshade in 1973. Thirty shapes could be assembled in twenty-one combinations. The series was appropriately called "IQ Assemblies".* ARP

② *Folded wax paper shades were popular in the 1940s and 1950s. This elegant example is by Kaare Klint.* ARP

③ *Pear-shaped pendant glass shades by Osram (GEC) Ltd, 1964.* ARP

④ *Uplighters of various kinds found favour in the 1980s. Art Deco meets High Tech in "Vega" by Mr Light, 1987.* ARP

⑤ *Many 1950s design forms aspired to be space rockets. This 1953 fitting by J.M. Barnicot was ready for blast-off in Coronation year.* ARP

⑥ *New plastics helped to make light fittings transparent and safe in the 1960s, as shown in this pendent light by Troughton & Young, 1963.* ARP

⑦ *Candles became popular in the late 1980s, instigating a new generation of sconces and chandeliers. This wall sconce is by Habitat, 1995.* HABI

⑧ *Pleated fabric shades as a fixture at Farnley Hey, Yorkshire, 1955, a classic of 1950s design in Britain.* PO

⑨ *Spotlights come track or wall-mounted, like this example from Erco, 1980.* ERC

⑩ *Bulbous forms were popular in the 1970s, for example this wall-mounted extendible fitting in polished aluminium by Dorothee Maurer-Becker.* ARP

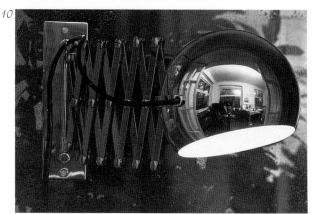

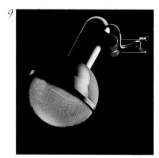

Woodwork

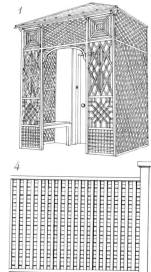

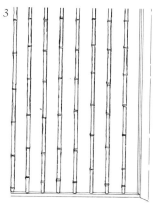

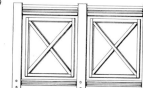

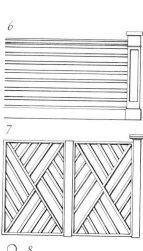

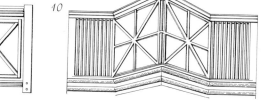

① *This porch by British architect Quinlan Terry has Regency overtones.*

② *An all-wood house by Venturi, Scott Brown and Associates. It revives the American Shingle style popular for seaside resort houses of the 1880s.* VE

③ *Bamboo poles, used to screen a stair landing window, 1950s.*

④ *A detail of trelliswork, used as a boundary fence.*

⑤ *Timber louvres are used to great effect in Stephenson Somerville Bell's extension to a house at Alderley Edge, Cheshire, 1995, uniting natural materials with the openness of High-Tech.* STE

⑥ *A clapboard fence, double-lapped for interest, 1970.*

⑦ *Another wooden fence, of geometric design, 1970.*

⑧ *Fence posts from the American periodical* Houses for Homemakers, *1945.*

⑨ *A gallery balustrade.*

⑩ *In a house in Greenwich, Connecticut: a staircase landing with prow-like projection.*

Wood is easily worked, and lends itself to the creation of decorative effects without great expense. The degree to which traditional carpentry skills have survived in an age of mass production varies widely from region to region. Inside the house, high-quality or unusual woods are often used as a luxury surface.

The woodworking tradition of the United States, denied through the Modernist period, began to flourish again with Post-Modern variants on the shingle style. The house made completely of wood, which had been reinterpreted in the Modern Movement, returned to something more like its original form, using skills that had never died out. Balconies, porches, fences and gateways all reappear as practical, elegant embellishments, even though their design might now carry overtones of irony or whimsicality. Sawn and turned details are easy to make to order, and can be used for fencing, balusters and the like. Georgian designs for latticework in the Chinoiserie taste are sometimes reinterpreted for porches and entrances.

The revival of interest in the Arts and Crafts movement and related aesthetics has led to creative design in wood in a style that can run all through the house. The details of C.R. Mackintosh, C.F.A. Voysey and Frank Lloyd Wright, for example, have proved comparatively easy to copy for a multitude of purposes.

LIGHTING

WOODWORK

BRITISH VERNACULAR

By the middle of the 17th century, many houses were built with two rooms per story, with a central entrance and staircase – an arrangement that originated in the timber houses of southeast England at the start of the 16th century, and was later adapted for stone. This 17th-century house in the village of Sulgrave, Northamptonshire, in the English Midlands, has been extended at the far end, spoiling its symmetry but not its appearance. It is built in fine local oolitic limestone, golden in hue but streaked brown in places by iron deposits. The windows have hoodmoulds of a type that originated in the Middle Ages, but used in the Midlands until well into the 18th century. Despite the fine masonry, the roof is thatched, not tiled – a local practice which died out later in the 17th century. AQ

British vernacular architecture embraces a bewildering array of different styles, apparent in thousands of houses built between the later Middle Ages and the Industrial Revolution – roughly the period 1350-1800. These styles reflect both cultural and physical differences across many distinct regions.

The Norman Conquest of 1066 laid the foundations of peace and political stability which eventually made a significant number of peasants and merchants wealthy enough to afford the luxury of a permanent house. Ordinary houses had previously fallen to pieces after only a generation or so. Now, people turned to an expanding group of craftsmen – masons, carpenters, bricklayers, plasterers, tylers (who made or laid tiles), glaziers and so on – who learned their skills locally, through example. Depending on local resources for their building materials, they developed their own methods, and these became the basis for the rich variety of vernacular styles, which differed not only in materials but also in the way in which those materials were exploited for decoration.

Once they had evolved, particular styles tended to remain current for several generations at least, with the consequence that vernacular houses are often difficult to date. The habit of adding to dwellings by a series of accretions over the years makes the process of dating harder still.

Although vernacular idioms could reflect the fashionable styles that were applied nationally to the houses of the wealthy, the need to economize brought adaptations. The cost of fetching building materials from afar was generally too high for ordinary dwellings, so local materials would be used instead, and this often imposed certain design restrictions. Moreover, the local craftsman's knowledge of high design might extend only as far as a naive understanding of a limited number of houses already considered old-fashioned in higher circles. A hardy conservatism ruled, but this did not cramp the imagination.

Regional differences were determined not only by the availability of local materials, but also by the uneven attainment of wealth among ordinary people. The long-established concentration of wealth in the south and east of England led to the early development of vernacular houses there. However, in areas where the landlord was acquisitive, peasants (or yeomen, as they came to be called) and merchants did not have a share of this wealth; and conversely there were many ostensibly poorer localities where yeomen could flourish and hence build good, though modest, houses. A combination of infertile land and overbearing landowners could inhibit vernacular architecture altogether. Social and political circumstances favoured the yeomen of Kent above all others. They were celebrated for their wealth long before the end of the Middle Ages. Thousands of their medieval timber-framed houses still survive, and many of them are large. In Devon, by contrast, great landlords tended to monopolize the wealth, and yeomen's houses were mostly modest. In some parts of the Pennines in the north of England, where yeomen profited from new domestic industries, especially weaving, there is evidence of them starting to build permanent houses in stone towards the end of the Middle Ages.

Less than two hundred years separate these six yeoman houses. They are arranged here in a way that corresponds approximately with their location.

① A farmhouse, Heapey, Lancashire, built in 1696 of hard Pennine millstone grit. The stone tiles of the roof are in the same material. The form of this house, with one main room and two subsidiary rooms on each floor, is typical of the west side of the Pennines. AQ

② A farmhouse, at Sowerby, West Yorkshire, built in 1662 on the more lavish scale typical of its region, with characteristic tiers of mullioned windows, stepped in the upper floor. Again the material is millstone grit. AQ

③ A small timber-framed house at Stoneleigh, Warwickshire, built c.1500 by a yeoman only just wealthy enough to build at all. The house was later rewalled with a brick infill. The heavy curved timbers are known as crucks. The cruck method is normal in central and northern England and most of Wales but is not found in eastern or southeast England. AQ

④ These are relatively poor stone cottages, with earthen walls and thatched or pantiled roofs. Thimbleby, Lincolnshire. AQ

⑤ A house at East Chinnock, Somerset, 1637, showing to good effect the local oolitic stone, with matching stone tiles, which the affluent local yeomenry could afford. AQ

⑥ Built at least a century earlier, of good oak, a farmhouse at Northiam, East Sussex, with decorative close-studding and clay tiles on the roof. AQ

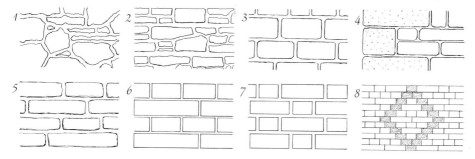

① to ④ Stone could be laid in three main ways, shown in the first three illustrations here: irregularly, as rubble; in rough courses; or in regular courses. The last illustration shows regular laying with larger, finely cut blocks at the corners, forming quoins (cornerstones). The corners of a building were often worked by more skilled craftsmen.

⑤ to ⑧ Bricks could be laid with their long sides (stretchers) and short sides (headers) facing outwards in an irregular pattern; or with courses of stretchers and headers alternating to form "English bond"; or with stretchers and headers alternating in each course to form "Flemish bond". Patterns of diapering were formed by mixing vitrified bricks among plain bricks.
⑨ As brick became more popular than exposed timber framing toward the end of the 17th century, many framed houses were re-clad with tiles hung on battens nailed to the frame. Particularly in the 19th century, the tiles could be decoratively shaped.

⑩ A less expensive way to finish a timber-framed wall was to clad it with weatherboarding. The boards could overlap, or be rebated leaving a groove between each layer. Usually, the softwood boarding was painted white.
⑪ In eastern counties of England a popular form of decoration was pargeting – incised or raised patterns in the plaster covering of a framed building. This tendril and flower design is from Clare, Suffolk.
⑫ A brick and flint house, Sussex. Flint was often used in south and east England. AQ

The complex patterns of local building materials are part of the inexhaustible fascination of vernacular houses. In the south and east of England, in the west Midlands and the eastern half of Wales, and in the lowland parts of Yorkshire and Lancashire, the earlier houses are of timber. Much effort went into decorating their frames, and this encouraged significant differences between the regions. By 1700 building in timber had been susperseded by building in brick, and localized styles of decoration were followed in the laying of brickwork and the raising of imposing chimney stacks.

The highland parts of England (notably the west and the north) and much of Wales and Scotland have plentiful stone. Because this stone is hard on the chisel, carving had to be restricted to prominent places such as doorways. Only where there was plentiful stone of high quality – for example, on the band of Jurassic limestone crossing England diagonally from Dorset to Yorkshire – could masons achieve greater feats of carving on vernacular houses. Even then, cost restricted their efforts.

In eastern England a distinctive form of decoration is pargeting – the use of incised or raised patterns on the plaster covering of a timber-framed house. Usually, this took the form of regularly repeated geometric shapes, but occasionally the pattern could be more ornate. Some examples even extend to figurative compositions, achievements of arms, or exotic patterns covering whole walls, which could be painted in bright colours to give them greater prominence.

Another form of decorative patterning on exterior walls stems from a combination of different building materials. For example, there is a tradition of combining flints (irregular lumps of silica) with bricks in south and east England. Cobbles or pebbles are also found in patterns with brickwork.

The Industrial Revolution, which made it possible for building materials to be transported inexpensively, brought an end to vernacular styles, although in the North they hung on until well into the 19th century. There was a vernacular revival in the mid-19th century, but this was little more than the donning of fancy dress. The inventive vigour that had characterized vernacular building for centuries proved to be inimitable, which is perhaps why the authentic country cottage or farmhouse continues to exert such a hold on the popular imagination.

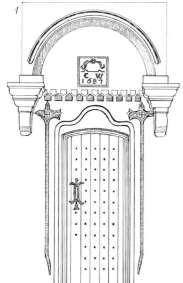

DOORS

① *Stone houses in the Yorkshire Dales from the later 17th and early 18th centuries often have elaborate doorways, with curves and scrolls, as well as the date and the initials of the owner.*

② *From a farmhouse in the Pennines, Yorkshire: the head of this door has an inscription and roundels.*

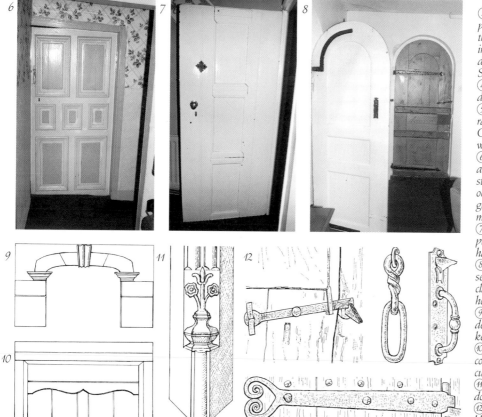

③ *Southern England came to prefer a sober if naive version of the prevailing national style, as in this classically inspired doorway at Burwash, East Sussex, c.1708. DM*

④ *Another classical idea was a doorhead in a shell shape. LL*

⑤ *In the poorest districts where rainfall was high, such as Cumbria, a plain enclosed porch was thought necessary.*

⑥ *On internal doors, battens and planks, and later rails, studs and panels, were made occasion for display. The panel grouping here is unusual. The mouldings are naively treated. LL*

⑦ *In this late 17th-century plank door, the centre section has been panelled. LL*

⑧ *Simple doors, but with semi-circular heads reflecting classical taste. Strap hinges help hold the doors together. LL*

⑨ *An internal doorway with depressed arch and prominent keystone, southwest England.*

⑩ *Less important doorways could still have Gothic double curves.*

⑪ *Mouldings on the base of a door frame.*

⑫ *Door fittings allowed the blacksmith a show of ornament.*

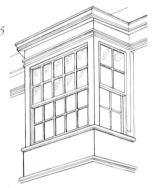

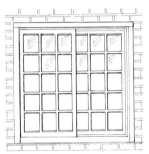

WINDOWS

① When glazing first became common toward the end of the 16th century, numerous arrangements of lights were devised, mostly based on setting them into large windows with mullions and transoms for support. This band of lights, with stone mullions, at New Thame, Saddleworth, Manchester, is of the later 17th century. AQ

② Two small windows, Swinithwaite, North Yorkshire, 1692. The right-hand one has had its mullion removed and a sash window inserted. AQ
③ The earliest opening windows were iron-framed casements. This 18th-century example is from Gloucestershire.
④ The use of lead cames to hold panes of glass in place may derive from the lattice

pattern of hazel wattles. This example is from East Sussex. DM
⑤ In seaside towns vertical sash windows were often fitted into projecting bays to take advantage of the view.
⑥ The alternative form of horizontally sliding sashes ("Yorkshire sliders") needs no counterweights, but the vertical seal may let rain in.

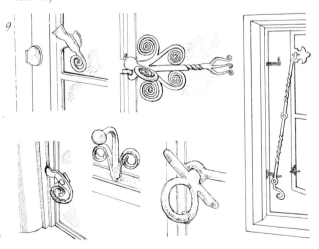

⑦ Window shutters were customarily used from ancient times. They simply folded back on vertical hinges. By the 18th

century, they were usually painted in pale colours to reflect light into the room. On larger houses they would be integrated

into schemes of panelling. LL
⑧ A rotating window: this method of opening gained ground in the 19th century.

⑨ Examples of 17th-century wrought-iron window hardware, including fasteners and stays.

WALLS
The internal wall finish added status to individual rooms and expressed their relative importance.

① *Timber-framed walls were finished with wattles inserted between timbers, and occasionally these were left uncovered, as in this example from Warbleton, East Sussex. Usually, however, they were plastered and limewashed, in which case the timbers of the frame, left visible, made an attractive pattern against the plain plastered sections.* DM

② *The space between the vertical timber studs could be filled with planks to differentiate an important room, as in this 17th-century partition between the main rooms in a house at Chetnole, Dorset.* AQ
③ *In the grander vernacular houses built toward the end of the 17th century, the timber framing could be covered by panelling, as illustrated by this house at Charlton Kings, Gloucestershire, dating from c.1740.* LL
④ *A less expensive approach was to make a partition with the timber studs positioned in such a way that they gave the impression of panelling. This example is from a mid 17th-century house in Avon, southwest England.*
⑤ *Stone, when well laid, has always been thought good enough for farmhouses, as in this house of c.1500 at Lettaford, North Bovey, Devon, where the projecting timber joists forming the ceiling of an inner room add to the decorative effect.* AQ

⑥ *Plastered walls could be pargeted inside as well as outside, or they could be finished with an overall herringbone pattern, as seen in this detail.* AQ
⑦ *Vigorous scrolled decoration on the dado of a panelled wall, from a farmhouse in southwest England, 1651. Similar patterns could also be used at a higher level of the wall, to make a frieze.* LL

CEILINGS

① *The first ceilings (as distinct from open roofs) had no decoration other than exposed joists, which were usually set close together in an ostentatious overuse of expensive*

materials. This example, from southwest England, is 16th-century. LL

② *The joists could run in both directions, at right angles, and have their undersides heavily moulded. Westfield, East Sussex.* DM

③ *Where the exposed joists were chamfered along their edges, the chamfers could end in a decorative flourish or chamfer-stop. This one has simple scroll motifs.* LL

④ *A similar treatment, with a chamfer-stop, would sometimes be executed in plaster, rather than in carved timber. This ceiling is from Thornbury, Avon, southwest England, and probably dates from the 1680s.* LL

⑤ *The whole of the ceiling could be plastered over and given raised or incised decorative patterns, like the plain segmental corner pattern in this example, from Warbleton, East Sussex.* DM

⑥ *A detail of elaborate but robustly worked floral decoration on a plastered ceiling, from a house in Thornbury, Avon. The grape motifs are in relief, contrasting with incised flowers and leaves.* LL

FLOORS

① *and* ② *The floors of vernacular houses were the least likely part to be decorated. Plain flagstones or soundly laid boards were the norm.* LL

③ *At ground level, regularly laid flagstones could be enhanced by patterns made from stone of different colours or mixed with smaller stones or bricks.* LL

④ *Small stones or even pebbles laid close together on edge to form intermingling circles, arcs and squares made the most interesting patterns, but they were hard to keep clean. This particular pattern is from Montgomeryshire, Powys, Wales.*

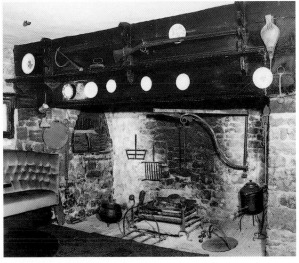

FIREPLACES

① The surround, hearth and ironwork – andirons, hooks for cooking pots, and equipment for turning spits as well as spit-tracks for supporting them – could be decorative as well as useful. The side of the hearth might contain an oven. Most of these features can be seen in this fireplace at Littleton, Avon. LL

② Hearths, especially in the north of England, were set within inglenooks containing seating, usually of wood but sometimes stone. LL
③ Sometimes a small oven was set over the hearth. From Oldbury on Severn, Avon. LL

④ This farmhouse fireplace, Bromley, near London, 1599, not only has a moulded surround but also a large overmantel with crude pilasters flanking a phoenix roundel – a grand feature to find in a modest house. AQ
⑤ The surround here is spanned by a timber hearth beam. This alone is heavily moulded, on its lower edge, but sometimes mouldings

run from a timber beam and turn downwards to run along the edges of the stone piers. LL
⑥ The moulding on this Devon stone fireplace runs all the way around. The niche high on the left was for a candle or taper. AQ
⑦ The use of fern-leaf patterns went back to medieval times; this example is from 1664.
⑧ Fluted Ionic pilasters, with cartouche.

⑨ A fireplace with initials, fleur-de-lys and the date, from Iron Acton, Avon.
⑩ Plain classical cornices with exaggerated proportions could equally serve.
⑪ By the 19th century, many farmhouses were content with plain surrounds. This one has vestigially classical brackets, contrasting with the elaborate factory-made range.

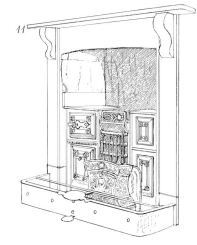

STAIRCASES

When upper rooms had little importance, as in the Middle Ages, stairs were simple, if not downright rough. Often there was just a simple ladder leading to a loft. These vertical access arrangements survive in many old farmhouses, usually adjoining the chimney stack and hidden behind a door. Sleeping upstairs was not universal until the 18th century. As houses became more spacious, stairs rose less steeply. Instead of being cramped in corners, they were given generous treatment, and ornamented as symbols of status.

① This plain spiral staircase dates from c.1600. LL
② A staircase with spiral balusters, from Pucklechurch, Avon, c.1680. LL
③ A panelled staircase with square newel posts, turned balusters and a moulded handrail, East Sussex, mid-18th century. DM
④ Classical piers used as the basis of balusters, 1686: a late example of misunderstood classical detailing of the Jacobean type. LL
⑤ A more ornate form of a similar design, c.1675. LL
⑥ The same pattern could be reduced to little more than wavy planks. Icklesham, East Sussex. DM

⑦ Turned balusters in an elegant three-per-step arrangement, from a farmhouse at Westerleigh, Avon, early 18th century. LL
⑧ A plain balustrade in a smaller house, early 18th century. LL
⑨ The tops of newel posts can be decorated, as in this example with crudely carved scrolls. LL

⑩ Balls or other rounded newel finials were more comfortable to grasp, as well as being visually attractive.

BUILT-IN FURNITURE

① and ② The ventilation holes set within or above cupboard doors could be carved into pleasing shapes, with scrolls or mock balustrading.

③ A North Yorkshire stone settle forms a "heck" to shield the fireplace area.

④ On the less elaborate type of dresser, the uprights did not go down to the floor. Probably 17th century.

⑤ In the 18th century, large cupboards were sometimes set into the fireplace wall. Some had drawers in their base.

⑥ Spice cupboards were set in the fireplace wall to keep their contents dry. Those of the 17th century can be elaborately decorated. This is an early 18th-century example from southwestern England.

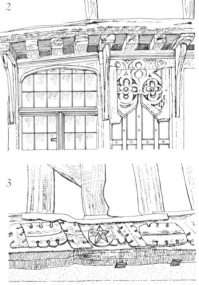

WOODWORK

① The framing of a timber-framed house could easily be decorated – either soberly, with studs set close together, or boldly, with patterns of arcs set within squares, some turned to make diamond shapes, as in this example from Gloucestershire, c.1600. LL

② The doorway of a timber-framed house could be treated decoratively, as in this house at Cerne Abbas, Dorset, with quatrefoil carving and roses incised deep into the doorhead. The joist ends, supporting the jettied (overhanging) upper floor, also contribute to the decorative effect.

③ Here, the bressumer, hiding the joist ends of a jettied house, is carved with a simplified pattern of oak leaves. Earls Colne, Essex.

④ Pendants, a relic of the Gothic style, were greatly admired on jettied houses in the 16th and early 17th centuries. This example, decorating a jettied gable, dates from 1621. DM

⑤ Naively classical scrolls and other patterns could be added to the brackets that supported the overhanging joists on a jettied house. DM

⑥ The corner posts on which jetties rested could be carved with grotesque figures. AQ

AMERICAN VERNACULAR

The Durie House, Bergen County, New Jersey. This early 18th-century house represents the Dutch building tradition as practised in the Hudson Valley, Long Island and northern New Jersey. Its gambrel roof profile is created by changing the angle of the wooden framing at a point below the ridge; the roof is then changed at yet another angle to create a porch supported on plain wooden posts. The flaring or "flying" eave suggests Flemish influence, which is often found mingled with Dutch styles. Small dormers light the upper-story bedroom spaces. Brick chimneys indicate the presence of large end-wall fireplaces. The exterior sheathing is wood – narrow clapboards on the walls and shingles on the roof. Steeply sloping roofs are characteristic of vernacular houses built to suit a northern climate. HABS

The term "Vernacular" is a much-disputed one, and in the United States is perhaps best understood to embrace a number of different types of architecture: buildings produced for lower budgets than those in the high style, and therefore exhibiting notable ethnic and regional characteristics; buildings made by traditional methods for rural or provincial clients; and buildings in which ethnic or regional traditions merge with current styles to create interesting hybrids. In the vernacular house there is likely to be a mix: some new ideas, some tradition.

The ethnic character of these houses originates from immigrant or often first-generation builders working with techniques and planning ideas that they learned from their countries of origin. Such methods may be preserved as valued traditions by subsequent builders – or sometimes they may be given up. The main ethnic influences derive from the first permanent colonial penetration of North America by European peoples – the Spanish in the 16th century, the French, Dutch and English in the 17th century, followed by the German and Scandinavian immigrants in the 18th and 19th centuries. Each tradition has contributed to the character of American vernacular houses.

Examples of the 17th-century vernacular are still standing, though few survive from the earliest period. At the other end of the time scale, the houses of our own century are more likely to participate in national (and therefore non-vernacular) culture by virtue of their mass-produced materials and the information networks that brought builders out of their insularity (although even modern manufactured housing shows

regional inflections once it is on the ground and inhabited).

Vernacular houses may be either owner-built or constructed by skilled craftspeople for clients. They may present a relatively rustic appearance, but may also exhibit fine finishes and attention to ornamental detail. Of course, the greatest number in the United States have disappeared, either because they were constructed as impermanent to begin with, or because owners have replaced them with something more imposing or up-to-date when improved resources allowed.

The regional characteristics of vernacular houses come from builders responding to the climate and topography of an area, and making use of local materials. In New England, with its severe winters, the favourite 17th- and 18th-century material was wood, used for framing houses and for exterior sheathing, sometimes combined with brick or stone for chimneys, footings or basements. Strongly sloping timber-framed roofs shed the snow and provide attic space. Dutch 17th-century settlers built houses using a series of heavy timber H-shaped frames, faced on the exterior with brick or stone. German builders of the 18th century in the Hudson River Valley and in Pennsylvania used stone for the body of the house and timber framing for the roof. Other German settlers, both northern (for example, in Wisconsin) and southern (North Carolina), chose half-timbered building techniques in the 18th and 19th centuries: a heavy timber frame was combined with an infill of clay, brick, or mud with straw. Sloping roofs might be tiled

① *The Jonathan Hager House, Hagerstown, Maryland, 1740. Stone was the preferred material of the Germans who settled in the area.* HABS
② *Brick construction gives an interesting pattern to the end-walls of this Dutch Hudson River Valley house.* HABS
③ *Moravians created a religious community at Old Salem, North Carolina,* beginning in the mid-18th century. *Old World half-timber construction was often clad in clapboarding.* HABS
④ *New England settlers created increasingly* symmetrical facades without the stepped-out upper story that is found on 17th-century predecessors. HABS
⑤ *A flat-roofed adobe house, Tucson, Arizona.* HABS

or shingled. Brick with a timber-framed roof was the preferred material for the large-scale house of the Chesapeake region, yet the small vernacular house – commonly a one-room structure – was made all of wood.

In the Mississippi Valley and Gulf Coast, 18th-century French settlements were constructed of buildings combining vertically placed timber posts with a stone or earth infill, often with a smooth rendered finish. Horizontal log construction with notched corners was also popular. A smooth finish is found in walls of the 17th- and 18th-century Spanish settlements of the Southwest, where the climate is hot and dry. Here builders made extensive use of adobe or mud-brick laid up in courses, with relatively flat roofs supported on wooden beams. Scandinavian settlers in the 19th-century Midwest used log construction techniques with corner notching; mud chinking filled in when there were gaps between the logs. On the prairies of the West, cut sod was used to create coursed walls, much as cut stone might be used elsewhere.

The impact of industrial techniques on building in the early 19th century, with mass-produced nails, powered sawmills, mail-order millwork and materials transported by the national rail network, did not immediately put an end to traditional vernacular building styles or methods. For newly arrived settlers of the mid-19th century, traditional methods and locally harvested materials continued to serve; not everyone in frontier settlements had the money or the access to railroad-transported materials to participate in mainstream building materials. However, vernacular styles were also expanded and "improved" by mass-produced materials, so that a hand-hewn log house might have a store-bought window. Perhaps the most far-reaching effect of the Industrial Revolution was in the spread of information. The widespread availability of printed materials containing advice on building techniques made stylish architectural details available to all builders, not just the elite. Throughout the 19th century, small, rural, inexpensive houses were made with fireplace, door and window details showing a familiarity with Greek Revival, Italianate or other styles popular in professional architects' repertoires, but adapted to local tastes.

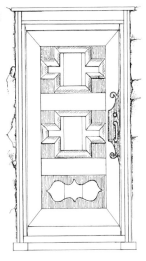

DOORS

① *Classical detailing in wood was used on many simple box-like houses of Colonial New England.* RS

② *The French tradition: glazed doors, with shutters, opening onto a porch (galerie), New Orleans.* HABS

③ *The inside of a front door from a Moravian farmhouse, Warren County, New Jersey.*

The split form and iron strap hinges are typical. HABS

④ *Graphic cut-out shapes, from an adobe house, Taos, New Mexico.*

⑤ *Half of an interior double door, 18th century; a round-arched style is peculiar to the Connecticut River Valley.*

⑥ *A "sheathing" door, Lancaster County, Pennsylvania, 18th century.*

⑦ *Folk renditions in wood of classical pilaster capitals, New England, late 18th century.*

⑧ *A Moravian wooden door latch, Pennsylvania, 1742.*

⑨ *This type of latch is operated from the outside by pulling the string; to secure the door, the string is simply pulled to the inside. Early 18th century.*

⑩ *A "Norfolk" latch, California, late 18th century. The shape of the latch and the ornamental border suggest it was made by a Mexican Indian.*

⑪ *An iron door knocker, from New Orleans, in a style familiar from French examples.*

⑫ *An early 19th-century door hinge from Pennsylvania, with double bird-necked curves.*

⑬ *An iron door latch made in a German settlement in the Valley of Virginia, mid-18th century.*

⑭ *An early 18th-century iron strap hinge, Virginia, with typical spade-shaped end.*

⑮ *This box lock from Connecticut uses metal, wood and leather elements.*

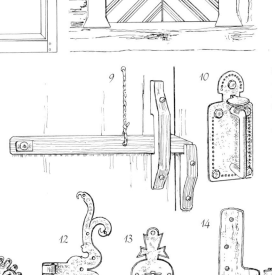

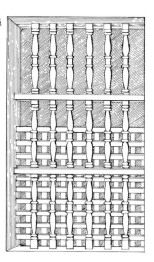

WINDOWS

① An early window, c.1700, Massachusetts.

② A typical window in an adobe house, New Mexico.

③ From a Colonial house in Deerfield, Massachusetts: a simple, elegant sash window. RS

④ A Spanish-style screen, St Augustine, Florida.

⑤ Small windows in a Wisconsin log house. In the most basic cabins, windows were closed by sliding boards or animal skins. HABS

⑥ A simple shutter catch, c.1800, from Massachusetts.

⑦ Shutter hardware: a typical bolt, shutter hook and hinge.

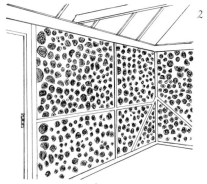

WALLS

① A "stovewood" wall, made of short lengths of cut logs laid in mortar. Wisconsin.

② The simple wall division of a Shaker interior, with base and peg boards.

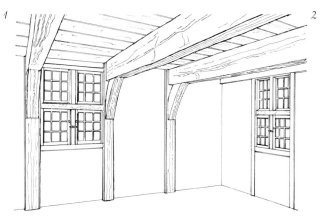

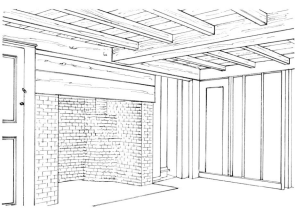

CEILINGS

American vernacular houses often have ceiling configurations that directly reflect methods of construction.

① The 17th- and 18th-century Dutch house was constructed using a series of "bents" or wood frames whose upper members are visible as deep ceiling beams connected to the wall by knee-braces. The diagram (below left) shows the ceiling members in the context of the structure as a whole.

② In this early New England kitchen (Dover, Massachusetts, 1701) a prominent "summer beam" crosses the middle of the room and rests on the brick chimney, at a right angle to the rest of the ceiling beams.

③ Occasionally the ceiling beams were given decorative treatment. This carved rosette is from Surry County, Virginia. The shaping of the beams is also noteworthy. *HABS*

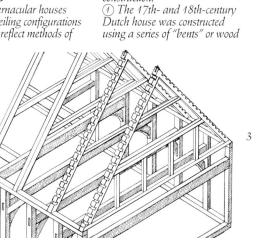

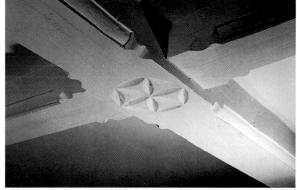

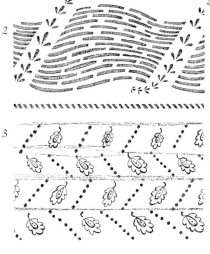

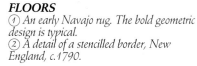

FLOORS

① An early Navajo rug. The bold geometric design is typical.
② A detail of a stencilled border, New England, c.1790.
③ Part of a painted oakleaf floor, New England, early 18th century. Pumpkin yellow was a favourite background colour.
④ A detail of a rug from Maine, early 19th century.

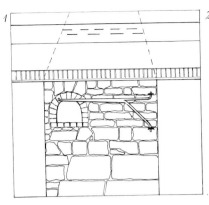

FIREPLACES

① *A fireplace in the kitchen of a Dutch house in Kerhonkson, New York, with an arched bread oven and a fireplace crane.*

② *Turned ornament on the fireplace frieze is a characteristic of Californian adobe houses.*

③ *A small fireplace opening framed by*

irregular stones with a modest wooden mantel shelf. Monterey, California. HABS

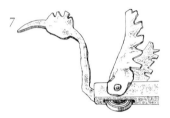

④ *This early 19th-century fireplace, North Carolina, features a rustic version of familiar classical motifs, with graining, marbleizing and decorative paintwork.*
⑤ *This is the basic type of fireplace (fogón) used in adobe houses in New Mexico. Because the fire chamber is small, short logs were used,*

arranged vertically.
⑥ *Andirons often took a basic animal form – reflecting the alternative term, "firedog".*
⑦ *A fireplace crane, from which a cooking pot was suspended, 18th century. It incorporates a pulley, for raising and lowering the kettle.*

STAIRCASES

Some form of staircase was necessary even for houses which had merely an unfinished attic above the ground floor.
① *In New Orleans and other hot-climate areas, exterior staircases were often used to reach the upper floor – and sometimes (for example, in some of the houses of St Augustine, Florida) there was also a staircase up to a flat roof. This is a New*

Orleans courtyard staircase, constructed simply out of wood. Seignouret House, c.1820. CRO
② *A wide wooden staircase from a Shaker dwelling house – that of the Church family, in Hancock, Massachusetts. The slender balustrade is typical. The Shaker dwelling house, designed to accommodate a "family" living in celibacy, had segregated dormitories with separate hallways and*

stairways for men and women. Varnishing of the handrail and balusters of the staircase was specifically allowed by the Millennial Law of the Shaker faith, codified in 1821. HABS
③ *A staircase from an adobe house in Monterey, California. The styling is relatively primitive, and the only decoration is a simple form of chamfering on the newel post. HABS*

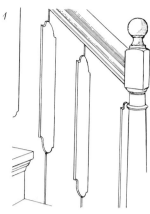

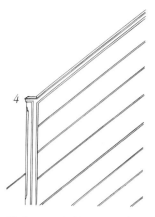

① *Simple cut-out designs could give a rhythm to a balustrade. This example is from North Carolina, c.1790.*

② *Sponge and line decoration on the risers. The treads, typically, are left plain.*
③ *An early 18th-century*

Connecticut staircase, which is partly boxed in with a panelled wall, surmounted by a balustrade.

④ *A more primitive approach, in which diagonally laid boards are used.*

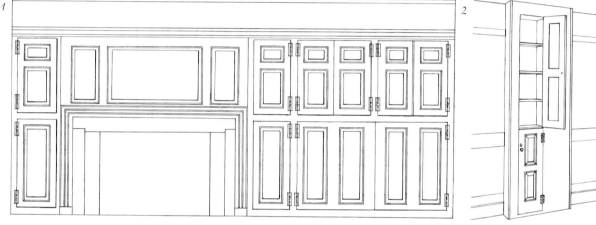

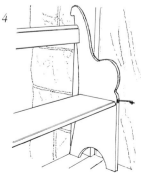

BUILT-IN FURNITURE
① *The use of small panelled cupboards on the fireplace wall is a typical Dutch Colonial feature.*
② *A late 18th-century Shaker cupboard: one of the earliest examples of Shaker built-in furniture.*
③ *A wall of built-in drawers and cupboards in the rigorous, unornamented Shaker*

woodworking style, providing stairwell storage. Hancock, Massachusetts. HABS
④ *Two typical porch benches from German Pennsylvania, late 18th century.*
⑤ *Box beds in the Dutch tradition were enclosed by panelling to conserve heat as well as keep the room tidy. The Jean Hasbrouck House, Ulster County, New York, 1712.*

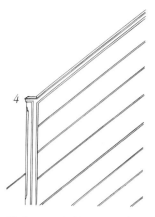

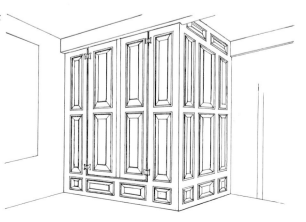

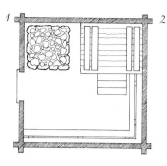

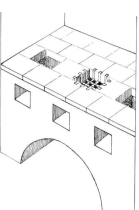

SERVICES

① *The sauna was an important element of the Wisconsin log house. It would be housed in a separate building, containing a stone oven and wooden benches.*
② *A Spanish stove, with "three-burner" top, from St Augustine, Florida, c.1800.*
③ *This is a Vermont version of the freestanding six-plate heating stove, early 19th century. This type of stove, which took its name from the number of cast-iron plates fitted together in its construction, was manufactured by the Pennsylvania Germans as early as c.1760. Later, ten-plate stoves were made which could also be used for cooking.*

④ *Shaker stoves are typically mounted on legs, which are mostly cast-iron (although they can also be wrought-iron with penny feet, or in cabriole (curved) form). The doors opened from left to right. This one dates from c.1780.*
⑤ *The five-plate or "jamb" stove was another Pennsylvanian German type. It shared a flue with a fireplace in the next room, as the cross-section (left) shows. The front would often be embellished with Biblical scenes and texts. The example here, with a date on it, shows a wedding feast.*

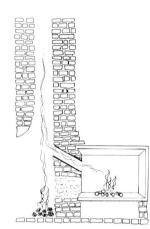

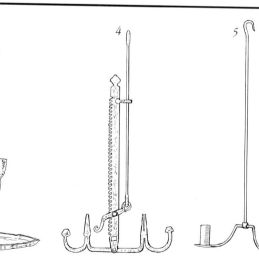

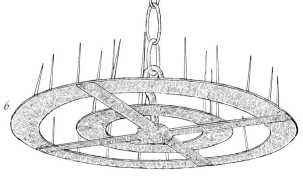

LIGHTING

① *Cylindrical lanterns of the 18th century were often decorated with piercing. Rectangular ones tended to be plainer.*
② *The Betty lamp was an improved form of grease lamp. This one has a combined spike and hook.*
③ *A hanging candleholder, wrought iron, 18th century. The ratchet mechanism was used to adjust the height.*
④ *A double rushlight holder, wrought iron, 18th century. The rushes were peeled, and the pith inside dried and oiled, before being fitted into the ends of the holder.*
⑤ *A two-candle hanging chandelier, with hook. Wrought iron, 18th century.*
⑥ *A chandelier of wrought iron. The candles were stuck on prickets. Late 18th century.*

METALWORK

① A selection of bootscrapers, dating from c.1790 to 1810. Bootscrapers were usually simply made in wrought or cast iron, and mounted next to the front door. All these examples are from New England.

② An ironwork grille, with cast decoration, set into the street door of a house on Chartres Street, New Orleans.

③ A main use of wrought iron in New Orleans was in balconies. Here, delicately repeating shapes of curved ironwork create a series of

pointed arches. Often, the balustrade would have an ornate central panel. Some balconies were carried around the corners of the house. The advent of cast iron columns encouraged a type of balcony that extended to the edge of the street, with a roof overhead. *HABS*

①

④ An elaborate double scroll bracket supporting a balcony: a typical feature of old New Orleans. *HABS*

2

3

4

1

2

3

4

5

WOODWORK

① A detail of a porch railing, made of flat wooden planks cut to give a curved, baluster-like profile. Casa de Pio Pico, Whittier, California.

② The Fernandez-Llambias House, St Augustine, Florida. The Spanish woodworking tradition gave rise to roofed balconies, about 5 feet (1.5m) wide. *HABS*

6

③ A typical St Augustine street balcony. The earliest existing balcony posts are square in section, with chamfers above the handrail.

④ A detail of a wooden lintel from a veranda (portal) of an adobe house, Taos, New Mexico.

⑤ In many New Orleans "shotgun" houses, round metal ventilators were set into the soffit, between the eaves brackets. *CRO*

⑥ Common forms of picket fence heads.

RESTORATION AND MAINTENANCE

The repair and restoration of historic buildings is a rewarding and responsible undertaking – and usually a time-consuming and complicated one. A specialist team is essential for all but the simplest of jobs. Architects should never be picked at random, but always through personal recommendation, or through organizations that have tackled similar projects. The same applies to builders and other craftworkers. Local and national conservation groups may be able to help in choosing the personnel. Historic buildings are usually subject to special building regulations or guidelines, depending on their age, importance and location: always check what is permitted with local bodies or preservation societies before undertaking any work.

DOORS

Front doors. The front door is an element that greatly affects the authenticity of a facade. Unfortunately front doors have not been well interpreted by commercial manufacturers. Front doors were designed as security barriers and the incorporation of glazing is a relatively modern phenomenon; so too is the "honest timber" look in panelled Georgian, Federal and Victorian doors, which would originally have been painted. Failure to renew the paintwork is the most likely cause of damage. Doors should be painted on all six faces: top and bottom, two edges, back and front. This prevents moisture intrusion, which causes expansion and contraction, and splitting and checking of wood panels. If the door is original, consider repair before replacement, but replace any door which is out of keeping. Search around architectural salvage establishments for a historic equivalent, or have the door made new to the right pattern by a competent carpenter.

Internal doors. Very often these will have been replaced by modern flush doors, or have had so many locks and other hardware changed over the ages that they will have been weakened. Existing panelled doors can be modified to provide fire-resistant qualities without altering their appearance too dramatically. Some pressed composite internal doors look acceptable when properly painted and often out-perform their modern wooden equivalents in dimensional stablility and strength. An ill-fitting door will be caused by: i) Expansion and loosening of joints. ii) Decay due to damp penetration. iii) Distortion through differing atmospheric conditions on each side. iv) Worn or loosened hinges and other hardware. v) Structural movement in the main building fabric. Rectify the cause before repairing or replacing a door. Use hot air guns or a solvent stripper to remove layers of old paint on old doors before repainting. Stripping by dipping can loosen and destroy old joints irretrievably. For cleaning down a waxed or French-polished wooden door, mix 4 parts vinegar, 4 parts turpentine, 4 parts raw linseed oil and 1 part methylated spirits. For feeding boarded hardwood doors for a natural finish, apply the following mixture until it can take no more: 50% raw linseed oil, 25% amyl acetate, 15% pure turpentine and 10% boiled linseed oil.

Hardware. A period door should have period fittings. Search for secondhand examples from shops and market stalls or use good reproduction items. If you have some existing patterns of ironware to be matched – simple latches, strap hinges and so on – they can often be made by local blacksmiths. Original latches and locks can be repaired by good locksmiths, who should also be able to reproduce the large, heavy-looking old keys. Wooden locks can be reproduced by encasing a "standard" metal rim lock with a wooden box surround.

PORTICOES, PORCHES AND VERANDAS

If you are lucky enough to have a portico as a grand front entrance, or a porch or veranda as an outside room, it will be well worth the expense of repair or replacement.

Repairs. The most common defect will be the penetration of dampness between the main building wall and the structure of the appendage. Metal flashing should be cut and properly sealed into the main wall, and fitted to the contours of the roof structure so that the finish is smooth.

Check the porch/veranda supports for signs of rot and deterioration. Weakness here is the prime cause of floors dropping and stress through the structure, which will lead to fractures, cracks and ultimately total collapse. Special epoxy mortars can be used to repair stone mouldings and columns, but beware of the differing weathering qualities which might make the repair more conspicuous and could cause the adjoining real stone to deteriorate more quickly.

Replacements. If the portico or porch structure is badly damaged certain elements will need to be replaced. Some firms reproduce columns and pediments in fibrous plaster or reproduction stone – consider these if their patterns fit the style. Fibreglass always looks and feels wrong. If the porch is beyond repair, a complete rebuild by a mason or carpenter may be the only answer. The original structure should be copied wherever possible, but if too little remains use a similar example from an old pattern book (many are published as reprints).

WINDOWS

No element in a facade denotes the age or character of a building more than the fenestration. It is therefore vital that repair or replacement is carried out sympathetically.

Repairs. If a window, whether wood or metal, is established as original, repair it wherever possible. Both its quality of construction and its materials (especially if wood) will be of a higher standard than is easily obtainable today. Often, deteriorated wood can be restored by removing the decay and then, using an epoxy filler, shaping it to the original pattern. This approach is suitable where the shape is visible or structurally important. Where neither is the case, remove deteriorated wood, then apply a coat of epoxy to seal the wood members. In many cases a good carpenter will be able to scarf in new pieces of wood or replace complete window elements more economically than a complete renewal. Remember that any open joint will let in moisture, and most fillers tend to trap damp rather than seal gaps.

Correct maintenance, especially regular repainting (at least every three years), is a prudent long-term saving. Hydraporous paint (which is waterproof but allows the wood to breathe) can save on preparation time and provide a longer life. Natural wood staining is a modern phenomenon, not found on historic fenestration. Rotten or cracked sills should be repaired or replaced. Damaged sash windows can have their weights, pulleys and cords easily removed and replaced. Use candle wax to ease runners and soften existing cords. If very thin glazing bars need replacing, a hardwood can be used for strength. Copy mouldings exactly: they provide historical accuracy.

Replacement. If a replacement is necessary because the original is beyond repair, use the original as a pattern for an *exact* copy. If the existing windows are not original, study architectural books and houses of similar age for patterns. Do not be tempted to use plastic-coated metal frames or other modern "maintenance-free" substitutes: they *never* look right.

Draught, noise and rattle. These are perhaps the most serious problems with old windows. All can be reduced dramatically (even in sash windows) by the introduction of draught strips/weatherstripping, preferably made of a spring bronze. Recommended application would be the top edge of the top rail, between the meeting rails of the top and bottom sash, and to the bottom of the bottom sash, as well as to the vertical jambs to ensure a weathertight installation. There are specialist suppliers who will also carry out this installation. Overcome the draughts before you even contemplate double glazing. If problems persist, consider permanently fixing some sashes to their frames and then sealing the joints; but only do this if sufficient ventilation can be achieved from the remaining sashes.

Double glazing. On some wooden and metal casement windows, double glazing can be achieved simply and without altering aesthetics. However, on some sash windows this will be a problem. Double glazing requires more than twice the rebate (channel or groove) to support the glass width, as the glass edge will need up to ½in (12mm) of silver foil seal; if the rebate is narrower, an unsightly overlap will be left; do not be tempted to increase the width of the glazing bars. Remember that the extra weight of double glazing can be difficult to balance with new sash weights. As an alternative to double glazing, good results can be achieved with proper draughtproofing, caulking and glazing. Consider secondary glazing or simple sheets of framed glass inside the windows for winter use only. Secondary glazing should be removed during the warmer months to prevent condensation damage.

SHUTTERS
External. Regular painting and maintenance are essential. Some plastic-coated or aluminium replacements can be aesthetically acceptable and are maintenance-free.

Internal. Internal shutters add a certain elegance to a room, but their practical use is often neglected. It is well worth the effort to make internal shutters operative again, as they improve security and provide excellent heat and sound insulation when closed. Well-maintained shutters and windows can be just as effective as double glazing for heat loss and noise reduction, but far less expensive and far more in character. Repaint shutters at least every five years. Take particular care of old shutter hardware, which is often ingenious in design and function.

GLASS
Windows of the 18th century had glass that was blown and spun rather than cast. With its slight flaws, spun glass (known as "crown" glass in Britain) creates interesting reflections which provide a depth to an original glazed facade. Old glass should be preserved wherever possible; it is easy to break and great care is needed, especially when stripping a window with a hot air gun. If a window is sent away to be repaired, make the point that you want the original glass to be used. Spun (crown) glass is now difficult to find, and expensive. A satisfactory and inexpensive substitute is "greenhouse" or "horticultural" glass, which is very poor-quality sheet glass. Reproduction Georgian-style "bottle panes" should never be used. Originally, such panes were used as an inexpensive method of glazing: they were the discarded centre part of a sheet of spun glass after the holding rod had been removed.

EXTERIOR WOODWORK
Elimination of dampness. The need to keep water and damp from entering timber is the main reason for maintenance and redecoration. Complicated repairs should be left to an expert. Pay special attention to the susceptible connection of timber to masonry. Always use good metal flashings to direct water well away from joints. If appropriate, modern sealants and mastics can be used to fill gaps and holes. Bear in mind that water trapped within unprotected wooden joints, or beneath a protective finish, where it cannot easily be dried by wind, will have devastating effect.

Painting. Wood is painted to retard or prevent water penetration and reduce movement caused by the effects of temperature and moisture. External woodwork should be regularly inspected and, depending on exposure, repainted at least every three to five years. If the paint has broken down, is cracking, blistering or flaking, it will have to be removed prior to redecorating. The same preparatory work will be required if old mouldings and details need to have their sharpness restored from the layers of old paintwork. Use a commercial paint stripper or a warm air torch to remove old paint, proceeding with great care. Never use a naked flame. Remember to neutralize solvent strippers prior to repainting. Existing paintwork in better condition should be washed with soap or detergent (non-alkaline) and rinsed thoroughly. Washing soda is good for removing grime. The surface should be rubbed with wet and dry abrasive paper, then rinsed clean and allowed to dry before coating.

INTERNAL WALLS

Failure of walls. An internal wall will either be structural (loadbearing) or a partition wall. It will be constructed of masonry or timber (or occasionally more primitive materials such as cob or adobe). A structural wall is seen to have failed when it is fractured or has dropped out of line. The cause should be carefully investigated, as the stability of the whole building may depend on it. If you have doubts, call in the experts. There is no point in embarking on any decorative restoration until the structure is sound.

Look for the following possible causes of failure: i) Alterations by previous owners which may have transferred additional weight onto certain structural elements. ii) Decay, causing weakness or failure in roof timbers, other walls or adjoining floor timbers. iii) Services excavation such as chasing or drilling for pipes.

The intrinsic failure of structural and partition walls, although not always so serious as external failure, should be diagnosed before repairing. Look out for: i) Failure of bonding of bricks or stone. Old lime mortar or even mud bedding might have turned to dust, with consequential loss of adhesion. ii) Infestation of timber studs and/or plaster lath by beetle, or from rot which is usually due to dampness. The cause of dampness *must* be eliminated before the wall is replaced or repaired.

Wall finish. Most old internal walls were plastered but some stone, cob or adobe walls might have been painted "fair-faced" – that is, onto an untreated surface. If redecorating unplastered walls, do not use a modern paint: a lime wash or distemper will not discolour so easily in the event of damp penetration or sweating, and will allow the masonry to breathe. Tap a plaster surface for hollow areas to see if its adhesion or the plaster laths have failed; remedial work will vary from filling small cracks to complete stripping and replastering. Very fine cracks can be dealt with as part of the redecorating process. Larger cracks should be widened to at least ½in (12mm), or to where the plaster is well adhered to the wall behind. Adjoining surfaces should be well wetted before filling with a quick-setting plaster such as plaster of Paris. An area of failed plaster and timber laths might need the laths replacing; alternatively a new "key" can be provided by inserting a galvanized expanded metal sheet fixed to adjoining

sound laths with galvanized nails or staples. Note the condition of the timber grounds or decks which may have been driven into masonry walls. These are wooden plugs or wedges which served as fixings for skirting boards/baseboards and dado rails. They can be a serious cause of rot and where possible should be renewed with non-ferrous fasteners.

For filling patches and replastering, three-coat work is still recommended, despite the availability of modern one-coat finishes. Use the plaster suggested for the particular application and the type of finish you require. For outside corners (for example, on a window reveal) use timber staff beads where appropriate: they have a groove running along them, which softens the appearance of the corners when plaster is applied. Alternatively, fix a screw or nail to a piece of wood to gouge out a groove to match that of an adjoining staff bead; do not use metal angle beads, which give too hard a look to the corners.

Wallpaper. Establishing the date of a wallpaper needs careful judgment of colours, composition and printing technique. Look for examples of any original wallpaper behind skirting boards/baseboards, architraves or recent plasterwork or panelling, or in built-in cupboards or closets. Preserve what you find – even if you do not intend to match designs; such fragments can be an interesting historic record. Old wallpaper glued onto plaster can be eased off with a flat-bladed knife. If the paper is attached to wood, this is more difficult: consider removing the wood as well to reduce possible damage. Paper can also by removed and layers separated by steaming, but this is a complicated process, and a conservation expert should be called in to advise.

If a historic reproduction is required, try to provide a sample which adjoins a cornice or dado, so that it includes any border; take a large enough area to include pattern repeats. In the past few years, a number of specialist firms have started to restore and match old wallpapers, and a good standard of reproduction is now available.

Tiles. These should provide a waterproof and maintenance-free surface, so the condition of existing old tiles must be good. If the removal of old tiles is required, careful levering and chipping away of the mortar behind is the safest method. If the tiles are valuable and difficult to remove, consider taking them off as a whole with all the plaster backing, and then remove this backing from the rear by careful chipping or with an angle grinder.

Old tiles had a thicker biscuit than their modern equivalents, and their glaze was opaque rather than clear. This would hide any dampness penetrating the tile from the joint or backing. Old tiles would be attached by a lime mortar. Clean old lime mortar from the glaze using a commercial acid cleaner. Chipped or glazed tiles are difficult and expensive to repair, and require specialist attention. Very small areas can be touched in with a clear epoxy varnish. Try using condensed milk to repair broken tiles – it sounds unlikely, but it works.

Antique markets and architectural salvage companies are a good source of old tiles. There are also tile suppliers who produce reproduction examples, and some will even supply tiles custom-made to individual designs. Some potters will also work to individual requirements, but skill is required to ensure a compatibility of glaze and biscuit.

DECORATIVE PLASTERWORK

The plaster mouldings of cornices and other ceiling decorations are an important ornamental feature, helping to set the style of a period house. Although expensive to repair and restore, original decorative plasterwork should be retained where at all possible. Plaster restoration is a very skilled craft, and for anything other than simple repair or paint removal, a specialist firm should be consulted.

Paint Removal. It is astonishing what layer upon layer of paint can hide. Cornices which look very ordinary can reveal, when the paintwork is stripped, the most intricate and attractive details. Removal of paint, however, is extremely laborious and slow (and therefore expensive if done by others). Distemper or lime wash can be carefully washed away with warm water and washing soda. Emulsion paint can be eased with the help of steam or methylated spirits. Oil-based paint will probably need a commercial stripping solvent, but start by experimenting on a small sample area and do not forget to neutralize before repainting. Proceed with even more care when you think that you are down to the initial surface: you might find an original colour wash. If you do, record this for your redecoration programme by matching on a colour chart.

Repairs. Cracks and small fissures can be fairly easily filled with proprietary plaster fillers or casting plaster. Originally, basic cornice sections were formed in situ by using a metal template pulled across the freshly plastered surface. Lengths of plaster to be repaired can be similarly formed or, more easily, cast in a mould on a bench and then applied. Enrichment such as acanthus leaves and modillions can be cast using latex or other moulds, a very skilled process.

Renewal. Sometimes whole rooms need to have the decorative plasterwork renewed. Choose your profiles carefully, either from similar-sized rooms of equal importance within the same house, or from reference books (such as this one) that show examples from the same period. Commercially made plastic or fibreglass sections should be avoided, as they are usually not of a correct profile or scale. Specialist suppliers of decorative plasterwork might, however, have suitable examples. These will probably be in fibrous plaster, a 19th-century development, which incorporated scrim and wood chips for strength and enabled lighter pieces to be made. Beware of too crisp or sharp a section if others in the house have had their edges worn by time.

PAINT

It is all too easy to ruin the effect of skilful repair or restoration by the inappropriate choice of paint colours, or the use of anachronistic finishes. As a general rule, avoid very glossy paints in all houses built before the 20th century. Pre-Georgian hardwood doors, exposed timber and the like would most probably have been left as natural wood (see DOORS for suggested finishes), but it is a misconception that natural wood was used thereafter. The stripped wood look is a modern taste, influenced by Scandinavian design. In Britain lead-based paint is still obtainable from specialist firms: it is used by purists seeking to achieve the authentic chalky white look in their woodwork. Lime wash and distemper have a similar soft feel to them, and are a suitable finish on walls which might be prone to damp. Modern vinyl emulsions do not look right in old buildings, but some firms produce a non-vinyl emulsion which has a suitable matt look and allows the surface to breathe.

Outside, the use of modern hydraporous paint can reduce preparatory work when redecorating. A permaglaze acrylic finish can add to the life of external paintwork by a year or two. It is always worth seeking advice from a good paint supplier – not just a local retailer.

FLOORS

Wood. Old wood floors will either be boarded or parquet. Floorboards will either be of hardwood such as oak or elm, or of softwood such as pine or spruce. If the floor is in good condition, its natural rich colours can create an attractive background for loose carpets and rugs. Piece in repairs with matching wood where possible – if butted boards have opened up leaving wide gaps, these can be glue-filled with tapered infill pieces. Old polish can be removed from hardwood floors by using the mixture described under DOORS. A polish suitable for wooden floors can then be applied; an electric floorpolisher is recommended for large areas. Pine floorboards can be enhanced by sanding and sealing. Remember to drive nails well home before sanding. If the floor is badly worn or pitted, sand diagonally with a coarse sandpaper before finishing with the grain. Floor sanders can be hired easily. You will need more sandpaper than you think, and use a mask to protect your lungs. It is an exhausting job to do thoroughly! An undesirable wood colour can be stained or even painted before sealing, but check the compatibility of the stain or paint with this final sealer. There are many wood floor sealers on the market, polyurethane or deoresinous being the most common. Beware of too shiny and plastic-looking a finish. Purists will remember that until the mid-18th century floorboards were scoured regularly with sand to clean them, and left untreated.

Stone flags. These are very hard-wearing, so little maintenance should be necessary. They can sometimes be lifted and relaid on a new damp-proof course, but number the flags first, and make a plan of how they fit together. Make sure the joints are not too wide, and point them with a fine sand/cement mortar. Seal old slates and other porous stones, after thoroughly cleaning off dirt and grease, with 1 part boiled linseed oil to 4 parts turpentine – cover with brown paper and leave for 2-3 days; do not walk on them. Sweep and water-wash to keep clean.

Linoleum. This is the original synthetic floor finish which is made of ground cork, wood, flour, linseed oil and resins, with a jute or hessian backing. It is unstable if water gets beneath the surface, and it is sensitive to alkalis. Linoleum should not be sealed, but can be polished with an emulsion polish.

Carpet. Expert advice is needed for restoration. Note that *any* colour of carpet can be made to special order, and at not too fantastic a price.

FIREPLACES

Marble fireplaces were common during the Georgian/Federal era. Sometimes these are found to be painted over: to clean, use a solvent stripper with care and try a sample area first. Discoloured marble can be cleaned with the application of a mix of equal parts of a soft soap, quicklime and caustic potash left for several days before wiping off. To polish marble, mix 2 parts finely sieved washing soda, 1 part pumice stone and 1 part chalk with sufficient water to make a paste; rub on and leave for a few hours before washing off with soap and water. Milk can also be used to tone up a polished marble fireplace.

Wooden fireplaces may show very intricate ornamentation. This is not necessarily carved but can be moulded in a composition of artificial wood and then painted over. To reveal the detail of fine ornamentation, strip paintwork with great care so as not to damage these compositions: they are very delicate and may, in fact, be held together by the paint layers.

Cast-iron fireplaces were common in the latter part of the 19th century. Restoration of damaged pieces is difficult, and specialists should be consulted. Fire grates, including dog grates and register grates, pose their own particular problems, often associated with distortion by heat. If badly damaged, complete replacement may be more appropriate.

Cracked fire bricks should be either replaced or repaired with fireproof cement. If the hearth is defective, check that its bed is sound. Hearths should be set on a good layer of incombustible material – not the wooden floor. It may be necessary to trim floor joists and insert concrete. More historic houses are lost because of fire caused by defective hearths or chimneys than from any other cause. Check fireplaces and chimneys very thoroughly before use.

STAIRCASES

The staircase will normally be made from wood or stone with a metal or wood balustrade. Repairs to woodwork, necessary because of collapse, wear, worm or fungal attack, can be made by a good carpenter. Check and repair the wooden strings and bearers thoroughly before dealing with the more visible parts. Repairs to stone stairs are more difficult and will probably require specialist help. Worn treads and damaged nosings can be repaired with new stone indents set into pockets and bedded in epoxy mortar – or a plastic repair can be made using a mixture of epoxy mortar or resin and crushed stone, with a copper wire reinforcement if necessary. Avoid all feather edges in any repair. A step damaged around the metal baluster can be repaired by cutting back and setting in a new section of matching stone, using non-ferrous dowels and epoxy resins.

If a wooden stair requires extensive repairs and does not contain very elaborate woodwork, it is often more sensible to replace it rather than patch it temporarily. If you choose to replace the staircase, special features such as the original handrail or balusters can always be incorporated into the replacement, or similar examples can be purchased from architectural salvage yards. Some commercially made handrails and balusters are acceptable for less important stairs, but the original examples cannot be bettered, and should be copied where possible.

JOINERY AND MOULDINGS

Repair original joinery wherever possible. If a building has lost its original joinery and mouldings, you are faced with the rather daunting and expensive task of restoring its character by careful reinstatement. Architectural salvage firms can be a source of historically suitable items, or alternatively they can be made new. Visit similar houses for patterns. Unfortunately, commercial joinery and mouldings are usually unsuitable: they are often relatively crude and historically inaccurate.

The complexity of joinery and mouldings – architraves, skirting boards/baseboards, dadoes, and the like – should correspond directly to the size and social significance of the rooms. Beware of purchasing an example which looks acceptable in its large showroom but might look totally out of scale in your own house.

Mouldings and joinery pieces should be used with restraint – not to change the character of a building, but rather to enhance the inherent style and historical personality.

SERVICES

Stoves and ranges. Restoring and using old stoves and ranges has recently become popular. When buying from a salvage company, carefully evaluate the appearance of the appliance. The working parts are more easily replaced and will probably have to be serviced or adapted by a specialist in any case. Early stoves contained a lot of cast iron finished in nickel plating or painted enamel. Although the plating can be removed and recoated, it can be difficult to locate a specialist who will do this, and the process is expensive. Touching up enamel with a matching paint (fill first with an auto-body filler) can hide the larger defects; minor scratches and dents can be left. Re-porcelaining is expensive, and colours can be hard to match.

Rust can be a problem, affecting not only aesthetics but also the working parts of the appliance; check thoroughly, especially the oven and fuel box walls.

Radiators. It is worth considering the reinstallation of old radiators in period buildings if the original models have been replaced. They can often be located in architectural salvage stores; alternatively, make enquiries at local demolition firms. Examine carefully for rust, especially around the connections: if possible, check them all with a water test, or, failing that, with the less reliable air pressure test. Beware of incompatible metals when connecting old radiators to a modern system – your plumber should be able to advise you.

Manufacturers are becoming much more aware of radiator design, so choose your fixtures carefully when having a new system installed. Do not just leave it to your plumber's preference. If you have to install radiators in a beautifully proportioned room, consider boxing them in or hiding them under window seats, but remember that some efficiency will be lost. Never allow a radiator to rise above chair-rail level, unless you are designing it as a feature of the room.

Pipework. It is most probable that with any period house renovation you will need to rewire and replace old pipes. Remove old services with care. It is often better to leave some in situ but disconnected, rather than risk damaging surrounding surfaces. Where possible, use the old pipe runs when laying new services to save on notching joists or chasing walls.

Sanitary fixtures. Old bathtubs, basins and other sanitary wares are readily available from architectural salvage stores, and can sometimes be acquired from demolition sites. New cast-iron bathtubs are becoming more difficult to obtain, but the condition of old ones is often good enough for re-use.

Re-enamelling of a bathtub can be done by a specialist firm, either in situ or more effectively if the appliance is taken away. Old chips and cracks in porcelain can be sealed with Superglue but touching up with paint is nearly always noticeable.

Old taps/faucets add character. They can easily be re-chromed or brass-plated, and most plumbers should be able to integrate them into your system. Be careful when removing old taps/faucets from sanitary fixtures as they were often bedded on a putty which, if old and well set, can be harder than the surrounding porcelain and may cause this to crack.

LIGHTING

Have all old fixtures checked by an electrician for safety before using. Old lights can be adapted to modern safety standards; alternatively, good quality reproductions are now available from a number of specialist firms. Fitting old brass switches can be complicated, requiring a conduit for earthing; again, there are modern reproductions which will comply with current safety standards.

METALWORK

Repainting. Decorative wrought- and cast-iron work, as found on balconies and railings, will often be rusted, but not as badly as may at first appear: rust occupies seven times the volume of unoxidized iron. All ironwork should be painted both for decoration and for protection against corrosion. The old paint surface must be wire-brushed or scraped, and all loose paint and rust removed completely. Burn off old paint or use a solvent-type stripper, cleaning thoroughly with turpentine or paint thinner followed by plenty of water. Build up the layers of new paint in accordance with the manufacturer's instructions. The application of two coats of rustproofing primer is far preferable to an extra top coat.

Repairing. Retain as much original ironwork as possible. If the replacement of parts is essential, use like materials. Be careful with cast iron, as it is particularly brittle and will easily fracture if subjected to tensile stress. Fractures in structural elements can be repaired by electrically welding, but make sure all welds are continuous and are ground smooth before repainting. Make sure that any welding will not restrict natural thermal and structural movement; if this is a danger, an alternative is the use of plates and splints.

Rainwater goods. Gutters and down pipes/downspouts are traditionally cast in iron, lead or copper, and when well maintained they have a long life. The recent introduction of plastic, aluminium and even fibreglass rainwater goods provides inexpensive and tempting alternatives, which the preservation-minded will prefer to avoid. An acceptable compromise for some is to use traditional materials for clearly visible down pipes/downspouts, and modern materials at higher levels. Note that some profiled guttering is an essential part of an eaves cornice, and that the profile should be retained when replacing.

SECURITY

Today the theft of architectural items is becoming a very serious concern. Take special precautions to secure and insure an empty building. Before restoration work begins, box in special features such as fireplaces, as protection against damage and prying eyes. Photographing and measuring these items is always advisable to help with identification in the event of theft.

Peter Sutton, the contributor of this essay, is a partner with Anthony Harrison of the Harrison Sutton Partnership, Fore Street, Totnes, Devon, England. Their architectural practice specializes in the restoration of historic buildings, including properties belonging to the National Trust and English Heritage.

BIOGRAPHIES

The following is a selective list of short biographies of indexed architects, designers and others who were significant to the development or dissemination of a style discussed in the text.

Aalto, Alvar (1898 - 1976). Finnish architect and designer. A master of the Modern Movement, he designed highly individual buildings that expressed a great sensitivity to site. His early work included some of the first Rationalist buildings in Scandinavia, notably the influential Sanatorium (1929 - 32) at Paimio, a crisp, white building with strip windows and cantilevered balconies. He later moved away from the machine aesthetic, expressing his strong feelings for materials in the use of timber (e.g. Finnish Pavilion, Paris, 1937) and developing a free-form approach (e.g. Finnish Pavilion, New York World's Fair, 1939). After 1945 he developed his distinctive form of Modernism, with curved walls, angular pitched roofs, extensive use of brick and timber and awareness of environmental context, as seen in Baker House (1946-9), MIT, Cambridge, Massachusetts; the Town Hall (1952), Säynätsalo; the Cultural Centre (1958), Helsinki; and the Vuoksenniska Church (1958), Imatra. Aalto is also well known for furniture designs exploiting moulded plywood shapes (e.g. the bentwood Paimio chair, 1933, and cantilevered chairs in laminated wood, 1946); he continued to produce furniture through his company Artek all his life.

Ackermann, Rudolf (1764 - 1834). English publisher, of German birth. He worked as a coachmaker in Europe and in London, where he moved to in about 1783. In 1795 he established a book and print shop in London, the Repository of Arts. He subsequently published the *Repository of Arts* (1809-28), an influential periodical covering art, architecture, interior design, fashion, science and other subjects. Contributors included J. B. Papworth and A. C. Pugin. Furniture designs published in the *Repository* in 1822 were later reprinted as *Fashionable Furniture* (1823). The *Repository* was mainly dedicated to the classical style until 1825, when Pugin began to contribute Gothic designs.

Adam, Robert (1728 - 92). Scottish architect and designer. He was one of the two most important architects in England in the late 18th century (with William Chambers, his archrival). The son of a leading Scottish architect, Adam went on a Grand Tour to Italy (1754-8), where he studied classical architecture; he also surveyed Diocletian's palace at Split. In 1758 he set up practice in London, later joined by one of his brothers, James Adam. Early work included the classical, columned Admiralty Screen (1759-60), London, and many house interiors in which Adam perfected his light and elegant Neo-classicism. This contrasted sharply with both the heavier Palladian style that preceded it and with the Greek Revival that followed. Adam's best-known country-house designs include Harewood House (1759-71); Kedleston Hall (from 1759); Syon House (1760-69); Osterley Park (1765-80); Luton Hoo (1766-74); Newby Hall (1767-85); and Kenwood House (1767-9). They were followed from the late 1760s by many fine London town houses. In all he integrated the decorative arts into new schemes with contrasting plan shapes derived from antiquity (e.g. the basilican hall, the rotunda, and coffered apses screened by columns). His decorative approach included flat grotesque panels and pilasters, elaborate colour schemes and delicate painted ornament, with urns, swags and ribbons. Adam also designed some large buildings in Edinburgh (e.g. the University, begun 1789) and some picturesque castles (e.g. Culzean Castle, 1777-92), where he contrasted rugged exteriors with delicate, refined interiors. The Adam style was widely disseminated through *The Works in Architecture of Robert and James Adam* (1773-8, 1779, 1822). Adam's ornament became increasingly mannered towards the end of his career and was much criticized in the first half of the 19th century. An Adam Revival began after the London Exhibition of 1862.

Adam, Robert (b 1948). English architect. He trained at the Polytechnic of Central London (1967-73) and then studied in Rome for a year. In 1977 he moved to Winchester and began designing classical revival buildings, particularly in the Georgian style, which he adapted to modern technology. He is also associated with the polemic between Modernists and Classicists surrounding the Prince of Wales and is involved with the Prince's Institute of Architecture.

Ashbee, C. R. (1863 - 1942). English architect and designer. He was strongly influenced by the ideas of John Ruskin and William Morris, particularly those on social reform. In 1888 he founded the Guild and School of Handicraft in London's East End. The School closed in 1895 but the Guild continued for many years as an important centre for the ideals of the Arts and Crafts Movement, producing furniture, metalwork, jewellery, enamelling and printing. Ashbee created some influential designs (e.g. simple Arts and Crafts jewellery and silverware). Among his surviving buildings are some houses (1898-9) in Cheyne Walk, London, with picturesque vernacular massing. He also completed many restoration projects in Chipping Campden, where he moved the Guild in 1902. He helped introduce Frank Lloyd Wright's ideas into Europe after meeting him in 1900. He also wrote several books, including *A Book of Cottages and Little Houses* (1906), *Craftsmanship in Competitive Industry* (1908), and *Modern English Silverwork* (1909).

Audsley, George Ashdown (1838 - 1925). Scottish architect and designer. In 1863 he set up practice with his brother William James Audsley in Liverpool. There they designed several churches, but Audsley is best known for his publications, many produced with his brother. *Cottage, Lodge and Villa Architecture* (c.1868) and a series of important books on Japanese art were followed by the pattern manuals *Outlines of Ornament in the Leading Styles* (1881) and *Polychromatic Decoration as Applied to Buildings in the Mediaeval Styles* (1882). In 1892 Audsley and Maurice Ashdown Audsley (possibly his son) published *The Practical Decorator and Ornamentist*, which was influential in the United States. He then moved to New York and continued publishing design books with his son Berthold Audsley.

Baillie Scott, M. H. (1865 - 1945). English architect and designer. He was a noted figure in the later stages of the Arts and Crafts Movement, when it acquired international influence and was seen as a precursor of early Modernism. Baillie Scott adopted a simple vernacular manner in his houses but developed a new kind of open spatial planning, with living rooms focused around a massive inglenook fireplace and orientated to the garden instead of the street. His finest houses include Blackwell, Bowness (1898); The White House, Helensburgh; and The Garth, Cobham (1899). His simple, unornamented furniture, metalwork and wallpaper designs, often using brilliant colour, were shown at the Arts and Crafts Exhibition in London in 1896. He became well known in Europe through his articles in *The Studio* from 1895 and for his interiors at the Grand Duke of Hesse's palace at Darmstadt (seat of the artists' colony founded in 1899). He also produced influential houses for Hampstead and Letchworth garden cities (1904-9). He published his early work in the book *Houses and Gardens* (1906). His later work, published in *Houses and Gardens* (1933), was less distinctive.

Behrens, Peter (1869-1940). German architect and designer. One of the key figures in the development of the early Modern Movement, he was involved in many of the progressive artistic groups founded around the turn of the 19th century. He initially studied painting, exhibiting throughout the 1890s. He then began to produce designs for graphics and the decorative arts. In 1899 he joined the artists' colony at Darmstadt, where he designed his own house. He is best known for his work as designer-architect (1907-14) for AEG in Berlin, where he introduced the concept of integrated corporate design covering advertising, graphic design, industrial products and buildings. His famous AEG Turbine Factory (1909), Moabit, combined a monumental, symbolic design with modern steel and glass technology, and is an icon of the early Modern Movement. He also designed typefaces, book-bindings, logotypes, glassware, cutlery, fabrics and furniture. In his later buildings he turned to classicism (e.g. German Embassy, St Petersburg, 1911), Expressionism (e.g. I. G. Farben Office Building, Hoechst, 1924), and then the International Style. All the great architects of the Modern Movement – Walter Gropius, Mies van der Rohe and Le Corbusier – worked in his office between 1908 and 1911.

Benjamin, Asher (1773-1845). American architect. Through his pattern books he was influential in the dissemination of the Neo-classical and Greek Revival styles in the United States. After an early career as a house-carpenter, when he worked on Charles Bulfinch's Connecticut State House at Hartford (1795), he produced *The Country Builder's Assistant* (1797). This, the first American builder's guide, drew on the publications of William Pain (who popularized the Adam style) but was adapted to American usage. In 1806 he produced (with Daniel Raynerd) *The American Builder's Companion*, which was influenced by Bulfinch's Federal style. It was immensely popular through several revisions during the next 20 years, when he added a variety of new sources, including William Chambers. Benjamin also developed an architectural practice in Boston in 1806-10, building three churches, the Exchange Coffee House and several fine houses on Beacon Hill. His next books, *The Practical House Carpenter* (1830) – which became the most popular American architectural book of the 19th century – *The Practice of Architecture* (1833) and *The Builder's Guide* (1838), promoted the new Greek Revival style.

Bing, Samuel (1838-1905). German decorative arts dealer. After working in a ceramics factory in Germany, he moved to Paris in 1871 and opened his first shop there. He travelled to China and Japan in 1875, then opened another shop in Paris to sell objects from the Far East. Louis Comfort Tiffany was one of his customers and he subsequently became Tiffany's European distributor. At the end of 1895 he opened a new shop in Paris called L'Art Nouveau, which displayed glass, graphic designs, metalwork, jewellery, wallpaper, fabrics and furniture. Artists represented included Tiffany, Emile Gallé, Aubrey Beardsley, René Lalique, Walter Crane, William Morris, C. F. A. Voysey and Henry Van de Velde. Bing had his own pavilion at the Paris Exposition of 1900 and played an important role in the dissemination of contemporary styles.

Breuer, Marcel (1902-81). Hungarian architect and designer, active in Germany, England and the United States. A pioneer of the European Modern Movement, he studied and taught furniture design at the Bauhaus in Weimar (1920-24) and Dessau (1925-8). There he developed new, functional forms using clear structural articulation, as in his famous Wassily chair (1925), one of the first tubular-steel chairs in general production; the B32 cantilevered tubular steel chair (1928); and simple modular storage systems. From 1928 he worked as an architect and interior designer in Berlin. In 1935 he moved to England and practised with the architect F. R. S. Yorke while continuing to design furniture (e.g. Isokon reclining plywood chair, laminated plywood nesting tables and stacking chairs). He then moved to the United States, teaching architecture at Harvard (1937-47) and practising with Walter Gropius (1937-41). Breuer's American houses combined modern forms with the use of timber and rough stonework (e.g. Breuer House, New Canaan, Connecticut, 1947). His later work included the Y-shaped UNESCO building in Paris (1953-8; with others) and the Whitney Museum of American Art, New York (1966).

Britton, John (1771-1857). English architectural writer. He is known for the several important books he published on the architectural history of England, which included carefully drawn plans and details as well as authoritative texts. Examples are *The Architectural Antiquities of Great Britain* (1807-26), *The Cathedral Antiquities of England* (1814-35) and *Illustration of the Public Buildings of London* (1825-8). In 1821-3 he published *Specimens of Gothic Architecture*, prepared with A. C. Pugin. His accurate records of medieval architecture provided a highly useful model for Gothic Revivalists.

Bulfinch, Charles (1763-1844). American architect. He was an influential exponent of the Federal or Adam style, acquiring a national reputation that popularized the style throughout the United States. After a two-year tour of Europe (1785-7), he designed several churches and the Connecticut State House (1795), Hartford. In 1795 he was commissioned to build the Massachusetts State House, Boston, one of the most important buildings of the period in the United States. In this he drew on London's Somerset House, completed by William Chambers only a decade before. The State House, with a colonnaded central projecting block and high dome, became a model for many state capitols thereafter. In 1799 Bulfinch obtained an administrative position with wide responsibilities, through which he helped to transform Boston. He designed many civic and commercial buildings (e.g. India Wharf, Boston, 1807; University Hall, Harvard, 1814; Massachusetts General Hospital, 1823) as well as houses, developing a rather plain style with attenuated Neo-classical details. His early churches, with tall belfries characteristically placed at the junction of porch roof and main roof, established a model for church design in the area. In 1817 Bulfinch took over as architect at the US Capitol, Washington, completing the work begun by Benjamin Henry Latrobe. This established his reputation.

Burlington, Richard Boyle, 3rd Earl of (1694-1753). English amateur architect and patron. He was the most influential promoter of the Palladian revival in England in the 18th century. Burlington adopted the style after the publication of Colen Campbell's *Vitruvius Brittanicus* and James Leoni's translation of Palladio's *Four Books of Architecture* in 1715. He then employed Campbell to take over the renovation of Burlington House from James Gibbs, and it became the first strictly Palladian building in London. Burlington visited Italy to study Palladio's buildings, and he acquired several original drawings by Palladio, as well as prints and books. He returned to England in 1719 with his protégé William Kent, who worked with him on many projects and whose *Designs of Inigo Jones* (1727) he financed. Burlington went on to design several Palladian buildings, notably Chiswick House, London (1725-9), his own villa, partly based on Palladio's Villa Rotonda; and the Assembly Rooms, York (1732), derived from Palladio's colonnaded Egyptian hall, which was in turn based on Vitruvius. Burlington's patronage assisted in the publication of many learned books, including a better translation of Palladio by Isaac Ware. These provided the models adopted in innumerable builders' pattern books that helped spread the Palladian idiom throughout Britain and the United States.

Campbell, Colen (1673-1729). Scottish architect. Together with Lord Burlington, he was one of the most influential proponents of the 18th-century Palladian revival. He established his reputation through the publication of *Vitruvius Britannicus* (1715-17), a collection of plans and illustrations drawn by him of houses built during the previous century or so. To these he added an introduction and some of his own designs promoting the work of Palladio and Inigo Jones in place of the Baroque. The great success of the book helped launch the Palladian revival and encouraged a wide general interest in architecture. Campbell's buildings included the new facade of Burlington House, Piccadilly, based on a palazzo design of Palladio's; some simple London town houses using Palladian proportions; and some notable country houses in which he adopted clearly recognizable elements such as the cubic hall and temple-front portico, providing easily reproducible models. Examples include Wanstead House, Essex (1720; destr.), and Houghton Hall, Norfolk (1722-9). His smaller Palladian villas include Stourhead, Wiltshire (1722), and Mereworth, Kent (c.1725), his own version of Palladio's Villa Rotonda.

Chambers, Sir William (1723-96). English architect and designer. His work, although less fashionable than Robert Adam's, was of equal importance in popularizing Neo-classical design in the second half of the 18th century. He also played an important role in the dissemination of exotic Chinese styles. Born in Sweden of Scottish parentage, he spent ten years in the Swedish East India Company (1739-49), where he was introduced to Chinese art and design. In 1749 he studied architecture in Paris, becoming familiar with French fashions, and in 1750-55 he undertook two extensive trips to Rome. In 1757 he became architectural tutor to the Prince of Wales (later George III), publishing his lessons and his designs as *A Treatise on Civil Architecture* (1759), one of the most influential books of its day. Chambers also worked for the Prince's mother, laying out Kew Gardens with a variety of exotic elements, (e.g. his famous Chinese Pagoda, 1763). His *Designs of Chinese Buildings, Furniture ...and Utensils* (1757) was influential for both garden design and chinoiserie. He became Architect of the King's Works in 1761 (jointly with Adam) and Surveyor-General in 1782. Chambers adopted various styles in his work, including French-Italian Neo-classicism (e.g. Casino at Marino House, Dublin, 1758-70); English Palladianism (e.g. Duddingston House, Midlothian, 1763); and Gothic (e.g. Milton Abbey, Dorset, 1776). His best-known work is Somerset House, London (1776-86), which showed the influence of Inigo Jones on the Strand front but French Neo-classicism in the courtyard. It also showed his skill as a designer of staircases and interiors, with some rooms being early English examples of the Louis XVI style.

Chippendale, Thomas (1718-79). English cabinetmaker. He was one of the most important cabinetmakers in London during the 1760s and 1770s. He opened premises in St Martin's Lane, then a centre of artistic life, in 1753. He designed furniture not only for his firm but also for his celebrated *Gentleman and Cabinet-Maker's Director*, first produced in 1754. The *Director* illustrated "household furniture" in styles ranging from Rococo to Chinese and Gothic. Popular among patrons and craftsmen, it showed a wider range of designs, including Neo-classical, in the third edition (1762). This was influential also in the United States and Europe, with copies acquired by Catherine II of Russia and Louis XVI of France. Chippendale's best furniture reflected the elegant Neo-classicical style of Robert Adam and William Chambers. He worked with Adam on a number of interiors, such as Harewood House, West Yorkshire. He also worked at other houses in Yorkshire (e.g. Nostell Priory, Aske Hall and Newby Hall); at Wilton House, Wiltshire; and at Petworth House, West Sussex. His son Thomas Chippendale the Younger, who took over after his father's death, is often considered more innovative; he produced some fine Neo-classical furniture for Stourhead (1797-1820).

Conran, Sir Terence (b 1931). English designer. He was immensely influential in introducing into the British mass market after World War II the concept of good quality modern design in furniture, textiles and homewares. In 1956 he formed the Conran Design Group, producing furniture and textiles for the commercial market. In 1964 he opened the first of his Habitat shops in London, using innovative displays to sell attractive, functional, reasonably priced furniture, fabrics, glassware and kitchenware to the domestic market. The designs were based on Scandinavian and Italian models, reproduced in affordable versions. The popularity of his designs led to the opening of about 50 Habitat shops in Britain and abroad in the next 20 years. London's Design Museum for mass-produced objects was sponsored (1989) by his Conran Foundation.

Cottingham, Lewis Nockalls (1787-1847). English architect and designer. He acquired an early knowledge of Gothic architecture through his work restoring medieval churches. Much of this knowledge was disseminated through his publications, including *Working Drawings of Gothic Ornaments* (1824), which contains fine illustrations. He also designed Gothic-style furniture (e.g. for Snelston Hall, Derbyshire, 1840s), classical interiors, and metalwork in both classical and Gothic styles. Some of the latter was published in his influential *Ornamental Metal Worker's Director* (1823; revised 1824), later issued as *The Smith's, Founder's and Ornamental Metal Worker's Director* (1845). His collection of casts, drawings and original Gothic fragments formed the basis of the Architectural Museum at Westminster (now in the Victoria & Albert Museum).

Crane, Walter (1845-1915). English painter, illustrator and designer. He achieved early fame as a popular book illustrator.

He then became a successful decorative designer, at first producing ceramics for Wedgwood and others. After meeting the leaders of the Arts and Crafts Movement, he began in the 1870s to produce designs for wallpaper, then embroideries, textiles, carpets, mosaics and stained glass. He was a founder-member of the Art-Workers' Guild (1884) and led the breakaway Arts and Crafts Exhibition Society (1888), which became influential in spreading abroad the ideas of the Arts and Crafts movement. Crane was also a teacher and wrote several influential books, including *The Claims of Decorative Art* (1892), *The Bases of Design* (1898), *Line and Form* (1900) – the latter two comprising his lectures at the Manchester School of Art – and *Ideals in Art* (1905). Many of his books were translated, and Crane had an established European reputation by the 1890s.

Davis, Alexander Jackson (1803-92). American architect. As one of the most influential architects in the United States in the middle of the 19th century, he helped popularize the Greek Revival and introduced picturesque Italianate and Gothic Revival forms. In 1829-35 and 1842-3 he worked in New York in partnership with Ithiel Town, designer of the Connecticut State Capitol (1827-31; destr.). Together they built two other monumental state capitols, at Indianapolis (1831-5; destr.) and Raleigh, North Carolina (1833-42), and the New York City Customs House (1833-42). They used Greek temple forms but usually added a central Roman Revival dome. Davis went on to work independently in a variety of styles, building classical institutions, Italianate villas and Gothic college buildings. He is perhaps best remembered for his picturesque country villas, some designed as rustic *cottages ornés* and many as castellated Gothic mansions, among the first of their type in the United States (e.g. Lyndhurst, Tarrytown, New York, 1838; for which he also made Gothic-style furniture). Davis was a fine draughtsman and introduced the use of romantic settings for his rendered drawings. He published some of his early designs in *Rural Residences, etc.* (1837). Many others appeared in A. J. Downing's popular books, including *Cottage Residences* (1842) and *The Architecture of Country Houses* (1850), which spread Davis's influence throughout the United States.

Downing, A. J. (1815-52). American landscape designer and rural architect. He is best known for his writings in the periodical *The Horticulturist* (1846-52) and in such books as *A Treatise on the Theory and Practice of Landscape Gardening Adapted to North America* (1841), *Cottage Residences* (1842) and *The Architecture of Country Houses* (1850). These books, among the first of their type in the United States, were mostly produced in collaboration with Alexander Jackson Davis, who prepared the illustrations, including many of his own recent villas and cottages, all shown in rural settings. They also drew on English sources (e.g. John Claudius Loudon). Downing's books were immensely successful and helped popularize the ideals of the Picturesque in the United States. In 1850 he established a practice with the English architect Calvert Vaux, which was among the first American firms to specialize in landscape design. Downing promoted the development of urban parks, for which Vaux, with Frederick Law Olmsted, later became famous.

Dresser, Christopher (1834-1904). Scottish designer and writer. He was an influential theorist on functional design in the 1860s and after. He was initially a respected lecturer and writer on the application of botany in the decorative arts. His first book on design was *The Art of Decorative Design* (1862). During the next 30 years he was a successful commercial designer of silverware, ceramics, glass, furniture, metalwork, wallpaper, carpets and textiles. His style was often abstract and geometric, with a concern for the honest use of materials, and he promoted machine production. Dresser also explored exotic forms. In 1876-7 he visited Japan, returning with art works collected for dealers, and he published the major work *Japan, Its Architecture, Art and Art Manufactures* (1882). Other influential books were *The Principles of Decorative Design* (1873) and *Modern Ornamentation* (1886).

Eastlake, Charles Locke (1833/6-1906). English designer and writer. Trained as an architect, he spent much of his professional career with the Institute of British Architects and the National Gallery, London. He is best known for his writings on design and ornament, notably *Hints on Household Taste in Furniture, Upholstery and Other Details* (1868). This featured his own designs influenced by the Arts and Crafts and Queen Anne styles, the honest expression of materials and construction, and the use of rectilinear, geometric ornament. It was particularly influential in the United States, where six editions were published (from 1872) and where a distinctive "Eastlake style" developed for furniture. It was later extended to architecture, particularly in California, where houses that were basically Queen Anne or Stick Style had curvilinear and turned ornament borrowed from furniture. Eastlake dissociated himself from both styles. His other writings included *A History of the Gothic Revival* (1872) and *Lectures on Decorative Art and Art-Workmanship* (1876).

Fry, E. Maxwell (1899-1987). English architect. He was an important pioneer of the Modern Movement in England in the 1930s. He turned to Modernism after meeting Wells Coates in 1932, and he was a founder-member of the MARS Group (1933) in support of Modernism. His best-known work of this period included private houses (e.g. Sun House, Hampstead, London, 1936) and several blocks of low-cost flats (e.g. Kensal House, North Kensington, London, 1936; with others), which were carefully planned and designed for standardized construction. In 1934-7 he was in partnership with Walter Gropius. After World War II, Fry and his wife Jane Drew and their partners carried out several large-scale educational buildings in West Africa, where they adapted Modernism to local tropical conditions and produced important, well-researched books on the subject (e.g. *Tropical Architecture in the Humid Zone*, 1956). Fry and Drew were influential in the appointment (1950) of Le Corbusier to design the new capital of the Punjab at Chandigarh, where they also worked.

Geddes, Norman Bel (1893-1958). American designer. His early career was as an influential stage designer, developing modern productions that integrated plays with scenery, lighting and costumes. About 1927 he took up industrial design, establishing the first specialist firm in the United States. He went on to develop futuristic projects based on the concept of aerodynamic streamlining. These included cars, buses, locomotives, ocean liners and airliners (one in the form of a massive aeroplane wing), as well as gas stoves, refrigerators, radios, interiors and window displays. His designs were popularized through his book *Horizons* (1932). His model of "Metropolis", the "City of Tomorrow" (1937), incorporated advanced ideas for traffic control, while his General Motors "Futurama" exhibit at the New York World's Fair (1939) was a vision of the high-rise city towers and freeways of the future. It inspired his *Magic Motorways* (1940), which was influential in the design of post-war American freeways

Gibbons, Grinling (1648-1751). English wood-carver. He is considered to be the most important English decorative carver, with a great virtuosity in naturalistic carving. Born in Rotterdam of English parents, he probably studied Dutch and Flemish still-life paintings, which may have inspired the richness of his later carvings of fruit and flowers. He moved to England c.1667 and was apparently "discovered" and introduced to Charles II by the diarist John Evelyn. Much of Gibbons's most important and sumptuous Baroque carving was carried out for the King, notably in the Royal Apartments at Windsor Castle, Berkshire, in 1677-82. He also worked at Kensington Palace, London, and at Hampton Court Palace. In 1693 he became Master Carver to the Crown, working under Surveyor-General Christopher Wren. At Wren's St Paul's Cathedral, London, he produced oak carvings in the choir (1696-7). Work for private clients included the well-known Carved Room (1692) at Petworth House, West Sussex, as well as architectural decoration in stone, marble and bronze (e.g. at Blenheim Palace, 1708-16). Other works produced by Gibbons or his workshop included statues and funerary monuments.

Gibbs, James (1682-1754). Scottish architect. He was the most important church architect in London in the early 18th century. He studied architecture with Carlo Fontana in Rome, and after returning to England in 1708 he became an influential exponent of the Baroque style. As Surveyor (1713-15) to the Fifty New Churches Commission in London he built St Mary-le-Strand (1714-23), the success of which led to his commission for St Martin-in-the-Fields, Trafalgar Square (1726), his best-known work. This has a temple-front portico topped by a steeple, which was much imitated. Its side windows feature the "Gibbs Surround" (window surrounds heavily rusticated with large blocks of stone), which was named after him. His private commissions included the Octagon Pavilion at Orleans House, Twickenham; Sudbrook Park, Petersham (both c.1720); and several ornamental buildings at Stowe (from 1726). His other important public buildings include the Radcliffe Camera, Oxford (1737-49), a domed rotunda form with echoes of Italian Mannerism. Gibbs was one of the first British architects to produce sculptural monuments (e.g. in Westminster Abbey). His *Book of Architecture* (1728), the first British book devoted to the work of a single architect, included designs for interiors and decorative elements as well as buildings. Together with his *Rules for Drawing the Several Parts of Architecture* (1732), it was highly influential, particularly in the United States, in continuing the popularity of his style.

Gill, Irving (1870-1936). American architect. He trained with Louis Sullivan in Chicago, then opened his own office in San Diego in 1896. His early buildings were influenced by the Shingle Style, but by about 1910 he had developed a remarkably simple, unornamented, geometric style, with flat roofs and plain, whitewashed surfaces softened by exterior planting. Examples include the La Jolla Women's Club (1912-14) and the Dodge House, Los Angeles (1914-16). This radical approach was at that time echoed only in the work of Adolf Loos in Vienna, not being generally adopted in Europe until the 1920s and 1930s. Gill's inspiration was probably Spanish architecture in California. He also favoured the use of reinforced concrete (then a new material) and developed prefabricated construction methods.

Greene & Greene. American architectural partnership formed in 1893 by Charles Greene (1868-1957) and his brother Henry Greene (1870-1954). Trained in carpentry as well as architecture, they were influenced by the Arts and Crafts ideals of John Ruskin and William Morris and by the timber architecture of Japan. They moved to California in 1893 and are best known for their development in the 1900s of the popular California bungalow – typically a low timber house with wide eaves, flat gables, shingle or timber cladding and verandahs (e.g. The Gamble House, Pasadena, 1909). The type was widely imitated, particularly in Australia. They later reverted to a stucco and tile Mediterranean idiom.

Griffin, Walter Burley (1876-1937). American architect. He worked with Frank Lloyd Wright in 1901-5 before setting up his own office with his wife, Marion Mahony Griffin, who produced some of the finest architectural drawings of the period. Griffin became known for a series of houses influenced by the Prairie school, with massive central fireplaces and split-level planning. These became increasingly rugged and cubic in form (e.g. Melson House, Mason City, Iowa, 1912), as distinct from Wright's work. Griffin is best known for his urban plan (1912) for Canberra, the new capital of Australia, which combined Beaux Arts ideas with a sensitivity to the local topography. He also designed some noted buildings in Australia in crystalline, abstract forms.

Gropius, Walter (1883-1969). German architect and designer. He was one of the most influential figures in the European Modern Movement, the theories of which he taught in the United States for 30 years. He was particularly interested in building for society and technology, advocating mass production. His early work included the Fagus Factory, Alfeld (1913), which introduced the glass curtain wall, and the Model Factory at the Deutsche Werkbund Exhibition, Cologne (1914); both were landmarks in the development of Modernism. In 1919-28 he was director of the Bauhaus, which became a focus of the European artistic avant-garde. His rectilinear steel and glass buildings for the Bauhaus at Dessau (1926) are clear statements of the purist International Style. Gropius was also prominent in the international modern architecture forum CIAM (from 1929) and designed prefabricated houses and blocks of flats for public housing projects. In 1934 he left Germany and went first to London, where he was in partnership with Maxwell Fry. He designed furniture for Isokon and built Impington Village College, Cambridgeshire (1936-9), a modern complex in brick, which became a model for later English work. In 1937 Gropius went to the United States and began his teaching career at Harvard, where he was later joined by Marcel Breuer. His own house (1938) at Lincoln, Massachusetts, a prismatic, flat-roofed building executed in timber, was one of the first modern houses in the state. After World War II he established TAC (The Architects' Collaborative) with a group of young architects, where he continued to have a strong influence.

Halfpenny, William (d 1755). English architect. He is best known as a prolific writer of architectural pattern books, which were enormously successful in England and North America. Among them was *Practical Architecture* (1724), one of the first books concerned with the Palladian revival. Others reflected a variety of styles from Baroque to Rococo and Gothic. They included *The Art of Sound Building* (1725); *New Designs for Chinese Temples* (1750), one of the first with Chinese designs; *Twelve Beautiful Designs for Farmhouses* (1750); and *The Country Gentleman's Pocket Companion* (1753), whose landscape settings anticipated the Picturesque.

Haviland, John (1792-1852). English architect, active in the United States. He went to Philadelphia in 1816, where he initially taught. His *Builder's Assistant* (1818-21) illustrated current architectural styles in England and was the first American book to show the Greek orders. Haviland went on to design some fine Greek Revival buildings in Philadelphia (e.g. Pennsylvania Institute, 1823, now Philadelphia College of Art; and the Franklin Institute, 1825, now Atwater Kent Museum). He also designed churches, as well as prisons with radiating panopticon plans, one in the form of a castellated Gothic fortress (the influential Eastern State Penitentiary, Philadelphia, 1825) and others in the form of Egyptian pylon buildings (e.g. Trenton, New Jersey, 1832).

Hope, Thomas (1769-1831). British amateur designer and patron. He was born in Amsterdam of a Scottish family and went on an extended Grand Tour (1787-95) to Europe and the Near East, later making further visits to Europe. In 1795 the family moved to England. Hope began to collect classical sculpture and pottery, and about 1800-04 he remodelled his mansion (destr.) in Duchess Street, London, as a house-museum, which he opened to the public. It had a Greek Room, with Greek Revival details and furniture inspired by designs on ancient pottery, which became influential in Regency design; an Indian Room; and an Egyptian Room, with Egyptian Revival furniture. This work was recorded in his *Household Furniture and Interior Decoration Executed from Designs by Thomas Hope* (1807). Hope wrote several other works on architecture and design. He promoted Greek Revival for urban designs but adopted the Picturesque in remodelling (1818-23) his 18th-century house Deepdene, near Dorking (destr.), which acquired an eclectic mix of elements.

Howard, Ebenezer (1850-1928). English theorist and amateur planner, who developed the principles of the influential garden city movement. His professional life was spent as a stenographer and he became a partner in the firm appointed by Parliament. At the same time, perhaps influenced by utopian writers of the United States where he lived in 1872-7, he was interested in the problems of urban crowding and rural depopulation. This led to his concept of the garden city, described in *Tomorrow: A Peaceful Path to Real Reform* (1898; revised as *Garden Cities of Tomorrow*, 1902) as an independent town of limited size, built as a satellite to a larger city but surrounded by a green belt of farmland, and planned in pleasant "rural" residential areas, with shopping, cultural and recreation facilities. In 1899 he founded the Garden City Association. The most important cities developed from his ideas are Letchworth (from 1903; by Parker & Unwin) and Welwyn Garden City, Hertfordshire (from 1920). His book was influential on planning theory elsewhere in Europe, especially in Germany, where a garden city movement was formed in 1902. Many new towns developed in England after 1945 also reflected his ideas.

Hunt, Richard Morris (1827-95). American architect. An eminent and prolific society architect, in his youth he spent 12 years in Europe (1843-55) and studied at the Ecole des Beaux Arts – the first American to do so. This gave him firsthand knowledge of the French Renaissance Revival, which he helped popularize in the United States. He is known for a series of increasingly opulent mansions for which he adopted a variety of styles, as seen in the Stick Style Griswold House, Newport, Rhode Island (1863); the Neo-classical Marble House, Newport (1892); the Italian Renaissance Revival The Breakers, Newport (1895); and the French

château style Biltmore House, near Asheville, North Carolina (1895), all for the Vanderbilt family. The most important of his commercial buildings in New York was the *New York Tribune* Building (1876; destr.), with a clock-tower and spire that made it the tallest building in the city for some years. He also designed the Beaux Arts entrance wing to the Metropolitan Museum of Art, New York (1894-1902). Hunt helped to establish professional building standards and a proper fee basis for architects; he also helped found the American Institute of Architects in 1857.

Jefferson, Thomas (1743-1826). American lawyer, statesman (President 1801-9) and architect. The author of the Declaration of Independence, he was also an influential architect (self-taught), introducing to the United States a robust Neo-classicism based on ancient Roman architecture and contemporary French Rationalism, which contrasted with the lighter Federal Style. For his own house, Monticello, Virginia (from 1770), he first designed an essentially Palladian building, but later additions transformed it into a largely single-storey classical villa in brick, with a pedimented garden portico and shallow dome. For the Virginia State Capitol, Richmond (1785-99), his design was derived from the ancient Roman Maison Carrée in Nîmes, to which he was introduced while in Paris as American Ambassador (1784-9). The Capitol was the first building in the United States designed in the form of a classical temple and was an important model for American public architecture of the period. Jefferson also influenced the planning of Washington through his knowledge of European cities and classical architecture. His design for the University of Virginia, Charlottesville (1817-26), as a group of separate faculty pavilions around a green, linked by colonnades, was possibly based on the Château of Marly, near Versailles. The Rotunda at the head of the green was based on the Roman Pantheon, halved in scale. Jefferson was an inventive designer, experimenting with geometric room shapes and practical ideas (e.g. for skylights, stairs and water closets).

Johnson, Philip (b 1906). American architect. One of the most prominent figures in 20th-century American architecture, he was, with Henry-Russell Hitchcock, instrumental in first exhibiting in the United States (1932) the buildings of the Modern Movement, including six American examples. They also co-authored the accompanying book, *The International Style: Architecture since 1922*, which coined the term "International Style" for architecture of the early Modern Movement. This he promoted in terms of its aesthetics, without the social context of the European work. He later produced an important exhibition and book (1947) on the work of Mies van der Rohe. The influence of Mies is apparent in Johnson's well-known Glass House, New Canaan, Connecticut (1949), and he worked with Mies on the glass curtain-walled Seagram Building, New York (1958). Thereafter his work has ranged from stripped classical (e.g. New York State Theater, 1964) to a series of large, late modern and Post-Modern office buildings, designed with others (e.g. the geometric, glass-clad Pennzoil Place, Houston, 1976, and the "Chippendale" pedimented AT&T Building, New York, 1983).

Jones, Inigo (1573-1652). English architect. He was immensely influential in introducing to England a rigorous interpretation of classical architecture, including the correct use of the orders. He made various journeys to Europe before 1606 and was initially known as a designer of court masques. In 1613/14 he went with Thomas Howard, 2nd Earl of

Arundel, on a Grand Tour to Italy, where he became one of the first Englishmen to study the buildings of Palladio and ancient Rome. In 1615 Jones became Surveyor of the King's Works, introducing his knowledge of classical and Renaissance architecture in such important and novel works as the Queen's House, Greenwich (1616-18; 1629-38), in the style of an Italian villa, and the Banqueting House, Whitehall (1622), in a Palladian style. He also introduced European urban planning principles at Covent Garden (1630-31), where he planned a piazza bounded by unified houses and arcades, with St Paul's Church at one end. The latter – the first wholly classical church in England – features a Tuscan portico, an original interpretation designed for the Protestant cause. He later remodelled St Paul's Cathedral with a classical exterior derived from Palladio and a huge Corinthian portico (1642; destr.). Jones's buildings were models for the Palladian revival initiated by Lord Burlington in the 18th century and were reproduced in several books (e.g. William Kent's *Designs of Inigo Jones*, 1727, and Isaac Ware's *Designs of Inigo Jones and Others*, 1731).

Kent, William (1685-1748). English painter, architect and designer. A noted and original figure in the early 18th century, he produced Italian Mannerist and Baroque decorative schemes and furniture, Palladian architecture, and early Gothick designs. He was also important in the development of the English landscape garden. Trained as a painter, he spent 10 years in Italy (1709-19). In 1719 he returned to England with Lord Burlington, with whom he produced the influential *Designs of Inigo Jones* (1727). He worked for Burlington as an interior decorator and won many prestigious positions through his influence, notably at Kensington Palace (1721-7), where he produced a unified decorative scheme in the Italian Mannerist style, with antique elements. He also worked at many large country houses in England, first on interior decoration, then architecture and garden design. Among them were Holkham Hall, Chiswick House, Esher Place, Houghton Hall, Rousham, Stowe and Claremont. The marble apsidal entrance hall at Holkham (1735), perhaps designed with Burlington and Thomas Coke, is one of the grandest classical interiors in England, with Ionic columns, a coffered ceiling and great staircase. In 1735 Kent became Master Mason and Deputy Surveyor in the Royal Office of Works, where he designed his most important buildings: the Treasury (1737) and Horse Guards (1748-59), Whitehall, London. These were influenced by the work of Inigo Jones as well as by Italian Renaissance and Baroque architecture. His work was popularized through John Vardy's *Some Designs of Mr Inigo Jones and Mr William Kent* (1744).

La Farge, John (1835-1910). American painter and designer. He became a respected painter of landscapes and still lifes, and he was an early collector of Japanese prints. In the 1870s he turned to the decorative arts. His interior decoration of H. H. Richardson's Trinity Church, Boston (1877), drew on both Renaissance and medieval sources, and integrated other arts, notably sculpture. It was the first such scheme by an established painter and helped to initiate the American Renaissance. Other commissions included murals in public buildings (e.g. St Thomas's Church, New York, 1878; Minnesota State Capitol, 1905; Baltimore Courthouse, 1907). La Farge also produced stained glass, sculpture and mosaic for private clients, mostly in New York and Newport, Rhode Island (e.g. the Vanderbilt family). He is known for inventing opalescent stained glass (1879), which was widely adopted, notably by Louis Comfort Tiffany, and was the United States' principal contribution to Art Nouveau. He also introduced Japanese motifs and floral designs for stained glass.

Lafever, Minard (1798-1854). American architect. Trained as a carpenter, he developed a successful architectural practice in New York, working in various revival styles. He designed several churches, including the Gothic Revival churches of the Saviour (1844; now First Unitarian Church) and Holy Trinity (1847), both Brooklyn, and the Egyptian Revival Whaler's Church, Sag Harbor (1844). He is better known for his builder's manuals, particularly *The Modern Builder's Guide* (1833) and *The Beauties of Modern Architecture* (1835). Based on British sources, notably *The Antiquities of Athens* (1762-1816) by James Stuart and Nicholas Revett, these were highly influential in promoting the Greek Revival style. His last book, *The Architectural Instructor* (1856), showed his eclectic later work, including Gothic and Italianate villas.

Langley, Batty (1696-1751). English architect and writer. He was a prolific and influential writer of architectural pattern books. He first worked as a gardener, becoming an early advocate of natural garden design, which he espoused in such books as *New Principles of Gardening* (1728). In this, as in most of his other publications, he drew heavily on the work of others. Langley was unsuccessful as an architect, but his books on classical architecture, with clear plates and construction details aimed largely at builders and craftsmen, helped instigate a reaction to the prevailing Palladianism of Lord Burlington. He is best known for his Gothic designs in *Ancient Architecture Restored* (1741-2; revised as *Gothic Architecture, Improved by Rules and Proportions*, 1747), which shows designs for both buildings and individual elements, such as chimney-pieces, doors and windows. He also included five "Gothick Orders", an attempt to establish proportional rules for Gothic that was ridiculed by scholarly authors. Langley's Gothic designs were among the first to be published and made available to a wider audience, and they were instrumental in popularizing the Gothic Revival in England and the United States.

Latrobe, Benjamin Henry (1764-1820). English architect, active in the United States. He was one of the best-known exponents of Neo-classicism in the United States. He studied in Germany and worked in England, coming into contact with the latest European Neo-classical fashions (especially the ideas of the French Rationalists and John Soane) before moving to the United States in 1795. The first fully trained architect to work in the United States, he established his reputation with the Bank of Pennsylvania, Philadelphia (1798; destr.), which featured a central domed cubic hall with Ionic porticoes. He also designed waterworks (in Philadelphia and, later, New Orleans) and the first Gothick house in the United States (Sedgeley, Philadelphia, 1799; destr.), with rather superficial details. His most famous surviving projects are the US Capitol, Washington (1803-17), where he altered William Thornton's design and invented a "corn cob capital"; and his Roman Catholic Cathedral, Baltimore (1804-18), with a temple front, shallow dome and heavy Roman classical details. He was close to Thomas Jefferson and advised on the latter's University of Virginia. Many of Latrobe's other works were demolished, but his influence continued through his pupils Robert Mills and William Strickland.

Le Corbusier (1887-1965) [Charles-Edouard Jeanneret]. French architect, painter and designer, of Swiss birth. He was the dominant figure in the Modern Movement from 1920 until his death. After training as a metal engraver, he worked with Auguste Perret in Paris (1908-9) and Peter Behrens in Berlin (1910), then travelled widely in Europe. In 1917 he moved to Paris, joined the artistic avant-garde and took up painting. He also began to edit the radical art journal *L'Esprit Nouveau*. In several essays (some later published as *Vers une architecture*, 1923), he elaborated the theory behind his architecture of this period: omission of all historical precedent; adherence to rational design ("a house is a machine for living in"); industrialization; and the "five points of a new architecture": *piloti* to raise the building off the ground, roof terraces, a free plan, free facade composition, and continuous ribbon windows. This was expressed in a series of crisp, white villas that became icons of the Modern Movement (e.g. Villa Stein, Garches, 1928; Villa Savoye, Poissy, 1930). By the late 1920s Le Corbusier was in the forefront of international Modernist developments, involved with the Weissenhofsiedlung, Stuttgart (1927) and mass-produced housing, entering the major international competitions and promoting highly mechanized urban planning schemes that dominated the international modern architecture forum CIAM in 1933 and after. In 1945 Le Corbusier began to develop a new aesthetic based on the bold expression of raw, board-marked concrete (*béton brut*), which later inspired the Brutalist school in Britain. It was used in the Unité d'Habitation, Marseilles (1945-52), which has two-storey apartments with shopping streets, communal services and a roof garden, the proportions of which were designed according to his Modulor system (1950). He also began to employ an individual approach to design in contrast to his earlier search for utopian, universal prototypes. He produced some poetic buildings, notably the sculptural Notre-Dame-du-Haut, Ronchamp (1950-55); the brick and concrete-vaulted Maisons Jaoul, Neuilly-sur-Seine (1951-5); the cellular, cloistered monastery of Ste Marie-de-la-Tourette, Eveux-sur-l'Arbresle (1955-9); and the Carpenter Center for the Visual Arts, Cambridge, Massachusetts (1963), which brought together many of his lifelong concerns. At Chandigarh, the new capital of the Punjab, he produced dramatic sculptural forms, mostly in reinforced concrete, for the principal government buildings (1951-62) and houses at Ahmedabad (1954-6) featuring his characteristic *brises-soleil*. Le Corbusier was a tireless promoter of his ideas, exhibiting and publishing his work from 1930. He lectured widely and employed many students in his office, who later helped spread his influence around the world.

Loos, Adolf (1870-1933). Austrian architect. Regarded as one of the most important early pioneers of the European Modern Movement, he developed a rational, unornamented architecture a decade before it was widely adopted in Europe. After a three-year visit to the United States (1893-6), he became a strident critic of the luxuriant styles of turn-of-the-century Vienna, advocating a simple, functional approach that rejected superfluous ornament. His early work in Vienna included some elegant interiors (e.g. the Café Museum, 1899; and the American Bar, 1908), in which rich materials such as marble and wood veneers were used in place of ornament. He is best known for the plain Goldman & Salatsch Building (1910; "Looshaus") and some private houses in Vienna: the Steiner House (1910), Horner House (1912) and Scheu House (1913). In these he introduced reinforced concrete, flat roofs, cubic, white forms and free, open plans. Loos's influence was most strongly felt through his writings, notably his famous essay "Ornament and Crime", which was widely circulated. He was also known for his entry to the *Chicago Tribune* tower competition (1922), showing a skyscraper in the form of a giant Doric column. In the early 1920s Loos became Chief Architect to the housing department of Vienna. He also built other influential houses: the Müller House, Prague (1930), was one of the first with a split-level design.

Lubetkin, Berthold (1901-90). British architect, of Russian birth. He designed some of the best-known early Modern buildings in Britain. He studied and worked in Moscow, Berlin and Paris, coming into contact with the European avant-garde and the social ideals of the Modern Movement. In 1931 he moved to London and formed a cooperative practice, Tecton (1932-8), which built the influential Highpoint blocks of flats at Highgate (1936, 1938), Finsbury Health Centre (1938), and structures at London Zoo, including the sculptural Penguin Pool (1934). The sophisticated concrete structures of these buildings gave him an international reputation.

Lutyens, Sir Edwin (1869-1944). English architect. He is best known for his many fine, traditional-style houses. The early ones, influenced by the Arts and Crafts vernacular, were among the best (e.g. Deanery Garden, Sonning, 1899-1902). They were romantic compositions of gables and chimneys, and many had gardens designed by Gertrude Jekyll, for whom Lutyens had built Munstead Wood, Godalming (1896). Later houses featured more eclectic styles (e.g. the classicizing Heathcote, Ilkley, 1906; and the castellated Castle Drogo, Devon, 1910-30). His most important public work was his monumental Beaux Arts plan for New Delhi (1912), the new capital of India, where he built the Viceroy's House (1912-30). He is also known for some impressive war memorials, notably in Whitehall (1920), and at Thiepval (1927-32); and for the neo-Georgian British Embassy, Washington (1928).

McKim, Mead & White. American architectural partnership formed in 1879 by Charles F. McKim (1847-1909), William Mead (1846-1928) and Stanford White (1853-1906). The most prolific and influential firm of its time, it produced grand classical buildings that established the idea of the "American Renaissance" in the United States at a time when the nation was becoming a world power. The firm made its reputation with several houses in Newport, Rhode Island, mostly in a Queen Anne or Shingle style (e.g. Isaac Bell Jr House, 1881-2), with isolated Colonial Georgian details. In the mid-1880s its work became more overtly historicist, adopting French and Italian Renaissance styles (e.g. the Italian Renaissance Villard Houses, New York, 1886), as well as Gothic Revival. The firm's mature style (from the late 1880s) featured a monumental classicism, promoted as the most appropriate style for the United States, which they saw as a product of the 16th-century Renaissance world. They drew on a variety of classical and Renaissance sources, as in the palazzo-style Boston Public Library (1887-95) and the Neo-classical Rhode Island State Capitol, Providence (1891-1903). Their Columbia University, New York (1893-4), was influenced by Thomas Jefferson's University of Virginia. Many artists were employed in the interior decoration of these buildings. McKim, Mead & White's classicism, opposed by the rationalist Chicago school, triumphed at the 1893 World's Columbian Exposition in Chicago. The office was an important training ground for architects, while *A Monograph of the Work of McKim, Mead and White* (1915) was influential in architectural schools for another 25 years.

Mackintosh, Charles Rennie (1868-1928). Scottish architect and designer. The most important figure in the British Art Nouveau movement, he developed a geometric, stylized approach that was influential among Secession artists in Europe. His best-known projects include the Glasgow School of Art (1896-1909), where he introduced continuous glazing on one facade and a remarkable structural interior for the library; fine interiors for four tea-rooms in Glasgow (e.g. Willow Tea-Rooms, 1903); and Hill House, Helensburgh (1904). In the interiors at Hill House the stylized Art Nouveau decoration is reflected in stencilled wall friezes, carpets, stained glass, metalwork and furniture in a fully unified scheme. His designs feature attenuated rectilinear forms contrasted with squares and delicately coloured floral motifs, and white-painted walls contrasted with wood panelling. The plain, rugged exterior of the house reveals influences from Scottish architecture and the work of C. F. A. Voysey. Together with Margaret Macdonald (whom he married in 1900), and her sister and future husband, Mackintosh exhibited graphic designs and paintings in London at the Arts and Crafts Society (1896). This led to an article in *The Studio*, an invitation to design exhibits at the Vienna Secession (1900) and Turin (1902), and a European reputation. In London after 1916 he produced some fine textile designs.

Marot, Daniel (1661-1752). French architect and designer, active in the Netherlands. He was immensely influential in spreading the Baroque style of Louis XIV to the Netherlands and to England. He initially worked in Paris as an engraver. After the revocation of the Edict of Nantes in 1685, he fled to the Netherlands, where his knowledge of contemporary French fashions led to a successful career as a court designer, unifying interiors and architecture in a manner hitherto unseen. His most important designs were produced for the royal summer residence Het Loo (from 1690) and the Binnenhof, The Hague (1698). He also worked at Hampton Court (1694-7) following the accession of William and Mary, introducing his ideas to England. Around 1703 he began to publish new engravings of his designs for buildings, interiors, furniture, metalwork, sculpture and gardens, which form an important record of the Louis XIV style. This led to several architectural works in The Hague, where he built impressive town houses as well as extensions to the Huis ten Bosch.

May, Hugh (1621-84). English architect. Following exile in the Netherlands and France, he returned to England upon the Restoration and received various official appointments. He is known for the introduction of a simple classicism influenced by contemporary Dutch work, often in brick with stone details and Palladian motifs, such as a central pedimented frontispiece with pilasters. His most important surviving work in this style is Eltham Lodge, Kent (1664). His Baroque state rooms at Windsor Castle (1675-84, with Grinling Gibbons and the painter Antonio Verrio; most destr.) were highly influential, as were May's medieval-style exteriors at Windsor, designed to harmonize with the original work. They inspired the castellated style adopted by John Vanbrugh in the 1720s and by later architects of the Picturesque movement.

Mies van der Rohe, Ludwig (1886-1969). American architect and designer, of German birth. One of the three masters of the European Modern Movement (with Le Corbusier and Walter Gropius), his sophisticated glass curtain-wall structures had enormous impact on 20th-century architecture around the world. He was trained in the building crafts and gained an appreciation for classicism through work in Peter Behrens's office. In the 1920s he began to explore the potential of new building materials in his famous visionary drawings for glass skyscrapers and concrete office buildings (1921-3). He directed the Weissenhofsiedlung at Stuttgart (1927), an exhibition of houses and flats by radical modernists that came to be seen as the defining moment in the creation of the International Style. There Mies also showed his cantilevered steel chairs. His German Pavilion at Barcelona (1929), one of the most influential buildings of the 20th century, was a pure statement of his approach, with an open plan, glass and marble-clad walls suspended between floor and roof planes, and finely detailed steel columns. He continued to design furniture (e.g. an S-shaped cantilever chair and his celebrated X-frame Barcelona chair) and was briefly director of the Bauhaus (1930-32). In 1938 he moved to Chicago and began to teach at the Illinois Institute of Technology, where he had an enormous influence on generations of students; he also designed a new campus and buildings. Here and in his famous steel and glass pavilion, the Farnsworth House, Plano, Illinois, (1945-50), he continued to evolve his minimalist style, later refined in some high-rise buildings that epitomized the International Style after 1950 (e.g. Lake Shore Drive Apartments, Chicago, 1951; Seagram Building, New York, 1958, both produced with others). His approach, adopting deliberately flexible open planning and universal construction methods, was adopted by innumerable architects but perhaps most notably by Skidmore, Owings & Merrill. In less skilled hands it was often debased and inappropriately used, and it was heavily criticized by Post-Modernists.

Mills, Robert (1781-1855). American architect. An important exponent of Neo-classicism, he considered himself to be the first native-born and native-trained architect in the United States. Influenced by Thomas Jefferson and Benjamin Henry Latrobe, with whom he worked in 1803-8, he designed some robust circular or octagonal Neo-classical churches based on the Roman Pantheon, with shallow domes and pedimented porticoes (e.g. Monumental Church, Richmond, Virginia, 1817). His reputation was made with the Washington Monument, Baltimore (1813-42), the first monumental column erected in the United States. In South Carolina in 1820-29 he developed fireproof construction using masonry vaulting, as seen in the Palladian-inspired Insane Asylum, Columbia (1827), and County Record Building, Charleston (1827; now South Carolina Historical Society). In 1830 Mills moved to Washington, where his most significant work was the fireproof Federal Treasury, Washington (1836-42), one of the United States' finest Greek Revival office buildings, with a long Ionic colonnade and a modular, vaulted plan reflecting French Rationalism. Mills also designed the Washington Monument in Washington (1833-84); although his scheme was not fully realized, this obelisk remains one of the world's tallest masonry structures and the United States' most famous monument.

Morris, William (1834-96). English designer and writer. He was instrumental in developing the philosophies of the Arts and Crafts Movement. Influenced by the ideas of John Ruskin, he believed that the arts could be used to create a better world for all. He spent a short time training as an architect with the Gothic Revivalist G. E. Street, where he met Philip Webb. He then turned to painting and design. In 1859 he commissioned Webb to build The Red House, Bexleyheath, Kent, a simple, picturesque, vernacular brick building regarded as the first house of the Arts and Crafts Movement. Morris decorated the house with his friends, and in 1861 he established a cooperative design firm, producing stained glass, furniture, tiles and wallpaper. Morris was most skilled as a designer of wallpaper, textiles and, later, carpets, creating marvellous patterns based on natural forms. The firm's products were influential in reviving interest in the decorative arts and interior design among artists and architects. In 1877, in opposition to contemporary restoration techniques, Morris founded the Society for the Protection of Ancient Buildings, which marked the start of the British environmental movement. In the 1880s he began to publish his lectures and essays (e.g. *Hopes and Fears for Art*, 1882). His influence was enormous, as seen in organizations formed in the 1880s (e.g. by C. R. Ashbee). His last endeavour was the foundation of the Kelmscott Press (1891), for which he designed typefaces and book decorations.

Nash, John (1752-1835). English architect. He was the most important architect of the English Picturesque and Regency, influencing English domestic design and helping to change the face of London. His early work included some speculative London houses (1777-82) in stucco, a material that later became widespread in London. In the 1790s and 1800s he was a successful country-house architect, initially (1796-1800) with Humphry Repton, and he developed asymmetrically planned houses to complement the Picturesque landscapes in which they were set. He built both Italianate villas (e.g. Cronkhill, Shropshire, 1802) and castellated mansions (e.g. Luscombe, Devon, 1800). In smaller houses he used rustic *cottage-orné* and thatched forms, as at Blaise Hamlet, Henbury (1811), a model for future housing estates. In 1806 Nash obtained a minor official post that led to his great works in London. He developed Regent's Park with a series of Neo-classical crescents and terraces with palatial stuccoed facades (1811-28) as well as some villas and cottages in Park Village (begun 1825), the whole forming a prototype of the garden suburb. He also planned Regent Street (from 1812) as a grand, processional route from Regent's Park to the residence of the Prince Regent (later George IV), transforming the West End of London. He built All Souls, Langham Place (1825), as a focal point in the plan; and he designed Carlton House Terraces (1826), St James's Park and Trafalgar Square. For the Prince Regent, Nash designed the onion-domed Royal Pavilion, Brighton (1815-22), with Chinese ornament. Less successful was his conversion of Buckingham House (1825-30) into a royal palace, with a triumphal arch at its gate (Marble Arch, moved to Hyde Park in 1851). On the death of George IV (1830), Nash was dismissed and Buckingham Palace completed by others.

Neutra, Richard (1892-1970). American architect, of Austrian birth. An influential exponent of the European Modern Movement in the United States, he was known for his ability to link its machine aesthetic to the California landscape. Like his compatriot Rudolph Schindler, he was influenced by the work of Frank Lloyd Wright as well as by Adolf Loos. He moved to the United States in 1923, worked in Chicago and then in 1924 spent some months with Wright before joining Schindler in Los Angeles. He achieved renown for his Lovell House (Health House) in the Los Angeles hills (1929), a setting that dramatized the rectilinear steel, glass and concrete structure, with terraces overlooking the views. Neutra went on to design schools, apartments and houses, among the finest being his own multiple-level house at Silver Lake (1933; 1964), the Josef von Sternberg House, Los Angeles (1936), and the Kauffman House, Palm Springs (1946), an elegant composition of window, wall and roof planes recalling the work of Mies van der Rohe but brilliantly sited against a mountain backdrop. In his later houses he began to use pitched roofs, timber, brick and rubble stone. In the 1950s Neutra worked on several large commissions with others.

Nicholson, Peter (1765-1844). Scottish architect. Initially trained as a cabinetmaker, he became a successful architect in Glasgow, building several houses and planning the town of Ardrossan. In 1810 he set up practice in London. He is best known for his many publications, on mathematics and perspective as well as architecture. First published were *The New Carpenter's Guide* (1792) and *Principles of Architecture* (1795-8). These and later books were very influential, providing construction details for buildings (e.g. *New Practical Builder and Workman's Companion*, 1823; *Carpenter, Joiner & Builder's Companion*, 1846) and for furniture (*Practical Cabinet-Maker, Upholsterer and Complete Decorator*, 1826-7).

Palladio, Andrea (1508-80). Italian architect. He is renowned as one of the great architects of the High Renaissance, whose buildings achieved an enduring and widespread influence. He trained as a mason in Vicenza, where he came into contact with influential patrons with classical learning who encouraged his study of antiquity. From this he first attempted to derive a contemporary form of villa architecture, combining elements from ancient Roman buildings with influences from the local vernacular. Palladio gradually perfected this ideal in a series of celebrated rural villas, in which a prestigious formal appearance was united with their functional role at the centre of agricultural estates. Most of his mature villas have pedimented temple fronts (some attached, some projecting, some recessed, some in two storeys and some with a giant order) and tripartite elevations. Most are also linked with their surroundings by embracing wings, open arcades and porticoes, or great flights of steps. Famous examples include Villa Barbaro, Maser (1558); Villa Emo, near Treviso (begun c.1559); and the enormously influential Villa Rotonda, near Vicenza (begun 1565/6), with four great porticoes linking it to the landscape. For his urban palazzi in Vicenza, Palladio adopted more formal Renaissance solutions to facade design, often adopting a giant order (e.g. Palazzo Valmarana, 1565-71), but he also experimented with open loggias (Palazzo Chiericati, c.1580). Meanwhile his public reputation was established with his brilliant reconstruction of the loggia surrounding the medieval town hall of Vicenza (Basilica, begun 1548). He also designed important churches in Venice, refining a vocabulary of interlocking pediments (e.g. S Giorgio Maggiore, begun 1566; Il Redentore, begun 1576). The elegance and the clear spatial composition of Palladio's domestic work were considered ideal for aristocratic house and villa design, mediating between the bourgeois and the princely. This was the stimulus for the success of the 18th-century Palladian revival, particularly in England, Ireland and the United States. His theories and work achieved widespread influence through his own *Quattro libri dell'architettura* (1570), first translated into English by James Leoni in 1715, as well as through *Idea dell'architettura universale* (1615) by his follower Vincenzo Scamozzi.

Papworth, J. B. (1775-1847). English architect and designer. A prolific and successful practitioner, he was influential in disseminating the ideas of the Picturesque through his publications. As an architect he designed in a variety of styles and worked on country houses, suburban villas and garden buildings (e.g. at Claremont, 1817). He was also involved in planning suburban estates (e.g. Lansdowne Place, Cheltenham, 1829), and he was known as a pioneer of cast-iron. He contributed designs for cottages and ornamental buildings to Rudolf Ackermann's *Repository of Arts*, which were reprinted as the immensely popular *Rural Residences* (1818) and *Hints on Ornamental Gardening* (1832). He also designed furniture, silver and stained glass.

Parker & Unwin. English architectural partnership formed by Barry Parker (1867-1947) and Raymond Unwin (1863-1940) and active from 1896 to 1914. They were pioneers of modern town planning principles, best known for their influential designs for Letchworth Garden City (from 1904) and Hampstead Garden Suburb, London (from 1905). Their early work was influenced by the Arts and Crafts Movement. In 1901 Unwin became involved with the Garden City Association and was commissioned to build a model housing estate for the Rowntree Company at New Earswick, near York (from 1902). His theories on housing design were published in *Cottage Plans and Common Sense* (1902). In 1903 he was invited by Ebenezer Howard, founder of the garden city movement, to help find a site for the first garden city, which Unwin was subsequently commissioned to plan at Letchworth. Surrounded by farmland, it was designed with tree-lined roads and cottage houses grouped around greens or cul-de-sacs. It was zoned for different uses, including an industrial estate, and was influential on the formulation of the Town Planning Act of 1909. Hampstead Garden Suburb had a wider range of housing types, many designed by Parker & Unwin (e.g. Reynolds Close, 1910-11). Unwin's book *Town Planning in Practice* (1909) became a standard work, and his ideas were highly influential, particularly in Germany. He went on to work for the government in housing and planning. Parker continued to practise, developing Wythenshawe, Manchester, with landscaped roads suitable for cars.

Pugin, A. W. N. (1812-52). English architect and designer. The most influential proponent of the Gothic Revival in England, he was instrumental in its adoption almost universally for Christian church building in the 19th century. His father, the architect A. C. Pugin, was noted for his books devoted to Gothic (e.g. *Specimens of Gothic Architecture*, 1821-3; *Pugin's Gothic Furniture*, 1827). The young Pugin worked on these books and in 1827 was given a commission to design Gothic furniture for Windsor Castle. In 1832 he began to study medieval architecture in Britain and Europe. His dedication to Gothic as the only true and beautiful architecture was confirmed by his conversion to Catholicism (1835), and he gained an early reputation for polemic in *Contrasts* (1836), a comparison of fine medieval buildings with poor 19th-century counterparts. In 1837 he began an independent practice, building several Catholic churches in Early English, Decorated and Perpendicular styles (e.g. St George's Cathedral, Southwark, London, 1848; St Augustine, Ramsgate, 1845-51; and St Giles, Cheadle, 1846). His churches often suffered from funding shortages but were more archaeologically correct than earlier Gothic designs, and he made a point of reintroducing rood screens. He continued to design Gothic furniture and decorative arts, including metalwork, stained glass, wallpaper, carpets and tiles. He is best known for his rich Gothic-inspired interiors and fittings (1844-51) for the new Gothic Revival Houses of Parliament by Charles Barry. Pugin's influence was widely disseminated through his writings, such as *Gothic Furniture in the Style of the 15th Century* (1835); *The Glossary of Ecclesiastical Ornament and Costume* (1844), which was instrumental in reintroducing many objects in church ritual; and *True Principles of Pointed or Christian Architecture* (1841), which showed an understanding of Gothic structure and adopted a protofunctionalist approach to design.

Repton, Humphry (1752-1818). English landscape designer. He was an important exponent of "natural" landscape design, which sought to enhance the character of an existing site. He developed the approach of Capability Brown a generation before by adding gardens (increasingly formal) closer to the house and uniting Picturesque landscape effects to "utility and convenience". In 1796-1800 he was in partnership with John Nash, and they produced some of the first schemes for asymmetrically designed houses complemented by Picturesque siting and landscaping (e.g. Luscombe Castle, Devon, 1800). Repton subsequently worked with his architect-son John Adey Repton, producing a number of important designs in an early Gothic Revival style ("Queen Elizabeth's Gothic"). He also designed suburban villas himself. His most important later schemes were executed at Woburn (1804), Uppark (1810), Sheringham (1812) and Endsleigh (1814). Repton was known for his "Red Books" in which he reported on a site and illustrated his proposals, using overlays to show the site before and after its improvement. His influential ideas and designs were published in such books as *Sketches and Hints on Landscape Gardening* (1795), *Observations on the Theory and Practice of Landscape Gardening* (1803) and *An Enquiry into the Changes of Taste in Landscape Gardening* (1806).

Richardson, Henry Hobson (1838-86). American architect. One of the most original architects of his day, he is known for his creation of the influential "Richardsonian Romanesque" style, which was distinctively American and marked a move away from historicist European styles. This approach first appeared in his Brattle Square Church, Boston (1873), and was perfected in Trinity Church, Boston (1873-7), built in massive, rock-faced stone, with squat, pyramidal proportions and round arches. The building made Richardson's reputation and was widely copied. He went on to adapt the style to a variety of building types, progressively removing historicist detail except for typical deep Syrian arches at the entrances. Notable examples include libraries (e.g. Crane Library, Quincy, 1883), railway stations and the Allegheny County Courthouse and Jail, Pittsburgh, 1888). Most famously, it was also adapted to commercial architecture in the monumental Marshall Field Store, Chicago (1887; destr.), with an internal iron frame and plain, rock-faced masonry facades with huge arches. This building had a particular influence on the Chicago school and is considered an important step in the development of rational modernism. Richardson was also known for his Shingle Style houses, where he used shingles to clad the entire exterior and centred plans around large living halls (e.g. Stoughton House, Cambridge, Massachusetts, 1883).

Ruskin John (1819-1900). English painter and writer. He was one of the most important art critics of the 19th century, influencing both the Gothic Revival and the later Arts and Crafts Movement. A prolific writer on many subjects, particularly painting, he attempted in his architectural writings to derive principles for design and to establish the pre-eminence of Gothic. An important early work, *The Seven Lamps of Architecture* (1849), established the principles of Sacrifice (to the finest and most beautiful works), Truth (to materials and construction), Power (of composition), Beauty (inspired by Nature), Life (inspired by hand manufacture), Memory (built for longevity) and Obedience (to a list of approved Romanesque or Gothic styles). *The Stones of Venice* (1851-3), a detailed study of the architecture of Venice, was influential in popularizing Venetian Gothic details and polychrome brickwork. It also contained a widely read chapter on the value of hand craftsmanship, which helped establish much of the theory later espoused by William Morris and the Arts and Crafts Movement.

Schindler, Rudolph (1887-1953). American architect, of Austrian birth. One of the pioneers of Modernism in the United States, he was influenced by Adolf Loos. In 1914 he moved to Chicago, joining Frank Lloyd Wright's office in 1916. He opened his own office in Los Angeles in 1921 and began to design revolutionary houses that were among the earliest American buildings in the International Style. Among the best known are the Schindler House, Hollywood (1922), with an innovative concrete tilt-up slab construction and a series of terraces extending the living areas of the house; and the Lovell Beach House, Newport Beach (1925-6), a dramatic structural composition of concrete frames and wall planes, with complex interior spaces. He worked for a short time with Richard Neutra, a fellow expatriate, then went on to develop his style in a series of houses, many designed for splendid hilltop sites (e.g. Fitzpatrick House, Hollywood, 1936). His work was usually distinguished by complex structural expression, often using timber cladding.

Shaw, R. Norman (1831-1912). British architect. One of the most prolific and successful architects of the later 19th century, he produced influential buildings in a variety of styles, notably Queen Anne Revival, that helped to break the dominance of High Victorian historicism. He worked for G. E. Street (1859-62) and began as a committed medievalist, designing strict Gothic Revival churches. For domestic work he and his close friend W. E. Nesfield developed the picturesque Old English style (e.g. Cragside, Northumberland, 1869-85, where he designed furniture and interiors). For London buildings he adopted the Queen Anne Revival, using red brick, white stone details and Dutch gables (e.g. Lowther Lodge, Kensington, 1875; now Royal Geographical Society). Both Queen Anne and Old English houses were built at Bedford Park, London's first garden suburb (1877-80), while New Scotland Yard, London (1890), and the White Star Line Offices, Liverpool (1898), reflect Scottish castles. Later work was more classicizing (e.g. the Baroque Revival Piccadilly Hotel, 1905-8). Shaw used iron frames to achieve independent planning or cantilevered facades, and Portland House, London (1908), his last building, introduced reinforced-concrete. Each of his different styles found a multitude of followers and strongly influenced the Arts and Crafts Movement.

Soane, Sir John (1753-1837). English architect. Regarded as Britain's most original architect, he evolved an individual, abstract form of Neo-classicism that was reduced to geometric forms and attentuated details. The son of a bricklayer, he trained with George Dance and worked for Henry Holland in 1772-7 before travelling to Italy on the Royal Academy scholarship. In his early career he built some small classical houses but soon began to introduce innovative interiors with top-lit umbrella domes (e.g. at Wimpole Hall, Cambridgeshire, 1791). His best-known works included the Bank of England (1788-1823; destr.), which included the massive, cruciform Stock Office, with plain barrel vaults and groin vaults, top-lit through a shallow central dome and lunettes. Similar ideas were also explored at Soane's finest country houses, Tyringham, Buckinghamshire (1793-7; altered), and his own house, Pitzhanger, Ealing (1800-04). His London house at 13 Lincoln's Inn Fields (1812-24) was, like Thomas Hope's, designed as a house-museum to contain his collection of casts, fragments, urns, sculpture, paintings and books. It has an interlocking plan of rooms with contrasting lighting effects. For his famous Dulwich College Picture Gallery, London (1811-14), Soane designed a primitivist composition in plain brick, with receding planes, simple

arches and minimal, abstract ornament. His style was criticized by academic architects of the later 19th century but received renewed recognition in the 20th.

Street, G. E. (1824-81). English architect. He was a prominent Gothic Revivalist in the more eclectic period following A. W. N. Pugin. In 1844-9 he worked for George Gilbert Scott I, then set up his own office and began a largely ecclesiastical practice. In 1850 he became Diocesan Architect in Oxford (later also in York, Winchester and Ripon) and elaborated his theories on the development of church design in *The Ecclesiologist* (1850-53). At the same time he began to travel regularly on the Continent, publishing *Brick and Marble in the Middle Ages* (1855) on North Italian architecture and *Some Account of Gothic Architecture in Spain* (1865). The former helped popularize polychromatic brickwork, which Street used in his first important work in London, St James the Less, Westminster (1859-61). He also designed church furnishings, stained glass, metalwork, woodwork and tile pavements. His secular work included some houses in a variety of styles (e.g. the Old English Holmdale, Holmbury St Mary, 1876). He remains best known for his Royal Courts of Justice, London (1868-82), where he used 13th-century Gothic forms for an important secular building, combined in a newly picturesque composition. He had a considerable influence on younger architects, many of whom worked in his office (e.g. Philip Webb, R. Norman Shaw and William Morris).

Strickland, William (1788-1854). American architect. A pupil of Benjamin Henry Latrobe, he became an influential proponent of the Greek Revival in American public architecture. He first achieved renown with his Second Bank of the United States, Philadelphia (1818-24), which has two Greek Doric porticoes modelled on the Parthenon. The purest Greek Revival building in the United States at the time, it was highly influential. In 1825 Strickland visited Britain to study British transport systems (published as *Reports on Canals, Railways, Roads, and Other Subjects*, 1826); this helped introduce the latest British technology to the United States. British Neo-classical influences can be seen in buildings he designed in Philadelphia in the next few years, including the Naval Asylum (1826-33), with cast-iron balcony columns; and the Philadelphia Merchants' Exchange (1832-4), with a semicircular colonnaded portico topped by a tall lantern. The Tennessee State Capitol, Nashville (1844-59), built on an elevated site, has Ionic porches on all sides and a tall lantern on the roof. He also designed the Egyptian Revival First Presbyterian Church, Nashville (1851).

Sullivan, Louis H. (1856-1924). American architect and designer. A leading influence in the Chicago school in the 1890s, he was at the forefront of the search for a new rational architecture, which he articulated with delicate, organic ornament. He worked with the engineer Dankmar Adler in Chicago from 1879 to 1895. Their first important work, the Auditorium Building (1889), Chicago, was strongly influenced by Richardsonian Romanesque. In their first steel-framed structure, the Wainwright Building, St Louis (1890-91), Sullivan introduced his well-known theory of facade design based on a classical order: a vertical "shaft" of identical office floors between a "base" for public areas and an "entablature" for plant rooms, with ornament on spandrels, friezes and cornices. This approach was refined in the Guaranty Building, Buffalo (1894-5). In Sullivan's last commercial structure, the lower-rise Carson, Pirie & Scott Store, Chicago (1899-1901), the facade was determined by the structural grid while the decoration was reduced to a minimum. Sullivan published several expressive writings on his architectural theories (e.g. *Kindergarten Chats*, 1902-3) and, later, his *System of Architectural Ornament* (1924). He was highly influential among the younger architects (including Frank Lloyd Wright) who comprised the Chicago school and led the opposition to the Beaux Arts styles. Sullivan's late works included several massive, ornamented bank buildings in small Midwestern towns, and the Bradley House, Madison (1909).

Swan, Abraham (fl 1745-68). English architect. He trained as a carpenter and joiner but remains known for his influential publications illustrating designs for Palladian buildings and Rococo interiors. Among them were *The British Architect: Or the Builder's Treasury of Staircases* (1745), a 1775 edition of which was the first architectural book printed in North America; *A Collection of Designs in Architecture* (1757); *One Hundred and Fifty New Designs for Chimney Pieces* (1758); and *The Carpenter's Complete Instructor in Several Hundred Designs* (1768). These were very successful in North America, with several in circulation before 1776.

Tiffany, Louis Comfort (1848-1933). American designer and painter. The son of Charles Louis Tiffany, founder of the famous New York jewellers, Tiffany trained as a painter in the United States and Paris. In the late 1870s he turned to the decorative arts. He experimented with stained glass techniques, designing geometric patterns and landscape scenes in brilliant colours and rippling effects. He established a successful design firm (1879-83), which created several eclectic interior schemes (e.g. at the White House, Washington, 1883) influenced by the British Arts and Crafts and Aesthetic movements. In 1885 he set up Tiffany Glass, producing flowing Art Nouveau designs (e.g. table lamps) and inventing new iridescent glass and a rough "Lava" glass. Tiffany exhibited at Samuel Bing's shop in Paris and at the exhibitions in Chicago (1893) and Paris (1900). He also designed some houses, including the eclectic Laurelton Hall, Oyster Bay (1902-4; destr.), where he set up an artistic foundation.

Town, Ithiel (1784-1844). American architect. He was one of the pioneers in the Greek Revival in the United States. His early work included the Trinity Church, New Haven (1814), in a Gothick style. In 1816 he became involved with bridge construction, inventing a successful lattice bridge truss (1820). His later buildings were resolutely Greek Revival, seen in houses (e.g. Bowers House, Northampton, 1826) and the Connecticut State Capitol, New Haven (1827-31; destr.), in pseudo-peripteral Doric style. After a European tour, when he began his extensive collection of books and prints, he went into partnership (1829-35) with Alexander Jackson Davis, with whom he created some of the grandest Greek Revival buildings in the United States: the Indiana State Capitol, Indianapolis (1831-5; destr.), where a Greek Doric temple form was topped by a monumental Roman dome; North Carolina State Capitol, Raleigh; New York Customs House (both 1833-42); the Ionic French Church du Saint Esprit, New York (1831-4); and many smaller buildings. Town was later involved with further bridge projects, but he worked with Davis on competition plans for the Illinois State Capitol in 1837 and on revisions to plans for the Ohio State Capitol, Columbus (1839).

Venturi, Robert (b 1925). American architect and designer. He is a pioneer of Post-Modernism, in which he has sought alternatives to the uniformity of the International Style. This was first explored in the Vanna Venturi House, Chestnut Hill,

Pennsylvania (1962; with John Rauch), which incorporates an eclectic mix of elements, including a split-pediment gable inspired by the Italian Baroque, and ribbon windows and a spatial plan inspired by Le Corbusier. In his influential books *Complexity and Contradiction in Architecture* (1966) and *Learning from Las Vegas* (1972; with others) he promoted an ambiguous, symbolic stylistic vocabulary embracing "memory" and the ordinary instead of the utopian visions of Modernism. This can be seen in his fire stations ("decorated sheds") at Columbus, Indiana (1966) and New Haven (1974). Other work reinterpreted the Shingle Style in exaggerated form (e.g. Trubeck and Wislocki houses, Nantucket Island, 1970). The classical tradition was used for such public buildings as the National Gallery extension, London (1987-91), "deformed" by the impact of modern culture. With Rauch and his wife Denise Scott Brown, Venturi also works on exhibition and product design, producing furniture, textiles and homewares.

Voysey, C. F. A. (1857-1941). English architect and designer. He was one of the most influential figures in the domestic revival in the later English Arts and Crafts Movement, producing houses that have been seen as precursors to Modernism. His early work included wallpaper and textile patterns (1883), which he continued to design all his life. From 1888 he produced a series of modest country houses combining functionalism, economy, free, convenient planning and harmony with the surroundings. In contrast to the picturesque compositions of the earlier Queen Anne Revival, his houses had a simple, abstract, astylar approach, with basically rectangular volumes, pitched roofs and horizontally grouped windows. They were often boldly modelled with gables, buttresses and chimneys, with their plain surfaces rendered in pebbledash, as at Perrycroft, near Malvern (1893), and the Sturgis House, Hog's Back, near Guildford (1896). The latter, a long, low building, has a large, asymmetrical gable at one end and long bands of windows. His best-known house is The Orchard, Chorleywood (1899-1900), with twin gables. Voysey designed all the interior fittings, furniture, fireplaces, metalwork, wallpaper and textiles. His furniture was plainer and lighter than most Arts and Crafts designs, and he made several designs for machine production. Voysey's houses, which have been compared to contemporary work by Frank Lloyd Wright, inspired countless house builders in the 1920s and 1930s, and his approach was reflected in the work of Parker & Unwin.

Walpole, Horace (1717-97). English amateur architect and writer. He is principally known for his role in promoting the Gothic Revival at his house Strawberry Hill, Twickenham, London (1753-76), which he bought in 1749. In 1750, with his friends the amateur architects John Chute and Richard Bentley, he formed a "Committe on Taste" to help him in its remodelling. Professional architects, notably Robert Adam and James Essex, were also later involved, but Walpole selected the designs, borrowing extensively from medieval cathedrals as well as from architectural pattern books. The first (eastern) part of the house, was designed with classicizing Gothick elevations. Later work included a round castellated tower at the south-west corner and a freely planned western extension. The use of historical precedent was extended to the design of interior fittings, such as chimney-pieces, screens, doors, furniture and wallpaper. Strawberry Hill was the first principal monument of the Gothic Revival and was popularized through *A Description of the Villa of Mr Horace Walpole at Strawberry Hill* (1774, 1784) and Walpole's Gothic novel *The Castle of Otranto* (1765).

Its antiquarian approach was a model for the later Gothic Revival, and the asymmetrical composition was a model for the Picturesque movement.

Walter, Thomas Ustick (1804-87). American architect. He was one of the leading architects in the middle of the 19th century. He initially trained as a bricklayer with his father, who built William Strickland's Greek Revival Second Bank, Philadelphia. He set up on his own in 1831 and was immediately successful, building the fine Greek Revival Girard College for Orphans, Philadelphia (1833-48). This gave him a national reputation and led to a large number of designs for simple, monumental buildings mostly based on the Greek temple form. In 1851 he was appointed to design extensions to the Capitol, Washington, where he built a large new building with Greek Revival colonnades, porticoes and ornament. As a focus to the complex he added a huge dome to the original Capitol building; the dome is Baroque in silhouette, supported on a tall, colonnaded drum, and was built in cast iron. Completed at the end of the Civil War, it became a symbol of national unity and was much imitated. It also acted as a stimulus to the developing iron industry.

Webb, Philip (1831-1915). English architect and designer. Together with R. Norman Shaw, he was one of the most influential architects of the 19th-century English domestic revival, turning away from the High Victorian historicist styles in search of the "absence of style". While working in the office of the Gothic Revivalist G. E. Street in 1854-9 he met William Morris, his lifelong friend, who commissioned him to build The Red House, Bexleyheath (1859-61). This is generally considered to be the first house of the Arts and Crafts Movement, in which Webb introduced a local red-brick traditional vernacular that he considered most appropriate to the English climate, the local environment and current building practices. The picturesque composition, emphasized by deep porches and steep roofs, was determined by the arrangement of the rooms. Webb subsequently became involved in the cooperative Morris set up to produce decorative arts, for which he designed fireplaces, glass, metalwork and influential Gothic-style furniture. Some of Webb's later houses were more symmetrical, with gables and tall chimneys, and some were designed as fortified houses (e.g. Standen, East Grinstead, 1891-4). His few non-domestic works included the Bell Brothers' office building, Middlesbrough (1891), for which he adopted the Queen Anne Revival, with curved parapets. Webb was also an early conservationist, working with Morris's Society for the Protection of Ancient Buildings.

Wren, Sir Christopher (1632-1723). English architect. One of the greatest of all English architects, he designed some of the most important and influential buildings of the English Baroque. Until after his 30th year he was involved in scientific studies, becoming adept in geometry and being appointed Professor of Astronomy in London (1657) and Oxford (1661). His skill at mathematics and scientific invention may have led to his involvement in architecture as a gifted amateur, designing the Sheldonian Theatre, Oxford, and Pembroke College Chapel, Cambridge (both 1663). In 1665-6 he visited Paris and studied classical and Baroque buildings. This experience served him well after the Great Fire of London (1666), when he became Commissioner for Rebuilding and then Surveyor of the King's Works (1669). He was involved in the design of 51 new parish churches, in which he introduced a classical approach that had almost no precedent in England (e.g. St Stephen, Walbrook, 1672-87). He also invented classical steeples (e.g. St Mary-le-Bow, Cheapside, 1670-77). His masterpiece, St Paul's Cathedral (1675-1709), is a scholarly essay in Italian Baroque classicism, dominated by a great, innovative hemispherical dome. Wren's important royal works introduced a simple Dutch-inspired classicism in brick and stone at the Royal Hospital, Chelsea (1682-9); a monumental French classicism in brick and stone at Hampton Court Palace (1689-1701); and a dramatic Baroque composition with perspective effects at the Royal Naval Hospital, Greenwich (1695-1735; completed by others). Wren also built other important works at Cambridge and Oxford (e.g. the upper part of Tom Tower, Christ Church, 1681-2, in which he adopted a classicizing Gothic).

Wright, Frank Lloyd (1869-1959). American architect and designer. He was one of the great masters of the 20th century and remains widely admired, but he worked in a highly individual manner, consistently evolving original solutions that had relatively little influence on mainstream architectural currents. After working for Louis Sullivan in Chicago (1888-93), he began to develop an increasingly abstract approach to design, which culminated in his first innovative buildings, the Larkin Office Building, Buffalo (1903-6; destr.), Unity Temple, Oak Park, Illinois (1905-8), and his famous Prairie houses of 1901-13 (e.g. Willitts House, Highland Park, Illinois, 1902; Robie House, Chicago, 1908-10). These houses introduced asymmetrical plans extending out into garden terraces but anchored by a massive fireplace; horizontal lines were emphasised by widely overhanging roofs, bands of windows and projecting bases. A more decorative approach was heralded in Midway Gardens, Chicago (1913; destr.), and the Imperial Hotel, Tokyo (1916-22; destr.), where he used prismatic surface decoration. This approach continued in the 1920s in some cubic, concrete-block houses, where textile-like patterns were cast into the blocks (e.g. Millard House, Pasadena, California, 1923). In 1935 Wright began another stage in his career with Fallingwater, near Pittsburgh, Pennsylvania (1935), a dramatic, modernist composition of stone walls and concrete terraces cantilevered over a waterfall. He went on to develop the plain, rectilinear Usonian house as a simple low-cost version of the Prairie house, eventually building more than 100. In his non-residential architecture he developed an increasingly geometric approach, using circular forms in the Johnson Wax buildings, Racine, Wisconsin (1938, 1944-50), and in the spiral Guggenheim Museum, New York (1943, 1959). He also used triangular grids, and floors cantilevered from a central spine (e.g. Harold Price Tower, Bartlesville, Oklahoma, 1956). For many of his buildings Wright designed the furniture and fittings, from geometrical stained glass, complex bookcases and upholstered settles to metal office furniture and filing cabinets. His work was first extensively published in 1910 in Berlin, and it was admired by many architects of the emerging Modern Movement. He had a greater influence over pupils at the Taliesin teaching communities he established, initially at Spring Green, Wisconsin (1932), and later also near Phoenix, Arizona (Taliesin West, 1938). He lectured widely in the 1930s, publishing some of his lectures as *Modern Architecture* (1931); other books included *The Disappearing City* (1932), *The Future of Architecture* (1953) and *The Natural House* (1954).

GLOSSARY

abacus: in classical architecture, the flat slab topping a capital.

acanthus: a carved ornament of conventionalized, serrated leaves, used on Corinthian and Composite columns and mouldings.

achievement: in heraldry, the complete display of a coat-of-arms, with shield, helmet, crest and motto.

acroterion: an ornamental cornerpiece or cresting.

Adamesque: in the Neo-classical style pioneered in Britain by the Adam brothers in the second half of the 18th century.

adobe: unbaked brick, dried by the sun, as used for house-building in the south-western United States.

aedicule: literally, a "little house", used to frame a niche or door or window opening, usually created by two columns or pilasters with a lintel or pediment above.

Anaglypta: a compressed lightweight moulded wallpaper, a less expensive version of Lincrusta.

andiron: see **firedog**

anthemion: a classical ornament featuring a repeating pattern of honeysuckle flowers and foliage.

arcade: a range of arches supported on piers or columns.

architrave: the moulded frame around a door or window opening; in classical architecture, the lowest member of an entablature.

area: an enclosed outdoor space below ground level that brings light and ventilation to an inner part of a building such as a basement.

ashlar: squared-off blocks of stone used in building.

astragal: a semi-circular moulding often shaped like a series of beads or an alternating series of beads and reeds. Also used as a synonym for glazing bar.

balconette: a small window balcony often fitted with flowerpot holders.

balloon framing: a simple method of timber-framed construction, common in the United States.

baluster: a short, usually turned post; a banister.

balustrade: a series of balusters supporting a rail or coping.

bargeboard: A wide, flat board which seals the space below the roof, between the tiles and the wall on a gable end. Bargeboards often have decorative carving or pierced decoration. Also called a vergeboard.

barrel-and-groin vaulting: a vault formed by two identical tunnel-shaped vaults intersecting in the middle; also called tunnel-and-groin vaulting.

barrel vault: a straight, continuous arched vault or ceiling in tunnel form, either semi-circular or semi-elliptical in profile.

baseboard: see **skirting board**

batten door: a door made from vertical boards joined together with two or more horizontal boards nailed on to their back sides.

bay window: a projection with a window on a house facade. It may be curved (bow window) or angular (canted) in plan. See also **oriel**.

beaded moulding: a small curved moulding decorated by a series of beads.

blind arch: an arch attached to wall or other surface, for decoration.

boiserie: wood panelling decorated with carvings in shallow relief.

bolection moulding: a moulding covering the uneven joint made by two members of different sizes, especially popular for fielded panelling in the late 17th and 18th centuries.

boss: a projecting ball, knob or similar ornament, often carved, that is found at the intersection of ribs in a vault or ceiling.

boxwinder: a staircase built into the space next to the chimney flue and hidden behind a door in the fireplace wall; it was common in small, fine houses in the United States in the 18th and early 19th centuries.

breakfront: having a protruding central section.

bressumer: a large horizontal beam that spans a fireplace or other opening; also, the main horizontal rail in a timber-framed house.

Betty lamp: an American boat-shaped lamp, fuelled by oil.

broken pediment: a pediment with a gap in the crown, sometimes filled with an urn or other motif. A broken-bed pediment has a gap in the base.

Brussels carpet: a flat-weave carpet with a looped, uncut pile.

cames: cast lead strips, usually of "H" section and soldered into place, used to fix small panes of glass in windows.

cantilever: a beam or structure projecting horizontally beyond its support, supported by leverage, by the weight of the structure on its enclosed end.

capital: the head or top part of a column or pilaster.

carreaux d'octagones: a floor pattern in which small black diamonds are laid at the intersections of slabs of lighter-coloured stone.

cartouche: a panel or tablet in round or oval form, often used for an inscription or coat of arms.

caryatid: a human figure, usually female, supporting an entablature. Male figures were termed atlantes.

casement: a window frame hinged on one side so that it swings out or in to open.

castellation: a short wall topped with alternating indentations and raised portions; also called a battlement.

cavetto: a concave moulding, of approximately quarter-circle section, typically used in ceiling cornices.

chair rail: a wall moulding that tops the dado and prevents chairs pushed against the wall from damaging the surface; also called a dado rail.

chamfer: the surface created by cutting off the corner of a square block of wood, stone, etc, usually at a 45° angle.

cheeks: the sloping sides of a fireplace opening.

chimney breast: the stone, brick or cement structure that projects into a room and contains the fireplace flue.

chimneypiece: a fireplace surround and its overmantel.

Chinoiserie: a European interpretation of Chinese art, popular from the late 17th to the 19th century.

chintz: a printed cotton with a glazed finish.

churrigueresque: a Spanish and Mexican decorative style of the early and mid-18th century characterized by lavish surface ornamentation.

clapboarding: the overlapping wedge-shaped boards forming the external covering of a timber-framed structure.

closed-string: the term applied to a staircase whose profile of treads and risers is covered at the side by a string, or sloping member which supports the balustrade.

Coade stone: an ornamental artificial stone manufactured by the company founded by Eleanor Coade in England during the late 18th and early 19th centuries, and used for a wide variety of urns, statues and architectural ornaments.

cob: a building material, consisting of clay mixed with chopped straw; British.

coffered ceiling: a ceiling in which the beams and cross-beams leave a regular pattern of square or multi-sided sunken panels, or coffers, each of which is often decorated with moulded, carved or painted decoration.

colonnade: a range of columns supporting either arches or a straight entablature.

column: a vertical member, circular in section, and normally with a gentle taper (entasis). In classical architecture, it is composed of a base, shaft and capital.

colza lamp: a lamp with a double cylinder that burns rapeseed, or colza, oil or another vegetable or animal oil; popular in the early 19th century.

Composite: one of the classical Orders

of architecture. The capitals of the columns combine Corinthian acanthus leaves with Ionic volutes (scrolls).

console: a decorative scroll-shaped bracket.

composition: an amalgam made from paper or wood pulp, with whiting and glue. Used for applied decoration.

console table: a side table supported against a wall only by consoles; many are elaborately carved and gilded and have marble tops.

coping: a cap or covering on top of a wall.

corbel: a projecting stone or timber block, often carved, supporting a horizontal member such as a beam.

Corinthian: the latest and most ornate of the classical Orders of architecture. The column is slender, and usually fluted, the capital elaborately carved with acanthus leaves.

cornice: a projecting moulding located where the ceiling or roof and wall meet; in classical architecture, the projecting top of an entablature.

cottage orné: a self-consciously rustic dwelling, often thatched.

cove: a large concave moulding between wall and ceiling.

coved ceiling: a ceiling that meets the walls at a large concave moulding, or cove.

cresset: a metal cup or basket, on a pole or hanging down, filled with a flammable substance which is burned as a source of light.

cresting: a decorative top border on a screen, wall or roof.

crocket: a decorative leaf carving jutting out at regular intervals on the sloped edges of gables, spires and canopies in Gothic architecture.

crown glass: an early form of window glass, cut from blown discs.

crown moulding: an alternative term for cornice.

cruck: one of a pair of large curved structural timbers, forming the end-walls of some timber-framed houses.

crumb cloth: a cloth temporarily laid over a floor or carpet to catch spills and crumbs.

cupola: a dome, usually small, topping a roof or turret.

curb: the fixed framework that encloses a raised fireplace hearth.

curtail step: the bottommost step in a flight, with a curved end to the tread.

cusps: the projecting points formed where foils meet in Gothic tracery.

cyma: a double-curved profile, convex above and concave below, or vice versa.

dado: the lower wall surface, from the chair rail down to the skirting board/baseboard.

dado rail: see **chair rail**.

deal: wood planking; also a soft wood, usually fir or pine.

dentil: one of a series of small blocks used to form an ornamental row, used primarily in Corinthian, Ionic and Composite mouldings; the collective term is dentillations, or a dentillated cornice.

diaperwork: an overall pattern of small repeated motifs, usually of diagonal, lozenge form.

distemper: water-based paint.

dog grate: a freestanding basket grate, for a fireplace.

dog-leg stair: two flights of stairs parallel to each other with a half-landing in between.

doorcase: the wooden, stone or brick framework around a hinged door.

Doric: the earliest and plainest of the classical Orders. Doric columns usually have no base; the shaft is thick and broadly fluted, the capital spare and unornamented.

dormer: a roofed projection set into the slope of a roof, usually containing a window.

drab: a light greyish-brown or greenish-brown colour, popular for Georgian paintwork.

drugget: a sturdy fabric floor covering, used to protect boards or a better carpet from wear.

eaves: that part of a sloping roof which overhangs the wall.

eaves cornice: a decorative wooden cornice popular in the late 17th and early 18th century.

ebonized: wood stained and polished black to simulate ebony.

echinus: a moulding similar to an ovolo, beneath the abacus of a Doric capital.

egg-and-dart moulding: a decorative moulding carved with a series of alternating rounded ovals and arrowheads.

electrolier: an electric chandelier or pendant light.

elevation: one of the external faces of a building; also, an architect's drawing of a facade, set out to scale.

embrasure: a door, window or similar opening whose sides are slanted so that the inside is wider than the outside.

encaustic tiles: earthenware tiles patterned with inlays of coloured clay slips.

engaged column: a column or half-column attached to a wall.

English bond: a form of brickwork, in which courses of headers alternate with courses of stretchers.

entablature: in classical architecture, the top of an Order, made up of an architrave, frieze and cornice.

escutcheon: a metal plate around a keyhole.

faïence: tin-glazed earthenware.

fanlight: a window above a door, usually semi-circular, with glazing bars radiating out like a fan. Also termed a transom window in the United States.

fascia: a plain horizontal band in an entablature.

fender: a screen or guard in front of a fireplace to prevent hot coals from damaging the surrounding floor or carpet.

fenestration: the arrangement of windows in a building.

festoon: see **swag**.

field: the upper part of a wall, between the frieze or cornice and the dado.

fielded panel: a panel with a plain raised centre.

fillet: a flat, square moulding between other bands of moulding; also, the narrow surface between flutings in the shaft of a column.

finial: an ornament on top of a spire, pinnacle, gable, etc.

fireback: a thick iron plate placed at the back of a hearth to protect the wall and reflect heat into the room.

firedog: one of a pair of supports for logs in a fireplace; also called andiron.

fire irons: fireplace tools, usually a shovel, poker and tongs.

Flemish bond: a form of brickwork in which, on each course, headers and stretchers alternate.

flight: a series of stairs not interrupted by a landing.

floorcloth: canvas sheeting painted to look like a more expensive floor covering such as a carpet, parquet or tile, and heavily varnished.

fluting: shallow vertical grooves on the shaft of a column.

foil: a lobe or leaf-shaped curve formed between cusps inside an arch or circle.

foliate: decorated with carved leaves.

forecourt: a court or courtyard at the front of a building.

French doors: a pair of casement windows that reach to the floor and are hinged on the outer edges so that they open in the middle.

French windows: see French doors.

fret: a band of horizontal and vertical lines forming a geometrical pattern, such as the key or meander pattern.

frieze: the middle section of an entablature; a panel below the upper moulding or cornice of a wall.

gable: that part of the wall immediately under the end of a pitched roof, cut into a triangular shape by the sloping sides of the roof.

gallery: a mezzanine supported over the primary interior space of a building; also, a long room used originally for outdoor exercise and later for the display of pictures.

gambrel roof: a roof with a double pitch, resembling a mansard roof.

gasolier: a gas-burning chandelier.

Gibbs surround: a rusticated door or window surround with alternating large and small blocks of stone; named after the British architect James Gibbs (1682–1754).

girandole: a branched candleholder with a back-plate fixed to a wall or overmantel.

glazing bars: the bars, usually of wood, that hold panes of window glass in place. Also termed astragals.

gougework: an ornamental woodwork pattern made with a rounded chisel.

grate: a metal open basket in which coal or wood is burned in a fireplace.

Greek key pattern: a geometrical decoration made of continuous right-angled lines; also called Greek meander.

Greek meander see **Greek key pattern**.

groin: the ridge formed where vaulted surfaces intersect.

guilloche: decoration of interlaced bands, forming a pattern of circles or loops.

guttae: small drop-like projections usually carved beneath the triglyphs on Doric architraves.

half-landing: a landing half-way up a flight of stairs.

half-lap joint: the joint between two pieces of wood that have been halved together, resulting in a flat surface.

half timbering: a construction method in which vertical and horizontal timbers make up the frame of the wall, which is then filled in with lath and plaster (nogging), sticks and mud or clay (wattle and daub), stone, or brick.

header: a brick laid so that only its short face is visible.

hearth: the floor of a fireplace, usually extending out into the room.

herm: a head or bust on a rectangular pillar.

hipped roof: a roof with four sloped sides.

hob: a ledge on the back or side of a fireplace or grate for warming a pot or kettle.

hob grate: a cast-iron grate in which the fire basket is supported off the ground, between two flat hobs. The flat front is usually cast with shallowed ornament or reeding. Termed a Bath stove in the United States.

hoodmould: a projecting moulding above a door, window or other opening to protect it from rain; also called a drip mould or label.

impost: the block set into a wall or above a column, from which an arch springs.

incised: deeply engraved or carved.

inglenook: a recessed space beside a fireplace, usually housing a bench.

ingrain carpet: an inexpensive pileless carpet. Also known as a Scotch or Kidderminster carpet.

Ionic: one of the classical Orders of architecture, characterized by fluted columns and prominent volutes on the capitals.

Italian moulding: a heavy, wide moulding that usually surrounds a fireplace; a type of bolection moulding.

jamb: the straight vertical side of a doorway, arch or window.

japanned: painted and varnished in imitation of Oriental lacquer work.

jettied: a term describing a timber-framed building whose upper story overhangs the lower story.

jib door: a concealed door flush with the wall and usually decorated to match it.

joinery: finished woodwork, such as

that used on doors, windows and stairs.

joists: horizontal timbers laid parallel as a base for the floorboards.

keystone: the central stone in the curve of an arch or vault.

label: see **hoodmould**

leaded lights: small panes of glass set into cames (lead strips) to form a window.

lights: in a window, the openings between mullions; more generally, panes.

Lincrusta: An embossed wallpaper intended to be painted and varnished; popular from the late 19th century.

linenfold panelling: wooden panelling in which the individual panels are carved with a motif like the vertical folds of linen, from the Tudor period.

linoleum: a floor covering made of compressed cork, ground wood and linseed oil backed by burlap or strong canvas.

lintel: a supporting wood or stone beam across the top of an opening such as that of a door or window.

loggia: a pillared gallery that is open on at least one side.

louver: one of a series of overlapping slats (for example, in window shutters).

lunette: a semi-circular opening, as in a lunette window.

lustre glass: an iridescent glass, of the type made by Tiffany in the United States.

mansard roof: a roof with two slopes, the lower almost vertical to allow extra roof space for the attic rooms.

mantel: the frame surrounding a fireplace; often used to denote just the shelf (mantel shelf).

marbleized: painted or stained to resemble marble.

medallion: see **rose**

metopes: the plain or carved square spaces between the triglyphs in a Doric frieze.

millwork: mass-produced woodwork.

modillion: a small ornamental bracket used in a series to support the upper part of a Corinthian or Composite cornice.

moiré: a fabric or wallpaper, usually silk, that has been treated so that it has a watered or wavelike look.

moulding: a decorative contour, in wood or stone.

mullion: an upright bar that vertically divides a window or other opening.

muntin: the subsidiary vertical member of the frame of a door, window, panel, etc.

newel post: the post at the end of a staircase, usually attached to both the handrail and the string; on a circular staircase, the central post around which the stairs curve.

nogging: the brickwork between the timbers in a timber-framed building.

nosing: the rounded edging of a stair-

tread, overhanging the riser.

oculus: a circular opening in a wall or in the top of a dome.

ogee arch: a pointed arch formed by two reversed curves, slightly S-shaped in profile.

open-string: the term applied to a staircase whose profile of treads and risers is visible from the side (that is, not closed off by a string). The treads support the balustrade.

orangery: a greenhouse or other such glassed structure where oranges and other tender plants are grown.

Order: in classical architecture, a particular style of column and entablature, each with its own distinctive proportions and detailing. The Five Orders are Doric, Ionic, Corinthian, Tuscan and Composite. The first three are derived from ancient Greek architecture; Tuscan and Composite are Roman adaptations of the earlier Greek models.

oriel: a bay window on an upper floor.

overdoor: a decorative section above a door, often panelled or containing a painting.

overmantel: a decorative treatment above a fireplace, often incorporating a painting or mirror.

overthrow: an ironwork hoop supporting a lantern, forming an arch in front of the street door of a house.

ovolo moulding: a wide convex moulding, often called a quarter-round because it forms a quarter-section of a circle.

palisade: a strong wooden fence.

Palladian style: an interpretation of the classical style developed by Andrea Palladio (1508-80), the Italian architect. Palladianism was revived in England in the early 18th century by Lord Burlington and Colen Campbell and influenced American architecture in the late 18th century.

Palladian window: see **Venetian window**

palmette: a decorative motif based on the fan-shaped leaf of a palm tree.

pantile: a roofing tile, S-shaped in section.

papier mâché: an inexpensive lightweight material made from paper pulp, used to form various items of interior embellishment.

parapet: a low wall surmounting the exterior wall of a building.

pargeting: ornamental plasterwork on walls and ceilings, most notably on the exterior of timber-framed buildings and often in the shape of figures and vines.

parquetry: small pieces of coloured hardwood made into a geometric floor pattern.

patera: a small oval or round ornament in classical architecture, often decorated with flowers or leaves.

pebbledash: a form of rough external wall rendering, with pebbles set into cement.

pediment: a low-pitched gable across a

portico, door or window; any similar triangular decorative piece over a doorway, fireplace or other feature. A pediment that is open on top is called a broken pediment.

pendant: an ornament hanging down from a ceiling, staircase, etc.

pendentive: a concave triangular corner vault that supports a dome above a square room.

piano nobile: the principal floor of a house, containing the reception rooms.

piazza: an American term for a broad veranda.

picture rail: a moulding on the upper part of a wall from which pictures are hung.

Picturesque: a term describing the 18th and early 19th-century Romantic taste for asymmetric, rustic features, such as *cottages ornés*.

pier: a solid vertical element of a wall between openings such as windows; the support for a lintel or arch. Also, a heavy masonry support used, for example, at either side of a gate.

pier glass: a tall, narrow mirror hung between two windows.

pilaster: a flat rectangular classical column fixed against a wall, or used to frame a doorway, fireplace, etc.

pintle: the pin or bolt that fits inside a hinge.

plinth: the projecting base of a wall or column.

porphyry: a hard, fine-grained dark red or purple rock flecked with white crystals embedded in it; also, grey and green igneous rocks of similar texture.

porte-cochère: a porch wide enough to allow access for a carriage.

portico: a roofed entrance porch, often with columns.

pulvinated: with a convex profile; the term usually describes a frieze.

purlin: a long horizontal member of a timber-framed roof, forming an intermediate support for the rafters.

putti: cherubs or young boys used as a subject in Italian Renaissance decoration.

quarry: a small square- or diamond-shaped pane of glass used in leaded windows.

quarry tile: an unglazed floor tile.

quatrefoil: a four-lobed circle or arch formed by cusping.

quirk: a V-shaped groove along a moulding or between moulding joints.

quoins: the dressed (finished) stones at the corners of a building.

rabbeted: two members joined together by interlocking grooves cut into each; also spelled rabbeted.

rail: a horizontal member of the frame of a door, panel, etc.

rebate or **rabbet**: a channel or groove cut into a surface edge (usually of wood) to receive another member.

reeding: a form of decoration formed by narrow convex mouldings in parallel strips divided by grooves.

register grate: a fire grate with a moveable iron plate in the flue to regulate the updraught.

repoussé: a pattern in relief, usually made by hammering thin metal from behind.

reveal: the inner surface of a doorcase or window opening, between the edge of the frame and the outer surface of the wall at right angles to it. The corresponding space above is the soffit.

rinceau: an ornament of scrolled foliage, usually vine leaves.

riser: the vertical surface of a step.

rocaille: the shell and irregular stone decoration popular in the Rococo style.

Roman cement: a patented plaster, similar to stucco.

rose: on a plaster ceiling, a moulded, radiating feature with a pendant light suspended from its centre; called a medallion in the United States.

rosette: any rose-shaped ornament.

roundel: a round flat ornament or a small round window.

row house: see **terraced house**

rubbed brick: the term used for carved brickwork.

rustication: masonry cut in large blocks separated by deep joints, used to give a bold, exaggerated look to the lower part of an exterior wall, or to frame a door or window.

sash window: a window formed with sashes – that is, glazed wooden frames which slide up and down in vertical grooves by means of counterbalanced weights. The standard form has two moveable sashes and is termed a "double-hung sash".

saucer dome: a shallow dome.

scagliola: a decorative finish imitating marble made from hardened and polished plaster and marble chips.

sconce: a wall bracket for holding a light source, particularly candles.

Scotch carpet: see **ingrain carpet**.

scotia: a concave moulding, as used at the base of a column between torus mouldings.

serliana: see **Venetian window**

shaft: the main vertical part of a column between the base and the capital; also, in medieval architecture, one of a cluster of thin columns that together form a pillar on a door or window surround.

shingle: wooden tiles used to clad exterior walls, especially in American Shingle-style houses.

sill: the horizontal ledge at the bottom of a window frame.

skirting board: the flat moulding running around the base of a wall; called a baseboard in the United States.

slip: a strip or long, thin piece of wood; also, a fascia (often marble or tiles) set into a fireplace surround.

soffit: the underside of a beam, arch or other architectural element; also, the reveal of the head of a door or window.

spandrel: the approximately triangular space between the curve of an arch and the rectangular frame above it; also, the space between two arches and the horizontal cornice that runs above them.

spindle: a thin, turned column of wood, as used in series in staircase screens and the like.

splayed: sloping or bevelled, usually referring to a door, window or fireplace opening that has slanting sides.

spline joint: the joint made when grooved boards are connected by a strip of wood.

stair-end: on an open-string stair, the face formed between the riser and the tread. Also, the cut-out or carved decorative element applied to this space. Sometimes also called a tread-end.

standard: an upright support or base.

stile: a main vertical member of the frame of a door, panel, etc.

stoop: in the United States, a small platform with steps leading up to it at the entrance of a building.

stop-chamfer: a triangular termination to a chamfer, bringing a three-sided form back to a right angle. A popular feature in early English and Victorian architecture.

strapwork: decoration formed by interlaced strips, either applied or carved in wood, stone or plaster. Often used in screens and on ceilings and cornices.

stretcher: a brick laid so that only its long face is visible.

string: one of the two sloping members that hold the ends of the treads and risers in a staircase.

stucco: a fine cement or plaster used on the surface of walls, mouldings and other architectural ornaments. By the 19th century, stucco is generally used as a term for exterior rendering.

studs: the upright timbers in a timber-framed building.

summer beam: a principal rafter or load-bearing beam, usually spanning the width of a room.

swag: a piece of fabric draped between two supports; a carved or painted decoration resembling such a fabric; or a garland of ribbons, flowers, fruit and/or foliage; also called a festoon.

swan's-neck pediment: a type of broken pediment with S-shaped curves, like two swans' necks facing each other.

terraced house: a house that forms one of a whole straight or curving line of at least three such houses attached to each other. Known as a row house in the United States.

terracotta: unglazed, fired clay used for tiles, architectural ornament, garden pots, etc.

terrazzo: a polished finish for floors and walls consisting of marble or stone chips set into mortar.

thatch: a roof covering of tightly packed straw or reeds.

tongue-and-groove: a method of joining wood so that the edge of one board has a tongue, or lip, that fits into a groove on the edge of another board.

torus: a large convex moulding, semi-circular in profile; originally the principal element of the column base.

tracery: an ornamental arrangement of intersecting ribwork, usually in the upper part of a Gothic window, forming a pierced pattern. If applied to a solid wall surface, known as blind tracery.

transom: the horizontal member across the top of a door, or across the top or middle of a window.

transom light: in the United States, a window or pane above a door, whether rectangular or arched (known as a fanlight in Britain); also, a window that is hinged along its top edge.

tread: the horizontal surface of a step.

tread-end: on an open-string stair, the triangular face formed between the riser and the tread. Also called the stair-end.

trefoil: a three-lobed circle or arch formed by cusping.

trelliswork: an open pattern of interwoven strips, usually of wood but sometimes metal; also called latticework.

triglyphs: the grooved projecting blocks between the metopes in a Doric frieze.

trompe l'oeil: a decorative effect, such as a painting of architectural detail or a vista, that gives the illusion of reality.

trophy: an ornamental carving of arms and/or armour, musical instruments or other implements arranged as a decorative motif.

truss: a wooden framework in the shape of a bridge or large bracket, used to support timbers, such as those in a roof.

tunnel-and-groin vaulting: see **barrel-and-groin vaulting**

turkey carpet: an English-made carpet in the Turkish style, characterized by bold colours, especially red and blue, and geometrical patterns of stylized living forms such as flowers and fruits, often with a border.

tympanum: the semi-circular space between a lintel of a door or window and the arch above it; also, the usually triangular space within the mouldings of a pediment.

vellum: a fine parchment made from calf, kid or lamb skin; also, a heavy cream-coloured paper resembling such parchment.

veneer: a thin slice of wood cut from the solid, applied as a decorative surface to a more common wood.

Venetian window: a window with a central arched section flanked by two tall, narrow rectangular sections. Also called a Palladian window or serliana.

veranda: a roof-covered but otherwise open gallery, porch or balcony supported by posts.

vergeboard: see **bargeboard**

vernacular: a term describing humble, often rural architecture, with little or no stylistic pretension, or in a purely regional style, or in a manner based on a naive misunderstanding of high-style architecture.

Vitruvian scroll: a classical frieze ornament, made up of a series of wave-like scrolls; also called a running dog.

volutes: in classical architecture, spiral scrolls, most characteristically forming the capital of a Greek Ionic column. Also, scroll-shaped supporting members strengthening a wall or serving as brackets.

voussoir: one of a number of wedge-shaped radiating stones or bricks used to form an arch or vault.

wainscot: the simple, early form of wooden panelling, either full height or on the lower half of a wall; also called wainscotting. The term is also applied to the oak or other timber used for panelling.

weatherboarding: see **clapboarding**

wicket: a small door set into a larger door or gate.

widow's walk: a rooftop platform or narrow walkway, often used as a lookout for incoming ships on 18th and 19th-century New England coastal houses.

Wilton carpet: a carpet that has a looped pile cut to give it a soft finish.

DIRECTORY OF SUPPLIERS: BRITISH

Architectural antiques and good-quality reproduction items are now available from an increasing number of suppliers. The following list is intended to cover most restoration requirements, but further information will be included in specialist magazines.

ARCHITECTURAL SALVAGE

Antique Fireplace Warehouse
194-200 Battersea Park Road,
London SW11 4ND
(0171) 627 1410
Fax: (0171) 622 1078
Antique fireplaces, many in marble, from Georgian chimneypieces to Victorian mantels.

Architectural Antiques
Ley Farm,
Alswear Old Road,
Queens Nympton,
nr South Moulton,
Devon EX36 4LE
(01769) 573342
Fax: (01769) 574363
Although much of their stock is more suitable for restaurants, bars and other public places, some items are appropriate for home restoration.

Architectural Antiques
351 King Street,
London W6 9NH
(0181) 741 7883
Fax: (0181) 741 1109
Wide range of antique and reproduction marble fireplace surrounds, also installation and restoration of antique and new marble.

Architectural Heritage
Taddington Manor,
Taddington,
nr Cutsdean,
Cheltenham,
Gloucestershire GL54 5RY
(01386) 584 414
Fax: (01386) 584 236
Suppliers of a large collection of authentic antique panelled rooms, chimneypieces, stained and leaded glass panels and windows, wrought- and cast-iron gates, period doors and other interior and exterior items.

Au Temps Perdu
5 Stapleton Road,
Bristol BS5 0QR
(0117) 955 5223
Architectural salvage, antiques and building materials, mostly from France. Many items restored. Shipping and installation can be arranged.

Baileys Architectural Antiques
The Engine Shed,
Ashburton Industrial Estate,
Ross on Wye,
Herefordshire HR9 7BW
(01989) 563015
Fax: (01989) 768172
A large and changing inventory of decorative architectural items for the house, both authentic and reproduction, such as doors, fireplaces and mantelpieces, gates, panelling, bathroom fittings, hardware, tiles and lighting.

Brighton Architectural Salvage
33 Gloucester Road,
Brighton,
Sussex BN14 4AQ
(01273) 681656 (Tel/Fax)
Restored architectural antiques, including fireplaces, doors, stained glass, panelling and cast-iron balcony railing.

Conservation Building Products
see Building Materials

Crowther of Syon Lodge
Syon Lodge,
Busch Corner,
London Road,
Isleworth,
Middlesex TW7 5BH
(0181) 560 7978/7985
Fax: (0181) 568 7572
Carefully restored fine antiques from around the world. Specialist in garden statuary but also handles antique fireplaces, panelled rooms and wrought-iron gates.

Dorset Reclamation
see Building Materials

**The London Architectural
Salvage and Supply Co. Ltd**
St Michael's,
Mark Street,
London EC2A 4ER
(0171) 739 0448
Fax: (0171) 729 6853
A great selection of panelling, fireplaces, flooring and other decorative details in wood, stone and marble.

Moochers
590 Warwick Road,
Tyseley,
Birmingham B11 2HJ
(0121) 680 7445
Architectural antiques of all kinds with nationwide delivery; restoration services include complete fireplace fitting and decorative paint finishes and marbling to surrounds and interiors.

Victorian Pine Save a Tree
298 Brockley Road,
Brockley,
London SE4 2RA
(0181) 691 7162
Reclaimed architectural components and pre-1920s items such as shutters, spindles, handrails, newel posts, panelling and especially hardwood doors.

Walcot Reclamation
108 Walcot Street,
Bath BA1 5BG
(01225) 444 404
Fax: (01225) 448 163
A large selection of architectural antiques and building materials of all types from all periods: salvaged bricks and tiles, pavers, chimney pots, timber and flooring, doors and windows, ironwork, period bathrooms, fireplaces, gates and panelling. Restoration work also done.

BATHROOMS

W. Adams and Sons Ltd
Unit 6, Credenda Road,
Bromford Road Industrial Estate,
West Bromwich B70 7JE
(0121) 553 2161
Antique and Georgian-style bathroom taps and matching accessories for basins, bidets, baths and showers.

Architectural Components
see Doors

Barwill Traditional Taps
Barber Wilsons and Co. Ltd,
Crawley Road,
Wood Green,
London N22 6AH
(0181) 888 3461
Fax: (0181) 888 2041
Long-time manufacturers of traditional bathroom and kitchen fittings in non-tarnish brass, unplated polished brass, nickel plate and conventional chrome.

Czech and Speake
244-254 Cambridge Heath Road,
London E2 9DA
(0181) 980 4567
Fax: (0181) 981 7232
Period bathroomware including porcelain freestanding and inset rolltop tubs, WCs, bidets and basins. Edwardian fittings in uncoated brass, non-tarnish brass, chromium plate and nickel plate. Many accessories such as hooks, towel rails, soap dish holders and cistern levers.

Heritage Bathrooms
Unit 1A, Princess Street,
Bedminster,
Bristol BS3 4AG
(0117) 963 9762
Fax: (0117) 923 1078
Victorian and Edwardian reproduction bathrooms; baths, washbasins, water closets, bidets and cabinets in pine and mahogany.

Miscellanea of Churt
Crossways,
Churt,
Farnham,
Surrey GU10 2JA
(01428) 714 014
Fax: (01428) 712 946
Maker of custom-design and reproduction period bathroom- and kitchen-ware. Also supplies bathroom accessories.

Original Victorian Bathroom Co.
Potovens Bathroom Centre,
38 Potovens Lane,
Lofthouse Gate,
Wakefield,
West Yorkshire WS3 3TS
(01924) 824 246
Fax: (01924) 820 237
Fully restored cast-iron rolltop baths. Also new and original period pottery and fittings.

Scottwood of Nottingham
see Built-in Furniture

Smallbone
see Kitchens

Stiffkey Bathrooms
The Chapel,
Stiffkey,
Norfolk NR23 1AJ
(01328) 830099
Fax: (01328) 830005
Restorer of antique sanitaryware, including showers, baths, basins, taps and toilets. Also supplies original and period accessories.

Winther Browne
see Woodwork and Joinery

BUILDING MATERIALS

Arundel Stone
62 Aldwick Road,
Bognor Regis,
West Sussex PO21 2PE
(01243) 829 151
Fax: (01243) 860 341
Reconstructed stone balustrading and architectural stonework for restoration projects.

Au Temps Perdu
see Architectural Salvage

Cathedral Works
Terminus Road,
Chichester,
West Sussex PO19 2TX
(01243) 784 225
Fax: (01243) 813 700
Specialist in stone masonry, restoration, conservation and stone carving.

Conservation Building Products
Forge Works,
Forge Lane,
Cradley Heath,
Warley,
West Midlands B64 5AL
(01384) 569551
Fax: (01384) 410625
Suppliers of reclaimed and new building materials for restored and period buildings, incl. doors, bricks, roofing materials, timbers, flooring, mouldings, fireplaces and accessories.

Dorset Reclamation
Cow Drove, Bere Regis,
Wareham, Dorset BH20 7JZ
(01929) 472 200
Fax: (01929) 472 292
Reclaimed traditional building materials and architectural antiques of all sorts including bricks, interior and exterior flagstones, tiles, boards and planks, finials, stones and cobbles, doors, hand rails, bathroom fittings, fireplaces and kitchen sinks.

UK Marble
21 Burcott Road,
Hereford HR4 9LW
(01432) 352 178
Fax: (01432) 352 112
Marble and granite for bathrooms, floors, worktops, decorative borders and panels, fireplaces, mouldings and the like.

Victorian Lace
Units U3 and S7
Rudford Industrial Estate,
Ford, Arundel,
West Sussex BN18 0BE
(01903) 731 030
Fax: (01903) 731 031
Decorative structural columns in cast aluminium and cast iron for porches, staircases, balustrading, decorative panels, railings and gates. Also makers of glazed canopies.

York Handmade Brick Co.
Forest Lane,
Alne,
North Yorks. YO6 2LU
(01347) 838886
Fax: (01347) 838885
Manufacturers of handmade bricks and terracotta floor tiles.

BUILT-IN FURNITURE

Archer and Smith Ltd
Manor House,
Chiseldon,
Swindon SN4 0LN
(01793) 740 375
Fax: (01793) 741 110
Maker and designer of reproduction period and custom-design furniture.

Artisan Period and Victorian Joinery
see Woodwork and Joinery

Ashley Stocks Furniture Ltd
Units 9 and 10,
Parkfield Trading Estate,
Culvert Place,
London SW11 5BA
(0171) 627 1222
Fax: (0171) 622 1053
Traditional-style made-to-measure kitchens, wardrobes and bookcases in natural wood and painted finishes.

Bylaw Ltd
The Old Mill,
Brookend Street,
Ross-on-Wye,
Herefordshire HR9 7EG
(01989) 562 356
Fax: (01989) 768 145
Maker of traditional solid oak and fruitwood furniture. Interior work includes solid-oak staircases, doors and panelling.

Hygrove Kitchens
see Kitchens

Japac Designs
St Saviour's Church,
Whitstable Road,
Faversham,
Kent ME13 8BD
(01795) 537 062 (Tel/Fax)
Makers of fitted furniture, sliding sash windows and staircases built to specification.

S. and H. Jewell Ltd
26 Parker Street,
London WC2B 5PH
(0171) 405 8520
Supplier of Queen Anne, Georgian, Regency, Victorian and Edwardian furniture.

John Ladbury and Co.
Unit 11,
Alpha Business Park,
Travellers Close,
Welham Green,
Hatfield,
Hertfordshire AL9 7NT
(01707) 262966 (Tel/Fax)
Maker of fitted furniture for traditional-style kitchens, bedrooms and studies.

Scottwood of Nottingham
Dabell Avenue,
Blenheim Industrial Estate,
Bulwell,
Nottingham NG6 8WA
(0115) 977 0877
Fax: (0115) 977 0367
Makers of fitted bathrooms, kitchens and bedrooms in pine and hardwoods in a variety of finishes.

Smallbone
see Kitchens

Yeo Valley Joinery
see Staircases

CEILINGS

Aristocast Originals Ltd
see Walls

Wheatley
Avonvale Studio Workshops,
Avonvale Place,
Batheaston BA1 7RF
(01225) 859 678 (Tel/Fax)
Ornamental plasterwork for ceilings and walls, including cornices, ceiling centres, niches, plaques, panel moulding, columns and fireplace surrounds. Will also fit items and do restoration work on existing plasterwork.

Winther Browne
see Woodwork and Joinery

CONSERVATORIES

Amdega Conservatories
Faverdale,
Darlington,
Co. Durham DL3 0PW
(01325) 468 522
Fax: (01325) 489 209
Conservatories and porches in period styles. Also conservatory blinds, fans and flooring, and summer houses, gazeboes and greenhouses. Has available a design service that will design and build to order.

Fairmitre Thames Valley
28 Kennylands Road,
Sonning Common,
Reading,
Berkshire RG4 9JT
(01734) 723 380
Custom-made modern and traditional conservatories and other small outdoor structures.

David Fennings Conservatories
Unit 3a,
Sunrise Park,
Higher Shaftesbury Road,
Blandford,
Dorset DT11 8ST
(01258) 459259
Fax: (01258) 459305
Supplier of Victorian and Edwardian conservatories and accessories.

The Original Box Sash Window Company
see Windows

Room Outside
Lakeside House
Quarry Lane,
Chichester,
West Sussex PO19 2NY
(01243) 776 563
Fax: (01243) 776 313
A range of modular elements for modern and traditional conservatories that allow you to choose sizes, finishes, types of glazing and other detailing.

Rutland County
'Snowhill' Preston,
Oakham,
Rutland,
Leicestershire LE15 9NJ
(01572) 737 502
Fax: (01572) 737 602
Maker of tailor-made conservatories and orangeries.

Vale Garden Houses Ltd
Melton Road,
Harlaxton, nr Grantham,
Lincolnshire NG32 1HQ
(01476) 64433
Fax: (01476) 78555
Designer and manufacturer of traditional conservatories and garden rooms.

DOORS

Architectural Components
4-8 Exhibition Road,
London SW7 2HF
(0171) 584 6800
Fax: (0171) 589 4928
Manufacturers of door fittings in Victorian, Georgian and Regency styles. Also cupboard, bathroom and furniture fittings, electrical plates and locks.

Aristocast Originals
see Walls

Barron Glass
see Windows

Brassart
Regent Works,
78 Attwood Street,
Lye, Stourbridge,
West Midlands DY9 8RY
(01384) 894 814
Fax: (01384) 423 824
Door fittings and electrical wall plates made from hand-made castings in a number of traditional styles. Finishes in polished brass, chrome plate and satin chrome; French lacquered gilt and gold plate available in some styles.

Classic Designs
Unit 15C,
Bilton Industrial Estate,
Humber Avenue,
Coventry CV3 1JL
(01203) 431 040/431 115
Fax: (01203) 443 104
Custom-designed doors and windows handmade from hardwoods in traditional designs.

Clayton-Munroe Ltd
Kingston,
Staverton, Totnes,
Devon TQ9 6AR
(01803) 762 626
Fax: (01803) 762 584
Manufacturers of 17th-century hand-forged door hardware and fittings.

T.J. Harwood and Co. Ltd
Harrison Street,
Briercliff,
Burnley BB10 2HP
(01282) 451110
Fax: (01282) 451160
Georgian, Victorian and other period styles of reproduction door hardware in brass, porcelain and cast iron.

'In' Doors Ltd
Invicta Works,
Mill Street,
East Malling,
Kent ME19 6BP
(01732) 841 606
Fax: (01732) 870 016
Suppliers of original old solid pine doors as well as glazed doors with plain and stained glass and cupboard doors.

B. Lilly and Sons Ltd
Baltimore Road,
Birmingham B42 1DJ
(0121) 357 1761
Fax: (0121) 357 9029
A small line of antique door handles in polished brass and brown relieved finish.

Mackinnon and Bailey
72 Floodgate Street,
Birmingham B5 5SL
(0121) 773 5827
Fax: (0121) 766 6072
Manufacturers of fittings for doors, windows, and cupboards in polished brass, chromium plate and satin chromium plate. Also make hooks, plates, brackets and ventilators.

The Original Box Sash Window Company
see Windows

Syntonic Joinery
see Woodwork and Joinery

Victorian Pine Save A Tree
see Architectural Salvage

FIREPLACES

Acquisitions
4-6 Jamestown Road,
London NW1 7BX
(0171) 485 4955
Fax: (0171) 267 4361
Original and reproduction Victorian and Edwardian fireplaces, gas- and coal-effect fires and accessories.

Amazing Grates
61-63 High Road,
East Finchley,
London N2 8AB
(0181) 883 9590
Fax: (0181) 365 2053
Manufacturers of reproduction fireplace settings and suppliers of original period chimneypieces and insert grates. Stock includes wood, stone and marble mantels, fireplace tiles, and a wide range of accessories. Also restores original fireplaces.

Architectural Antiques (London)
see Architectural Salvage

Aristocast Originals Ltd
see Walls

Baileys Architectural Antiques
see Architectural Salvage

Campbell Ceramic Fireplace Tiles
H. and R. Johnson Tiles Ltd,
Highgate Tile Works,
Tunstall, Stoke-on-Trent,
Staffordshire ST6 4JX
(01782) 575 575
Fax: (01782) 577 377
Victorian reproduction fire tile panels, decorative borders and insets and cordinating hearth tiles.

Chiswick Fireplace Company
68 Southfield Road,
Chiswick,
London W4 1DB
(0181) 995 4011
Fax: (0181) 995 4012
Supplier of Victorian and Edwardian fireplaces. Also restores antique fireplaces.

Dowding Metalcraft Ltd
Mulberry Road,
Canvey Island,
Essex SS8 0PR
(01268) 684 205 (Tel/Fax)
Manufacturers of reproduction fire grates and fenders for wood, coal, gas and electric fires.

Fireplace Designers
18 Chepstow Corners,
Pembridge Villas,
Notting Hill,
London W2 4XE
(0171) 229 8843
Fax: (0171) 229 8864
Supplier of antique, period and reproduction fireplaces and fireplace accessories.

Firestyle Chimneypieces
158 Upminster Road,
Upminster,
Essex RM14 2RB
(01708) 456 895
Fax: (01708) 477 994
Handcrafted marble chimneypieces in several classical and period designs; also fireplace inserts and a fitting service available.

Grahamston Iron Co.
see Ironwork

Hallidays
The Old College,
Dorchester-on-Thames,
Oxfordshire OX9 8HL
(01865) 340 028/340 068
Fax: (01865) 340 1149
Specializing in hand-carved Baltic pine reproduction mantelpiece designs of the Regency, Georgian, Victorian and Edwardian periods. Complementary marble slips, hearths, firegrates, fenders and other accessories, both reproduction and authentic antique; also wood panelled rooms and cabinet furniture.

Overmantels
66 Battersea Bridge Road,
London SW11 3AG
(0171) 223 8151
Fax: (0171) 924 2283
Overmantel gilt mirrors reproduced from Victorian, Regency, Georgian and French period originals. Also makers of custom-designs.

Petit Roque
5A New Road,
Croxley Green, Rickmansworth,
Hertfordshire WD3 3EJ
(01923) 779 291
Fax: (01923) 896 728
Suppliers of Georgian and Regency style mantelpieces in hand-carved pine and polished sheet marble. Coloured marbles and granites may be specially ordered. Also cast-iron, wrought iron and brass grates and other accessories for wood- and coal-burning fireplaces.

Renaissance Mouldings
262 Hansworth Road,
Hansworth,
Sheffield S13 9BS
(0114) 244 6622
Fax: (0114) 261 0472
Maker of period-style fireplaces and mouldings.

Tatters of Tysley Ltd
Swallows Barn,
Meer End, nr Kenilworth,
Warwickshire CV8 1PW
(01676) 535 989 (Tel/Fax)
Supplier, restorer and fitter of antique fireplaces.

Mr Wandle's Workshop
200-202 Garratt Lane,
London SW18 4ED
(0181) 870 5873
Suppliers and restorers of authentic Victorian cast-iron fireplaces, grates and accessories. Also Victorian kitchen ranges and stoves.

Winther Browne
see Woodwork and Joinery

FLOORS

John Burgess Tiles
Unit B25, Maws Craft Centre,
Jackfield, Shropshire TF8 7LS
(01952) 884 094
Reproduction Victorian and Art Nouveau ceramic wall and floor tiles.

Crucial Trading Ltd
77 Westbourne Park Road,
London W2 4BX
(0171) 221 9000
Fax: (0171) 727 3634
Natural floor coverings in a range that includes seagrass, coir, sisa, rush and medieval matting.

S. Frances
82 Jermyn Street,
St James's,
London SW1Y 6JD
(0171) 976 1234
Fax: (0171) 930 8451
Antique carpets, textiles and tapestries.

H. and R. Johnson Tiles Ltd
see Walls

Original Style
Falcon Road,
Sawton Industrial Estate,
Exeter,
Devon EX2 7LF
(01392) 216 923
Fax: (01392) 219 932
Ready-moulded Victorian geometric floor tiles and wall tiles in Victorian and Art Nouveau styles.

The Original Tile Company
see Walls

Paris Ceramics
583 Kings Road,
London SW6 2EH
(0171) 371 7778
Fax: (0171) 371 8395
Specialists in restoring and fitting antique terracotta and stone floors from France. Also suppliers of new Spanish terracotta floor tiles, Blue English limestone and unglazed decorated floor tiles in a variety of styles. Several wall tiles from Spain, Holland and France, some made from antique patterns.

Treamlod Tillery
Ambleston,
Haverfordwest,
Dyfed SA62 5DQ
(01437) 741 541
Maker of medieval and Victorian encaustic floor tiles. Also makes custom-designs, restores and replaces original tiles.

Woodward Grosvenor and Co. Ltd
Stourvale Mills,
Green Street,
Kidderminster DY10 1AT
(01562) 820020
Fax: (01562) 820042
Carpet makers, archivists, will reproduce any pattern to commission.

York Handmade Brick Co.
see Building Materials

IRONWORK

Ballantine Boness Iron Co.
Links Road, Bo'ness,
West Lothian,
Scotland EH51 9PW
(01506) 822 721/281 281
Fax: (01506) 827 326
Manufacturer and fitter of ornamental cast-iron panels for railings, balconies, gates and stairways.

J.D. Beardmore and Co. Ltd
3-5 Percy Street,
London W1P 0EJ
(0171) 637 7041
Fax: (0171) 436 9222
A large selection of period reproduction designs: decorative grilles, electrical fittings, door and cabinet furniture, locks.

Britannia
Old Coach House,
Draymans Ways,
Alton,
Hampshire GU34 1AY
(01420) 84427
Fax: (01420) 89056
Large range of Victorian cast-iron work for balconies, spiral and straight staircases and the like. Also restoration and repair work and custom-made designs from original castings.

Capricorn Architectural Ironwork
Tasso Forge,
56 Tasso Road,
London W6 8LZ
(0171) 603 1282
Fax: (0171) 603 1283
Designers and makers of hand-forged architectural and artistic fittings. All the work, done by a collective of local blacksmiths, is commissioned and includes among other things railings, balconies, straight and spiral staircases and gates. Also restores original ironwork.

The Cast Iron Shop (R. Bleasdale Spirals)
394 Caledonian Road,
London N1 1DW
(0171) 609 0934
Traditional British, French and American ironwork reproductions in a wide range of patterns and styles: spiral and straight staircases, railings, balconies, room dividers and window boxes.

Clayton-Munroe Ltd
see Doors

Grahamston Iron Co.
Broomside Works,
Hillview Road,
Highbonny Bridge,
Stirlingshire FK4 2EN
(01324) 814604
Fax: (01324) 815759
Ironfounders and enamellers of fireplace inserts, grates, stoves and kitchen cookers.

Southwell Stockwell Ltd
3-7 Holly Road,
London SE15 5DQ
(0171) 635 0950
Fax: (0171) 277 9591
*Fabricate and fit cast-iron work from
reproduced Georgian and Victorian
patterns and moulds for railings,
window guards, bootscrapers, gates
and spiral staircases; also refurbish
original ironwork.*

Traditional Gates and Railings
Unit P701,
Royal Ordnance Site,
Furston Road,
Waltham Abbey,
Middlesex EN9 1AY
(01992) 762 750
Fax: (01992) 762 756
*Manufacturers of traditional-style
gates and railings to almost any size
either for self-fit or installation by their
fitters.*

KITCHENS

Crabtree Kitchens
The Twickenham Centre,
Norcutt Road,
Twickenham,
Middlesex TW2 6SR
(0181) 755 1121
Fax: (0181) 755 4133
*Handmade, solid-wood kitchens in
pine, oak and ash, finished with
lacquer and wax polish, or painted in
styles inspired by Biedermeier faux
bois, trompe l'œil and faux marbling.*

Henslowe and Fox
Commodore Kitchens Ltd,
Acorn House,
120 Gumley Road,
Grays,
Essex RM20 4XP
(01375) 382 323
Fax: (01375) 394 955
*Builders of fitted kitchens developed
from traditional period designs in
limed oak. Also available by special
order in natural, honey and white
painted, as well as in a pigmented
glaze in five different broken paint
finishes typical of many 18th-century
interiors*

Hygrove Kitchens
152-4 Merton Road,
Wimbledon,
London SW19 1EH
(0181) 543 1200/6520
Fax: (0181) 543 6521
*Custom-built wood kitchens in both
antique and traditional finishes and a
variety of painted designs. Also a
selection of fitted bathroom and
bedroom furniture available.*

Japac Designs
see Built-in Furniture

Harvey Jones Kitchens
57 New Kings Road,
London SW6 4SE
(0171) 731 3302
Fax: (0171) 371 0735
*Traditional painted kitchen
specialists.*

Kitchen Art
5-6 The Centre,
The Broadway,
Beaconsfield Road,
Farnham Common,
Buckinghamshire SL2 3PP
(01753) 646 631
Fax: (01753) 644 144
*Fitted and freestanding kitchens, both
standard and custom-built. The
original range is a traditional, all-
timber design.*

John Landbury and Co.
see Built-in Furniture

Miscellanea of Churt
see Bathrooms

Plain English
The Tannery,
Combs,
Stowmarket,
Suffolk IP14 2EN
(01449) 774 028
*Specialist in fitted kitchens for period
houses.*

Robinson and Cornish
Southay House,
Oakwood Close,
Barnstaple,
Devon EX31 3NJ
(01271) 329 300
Fax: (01271) 328 277
*Specialist in custom-design kitchens
for period houses.*

Scottwood of Nottingham
see Built-in Furniture

Smallbone
Hopton Industrial Estate,
London Road,
Devizes,
Wiltshire SN10 2EU
(01380) 729 090
Fax: (01380) 727 771
*Handcrafted kitchen, bedroom and
bathroom furniture in a wide range of
traditional and period styles and
finishes.*

Wood Workshop
28 Chestnut Road,
London SE27 9LF
(0181) 670 8984
*Builders of fitted kitchens in many
hardwoods and several styles,
including some of the Victorian period
(and the Arts and Crafts Movement)
and 1930s Art Deco.*

KITCHEN STOVES

Aga
Glynwed Consumer
and Building Products Ltd,
PO Box 30, Ketley,
Telford,
Shropshire TF1 4DD
(01952) 642 000
Fax: (01952) 641 961
*Distributors of the well-known Aga
cooker based on the design of Nobel
prize-winning Swedish physicist Dr
Gustav Dalen, in the early 1920s.
The 2- and 4-oven cookers can be
fuelled by off-peak electricity, natural
or propane gas, oil or solid fuel.*

Coalbrookdale
Glynwed Consumer
and Building Products Ltd,
PO Box 30, Ketley,
Telford,
Shropshire TF14DD
(01952) 642 000
Fax: (01952) 641 961
*Cast-iron stoves that burn wood, coal
and peat for heat and hot water.*

Country Cookers
5 Sherford Street,
Bromyard,
Hertfordshire HR7 4DL
(01886) 884 262
Fax: (01886) 884 461
*Suppliers of reconditioned Aga
cookers.*

Godin
Morley Marketing,
Marsh Lane, Ware,
Hertfordshire SC12 9QB
(01920) 468 002
Fax: (01920) 463 893
*These coal- and wood-burning and
gas-fired stoves have been made in
France since the end of the last century
and are finished in antique colours.
Suitable for Victorian and Edwardian
settings and conservatories.*

Grahamston Iron Co.
see Ironworks

The Hotspot
53/55 High Street,
Uttoxeter,
Staffordshire ST14 7JQ
(01889) 565 411
Fax: (01889) 567 625
*Distributors of cast-iron wood- and
coal-burning stoves, some in period
styles.*

Stanley Super Star
Stanley Cookers GB Ltd,
Gledrid Industrial Park,
Chirk,
Clwyd LL14 5DG
(01691) 772 922
Fax: (01691) 773 552
*Gas, oil and multi-fuel combination
cookers and central heating units.*

Mr Wandles Workshop
see Fireplaces

LIGHTING

Albert Bartram
177 Hivings Hill,
Chesham,
Buckinghamshire HP5 2PN
(01494) 783 271 (Tel/Fax)
*Reproduction pewter 17th-century
chandeliers and wall sconces; they are
supplied to take candles but may be
wired for electricity.*

Chelsom Ltd
Heritage House,
Clifton Road, Blackpool,
Lancashire FY4 4QA
(01253) 791 344
Fax: (01253) 791 341
*Suppliers of a wide range of
contemporary and reproduction
lighting for both indoor and exterior
use, including table lamps and wall
lights, chandeliers and lanterns.
Many styles are represented:
Georgian, Regency, period American,*

*Art Deco, Art Nouveau, Victorian and
traditional English designs. While
brass is the most common finish, some
items are available in up to a dozen
other finishes.*

Danico Brass Ltd
31-33 Winchester Road,
Swiss Cottage,
London NW3 3NR
(0171) 483 4477
Fax: (0171) 722 7992
*Supplier of traditional modern
electrical accessories, including
Georgian, Regency and Victorian
styles.*

Forbes and Lomax Ltd
205B St John's Hill,
London SW11 1TH
(0171) 738 0202
Fax: (0171) 738 9224
*Suppliers of electric light switches and
sockets for period houses, including
the Invisible Light Switch, which is
similar to 1930s glass switches, and
antique bronze satin chrome switches.*

Jones
194 Westbourne Grove,
London W11
(0171) 229 6866 (Tel/Fax)
*Large collection of restored antique
lighting, fittings and shades from
1860 to 1960. The collection includes
converted Victorian gas fittings, Art
Nouveau and Art Deco lighting.*

Sugg Lighting
Sussex Manor Business Park,
Gatwick Road, Crawley,
West Sussex RH10 2GD
(01293) 540 111
Fax: (01293) 540 114
*Reproduction lanterns and wall and
hanging lamps suitable for gas or
electricity in Victorian and Edwardian
styles.*

Wilchester County
The Stables, Vicarage Lane,
Steeple Ashton, nr Trowbridge,
Wiltshire BA14 6HH
(01380) 870 764
*Specialists in reproduction American
primitive lighting.*

**Christopher Wray's Lighting
Emporium**
600 Kings Road
London SW6 2DX
(0171) 736 8434
Fax: (0171) 731 3507
*Contemporary and reproduction
lighting of all kinds, also parts and
accessories in their showrooms and
through the catalogue.*

STAIRCASES

Ballantine Boness Iron Co.
see Ironwork

Britannia
see Ironwork

Bylaw Ltd
see Built-in Furniture

The Cast Iron Shop
see Ironwork

Miller Shop Fitting
Unit 2, St Clements Centre,
St Clements Road,
Nechells, Birmingham B7 5AF
(0121) 322 2272
Fax: (0121) 327 0920
*Manufacturers of custom-built curved
staircases, handrails and ballusters,
and oak panelling. Also traditional
weight sliding sash windows.*

Southwell Stockwell Ltd
see Ironwork

Winther Browne
see Woodwork and Joinery

Yeo Valley Joinery
Church House,
Broad Street,
Congresbury,
Avon BS19 5DG
(01934) 833 660
Fax: (01934) 877 660
*Fine, custom-designed and
-built period staircases with hand-
carved traditional handrail work and
turned hardwood or cast-iron
balustrade; also fitted furniture and
other architectural features.*

WALLS

Aristocast Originals Ltd
14A Orgreave Close
Dorhouse Industrial Estate,
Hansworth,
Sheffield S13 9NP
(0114) 269 0900
Fax: (0114) 269 0955
*Georgian- and Victorian-style feature
plasterwork: mouldings, niches,
ceiling centres, fire surrounds, door
surrounds and canopies, columns and
beams.*

Alexander Beauchamp
Vulcan House,
Stratton Road,
Gloucester GL1 4HL
(01452) 384959
Fax: (01452) 385417
*Hand-printed wallpapers and fabrics,
based on archival designs dating from
1680.*

John Burgess Tiles
see Floors

Kenneth Clark Ceramics
The North Wing,
Southover Grange,
Southover Road,
Lewes, East Sussex BN7 1TP
(01273) 476 761
Fax: (01273) 479 565
*Many wall tiles and ceramic murals
of unique design, both those in stock
and those individually designed and
decorated. Notable are reproductions
of William de Morgan Victorian tiles.*

Colefax and Fowler
39 Brook Street,
London W1Y 2JE
(0171) 493 2231
Fax: (0171) 355 4037
*Reproduction 18th- and 19th-century
wallpapers.*

Belinda Coote
29 Holland Street,
London W8 4NA
(0171) 937 3924
Fax: (0171) 376 1027
*Reproduction antique tapestries copied
from European originals, all hand-
finished in a variety of sizes. Also
contemporary tapestries, cushion
covers, tapestry fabrics, paisley and
handpainted firescreens.*

WG Crotch Ltd
10 Tuddenham Avenue,
Ipswich, Suffolk IP4 2HE
(01473) 250 349
Fax: (01473) 213 180
*Manufacturers of fibrous plaster
mouldings, overmantels, console
brackets, ceiling roses, etc.*

Decorative Tile Works
Jackfield Tile Museum,
Ironbridge,
Telford,
Shropshire TF8 7AW
(01952) 884 124
Fax: (01952) 884 487
*Specialists in the reproduction of 19th-
century English tiles.*

Fine Art Mouldings Ltd
Unit 6,
Roebuck Road Trading Estate,
Roebuck Road,
Hainault, Ilford
Essex IG6 3TU
(0181) 502 7602
Fax: (0181) 502 7603
*Producers of decorative plasterwork for
classical, Tudor and Regency interiors.*

Hamilton Weston Wallpapers Ltd
18 St Mary's Grove,
Richmond,
Surrey TW9 1UY
(0181) 940 4850
Fax: (0181) 332 0296
*Specialists in reproduction original
18th- and 19th-century wallpaper
designs.*

AE Houghton and Son Ltd
see Woodwork and Joinery

H. and R. Johnson Tiles Ltd
Highgate Tile Works,
Tunstall,
Stoke-on-Trent ST6 4JX
(01782) 575575
Fax: (01782) 577377
*Maker of ceramic wall and floor tiles
for period and restoration projects.*

Original Style
see Floors

The Original Tile Company
23A Howe Street,
Edinburgh EH3 6TF
(0131) 556 2013
Fax: (0131) 558 3172
*A wide range of wall and floor tiles:
terracotta, natural stone and marble
tiles. Also handpainted tiles, both
imported and those done by their own
artists, including the Art Nouveau
selection inspired by Charles Rennie
Mackintosh. Restoration and
reproduction of broken or missing old
tiles including a tile fitting service.*

Osborne and Little
304-308 Kings Road,
London SW3 5UH
(0171) 352 1456
Fax: (0171) 351 7813
Reproduction traditional wallpapers.

Paris Ceramics
see Floors

Sanderson
112-120 Brompton Road,
London SW3 1JJ
(0171) 584 3344
Fax: (0171) 584 8404
*Reproduction period wallpapers;
19th-century archive designs include
those of William Morris.*

Watts and Co.
7 Tufton Street,
Westminster,
London SW1P 3QE
(0171) 222 2893
Fax: (0171) 233 1130
*Wallpapers and paper borders hand-
printed from authentic traditional
designs. Special commissions taken.*

Winther Browne
see Woodwork and and Joinery

Zoffany Ltd
Talbot House,
17 Church Street,
Rickmansworth,
Hertfordshire WD3 1DE
(01923) 710680
Fax: (01923) 710694
*Makers of wallpaper in Georgian,
Regency and Victorian designs, based
on their archive.*

WINDOWS

The Art of Glass
Manor Farm Craft Centre,
Wood Lane,
Earlswood,
Solihull B94 5JH
(01564) 703992
*Designer, painter, maker and restorer
of traditional stained and architectural
glass work.*

Barron Glass
Unit 4, Old Coalyard Farm Estate,
Northleach,
Gloucestershire GL54 3HE
(01451) 860 282
Fax: (01451) 860 275
*Maker of period etched and
enamelled glass, and suppliers of
period doors.*

Classic Designs
see Doors

Copycats
The Workshop
29 Maypole Road
Ashurst Wood East
East Grinstead
West Sussex RH19 3QN
(01342) 826 066
*Restoration and replacement of
traditional box sash windows.*

Goddard and Gibbs Studios
41-49 Kingsland Road,
London E2 8AD
(0171) 739 6563
Fax: (0171) 739 1979
*Specialists for over 100 years in the
fabrication and installation of stained
and decorative glass.*

Japac Designs
see Built-in Furniture

The London Shutter Company
18 Brockenhurst Road,
Ascot,
Berkshire SL5 9DL
(01344) 28385
Fax: (01344) 27575
*Both internal and exterior wooden
shutters in hard and soft woods, with
an oiled or painted, or handpainted,
finish.*

Mackinnon and Bailey
see Doors

Miller Shop Fitting
see Staircases

**The Original Box Sash Window
Company**
The Joinery, Unit 10,
Bridgewater Way,
Windsor, Berkshire SL4 1RD
(01753) 858 196
Fax: (01753) 857 827
*Box sash windows in traditional
designs made with pulleys and sash
cords and also casement windows,
with single or double glazing and
finished with wax, stain or white
paint. Also available are custom-
made exterior doors and door/window
screens in all period styles.*

Sashy and Sashy
5 Phoenix Lane,
Ashurst Wood,
Forest Row,
East Sussex RH19 3RA
(01342) 823 408
Fax: (01342) 823 745
*Sash window restorations and
replacements.*

Syntonic Joinery
see Woodwork and Joinery

Winther Browne
see Woodwork and Joinery

WOODWORK AND JOINERY

**Artisan Period and Victorian
Joinery**
Grange Farm,
Buxshalls Hill,
Lindfield,
Sussex
(01444) 484 491 (Tel/Fax)
*Traditional handmade joinery,
windows, doors, panelling, fitted and
freestanding cupboards, bookcases
and kitchens.*

Bylaw Ltd
see Built-in Furniture

AW Champion Ltd
Champion House,
Burlington Road, New Malden,
Surrey KT3 4NB
(0181) 949 1621
Fax: (0181) 949 0271
Suppliers of a large range of period mouldings including skirtings, architraves, dados, picture rails, beads and sash materials. Will also custom-make mouldings to match.

AE Houghton and Son Ltd
Common Road,
Dunnington,
York Y01 5PD
(01904) 489 193
Fax: (01904) 488 730
Restorers of antique furniture, panelling and joinery.

JAK Products
Glebe Cottage,
Hunsingore, nr Wetherby,
North Yorkshire LS22 5HY
(01423) 358216
Fax: (01423) 358050
Wood turnings for balusters, newels, columns and furniture parts.

Japac Designs
see Built-in Furniture

JSR Joinery Ltd
Woodpecker Court,
Poole Street,
Great Yeldham,
Halstead,
Essex CO9 4HN
(01787) 237 722
Fax: (01787) 237 294
Custom-made joinery for listed buildings, period houses and barn conversions.

Miller Shop Fitting
see Staircases

Syntonic Joinery
4 Woodville Road
Thornton Heath
Surrey CR7 8LG
(0181) 778 7838
Fax: (0181) 653 9449
Custom-made architectural details and cabinet work, also curved doors and windows.

Winther Browne
Nobel Road,
Eley Estate,
London N18 3DX
(0181) 803 3434
Fax: (0181) 807 0544
Specialize in timber beams. Also make decorative wood carvings and mouldings for doors, windows, walls, ceilings, staircases, panelled rooms, and mantels. Most of the items are made in pine and mahogany but other timbers may be specially ordered. Special items not in the catalogue can be commissioned.

Yeo Valley Joinery
see Staircases

**OTHER USEFUL
ADDRESSES/SOURCES**

British Ceramic Tile Council
Federation House,
Station Road,
Stoke-on-Trent ST4 2RU
(01782) 747 147
Information on the installation of ceramic tiles.

British Decorators' Association
6 Haywra Street,
Harrogate HG1 5BL
(01423) 567292/3
Over 3,000 member firms, many of which specialize in the decoration of period homes.

British Wood Preserving and Damp Proofing Association
6 Office Village,
4 Romford Road,
London E15 4EA
(0181) 519 2588
Free advice and literature on problems concerning timber preservation and flame retardation.

Building Conservation Trust
Apartment 39,
Hampton Court Palace,
East Molesey KT8 9BS
(0181) 943 2277
Educational charity promoting the good maintenance of buildings of all styles and ages. Permanent exhibit on home improvement and maintenance.

Building Employers Confederation
82 New Cavendish Street,
London W1M 8AD
(0171) 580 5588
Lists of stonemasons, painters and decorators available for work.

Cadw-Welsh Historic Monuments
2 Fitzalan Road,
Cardiff CF2 1UY
(01222) 500 200
Awards grants for repairing historic buildings in Wales.

Chartered Institution of Building Services Engineers (CIBSE)
Delta House,
222 Balham High Road,
London SW12 9BS
(0171) 675 5211
Free advice on plumbing, heating and ventilation.

Chartered Society of Designers
29 Bedford Square,
London WC1B 3EG
(0171) 631 1510
Many interior designers among its 8,000 members; information service and library.

Civil Trust
17 Charlton House Terrace,
London SW1Y 5AW
(0171) 930 0914
Promotes the protection and improvement of the environment in relationship to conservation and restoration projects.

English Heritage
Chesham House,
30 Warwick Street,
London W1R 5RD
(0171) 973 3000
Advice on restoration and preservation; grants available for repairing historic buildings in England.

The Georgian Group
6 Fitzroy Square,
London W1P 6DX
(0171) 387 1720
Advice on restoration and repair of Georgian buildings.

The Guild of Master Craftsmen
166 High Street,
Lewes,
Sussex BN7 1XU
(01273) 478 449
Trade association with member craftsmen available for restoration work; information service and library.

Historic Buildings Council for Scotland
Longmore House,
Salisbury Place,
Edinburgh EH9 1SH
(0131) 668 8600
Awards grants for repairing historic buildings in Scotland.

Historic Houses Association
2 Chester Street,
London SW1X 7BB
(0171) 259 5688
Association of owners and guardians of historic houses, parks and gardens; information service and seminars.

The National Trust
36 Queen Anne's Gate,
London SW1
(0171) 222 9251
Membership organization promoting the restoration and maintenance of period properties of historic significance.

The National Trust for Scotland
5 Charlotte Square,
Edinburgh EH2 4DU
(0131) 226 5922
Member organization promoting the preservation and care of places of natural, historic or architectural interest in Scotland.

Paint Research Association
Waldegrave Road,
Teddington,
Middlesex TW11 8LD
(0181) 977 4427
Literature available on paints, pre-treatment products and masonry coatings.

Royal Commission on the Ancient and Historical Monuments in Wales
Crown Building
Plascrug
Aberystwyth SY23 1NJ
(01970) 621200
Answers queries from the general public concerning the age, type and function of buildings.

Royal Commission on the Ancient and Historical Monuments of Scotland
John Sinclair House,
16 Bernard Terrace,
Edinburgh EH8 9NX
(0131) 662 1456
Extensive collection of pictorial and documentary material relating to Scottish ancient monuments and historical buildings.

Royal Commission on the Historical Monuments of England
National Monuments Record Centre,
Kemble Drive,
Swindon SN2 2GZ
(01793) 414 600
Maintains inventories of ancient and historic monuments connected with the culture and condition of the life of people in England; publications available from HMSO.

Royal Incorporation of Architects in Scotland
15 Rutland Square,
Edinburgh EH1 2BE
(0131) 229 7205
2,700 member architects in Scotland.

Royal Institute of British Architects (RIBA)
66 Portland Place,
London W1N 4AD
(0171) 580 5533
22,000 member architects: Directory of Practices available; library.

Royal Institute of Chartered Surveyors (RICS)
12 Great George Street,
Parliament Square,
London SW1P 3AD
(0171) 222 7000
69,000 members; information service and library.

The Society for the Protection of Ancient Buildings
37 Spital Square
London E1 6DY
(0171) 377 1644
Publishes technical bulletins on repairs of historic buildings; provides names of architects and others specializing in restoration work.

The Victorian Society
1 Priory Gardens, Bedford Park,
London W4 1TT
(0181) 994 1019
Promotes the preservation of Victorian and Edwardian buildings.

PERIODICALS OF INTEREST:

Architectural Design
Building Design
Country Homes and Interiors
Country Life
Country Living
Elle Decoration
English Heritage Magazine
Essential Kitchen, Bathroom and Bedroom Magazine
Historic House
Historic Houses, Castles and Gardens Annual
Home
Home Flair
Homes and Antiques
Homes and Gardens
Homes and Ideas
House and Garden
House Beautiful
Individual Homes
Kitchens, Bedrooms, Bathrooms
National Trust Magazine
Period House
Period House and its Garden
Period Living and Traditional Homes
Victorian Society Annual
World of Interiors

DIRECTORY OF SUPPLIERS: AMERICAN

This list includes many of the best and most widely-distributed suppliers of home furnishings products, but is by no means complete. Not only are literally hundreds of companies making fine products for interiors, but the field is rapidly growing. Magazines devoted to interior restoration, preservation and style are rich sources of craftspeople and manufacturers.

Most of the companies below produce catalogs which they distribute either free or at moderate cost. The catalogs themselves are often full of good ideas for restoration projects.

Manufacturing sources normally sell only to retail outlets. If you write or call, they will identify the source nearest you.

Sources which sell to the trade only may allow you to visit their showrooms; many have catalogs or brochures. To buy from these sources, however, it will be necessary to use the services of a decorator or architect.

ARCHITECTURAL SALVAGE YARDS

Antiquarian Traders
9031 West Olympic Blvd.,
Beverly Hills,
CA 90211
(310) 247-3900
and
399 Lafayette Street,
New York,
NY 10003
(212) 260-1200
Antique architectural elements, lighting and furniture on both coasts.

Architectural Accents
2711 Piedmont Road,
Atlanta,
GA 30305
(404) 266-8700
Old and reproduction architectural elements.

Architectural Antiques
121 East Sheridan Avenue,
Oklahoma City,
OK 73104
(405) 232-0759
Architectural salvage.

Architectural Antiques Exchange
715 North Second Street,
Philadelphia,
PA 19123
(215) 922-3669
Old house and building parts.

Architectural Antiques, Inc.
801 Washington Avenue North,
Minneapolis,
MN 55401
(612) 332-8344
Architectural salvage & reproductions.

Architectural Antiquities
Harborside,
ME 04642
(207) 326-4938
Old house parts, hardware, lighting.

The Architectural Bank
1824 Felicity Street,
New Orleans,
LA 70113
(504) 523-2702
Old and reproduction shutters, fireplaces, hardware.

Berkeley Architectural Salvage
2741 Tenth Street,
Berkeley,
CA 94710
(415) 849-2025
Salvage hardware and new stock.

Sylvan Brandt
651 East Main Street,
Lititz,
PA 17543
(717) 626-4520
Flooring, windows, doors, hardware, log houses.

By-Gone Days Antiques
3100 South Boulevard,
Charlotte,
NC 28209
(704) 527-8718
Architectural salvage.

Coronado Wrecking & Salvage
4200 Broadway South East,
Albuquerque,
NM 87105
(505) 877-2821
Old house parts.

Elizabeth Street
210 Elizabeth Street,
New York,
NY 10012
(212) 941-4800
Outdoor and garden objects, fountains.

The Emporium
2515 Morse Street,
Houston,
TX 77019
(713) 528-3808
Salvage and reproduction elements for old houses.

Gargoyles
512 South Third Street,
Philadelphia,
PA 19147
(215) 629-1700
Decorative and architectural house elements.

Great Gatsby's
5070 Peachtree Industrial Boulevard,
Atlanta,
GA 30341
(404) 457-1905
Large selection of architectural antiques and reproductions.

Irreplaceable Artifacts of North America, Inc.
14 Second Avenue,
New York,
NY 10003
(212) 777-2900
Interior and exterior elements from New York and surroundings.

Lost City Arts
275 Lafayette Street,
New York,
NY 10012
(212) 941-8025
Architectural lighting, advertising signs, elements of demolished buildings.

Materials Unlimited
2 West Michigan Avenue,
Ypsilanti,
MI 48197
(313) 483-6980
Salvage plus new architectural materials, antique furniture and accessories.

Nostalgia Architectural Antiques
307 Stiles Avenue,
Savannah,
GA 31401
(912) 236-8176
Doors, windows, fireplaces. All old and new building and decorating materials and lighting.

Ohmega Salvage
2407 San Pablo Avenue,
Berkeley,
CA 94702
(510) 843-7368
Authentic hardware and architectural elements. Will search for particular needs.

The Renovation Source
3512 North Southport,
Chicago,
IL 60657
(312) 327-1250
All elements needed for restoration and renovation.

United House Wrecking
535 Hope Street,
Stamford,
CT 06906
(203) 348-5371
Old and reproduction house parts, windows, doors, garden ornaments.

Urban Archaeology
285 Lafayette Street,
New York,
NY 10012
(212) 431-6969
Doors, windows, fireplaces, exterior ornament.

Urban Artifacts
4700 Wissahickon Avenue,
Suite 111,
Philadelphia,
PA 19144
(800) 621-1962
Fireplaces, doors, stained and beveled glass.

Dennis C. Walker
PO Box 309,
Tallmadge,
OH 44278
(216) 633-1081
Historic building materials: beams, flooring, stone, mantels, doors, dismantled buildings.

DOORS AND WINDOWS

Allied Window, Inc.
2724 West McMicken Avenue,
Cincinnati,
OH 45214
(800) 445-5411,
(513) 559-1212
Invisible storm windows, inside or outside.

American Heritage Shutters, Inc.
6655 Popler Street,
Suite 204,
Germantown ,
TN 38138
(901) 751-1000
Interior and exterior shutters

Andersen Windows
Box 3900,
Peoria,
IL 61614
(800) 426-4261
Windows, glazed doors, skylights.

Architectural Components
26 North Leverett Road,
Montague,
MA 01351
(413) 367-9441
Pediment doorways, palladian windows, sashes, all woodworking services.

Artistic Glass
2112 Dundas Street West,
Toronto,
Ontario M6R 1W9
Canada,
(416) 531-4881
Tempered glass doors, windows, skylights, room dividers.
To the trade only.

The Atrium Door & Window Company
PO Box 226957,
Dallas,
TX 75222-6957
(214) 634-9663
Doors, windows, exterior hardware.

S. A. Bendheim Co., Inc.
61 Willett Street,
Passaic,
NJ 07055
(800) 221-7379,
in NJ (201) 471-1733
Restoration glass made using the original cylinder method.

Blenko Glass Company
Box 67,
Milton,
WV 25541
(304) 743-9081
Handblown reproduction glass.

Grand Era Reproductions
PO Box 1026J,
Lapeer,
MI 48446
(313) 664-1756
Victorian, colonial, Cape Cod style screen/storm doors.

Historic Shutter & Restoration, Inc.
5700 Fourth Avenue,
Key West,
FL 33040
(305) 296-6332
Custom manufacturing and complete shutter restoration.

Historic Windows
PO Box 1172,
Harrisonburg,
VA 22801
(540) 434-5855
Wooden interior shutters.

Hope's Landmark Products Inc.
PO Box 580,
95-99 Jamestown Avenue,
Jamestown,
NY 14702-0580
(716) 665-6223
Window hardware such as casement operators and scroll handles.

Jennifer's Glass Works
6767 Peachtree Industrial Blvd.,
Norcross,
GA 30092
(404) 447-4878
Leaded, beveled and stained glass; window and door millwork.

Kenmore Industries
One Thompson Square,
PO Box 34,
Boston,
MA 02129
(617) 242-1711
Exterior doors, windows.

Lamson-Taylor Custom Doors
3 Tucker Road,
South Ackworth,
NH 03607
(603) 835-2992
Custom wood doors.

Marvin Windows & Doors
Warroad,
MN 56763
(800) 346-5128
in MN (800) 552-1167
in Canada (800) 263-6161
Woodframed doors, windows, skylights.

Morgan Products Ltd.
500 Park Plaza,
Box 2446,
Oshkosh,
WI 54903
(800) 766-1992
Wooden doors and windows in all styles; a new line includes leaded, beveled panes.

National Windows
2201 North 29th Avenue,
Birmingham,
AL 35207
(205) 252-7157
Windows in all styles.

The Old Wagon Factory
PO Box 1427,
Clarksville,
VA 23927
(804) 374-5787
Victorian storm/screen doors, gingerbread ornaments, garden gates.

Pella Corporation
100 Main Street,
Pella,
IA 50219
(800) 547-3552
All windows and doors, including the Architects Series.

Shuttercraft
282 Stepstone Hill,
Guilford,
CT 06437
(203) 453-1973
Wooden interior shutters.

Touchstone Woodworks
Department E.S.,
PO Box 112,
Ravenna,
OH 44266
(216) 297-1313
Victorian style screen/storm doors.

Velux-America Inc.
PO Box 5001,
Greenwood,
SC 29648-5001
(800) 283-2831
Windows, skylights.

Weathershield Mfg.
PO Box 309,
Medford,
WI 54451
(800) 477-6808

The Woodstone Company
Patch Road,
PO Box 223,
Westminster,
VT 05158
(802) 722-4784
Custom-made exterior doors, windows.

FABRICS

Baker, Knapp & Tubbs
917 Merchandise Mart,
Chicago,
IL 60654
(312) 329-9410
Fabrics for use in traditional settings. To the trade only.

John Boone Inc.
979 Third Avenue,
New York,
NY 10022
(212) 758-0012
Fabrics, wallcoverings and trimmings. To the trade only.

Boussac of France, Inc.
979 Third Avenue,
New York,
NY 10022
(212) 421-0534
French fabrics. To the trade only.

Brunschwig & Fils
979 Third Avenue,
New York,
NY 10022
(212) 838-7878
Fabrics, wallcoverings, many documentary in source. To the trade only.

Calico Corners
203 Gale Lane,
Kennett Square,
PA 19348-1764
(800) 777-9933 for store locations
Nationwide chain of discount shops carrying fine fabrics. Also mail-order catalog.

Manuel Canovas, Inc.
979 Third Avenue,
New York,
NY 10022
(212) 752-9588
Fax: (212) 935-0619
French fabrics. To the trade only.

Clarence House Imports
211 East 58th Street,
New York,
NY 10022
(212) 752-2890,
Fax: (212) 645-8060
Traditional imported furnishing fabrics and wallcoverings. To the trade only.

Cowtan & Tout
979 Third Avenue,
New York,
NY 10022
(212) 753-4488
Traditional furnishing fabrics and wallcoverings, including Colefax & Fowler, Jane Churchill. To the trade only.

The Fabric Outlet
30 Airport Road,
Airport Executive Plaza,
West Lebanon,
NH 03784
(800) 635-9715
Discount designer fabric.

Fabrics First
PO Box 3359
Grand Rapids,
MI 49501-3359
(800) 627-2526
Fabric catalog — they will make up window treatments and pillows to order.

Fonthill, Ltd.
979 Third Avenue,
New York,
NY 10022
(212) 755-6700
Fabrics and coordinating wallcoverings. To the trade only.

Greeff Fabrics
210 Madison Avenue,
New York,
NY 10016
(212) 223-0357
Fabrics and wallcoverings, including Winterthur Collection. To the trade only.

Hinson & Company
979 Third Avenue,
New York,
NY 10022
(212) 475-4100
Fabrics, wallpaper, decorative accessories, lighting. To the trade only.

Houles
8584 Melrose Avenue,
Los Angeles,
CA 90069
(213) 652-6171,
Fax: (213) 652-8370
French imported drapery and upholstery trimmings. To the trade.

Christopher Hyland Inc.
979 Third Avenue,
New York,
NY 10022
(212) 688-6121,
Fax: (212) 688-6176
Imported English fabric and wallcovering including Watts & Co., Gainsborough Silk Weavers, Timney-Fowler. To the trade only.

Kravet
225 Central Avenue South,
Bethpage,
NY 11714
(516) 293-2000
Fabrics including the Mark Hampton collection. To the trade only.

Lee/Jofa
800 Central Blvd.,
Carlstadt,
NJ 07072
(201) 438-8444,
Fax: (201) 438-7034
Fabrics and wallcoverings. To the trade only.

Marvic Textiles
979 Third Avenue,
New York,
NY 10022
(212) 371-4333
Fine traditional fabrics. To the trade only.

Christopher Norman, Inc.
504 East 74th Street,
New York,
NY 10021
(212) 879-6559
Fabric, wallcoverings, furniture, lighting. To the trade only.

Osborne & Little
979 Third Avenue,
New York,
NY 10022
(212) 751-3333
Fabrics and wallcoverings imported from England and France; Nina Campbell, Designers Guild, Fardis lines. To the trade only.

Pierre Deux
870 Madison Avenue,
New York,
NY 10021
(800) 7-PIERRE
French furnishing fabrics distributed through Pierre Deux shops nationwide.

Raintree Designs
979 Third Avenue,
New York,
NY 10022
(800) 422-4400
Manufacturers of the Victoria Morland fabrics and wallcoverings widely distributed at retail.

Arthur Sanderson & Sons
979 Third Avenue,
New York,
NY 10022
(212) 319-7220
Traditional English fabrics and wallcoverings including William Morris designs. To the trade only.

Scalamandré
300 Trade Zone Drive,
Ronkonkoma,
NY 11779
(516) 467-8800
Specialists in fabrics for historic restorations. To the trade only.

F. Schumacher & Co.
79 Madison Avenue,
New York,
NY 10016
(800) 523-1200
(212) 213-7900
Traditional fabrics, wallcoverings, carpets. To the trade only.

Silk Surplus
235 East 58th Street,
New York,
NY 10022
(212) 753-6511
Discount fabrics and trimmings, many from Scalamandré.

FIREPLACES AND STOVES

Danny Alessandro, Ltd.
Edwin Jackson, Ltd.,
307 East 60th Street,
New York,
NY 10022
(212) 759-8210
Antique and reproduction fireplaces and accessories.

Bryant Stove Works, Inc.
RFD2 Box 2048,
Rich Road,
Thorndyke,
ME 04986
(207) 568-3665
Victorian-style woodstoves and cookstoves, coal stoves, player pianos.

Buckley Rumford Fireplace Co.
PO Box 21131,
Columbus,
OH 43221
(614) 221-6131
Efficient fireplace inserts; plans, kits, components and fully-installed units.

Classic Cast Stone of Dallas, Inc.
3162 Miller Drive North,
Garland,
TX 75042-7759
(214) 276-2000
Cast stone fireplaces and architectural elements. To the trade only.

The Country Iron Foundry
PO Box 600,
Paoli,
PA 19301
(610)296-7122,
Cast iron firebacks.

Draper & Draper, Ltd.
200 Lexington Avenue,
New York,
NY 10016
(212) 679-0547
Handcarved reproduction American-style mantels.

Elmira Stove Works
22 Church Street,
Elmira,
Ontario N3B 1M3
Canada,
(519) 669-5103
Fireplace inserts, woodstoves, cookstoves

Hallidays America Inc.
PO Box 731,
Sparta,
NJ 07871-0731
(201) 729-8876
Antique and reproduction mantels from England, distributed through Beacon Hill showrooms to the trade.

Mantels of Yesteryear, Inc.
70 West Tennessee Avenue,
PO Box 908,
McCaysville,
GA 30555
(706) 492-5534
Antique mantelpieces to the trade.

Rais & Wittus, Inc.
Hack Green Road,
Pound Ridge,
NY 10576
(914) 764-5679
Distributors of the Swedish Rais woodstove.

Readybuilt Products
1701 McHenry Street,
Baltimore,
MD 21223,
(301) 233-5833
Manufacturers of mantelpieces, heater fireplaces, gas/electric logs.

Royal Crown European Fireplaces
333 East State Street, Suite 206,
Rockford,
IL 61104
(800) 373-2042
Swedish-style ceramic stoves burning wood or natural gas.

FLOORS

ABC Carpet & Home
888 Broadway,
New York,
NY 10003
(800) 888-7847,
in NY (212) 473-3000
A fabulous store with every style of old and new rugs, carpeting, furniture, home accessories.

Aged Woods
First Capital Wood Products, Inc.,
2331 East Market Street,
York,
PA 17402
(800) 233-9307,
in PA (717) 840-0330
Antique wood floor boards, ceilings, wall paneling.

Albany Woodworks
PO Box 729,
Albany,
LA 70711,
(504) 567-1155
Antique pine flooring, moldings, paneling, doors, stairtreads.

American Olean Tile Co.
1000 Cannon Avenue,
PO Box 271,
Lansdale,
PA 19446-0271
(215) 855-1111
Tiles for floors, walls, kitchens, baths.

Authentic Pine Floors Inc.
4042 Highway 42,
PO Box 206,
Locust Grove,
GA 30248
(800) 283-6038
4-inch to 12-inch pine flooring.

Doris Leslie Blau
15 East 57th Street,
New York,
NY 10022
(212)759-3715
Fine antique carpets and textiles.

J. R. Burrows & Co.
PO Box 522,
Rockland,
MA 02370
(617) 982-1812
American representative of Woodward Grosvenor & Co. of England. William Morris and other archival patterns. Scottish lace, late 19th century wallpaper patterns.

Carlisle Restoration Lumber
Box 606D,
Stoddard,
NH 03464
(603) 446-3937
Wood for wide-board floors, wall paneling.

Chevalier, Inc.
11 East 57th Street,
New York,
NY 10022
(212) 750-5505,
Antique tapestries & rugs, restoration and cleaning.

Conklin's
R.D. #1, Box 70,
Susquehanna,
PA 18847
(717) 465-3832
Barnwood weathered over decades, random-width planks and flooring, hand-hewn beams. To the trade.

Country Floors Inc.
15 East 16th Street,
New York,
NY 10003
(212) 627-8300
Vast selection of floors in all materials. Several trade showrooms nationwide.

Designs in Tile
PO Box 358,
Mt. Shasta,
CA 96067
(916) 926-2629
Historic reproductions in many styles such as; Art Deco, Gothic Revival, William De Morgan, Arts & Crafts.

Elon Tile
150 East 58th Street
New York,
NY 10155
(212) 759-6996
Tiles for floors, kitchens, baths.

Edward Fields Carpetmakers
232 East 59th Street,
New York,
NY 10022
(212) 310-0400
Custom carpets. To the trade only.

Goodwin Lumber Company
Rt. 2, Box 119-AA,
Micanopy,
FL 32667
(800) 336-3118, or (904) 373-9663
Heart pine flooring, lumber for cabinetry.

Harris-Tarkett Inc.
2225 Eddie Williams Road,
PO Box 300,
Johnson City,
TN 37605-0300
(800) 842-7816
Hardwood flooring in plank and parquet; pine flooring.

The Italian Tile Center
Italian Trade Commission,
499 Park Avenue,
New York,
NY 10022
(212) 980-1500
Information on Italian tile manufacturers and distributors in the US.

The Joinery Co.
PO Box 518,
Tarboro,
NC 27886
(919) 823-3306
Heart pine for flooring, paneling, stair parts, cabinetry.

Kentucky Wood Floors
4200 Reservoir Avenue,
Louisville,
KY 40213
(502) 451-6024
Wood floors

Patterson, Flynn & Martin, Inc.
979 Third Avenue,
New York,
NY 10022
(212) 751-6414
Carpets and rugs including Colefax & Fowler and Stockwell from England. To the trade only.

Mountain Lumber
Route 2 Box 43-1,
Ruckersville,
VA 22968
(804) 985-3646
Antique heart pine.

Sandy Pond Hardwoods
921-A Lancaster Pike,
Quarryville,
PA 17566
(717) 284-5030
Tiger and bird's-eye maple, curly ash, oak, cherry, birch lumber and flooring.

Stark Carpet Corporation
979 Third Avenue,
New York,
NY 10022
(212) 752-9000
Antique and custom-made carpets. To the trade only.

Tiresias, Inc.
PO Box 1522,
Orangeburg,
SC 29116
(803) 534-8478
Wood floors, fireplaces, moldings.

Thos. K. Woodard
799 Madison Avenue,
New York,
NY 10021
(212) 988-2906
Early American-style carpets and runners; quilts.

HARDWARE

American Home Supply
PO Box 697,
Campbell,
CA 95009
(408) 246-1962
Solid brass reproduction hardware.

Anglo-American Brass Co.
PO Box Drawer 9487,
San Jose,
CA 95157-9487
(408) 246-0203
Manufacturers of exterior and interior hardware in many styles. Lamps, shades and furniture hardware.

Ball and Ball
463 West Lincoln Highway,
Exton,
PA 19341
(610) 363-7330
Exterior hardware, interior hardware, lighting.

Monroe Coldren & Sons
723 East Virginia Avenue,
West Chester, PA 19380,
(610) 692-5651
Original iron and brass hardware

Crawford's Old House Store
301 McCall, Room 907,
Waukesha,
WI 53186
(800) 556-7878,
(414) 542-0685
Reproduction Victorian hardware.

Crown City Hardware
1047 North Allen Avenue,
Pasadena,
CA 91004
All restoration hardware.

Elephant Hill Ironworks
Rte. 1, Box 168,
Tunbridge,
VT 05077
(802) 889-9444
Hand-forged iron latches, hinges, fireplace cranes, jamb hooks.

Liz Gordon
Los Angeles,
CA
(800) 939-9003
Antique and reproduction hardware from mid-1800s to Bakelite.

P.E. Guerin
21-23 & 25 Jane Street,
New York,
NY 10014
(212) 243-5271
Manufacturers and importers of door and plumbing hardware. To the trade only.

Historic Housefitters Co.
Farm to Market Road,
Brewster,
NY 10509
(914) 278-2427
Brass and iron handmade hardware.

The Home Book
628 Santa Cruz Avenue,
Menlo Park,
CA 94025
Catalog of hardware, tools, lighting, plumbing fixtures, furniture and accessories mostly contemporary in style.

Hundley Hardware
617 Bryant Street,
San Francisco,
CA 94107
(415) 777-5050
Door, furniture and bathroom hardware.

Kayne & Son Custom Forged Hardware
76 Daniel Ridge Road,
Candler,
NC 28715
(704) 667-8868
Hooks, brackets, custom forging.

Kemp & George
9180 Lesaint Drive,
Fairfield,
OH 45014
(800) 343-4012
Mail order exterior door hardware, ceilings, moldings, lighting, kitchen sinks, bath hardware.

Kraft Hardware
306 East 61st Street,
New York,
NY 10021
(212) 838-2214
Wide range of architectural, bath and furniture hardware. To the trade only.

Brian F. Leo
7532 Columbus Avenue, South,
Richfield,
MN 55423
(612) 861-1473
Custom fabricator of hardware, architectural ornament and cast-metal specialties.

Liz's Antique Hardware
435 South La Brea Avenue,
Los Angeles,
CA 90036
(213) 939-4403
350,00 pieces of old hardware in all styles from Victorian to Deco.

Paxton Hardware Ltd.
7818 Bradshaw Road,
Upper Falls,
MD 21156
(410)592-8505
Distributors of door and furniture hardware and lamp parts.

Plexacraft Products, Inc.
5406 San Fernando Road,
PO Box 3722,
Glendale,
CA 91201
(818) 246-8201
Exterior and interior hardware.

The Renovator's Supply
Millers Falls,
MA 01349
(800) 659-2231
Mail order exterior hardware, interior hardware, stairs, fireplaces, bath and kitchen hardware, bath sinks.

Tremont Nail Company
8 Elm Street,
PO Box 111,
Wareham,
MA 02571
(508) 295-0038
Steel cut nails for historic restoration; hardware.

Virginia Metalcrafters
1010 East Main Street,
PO Box 1068,
Waynesboro,
VA 22980
(540)949-9400
Hardware, lighting, fireplace accessories from a number of historic restorations: Colonial Williamsburg, Historic Newport, Old Sturbridge Village, Mystic Seaport.

Williamsburg Blacksmiths
PO Box 1776,
Williamsburg,
MA 01096
(413) 268-7341
Quality wrought iron hardware.

Wood's Metal Studios
6945 Fishburg Road,
Dayton,
OH 45424
(513) 233-6751
Reproduction iron latches, shutter hardware, pot racks.

Woodbury Blacksmith & Forge Co.
PO Box 268,
Woodbury,
CT 06798
(203) 263-5737
Early American wrought iron hardware.

KITCHEN AND BATH CABINETRY

Allmilmo Corporation
70 Clinton Road,
PO Box 629,
Fairfield,
NJ 07004
(201) 227-2502
Kitchen and bath cabinets.

Alno Network USA
One Design Center Place, #643,
Boston,
MA 02210
(616) 482-5592
Kitchen cabinetry

Downsview Kitchens
2635 Rena Road,
Mississauga,
Ontario L4T 1G6
Canada
(905) 677-9354 for nearest showroom
Kitchen cabinetry through designers.

Beverly Ellsley Collection
175 Post Road West,
Westport,
CT 06880
(203) 454-0503
Handcrafted kitchen cabinets.

The Kennebec Company
1 Front Street,
Bath,
ME 04530
(207) 443-2131
Handcrafted wooden cabinetry.

Merillat Industries, Inc.
PO Box 1946,
Adrian,
MI 49221
(800) 624-1250
Kitchen and bathroom cabinets.

Christopher Peacock Bespoke English Cabinetry
151 Greenwich Avenue,
Greenwich,
CT 06830
(203) 862-9333
Kitchen cabinets in the English tradition. Brochure.

Poggenpohl USA Corp.
8010 Woodland Center, Suite 400,
Tampa,
FL 33614
(305) 923-2688
Kitchen and bathroom cabinets.

Rutt Custom Kitchens
PO Box 129,
1564 Main Street,
Goodville,
PA 17528
(215) 445-6751
Kitchen cabinets.

SieMatic Corporation
886 Town Center Drive,
Langhorne,
PA 19047
(215) 750-1928
Kitchen cabinetry, including Smallbone.

Wellborn Cabinet Inc.
38669 Hwy. 77,
PO Box 1210,
Ashland,
AL 36251
(800) 336-8040
Wooden cabinets for kitchen, bath.

Wood-Mode
Kreamer,
PA 17833
(800) 635-7500
Kitchen cabinets.

LIGHTING

Marvin Alexander, Inc.
315 East 62nd Street,
New York,
NY 10021
(212) 838-2320
Fine antique chandeliers and wall sconces. To the trade.

Authentic Designs
The Mill Road,
West Rupert,
VT 05776-0011
(802) 394-7713
Early American and Colonial reproduction lighting fixtures.

B & P Lamp Supply, Inc.
843 Old Morrison Highway,
McMinnville,
TN 37110
(615) 473-3016
Early American and Victorian reproduction lamps, lamp parts, shades, bulbs.

Brandon Industries
1601 West Wilmeth Road,
McKinney,
TX 75069
(214) 542- 3000
Sconces, lamp posts, mailboxes.

Brass Line
5935 South Broadway,
Tyler,
TX 75703
(903) 561-1111
Reproduction lighting from American, English, and French originals.

City Lights
2226 Massachusetts Avenue,
Cambridge,
MA 02140
(617) 547-1490
Large stock of antique fixtures and lamps.

A. J. P. Coppersmith & Co.
20 Industrial Parkway,
Woburn,
MA 01801
(617) 245-1223
Indoor and outdoor lighting.

Conant Custom Brass
PO Box 1523T,
Burlington,
VT 05402
(802) 658-4482
Solid brass and polished chrome reproduction lighting and hardware.

Hammerworks
6 Fremont Street,
Worcester,
MA 01603
(508) 755-3434
Handmade Colonial reproduction chandeliers, sconces, lanterns in copper, brass, iron, tin

Hurley Patentee Lighting
464 Old Rt 209,
Hurley,
NY 12443
(914) 331-5414
Reproduction early lighting, either candle-lit or electrified. Hurricane shades, brackets, candles, bulbs.

Iron Apple Forge
Routes 263 & 413,
PO Box 724,
Buckingham,
PA 18912
(215) 794-7351
Wrought iron chandeliers and ironwork.

Just Bulbs
936 Broadway,
New York,
NY 10010
(212) 228-7820
Every sort of light bulb: quartz halogen, globes, candle bulbs.

King's Chandelier Company
Highway 14, PO Box 667,
Eden (Leaksville),
NC 27288
(910) 623-6188
Crystal chandeliers and sconces.

Lighting Specialist, Inc.
4103 San Fernando Road,
Glendale,
CA 91204
(818) 240-3913
Antique chandeliers, wall sconces and lamps. To the trade.

Gates Moore
River Road, Silvermine,
Norwalk,
CT 06850
(203) 847-3231
Reproductions of antique lighting.

Nesle
151 East 57th Street,
New York,
NY 10022
(212) 755-0515
Antique and reproduction chandeliers, sconces and lamps. To the trade only.

Progress Lighting
101 Corporate Drive,
Spartanburg,
SC 29303-5007
(803) 599-6000
Indoor and outdoor lighting.

Rejuvenation Lamp & Fixture Co.
1100 South East Grand Avenue,
Portland,
OR 97214
(503) 230-1900
Reproduction lighting; especially strong in arts-and-crafts styles.

Roy Electric Co., Inc.
1054 Coney Island Avenue,
Brooklyn,
NY 11230
(800) 366-3347,
in NY (718) 434-7002
Antique & reproduction Victorian and turn of the century lighting; antique and reproduction plumbing fixtures, parts.

The Saltbox
3004 Columbia Avenue,
Lancaster,
PA 17603
(717) 392-5649
Reproductions of indoor and outdoor lighting, mainly 18th century.

Versailles Lighting, Inc.
224 West 30th Street, 9th Floor,
New York,
NY 10001
(212) 564-0240
Antique chandeliers and sconces. To the trade.

Victorian Lighting Works
251 South Pennsylvania Avenue,
PO Box 469,
Centre Hall,
PA 16828
(814) 364-9577
Victorian-style lighting fixtures.

METALWORK

AA Abingdon Affiliates, Inc.
2149 Utica Avenue,
Brooklyn,
NY 11234
(718) 258-8333
Tin ceilings, moldings.

Architectural Iron Company
Box 126, Route 6 West,
Milford,
PA 18337
(717) 296-7722,
(212) 243-2664
Wrought and cast iron fences and restoration.

Cassidy Bros. Forge, Inc.
U.S. Route 1,
Rowley,
MA 01969-1796
(508) 948-7303
Custom architectural ironwork.

Chelsea Decorative Metal Co.
9603 Moonlight Drive,
Houston,
TX 77096
(713) 721-9200
Embossed metal ceilings.

Erie Landmark Company
4449 Brookfield Corporate Drive,
Chantilly,
VA 22021-1642
(800) 874-7848
National Register plaques, metal signs and logo medallions.

Mike Shaffer, Blacksmith
Mountain Forge,
1155 Dantel Court,
Stone Mountain,
GA 30083
(770) 469-2680
Custom ornamental iron work, hand forgings.

Monte Haberman
1202 East Pine Street,
Placentia,
CA 92670
(714) 993-4766
Hand-forged fence parts, lamps.

The Iron Shop
PO Box 547,
400 Reed Road,
Broomall,
PA 19008
(610) 544-7100
Aluminum spiral staircases in cast-iron style.

Moultrie Manufacturing Company
PO Drawer 1179,
Moultrie,
GA 31768
(800) 841-8674,
(912) 985-1312
Fences, furniture, fountains, statuary.

W. F. Norman Corp.
P. O. Box 323,
Nevada,
MO 64772
(800) 641-4038,
in MO (417) 667-5552
Steel ceilings, moldings, all kinds of ornaments, weathervanes, finials.

Robinson Iron
Box 1119,
1856 Robinson Road,
Alexander City,
AL 35011-1119
(205) 329-8486
Cast iron lighting, fountains and statuary.

Steptoe & Wife Antiques, Ltd.
322 Geary Avenue,
Toronto, Canada M6H 2C7
(416) 530-4200
Cast iron spiral stairs.

Stewart Iron Works Co.
PO Box 2612,
20 West 18th Street,
Covington,
KY 41012-2612
(606) 431-1985
Fences and gates in Victorian/Edwardian styles.

Wind & Weather
The Albion Street Water Tower,
PO Box 2320,
Mendocino,
CA 95460
(800)922-9463,
(707) 937-0323
Weather vanes, sundials, weather instruments, cupolas.

PLUMBING

American-Standard
PO Box 6820,
Piscataway,
NJ 08855
(800) 821-7700
Kitchen and bath fixtures.

Bates & Bates
3699 Industry Avenue,
Lakewood,
CA 90712
(213) 595-8824,
(800) 726-7680
Bath fixtures and hardware. To the trade only.

Eljer Plumbingware
17120 Dallas Parkway,
Dallas,
TX 75248
(800) 42-ELJER
Bathroom fixtures.

Kohler Co.
Highland Drive,
Kohler,
WI 53044
(800) 4 KOHLER
Kitchen and bath fixtures.

Sherle Wagner International
60 East 57th Street,
New York,
NY 10022
(212) 758-3300
Exclusive bathroom fixtures and hardware.

Waterworks
237 East 58th Street,
New York,
NY 10022
(800) 899-6757 for catalog
Elegant bath fixtures in traditional styles. To the trade.

WALLS, CEILINGS AND MILLWORK

Anaglypta & Lincrusta
To find local dealers:,
East Coast (800) 824-4777,
West Coast (800) 992-8700
Embossed wallcoverings and borders in classical and Victorian patterns.

Anthony Wood Products
PO Box 1081,
Hillsboro,
TX 76645
(817) 582-7225
Balusters, finials, porch posts, fretwork, brackets, corbels.

Architectural Paneling, Inc.
979 Third Avenue,
New York,
NY 10022
(212) 371-9632
Paneling, moldings, fireplaces; all made to order and to the trade only.

Arvid's Historic Woods
2500 Hewitt Avenue,
Everett,
WA 98201
(800) 627-8437,
(206) 252-8374
Wood moldings, corbels, fireplaces.

Bendix Mouldings, Inc.
37 Ramland Road South,
Orangeburg,
NY 10962
(800) 526-0240
Wood, metal and plastic moldings.

Joseph Biunno
129 West 29th Street,
New York,
NY 10001
(212) 629-5630
Carved finials which may be used as newel posts.

Blue Ox Millworks
Foot of X Street,
Eureka, CA 95501,
(800) 24-VICKY
Historically accurate millwork: moldings, balusters, finials, handrails.

Bradbury & Bradbury
PO Box 155-C,
Benicia,
CA 94510
(707) 746-1900
Victorian wallpapers, handprinted borders, friezes, ceiling papers.

Cabot Stains
100 Hale Street,
Newburyport,
MA 01950
(800) 877-8246
Stains and sealers in wood hues and colors including white.

Chadsworth, Inc.
PO Box 53268,
Atlanta,
GA 30355
(404) 876-5410
Architectural wooden columns for interior and exterior.

Constantine's
2050 Eastchester Road,
Bronx,
NY 10461
(212) 792-1600
Many kinds of paint including milk paint.

Craftsman Lumber Company
436 Main Street,
Box 222J,
Groton,
MA 01450
(508) 448-6336
Kiln-dried lumber for paneling, moldings, floors, dual wainscoting.

Cumberland Woodcraft Co., Inc.
PO Drawer 609,
Carlisle,
PA 17013
(800) 367-1884,
in PA (717) 243-0063
Wood corbels, brackets, moldings, staircase parts, paneling, lattice, porch parts.

Decorators Supply Corp.
3610 South Morgan Street,
Chicago,
IL 60609
(312) 847-6300
Moldings, brackets, capitals, fireplaces.

Driwood
PO Box 1729,
Florence,
SC 29503
(803) 669-2478
Wall paneling, moldings, stairs, fireplaces.

Eisenhart Wallcovering Co.
400 Pine Street,
Hanover,
PA 17331
(717) 632-5918
Traditional wallcoverings widely distributed at retail.

Empire Woodworks Co.
PO Box 407,
Johnson City,
TX 78636
(210) 868-7520
Interior and exterior gingerbread.

Raymond Enkeboll Designs
16506 Avalon Boulevard,
Carson,
CA 90706
(310) 532-1400
Carved wood architectural moldings and fireplaces. To the trade only.

Evergreene Painting Studios, Inc.
635 West 23rd Street,
New York,
NY 10011
(212) 727-9500
Architectural painting and murals for public and private buildings.

Fe Fi Faux Inc.
337 South Davis Street,
Greensboro,
NC 27401
(910) 272-3289
4-day workshops in all faux finishes.

Fisher & Jirouch Co.
4821 Superior Avenue,
Cleveland,
OH 44103
(216) 361-3840
Handcrafted plaster ornaments, moldings, friezes.

Gold Leaf Studios
PO Box 50156,
Washington,
DC 20091
(202) 638-4660
Expert restoration of architectural gilding and picture frames.

Gracie, Inc.
1010 Lexington Avenue,
New York,
NY 10021
(212) 861-1150
Antique wallpapers and reproductions in antique style. To the trade.

Haas Wood & Ivory Works, Inc.
64 Clementina,
San Francisco,
CA 94105
(415) 421-8273
Stock and custom millwork, moldings, balusters, porch parts.

Hosek Manufacturing Company, Inc.
4877 National Western Drive, Suite 205,
Denver,
CO 80216
(303) 298-7010
Plaster and fiberglass moldings, ceilings, exterior columns, fireplaces.

Hyde Park Fine Art of Mouldings, Inc.
2916 40th Avenue,
Long Island City,
NY 11101
(800) 843-3015,
(718) 706-0504
Plaster moldings, fireplaces and architectural ornament.

Jennifer's Glass Works
1151 Hammond Drive,
Atlanta,
GA 30346
(770) 393-0981
Leaded, beveled and stained glass; windows and door millwork.

Dimitrios Klitsas, Fine Wood Sculptor
378 North Road,
Hampden,
MA 01036
(413) 566-5301
Hand woodcarving for private, corporate and ecclesiastical applications.

Mad River Woodworks
PO Box 1067,
189 Taylor Way,
Blue Lake,
CA 95525-1067
(707) 668-5671
Wood moldings, paneling, porch parts, stairs, gazebos.

MB Historic Decor
PO Box 880,
Norwich,
VT 05055
(802) 649-1790
Historically accurate wall and floor stencils in New England style.

Mendocino Millwork
Box 669,
Mendocino,
CA 95460
(707) 937-4410
Moldings, porch parts, doors, shingles.

Benjamin Moore Paints
51 Chestnut Ridge Road,
Montvale,
NJ 07645
(201) 573-9600
Historical Collection colors. Widely distributed in paint stores.

Moyner & Shepherd Joyners Inc.
122 Naubuc Avenue,
Glastonbury,
CT 06033
(203) 633-2383
Paneling, moldings, windows, doors, entryways, old glass.

Old-Fashioned Milk Paint Company
Box 222,
Groton,
MA 01450
(508) 448-6336
Milk-based paint in authentic colors for walls, furniture, stenciling.

Orac Decor
Outwater Plastic Industries,
4 Passaic Street, Dock No. 1,
Door #5,
Wood-Ridge,
NJ 07075
(800) 888-0880,
in NJ, (201) 340-1040,
High density polyurethane moldings, wall lights, columns, niches.

Pagliacco
PO Box 225,
Woodacre,
CA 94973
(415) 488-4333
Victorian style turnings and millwork and columns, interior and exterior.

Garry R. Partelow
PO Box 433,
34 Lyme Street,
Old Lyme,
CT 06371
(203) 434-2065
Custom wood turnings, balusters, newel posts, fluting, spiral rope twist, furniture parts.

Paxwell Painting Studios
223 East 32nd Street,
New York,
NY 10016
(212) 725-1737
Decorative painting, murals.

Pratt & Lambert
75 Tonawanda Street,
Buffalo,
NY 14207
(716) 873-6000
Early Americana colors from Henry Ford Museum and Greenfield Village. Widely distributed in paint stores.

San Francisco Victoriana
2070 Newcomb Avenue,
San Francisco,
CA 94124
(415) 648-0313
Wood molding, plaster ornament, ceiling roses, cornices, swags, capitals, Crown Anaglypta embossed wallcovering, antique embossed wallpaper borders.

A. F. Schwerd Manufacturing Co.
3215 McClure Avenue,
Pittsburgh,
PA 15212
(412) 766-6322
Wooden columns and capitals for interior and exterior use.

Sheppard Millwork, Inc.
21020 70th Avenue, W.,
Edmonds,
WA 98020-6701
(206) 771-4645
Molding, interior doors, stairs, fireplaces.

The Sherwin-Williams Company
101 Prospect Avenue,
Cleveland,
OH 44115
(800) 321-1386
Interior and exterior paints and stains including Preservation Palette authentic exterior colors from Colonial to the 1970s.

Silverton Victorian Millworks
PO Box 2987,
Durango,
CO 81302
(303) 259-5915
Molding, porches, exterior doors and windows, stairs, fireplaces.

Stone Legends
301 Pleasant Drive,
Dallas,
TX 75217
(214) 398-1199
Cast stone architectural elements and columns. To the trade.

Stromberg's Architectural Stone
I 30 West,
Greenville,
TX 75401
(903) 454-0904,
Cast stone moldings, fireplaces, columns, balustrades, fountains.

Trend Lines
170 William Street,
Chelsea,
MA 02150
(617) 887-0153
Milk paint.

Tania Vartan Studio
970 Park Avenue,
New York,
NY 10028
(212) 744-6710
Murals, trompe l'oeil, faux finishes.

Vintage Wood Works
Highway 34,
Box R. #3052,
Quinaln,
TX 75474
(903) 356-2158
Moldings, porches, shingles, doors, stairs, gazebos.

J. P. Weaver Co.
941 Airway,
Glendale,
CA 91201
(818) 841-5700
Fine wood moldings, paneling, ornament; also books and videos on architectural ornament.

Worthington Group, Ltd.
PO Box 868,
Troy,
AL 36081,
(800) 872-1608
Moldings, trim, doors.

OTHER USEFUL ADDRESSES/SOURCES

The National Trust for Historic Preservation
1785 Massachusetts Avenue,
North West,
Washington, DC 20036,
(202) 673-4000
A membership organization which preserves historically important buildings, publishes Historic Preservation *magazine, publishes books via the Preservation Press, sells books by mail, and operates the Historic Houses Association, an information center for those interested in old houses.*

Urban Center Books
The Villard Houses,
457 Madison Avenue,
New York, NY 10022,
(212) 935-3595
Comprehensive architecture and design bookshop, located in the historic building which also houses the Municipal Art Society, one of New York's main preservation organizations.

New York Landmarks Conservancy
141 Fifth Avenue,
New York, NY 10010,
(212) 995-5260
A private organization dedicated to preservation, publishers of The Restoration Directory, *a guide to services in the New York Area.*

Local historical and preservation societies are the most valuable resources for authentic information about the many variations in architecture around the country. The invaluable *Directory of Historical Organizations in the United States and Canada* is in its 14th edition, published 1990, and should be available in public libraries or from

the publisher, the American Association for State and Local History, 530 Church Street, Suite 600, Nashville, TN 37219, (615) 255-2971. The book costs $79.95 plus $3.50 shipping and handling.

SCHOOLS & UNIVERSITIES

Most universities have courses in historic style and preservation, usually in the departments of architecture and fine arts. Many courses are available through extension or adult education programs. State and local historical societies very often have associated courses. The National Trust also offers opportunities to take part in research programs.

Schools teaching the crafts associated with preservation such as special paint finishes and gilding exist in many locations. The most famous of all such schools, drawing students from all over the country, is The Isabel O'Neil Foundation, 177 East 87th Street, New York, NY 10128, (212) 348-2120. Ex-O'Neil students have set up schools in many other towns.

Craftsmen often take on apprentices. Art schools sometimes teach wood carving as well as painting. The best way to find out about opportunities near you is through local papers and art and craft shows.

MAGAZINES AND BOOKS

Architectural Digest, Colonial Homes, Country Living, Country Home, Elle Decor, Fine Homebuilding, Historic Preservation, House Beautiful, House & Garden, Metropolitan Home, Old-house Journal, Southern Accents, Southern Living, Traditional Homes

Carley, Rachel, *The Visual Dictionary of American Domestic Architecture,* Henry Holt, New York, 1994; Garrett, Wendell, *Classic America and Victorian America,* Rizzoli, New York, 1992; Gottfried & Jennings, *American Vernacular Design 1870 - 1940,* Van Nostrand Reinhold, New York, 1985; Greene, Fayal and Bonita Bavetta, *The Anatomy of a House,* Doubleday, New York, 1991; Harris, Cyril M., *Dictionary of Architecture and Construction,* McGraw-Hill, New York, 1993; Highsmith, Carol M. and Ted Landphair, *America Restored,* Preservation Press, Washington, DC, 1995; Kennedy, Roger G., *Greek Revival America,* Stewart, Tabori & Chang, New York, 1989; Kitchen, Judith L., *Caring for Your Old House,* Preservation Press, Washington, DC, 1995; McAlester, Virginia and Lee, *A Field Guide to American Houses,* Knopf, New York, 1984; Miller, Martin & Judith, *Period Details,* Crown Publishers, New York, 1987; Poppeliers, John, S. Allen Chambers, Jr., and Nancy B. Schwartz, *What Style Is It?,* Preservation Press, Washington, DC, 1983; Praz, Mario, *Interior Decoration,* Thames and Hudson, New York, 1982; Savage, Beth L., Editor: *African American Historic Places,* Preservation Press, Washington DC, 1995; Thornton, Peter, *Authentic Decor,* Viking Press, New York, 1984.

BIBLIOGRAPHY

Abercrombie, Patrick, *The Book of the Modern House,* Hodder and Stoughton, London, 1939

Adams, Steven, *The Arts and Crafts Movement,* Apple Press, London, 1987

Adams, William Howard, *Jefferson's Monticello,* Abbeville, New York, 1983

Adburgham, Alison, *Liberty's: The Biography of a Shop,* Alan and Unwin, London, 1975

Airs, Malcolm, *Tudor and Jacobean: A Guide and Gazetteer,* The Buildings of Britain series, Barrie and Jenkins Ltd, London, 1982

Albrecht, Donald, *Designing Dreams: Modern Architecture in the Movies,* Thames and Hudson, London, 1987

Allwood, John, *The Great Exhibitions,* Studio Vista, London, 1977

Amery, Colin (ed.), *Period Houses and their Details,* Butterworth Architecture, London, 1974
Three Centuries of Architectural Craftsmanship, Butterworth Architecture, London, 1977

Anderson, T. J., E. M. Moore, and R. W. Winter *California Design 1910,* California Design Publications

Andrews, Wayne, *Architecture in Early New England,* Stephen Greene Press, Brattleboro, Vermont, 1973

Artley, A. (ed), *Putting Back the Style,* Evans Brothers, London, 1982

Aslet, Clive and Alan Powers, *The National Trust Book of the English House,* Viking, New York 1985, Penguin Books Ltd, England, 1986

Aslin, Elizabeth, *The Aesthetic Movement,* Ferndale, London, 1969
E. W. Godwin Furniture and Interior Decoration, John Murray, London, 1986

Barrett, Helena, and John Phillips, *Suburban Style, The British Home 1840-1960,* Macdonald Orbis, London, 1987

Battersby, Martin, *The World of Art Nouveau,* Arlington Books, London, 1968
The Decorative Twenties, Studio Vista, London, 1969
The Decorative Thirties, Studio Vista, London, Walker and Co., New York, 1971

Bayer, Patricia, *Art Deco Source Book,* Phaidon, Oxford, 1988

Beard, Geoffrey, *Decorative Plasterwork in Great Britain,* Phaidon, London, 1975
Craftsmen and Interior Decoration in England 1660-1820, J. Bartholomew, Edinburgh, 1986

Belcher, John, and Mervyn E.

Macartney, *Later Renaissance Architecture in England,* 2 vols, Batsford, London, 1901

Blom, Benjamin, *A Monograph of the Works of McKim Mead and White 1879-1915,* New York, 1973

Blomfield, Sir Reginald, *History of Renaissance Architecture in England,* 2 vols, George Bell and Son, London, 1897

Boris, Eileen, and Wendy Caklan, *The Art that is Life – The Arts and Crafts Movement in America 1875-1920,* Boston Museum of Fine Arts, Boston, 1987

Brandon-Jones, John, et al, *C. F. A. Voysey: Architect and Designer 1857-1941,* Lund Humphries, London, 1978

Brooks, H. Allen, *The Prairie School: Studies from the Western Architect,* Van Nostrand Reinhold, Toronto, 1972

Brown, Patrick, *South West England,* Morland Publishing, Ashbourne, 1981

Brown, Roderick (ed.), *The Architectural Outsiders,* Waterstone, London, 1985

Brunhammer, Yvonne, *The Nineteen-Twenties Style,* Hamlyn, London, 1969

Brunskill, R. W., *Illustrated Handbook of Vernacular Architecture,* Faber and Faber Ltd, London, 3rd edn, 1987

Burke, Doreen Bolger, et al, *In Pursuit of Beauty,* The Metropolitan Museum of Modern Art/Rizzoli International Publications, Inc., New York, 1986

Bush, Donald J., *The Streamlined Decade,* New York, 1975

Byrne, A., *London's Georgian Houses,* Georgian Press, London, 1986

Calloway, Stephen, *Twentieth Century Decoration,* Weidenfeld and Nicholson, London/Rizzoli International Publications, Inc., New York

Calloway, Stephen, and Stephen Jones, *Traditional Style: How to Recreate the Traditional Period Home,* Pyramid Books, London, 1990

Carrington, Noel, *Design in the Home,* Country Life, London, 1933

Cerwinske, Laura, *Tropical Deco: The Architecture and Design of Old Miami Beach,* Rizzoli, New York, 1981

Chambers, James, *The English House,* Methuen/Thames Television International, London, 1985

Clark, Robert Judson, *The Arts and Crafts Movement in America 1876-1916,* Princeton University Press,

New Jersey, 1973

Condit, Carl Wilbur, *American Building: materials and techniques from the first colonial settlements to the present,* University of Chicago Press, Chicago and London, 1982

Conner, Patrick, *Oriental Architecture in the West,* Thames and Hudson, London, 1979

Cook, Olive, and Edwin Smith, *English Cottages and Farmhouses,* Thames and Hudson, London, 1954

Cooper, Nicholas, *The Opulent Eye,* Butterworth Architecture, London, 1976

Crane, Walter, *The English Revival of Decorative Art,* 1892 *Ideals in Art,* London, 1905

Creighton, Thomas H., and Katherine M. Ford, *Contemporary Houses – evaluated by their owners,* Reinhold Publishing Corp., New York, 1980

Croft-Murray, Edward, *Decorative Painting in England 1537-1837,* 2 vols, Country Life Books, Feltham, 1970

Cruickshank, Dan and Peter Wyld, *London: The Art of Georgian Building,* Butterworth Architecture, London, 1975

Cunnington, Pamela, *How Old is Your House?,* Alpha Books, Sherborne, 1988

Davie, W. Galsworthy, *Old English Doorways,* Batsford, London, 1903

Davies, Karen, *At Home in Manhattan; Modern Decorative Arts 1925 to the Depression,* Yale University Press, New Haven, 1983

Davis, Terence, *John Nash, The Prince Regent's Architect,* Country Life, London, 1966
The Gothick Taste, David and Charles, 1974

Downes, Kerry, *English Baroque Architecture,* A. Zwemmer Ltd., London, 1966

Dutton, R., *The English Interior 1500-1900,* Batsford, London, 1948
The Age of Wren, Batsford, London, 1951

Eames, Penelope, *Furniture in England, France and the Netherlands from the Twelfth to the Fifteenth Century,* Furniture History Society, London, 1977

Edis, Robert W., *Decoration and Furniture of Town Houses,* Kegan Paul, London, 1881

Edwards, R. (ed.), The Connoisseur Period Guides: *Tudor 1500-1603; Stuart 1603-1714; Early Georgian 1714-1760; Late Georgian 1760-*

1810; Regency 1810-1830; Early Victorian 1830-1860, London, 1976-1978

Field, Wooster Bard, *House Planning,* McGraw Hill, New York and London, 1940

Fisher, Richard B., *Syrie Maugham,* Duckworth, 1970

Fleming, John, Hugh Honour and Nikolaus Pevsner, *The Penguin Dictionary of Architecture,* Penguin Books Ltd, England, 2nd edn 1972

Ford, James, and Katherine Morrow Ford, *The Modern House in America,* Architectural Book Publishing Company, New York, 1940

Forman, Henry C., *Early Manor and Plantation Houses of Maryland,* Easton, Maryland, H. C. Forman, 1934
Maryland Architecture: A Short History from 1634 through the Civil War, Tidewater Publishers, Cambridge, Maryland, 1968

Fowler, John, and J. Cornforth, *English Decoration in the Eighteenth Century,* Barrie and Jenkins, London, 1978

Frankl, Paul, *Space for Living* from *New Dimensions,* Payson and Clarke, New York, 1928

Garner, T., and A. Stratton, *Domestic Architecture of England during the Tudor Period,* 2 vols, Batsford, London, 2nd edn 1929

Gilbert, Christopher, et al, *Country House Floors 1660-1850,* Leeds City Art Galleries, 1987 *The Fashionable Fire Place 1660-1840,* Leeds City Art Galleries, 1985

Gilliat, Mary, *English Style,* Bodley Head, London, 1967

Gillies, Mary Davies, *McCall's Book of Modern Houses,* Simon and Schuster, New York, 1951

Gillon (Jnr), Edmond V., *Early Illustrations and Views of American Architecture,* Dover Publications Inc., New York, 1971

Gillon (Jnr), Edmond V., and Clay Lancaster, *Victorian Houses – A Treasury of Lesser-known Examples,* Dover Publications Inc., New York/ Constable, London, 1973

Girouard, Mark, *Robert Smythson and the Architecture of the Elizabethan Era,* Country Life, London, 1966
Sweetness and Light – The 'Queen Anne' Movement, 1860-1900, Oxford University Press, 1977
Life in the English Country House: A Social and Architectural History, Yale University Press, New Haven and London, 1978

Glancey, Jonathan, *New British*

Architecture, Thames and Hudson, London, 1989

Glassie, Henry, *Folk Housing in Middle Virginia: A Structural Analysis of Historic Artifacts*, University of Tennessee Press, Knoxville, 1975

Gloag, J., *Early English Decorative Detail*, Tiranti, London, 1965

Godfrey, Walter H., *The English Staircase*, London, 1911

Goodnow, Ruby Ross, *The Honest House*, The Century Co., New York, 1914

Gotch, J. Alfred, *Architecture of the Renaissance in England*, 2 vols, Batsford, London, 1894

Grief, Martin, *Depression Modern; The Thirties Style in America*, Universe Books, New York, 1975

Guild, Robin, *The Complete Victorian House Book*, Sidgwick and Jackson, London, 1989

Hamlin, Talbot, *Greek Revival Architecture in America*, Oxford University Press, 1944

Handlin, David P., *American Architecture*, Thames and Hudson, London, 1985

Harris, John, *English Decorative Ironwork 1610-1836*, Tiranti, London, 1960

Harris, John, and Jill Lever, *Illustrated Glossary of Architecture*, Faber and Faber, 1966

Haslam, Malcolm, *In the Nouveau Style*, Thames and Hudson, London, 1989

Herman, Bernard, *Architecture and Rural Life in Central Delaware*, University of Tennessee Press, Knoxville, 1987

Hill, Oliver, and John Cornforth, *English Country Houses: Caroline 1625-1685*, Country Life Ltd, London, 1966

Hills, Nicholas, *The English Fireplace – Its Architecture and the Working Fire*, Quiller, London, 1983

Hoever, O., *A Handbook of Wrought Iron from the Middle Ages to the end of the Eighteenth Century*, Thames and Hudson, London, 1962

Hoffmann, Donald, *Frank Lloyd Wright's Robie House: The Illustrated Story of an Architectural Masterpiece*, Dover Publications, Inc., New York, 1984

Hope, Alice, *Town Houses*, Batsford, London, 1963

Howarth, Thomas, *Charles Rennie Mackintosh and the Modern Movement*, Routledge and Kegan Paul, London 1952

Howells, John M., *The Architectural Heritage of the Piscataqua: Houses and Gardens of the Portsmouth District of Maine and New Hampshire*, Architectural Book

Publishing Co., New York, 1965

Hussey, Christopher, *Early Georgian English Country Houses*, Country Life, London, 1955

Hussey, Christopher, and John Cornforth, *English Country Houses Open to the Public*, Country Life, London, 4th edn. 1964

Ingle, Marjorie I., *The Mayan Revival Style: Art Deco Mayan Fantasy*, Peregrine Smith, Inc., Salt Lake City, 1984

Ison, Walter, *The Georgian Buildings of Bristol*, Faber and Faber, London, 1952/1978

Jackson, Alan, *Modern Over Miami*, 1937

Jencks, Charles A., *Language of Post Modern Architecture*, Academy Editions, London, 1987

Johnson, Diane Chalmers, *American Art Nouveau*, Harry N. Abrams, Inc., New York, 1979

Jourdain, Margaret, *English Interiors in Smaller Houses – from the Restoration to the Regency 1660-1830*, Batsford, London, 1923
English Decorative Plasterwork of the Renaissance, Batsford, London, 1926
English Interior Decoration 1500-1830, Batsford, London, 1950

Kaplan, Sam Hall, *LA Lost and Found; An Architectural History of Los Angeles*, Viking, Harmondsworth, 1987

Kaplan, Wendy, *"The Art that is Life": The Arts and Crafts Movement in America 1875-1920*, Little, Brown and Co., New York, 1987

Karp, Ben, *Ornamental Carpentry on Nineteenth-Century American Houses*, Dover Publications, Inc., New York, 2nd edn, 1981

Kaufmann (Jnr), Edgar, *Fallingwater: A Frank Lloyd Wright Country House*, Architectural Press, London, 1986

Kaufmann, Henry, *Early American Ironware: Cast and Wrought*, Charles E. Tuttle, Rutland, Vermont, 1966

Kelly, A., *The Book of English Fireplaces*, Country Life Books, Feltham, 1968

Kelly, Frederick, *Early Domestic Architecture in Connecticut*, Yale University Press, New Haven, 1924

Kenna, Rudolph, *Glasgow Art Deco*, Drew, Glasgow, 1985

Kennedy, Roger G., *Greek Revival America*, National Trust for Historic Preservation/Stewart Tabori and Chang, New York, 1989

Kimball, Sidney Fiske, *Domestic Architecture of the American Colonies and the Early Republic* Dover Publications Inc., New York, 1966

Klein, Dan, et al, *In the Deco Style*,

Rizzoli Publications International, Inc., New York, 1986

Lambton, Lucinda, *Vanishing Victoriana*, Elsevier Phaidon, Oxford, 1976

Langdon, Philip, *American Houses*, Stewart, Tabori and Chang, Inc., New York, 1987

Lesieutre, Alain, *The Spirit and Splendour of Art Deco*, Paddington Books, New York and London, 1974

Lewis, Arnold, et al, *The Opulent Interiors of the Gilded Age*, Dover Publications, Inc., New York, 1987

Lipman, Jean, and Alice Winchester, *The Flowering of American Folk Art (1776-1876)*, Viking, New York, 1974

Lister, Raymond, *Decorative Wrought Ironwork in Great Britain*, G. Bell and Sons, London, 1957
Decorative Cast Ironwork in Great Britain, G. Bell and Sons, London, 1960

Lloyd, Nathaniel, *A History of the English House: from Primitive Times to the Victorian Period*, Architectural Press, London, 1931
A History of English Brickwork, H. G. Montgomery, London, 1936

Loth, Calder, and Julius Trousdale Sadler (Jnr), *The Only Proper Style: Gothic Architecture in America*, New York Graphic Society, Boston, 1975

Lynn, Catherine, *Wallpaper in America, from the 17th century to World War I*, Norton, 1980

Maass, John, *The Gingerbread Age*, Rinehart and Co. Ltd., 1957
The Victorian Home in America, Hawthorn Books, Inc., 1972

McAlester, Virginia and Lee, *A Field Guide to American Houses*, Alfred A. Knopf, New York, 1990

Macarthy, Fiona, *All Things Bright and Beautiful – Design in Britain 1830 to Today*, Alan and Unwin, London, 1972

MacQuoid, Percy, and Ralph Edwards, *The Dictionary of English Furniture*, Country Life Ltd, London, 1924-27 3 vols, 1954 3 vols
A History of English Furniture, Victoria and Albert Museum, London, 1955

Marshall, H. G. Hayes, *Interior Decoration Today*, F. Lewis Ltd, 1938

Mercer, Henry, *The Bible in Iron; or the Pictured Stoves and Stove Plates of the Pennsylvanian Germans*, Poylestown, Pa Bucks County Historical Society, 1914

Metcalf, Pauline C., *Ogden Codman and the Decoration of Houses*, David R. Godine Publisher, 1988

Miller, Duncan, *Interior Decorating*, "How to do it" series, No. 13, The Studio Publications, London, 1937

Morningstar, Connie, *Flapper*

Furniture and Interiors of the 1920s, Wallace-Homespar Book Co., 1971

Morrice, Richard, *Stuart and Baroque: A Guide and Gazetteer*, Buildings of Britain series, Barrie and Jenkins Ltd, London 1982

Morrison, Hugh, *Early American Architecture; from the first colonial settlements to the national period*, Dover Publications Inc., New York/ Constable, London, 1987

Moss, Roger W., *Lighting for Historic Buildings: A Guide to Selecting Reproductions*, The Preservation Press, National Trust for Historic Preservation, 1988

Muthesius, Stefan, *The English Terraced House*, Yale University Press, New Haven and London, 1982

Naylor, Gillian, *The Arts and Crafts Movement*, Studio Vista, London, 1971

Newsom, Samuel, and Joseph C., *Picturesque Californian Homes*, Hennessey and Ingalis, Inc., Los Angeles, 1978

Oman, C., and Jean Hamilton, *Wallpapers: A History and Illustrated Catalogue of the Collection of the Victoria and Albert Museum*, P. Wilson/ Sotheby Publications, London, 1982

Orr, Christina, *Addison Mizner: Architect of Dreams and Realities*, Norton Gallery of Art

Osborne, A. L., *Dictionary of English Domestic Architecture*, Country Life, London, 1954

Owsley, David, and William Rieder, *The Glass Drawing Room from Northumberland House*, Victoria and Albert Museum, London, 1974

Patmore, Derek, *Modern Furnishing and Decoration*, The Studio Publications, London, 1936
Colour Schemes and Modern Furnishing, The Studio Publications, London, 1947

Pearce, David, *London's Mansions*, Batsford, London, 1986

Powers, Alan, *Oliver Hill Architect and Lover of Life 1887-1968*, Mountain Publications, London, 1989

Quiney, Anthony, *Period Houses: A Guide to Authentic Architectural Features*, George Philip Ltd, London, 1989

Ramsay, Stanley C. and J.D.M. Harvey, *Small Georgian Houses and Their Details 1750-1820*, Butterworth Architecture, London, 1977

Robertson, Alan, *Architectural Antiques*, Unwin Hyman, 1987

Robertson, E. G. and J., *Cast Iron Decoration*, Thames and Hudson, London, 1977

Robinson, John Martin, *Latest Country Houses*, Bodley Head, London, 1984

Rowan, Alistair, *Garden Buildings*, Country Life, Feltham, 1968

Saint, Andrew, *Richard Norman Shaw*, Yale University Press, New Haven, 1976

Schmidt, Carl F., *The Victorian Era in the United States*, New York, 1971

Scully, Vincent J., *The Shingle Style and The Stick Style*, Yale University Press, New Haven/Oxford University Press, London, 2nd edn 1971
The Architecture of the American Summer: The Flowering of the Shingle Style, Rizzoli International Publications, Inc., New York, 1989

Scully, Vincent, and Antoinette Downing, *The Architectural Heritage of Newport, Rhode Island 1640-1916*, Bramhall House, New York, 1967

Sergeant, John, *Frank Lloyd Wright's Usonian Houses: the case for organic architecture*, Whitney Library of Design (Watson-Guptill Publications), New York, 1975

Service, Alastair, *Anglo Saxon and Norman: a guide and gazetteer*, The Buildings of Britain series, Barrie and Jenkins Ltd, London, 1982

Shopsin, William C. and Mosette Glaser Broderick, *The Villard Houses*, Viking/Municipal Art Society, New York, 1980

Shuffrey, L. A., *The English Fireplace*, Batsford, London, 1912

Sitwell, Sacherville, *British Architects and Craftsmen*, Batsford, London, 1945

Smithells, Roger, and S. John Woods, *The Modern Home*, F. Lewis, Benfleet, 1936

Sonn, Albert, *Early American Wrought Iron*, 3 vols, Charles Scribners and Sons, 1928

Spencer, I., and A. Brown, *The Prairie School Tradition*, 1979

Staebler, Wendy W., *Architectural Detailing in Residential Interiors*, Whitney Library of Design (Watson-Guptill Publications) New York, 1990

Stevens, John Calvin, and Albert Winslow Cobb, *American Domestic Architecture*, The American Life Foundation and Study Institute, The Library of Victorian Culture, Watkins Glen, New York, 1978

Stickley, Gustav, *The Best of Craftsman Homes*, Peregrine Smith, Inc., Santa Barbara, 1979

Stillman, Damie, et al, *Decorative Work of Robert Adam*, Tiranti, London, 1966
Architecture and Ornament in Late 19th Century America, University of Delaware, 1981

Strattan, Arthur, *The English Interior*, Batsford, London, 1920

Summerson, John, *The Classical Language of Architecture*, Thames and Hudson, 1980
Georgian London, Barrie and Jenkins Ltd, London, 1988

Sykes, C. S., *Private Palaces*, Chatto and Windus, London, 1985

Thornton, Peter, *Seventeenth-Century Interior Decoration in England, France and Holland*, Yale University Press, New Haven, 1978
Authentic Decor: The Domestic Interior 1620-1920, George Weidenfeld and Nicolson Ltd, London, 1984

Todd, Dorothy and Raymond Mortimer *The New Interior Decoration*, Batsford, London, 1929

Turnor, R., *The Smaller English House*, 1952

Uecker, Wolf, *Art Nouveau and Art Deco Lamps and Chandeliers*, 1986

Wallace, Philip B., *Colonial Ironwork in Old Philadelphia: the craftsmanship of the early days of the republic*, Dover Publications, Inc., New York/Constable, London, 1970

Waterman, Thomas, and John Barrows, *Domestic Colonial Architecture of Tidewater Virginia*, Charles Scribners and Sons, New York, 1932

Watkin, David, *Regency: A Guide and Gazetteer*, The Buildings of Britain series, Barrie and Jenkins Ltd, London, 1982

Welles-Cole, Anthony, *Historic Paper Hangings*, Leeds City Art Galleries, 1983

West, Trudy, *The Fireplace in the Home*, David and Charles, Newton Abbot, 1976

Whinney, Dr. Margaret, *Home House No. 20 Portman Square*, Country Life/Hamlyn, Feltham, 1969

Willis, Royal Barry, *Houses for Homemakers*, 1945

Wilson, M., *William Kent: Architect, Designer, Painter, Gardener 1685 – 1748*, Routledge and Kegan Paul, London, 1984

Wilson, Richard Guy, *McKim, Mead and White Architects*, Rizzoli, New York, 1983

Wise, Herbert H., *Attention to Detail*, Perigee Books, New York, 1979

Yerbury, F. R., *Georgian Details of Domestic Architecture*, London, 1926

Yorke, F. R. S., *The Modern House*, Architectural Press, London, 1934
The Modern House in England, Architectural Press, London, 1937

Dover reprints

Historic architectural pattern books and catalogues are reprinted by a number of publishers, most notably Dover Publications, Inc., whose list includes the following:

The American Builder's Companion, R.

P. and C. Williams, 6th edn 1827, reprinted New York, 1969

The Architect, or Practical House Carpenter (1830), L. Coffin, Boston, 1844, reprinted New York, 1988

The Architecture of Country Houses, A. J. Downing, New York, reprinted 1969

Authentic Victorian Stoves, Heaters, Ranges, Etc., Floyd, Wells and Co., Royersford, 1898, reprinted New York, 1988

Bicknell's Victorian Buildings: Floor Plans and Elevations for 45 Houses and Other Structures, A. J. Bicknell and Co., New York, 1878, reprinted New York, 1979

Country Houses and Seaside Cottages of the Victorian Era, William T. Comstock, New York, 1883, reprinted New York, 1989

Early Connecticut Houses: An Historical and Architectural Study, Norman Isham et al., New York, 1900, reprinted New York 1965

Gerald K. Geerlings Wrought Iron in Architecture: An Illustrated Survey, Charles Scribner's Sons, New York and London, 1929, reprinted New York, 1983

Greek Revival Architecture in America, Talbot Hamlin, Oxford University Press, London, 1944, reprinted New York, 1964

Montgomery Ward and Company, Catalogue no. 57, Spring and Summer 1895, reprinted New York, 1969

Mott's Illustrated Catalog of Victorian Plumbing Fixtures for Bathrooms and Kitchens, The J. L. Mott Iron Works, New York, 1888, reprinted New York 1987

Picture Book of Authentic Mid-Victorian Gas Lighting Fixtures, Mitchell, Vance and Co., 1876, reprinted New York, 1984

Roberts' Illustrated Millwork Catalog: A Sourcebook of Turn of the Century Architectural Woodwork, E. L. Roberts and Co., Chicago, 1903, reprinted New York, 1988

Sears, Roebuck Home Builder's Catalog, Sears, Roebuck and Co., Chicago, 1910, reprinted New York, 1990

Sloan's Victorian Buildings, E. S. Jones and Co., Philadelphia, 1852, reprinted New York, 1980

Turn-of-the-Century Houses, Cottages and Villas, R. W. Shoppell et al., Shoppell's catalogues, 1880-1900, reprinted New York, 1983

Victorian Cottage Residences, Andrew Jackson Downing, reprinted New York, 1981

Victorian Domestic Architectural Plans and Details, William T. Comstock, New York, 1881, reprinted 1987

A Victorian House Builder's Guide,

George. E. Woodward, New York, 1869, reprinted New York, 1988

Victorian Patterns and Designs in Full Colour, George Ashdown Audsley and Maurice Ashdown Audsley, New York, reprinted New York, 1988

Readers are advised to visit one of the Dover bookshops:
18 Earlham Street, London WC2; tel. (071) 836 2111
180 Varick Street, New York, NY 10014; tel. (212) 255 3755

Reprints from other publishers

A Suburban House and Garage, The White Pine Series of Architectural Monographs, vol. 2, No. 4, August 1916

A White Pine House, The White Pine Series of Architectural Monographs, vol. 3, No. 4, August 1917

A White Pine House for the Vacation Season, The White Pine Series of Architectural Monographs, vol. 4, No. 4, August 1918

Illustrated Catalogue of American Hardware of the Russell and Erwin Manufacturing Company, 1865, The Association for Preservation Technology, 1980

Palliser's American Architecture or Everyman: A Complete Builder, Palliser, Palliser and Co. Architects, J. S. Ogilvie, New York, 1888 *New Cottage Homes and Details*, Palliser, Palliser and Co. Architects, Da Capo Press, New York, 1975

Victorian Architectural Details – Two Pattern Books, Marcus Fayette Cummings and Charles Crosby Miller, originally published as *Architecture Designs for Street Fronts, Suburban Houses and Cottages*, S. Bailey and Eager, Ohio, 1868, and *Cummings' Architectural Details*, Orange Judd and Company, New York, 1873, reprinted American Life Foundation and Study Institute, Watkins Glen, New York, 1978

Victoriana – Floor plans and Renderings from the Gilded Age, Eugene Mitchell, Van Nostrand Reinhold Co., 1983

Victorian Home Building: A Transcontinental View, E. C. Hussey, originally published as *Home Building: A Reliable Book of Facts*, Leader and Van Hoesen, New York, 1876, reprinted American Life Foundation, Watkins Glen, New York, 1976

Villas and Cottages, Calvert Vaux, Harper and Brothers, New York, 1857, reprinted Da Capo Press, New York, 1968

Woodward's National Architect, George E. Woodward, New York, 1869, reprinted Da Capo Press, New York, 1975

ACKNOWLEDGMENTS

The following architectural consultants are gratefully acknowledged for their advice and good offices: Dr N. Alcock, Leamington Spa, England; John Biggs, Bournemouth, Dorset; Merill Carrington, London; Dr Christopher Currie, Institute of Historical Research; A. Stuart Gray, Hampstead Garden Suburb, England; Linda Hall, Middlesex; Ruth H. Kamen, Royal Institute of British Architects, London; Paul F. Miller, Newport, Rhode Island; Tom Savage, Charleston, South Carolina; Wendy Potts, Bournemouth, England; John Stubbs, New York City; Peter Sutton, Totnes, England; Penny Thompson, Russell-Cotes Art Galley and Museum, Bournemouth, England; Mark Wenger, Williamsburg, Virginia

Thanks are due to Kuo Kang Chen for help with the artwork projections on combined photo/artwork images

Invaluable research help was provided by: Laura Arnette, Peter Bejger, Fayal Greene, Carol Hupping, Caroline Russell, James Elliott Benjamin, Francis Graham, Melanie Mills, Deirdre Nolan, Emma Rance, Lee Roberts, Jeff Wilkinson

The following kindly allowed their own photographs to be used in this book: Andrew Adams, James Elliott Benjamin, Mike Brown, Stephen Calloway, Elizabeth Cromley, Philip Dole, Kim Furrokh, Mike Gray, Linda Hall, David Martin, Alan Powers, Anthony Quiney, Peter Sutton, Simon Thurley, Sarah Polden, Robert Saxton, Katie True

Substantial help of various kinds was also provided by: Sarah Boothby; Camilla Costello; Diana Lanham (National Trust, London); Francesca Scoones (National Trust, London)

The Directory of Suppliers was compiled by Carol Hupping and Emma Shackleton (Britain) and Fayal Greene (United States)

The publishers and general editor are especially indebted to those individuals and institutions who allowed photographer Kim Sayer to photograph inside their houses. In the photo credits below, owners have not always been specified: some preferred to remain anonymous. The code letters relate to the codes used in the captions throughout the book. As well as houses and house owners, the list identifies those who allowed their own photographs to be used for reproduction; some of the codes refer to historic books in private collections which were specially photographed by Ian B. Jones. The letter © after a name indicates the copyright holder of the photograph, in cases where copyright does not belong with the publishers

PHOTO CREDITS

A Batty Langley, *A Sure Guide to Builders*, 1729

AA Andrew Adams ©

AB Asher Benjamin, *The Architect, or Practical House Carpenter*, 1830

ABA Asher Benjamin, *The American Builder's Companion*, 6th edn, 1827

AC Anaglypta, illustrated catalogue, 1926

ACG T. Mawson, *The Art and Craft of Garden Making*, Batsford, London, 4th edn, 1912

AD Crooked Pightle, Crawley, nr. Winchester (Robert Adam); thanks to Robert Adam, Winchester Design (Architects)

AE A. Emanuel and Son Ltd, general catalogue, 1901, London

AG *Gas, The National Fuel*, Ascot Gas Water Heaters Ltd, London, 1935

AH Avenue House, Ampthill Bedfordshire; thanks to Simon Houfe

AHH Abraham Hasbrouck House, New Paltz, New York; courtesy of the Huguenot Historical Society ©

AJD A.J. Downing, *Cottage Residences*, 1873 edn

AK Rudolf Ackermann, *Repository of Arts, Literature, Fashions Etc*, London, early 19th century

AL Ashley Hall School, Charleston, South Carolina (Patrick Duncan House)

AM Courtesy of the Ashmolean Museum, Oxford ©

AOH *About Our Homes*, 8th edn

AP Andrea Palladio, *First Book of Architecture*, translated by Godfrey Richards, London, 11th edn, 1729

APR Architectural Press, London ©

AQ Anthony Quiney ©

AR *The Ideal Fitter*, American Radiator Company, 1904

ARC Richard Bryant ©/Arcaid

AS Abraham Swan, *The British Architect*, 1758 edn

ASA Abraham Swan, *A Collection of Designs in Architecture*, 1757

AT R. Lugar, *Architectural Sketches for Cottages, Rural Dwellings and Villas*, London, 1823

B Batty Langley, *The Builder's Compleat Assistant*, 1738

BA James Gibbs, *A Book of Architecture*, London, 2nd edn, 1739

BAN Bang & Olufsen, c/o Munro & Forster Communications, London

BB Bishopsbarn, York; thanks to Major and Mrs Lane

BC Prof. H. Adams, *Building Construction*, Cassell, London

BE Berry's Electric Ltd, *Berry's Heating of Today*, London

BF *Beautiful Rooms*, The Wallpaper Manufacturers Ltd, Manchester, c.1910

BG Belling Electric Heating and Cooking, illustrated catalogue, Enfield, Middlesex, 1958

BH Courtesy of Glynn Boyd Harte, Dolphin Studio ©

BHL Belton House, Lincolnshire; courtesy of The National Trust ©

BI A.J. Bicknell and Company, *Bicknell's Village Builder and Supplement*, 1878

BIL Biltmore Estate, Ashville, North Carolina ©

BJ Batty Langley, *The Builder's Jewel*, London, 1746

BJB Bayliss, Jones and Bayliss, illustrated catalogue of iron handles, fencing, field and entrance gates, Wolverhampton, 1891

BL Batty Langley, *Builder's and Workman's Treasury of Designs*, 1770 edn

BM *The Builder's Magazine*, 2nd edn, London, 1779

BO New York; thanks to Raf Borello

BOD Courtesy of the Bodleian Library, Oxford ©

BP Boulton and Paul, general catalogue, 1898

BR Burbage Road, London; thanks to Barbara Cantor

BRI Britannia Domestic Appliances

BS John Bolding and Sons Ltd, catalogue, London, c.1925

BT Bennett's "Tungit" Wood Flooring Company, catalogue, London

BU *Builder's Practical Director*, published by J. Hagger, London, c.1865

BUL Bulthaup

BV The "Boyle" System of Ventilation, catalogue, London, 1899

BW Bartow-Pell Mansion, Bronx, New York

C Chastleton House, Oxfordshire; thanks to Mrs A. Clutton-Brock

CA Carron Company, architect's catalogue, 1913

CAF Chicago Architecture Foundation

CB Isaac Ware, *The Complete Body of Architecture*, London, 1756

CBA Cotterell Bros, *Wallpapers, Latest Designs in stock*, catalogue, Bristol, 1914

CBB Cotterell Bros, catalogue, Bristol, 1937

CC Catesby's *Cork Lino, Attractive Patterns*, catalogue, London, c.1925

CF Carter and Co. Ltd, Carters Fires, catalogue, Poole, Dorset, c.1929

CG M.F. Cummings, *Cummings' Architectural Details*, New York, 1873

CH C. Hindley and Son, catalogue, London, c.1880

CHS/B Chicago Historical Society/ Hedrich-Blessing ©

CHS/H Chicago Historical Society/ Ken Hedrich, Hedrich-Blessing ©

CI Courtesy of Christie's, London ©

CJ C. Jennings and Co. Ltd, price list, c.1910

CK William T. Comstock, *Modern Architectural Designs and Details*, New York, 1881

CL G.A. and W.J. Audsley, *Cottage, Lodge and Villa Architecture*, c.1860

CM *The Contractor's, Merchant's and Estate Manager's Compendium*, London, 1900

CN Casa Nueva, Los Angeles; thanks to Max A. van Balgooy, Workman and Temple Family Homestead Museum

CN/A Andreas von Einsiedel © House and Garden, Condé Nast, UK

CN/B Michael Wickham © House and Garden, Condé Nast, UK

CNY Courtesy of Christie's, New York ©

CO Carron Company, catalogue, Stirlingshire, Scotland, c.1895

COL Colchester Museum, Essex; thanks to Oliver Green

CP John Britton, *The History and Description of Cassiobury Park*, London, 1837

CR Cragside, Northumbria; courtesy of The National Trust ©

CRO Elizabeth Cromley ©

CS Derek Patmore, *Colour Schemes and Modern Furnishing*, The Studio, London, 1945

CT Courtesy of The Charleston Museum, Charleston, South Carolina ©

CU George Smith, *Cabinet-Maker's and Upholsterer's Guide*, 1826

CV Cliveden, Germantown Avenue, Philadelphia, Pennsylvania; a co-stewardship property of the National Trust for Historic Preservation

CW Cooper Hewitt Museum, New York City (Andrew Carnegie Mansion)

CWF Courtesy of Colonial Williamsburg Foundation ©

D Doulton and Company, illustrated catalogue, London, 1887

DA Doulton and Company Ltd, catalogue, 1904

DAV Richard Davies ©

DB Debenham House, London; courtesy of the Richmond Fellowship ©

DC Spitalfields, London; thanks to Dan Cruickshank

DD J. Aldam Heaton, Designer and Decorator, catalogue, London, c.1885

DE Abraham Swan, *Designs in Architecture*, 1757

DF D.F. Company Ltd, catalogue, 1910

DG The Davis Gas Stove Co. Ltd, *Up-to-date Gas Heating Stoves*, catalogue, London, 1901

DH Drayton Hall, Charleston, South Carolina, a property of the National Trust for Historic Preservation; thanks to Christine Castaneda

DHH Drayton Hall, Charleston, South Carolina/Gene Heizer ©

DK Courtesy of Dickens' House, Doughty Street, London

DM David and Barbara Martin, Robertsbridge, Sussex ©

DO G.A. and M.A. Audsley, *The Practical Decorator and Ornamentist*, Blackie, Glasgow, 1892

DR David Rowell and Company, illustrated catalogue, Westminster, London, c.1900

DS Spitalfields, London; thanks to Denis Severs

EA Lewis F. Day, *Every-day Art*, B.T. Batsford, London, 1882

EB "Evered" Brassfoundry, illustrated catalogue, Birmingham, c.1910, updated 1925

EC Eagle Combination Grates, catalogue, Birmingham, c.1935

ECR Benjamin Count of Rumford, *Essays*, 5th edn, vol. I, London, 1800

EG Willow Road, London (Ernö Goldfinger); thanks to Ursula Goldfinger

EH Edward Hoppus, *The Gentleman's and Builder's Repository*, 1738

EL Ebnall House, Shrewsbury; thanks to Dr Gordon Rose

EO Henry Shaw, *Examples of Ornamental Metal Work*, 1836

EP E.L. Tarbuck, *The Encyclopaedia of Practical Carpentry and Joinery*, London, c.1860

ER Erco Lighting Ltd.

ES The Elms, Newport, Rhode Island; courtesy of the Preservation Society of Newport Country; thanks to Monique Panaggio

EST Peter Aaron ©/Esto

FG Frances Goodwin, *Domestic Architecture*, vol. 3, 2nd edn, 1843

FH Forest Hills, Queens, New York; thanks to Rosalind Esakoff

FL Floyd, Wells and Company, Royerford, Pennsylvania, catalogue, c.1898

FO Dobbie and Forbes and Company, catalogue, Larbert, Scotland, c.1910

FP F. Pratten and Company Ltd, catalogue no. 42, Bath, 1936

FR S. Franses Ltd ©, 82 Jermyn St, St James's, London SW1

FRE Michael Freeman ©

GB Gaillard-Bennett House, Charleston, South Carolina

GBV *Regolla delli Cinque Ordini D'Architettura di M. Giacomo Barozzio da Vignola*, 1620

GE The Grange, Drexel Hill, Philadelphia, Pennsylvania; thanks to Mrs Ackerman

GEC General Electric Company, complete catalogue, vol. III, London, 1911-12

GF George Farmiloe and Sons, general catalogue, London, 1891

GFB George Farmiloe and Sons Ltd, catalogue no. 9, London, 1901

GG Gamble House, Pasadena (Charles and Henry Greene); thanks to Ted Bosley

GH Gibbons Hinton and Company Ltd, tile catalogue, Brierley Hill, South Staffordshire, c.1905

GJ G. Jackson and Sons Ltd, *Fireplaces*, London, c.1935

GJA George Jackson and Sons, *Examples of Architectural Ornaments*, 2 vols, London, 1889

GL Gravel Lane, Houndsditch, London

GPB *Leadwork by George P. Bankart*, catalogue, Nottingham, c.1910

GR John P. White, *Garden Furniture and Ornament*, catalogue, Bedford, c.1908

GS Gardiner, Sons and Company Ltd, Bristol, illustrated catalogue, c.1900-05

GV Argyle Square, London; thanks to Gavin Stamp

GW George Williams House, Charleston, South Carolina (Calhoun Mansion)

H *Furniture by Harrods*, catalogue, c.1910

HA Hale House, by permission of Heritage Square Museum, Los Angeles, California

HABI Habitat UK

HABS Historic American Building Survey, Library of Congress, Washington D.C.

HB Hedrich Blessing Photographers/Jon Millar, Illinois ©

HD H. and C. Davis and Company, *Pattern Book of Best Cast Brass Foundry*, London, 1888

HE *Health and Healthy Homes,* The Sanitary Engineering and Ventilation Company, London, 1877

HEG H.E. Gaze Ltd, catalogue, c.1920

HEI Thomas A. Heinz, Illinois ©

HF Thomas Hope, *Household Furniture and Interior Decoration,* 1807

HG M.H. Baillie Scott, *Houses and Gardens,* London, 1906

HH Courtesy of Home House, Portman Estate, London

HHF W. Shaw Sparrow, *Hints on House Furnishing,* 1909

HHH Hammond-Harwood House, Annapolis, Maryland ©

HI C.L. Eastlake, *Hints on Household Taste,* Longmans, London, 1872

HJJ *Description of The House and Museum of Sir John Soane,* London, 1836

HL The Hill House, Helensburgh, Scotland; courtesy of the National Trust for Scotland

HP Huncoat Plastic Brick Terracotta Works, catalogue, Accrington, c.1910

HS Hampton and Son, illustrated catalogue, London, 1892

HSA Hampton and Son, London, illustrated catalogue, London, c.1910

HSMC Courtesy of Historic St Mary's City, Chesapeake, Maryland ©

IN William Ince and Thomas Mayhew, *The Universal System of Household Furniture,* 1759-62

IJT I. and J. Taylor, *Ornamental Iron Work,* 1795

IW Isaac Ware, *The Complete Body of Architecture,* 1756

JB Messrs Johnson Bros and Company, *Studies of Wrought Iron Entrance Gates,* catalogue, London, May 1873

JBE James Elliott Benjamin ©

JC John Carwitham, *Various kinds of Floor Decoration represented both in Plano and Perspective Being useful Designs for Ornamenting the Floors of Halls, Rooms, Summer Houses, etc. Whether in Pavements of Stone, or Marble, or with Painted Floor Cloths. In Twenty four Copper Plates,* 1739

JE The Thematic House, London (Charles Jencks)

JG John Goldicutt, *Specimens of Ancient Decorations from Pompeii,* 1825

JM James Malton, *An Essay on British Cottage Architecture,* 1798

JNP John Plaw, *Rural Architecture,* 1794

JO Peter Blundell Jones ©

JP John Plaw, *Ferme Ornée,* 1795

JS S.C. Johnson and Son Ltd, *The Proper Treatment for Floors, Woodwork and Furniture,* 1924

JW John Wright and Company Ltd, leaflet, Birmingham

KE Robert Kerr, *The Gentleman's House,* John Murray, London, 1871

KF Courtesy of Kenmore Association, Fredericksburg, Virginia ©

KH Courtesy of Keats' House, Hampstead, London

KT Katie True, New York ©

KW Kentish Wallpaper Company, *Artistic Wallpapers,* sample book, 1932

L Liberty's Solid Oak Panelling, catalogue, Regent Street, London, c.1910

LF Louis G. Ford, catalogue no. 41, Eastbourne, c.1935

LG Leighton House, London (Royal Borough of Kensington and Chelsea); thanks to Joanna Banham

LH Longfellow House, Cambridge, Massachusetts; courtesy of Eastern National Park and Monument Association ©

LHT Courtesy of the Lamport Hall Trust ©

LL Photo by Linda Hall, Middlesex ©

LIF Sir John Soane Museum, Lincoln's Inn Fields, London

LP *Laxton's Price Book,* London, 1878

LSH Courtesy of Linley Sambourne House, London

LV Lavenham, Suffolk

M Courtesy of The Minories Art Gallery, Colchester, Essex

MA Metal Agencies Co. Ltd, catalogue no. 56, Bristol, 1932

MAA Metal Agencies Co. Ltd, catalogue no. 66, Bristol, 1937

MAB Floor design, Maggie Angus Berkowitz

MB *Mason's Bricklayer's, Plasterer's and Decorator's Practical Guide,* James Hagger, London, c.1865

MC Macfarlane's Castings, catalogue, 6th edn, 2 vols, Glasgow, 1882

MCA Macfarlane's Castings, catalogue, 7th edn, vol. I, Glasgow, 1907

MCG Norman McGrath

MD C. Middleton, *Designs for Gates and Rails,* 1806

ME Messenger and Company Ltd, catalogue, Loughborough, c.1910

MH *Modern House Construction,* ed. G. Lister Sutcliffe, vol. I, Gresham Publishing Company, 1909

MHA James Ford and Katherine Morrow, *The Modern House in America,* Architectural Book Publishing Company, Inc., New York, 1940

MI Milton Castings, MacDowall, Steven and Company Ltd, catalogue, London, c.1900

MID G.A. Middleton, *Modern Buildings,* vol. II, Caxton Publishing Company, London

MJ Morris-Jumel Mansion, New York; thanks to Susannah Elliott

MJB Mike Brown ©

ML/B Minard Lafever, *The Modern Builder's Guide,* 1833; courtesy of the Charleston Library Society, Charleston, South Carolina ©

ML/C Minard Lafever, *Beauties of Modern Architecture,* 1835; courtesy of the Charleston Library Society, Charleston, South Carolina ©

MM Michael Main Ltd, Architectural Antiques ©, The Old Rectory, Cerrig-y-Drudion, Corwen, North Wales LL21 0RU

MO Moulton Manor, Richmond, Yorkshire; thanks to Captain Vaux

MOR Michael Moran, New York ©

MOT J.L. Mott Iron Works, New York and Chicago catalogue G, 1888

MOU Kate Mount ©

MP Mount Pleasant, Philadelphia; thanks to Philadelphia Museum of Art

MR Marble Hill House, Twickenham, Middlesex

MT Minton Hollis and Company, Minton Tiles, catalogue, Stoke-on-Trent, 1910

MU Moulton Hall, Richmond, Yorkshire; thanks to the Hon. John and Lady Eccles

MV Mount Vernon Ladies Association of the Union, Virginia ©

MX Joseph Moxon, *Mechanick Exercises,* 1703

MY Courtesy of the Museum of the City of New York ©

NA Newport Art Museum, Newport, Rhode Island (Griswold House); thanks to Mark Simmons

NB N. Burst and Company, lighting catalogue, London, c.1900

NC Nicholls and Clarke Ltd, ironmongery catalogue No. 11, London, 1906

NCA Nicholls and Clarke Ltd, catalogue, Shoreditch, London, 1912

NE Nico Electric Lighting, catalogue, 1930-31

NH Newby Hall, North Yorkshire

NHH Nichols-Hunter House, Newport, Rhode Island; courtesy of the Preservation Society of Newport County

NN Peter Nicholson, *The New Practical Builder,* 1825 edn

NP J. Molinson, *New Practical Window Gardener,* Groombridge and Son, London, 1877

NR Nathaniel Russell House, Charleston, South Carolina; thanks to J. Thomas Savage

NW Newmarket Palace, Cambridgeshire ©

O Olana, Hudson River Valley, New York; thanks to James Ryan

OB O'Brien Thomas and Company, catalogue, Rotheram, London, 1911

OC Octagon, Orleans House

OE Claygate Brickfields Ltd, *Old English Fireplaces,* catalogue, Surrey, 1929

OH H. J. Jennings, *Our Homes and How to Beautify Them,* 2nd edn, Harrison and Sons, London, 1902

OL Landfall, Poole, Dorset (Oliver Hill); thanks to Dr and Mrs C.E. Upton

OM Old Merchants House, New York; thanks to Elizabeth Churchill Cattan

OU Sussex, England (John Outram)

OUP Based on a plan in R.T. Guntler's *The Architecture of Sir Roger Pratt*, Oxford University Press

OV Barley Splatt, Cornwall (Graham Ovenden); thanks to Graham Ovenden

P Paycockes, Coggeshall, Essex; courtesy of the National Trust ©

PA Palliser and Company, *Palliser's American Architecture*, New York, 1888

PB Peter Nicholson, *Practical Builder*, London, 1822

PC A. W. N. Pugin, *True Principles of Pointed and Christian Architecture*, London, 1841

PD Philip Dole, Oregon ©

PE Sydney Perks, *Residential Flats*, B.T. Batsford, London, 1905

PP Pryke and Palmer, illustrated catalogue, London, 1896

PPA Pryke and Palmer, illustrated catalogue, London, 1906

PL William Salmon, *Palladio Londiniensis*, London, 8th edn, 1773

PO Alan Powers ©

PR Private collection

PS Peter Sutton ©

PW Parker, Winder and Achurch Ltd, The "Devon" Fire, catalogue, Birmingham, c.1920

RA *The Works in Architecture of Robert and James Adam*, 3 vols, 1778

RB Rowe Bros and Company Ltd, Builders' Ironmongery, illustrated catalogue, Birmingham, 1935

RBA Rowe Bros and Company Ltd, catalogue, Bristol, 1937

RC Russell-Cotes Art Gallery and Museum, Bournemouth ©; thanks to Penny Thompson

RE Richard Elsam, *The Practical Builders's Perpetual Price Book*, 1825

RG Thanks to Roderick Gradidge, Elliot Road, Chiswick

RH Red House, Bexleyheath, near London; thanks to Mr and Mrs Edward Hollamby

RIBA Royal Institute of British Architects, London ©

RL Robert Lewis and Company, "Anaglypta" relief decorations, catalogue, Cardiff

RO E.L. Roberts and Company, general catalogue, Chicago, 1903

ROC Paul Rocheleau, Richmond, Massachusetts ©

RR J.B. Papworth, *Rural Residences*, London, 1818

RS Robert Saxton ©

RU Shirley Hibberd, *Rustic Adornments*, London, 1857

S *The Studio*, Special Summer Number, 1901: Modern British Domestic Architecture and Decoration

SA Sarum Chase, London

SAL Courtesy of Salve Regina College, Newport, Rhode Island (Watt Sherman House)

SB Steven Bros and Company, section III, Rain Water "Plumbing" Sanitary Castings catalogue, c.1885

SC Sandeman and Company, illustrated catalogue of general brass foundry, London, 1895

SCA Courtesy of Scalamandré, New York ©

SCY Stephen Calloway ©

SE Sebastiano Serlio, *The First Book of Architecture*, printed for Robert Peake, London, 1611

SF L.N. Cottingham, *The Smith and Founder's Director*, London, 1824

SG Sam Gratrix Jnr and Brothers Ltd, illustrated catalogue of brass fittings, Manchester, 1911

SH Strawberry Hill, Twickenham, Middlesex; thanks to St Mary's College

SHU Julius Shulman, Los Angeles, California ©

SI John Simpson & Partners, London

SK Sears, Roebuck and Company, *Our Special Catalog for Home Builders*, Chicago, 1910

SM St Martin's, Oxford; thanks to Ben Lenthall

SN Samuel Sloan, *The Model Architect*, E.S. Jones and Company, Philadelphia, 1852

SO Courtesy of Sir John Soane's Museum, London ©

SP Sarah Polden ©

SR West Hollywood, California (Rudolph Schindler); thanks to Robert Sweeney

SS Selden and Son, illustrated trade catalogue, June 1902, London

ST Stencil House, Shelburne Museum, Shelburne, Vermont ©, photograph by Ken Burris

STE Stephenson/Bell, Architects and Planners

SU Sutton House, Hackney, London; thanks to Mike Gray ©

SUM Drawing by Alison Shepherd ©, reproduced in John Summerson's *Georgian London*, Barrie and Jenkins, 1988 edn

SUT G. Lister Sutcliffe, ed., *Modern House Construction*, London, 1909

SV John Ruskin, *The Stones of Venice*, vol. I, 4th edn, George Allen, 1886

SW G. Jennings, The South Western Pottery, catalogue, 1874

TA Sebastian le Clerc, *A Treatise of Architecture*, London, 1724

TAL B.J. Talbert, *Examples of Ancient and Modern Furniture etc.*, R.O. Rickatson, 1876

TB Christopher Dresser, *Truth, Beauty, Power; Principles of Decorative Design*, 2nd edn. Cassell, Petter and Galpin, London

TC Tynecastle, illustrated catalogue, Edinburgh, c.1900

TCH Thomas Chippendale, *The Gentleman and Cabinet Maker's Director*, 3rd edn, 1762

TCM W. Young, *Town and Country Mansions*, London, 1879

TE Tenement House, Glasgow; courtesy of the National Trust for Scotland

TG The Studio, Highgate, London (Tayler and Green); thanks to S. O'Rhiordan

TH Thorpe Hall, Northamptonshire; courtesy of the Sue Ryder Organization

TI *Timber Homes by Bolton and Paul Ltd*, Norwich, c.1937

TL Taylor and Law Bros, Mouldings, Architraves, Skirtings etc, catalogue, Bristol, c.1890

TP Thomas Parsons and Sons, *Ornamental Decoration*, London, 1909

TW T. and W. Farmilow Ltd, catalogue, London, 1909

TY Simon Thurley ©

UD *Universal Design Book*, Chicago, 1903

UI Courtesy of the Ukrainian Institute, New York

VC *Villa and Cottage Architecture*, Blackie and Son, Glasgow, Edinburgh and London, 1869

VE Stony Creek, Connecticut (Venturi, Scott Brown and Associates); thanks to Mr and Mrs George Izenour

WA Warne's Rubber Flooring and Tiling, Barking, Essex, c.1937

WC William Cooper, general catalogue, London, 1893

WD *Woodward's National Architect*, New York, 1869

WF Wallpaper catalogues, by courtesy of Warner Fabrics

WG Waring and Gillow, general catalogue, London, c.1910

WGE Waring and Gillow Ltd, *The Carpet Book*, London, c.1910

WH Winslow Hall, Buckinghamshire; thanks to Sir Edward and Lady Tomkins

WHP William Halfpenny, *The Modern Builder's Assistant*, 1742

WI Photo by Wildlife Matters, Battle, Sussex ©

WL *Souvenir of Wickham Hall, Kent*, 1897

WM Courtesy of William McDonough Architects, New York ©

WN Manders Brothers Ltd, Winslow Wallpapers, catalogue, 1952-3

WO Courtesy of Woodward Grosvenor and Co. Ltd, Kidderminster; thanks to Geoffrey C. Smith

WP William Pain, *Practical House Carpenter*, 1766

WPB William Pain, *The Practical Builder*, 4th edn, 1779

WT Woodland Terrace, Philadelphia, Pennsylvania; thanks to Lauren Leatherbaum and Bill Owen

WW William Wood and Son Ltd, catalogue, Taplow, Buckinghamshire

YM Young and Marten, catalogue of builders' requisites, 1910

YMA Young and Marten Ltd, catalogue, London, c.1910

YH Yaffle House, Dorset; thanks to Peter Holguette

YS John Reid, *The Young Surveyor's Preceptor*, 1848

INDEX